The American

Secondary School

TEXTBOOKS IN EDUCATION
William H. Burton, *Consulting Editor*

An Approach to Guidance, by Edna Dorothy Baxter.

Growth and Development of the Preadolescent, by Arthur Witt Blair and William H. Burton.

The Diagnosis and Treatment of Learning Difficulties, by Leo J. Brueckner and Guy L. Bond.

Student Teaching in the Elementary School, 2nd ed., by James R. Burr, Lowry W. Harding, and Leland B. Jacobs.

Guidebook for Elementary Student Teachers, by Isabel Miller, George E. Dickson, and Loren R. Tomlinson.

The Guidance of Learning Activities, 2nd ed., by William H. Burton.

Supervision, 3rd ed., by William H. Burton and Leo J. Brueckner.

Education and Morals, by John L. Childs.

Public Education in America, by George R. Cressman and Harold W. Benda.

The Third Curriculum, by Robert W. Frederick.

Educational Psychology, by Karl C. Garrison and J. Stanley Gray. Also accompanying *Workbook,* by Karl C. Garrison, Ira E. Aaron, and Joseph C. Bledsoe.

Introduction to Educational Research, by Carter V. Good.

Methods of Research, by Carter V. Good and Douglas E. Scates.

Human Relations in School Administration, by Daniel E. Griffiths.

Guidance in Democratic Living, by Arthur Hollingshead.

The Guidance Function in Education, by Percival W. Hutson.

Early Elementary Education, by Myrtle M. Imhoff.

The Child and His Curriculum, 2nd ed., by J. Murray Lee and Dorris May Lee.

The Child and His Development, by J. Murray Lee and Dorris May Lee.

The Preadolescent, by Mary Jane Loomis.

Changing the Curriculum, by Alice Miel.

Teaching Adolescents in Secondary Schools, by Harry N. Rivlin.

The American Secondary School, by L. O. Taylor, Don R. McMahill, and Bob L. Taylor.

Education and the Democratic Faith, by Ephraim Vern Sayers and Ward Madden.

Statistical Methods in Educational and Psychological Research, by James E. Wert, Charles O. Neidt, and J. Stanley Ahmann.

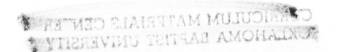

The American Secondary School

L. O. TAYLOR
formerly University of Omaha

DON R. McMAHILL
Omaha Technical High School

BOB L. TAYLOR
San Francisco State College

New York

APPLETON - CENTURY - CROFTS, INC.

PICTURE CREDITS

INVITATIONS AND NAME CARDS: *Tiffany & Co.* and *B. Altman & Co.,* New York

PHOTOGRAPHS OF TABLE SETTINGS, p. 119: *Towle Silversmiths,* Newburyport, Mass.

Preface

We are in the midst of a renaissance of considerable proportions in the United States. At such times, the secondary school, which is usually conservative, will be subject to the criticism that it has failed to modify its program in accordance with the demands of the time. In this book, the authors have recognized this situation. We have proposed a program in agreement with the consensus of specialists in secondary education. This program depicts our American heritage as it is currently reflected, with such essential modifications as the needs of our time seem to require.

There are four factors which determine the form that secondary education should assume: (a) the purposes of the high school as they are related to the nature of the students and the character of our culture, (b) the quality and flexibility of the high school curriculum, (c) the nature of certain contemporary problems in secondary education and their relationship to student development and teacher competency, and (d) the quality of service provided by the school for its youth. Accordingly, this volume has been divided into four parts. Part I is concerned with the identification of the aims and purposes of the high school. Specifically, it deals with the characteristics of our youth and of the American secondary school as an institution which has been shaped by our evolving culture. Part II is devoted to a consideration of the means and the materials by which the purposes of the high school can be achieved. There is an explanation of how the curriculum of the American high school has developed. Proposals have been made for the modification of the curriculum to better adapt it to the role of the high school in our contemporary culture. Part III is allotted to the presentation of five significant problems in secondary education. In providing a type of education adapted to all American youth, certain very difficult problems have become prominent, especially for the beginning teacher. A study of these problems provides a more complete interpretation of the principles of secondary education developed in Parts I and II. As students wrestle with these problems, they comprehend the principles of secondary education more fully and expand and fix them. Part IV deals with certain assumptions for improving service to youth. These assumptions seem entirely justified if it is realized that both the state and the national government need to protect our youth from practices that permit a poor quality of education to be provided. Too often today, our youth are being cheated because of the quality of education furnished by the local community.

This volume was written as a textbook for the first course in secondary education taken by the pre-service teacher. All of the authors have had extensive experience as high school teachers; two of them have taught principles of secondary education and supervised student teaching on the college level; one has been highly successful in guiding many pre-high-school teachers in the acquisition of initial skills in his classroom. The principles emphasized in this book are a product of wide practical experience, as well as extended study of secondary education. The book should be helpful to in-service teachers and citizen study groups. It should serve as a source book in secondary education for administrators, supervisors, and teachers.

L. O. T.
D. McM.
B. L .T.

Contents

Preface v

PART I: FREEDOM'S HERITAGE

1. **The Role of the American Secondary School** 3
   The Role of the High School in Maintaining Our Democracy 4
   The American High School from Then to Now 9
   Understanding the High School Student 11
   What Are the Objectives of the High School? 18

2. **Education and Culture in a Democratic Society** 26
   Our Heritage Adjusts to Changes in the Economy 26
   Our High Schools and the State 31
   Some Fundamental School-Society Relationships 36
   Extending Democracy 39

3. **Persistent Conflicts Within Our Culture about High School**
   Education 47
   Continuing Crosscurrents in American Education Since 1607 47
   Sources of Major Criticisms of the High School 52
   Education and Research in Today's School 61
   A Defense Against Criticism 67
   The Critics and "Operation Stork" 70
   Summary 71

4. **Reorganization of the High School to Serve All Youth** 75
   The Reorganization Movement 75
   Agitation for Improvement 77
   Forms of Organization 85
   The Organization of the Secondary School Is Being Adapted to the
     Characteristics of Youth 87
   Keeping All American Youth in High School 89
   The High School—A Common School 95
   What Practical Proposals Can Be Made for Retaining All Teen-
     Agers in High School until Graduation? 101

5. **The Teacher and Society** 105
   A High Professional Calling 105
   Desirable Traits for Professional Teachers 109
   Teacher and Community Adjustments 113
   Policies and Programs Constantly Change 119
   Gnothi Seauton—Know Thyself—and Thy Children 123
   Summation 123

PART II: THE MODERN CURRICULUM

6. **The High School Curriculum** **129**
   The Curriculum in Early Cultures 129
   Motives for Curriculum Development in the United States 133
   The Curriculum and the Purposes of the High School 140
   A More Meaningful Organization of the Curriculum 145
   A Brief Summary 151

7. **The Common Learnings or General Education** **155**
   How Education for All Came to the High School 155
   The Need for a Program to Provide for Different Mentalities 157
   The Nature of the Common Learnings Program 159
   Illustrations 161
   Summary 168

8. **Special Learnings** **171**
   The Classical Curriculum—American Version 171
   The Vocational Program 185

9. **Developing the Curriculum in the Classroom** **197**
   Old Ways Versus New Ways 198
   The Unit or Laboratory Method 202
   Planning and Developing a Subject 212
   Modernizing Study 216

10. **Learning Through Student Activities** **222**
    The Activity Movement 223
    How Student Activities Develop 226
    The Kinds of Student Activities 232
    An Integral Part of the Instructional Program 238

11. **Utilizing Instructional Materials** **243**
    Instructional Resources, Aids, and Materials 244
    The Selection of Instructional Materials 248
    Aids and Resources for Growth 253
    Suggested Sources of Resources and Materials 257
    Summary 259

PART III: SOME SIGNIFICANT PROBLEMS IN SECONDARY EDUCATION

12. **Reporting Student Progress** **265**
    Recognition of and Adjustment to Individual Differences 265
    Modernizing Marks and Marking 270
    Modernizing Reports to Parents 277
    Characteristics of Good Reporting 280

13. **The Slow and the Rapid Learner** **288**
    The Problem 288
    Heterogeneous and Homogeneous Grouping 293
    The Slow Learner 295

The Rapid Learner 298
Retarded, Gifted, and Talented Learners 302

14. **The Improvement of Reading** **310**
The Nature of the Reading Problem 310
How to Improve Reading 311
Some Essential Reading Skills and Abilities 314
Diagnostic and Remedial Procedures 317
An Outline of the Reading Program 320

15. **Guidance and the Teacher** **329**
Guidance in the High School 329
Guideposts to Guidance and Counseling 334
Guidance Techniques 336
Script for a Guidance Program 346
School and Teacher Follow Through 348

16. **Discipline and Adjustment to School Life** **352**
What Is the Problem? 352
The Causes of Discipline Problems 354
Growth toward Maturity 360
Favorable Conditions for Good Work in the Classroom 363
Factors Affecting Adjustment to School Life 367

PART IV: BETTER SERVICE FOR YOUTH

17. **Improving School and Community Relations** **377**
Public Relations—a Business Principle for Schools 377
Advertising—a Business Principle for Schools 380
School Publicity Should Not Be Spasmodic 385
What Is Meant by Good Public Relations? 389
A Program for Public Relations Action 391

18. **More Than a Student and a Log** **395**
The Needs of Youth Should Determine the Nature of the Program
Provided 396
Provisions for Special Services 400
Better Instructional Tools for Better Teaching 407
Better Service to Older Adolescents Who Are Low in Academic
Ability and Social Status 409

19. **Leadership for Learning** **416**
What Is Leadership for Learning? 416
Characteristics of Leadership of the Secondary School 419
Leadership for Learning in the Classroom 430

20. **Equalization of Education Opportunities** **435**
Old Ways Versus New Ways 435
How to Provide Equal Educational Opportunity for All Youth 442
A Superior High School for All Youth 448
Characteristics of a Superior High School 451

21. **What Is Better for Youth?** **456**
Assumptions as to What Is Better for Youth 456
Youth and Our Technological Revolution 468
Parents, Too, Wrestle with the Problem 475
Index 483

Charts, Figures, Tables

CHARTS

1. Some Forces That Have Operated to Produce Reorganization and Improvement in the High School 79

2. A Comparison of Old and New Educational Concepts 84

3. Some Pros and Cons of Merit Pay Plans 113

4. Political Concepts, Forces, People, and Events That Created a Favorable Climate for a Public-Supported School System 135

5. Subjects of Study in Public High Schools, 1891 139

6. An Opinionnaire on Some Issues in Public Education 143

7. A Comparison Between the Academic and the Functional Curriculum Approach 144

8. Patterns of Curriculum Organization in Our Contemporary Secondary Schools—Arranged According to Effectiveness 146

9. Old and New Methods of Selecting Curriculum Content 148

10. Stages in the Process of Getting Meaning from What Is Taught 151

11. The Curriculum of a Modern High School 165

12. The Common Learnings Course of Study 167

13. The Old Versus the New 198

14. Three Methods for Developing the Secondary School Curriculum in the Classroom 213

15. Social Activities in a Typical High School 227

16. A Few Procedures for the Evaluation of Personality 271

17. The Common Numerical Systems 274

18. Pre-modern Versus the Modern Statements of Educational Objectives 279

19. Contrast in Methods of Teaching Slow and Rapid Learners 301

20. Illustrative List of Talents with Clues 306

21. Differences in Emphasis with Respect to the Improvement of Reading 312

22. Guideposts to Guidance and Counseling 335

23. Homeroom Guideposts 341

24. Teachers' Deficiencies Which Cause Discipline Problems 356

25. List of Essential Routines 365

26. Methods for Checking Disruptive Behavior in a Classroom 367

27. An Analysis of Two Types of Leadership 427

28. Pros and Cons of Federal Aid to Education 441

29. Comparison of the Stands of Business and Labor on Public Education 449

30. Sample Teaching Assignments in 18 States, Alaska, the District of Columbia, and Hawaii 461

31. Factors Affecting Change 469

32. Typical Educational Issues Within the Profession 472

33. Conservative Proposals and Their Probable Effect on the Program of the Contemporary High School 473

34. Liberal Proposals and Their Probable Effect on the Program of the Contemporary High School 474

FIGURES

1. Showing the Trends in High School Reorganization from 1890 to 1950   86

2. The Probable Distribution of Intelligence Quotients in a Comprehensive High School 174

TABLES

1. Growth in Enrollments in the High School, 1880 to 1958-59 11

2. The Work of National Commissions, 1918-1959, on the Improvement of High School Objectives and Proposals for Achieving Objectives 20

3. Summary of Studies of Reading Achievement 66

4. Distribution of High Schools in the United States, 1949 87

5. Youth Population of the United States, 12 to 20, and Youth Population in High School 88

6. Number of High School Graduates 17 Years of Age Compared with Population Peers (Continental United States, 1870 to 1950).... 89

7. A Summary of Some Factors Related to Early School Leavers from Six Studies of the Problem 90

8. Survival Rates, Ninth Grade Through High School Graduation, in Public and Non-Public Schools, 1948-49 Through 1951-52 92

9. Secondary School Enrollment by Grades, 1953-54 96

10. Showing the Age Limits for Compulsory Attendance in the Various States and Territories of the United States, 1957 97

11. Developments of High School Subjects of Study 137

12. New High School Subjects Accepted for College Entrance, 1860-1890 137

13. Comparing the Subject Areas of the College Preparatory (1893) with the Subject Areas of the Modern High School Curriculum (1949) 182

14. A Study of Intellectual Aptitude in a Comprehensive High School .. 269

15. Student Identification of Their Class Roles 343

16. Follow-up Survey of the Graduates of a Midwestern Comprehensive High School 349

17. A Comparison of Income and Educational Investments by Five States Making the Greatest and Five States Making the Least Educational Investments 441

18. Proportion of Revenue for Public Education, Elementary and Secondary, Derived from Federal, State, and Local Sources over a Two-Year Period 446

PART I

Freedom's Heritage

Chapter 1

THE ROLE OF
THE AMERICAN SECONDARY SCHOOL

As a society becomes more complex . . . it is found necessary to pro-vide a special social environment which shall especially look after nurturing the capacities of the immature.—JOHN DEWEY, *Democracy and Education*

All societies establish institutions for the formal instruction of the young. Why is this so? And why are the people within a state willing to tax themselves in order to provide good schools? How do schools help to make a nation strong?

Every nation uses its schools to instruct its youth in the common beliefs and principles of its people. The United States of America is a democratic state; our people believe in democracy. Hence, part of the role[1] of the American secondary school is to teach the principles and beliefs held in common by all Americans. It is this body of common beliefs and principles which has made America stable, strong, and powerful. It was for this primary purpose that education at public expense was established in our country. Because some students do not continue beyond high school and because the younger children are too immature to understand the total concept of our democracy, the secondary school has the major obligation for instructing in citizenship.

In our time, Communist Russia has demonstrated that a system of public education is important to the power of a state. They have staffed their schools with competent teachers who are politically reliable, that is, teachers who sincerely believe and teach the communist doctrine. All youth are required to attend these schools and are indoctrinated with the beliefs and principles of the Communist Party. Thus, in Communist Russia, public education has been an important factor in the building of a stable, powerful, communist state.

[1] Some synonyms for *role* are *task, work, function, service,* and *duty.*

THE ROLE OF THE HIGH SCHOOL IN MAINTAINING OUR DEMOCRACY

"Pray," said Lycurgus, "do you first set up a democracy in your own house."—PLUTARCH.

In order to preserve itself, a society must be an integrated organic whole. Democracy depends for its very continuance upon a citizenry that holds common ideals and values and that recognizes common responsibilities and obligations. The high school as an institution established by society is in part responsible for the transmission of this social inheritance and wholly responsible for its re-enforcement. While some excellent groundwork is laid from the first grade up, on citizenship problems within the experience and maturity of the pupils, the ages 14 to 18 are the most productive for achieving a more mature understanding of the ideals and principles upon which the American state rests.

Students come to the high school from all types of homes and backgrounds. Without a systematic attempt to teach the ideals of our democratic society, it cannot be assumed that our citizens will be like-minded. A real test of the high school's accomplishments is the kind of citizens it provides the state. The basic beliefs and values which have made us a nation have come to be known as democracy's own; hence, we believe that such beliefs and values must persist if our democracy is to be preserved.

Sometimes the method used to develop common ideals among high school students is bluntly called "indoctrination by the use of propaganda." In the recent wave of attacks against the public school, this method has been proposed by such men as Merwin K. Hart[2] who want to tell young men what is right and see to it that they have no opportunity to discuss the issue or hear it in any other way. This method of indoctrination selects the necessary facts to create a one-sided impression, omits certain truths, and gives no more than a single side for any case. As a matter of contrast, we will favor the American Way throughout this text, for we believe in it. This treatment supports the free use of intelligence and condemns indoctrination in the area of controversial issues.

We in America know how to secure common ideals if we really desire to do so. That was demonstrated during World War II. The American public is well aware that an apparatus may be set up to infiltrate American institutions, and every professionally-minded school employee is on the constant alert against it. Our public schools are relatively free from any hint of such infiltration, yet it is apparent that the time has arrived

[2]Association for Supervision and Curriculum Development, *Forces Affecting American Education,* 1953 Yearbook (Washington, D.C., National Education Association, 1953), p. 55.

for greater emphasis to be placed upon common American ideals. With the support of the public, the American high school can strengthen the common ideals and values which we hold dear, but it remains for the high schools to agree upon a program for the achievement of these worthy goals.

Identifying Some Guideposts of Democracy. What concepts of democracy should the high school seek to preserve? In American democracy there is a set of principles which indicate the relationship of the individual to the group. These guideposts to democratic living apply to the classroom, the school, the community, and the nation. We suggest the following guideposts:

1. Every person is regarded as worthy of developing his potentialities, and his importance and contributions to the group must be recognized. Each can be of value to the school, the community, and the nation. In such a healthy mental climate, the school can assist each student in finding himself and can give him confidence of being worthy of respect. It is through his strengths and not through his weaknesses that the learner will make his contributions as a citizen.

2. Differences in opinions, abilities, and interests among individuals are valued. Of course, common beliefs and ideals are essential to the integration of the school and the nation. But a diversity of interests and abilities provides the strength for carrying on the many and varied activities required in the modern world. In both school and nation, a diversity of opinions, abilities, and interests makes for stability and adds zest to living. All individuals are valued because of what they can do.

3. A democratic society is characterized by an ever-widening concern and responsibility for others—their welfare—and for the social consequences of one's actions. This is a critical guidepost for living in a democracy. Research on this problem shows an interesting fact: it has been determined on several occasions that student sensitivity to individual rights is very strong while willingness to discharge obligations is definitely weaker. In schools employing modern methods of teaching, the willingness to discharge obligations is considerably stronger.

4. In a democracy the control comes from within the group concerned, not from the outside. Group participation in making policies and rules that affect individuals in the group is basic for our democratic freedom. Our country was formed out of a rebellion against autocratic government; the right to participate in making laws for themselves is fundamental to the liberty of any people. This principle is accepted and practiced in the good American home.[3] Many high school teachers have found that planning with a class creates a much more favorable social climate, promotes a much better understanding of the democratic proc-

[3] G. G. Jenkins, H. Shacter, and W. W. Bauer, *These Are Your Children* (Chicago, Scott, Foresman & Company, 1953), Ch. 12.

esses, and helps students to grow toward responsible citizenship. Some interesting conflicts occur, however, when the authoritative teacher suddenly thrusts democratice methods and mutual planning into the traditional curriculum. Joan Dunn[4] wrote, "I found it impossible to build any kind of lesson on their interests because their interests are too few . . ." Without desire and ability on the part of the teacher, there can be no democracy within the group, no mutual planning, and—as Miss Dunn admitted—very little of anything.

5. The democratic method requires uncovering all of the facts and arriving at intelligent decisions co-operatively. Practice in making intelligent decisions in the classroom is a counterpart to the way it has been done by small American communities in the past and is being done today in civic meetings and in labor unions. Having acquired this experience, the young citizen is better prepared to apply the principle in meeting his adult responsibilities. In addition, knowing how decisions are made among democratic Americans, the young citizen is less susceptible to the propaganda devices of selfish promoters.

To make these guideposts stand out still more, apply the reverse of each, and you will marvel at how far away from American democracy it is possible for some high schools to travel. It is one thing to become reminiscent, but quite something else to suggest that a return to the "good old days" would solve the problems of the present age. Here, to illustrate, is what Frederick Lewis Allen[5] had to say regarding our yesterdays. It was a time when the average annual income of Andrew Carnegie was some 10 million dollars as opposed to that of the average worker who did well to make four hundred dollars.

In short, Andrew Carnegie's annual income was at least 20 thousand times greater than that of the average American workman. There you have the basic contrast. Andrew Carnegie was one of the very wealthiest men of his day, but many others had incomes in the millions. And their way of life showed it.

Typical of those who criticized the public schools is the following writer who apparently yearns for a return to the methods of the "good old days":

I went to an old-fashioned school . . . I don't remember the school's ever being interested in our psyches or our future lives, or worrying about us as people in any self-consciously pedagogical way . . . I and my friends have some of the (most amazing) psyches you ever saw, all because we wasted our formative years, with nothing to show for it but an awful lot of Latin.[6]

In the time of and previous to Carnegie, the tempo of life was slower

[4] Joan Dunn, *Retreat from Learning* (New York, David McKay Co., Inc., 1955), p. 131.

[5] Frederick L. Allen, *The Big Change* (New York, Harper & Brothers, 1952), p. 4.

[6] Hortense Calisher, "Reeling, Writhing—Grouping," *The Reporter* 13:37-41 (September 8, 1955).

and the problems of citizenship were less complex. For the most part the students in the high school then were a more select group and could grasp more easily the citizenship problems of the day. Now, with all or nearly all youth in high school, with a vastly expanded school population, and with the United States faced constantly with serious world crises, the problems of the teacher are more complex. To help students grasp the problems of our day, the teacher must be skilled in leading discussions and helping student groups reach valid decisions on social, economic, and political problems. Now, it is no more possible to preserve our democracy through a continuance of the school methods employed in Carnegie's time than to compete in the contemporary steel market with the production methods then used. Society has undergone a change; the schools have matured to meet the demands created by social change.

The Responsibility of Society. Far too often, it is assumed that society's only part in the perpetuation of public schools (and preservation of our democracy) lies in footing the bills. This is reflected in the attitude of the citizen who will say, when solicited for help in a juvenile program, "Sure, count on me! How much money do you want?" Surely, the social structure of the home is based upon far more than money assets. Surely, the schools need far more than money to achieve worthy goals.

Many comparisons have been made between wages paid the bricklayer, the bartender, or the insurance salesman and those paid to teachers in various regions of the United States. It seems clear that money should not be the sole reason for entering the profession: the beginning teacher in most cases will not receive as much pay per hour as the skilled workman. There are other reasons for teaching, however, and society can provide the following three without the collection of additional tax dollars.

Status may be given to the profession of teaching. One who is accorded this mark of respect is permitted to use his best judgment in solving the many problems that arise each hour and each day of the school year. If the teacher has status, he regulates his personal affairs and his school affairs in terms of the best outcome for youth, society, and himself. It follows that a teacher with status will never be ordered to undertake any activity which he feels is unworthy. He will not be exploited by his superiors, by the community, nor by his students.

Tenure may be granted to those teachers who, after a period of service, demonstrate that they are competent, good youth leaders, and desirable agents of the community. Tenure provides security in position during efficient service and protection against arbitrary acts of the administration, board of education, and the community. It removes the need for reelection each year, but does not necessarily insure life-long employment. It does insure that the teacher has a right to appear before his school board, with or without counsel, prior to his official dismissal. The flaunting of their tenure in the face of suggestion for improvement and growth by some inefficient teachers has caused the public to become somewhat less than wholehearted in its support. Nevertheless, if teachers, as a group, will recognize that efficient service and continued growth to an observable degree is the only valid basis upon which tenure can be maintained, it is no doubt here to stay.[7]

Authority may be accorded to the teacher who, morally and legally, may be called upon to act in *loco parentis.* In his daily contacts with students he must have the right to direct student behavior for the general good of all.

Status, tenure, and authority are all symbols of recognition bestowed upon an individual or a group by society. Good school communities grant these to good teachers. Teachers, being human, glory in these symbols of reward conferred by the school community. However, other school communities, lacking insight, remain immune to the use of such social symbols. Perhaps, the basic difficulty with these latter communities is that they do not know that teaching, when effectively done, is a professional activity requiring aptitude and many acquired competencies. Such communities believe that anyone can teach. Hence, they employ poorly qualified teachers and accord them no symbols of recognition. Because such teachers are unable to successfully instruct youth in how to recognize, analyze, and understand so as to make wise decisions as citizens, these teachers are in reality expensive. Furthermore, their pupils are being cheated.

These are elements which society often overlooks in the struggle to keep school faculties strong and equal to the new challenges of modern education. Nevertheless, the teachers who have earned and been granted professional recognition, that is, status, tenure, and authority, will not be on the defensive over such matters as methods and discipline.

Many parents have unpleasant memories of school, and many have been "burned" by the school, as Hymes has indicated.[8] These facts are made crystal clear each June by the rash of cartoons which depict children enthusiastically singing "No more pencils, no more books, no more teacher's nasty looks" as they erupt from the doors of the school. These cartoons are drawn by people who are from the same age group as the school-children's parents. The cartoons reveal, with many exceptions, the fears and hates that were acquired a generation ago by the parents of today's school children. These cartoons are enjoyed by parents because they release through laughter those remembered hates and fears.

Because of these unpleasant memories, some parents may readily be exploited by any individual or group seeking to discredit public education. Even though the parents may sincerely believe in education and the current offerings, their negative attitudes can lead them to give credence to such statements as these:

[7] William H. Burton, and Leo J. Brueckner, *Supervision: A Social Service,* 3rd ed. (New York, Appleton-Century-Crofts, Inc., 1955), pp. 113-115. (This is a paraphrase.)

[8] James L. Hymes, *Effective Home-School Relations* (Englewood Cliffs, N. J., Prentice-Hall, Inc., 1953), pp. 41-43.

All educators have their heads in the clouds: "You ought to meet a payroll. Then you would know what life is about. You would not treat these youngsters with kid gloves. You would get them ready for life."

A business man wants more competition in the schools; he blames us for stressing co-operation too much. A workingman wants more discipline with rigid rules and harsher punishment. It's a tough life and these kids have to learn to take it.

THE AMERICAN HIGH SCHOOL FROM THEN TO NOW

From colonial times to now, a central theme—the common man's dream of a people's college for youth and adults—has been woven into the social heritage of America as a continuous strand. Also, from then until now, there has been a persistent struggle over this issue—between those who would reserve the high school for the elite and for college preparation only and those who would maintain the high school for preparation for life, as well as for college. Even now, most of the criticism of secondary education comes from the adults who seek to restrict high school education to the elite.

The Latin Grammar School. This institution, established by the Massachusetts Bay Colony five years after its settlement in 1635, was the first public secondary school in the United States. A goodly number of the male members of this settlement were English gentry who had either attended or graduated from Cambridge College. They feared that learning would die with them when they were laid in their graves. Hence, they established the Latin grammar school to prepare young men for Harvard College (established 1636) by teaching them to read and write the Latin language. In establishing the Latin grammar school, the Puritans had imported an upper-class institution from England. The subjects taught were Latin, Greek, mathematics, and religion; however, the major emphasis was upon Latin. Although the Latin grammar school spread throughout the colonies, the enrollments in the school were always small, and the school itself was never popular.

The Academy. As brisk trade sprang up between the colonies and the mother country and as the population of the colonies grew, there was a demand for the teaching of such subjects as surveying, navigation, bookkeeping, and similar practical subjects. The Latin grammar school, which had been designed to prepare young men of the upper class for college, ignored these new needs. About 1750, Benjamin Franklin proposed a secondary school, an academy or a people's college, to teach those studies that "are most useful and most ornamental." The academy was a boarding school that proposed to teach whatever studies were in demand. All youth who desired to attend were afforded the opportunity. In setting up the early academies, there was a bitter fight with respect to the suitability of English as a study for a secondary school. It was claimed that English was not a classical language and was, therefore, unsuitable for a secondary school.

After the Revolutionary War the academy became a thriving institution that offered both practical and classical studies, and by 1850 there were more than six thousand academies with total enrollments of more than 250,000 students. It was the first American secondary school to be entirely free from denominational control, the first to offer courses of a practical nature, and the first to admit girls. However, as the academy began to take over the accepted role of the declining Latin grammar school, it also began to be selective as to the students it would admit, and therefore began around 1850 to lose its influence with the public. While the academy failed to keep pace with the advancing times, the American dream of equal educational opportunity was first manifested in the early academy.

The Public High School. In the meantime, a public high school, publicly supported and publicly controlled, was established in Boston in 1821. It was founded to meet the needs of the children of tradesmen and mechanics. The Board of Education was petitioned by them to provide a school for students who were graduating from the elementary school too young to go to work and who would profit by additional time spent in school. The idea spread to many communities, especially in the growing cities. The free public high school was dedicated to the proposition that secondary education should be a public enterprise, and that therefore the public should determine the studies to be offered. Thus, the American dream of a people's college for youth and adults began to materialize.

Though the high school was popular, certain big taxpayers and some private schools raised the question of its legality. In 1872, an injunction was brought against the Kalamazoo, Michigan, Board of Education prohibiting the payment of salaries to teachers. The court ruled in 1874 that there was nothing in either law or custom to prevent maintaining such a school. This case established the legal precedent which provided a solid foundation for the American dream. After this decision, the public high school experienced rapid growth as is shown in Table 1.

The facts, as shown in Table 1, reveal a modern miracle—the doubling of the high school enrollment each decade from 1880 to 1930. By late 1930, 73 out of every 100 young people between the ages of 14 and 18 were in high school. What better evidence of the realization of the American dream could be found? Under pressure from patrons to retain all youth in school, the high school responded by providing, as well as it could, a variety of studies for the very wide range of individual differences found among students in a rapidly changing industrial society. Whatever the public demanded, the high school tried to provide. The problem of money

Table 1. Growth in Enrollments in the High School, 1880 to 1958-59

YEAR	NUMBER OF STUDENTS ENROLLED	YOUTH POPULATION OF THE UNITED STATES AGED 14 TO 17	PER CENT OF YOUTH AGED 14 TO 17 ENROLLED
1880	110,277	4,056,867*	2.7
1890	202,963	5,119,653)	3.9
1900	519,251	6,116,795)	8.4
1910	915,061	7,220,298)	12.6
1920	2,181,216	7,736,000)**	28.2
1930	4,399,422	9,341,000)	47.0
1940	6,545,981	9,720,000)	67.3
1950	5,664,907	8,710,000)	65.3
1959	8,880,000	9,260,000***	95.3

* Estimated (Warren S. Thompson and P. K. Whelpton, *Population Trends in the U.S.A.*, New York [McGraw-Hill Book Co., 1933], p. 1.)
** *The Statistical Abstracts of the United States*, 1895, 1910, 1930, and 1952 (Washington, D.C., Government Printing Office, dates indicated).
*** "Growth in School Enrollments," *NEA Research Bulletin* 36:124-5 (December, 1958); "45 Million in School," *School Life* 41:8 (September, 1958).

for school support continued, for the public has never provided the financial support to finance the program it wanted.

Look again at Table 1. Note that the total enrollment for 1940 stood at seven million while the enrollment for 1950 reached only six million. Why? What caused this drop in enrollment during the 1940's? There are four probable causes. (1) The birth rate of the 1920's was somewhat above average while that of the 1930's was decidedly low.[9] Hence, fewer teen-agers were eligible for high school in the 1950's. But the proportion of youth in high school in 1950 was greater than in 1940. (2) In the 1930's, due to the depression, jobs were scarce and male adults were given preference. Many teen-agers attended high school who normally would have gone to work. (3) From 1945 to after 1950 the demand for goods and services greatly exceeded the supply. Both business and industry were in a period of boom. The supply of labor was short and the wage rate high. High wages had more appeal to many teen-agers than high school attendance. Many 14- to 18-year-olds who usually would have attended high school as a matter of course went to work. (4) Early marriages were in fashion. While this was probably only a minor cause, the total high school enrollment was reduced by it.

UNDERSTANDING THE HIGH SCHOOL STUDENT

Teen-Age Characteristics. Meet Mary and John, two typical teen-agers. Young people such as Mary and John are found in high school classes

[9] Warren S. Thompson and P. K. Whelpton, *Population Trends in the United States* (New York, McGraw-Hill Book Co., 1933), Ch. 7.

which usually range in size from 15 to 45 in all of the 27 thousand high schools of the United States. Mary and John, like all who attend American high schools, range in ages from 12 to 19. Each differs from the other, yet both have certain characteristics in common. They are both in a period of transition from childhood to adulthood. They are going through a phase of development called *adolescence* that is characterized by attitudes and behaviors which sharply differentiate them from children on one hand and adults on the other.

An axiom among carpenters is: *work with and not against the grain of the wood.*

An axiom among blacksmiths is: *strike while the iron is hot.*

An axiom among high school teachers is: *work with and not against teen-age nature.*

Success at any type of work requires that the individual, be he a professional man or a laborer, must understand the nature and characteristics of the material being processed. Charlton Ogburn, Jr., expressed this idea quite clearly when, in speaking about some of the men under his command, he said:

Each had something egging him on . . . Eve, the fresh-looking, blond boy from the Middle West, turned out to have the blessed gift of a Way with Mules.[10]

Certain high school teachers have the blessed gift of a *way with teenagers.* They seem to understand the characteristics of teen-agers and what makes them tick.

There comes a time in the life of every teen-ager when he feels impelled to learn certain things. In dealing with him at such a moment, we must take him as he is—not as what we would like him to be. Aside from his heritage, he is a product of his time, his culture, his peer group, his past and present status, and his social environment. Even teen-age behavior that is highly annoying is often necessary and appropriate for the individual involved. He is so constituted that gaining the respect of his peers, at this precise time, is more important to him than gaining the respect of his teacher.

Developmental Tasks of Teen-Agers. Since 1900 there has been a change in emphasis with respect to the purposes of the high school. To an older purpose, that of transmitting the heritage of the past, has been added the purpose of teaching students to live here and now in a rapidly changing world—and each of these purposes is considered equally vital. To achieve the newer purpose, greater emphasis is being placed upon understanding teen-age characteristics and contemporary American culture. The concept of the developmental task, a contribution by Robert

[10] Charlton Ogburn, Jr., "Merrill's Marauders," *Harper's Magazine* 214:29-44 (June, 1957).

J. Havighurst of the University of Chicago, has been widely accepted in recent years because of its simplicity in explaining teen-age characteristics. Havighurst has defined this concept as follows:

A developmental task is a task which arises at or about the same period in the life of each individual, successful achievement of which leads to his happiness and success with later tasks, while failure leads to unhappiness in the individual, disapproval by society, and difficulty with later tasks.[11]

Overstreet,[12] another widely recognized student of this problem, has stated it with a slightly different emphasis as follows:

Few schools have recognized that their central problem is that of helping young life to grow into mental, emotional, and social maturity. This recognition must come as our next great educational adventure.

American citizens and patrons of the high school, over the years, have phrased the same demand this way: *Give each youth the kind of education he can take—give each youth the kind of education that will be most profitable to him and to society.* As will be shown later in this text, there is a small, vocal group that would provide high school education only for a select few of the teen-agers. But the emphasis is clearly democratic—educate *all* youth.

What then are the implications of working *with* rather than *against* adolescent nature? In a contemporary situation such as ours, several answers could be given to this question. But, among professional people and the general public, more than 80 per cent[13] favor assisting teen-agers in achieving the developmental tasks which are pertinent to their age and development. Our society has assigned to the high school the function of helping adolescents to become more mature men and women—good citizens and productive workers, who are able to establish reasonable family relations in their new homes. Society, let us note, has not relieved the high school of the task of preparing these same young Americans for college entrance. There are some critics who do not understand this broad assignment.

What are these developmental tasks with which the modern school can help the teen-ager? The following six are frequently listed:

1. Accepting one's physique and using the body effectively.
2. Developing new relations with age mates of both sexes.
3. Gaining emotional independence of parents and others.

[11] Robert J. Havighurst, *Developmental Tasks and Education* (Chicago, University of Chicago Press, 1953), p. 8.

[12] H. A. Overstreet, *The Mature Mind* (New York, W. W. Norton & Company, Inc., 1949), p. 259.

[13] Harold C. Hand, *What People Think about Their Schools* (Yonkers-on-Hudson, World Book Co., 1948), p. 11.

4. Achieving assurance of economic independence; selecting and preparing for an occupation.

5. Developing civic competence and a sense of social responsibility.

6. Developing conscious values by which to live.[14]

The behavior of adolescents becomes much more understandable if this general framework is kept in mind.

There are two considerations to heed in any discussion of developmental tasks. First, all of these tasks are interrelated. Adolescents, usually, are attempting to achieve several of them at the same time. For example, one can not separate bodily changes that constantly occur from the efforts of the teen-ager to achieve new relationships. Second, while it is true that all adolescents must accept their own bodily changes, each will achieve this task in his own unique way. For one student it may be easily done while for another it may be very difficult.

As a pre-service teacher, you could profit by asking yourself these questions:

1. What behavior of a teen-ager reflects effort on his part to achieve the developmental tasks?

2. What are some of the consequences that may result when these developmental tasks are inadequately realized?

3. What might be the importance of time or stage of development in the achievement of any task?

4. How do these tasks differ in the upper, middle, and lower strata of our American society?

Guideposts to Understanding the Teen-Ager. Each of the developmental tasks provides a means, when studied, of understanding one phase of teen-ager characteristics. The six developmental tasks serve as guideposts to the interpretation of teen-age behavior. The achievement of these tasks is an essential for the teen-ager, the high school, and society. In the next few pages each of these tasks will be briefly analyzed.[15]

Accepting one's physique. Within limits heredity determines the physique of a teen-ager. But the American Way of Life sets the ideal as six feet tall and broad-shouldered for the boy and willowy and tall for the girl. Of course, every boy and girl expects to achieve the ideal. A too-great deviation from the standard, especially if there is unfavorable comment by adults, can cause frustration. Since worry will not change the physique, acceptance of self with pride is vital to teen-age welfare. A second organic problem of the teen-ager is rapid development of the reproductive organs which become mature some years before the teen-ager is accepted as an adult. Our mores tend to ignore this latter development even though its control is a difficult problem for the teen-ager. The

[14] There is no single source for this listing.

[15] For a more complete treatment see *Fostering Mental Health in Our School* by the Association for Supervision and Curriculum Development, and *Human Development and Education* by Robert J. Havighurst.

urge to use these new physical powers is strong; hence, adult guidance toward accepted adult ways can be of great service to the teen-ager as well as to society. To what degree might the qualified teacher be of value in helping to guide this developmental process?

The development of new heterosexual relations. Due to the pubertal changes described above, peer groups expand to include teen-agers of both sexes. Although acceptance requires conformity to the heterosexual standards of the expanded group, the need to be accepted is urgent, and all or nearly all desire to belong. The conflict between adolescents and those in authority or the older and the younger generations is so great that teen-agers feel compelled to band together in order to set their own standards as to clothing, language, entertainment, and stage idols. Many peer groups are held tightly together by the resentment of and threats from the authority exercised by adults. The clearly differentiated roles of men and women of an earlier generation have been fading. This probably tends to aggravate the perpetual conflict between the older and the younger generations and confuses some teen-agers. Some high schools co-operate with these peer groups in setting standards for better grooming and for an acceptable code of ethics. Such co-operation helps youth move toward maturity, and incidentally tends to reduce antagonism between teen-agers and adults. This poses a question to pre-service teachers. "How can you avoid this resentment of teen-agers toward adults?"

The achievement of emotional independence. Although at birth one is completely dependent upon adults and is emotionally irresponsible, one should, by maturity, be completely independent of adults and a responsible person. Being able to make and carry out a decision on one's own is a real achievement. Psychologists attribute much of the irresponsibility of soldiers in World War II to overdependence upon mothers.[16] Either overdominating or overprotective parents seem to be a cause of overly dependent teen-agers. But in homes where parents show affection, talk difficulties out with their children, and set limits as behavior guides, the gradual growth from dependency on parents to being independent of them takes place. Teen-agers from dominating or overprotective homes frequently transfer their repressed rebellion to the school. This is probably the cause for some of the most persistent disciplinary problems in the high school classroom.

Since emotionally immature parents are never likely to provide suitable environments for the emancipation of their teen-age children, help, if it comes at all, will come largely from the school. The teacher who is to give this help needs an insight into the cycle of human development from birth to maturity with special emphasis upon ages 12 to 18. He must understand how to help teen-agers learn to make and carry out decisions on their own.

[16] Edward A. Strecker, *Their Mothers' Sons* (Philadelphia, J. B. Lippincott Co., 1946), Ch. 2.

Achieving assurance of economic independence. Holding a job gives to a man status and recognition in his community. When a teen-ager can hold a regular job, he too is given status and recognition. To the community this is proof that the teen-ager is an adult or nearing adult status. A century ago, it was easy to get and hold a job. But more and more in today's world, getting and holding a job requires specific skills and abilities; in addition, the teen-ager is often required to have had some pre-job experience. Youth are prone to favor occupations which give prestige and which may be quite apart from the vocation for which they are best suited by temperament and aptitude. Who will provide this essential guidance? How can the regular classroom teacher help students become more realistic about preparing for a vocation? Since all or nearly all teen-agers are now in high school, many thoughtful citizens feel that the high school should provide: (1) expert help in the determination of aptitudes and competencies, (2) quality instruction in all subjects as a superior preparation for many types of work, and (3) an elective program in general vocational education as a means of acquiring some of the pre-job skills and competencies frequently demanded by employers.

The development of civic competence. This development—or the making of good citizens—is the one purpose of the high school about which there is almost universal agreement. The public school, and later the public high school, was established for this purpose. Students learn the meaning of democracy and the methods of democratic action through direct experience and in face-to-face relations.[17] In our world of today, communication, trade, and travel, as well as social and economic problems, are on a world-wide basis. We can no longer be a self-satisfied and self-contained nation. To vote wisely, our citizens must be informed on all of the great problems of our day. All of this is putting to the test our faith in the intelligence of the common man. It is probably true that the best years for developing in young people civic and economic understanding lie between 14 and 18.

Youth needs an understanding of the local community and the nation, as well as of all nations of the earth. To achieve this understanding, there must be some sacrifice on the part of youth as well as a degree of social reward. During World War II, when young men were given a place in the sun, they demonstrated their ability to grow and to serve when recognized and rewarded. The high school is ideally adapted for providing the type of recognition which can help teen-agers mature from self-centered individuals to young adults who recognize, accept, and practice social responsibility. How can this be done? Some students of this problem propose that the high school provide: (1) for teen-agers to participate in adult community life, in civic clubs, and in the campaigns and activities

[17] Educational Policies Commission, *Education for All American Youth—a Further Look*, rev. ed. (Washington, D. C., National Education Association, 1952), p. 84.

of the political parties; (2) for participation in community surveys and the follow-up of surveys aimed at the improvement of community life; (3) for a study of the history and literature of the local region and of the state and nation, especially to learn what has not yet been discovered about the community and nation; and (4) for ceremonials to inculcate true loyalty to the community and the nation.

The development of conscious values to live by. Man alone has achieved a set of ethical controls which characterize him as a good man and a good citizen. An individual can not live a good life except by following these ethical precepts which are usually called moral and spiritual values. He needs a sense of direction for his life, and some basis for making decisions that involve questions of morality. Christian ethics are an integral part of the American Way of Life. Youth must find a correct approach for establishing a relationship between "me and we" and "me and nature and nature's God." A long time ago, Socrates said that the unexamined life is not worth living. We are now living in a period of social unrest and confusion, which demands re-examination of our moral concepts. Even as recently as 1945, Landis noted that "we are now living in a time when moral values are in an ambiguous state."[18]

For certain young people, the school contributes significantly to moral development. One study of adolescent character reported a correlation of .74 between character (reputation) and school achievement.[19] Experiences that provide security usually result in a more willing acceptance of the existing moral code; but for many young people the school has failed, especially for those whose home standards vary greatly from those of the school.[20] Kentucky has carried on an experiment for some years now that seems to offer greater promise. Their experimental schools have found ways to emphasize moral and spiritual values as a part of the regular academic content. Thus, a teacher who felt a need to give emphasis to certain values brought them to light as a matter of course in presenting the usual subject matter. Hartford[21] has provided the following illustration of how this was done:

The leader of this course was a very capable young man. The program he had planned included Irving Berlin's "Give Me Your Tired, Your Poor." As the students learned to sing the song, they were thrilled deeply and at its conclusion the whole chorus applauded wildly.

[18] Paul H. Landis, *Adolescence and Youth* (New York, McGraw-Hill Book Co., 1945), Ch. 9.

[19] Robert J. Havighurst, and Hilda Taba, *Adolescent Character and Personality* (New York, John Wiley & Sons, Inc., 1949), p. 179.

[20] A. B. Hollingshead, *Elmtown's Youth* (New York, John Wiley & Sons, Inc., 1949), p. 176.

[21] Ellis F. Hartford, "A High School's Three Years of Experiment: Emphasis upon Moral and Spiritual Values," *The Clearing House* 27:515-522 (May, 1953).

The development tasks of youth are real. Helping teen-agers achieve them is a responsibility of the school and its teachers. Some of these tasks originate in the need of the organism to adjust to bodily changes. Others arise from the demands of society or the national culture. The achievement of all of these tasks is essential to the stability of the individual and thus to the stability of the state itself. The press and the public usually speak of the particular tasks that concern society and the nation as the "American Way of Life." In a very real sense, our study of the developmental tasks of youth is an introduction to the objectives of the high school which will be our next topic.

WHAT ARE THE OBJECTIVES OF THE HIGH SCHOOL?

"Make the high school practical." That is the opinion of the man on the street. Most laymen would accept this answer. High school teachers also would insist that this goal can not be achieved without great emphasis upon academic subject matter or the subjects necessary for college entrance. Even to Benjamin Franklin in 1750, this would have been a reasonable objective. There is nothing impractical about preparation for college entrance; nor is there wasted effort in preparing *not* to enter college. Thus, the high schools have a double objective, a dual obligation to society and society's children.

In *Learning the Ways of Democracy*, the Educational Policies Commission[22] stated the issue thus:

In every school three questions have to be answered . . . What is to be done? This is the problem of *purpose*. How is it to be done? This is the problem of *procedure*. Who is to do it? This is the problem of *personnel* . . . It is true, of course, that the ultimate source of authority for school policies is outside the school itself, namely the public which maintains and supports the school . . . But the school can go at least as far as the public wants it to go in educating youth.

A small minority, highly vocal, would have us believe that "frill" subjects (activity type courses such as home economics and industrial arts) have no place in the high school. There is confusion on the part of the public as to what should be taught. One superintendent of a large metropolitan school district said, "There's the rub. Education for every American boy and girl would be tremendously expensive. The public does not want to pay that kind of a bill—and prefers to hack away at what the high schools are attempting to do. If, by some miracle, education didn't cost us a dime, then I doubt that there would be much argument over *who* went to high school and *what* was in the curriculum."

[22] Educational Policies Commission, *Learning the Ways of Democracy* (Washington, D. C., National Education Association, 1940), Ch. 1.

Thus, the objectives of the high school must be kept in some harmony with what the public demands and what the public is willing to support.

The Task of Stating Over-All Objectives. Each high school must formulate its aims in accordance with the needs of youth—locally as well as nationally. Since 1918, a number of national commissions have wrestled with this problem. The National Commission on Secondary Education[23] in 1918 stated what should be the objectives of secondary education: (1) good mental and physical health, (2) the ability to read, write, compute, and communicate effectively, (3) the ability to establish and maintain a good home, (4) the ability to make a good living (vocational skills), (5) civic competence, (6) the ability to use leisure time wisely, (7) the ability to live an effective moral and spiritual life.

In the years since then, other national commissions have attempted to state these principles more concisely and to make proposals by which they might be achieved. They are listed for study in Table 2.

Perhaps more distinctly than any other group, the Educational Policies Commission, in *Education for All American Youth—a Further Look*, 1952 edition, has outlined a blueprint for the high school to follow. While its proposals for achieving the purposes outlined are considerably more liberal than those now prevailing in the American high school, they are similar to the objectives followed by the best schools of our time. The proposed program provides a balance between excessive individualism and extreme conformity. The Commission[24] gives much emphasis to how youth differ and what this means in providing a proper school program. To the Commission, the following statements indicated what youth have in common and what should be the purposes of the high school:

All youth are citizens now; all (or nearly all) will be qualified voters in the future; all require education for civic responsibility and competence.

All youth (or nearly all) are members of family groups now and will become members of other family groups in the future; all require an understanding of family relationships.

All American youth are now living in the American culture and all (or nearly all) will continue to do so in the future; all require an understanding of our culture.

All youth need to maintain their mental and physical health now and in the future; all require instruction to develop habits of healthful living, understanding of conditions which foster health, and knowledge of ways of preventing disease, avoiding injuries, and using medical service.

All American youth will be expected to engage in useful work and will need to work to sustain themselves and others; all, therefore, require occupational guidance and training, and orientation to current economic conditions.

[23] The Commission on Reorganization of Secondary Education, *Cardinal Principles of Secondary Education*, U. S. Bureau of Education Bulletin 35, 1918 (Washington, D.C., Government Printing Office, 1919), 32 pp.

[24] The Educational Policies Commission, *Education for All American Youth*, pp. 28-29.

All American youth have the capacity to think rationally; all need to develop this capacity and, with it, an appreciation of the significance of truth as arrived at by the rational process.

All youth must make decisions and take action which involves choice of values; all, therefore, need insight into ethical values. Particularly do they need to grow in understanding the basic tenet of democracy—that the individual human being is of surpassing worth.

Table 2. The Work of National Commissions, 1918-1959, on the Improvement of High School Objectives and Proposals for Achieving Objectives

DATE	COMMISSION AND REPORT	CONTRIBUTION
1893	The Committee of Ten, "Report of the Committee of Ten on Secondary School Studies"	Standardized the high school curriculum around the college-preparatory objective —brought order out of chaos but led to a fixed pattern hampering to needed change. Established a basis for the higher education of the common people. Instigated the practice of setting up national committees to deal with issues.
1918	Commission on the Re-Organization of the High School, "Cardinal Principles of Secondary Education"	Secondary education should be determined by the needs of society it serves, the character of the individuals, and the knowledge of educational theory and practice available.
1937	Committee on the Orientation of Secondary Education, "Functions of Secondary Education"	Functions: Integration; Satisfaction of Needs; Evaluation of the Social Heritage; Exploration of Interests, Aptitudes, and Capacities; Systematization and Application of Knowledge; Establishment and Direction of Interests; Guidance; Methods of Teaching and Learning; Retention and Direction of Learning.
1938	New York Regents Inquiry, "A Study of the High Schools" (H. T. Spaulding, "High School and Life")	One-fourth of the graduates not adequately prepared for citizenship; programs highly academic; drill and memorization dominate instruction; students unwilling to assume any responsibility for civic cooperation.
1939	The American Youth Commission (H. R. Douglass, "Secondary Education for Youth in Modern America")	Citizenship and home living in the broadest sense; recreational activities and the leisure side of life; vocational life; physical health; effective and healthy personality and individuality; development of such information, interests, and skills as will prepare young people for continued study in college and throughout life.
1940	The American Youth Commission, "How Fare American Youth?" "Youth Tell Their Story" "Equal Educational Opportunity"	Studies of youth during time of depression; constructive proposals for aiding youth during the depression.

DATE	COMMISSION AND REPORT	CONTRIBUTION
1942	The North Central Association of Colleges and Secondary Schools, "General Education in the American High School" (first such program)	General education is: (1) intended for everyone, (2) concerned with the whole personality, (3) concerned with individual's nonspecialized activities.
1944	The Educational Policies Commission, "Education for All American Youth" (revised in 1952)	The 10 imperative needs of youth; the 10 imperative needs of society.
1945	The Harvard Committee Report, "General Education in a Free Society"	The first assumption of responsibility for change by the college in 50 years. Recognized the need for both general and special education in U. S. A. The curriculum proposals, however, put emphasis upon the established academic subjects.
1946	Report of the John Dewey Society, "The American High School"	A yearbook of the society by eight able educators. Proposed three features that must be stressed if the high school is to serve youth well. These were the proposals: (1) resolve a list of issues so the high school lives up to its promise, (2) provide certain common experiences for all youth (common learnings), and (3) direct secondary education toward the achievement of these goals (goals listed and discussed)
1947	The United States Office of Education, "The Prosser Resolution" (The needs for life adjustment education)	Stated that the present high school meets adequately the needs of only a part of its students. Should make the high school truly a school for all—where the needs of none are neglected. General education and life adjustment education are similar in meaning though cultural integration may be given more emphasis through general education, while social integration will be given more emphasis through life adjustment education. Guidance, pupil personnel service, education for leisure time, consumer education, and citizenship are some of the services stressed by life adjustment education.
1959	The Conant Report, "The American High School Today"	Made these recommendations for improving the American public secondary school: eliminate the small high school, improve the counseling of students, provide a general education curriculum for all students, use ability grouping of students, identify college-bound youth, and provide a greater challenge for the gifted.

In the *10 imperative needs of youth* by the Educational Policies Commission and in the addition by the National Association of Secondary-School Principals of the *10 imperative needs of society*,[25] the purposes of the secondary school were made somewhat more complete. The question still may be asked, "What are the objectives of a high school education?" The imperative needs of youth and society should be the objectives of the secondary school. (Observe that neither the Educational Policies Commission nor the National Association of Secondary-School Principals specifically mentions academic subjects as such.)

The 10 imperative needs of youth. All youth have certain educational needs in common. All parents can agree that the school should meet these needs.

1. All youth need to develop salable skills and those understandings and attitudes that make the worker an intelligent and productive participant in economic life. To this end most youth need supervised work experience as well as education in the skills and knowledge of their occupations.

2. All youth need to develop and maintain good health and physical fitness and good mental health.

3. All youth need to understand the rights and duties of the citizens of a democratic society and to be diligent and competent in the performance of their obligations as members of the community and citizens of the state and nation and people of the world.

4. All youth need to understand the significance of the family for the individual and society and the conditions conducive to successful family life.

5. All youth need to know how to purchase and use goods and services intelligently, understanding both the value received and the economic consequences of their acts.

6. All youth need to understand the methods of science, the influence of science on human life, and the main scientific facts concerning the nature of the world and of man.

7. All youth need opportunities to develop their capacities to appreciate beauty in literature, art, music, and nature.

8. All youth need to be able to use their leisure time well and to budget it wisely, balancing activities that yield satisfaction to the individual with those that are socially useful.

9. All youth need to develop respect for other persons, to grow in their insight into ethical values and principles, and to grow in the moral and spiritual values of life.

10. All youth need to grow in their ability to think rationally, to express their thoughts clearly, and to read and listen with understanding.[26]

The 10 imperative needs of society. Modern society in the United States also has certain problems which all students must face, deal with, and

[25] National Association of Secondary-School Principals, *Planning for American Youth* (Washington, D.C., National Education Association, 1951), p. 9.
[26] Educational Policies Commission, *Education for All American Youth*, p. 216.

endeavor to solve. Youth should learn to understand and deal effectively with them.

1. Society needs to be organized and governed so that differences will be respected and peace and political ability shall prevail among nations.

2. Society needs a free economic system which supplies the basic needs of people without interruption.

3. Society needs to develop a condition which facilitates cooperation among labor, government, farmers, and industry; which promotes free discussion of differences; and which enables them to reach agreements for cooperative planning and action.

4. Society needs to make it possible for organized business and labor to share the benefits of production on terms reached by bargaining among themselves.

5. Society needs to provide opportunities for individuals to work continuously at living wages and enjoy security after they have passed their productive period in life.

6. Society needs to develop loyalty to the principles of democracy, to protect the individual freedom of thought and expression, to assure justice to all citizens, and to develop independent people free from harmful propaganda and uniformity.

7. Society needs to make it possible for people of all races, colors, and creeds to be respected with equal opportunities for work, legal protection, and education.

8. Society needs a strong, popular government to protect the welfare of all of its citizens from illegal practices or irresponsible groups.

9. Society needs to protect and replenish its natural resources so that they may not be wasted or exhausted.

10. Society needs to preserve the basic social institutions of the home and family and church and school so that fundamental social, moral, and spiritual values may be learned, cherished, and perpetuated.[27]

Not many Americans would challenge this listing which presents the combined thinking of representative educators of our time. But there is an active minority that questions the *program*. Every teacher must decide for himself whether this vocal minority is right in objecting to education for *all* American youth. What is best for youth and what is best for the American commonwealth?

"Education for all American youth" is representative of America as a whole and not of any particular high school. High schools are best operated on a partnership basis between the community and the faculty. If the high school staff understands or develops an understanding of the legitimate objectives of the enterprise, then the citizens of the community may come to realize those objectives. It would be foolish for a faculty to attempt to teach without full appreciation of objectives desired; it

[27] National Association of Secondary-School Principals, *op. cit.*, p. 8.

would be equally foolish to conduct a high school program without community understanding and acceptance of such objectives.

DISCUSSION PROBLEMS

1. Why is a secondary education of importance in the making of a citizen?
2. How does *indoctrination* differ from *education?*
3. From your own experiences, would you say that the public schools are keeping taxpayers adequately informed regarding needs, goals, and methods?
4. Advertising specialists often argue the merits of "single-blast" methods (full-page advertisements, full-hour radio-TV programs) as opposed to brief messages over a long period of time. Which do you think would be a preferable policy for the public schools?
5. It has been stated that 1958 would go down in history as the year when many Americans first expressed dissatisfaction with two of the things they had been proudest of—their automobiles and their schools. How do you interpret this with respect to the schools?
6. How does society's role in supporting the schools go beyond mere financial support?
7. Which of the "ten imperative needs of society" listed in this chapter might you rank as most urgent today? Would realistic "education for all American youth" actually solve this problem?
8. Why do high school principals ask, "Does he understand kids?" when inquiring about an applicant for a teaching position?

RELATED REFERENCES

ALLEN, Frederick L., *The Big Change* (New York, Harper & Brothers, 1952).

Association for Supervision and Curriculum Development, *Forces Affecting American Education,* 1953 Yearbook (Washington, D.C., National Education Association, 1953).

———, *Growing Up in an Anxious Age,* 1952 Yearbook (Washington, D.C., National Education Association, 1952).

BEARD, Charles A., *The Unique Function of Education in American Democracy* (Washington, D.C., The Educational Policies Commission, The National Education Association and the Department of Superintendence, 1937).

BENJAMIN, Harold, *The Saber-Tooth Curriculum* (New York, McGraw-Hill Book Co., 1939).

BURTON, William H., and BRUECKNER, Leo J., *Supervision: A Social Service,* 3rd ed. (New York, Appleton-Century-Crofts, Inc., 1955).

CASWELL, H. L., (ed.), *The American High School,* Eighth Yearbook of the John Dewey Society (New York, Harper & Brothers, 1946).

Commission on the Reorganization of Secondary Education, *Cardinal Principles of Secondary Education,* Bureau of Education, Bulletin 35, 1918 (Washington, D.C., Government Printing Office, 1919).

DOUGLASS, Harl R., *Secondary Education for Youth in Modern America,* Report of the American Youth Commission of the American Council on Education (Washington, D.C., 1937).

DRAKE, William E., *The American School in Transition* (Englewood Cliffs, N. J., Prentice-Hall, Inc., 1955).

DUGAN, Lucille, "How to Plan a Social Program in a Large High School," *Bulletin of the National Association of Secondary School Principals* 214:104-108 (November, 1955).

DUNN, Joan, *Retreat from Learning* (New York, David McKay Company, Inc., 1955).

Educational Policies Commission, *Education for All American Youth—A Further Look,* Revised (Washington, D. C., National Education Association, 1952).

Learning the Ways of Democracy (Washington, D. C., National Education Association, 1940).

HAND, Harold C., *What People Think about Their Schools* (Yonkers, N. Y., World Book Co., 1948).

HARTFORD, Ellis F., "A High School's Three Years of Experiment: Emphasis upon Moral and Spiritual Values," *The Clearing House* 27:515-22 (May, 1953).

HAVIGHURST, Robert J., *Developmental Tasks and Education* (Chicago, University of Chicago Press, 1953).

——, and TABA, Hilda, *Adolescent Character and Personality* (New York, John Wiley & Sons, Inc., 1949).

HOLLINGSHEAD, A. B., *Elmtown's Youth* (New York, John Wiley & Sons, 1949).

HORN, Gunnar, "Heaven Help the Adolescent," *Nebraska Educational Journal* 26:52-53 (February, 1946).

HYMES, James L., *Effective Home-School Relations* (Englewood Cliffs, N. J., Prentice-Hall, Inc., 1953).

JENKINS, G. G., SHACTER, H., and BAUER, W. W., *These Are Your Children* (Chicago, Scott, Foresman & Company, 1953).

KEPPEL, Francis, and WILSON, Sloan, "Goals for Schools," *Saturday Review* (September 10, 1955).

LANDIS, Paul H., *Adolescence and Youth* (New York, McGraw-Hill Book Co., 1945).

National Association of Secondary-School Principals, *Planning for American Youth* (Washington, D. C., National Education Association, 1951).

OGBURN, Charlton, Jr., "Merrill's Marauders," *Harper's Magazine* 214:29-44 (June, 1957).

OVERSTREET, H. A., *The Mature Mind* (New York, W. W. Norton & Company, Inc., 1949).

SPEARS, Harold, *The High School for Today* (New York, American Book Company, 1950).

STRECKER, Edward A., *Their Mothers' Sons* (Philadelphia, J. B. Lippincott Company, 1946).

THOMPSON, Warren S., and WHELPTON, P. K., *Population Trends in the United States* (New York, McGraw-Hill Book Co., 1933).

EDUCATION AND CULTURE
IN A DEMOCRATIC SOCIETY

We live today in a deeply troubled time.
—GEORGE S. COUNTS, *Education and*
American Civilization

OUR HERITAGE ADJUSTS TO CHANGES IN THE ECONOMY

It is a truism that education reflects the culture that supports it. Social and economic changes have come rapidly to our America, especially since 1900. In an age of machines, our culture has progressed more than that of any other nation—yet one element of our heritage, that of equality of educational opportunity, has persisted as an ideal despite tremendous changes in our economy and culture.

It is also a truism that our move from an agrarian to an industrial society has brought subtle changes in the family, the churches, and the attitude of every community toward its schools. Many of us are not aware that our moral and ethical values have also been modified in the process. Our ways of thinking and behaving are an integral part of our way of life. Let us here attempt to identify some of the major changes in our way of thinking and behaving. We have changed:

FROM	To
a society where relatively no unemployment existed	a society where mass unemployment is a constant threat
a culture where handicraft was dominant	a culture where mass production and the assembly line predominate—automation is moving in
a culture where every man was free to express his own opinion	a culture where economic power carries political power—those who own the machines also "own" the men who operate them, to a degree

FROM	To
a culture where great emphasis was put upon the older generation	a culture that puts great emphasis upon the young
a culture where the farm population dominated	a culture where the industrial population dominates
a culture where the young greatly predominated in numbers	a culture where the old predominate in numbers
a culture where the man was the breadwinner and the head of his household	a culture where it is acceptable for both husband and wife to work away from the home; both, more often than not, are head of the house
a relatively obscure nation—isolated and isolationist	the number one nation of the world in many respects

The Culture-Molding Process. Communities are improved when people and their incomes are improved. Both of these improvements are in a large measure an accomplishment of the public schools.[1] Teen-agers are people with potentials. In defiance of the deep-rooted myth that only the elite are worth educating, the public school takes youth from varying types of homes and sets up a favorable environment for learning. It introduces the teen-ager to a vastly expanded heritage that often is in great contrast to his narrow and restricted home and neighborhood. This is the phenomenon of the culture-molding process.[2] It helps each youth to interpret more accurately the life about him, and it guides him in his study of the social heritage. Literally, it is a culture-transmission process, and even the poorest excuse for a public school contributes some measure of good to this endeavor.

Public education is truly an investment in the safety and welfare of American democracy. The public school is our greatest means for realizing the dream of James Truslow Adams, "that dream of a land in which life should be better and richer and fuller for every man, with opportunity for each according to his ability or achievement."[3]

When Thomas Jefferson in 1787 declared, "educate and inform the whole mass of the people . . . ," he envisioned our American society hundreds of years to come. Public schools do, in this mid-twentieth century, educate the whole mass of the people. This has happened be-

[1] Earle U. Rugg, "Our Greatest Social Achievement," *Phi Delta Kappan* 38:69-74 (November, 1955).

[2] Francis J. Brown, *Educational Sociology*, 2nd ed. (Englewood Cliffs, N. J., Prentice-Hall, Inc., 1954), Ch. 11.

Harold Rugg and William Withers, *Social Foundations of Education* (Englewood Cliffs, N. J., Prentice-Hall, Inc., 1955), Ch. 2.

[3] James T. Adams, *The Epic of America* (Boston, Little, Brown & Co., 1931), p. 404.

cause of rather than despite the changes in our culture. What are some of the changes that have brought this about?

The impact of a changed economy, as we have stated, has quite naturally been reflected in the entire social structure. Schools have been forced to change because they are an essential part of society.

In 1880, one farmer was able to provide enough food for between four and five persons. By 1955, he had progressed so much that he was able to provide food for 18 persons. Some of his fellow farmers were no longer needed. They went to the cities, and today there are some 60 million workers employed in private and public occupations other than farming. The same soil is now, in a sense, nearly five times as productive through know-how and machine operations.

Such a change was bound to reach the very heart of the traditional farm family. For example, Old World methods demanded large families, with a premium of sorts on boys (farm hands) rather than girls; it was natural for even young children to do their share of the chores. They lugged wood, slopped the hogs, and ground the feed. Today, modern farms are heated by natural gas, fuel oil, or coal. There are machines to milk cows, feed hogs, and grind feed. One or two workers can do the daily chores and run the farm as well.

The following changes were listed in 1955 by Agriculture Secretary Benson:

1. In no other nation today do so comparatively few farmers produce food and fiber to feed and clothe so many.
2. Thirty years ago, an hour's take-home pay would buy five and one-half loaves of bread; now it buys 10 loaves.
3. An hour's take-home pay would buy three and one-half quarts of milk; now it buys seven.
4. Then it bought one and one-half pounds of steak; now it buys two.
5. Then it bought one and one-half pounds of chicken; now it buys three pounds.
6. An hour's take-home pay today buys three dozen oranges or nine and one-half cans of tomatoes—about three times as much as 30 years ago.

There is no question that agricultural research combined with the rapid application of machinery to the most difficult tasks have spurred great changes in our cultural patterns. No longer can it be said that "if you can't do anything else, you can always go into farming." Farming is now a science, and there is no place in it for the dullard. Farm management calls for skilled persons.

Morrill and Smith-Hughes Acts. As early as 1850, Pennsylvania State University and Michigan State College established agricultural experiment stations. In 1862, Abraham Lincoln signed the Morrill Act to allot federal funds for the support of an agricultural college in every state of our commonwealth. In most of the states, vigorous research on such problems as stock-breeding and crop-raising has gone on for nearly a century. The University of Minnesota in 1888 established an agricultural high school for farm boys who wished to make farming their way of life.

During World War I, a food shortage brought about the creation of the Smith-Hughes Act which was passed by Congress in 1917. By this legislation, Congress tried to stimulate the various states, through federal subsidy, to establish vocational agriculture departments in many high schools throughout the land. The effort was successful, and, because of the on-the-job methods employed by skilled teachers, many farmers came to accept scientific agriculture as a better way of life.

The change from traditional farming to scientific management came slowly. When fully analyzed, it is clear that the instruments which brought about this change were largely the agricultural college and the American high school. Although the income of many farmers has been greatly enhanced, the change is still incomplete, and by and large agriculture is, economically, a seriously depressed enterprise.

In an appraisal of the "goodness" of communities, Thorndike[4] shows with elaborate statistical proof that 85 per cent of community improvement comes from improving people and their incomes. Our examination of the improvement of farmers and their incomes indicates that the high school and college have played a magnificent role in making this possible.

Has business, too, profited because of the institution of education? Let us turn to this question.

Education and Business Interests. At the close of World War II, members of the United States Chamber of Commerce published the first of several studies related to public education. *Education—an Investment in People* revealed direct relationships between the number of years of schooling and the living standards achieved by adults. From the viewpoint of educators this was a simple truth, but to hardheaded leaders in the business world it represented a new key to continued prosperity. Schoolmen, who had been attacked for spending tax dollars without any apparent reason, now felt that another change had occurred, for with the honest support of business interests, every educational dream would soon be realized.

Continued research established the validity of *Education—an Investment in People*. It was catalogued by the Chamber of Commerce as a worthy publication and made available everywhere.[5]

The study revealed that the more a student is exposed to the finer

[4] Edward L. Thorndike, *Your City* (New York, Harcourt, Brace & Co., 1939), p. 17.

[5] Department of Education, Chamber of Commerce of the United States, 1615 H Street, N.W., Washington, D. C. Description: "A graphic summary of research data on (1) the relationship of the education levels of American people to per capita income, retail sales, magazine circulation, political activity, farm production, economic attitude and military service; (2) changes in population size, age distribution, education level and per capita income distribution in the last century; and, (3) current and predicted school conditions—enrollment, housing, teachers' salaries and financing. Useful in stimulating action on local educational levels."

things in life, the more he desires them for himself. In striving to obtain them—and they are not all material objects—he produces more. Certainly, the high school graduate produces more than the elementary school graduate. Because he is more productive, he receives more pay and is able to afford a better home and a finer automobile; his clothing, hobbies, and recreational habits are more costly—all of which is cheering news for the merchant who sells these items. In America, where opening the cornucopia of *things* leads to increased status, this formula was grasped and understood.

Certainly, material rewards are a basic part of the cultural life which we experience in America. It is good business for the Chamber of Commerce to press forward in aiding the schools. In addition to educational literature, local Chambers now provide films and other aids for the purpose of showing the American way of business in an attractive manner. Thomas A. Ballentine, 1955 Education Chairman of the United States Chamber of Commerce, assured the authors of this textbook:

I would like to assure you that the United States Chamber of Commerce will continue to press forward for good schools, staffed with well-trained teachers (adequately compensated).

It is difficult to determine to what extent a statement like the one above can be accepted as the real policy of an organization such as the United States Chamber of Commerce. Is it an equivocal statement? Certainly, within a few weeks after the letter was written, the United States Chamber of Commerce along with the National Association of Manufacturers, the Farm Bureau Federation, and various taxpayers' leagues joined in a propaganda campaign to defeat a bill in Congress which was designed to provide aid for the construction of school buildings. School-building programs had been cut to a minimum during World War II, and schools were then badly overcrowded—many schools were operating in double sessions. Also, there were too many pupils in most of the classrooms for efficient teaching, and teachers' salaries were too low to attract and keep enough competent teachers.

Furthermore, the brash efforts of some business groups to exploit children through the direct introduction of advertising into the classroom violates the principle that the school serves all segments of society. The public school could not survive without the support of the whole society which it serves; hence, it does not cater to special groups. Here and there, business interests have attempted to subsidize the publication of textbooks that were markedly favorable to a single side of a controversial issue. However, it is generally recognized that the school belongs to all of the people. Locally, business men usually accept this tenet and co-operate wholeheartedly with the schools. There are, of course, glaring exceptions.

Business-Industry-Education Days. An annual "holiday" for school employees, known as BIE Day, now serves to acquaint city-school teachers with behind-the-scene operations of banks, department stores, steel mills, packing houses, railroads, and similar vast enterprises that represent the core of our capitalistic economy. Through this innovation, which normally occurs during the week prior to the opening of the school term, teachers receive the full force of public relations planning—a friendly visit, a coffee break, a free lunch, audio-visual presentations, and personal chats with the top officers of management.

In the springtime, schools return the compliment and hold an EBI (Education-Business-Industry) Day for management and labor. The schools' open house brings as guests: bank presidents, who visit new and old buildings; industrial managers, who study school shop equipment and witness its operation; and various labor leaders, who may sit in social studies classes and observe lively debates on, perhaps, the problems of capital and labor.

Through such mutual visitations, America's key leaders are now sensing that there is something more than material culture offered by our system of free public education. This interest in the American heritage is demonstrating the worth of the schools; it also reveals what school population problems are and what must be done to meet them.

Now let us turn to another phase of education and culture in our democratic society. Have the schools been successful in fostering the interests and the support of the state?

OUR HIGH SCHOOLS AND THE STATE

What is the essential relationship between the high school and the state? Since ours is a democratic state and since the secondary school will reflect the type of government that supports it, public education in our society is, and should be, grounded in the spirit and tenets of democracy. What is the nature of our democracy?

Social organization is the grouping of individuals. A single individual may belong to a number of different groups, that is, religious, economic, and political, but it is the relation of the individual to the group which is important in determining the nature of the organization. Vital to democracy as a way of life is a regard for the value of the individual; however, this must not be so to the exclusion of a consideration for other individuals. In our democracy, a balance is maintained between the rights of the individual and the rights of others.

In *The Great Democracies*, Winston Churchill has hit upon something unique in the development of our American democracy. This is the frontier heritage. That the frontier should have reshaped the traits and institutions of those who experienced it is understandable.

By 1800 there were a million Americans west of the mountain ranges of the Alleghenies. From these new lands a strong, self-reliant Western breed took its place in American life. Modern American democracy was born and cradled in the valley of the Mississippi. The foresight of the first independent Congress of the United States had proclaimed for all time the principle that when new territories gained a certain population they should be admitted to statehood upon an equality with the existing partners of the Union. It is proof of the quality and power of the Westerners that eleven of the eighteen Presidents of the United States between 1828 and 1901 were either born or passed the greater part of their lives in the Valley of the Mississippi.[6]

How did these common men achieve the power indicated by Churchill? Counts[7] stated that they obtained these rights by: (1) the ownership of firearms to defend themselves and their families, (2) the possession of property, (3) extending suffrage to all, (4) fighting for a free public school, and (5) the right to worship in the church of their choice. Here on the American frontier a new balance was achieved between the rights of the individual and the rights of the group. The frontiersmen fought for and achieved the rights available only to the ruling class in Europe. This was an American dream to extend to all men the same rights as those held by privileged European classes.

The Relationship Between the High School and the State. Why has this American dream always been related to American education? A chief characteristic of American education is its effort to contribute directly to the "American dream of a land in which life should be better, richer, and fuller for each according to his ability or achievement . . . It is not a dream of motor cars only, but a dream of a social order in which each man and each woman shall be able to attain the fullest stature of which they are capable . . ."[8]

Although the American school is attended by all or nearly all American children, American education has not been planned and carried out to achieve the principles of American democracy with the same thoroughness that Nazi Germany did or Communist Russia is doing to make their political and social philosophies function. In nearly every other country in the world, the nature and quality of the educational program are determined at the seat of the national government. The program is formulated in specific directives and sent to all educational officers through the nation. The directives then are carried out in detail by the classroom teachers. In America, with minor exceptions, there are no national patterns imposed on education by the federal government. Each state sets up certain minimum requirements which all schools

[6] Winston Churchill, *History of the English Speaking People*, Vol. 4, *The Great Democracies* (New York, Dodd, Mead & Co., 1958), p. 133.

[7] George S. Counts, *Education and American Civilization* (New York, Bureau of Publications, Teachers College, Columbia University, 1952), p. 78.

[8] Adams, *op. cit.*, p. 404.

within the state must meet. Beyond these, the people in each local community determine the nature and the quality of the program which is provided for their children. This is a unique American contribution. It does make education flexibile enough to meet the varied needs of youth in a large nation such as ours. Hence, local leadership must be able and competent or the local program becomes fuzzy and wobbly.

The United States, as well as all other countries of the world, recognizes the need and accepts the responsibility for transmitting certain attitudes and behavior patterns to all pupils. But this is a highly local matter in our democracy. American high school teachers, through in-service education programs, prepare their own teaching guides in such areas as developing civic competence. Because each high school does adapt its program to the needs of local students and the demands of the local community, these teacher's guides vary in topic content and emphasis from one high school to another. However, in general, the citizenship education program includes the following types of activities: (1) living democratically in the high school, (2) extending civic activities into the community, (3) moving out in the state, national, and world scene, (4) developing competence in the study of public problems, (5) developing competence in political action, (6) building knowledge as a tool of civic competence, and (7) fostering loyalty to the principles and ideals of American democracy.[9]

Our Democratic State Is Based upon the Hebraic-Christian Faith. The Hebraic-Christian faith is at the very heart of our democratic way of life and is an integral part of our American culture. The precepts that comprise the faith have been created, as well as borrowed from other cultures, by the Hebrews and Christians. Although the public high school may not teach a secular religion, it must reflect the Hebraic-Christian ethics which have molded our way of life.

But in a democracy, a school must do more than reflect moral and spiritual values; it must take active steps to transmit the moral precepts. Both the school and the home need to work at the problem of guiding teen-agers in the recognition, the acceptance, and the practice of the rules for playing the game of life.

What are these principles by which men might live richer and fuller lives? These three are proposed:

1. *Homo sapiens* or man is a creature of supreme earthly dignity and worth. Each man has an equal right with other men to achieve to the limit of his capacity. A teacher recognizes every teen-ager as having dignity and being worthy of respect. Through teaching, one renders a service to mankind; hence, teachers, to a greater extent than most other occupational groups, probably practice a valid rule for

[9] Educational Policies Commission, *Education for All American Youth—A Further Look* (Washington, D. C., National Education Association, 1952), pp. 84-103.

establishing good human relations by "doing unto others as they would that others do unto them." Currently, there is some criticism of teachers for being too pliant or failing to help teen-agers achieve according to their potentialities. We quickly acknowledge that such possibilities exist and recognize that being too easy may harm rather than help students.

2. It is recognized that all men belong to the same human family; there is no superior race of men. Hence, neither color, nor race, nor creed in themselves make a human being inferior or superior. Given like environments and equal opportunities a man of any color, race, or creed can acquire a culture and reflect it in his daily life. However, this does not imply that all men are equal in capacity to achieve. Individual differences do exist among men as individuals, but the color of their skin, their creed, or their race as such is not a significant factor in acquiring a particular culture or in their ability to make a good high school record.

3. Men must be free to reach decisions on the basis of truth. Thomas Jefferson selected this passage as a motto for the University of Virginia, "and ye shall know the Truth and the Truth shall make you free." It is an expression of democratic faith. The search for truth is never-ending, and such research is now a part of our social heritage. A cure for cancer, a better hybrid corn, a reduction of smog in our cities, an improvement in human relations—all represent a quest for truth.

It has been said, "democracy asks that there be a search for truth; truth then stands on its own merits, accepted by men of good will who determine their course on the basis of fact rather than fancy."[10] What makes "right" right? After all, what is the right way in education, and what determines right from wrong? Free use of the intellect should indicate the proper course of education. One quite thorough and extensive study of Abrams[11] indicated that where college students sense that a devotion to certain values is expected of them or where a college course sets out to involve the student in a real-life situation of social or political action, colleges do appear to have a definite influence on students. On the high school level where the research has been much less extensive, one could expect similar findings.

But unless the truth, when found, is recognized, accepted, and used, the search has been in vain. If people do not like the truth, they just ignore it. It neither makes them free, nor enslaves them. However, there is some evidence to indicate that there are teachers who can and do build favorable attitudes toward both a search for truth and its accept-

[10] Paul B. Jacobson, *The American Secondary School* (Englewood Cliffs, N. J., Prentice-Hall, Inc., 1952), p. 73.

[11] Irving Abrams, "What Is Missing on the Campus," *The Phi Delta Kappan* 39: 310-313 (April, 1958).

ance when found. In cases such as this, the teacher himself is relatively free of bias; he has a highly favorable attitude toward searching for the related facts. He can guide a class with enthusiasm through the selection and organization of the related facts to the right answer or truth. Apparently, a highly important factor is the extent to which the members of the class, themselves, become involved as individuals in the search for truth. When they become so involved, they accept the truth when found.

Our Past Deeply Influences Our Concept of Education. America was settled by people who sought a better way of life—an escape from the tyrannies and restraints suffered by the European peasantry. They came to the New World at a time when John Locke and Jean-Jacques Rousseau were laying the intellectual foundation for popular rule—the theory that sovereignty belonged squarely in the hands of all the people.

America is a nation of many racial and national origins; we are a mixture of a number of the cultural patterns of the world. In the early periods, the colonists came from Northern European stock and were mostly Protestant by religion. After 1850, immigrants from all parts of the world were attracted to our shores. The schools took the children of these newcomers, taught them English, and made them good citizens. In time, the adult immigrant was given an opportunity to attend citizenship classes. Here today, we bring together Lithuanians and Russians, Germans and Jews, Swedes and Danes—all arch-enemies of each other from the Old World. Through the schools, they learn to live together as new Americans. But they inevitably cling to certain Old World concepts, particularly in family relationships. Some are as follows:

1. The male is superior to the female.
2. All children must work as early as possible.
3. All earnings must go into a single fund for the family.
4. Hunger is the first enemy to conquer.
5. Old World religions are superior.
6. Children must support the elders in the family.

The conflicts that abide in these deep loyalties are at the roots of many contemporary economic, social, and political problems in our culture. Most certainly they are reflected in our schools each day.

That America was settled by common people is on the record, but the fact that they had the initiative to cross an ocean and face the hardships of a wilderness indicates that a selection of a positive nature was taking place.[12]

Why did these common people rise to power? As developed by Counts, here are the factors:

1. They learned how to take life by the long rifle and Colt's revolver. In Europe they had been forbidden to use or own firearms or weapons.

[12] Counts, *op. cit.*, p. 74.

2. They achieved a large measure of economic power through the ownership of land. Social situations in Europe prevented this economic rise for most of them.

3. They achieved a large measure of political power through winning the right to choose their rulers. In Europe this right resided only in the upper classes.

4. They proclaimed the principle of human equality by nurturing the doctrine that the individual, regardless of ancestry or previous background, should be judged only by his own industry, talents and character. A man should be judged by what he is and what he can do and not by previous social status.

Early America was a free society of farmers and tradesmen. It was a pre-industrial society—a land of farm families in rural neighborhoods. The economy was based upon individual and private enterprise. Private property in the land and in the tools of production was the basic institution and most people pursued the same or similar occupations. As a rule, the people worked for themselves. Government played a very minor role in early America.

Out of this environment and way of life have come many deep-seated beliefs and attitudes that still persist. Some of them, in our present industrial age, need to be examined and adapted to our modern status. One might well ask this question, "What elements of our social heritage need to be held fast and transmitted to our children through the offices of the secondary school?"

SOME FUNDAMENTAL SCHOOL-SOCIETY RELATIONSHIPS

Our Democratic Society and the American High School. The high school will reflect in its program the society that supports it. Since ours is a democratic society, the high school program will promote the democratic way of life. A generation ago, Alexander Inglis[13] stated clearly the several implications to the proposal that the American high school conform to democratic ideals and organizations, as follows:

The school's obligation. To participate intelligently in American society one must: (1) be able to discharge one's responsibility as a voter and to carry one's burden of political responsibility, (2) be able to contribute to world services and world goods as much as one consumes, (3) behave in such a manner at leisure and at work as will not interfere with the interests of society at large nor violate the rights of other individuals in that society. The total educational provisions for the development of these three types of behavior, in a society such as the United States, has a prior claim upon curriculum, methods, and the objectives of the high school. Too much emphasis upon the education of the individual, especially upon the interests of the individuals, is contrary to the social function and character of the high school and opposed to the nature of American society.

[13] Alexander Inglis, *Principles of Secondary Education* (Boston, Houghton Mifflin Co., 1918), pp. 342-44.

Education for citizenship is necessary. In our type of evolutionary, democratic society, each individual must be prepared to participate, directly or indirectly, in the making of laws or the setting of custom. Because our economic and social life is constantly growing more complex, the need for social and civic education is very important and constantly increasing.

Education for participation in control and support of the public school. The political responsibility of citizens, which involves control of social institutions of a public nature, includes the responsibility for particpating in the direction and control of the public schools. The public school must not only prepare for democracy, it must be controlled and operated through democracy.

A statement of the Educational Policies Commission,[14] in 1940, added to Inglis' ideas, as follows:

Learn the ways of democracy in school through participation. In a democratic society such as ours, a youth should be trained for democracy not only by the materials of instruction but by providing opportunities for democratic living with his fellows and his teachers in the school as well as participation in the learning activities of himself and his fellows. The trend of the last 20 years extends this principle even farther to include democratic relationships as between administrators and teachers as well as between teacher and teacher.

Prepare students for changes in our evolutionary society. In times of rapid change in a society, such as ours, the school should prepare students not only to adjust to society as it changes but also to participate in learning the nature of the changes as they are taking place. For example, our high school students need help in adjusting to the atom bomb and the changes in our society that will result by its widespread use as a source of power. We need to help teen-agers anticipate changes that are coming.

Individual Interests and the Interests of Society. Usually, the welfare of the individual is not in conflict with that of society; thus, what is good for society is usually good for the individual. In America, the state is a political as well as a social device for achieving common ends, for advancing common welfare, and for benefiting the individual. In the totalitarian state this is not the case; there the individual exists only to serve the state. He has no rights or privileges except as the state grants them. With us the state acts to provide only such services as would be very difficult for the individual to furnish—common defense, provision for exports and imports, police protection, a supply of pure water, maintenance of street and roads, protection from impure foods and drugs, and others. Educating future citizens to best serve the state is educating them to serve themselves and others equally on matters common to the welfare of all. The interests of individuals are best served when all are educated in such a way as to participate as leaders and followers.

[14] Educational Policies Commission, *Learning the Ways of Democracy—A Casebook in Civic Education* (Washington, D. C., National Education Association and the American Association of School Administrators, 1940), p. 326.

Teachers are accused sometimes of failing to emphasize society's stake in education. Perhaps this is due to the fact that the interests of individual teachers are too closely bound up with the selfish interests of students and that there is no active pressure brought upon teachers to develop an alert program to serve the common interests of society. As professional people, teachers have the important responsibility to see that the interests of society are not subordinated to the direct and selfish classroom interests of students and teachers. Teachers and educators are the official agents and representatives of society.[15]

Teachers need to remember that the school in the United States is an institution provided for and supported by society. It is a social institution maintained for the purpose of helping to uphold the stability of society and of directing and accelerating its progress.

In America all individuals are taxed for the public school, even individuals who have no children and those who send their children to non-public schools. Individuals are also taxed according to wealth and income rather than according to the number of children they have in school. Upon no assumption other than that the school is a social institution established for the common welfare and for the interest of society could these practices be justified. In support of this, over and over again in the history of public education, it has been asserted that public education decreases the cost of crime. While citizens usually maintain that the school system does not exist for the benefit of the individual but for the common welfare, all are completely aware that both the public and the state benefit greatly by increased productivity of services, greater discrimination in voting and personal decisions, and the increased social effectiveness of the literate person.

The Relation of the School to Other Educational Agencies. The public school is only one among many educational agencies of our society. The home, the church, the press, the radio, the movies, and television are some of these agencies. When rapid changes take place in a society such as ours, it is necessary for teachers to be alert and to adapt and adjust the school's program to the changing society. As changes in industry cause changes in the home, it becomes necessary for the school to assume the responsibility for education formerly provided by the home. Indeed, this trend has been accepted all too readily by many homes, for the home still has a moral obligation to educate the young, despite social changes. Resources of the school are limited and budgets are geared to the needs of an earlier day; at what point should the school decline to offer added services?

For example, if one half of all mothers in a community are now working outside their homes, the school might extend its day from eight

[15] Harl R. Douglass, *Secondary Education* (New York, The Ronald Press Company, 1952), p. 60.

in the morning until five in the afternoon and add a nursery school. At what point does education become nothing more than mere baby-sitting? And should society still pay the costs of such added services?

One of the traits of human nature is the desire to secure "something for nothing," and it often becomes manifest in home-school relationships. Certainly, it is the obligation of the school to distinguish clearly between services that are educational and those that are not in setting up a school program. If society continues to change and if schools are asked to take more complete charge of all young people for a major part of the day, then society must be prepared to pay the added tax dollars.

EXTENDING DEMOCRACY

We hold these truths to be self-evident, that all men are created equal, they are endowed by their Creator with certain unalienable rights . . . That to secure these rights, Governments are instituted among men, deriving their just powers from the consent of the governed.

In the century and a half that has elapsed since Thomas Jefferson penned the above words, as a part of the Declaration of Independence, our culture has attempted to live up to the stated ideal. Americans generally will agree that one qualified for a job should be employed without regard for race, creed, or political belief. This expression of fairness does not necessarily commit Americans to follow it. We believe in democracy though many of us actually violate our beliefs in practice. Is democracy in America still growing?

Extending Democracy to All Minority Groups. Can it be done? The answer is neither an unqualified *no* nor an unqualified *yes*. However, the proposition that all men are created equal has been repeated in our time. On July 18, 1950, a UNESCO committee of experts on race relations reported: "There is no superior race. There is only one race, the human race or *homo sapiens*."[16] A thoughtful American anthropologist, Franz Boaz, expressed the same idea in 1890, but the UNESCO committee statement has the extensive research of the intervening years to support its finding in 1950. Even as some of us will still insist that our earth is flat and not round, so there is a vigorous minority who refuse to accept the proposition of racial equality.

In its decision to bar segregation in all areas of the American public school, the United States Supreme Court probably expressed the general attitude and desire of a majority of the American people.[17] But the

[16] UNESCO Committee on Race Relations, "The Scientific Basis for Human Relations," *The Phi Delta Kappan* 36:34-36 (October, 1954).

[17] Supreme Court Ruling, Brown versus Board of Education, 347, U. S. 483. Chief Justice Earl Warren commented: "In the field of public education, the doctrine of separate but equal has no place. Separate educational facilities are inherently unequal."

very fact that the Supreme Court was called upon for a decision reveals the strength of the minority. There is indeed discrimination against
the Negro in the Southeast and South; against the Mexican in the West
and Southwest; against the Oriental in the West; and against the
American Indian everywhere. In all parts of our nation, there are
those who greatly desire to extend discrimination. It is no longer a
sectional conflict; the accusing finger can be pointed at neither North,
South, East, or West as the culprit. All areas are guilty of practicing
discrimination.

It is not the purpose of this textbook to enter the controversy, but
the pre-service teacher needs to dwell seriously upon the issues. The
following observations may stimulate additional thinking.

Is this the American Way? The Emancipation Proclamation of Abraham Lincoln changed the economic base of the Southern States from one
of slavery to one of a free economy. Students of cultural evolution
know that dramatic changes come slowly. Even a much more simple
social problem, safety on our highways, is being solved very slowly
since it requires changes in *attitude*. The Negro has been living in
America for three centuries and knows no culture other than ours.
Legally, a century has passed since the transition from slavery to
citizenry began. It is relatively easy for law-abiding Americans to see
that many of the Negro race have risen to positions of prominence in
education, literature, law, scientific research, and social service. In
industry, the Negro has shown a capacity to develop the type of highly
technical skills needed for high productivity. This ready adaptation
to the American Way of Life is destined to lead gradually to full acceptance in all parts of the United States, even though all other means may
fail.

Does democracy include everyone? De-segregation for the Indian, the
Mexican, and the Oriental involves fewer persons than for the Negro,
but greater variation in cultural patterns and ways of life. Most of
the Mexicans, the Orientals, and the Indians are located in the western
part of the United States. The Indian no longer feels at home in the
continent where his forefathers hunted and fought and lived. Instead,
there are many indications that the Indian has come to feel that taking
on American ways is preferable to the narrow and restricted life of the
reservation. Seemingly, a time has arrived when the Indian is willing
to accept first-class citizenship.

Intellectual power varies in all races. The Mexican peon, in large
numbers, is a recent addition to America's minority groups. Higher wages
and better living conditions have attracted them to our agricultural areas,
and many have settled down to living in our way. Some teachers who
have worked with Mexican teen-agers believe them to be somewhat
less receptive to high school education than the native white or Negro.

But *by our own standards of culture*, we find the Mexican just as prominent in art, science, music, and sculpture as any other human. All races
provide their slow and rapid learners, as well as the gifted, and it is
not realistic to single out any segment and pretend that it represents the
whole. The marvel is that there are members of minority groups who
have achieved outstanding success despite their lack of opportunities and
their limited home backgrounds.

Do we fear economic strife? The following statement about the Oriental reveals two of the factors that operate in producing minority group
problems. Hicks states:

Japanese immigration into the United States, beginning about 1900, was a
source of friction. By 1906, the number of Japanese residents in the Pacific
States had reached about 75 thousand and they had begun to give native
Americans strenuous *competition* as day laborers and market gardeners. They
even bought land, and by swarming over it, *broke down the land values* of
neighboring tracts, and then bought still more. Racial antagonism was easily
stirred, and in 1906 the San Francisco board of education decided on separate
schools for Japanese children, a discrimination that was deeply resented by the
sensitive Japanese.[18]

While the factors causing tension with minority groups will vary,
economic competition and *breaking down of property values* are constant. By and large, all members of such groups are citizens of the United
States and have all the rights, the privileges, and the responsibilities of
Americans. One of these rights is equality of opportunity for free public
education.

Extension of Democracy Through Extension of Suffrage. Another tenet
of our American faith, as expressed by Thomas Jefferson, holds that
"governments . . . derive their just powers from the consent of the
governed." This means that in a democracy the citizens express their
will through suffrage or by casting a vote. Has there been an extension
of suffrage since the establishment of the American Republic?

It has been estimated that less than one-fifth of the entire male population enjoyed the right to vote in 1789.[19] At that time ownership of
property and the payment of taxes were prerequisites for voting. It
was almost a universal conviction that landless men and non-taxpayers,
who had no property or stake in the government, were unfit to help in the
making of laws and their administration.

But men and women who were discontented with their lot in the seaboard states moved to the relatively free lands on the frontier. And
there, democracy based upon manhood suffrage was born. Every man

[18] John D. Hicks, *The American Nation: A History of the United States from 1865
to the Present* (Boston, Houghton Mifflin Co., 1943), p. 360.
[19] Edward H. Reisner, *Nationalism and Education Since 1789* (New York, The
Macmillan Co., 1922), p. 330.

owned his homestead; a man was respected for what he could do; and social rank had no place. Every man had the right to vote, and he exercised it. As governments came into being, they were made much more responsible to the popular will than had been the case on the seaboard.

The older states felt the economic impact of this movement toward manhood suffrage. When men and women became dissatisfied with arbitrary decisions in local coastal areas, they joined in the move to the frontier.

A steady stream of emigrants made their way into the back country . . . in the regions West of the mountains. It is reported that even whole villages with their pastors and schoolmasters moved into the new land of promise. The older communities began to see in their loss of population and the rapid growth of the new sections not only economic decay, but the loss of representation in national affairs.[20]

One by one, the northeastern states established manhood suffrage. Extension of suffrage did not come to the southern states until after the Jacksonian political revolution. Manhood suffrage, even with all restrictions removed, to this day has not been completely achieved in the South.

In American history, 1829-1860 is known as the era of reform. To many women, such movements as anti-slavery, temperance, and the improvement of prisons and hospitals were highly essential for public welfare. But when able women appeared before groups to promote these reforms, they were ridiculed—women simply were not expected to do such things. Women such as Lucy Stone and Susan B. Anthony realized that to accomplish anything as reformers they must first achieve a more honorable position for themselves. Thus, the Women's Rights Movement was born, and one of the rights demanded was the extension of suffrage to all women. From 1870 to 1920, a continuous and strong campaign was waged by capable women for the extension of suffrage. The spark that set it off was the extension of suffrage to former slaves by the Fifteenth Amendment to the Federal Constitution. On August 26, 1920, just a half century after the campaign started, suffrage was extended to women by the Nineteenth Amendment. At that point, the development of civic competence through the high school program became equally as important for girls as for boys.

Restrictions on Suffrage. By recent count, however, 15 states require that the voter must pass a literacy test; five have a poll tax that must be paid before voting; and only two permit eighteen-year-old citizens to cast the ballot. In most states, registration of all or part of the voters is required. If literacy tests exist as such, it is implied that there are

[20] *Ibid.*, p. 333.

American citizens who cannot read and are, therefore, limited in their power to exercise suffrage. If the poll tax exists, it is also implied that there are some Americans who cannot afford a small fee for the privilege of voting. And if only two states, Georgia and Kentucky, permit teen-agers to vote, it may be assumed that the other 48 states are not quite satisfied with the ability of youth to make important decisions. What has this to do with the high schools?

Many secondary school teachers and administrators favor lowering the voting age to 18. They believe that students on the senior high school level are capable of passing the literacy tests and that almost all of them are earning enough money for payment of poll taxes. The simple act of registration can be done by any educated person, and literacy tests usually require the reading of a passage from the state constitution, something every high school senior might easily do.

But real participation in citizenship calls for active thinking and sound judgment on political issues. Legally, at 18, a youth can teach school, make contracts, operate a private business; more to the point, he is considered mature enough to wear his country's uniform and take part in military action. It seems equally important for him to take part and have some voice in determining the policies of his local and national government. The high school generally would welcome this extension of democracy so that teen-agers would have the right to vote. Through this, citizenship habits established early will continue as life-long habits. But, are eighteen-year-olds mature enough to vote? Are they experienced enough to judge political issues wisely? A goodly number of American citizens believe that they can be trusted with the suffrage. What is your opinion on this issue?

Threats to the Success of Democracy. Not all of the changes in our society have been on the credit side of the ledger. Some of them have been unfavorable to the growth and extension of democracy. In recent years, a few giant corporations have acquired assets greater than the whole of the United States at the time of the Civil War. Such corporations as U. S. Steel and General Motors have for several years in succession had an annual profit greater than the profits of all business in 1860. There is nothing necessarily evil in big business nor in big profits. The mass production of goods and services has cut the cost of production and of goods to the consumer. Materials and services are now available to many Americans where formerly only the well-to-do could afford them. But great wealth exerts an alarming influence upon the government, the press, radio, and television. Without the vast sums from advertising, the press, as we well know, could not survive; and without commercial sponsorship, radio and television would fold up. The most reputable magazines, with few exceptions, depend upon advertising copy from corporations to keep solvent.

The cost of campaigns for public office has become so great at the national level (and even on state levels for governorships) that without outside help, no persons other than wealthy men can afford to finance a strong campaign. Under present conditions, the campaigns are financed by commercial and business organizations on one hand—and labor unions on the other. Both sides are aware of the dangers here indicated, and both have suggested sharp limitations to be placed upon the amounts of money to be spent in political campaigning. It is realistic to assume that, should the present trend continue unchecked, our government will be completely dominated by pressure groups and forces. No longer will it be a government of the people, by the people, and for the people.

Furthermore, there are other threats to democracy that may be summarized as follows:

1. The lassitude of nearly half of our qualified voters in circumstances that permit universal suffrage.

2. The quirk that drives humans to follow the demagogue.

3. The immature acceptance of material well being as ample evidence of status and worthiness.

4. The tendency to give leadership full responsibility without mass support and assistance.

5. The attitude that cheating the government is justifiable; that payment of taxes is unworthy; that it is smart to get something for nothing.

These are attitudes that are not a credit to the American Way of Life. What might a high school staff do in the education of our future citizens to help them manifest decency in their attitudes toward each other and our government?

1. Give added emphasis to the ideals of the common welfare, of fair dealing, of honest and efficient government, and of democracy itself.

2. Provide for the continuous development of all pupils through a program of orientation to the problems that confront our democracy in the critical analysis of printed material and the spoken word and in clear and logical thinking about matters of economics and government.

The solution is to be found in educating all of our youth to desire the attainments and achievements of democratic ideals. They must be armed with the skills, habits, and understandings that will protect them from those influences which would prevent them from having knowledge of democracy and its blessings.

DISCUSSION PROBLEMS

1. The United States Chamber of Commerce supports the annual Business-Industry-Education Days and encourages the recognition of a teacher-of-the-year. Yet, this organization, along with the National Association of Manufacturers and the Farm Bureau Federation, opposes federal aid to education. Are these policies consistent?

2. What is meant by "guilt by association" and how have social forces capitalized upon this technique in the case of the schools?
3. Should all national issues be discussed in the classroom?
4. Can you cite examples, based on social change, of how your adolescence differed from that of your parents?
5. Why are educated workers essential to a modern industrial society?
6. How did the frontier heritage contribute to the development of American democracy?
7. Most American communities display cultural concepts which are importations from other cultures. Have you observed any in your community?
8. Do the interests of the individual and the society always agree. Should they?
9. Can we really extend democracy to all American minority groups?

RELATED REFERENCES

ABRAMS, Irving, "What Is Missing on the Campus," *The Phi Delta Kappan* 39:310-313 (April, 1958).

ADAMS, James T., *The Epic of America* (Boston, Little, Brown & Co., 1931).

BROWN, Francis J., *Educational Sociology*, 2nd ed. (Englewood Cliffs, N. J., Prentice-Hall, Inc., 1954).

CASWELL, Hollis L., *The American High School*, 8th Yearbook of the John Dewey Society (New York, Harper & Brothers, 1946).

CHURCHILL, Winston, *History of the English Speaking People*, Vol. 4, *The Great Democracies* (New York, Dodd, Mead & Co., 1958).

CONANT, James B., *Education and Liberty* (Cambridge, Mass., Harvard University Press, 1953).

COUNTS, George S., *Education and American Civilization* (New York, Bureau of Publications, Teachers College, Columbia University, 1952).

———, and LODGE, Lucia P., *I Want to Be Like Stalin* (New York, The John Day Company, Inc., 1947) (from the Russian text on pedagogy by B. P. Yesipov and N. K. Gonihorov).

Chamber of Commerce, Department of Education, *Investment in People* (Washington, D. C., The Chamber, 1955).

DEUEL, Leo, ed., *The Teacher's Treasure Chest: The Little Black Boys* (Englewood Cliffs, N. J., Prentice-Hall, Inc., 1956).

DOUGLASS, Harl R., *Secondary Education* (New York, The Ronald Press Company, 1952).

Educational Policies Commission, *Education for All American Youth—A Further Look*, rev. ed. (Washington, D. C., National Education Association, 1952).

Learning the Ways of Democracy—A Casebook in Civic Education (Washington, D. C., National Education Association and the American Association of School Administrators, 1940).

EDWARDS, Newton, and RICHEY, Herman G., *The School in the American Social Order* (Boston, Houghton Mifflin Co., 1947).

GITTLER, J. B., *Understanding Minority Groups* (New York, John Wiley & Sons, Inc., 1956).

HICKS, John D., *The American Nation: A History of the United States from 1865 to the Present* (Boston, Houghton Mifflin Co., 1943).

INGLIS, Alexander, *Principles of Secondary Education* (Boston, Houghton Mifflin Co., 1918).

JACOBSON, Paul B., *The American Secondary School* (Englewood Cliffs, N. J., Prentice-Hall, Inc., 1952).

LILIENTHAL, David E., *This I Do Believe* (New York, Harper & Brothers, 1949).

MACCONNELL, C. M., MELBY, Ernest O., and ARNDT, Christian O., *New Schools for a New Culture* (New York, Harper & Brothers, 1943).

REISNER, Edward H., *Nationalism and Education Since 1789; A Social and Political History of Modern Education* (New York, The Macmillan Company, 1922).

RUGG, Earle U., "Our Greatest Social Achievement," *The Phi Delta Kappan* 38:69-74 (November, 1955).

RUGG, Harold, and WITHERS, William, *Social Foundations of Education* (Englewood Cliffs, N. J., Prentice-Hall, Inc., 1955).

THORNDIKE, Edward L., *Your City* (New York, Harcourt, Brace & Co., 1939).

TYLER, Ralph W., "The Responsibility of the School for the Improvement of American Life," *School Review* 52:400-405 (September, 1944).

UNESCO Committee on Race Relations, "The Scientific Basis for Human Relations," *The Phi Delta Kappan* 36:34-36 (October 1954).

Chapter 3

PERSISTENT CONFLICTS

ABOUT HIGH SCHOOL EDUCATION

*The health of democracies, of whatever type and range, depends on
. . . electoral procedure . . . if the regime of the elections is successful,
if it is in accordance with reality, all goes well; if not . . . all goes wrong.*
—José Ortega y Gasset, *Revolt of the Masses*

Americans have seldom hesitated to criticize their Presidents, Congresses, and Supreme Courts, and frequently they have been highly critical of their ministers, schoolmasters, local politicians, newspapers, neighbors, wives, and husbands. Censure is a part of the American culture, and it reaches full force when the umpire calls Willie Mays "out on second!" Criticism, then, does not necessarily mean that any ethical code has been violated; it is merely a way of expression in this land.

CONTINUING CROSSCURRENTS IN AMERICAN EDUCATION
SINCE 1607

Americans are not alone in their desire to censure the activities of the school. Criticisms and changes have been continuous in curriculum and methods of teaching from the beginning of recorded history. Then as now, there were men who believed that the "good old ways" were to be preferred to the present practice with its uncertainty and its experimentation. The successions of criticisms and changes illustrate a fact of basic importance: the continuity of effort to bring curriculums into line with the greater knowledge of how youth learn and acquire the tribal or national heritage.[1]

Clay tablets representing some of the most ancient of civilizations (5,000 to 6,000 years ago) contain statements from irate taxpayers and parents that are similar to those being published in contemporary Amer-

[1] William H. Burton, and Leo J. Brueckner, *Supervision: A Social Process*, 3rd ed. (New York, Appleton-Century-Crofts, Inc., 1955), p. 689.

ican newspapers and magazines. In the intervening years, innovators of new movements such as Confucius, St. Augustine, and Rousseau reveal that the "old ways" were revered by many parents and taxpayers whenever changing times required the acceptance of new ways.

Conflicts Arise in the Colonial Period. Fate brought together in America Calvinists, Anglicans, Quakers, Catholics, and men and women from many different cultures and with diverse concepts about government, religion, and the function of the school in a society. Profound changes in the institutional life of colonial America and the ferment in this institutional life led men to think harder.[2] Similar profound changes have occurred in the United States since 1930 with similar results: we are thinking harder and harder about education today.

The turmoil over education during the colonial period produced these major conflicts: (1) an authoritarian concept of child nature *began* to be softened by a less severe attitude toward discipline and more careful attention being paid to the child as a person to be valued for himself, that is, the authoritarian versus the liberal conflict; (2) the exclusively classical and humanistic quality of secondary and higher education *began* to be widened to include practical and utilitarian goals, that is the classical and humanitarian versus the practical and utilitarian conflict; (3) the aristocratic and private character of education *began* to be challenged by a more democratic kind of education to be achieved by public control and support, that is, the public versus the private control conflict; (4) also, the trend of thought concerning the nature and purpose of colleges in the colonial period reflected a similar controversy, that is, the religious and classical versus the scientific and utilitarian conflict.

Battles over the Founding of a Public School System in the New Nation. In the years between 1779 and 1865, American society took on the characteristics which distinguished it from its European antecedents. The conflicts within the colonies over education continued under the republic along with new issues arising from the establishment of a new nation. Successions of issues and changes operated to produce national growth and development—conflicts led to struggles and struggles led to changes. The old colonial conflicts gradually brought about changes which in turn caused new conflicts to arise.

In 1779, Thomas Jefferson introduced a bill in the Virginia Assembly under the title, "For the More General Diffusion of Knowledge." The bill did not pass. It did, however, stir up a furor of bitter conflict. In defense of his bill, Jefferson proposed that in a free society public schools designed to serve the whole public must be under governmental direction and free

[2] See R. Freeman Butts and Lawrence A. Cremin, *A History of Education in American Culture* (New York, Henry Holt & Co., Inc., 1953), Chs. 3, 7, 11, and 15. (There are no direct quotes but some paraphrasing from these chapters for the next few pages.)

from religious, sectarian, or private control. Americans by no means were of one mind about this. Many opposing ideas about education vied for acceptance. Perhaps the four most controversial were: (1) universal education versus education for the few, (2) public tax support of education versus private support, (3) state control versus local or church control, and (4) elective versus prescribed courses.

From 1830 to 1850 every effort to establish an educational system such as we now know in the United States was bitterly contested; nevertheless, the movement succeeded. The need for citizens of a free society to be educated was accepted by nearly everyone; universal education was criticized only when it was associated with tax support or public control. On the other hand, a strong minority of citizens believed that the government must both support and control education in order to produce political enlightenment, patriotism, and equality of opportunity. During the latter part of this period, a strong movement arose to provide special professional education for teachers and to expand the school curriculum by making the subject content more practical. Please note that the conflicts about education persist. While changes in education occurred and were accepted by a larger and larger proportion of citizens, nearly identical criticisms, in a later period, were expressed again and again by a smaller portion of the population. When tensions in our nation increase, the demands for educational change become acute and shrill.

Controversy and Conflict over Education Rages on (1869 to 1918). As the Civil War came to a close the educational conflicts of the 1830's and 1840's, which had been pushed aside, came again to the fore. Education on elementary, secondary, and university levels had become an integral part of the American Way. While all had accepted education as an essential service to young citizens, not all were in agreement as to who should control and operate the schools. Controversy raged in the public press and at many public forums over the principal issues. The following is a brief summary of the major issues.

Equalizing educational opportunity. This was the age of dreamers.[3] One of these dreams was to make education equally available to all. Citizens, looking about, noted that many children were not in school, even though a school was near at hand. Hence, a movement was born— compulsory education. Parents must be compelled to send their children to school. Shortly, state legislatures began enacting compulsory education laws, and immediately there was an issue: it is the duty of parents to send their children to school, yet can the state so infringe upon the inviolable rights of parents? This is still an issue, though a less torrid one now than then.

[3] Stewart H. Holbrook, *Dreamers of the American Dream* (Garden City, N. Y., Doubleday & Company Inc., 1957). Provides a commendable discussion of the activities of some minority groups.

The Fourteenth Amendment to the Constitution had made Negroes both citizens and voters. Although the principle of equal educational opportunity was accepted generally, Americans divided into three groups on the issue of schools for Negroes: (1) Negroes are too stupid to learn, (2) there must be separate schools for Negroes and whites, and (3) there should be common schools for all. For races other than white or Negro, the issue was common schools for all versus segregated schools.

Public high school education. Is the high school a common school? Most citizens of the 1870's answered "no" with conviction. It had always been a school for the elect. However, boards of education did finance high schools from tax funds. The Kalamazoo Decision of 1874 settled the issue by ruling that boards of education could levy taxes for the support of the high school.

Can the high school offer other than academic courses? In this period of the 1870's to the 1890's, all past tradition opposed it; however, the academies had introduced practical subjects at the request of parents. Still, parents were pragmatists who wanted their sons and daughters to study practical as well as academic subjects. What parents wanted in a community school supported by parents, they could get. Hence, more and more practical subjects were introduced as additions to the academic program.[4] Of course, there were conflicts over this issue—bitter ones.

What is the purpose or purposes of the high school? Is its only purpose to prepare students for college? Or is it a many-purposed institution— to prepare students for college, for citizenship, for earning a living, for learning to co-operate with others? Gradually, but only with difficulty, was this issue resolved in part. The high school came to be accepted by most communities as a many-purposed institution. Yet, some of the severest criticisms of the 1950's have revolved around this issue.

Who should control and support the high school? Should the federal government both support and control the high school? A small minority group has always been in favor of placing our high schools under the control of the federal government. Should the federal government support the high school in part or entirely but without any control over it? A strong minority group believes this to be the proper relationship between the high school and the government. Should the federal government provide neither support nor control of the high school? In general, a sizeable majority has been able to maintain this as the correct relationship. Yet the size of this majority varies widely from time to time.

Incidentally, the same issues have prevailed as to state support and control. In the 1880's and 90's, the public opposed either federal control or state support; this issue has not been entirely resolved in the intervening time between then and now.

[4] Carter V. Good, *Dictionary of Education* (New York, McGraw-Hill Book Co., 1945). Defines *academic* as pertaining to the fields of English, foreign languages, history, economics, mathematics, and science.

Religious education in the high school was a burning issue during the latter part of the nineteenth century. However, no religious sect would permit religion to be taught in the public school. It remained an unresolved issue.

Finally, teacher education was accepted by the public and developed rapidly in this period. The public was impressed both by the improvement in teaching and the increased supply of capable teachers.

Crises, Critics, and Criticisms Flourish (1918 to the Present). Between the end of World War I and 1960, the United States has passed through a soul-searching depression, has fought World War II, and has occupied the position of a leader nation in the cold war between Communism and the Western Block of Free Nations. We have been and still are in a period of insecurity and uncertainty. The World War II draft revealed that one-fourth of our youth were physically unfit and that another one-tenth could not read simple instructions or do easy arithmetic. This was basic information, and the critics made the most of it. Isn't it natural to expect that the motives of the critics might involve (1) those who honestly believe that the schools could do better, (2) those who dislike paying taxes for any purpose, (3) special interest groups who would like to have the schools serve their own purposes, and (4) those who are really not informed about the schools they criticize? For two decades criticism of education, especially secondary education, has been rampant. The issues that stand out are the following:

Integration. Racial segregation has been a decidedly taut phase of this issue. In a unanimous decision, May 17, 1954, the Supreme Court ruled that racial segregation is unconstitutional.[5] Some changes favorable to integration[6] have occurred, and it is probable that integration will ultimately be established throughout our country.

Conflicts over support and control of education. This issue has been aptly stated in the form of a question, "Should America continue its experiment to maintain public and private systems side by side, should it give greater emphasis to public education, or should it encourage private institutions to become a major factor in American education?" Two Supreme Court decisions give a partial answer to this question. In Meyer vs. Nebraska,[7] 1923, and Pierce vs. Society of Sisters,[8] 1924, (Oregon) the Supreme Court ruled: (1) The state can compel children to attend school, and it can set up reasonable regulations. But it has no right to compel all children to attend a public school. (2) No tax in any amount can be levied to support religious activities. What conclusions should you draw from these two cases? Recently, there has been a vigor-

---

[5] Brown vs. Board of Education 347 U.S. 483 (1954).
[6] Integration—a common school for the children of all citizens.
[7] Meyer vs. Nebraska 262 U.S. 390 (1923).
[8] Pierce vs. Society of Sisters 268 U.S. 510 (1924), pp. 534-535.

ous movement among some religious groups, especially the Roman Catholics, to secure public assistance for support of parochial schools.

Federal aid to education. Research studies in recent years indicate that the quality of education, in part, is dependent upon the economic ability of a community or a state to finance education. Research also reveals that the economic capacity from state to state and from community to community varies widely. Naturally, a movement has developed to reduce these variations in the quality of education. Congress was urged to provide federal aid. Bills were prepared and had strong support, but they failed to pass. It has been charged that tension over aid to parochial schools and the segregation issue are the causes of the failure.[9]

Controversies over the Educational Program. A deluge of magazine articles, pamphlets, and books has descended upon us in recent years criticizing the public schools. Be not dismayed, for actually the schools are becoming better all the time. There was a good reason for some of the criticisms at the end of the severe depression and after World War II; there were improvements that needed to be made. Also, there is a striking paradox between the critics of the 1920's and those of today. Then, they were denouncing old-fashioned and worn-out methods of teaching. Learning from books was being devalued, and the fundamental skills of the 3 R's were being criticized, as well as the acquisition of factual information without understanding. The recent critics have done just the reverse. They have criticized the schools for neglecting the 3 R's, for soft pedagogy, for a too-limited use of books, and for too little emphasis upon memorization. Criticisms can not be taken literally; one must ask what are the basic values of the critic?

As one traces the conflicts and clashes over education from early Colonial times to now, one fact stands out—the issues are nearly identical and have been persistent throughout American history. These common and persisting issues are: (1) the classical and humanistic versus the practical and utilitarian, (2) universal education for all versus education for the favored, (3) state support and control of education versus private support and control, (4) professionalization of the teaching vocation versus treating it as a skilled trade, and (5) equalizing educational opportunity.

In the section that follows, the emphasis will be upon the critics and their criticisms. What are the conflicts that have caused these criticisms? What features of the high school are under fire?

SOURCES OF MAJOR CRITICISMS OF THE HIGH SCHOOL

Many high school teachers report that in their communities it is quite difficult to get students to take their work seriously. While many parents

[9] Butts and Cremin, *op. cit.*, pp. 534-538.

think that it is quite necessary for their teen-agers to complete high school—it is the expected thing—many of them care little about the quality of work done.

Ortega y Gasset has applied to this type of behavior the term, "Revolt of the Masses." Men and women in our democracies have taken over the power and the authority of the former nobility, but they have not accepted the duties and responsibilities which go with such authority. Ortega comments also that "the mass crushes beneath it everything that is different, everything that is excellent, individual, qualified, and select. Anybody, who is not everybody, runs the risk of being eliminated."[10]

Mass men and the children of mass men are not interested in civilization. They are only interested in anesthetics, motor cars, and other materialistic things. But this only confirms their lack of interest in civilization—they set no limits for themselves and feel under no obligation to society. The mass man is satisfied with himself exactly as he is. Is life worth living unless one puts effort into it? Has one lived fully until one passes beyond what one is to become what one might be? Must each of us meet fully the obligations that membership in society imposes upon one?

Conflicts over Values and Belief. As a man thinketh in his heart so is he. Firmly held values and beliefs are the foundations upon which personal integrity is built—they are the essentials for sound citizenship. When teachers report that students do not take school work seriously, they indicate that a conflict exists between students and teachers over values and beliefs. The statement above of Ortega about mass men versus the nobility indicates a conflict in values and beliefs between mass men and the nobility. To mass men, materialistic things alone are important; while to the noble, life is not worth living unless effort is put forth to achieve a purpose above crass material things.

Scott and Hill in *Public Education Under Fire*[11] related that almost every article or book attacking or defending the public school attempted to state the purpose of education—these statements reveal the beliefs and values held concerning education. The critics are in wide disagreement about educational values. Also, they found that the values and beliefs held by the critics were rarely in agreement with those held by the public. For example, many of the critics censure the school for not requiring students to memorize tables, formulae, and passages from the text to be recited verbatim during class recitations. Our contemporary school puts much more emphasis upon helping students solve problems and acquire understandings.

As a matter of fact, the public school is now managed by politically

---

[10] José Ortega y Gasset, *The Revolt of the Masses* (New York, W. Norton and Co., 1932), p. 88 (authorized translation from the original).

[11] C. Winfield Scott and Clyde M. Hill, *Public Education Under Fire* (Englewood Cliffs, N. J., Prentice-Hall, Inc., 1954), pp. 3-9.

appointed or elected school boards who are very sensitive to public pressure. It was not the theories of professional educators which instigated the great changes in education.[12] It was the demand of the public insistently voiced through every school board in the land. What the people wanted came to pass. For the most part, the critics are out of step with the general public. Actually, the books and articles being published are political devices, which use the school as a whipping post, to influence public opinion.

The Modern *versus* the Mechanistic Authoritarian Curriculum. It is well established that youth differ in needs, abilities, and interests, yet many critics of the public school demand a straight academic program for all and the expelling of those who are not capable of profiting from such an offering. The critics demand this in spite of the fact that the student is compelled to remain in school by both law and custom—furthermore, the employment regulations of industry decidedly limit the regular employment of youth under 18 years of age. The contemporary high school which serves us best reflects the goals of today's culture. Some of the critics are attacking the schools for not achieving the goals of a generation ago. In terms of the number now in our schools, more youth get more education—classic and vocational—than ever before.

However, let us not be too complacent about the high school as it is. An objective study of the criticisms will often give insights about neglected aspects. During the recent years, the American public has been doing just that. Public relations polls have indicated that more than 80 per cent of the American citizens were satisfied with American high schools as they were.[13]

For the most part, the critics would restrict the curriculum of the high school to offerings comprising only English, foreign language, history, economics, mathematics, and science—that is, a curriculum for the better-than-average student. This is not a curriculum appropriate for all youth—such a curriculum would include the academic subjects plus art, business education, common learnings, homemaking, industrial arts, health and physical education, music, and the social studies. Could it be that some of these critics were employed by certain organizations to create a public opinion unfavorable to the comprehensive high school? Since these critics do write fluently, they may, in part, be expressing a high degree of satisfaction with an academic curriculum, but it should be mentioned that an academic curriculum for a small elite group is much the cheaper program.

---

[12] Sloan Wilson, "Public Schools Are Better Than You Think," *Harper's Magazine* 211:29-33 (September, 1955).

[13] H. C. Hand, *What People Think About Their Schools: Value and Methods of Public Opinion Polling as Applied to School Systems* (Yonkers, N. Y., World Book Co., 1948).

Modern Methods of Teaching *versus* the More Formal Earlier Methods. What are the major differences between the more routine methods of a generation ago and the more flexible methods of today? In general, today we emphasize *participation of the student* in his own learning; formerly, we put much more emphasis upon memorizing from a book. Then, we were the stern taskmaster; today, we are the friend and helper of the learner. Then, the teacher did all the planning; now, to a much greater extent, *teacher and learner plan together.* Then, we followed the same instructional routine, day after day; now, we *employ many aids and devices* to introduce a greater variety of activities and learning experiences into the classroom. The public demanded a change that would keep all educable youth in school, and the result is much more meaningful to students who have a wide variety of scholastic aptitudes.

As an illustration, recently an extensive research program on how to improve instruction in mathematics and science was initiated in the high schools and universities. Shortly, teachers who had participated in this investigation returned to their classrooms with new teaching concepts. Almost immediately, students who had found mathematics boring and dull became interested in this field. Why did this happen? Largely because the instructor had changed his instructional program from a dull routine with emphasis upon memorizing and doing exercises to an inductive approach where the learner experienced the symbols and sought to grasp the relationships between them.

One comment from an experienced teacher was that modern methods are merely the introduction of free enterprise to the high school classroom.

Many teachers, through in-service education courses, have picked up ideas on how to teach more effectively. Because of such efforts and because of the public demand for better teaching, they have gradually modified their ways of teaching to be more in accord with the newer principles of how we learn.

Special Interest Groups *versus* Free Inquiry. It is not a simple matter to isolate each social virus that at times threatens, through sponsored criticism, the wholesome operation of the public schools. However, these common manifestations have been noted. Special-interest groups attempt to exploit every school member and facility as a source of profit and power, but keep the schools under harsh controls in the name of democracy, thrift, and tradition. Usual demands include limitations of academic freedom; approval of teacher candidates, textbooks, curriculum, school plants and sites; loyalty oaths (for teachers, but not for themselves); access to all school records; release of school time for their benefit; continuance of the college preparatory courses to the exclusion of all others; and the immediate expulsion of any school board member, college president, superintendent of schools, or teacher who fails to compromise or concede to these requirements.

More specifically, special-interest groups may be classified as follows.

Political influences. Schools may be forced to adopt a middle ground of inactivity by the extremes of conservativism or liberalism; world government or isolationism; pacifism or militarism. The whole issue of the United Nations, for example, can not be discussed or studied legally in certain school districts today, yet agents from foundations and colleges supported by anti-United Nations forces have free entry.

Religious influences. The natural rivalry between public and parochial schools is too often blemished by political manipulation and name-calling. Parochial publications on occasion take editorial stands in opposition to bond issues for public schools. Many teachers are hired only in terms of their religious faith. Parochial leaders overlook the tax-exempt status of church-held properties and warn that the public could never afford the education of all children in public schools.

Self-appointed guardians of the Constitution. This group openly opposes any interpretation or teaching of the United States Constitution other than its own. It exerts its influence by circulating lists of books, authors, publishers, and teachers who are not approved. Under suspicion is the teaching of German or Russian languages.

Truly subversive influences. Democracy has a tendency to defeat itself in permitting those who openly provoke unrest to remain unchecked. Here we must rely upon the F.B.I. to ferret out those who would ultimately deny freedom and the rights of man.

Big business and big unions. Curiously, business associations do not support the elevation of teacher salaries to professional status yet insist that such teachers yield a high-quality product; just as strange has been the failure of various unions to capitalize fully upon this anomaly. Both forces give extended lip service to education, provide reading material, films, and film strips, but generally tend to use the schools to promote jealous interests.

One-way press. Controversy has often been called the keynote to success in commercial journalism, and to this end the public schools are often utilized. The hack writer who must produce material of a sensational nature for the syndicated Sunday supplements has few qualms when it comes to name-calling. For him the school plants are never right —they are either "fire traps" or "palaces." Teachers are occasionally honored, but more often are "educationists," "eggheads," or "old maids." Teen-agers are either "delinquents" or "brains." In the local papers, school sports programs are fully exploited, pleas are made for postseason "charity" games, and some coaches are hired and fired according to the expressed will of the sports editor. In other columns, actual school needs and goals are too often buried beneath the froth that, in the publisher's judgment, constitutes the real news of the moment. Only rarely does a newspaper, such as the *New York Times,* afford a qualified and objective person as education editor. Similarly, magazines seem to count heavily upon controversy to stimulate sales among those who have more than a passing interest in school matters. A number of books have been printed, a few by reputable publishers, that brought a good profit through refinement of the Sunday supplement technique.

Americans tend to think about their schools just as the special-interest propagandist would have them think—in terms of stereotypes. These images are formed through use of time-honored techniques that include name-calling, generalities, letters to the editor, and outright manipulation of the truth. It is amazing that despite all such efforts to harass and harness the public schools so much real progress has been possible. The profession of education, we must remember, is the youngest of them all, and perhaps therein it has great strength and the ability to rise far above the levels to which special-interest groups would reduce it.

Teacher Education Is Steadily Improving *versus* Teacher Education Is Abominable. From the expressed criticism of teacher education institutions, one might think that emphasis is not upon what to teach but how to teach. That this assumption is fallacious is evident to anyone who examines the facts. Teachers' colleges do emphasize subject-matter content. Subject-matter content is essential for high school teachers, both in the sense of a broad liberal education and of competence in a subject-matter field.

The statement that the teachers' college undergraduate spends the *bulk* of his time learning teaching techniques, which is frequently made by many anti-educationists, is simply untrue. Actually, the typical undergraduate program of a secondary-school teaching candidate includes slightly less than one-fourth education classes and more than three-fourths academic courses. If the academic subjects are poorly taught or if prospective teachers are passed in subject-matter courses when they are not really competent, that is the responsibility of the liberal arts faculty.

Successful teaching in the American high school requires a good deal more than scholarship. If the liberal arts faculty will set requisite standards in academic scholarship for pre-teachers, the teachers' college will provide an equally adequate program in psychology and principles of teaching. Both types of preparation are equally imperative.

It is acknowledged that there are defects in professional education. The proliferation of courses in some colleges of education is disturbing; equally disturbing is the proliferation of courses in English and history in some liberal arts colleges. Many experiments in teacher education are currently under way in search of more effective methods for producing competent teachers. One type of experiment that has gained considerable recognition is the fifth-year program devoted entirely to an internship plus two summer terms in the study of principles of teaching for meeting certification requirements.

A crucial point about methods of teaching, however, still clouds this controversy. The issue is over methods of teaching versus techniques of teaching. Methods of teaching can be defined as the study of generalized procedures for facilitating learning, for maintaining socialized control, and for discovering and testing knowledge. We can state deliberately and sanely that the study of teaching methods includes much theoretical content which is every bit as important, as complex, and as intellectually respectable as any of the content material suggested by the critics as a substitute for the study of teaching methods. But this statement needs to be qualified in part. There is a difference between methods of teaching and techniques of teaching. Techniques are really ways of putting methods into operation. For example, methods of teaching would emphasize the importance of developing student interest in the subject to be learned. If an elementary teacher desired to get children interested in nutrition, she might have the children take care of pets in school and note the effects of different diets upon animal growth. This latter is a technique and is much more dependent upon practical learning experience than is the understanding of method. Techniques can be learned on the job—method can not.

Still, the question is sometimes raised, with *raised* eyebrows, "Is education a profession?" There are business and industrial leaders who would gladly accept the point of view that education is not a profession, in order to classify teachers as unskilled and thus reduce the cost of public education. Yet it is accepted generally by both the public and professional people that teaching in the public schools justifiably requires training far beyond that given in contemporary programs. Also, we should not forget that there is no question as to the professional status of the teacher in many countries.[14] To eliminate the controversy about teaching, there is probably one premise that teachers and public alike must accept. Only an occupation requiring *theoretical* training for practical efficiency can be regarded as a profession. Let us turn now to the two words that seem to be at the heart of the controversy over teacher education.

The two words *theoretical* and *practical* have caused confusion and muddled dispute over teacher education. In education, as in other professions, the theorist devises the basic principles which are used by the practitioner, in this case the teacher. Both the theoretical educator and the teacher in the classroom must have a grasp of theory. The theorist needs it to carry out research and to extend theory further; the classroom teacher needs it to carry out the practical task of getting the students interested in class work. The theorist and the practitioner represent

[14] Myron Lieberman, *Education as a Profession* (Englewood Cliffs, N. J., Prentice-Hall, Inc., 1956), p. 196.

divisions of labor which have as their ultimate and common purpose the improvement of practice. In the profession, the teacher in the classroom must draw heavily upon the theorist to be a successful teacher, and the theorist or professor of education must look to the teacher for the problems to be emphasized in research. A wise society will see to it that a proper balance is maintained between the resources expended upon each type of effort.

Preparation for College *versus* Meeting the Individual Needs of Students. This is essentially a conflict over values and beliefs. The criticisms about preparation for college come largely from the liberal arts college faculties. The representatives of this group—Bestor,[15] Fuller,[16] Smith,[17]—are all liberal arts college men. In general, these critics insist that the transmission of *the* social heritage is the function of the high school. Boards of education, who are the representatives of the parents, also accept the transmission of the social heritage as *one* function of the high school. Yet they add these other functions as also essential: physical fitness, vocational orientation, civic competence, and social adjustment. When pressed too hard on this issue, parents sometimes ask the college professors: "What taxes are you paying to support our high schools?" Should the high school be restricted, as was the high school of our fathers' fathers, to *the* sole function of transmitting the social heritage?

Nevertheless, there are weak spots in the public high schools, the private high schools, and the liberal arts colleges. There are students in the public high schools, the private high schools, and the liberal arts colleges who loaf, who are unable to spell or to use mathematics effectively, and who neither speak nor write in any of the foreign languages taught in these schools. There are also superior students in all of these schools who work hard, can spell, think accurately in mathematical symbols, and can both read and write in the foreign languages taught. In part, at least, some of the softness of the loafers is a product of the lush lives Americans live; indeed, few of us ever learn to live the rich and noble lives recommended by the liberal arts professors. Many of the loafers who will become graduates of either public or private high schools will also become graduates of the liberal arts colleges.

Equal Opportunity for All *versus* Discrimination in the Quality of Education Provided. Americans believe in equality of opportunity, irrespective of the economic status of the family.[18] To some Americans, education for all is education for none. Surely, they are men of little

[15] Arthur E. Bestor, *Educational Wastelands: Retreat from Learning in Our Public Schools* (Urbana, University of Illinois Press, 1953).

[16] Harry J. Fuller, "The Emperor's New Clothes," *Scientific Monthly* 72:32-41 (January, 1951).

[17] Mortimer Smith, *The Diminished Mind* (Chicago, Henry Regnery Co., 1954).

[18] James B. Conant, *The American High School Today* (New York, McGraw-Hill Book Co., 1959), pp. 5, 6.

faith who would educate only a favored few. In a setting where the able must test their powers, all can be more fully developed. Men who believe that education for all is education for none believe in a controlled economy, a controlled society, a controlled education—they do not really believe in free enterprise. The more competition we have, the better the top performers must become.

To improve American education or to reduce educational inequality, the United States must (1) reduce drastically the number of very small high schools, (2) eliminate incompetent teachers, (3) greatly increase tax allocations for education, (4) provide sufficient modern instructional facilities for teachers, (5) improve the quality of administrative leadership, and (6) reduce community conflicts over education (segregation greatly reduces the contributions that the gifted members of racial groups can make to American welfare).

Also, insofar as possible we need to equalize educational opportunities as between (1) rural and urban areas, (2) the slums and the better residential areas of our cities, (3) white students and segregated racial groups throughout America, (4) the states with low per capita income and those of high per capita income, and (5) learners of low, average, and high capacity (individualize the programs of students).

Many of the critics of education are looking backwards to an educational program which suited America of a generation ago instead of to a program for an age of automation and hydrogen power. Of course, current education will be greatly changed in helping students to adapt to automation and the hydrogen age. Men with vision predict that all must be educated to higher levels.[19]

To our critics European secondary education is ideal, especially the English type of secondary school. However, the *London Times*, March 1, 1959, page 6, states, "To be in a really healthy state, academic studies ought to fit people for jobs as well as giving them general education. . . . Mr. Geoffrey Lloyd, Minister of Education, is to be invited to attend a special meeting of the Conservative Back Bench M.P.'s. . . . Complaints have already been privately expressed that Ministerial approvals for the erection of comprehensive schools have been given excessively. Viscount Hailsham, Lord President of the Council, said . . . that there ought to be no over-riding of educational authorities unless it could be shown that they had forgotten the interests of the children and teachers in the interest of political dogma."

Automation and other modifications of industry are rapidly spreading over Continental Europe as well as the United States. These conditions require, at least, high school graduation of nearly all men employed in industry.

[19] Ernest O. Melby, *Education of Free Men* (Pittsburgh, University of Pittsburgh Press, 1955), Chs. 7 and 8.

Parent-School Co-operation *versus* **Divided Responsibility.** If critics would distort less and examine and state more realistically their objections to the discipline in today's schools, their diatribes about discipline would make more sense. As a matter of fact, adolescents do need adult support and control. If control is minimal and can be counted on, they feel more safe and secure. Youth are on the threshold of having to become completely responsible for their actions, and this step is frightening as well as tempting. Parents and teachers should be ready to give support when it is necessary without unduly emphasizing the guilt involved. In this contemporary period of lush living, parents have been somewhat lax and negligent, and they have failed to face issues firmly and immediately. Teachers too have been affected somewhat by the public attitude toward laxness. Yet they are often curbed in their control of adolescents by community attitudes and state laws.

Since parents and teachers are jointly responsible for disciplinary actions, some common understandings about behavior standards need to be established. Where parents and teachers have co-operated in formulating guide lines for accepted conduct, especially on moot questions, both parents and teachers can provide the necessary support without becoming annoyed or upset. When the behavior code is clear and concise, youth fall into line. In fact, most youth welcome such guide lines and observe them. Since youth want to be accepted by other youth as well as by adults, these guide lines serve them as controls and supports.

One constant factor among delinquents is an expressed hatred for parents and often for teachers as well. Here is one key to the whole problem of juvenile delinquency. Adolescents do need adult control and support. If they can count on both teachers and parents to provide a minimal control without terrible explosions and scenes, they feel safe and secure. However, teachers and parents must learn to co-operate in this control and support. The hatred some adolescents feel toward parents and teachers is natural, because their parents and teachers have let them down. The security which is a product of minimal discipline has not been provided. In their rantings about the type of punishment by which to replace the softness in the schools, many of the critics reveal a complete lack of understanding about how appropriate human relations are established.

EDUCATION AND RESEARCH IN TODAY'S SCHOOL

Horace Mann, America's greatest educational reformer and statesman, died 100 years ago. Yet, his enthusiasm to extend public education brought him into violent controversy with political and professional reactionaries. It was ever thus. Back in the sixteenth and seventeenth centuries Galileo and Francis Bacon came into violent conflict with the reactionaries of their time through the publication of certain research findings that are now recognized as essential first steps in science. We now recognize the contributions made to our civilization by the research of the past. Should not research also be employed for improving education?

The Role of Research in Education. The Russian Sputnik I, which was launched late in 1957, was an outcome of intense research and experimentation as was the American missile launched a few weeks later. The men who produced these missiles had learned about the universe by close observations. They had collected and studied facts and had arrived at principles as to the relations between these facts. Originated in the sixteenth century by Francis Bacon and others, this inductive procedure rather than the older deductive procedure of scientific investigation brought about the industrial revolution in Western civilization. New industrial machines for home, shop, road, and farm did not spring into existence full-blown. They were products of slow and painful research. There was first an idea; then the study and collection of facts; and then the relating of the facts to produce the new machine. The ultimate and crucial test of the completed machine was, "Does it work?" If the machine works, the proper relationships have been identified and properly integrated. But the impact of research on industry is an old story—it has been told over and over again. All of us know about the many new household appliances, automation, or the new wonder factories, the machines that dig ditches and the electronic computers.

Since the value and worth of the machines are known wide and far, critics of the machines lose face. It may be that the abundance of criticisms and critics reveals that our limited research in education has been highly successful. The limited contact of the layman with the improvements in education due to research makes him more gullible.

What these laymen do not seem to know is that such men as Arnold Gesell of Yale, Edward L. Thorndike of Columbia, William James of Harvard, Charles H. Judd of Chicago University, Franz Boaz of the Chicago Field Museum, Frank Freeman of the Universities of Chicago and California, G. Stanley Hall of Johns Hopkins, James McKeen Cattell of Columbia, Lewis M. Terman of Stanford, Kurt Lewin of Iowa U., Guy T. Buswell of Chicago and California, and hosts of others devoted their entire lives to experimentation and research to improve education. These men employed the same inductive approach in their research for sound instructional materials and the establishment of basic principles as do the men who perform research and experimentation in the physical sciences. When the instructional idea or the instructional material is clearly developed, it is tried out under normal classroom conditions to see if it works. If it does work, if it saves teacher time, it is accepted and used.

The noted educators mentioned above were creative and imaginative men. As they worked at their experimentation and research, they let their minds follow the direction indicated by their investigations. Each of these men cut through the doctrinaire tumult of the times and laid bare the ideas upon which we today build the discipline, education. Two concepts seem to be the most basic to the work of these educators: (1) the learner should experience rather than memorize,[20] and (2) the relations between things rather than the things themselves are of primary importance.[21]

This is what is meant by the impact of research on education. We know that research and experimentation made American industry the giant which it is. Also, the progress which education has made is largely due to the same approach. However, research and experimentation in education have been just a drop in the bucket to the research that is needed to make education function at its optimum efficiency. In part, at least, the critics of education have merely shown by their criticism their own ignorance, but one must not ignore the elements of truth which are present in many of the criticisms.

Research Reveals the Goodness of Today's Education. Are the results of today's teaching poorer than, as good as, or better than those achieved in the past? In general, the results are better than those achieved at any prior time in the history of the American secondary school. This has occurred despite the fact that more youth today attend school through their eighteenth birthday than at any previous time in our history. A few representative studies are cited below in support of the above statement.

Then and Now.[22] An early study of this question utilized a battery of examinations given to Boston school children in 1845. The same tests which had been administered to Boston children who completed the elementary school in 1845 were given to a large group of eighth-grade pupils from different sections of America in 1919. The comparison of test results was between the selected best of the 1845 Boston students and the unselected lower 40 per cent of comparable American students in 1919. The principal conclusions drawn from this study were: (1) the children of 1919 made higher scores on the thought questions and lower scores on the pure memory questions than the students of 1845, (2) this situation seemed to prevail all over America in 1919, and (3) the over-all efficiency of the 1919 instruction was superior to that of 1845.

An Evaluation of Modern Education.[23] Back in 1942 Leonard and

---

[20] Memorizing has a place in education, but its importance is second to that of relating and understanding.

[21] Harold Rugg, *Foundations for American Education* (Yonkers, N. Y., World Book Co., 1947), foreword.

[22] Otis W. Caldwell and Stuart A. Courtis, *Then and Now in Education* (Yonkers, N. Y., World Book Co., 1924), Ch. 7.

[23] J. Paul Leonard and Alvin C. Eurich, *An Evaluation of Modern Education* (New York, Appleton-Century-Crofts, Inc., 1942), preface.

Eurich headed a comprehensive report for the Society for Curriculum Study. In their preface, they stated, "As society changes so must education; as psychology improves its procedures, so must evaluation expand in scope and accuracy . . . A purpose of the report is to provide teachers, administrators, and laymen with the facts regarding the success of the school."

Cited by Leonard and Eurich is Wrightstone's[24] study comparing the performance of students from conventional high schools with students from newer-type high schools on a battery of achievement tests. The students were equated in a number of ways—that is, intelligence quotients, chronological age, grade level, and socio-economic status—to increase the validity of the study. The findings of the study indicated that the students from the newer-type schools equaled or surpassed the achievement of students from the conventional schools in their ability to recall facts of general science, biology, physics, chemistry, algebra, plane geometry, French grammar, French vocabulary, and Latin vocabulary. The ability to recall facts of Latin grammar was the only recall area reported in which the conventional-school children were significantly superior.

Did They Succeed in College?[25] This is the title of the fourth volume in the report on the Eight-Year Study. The question raised is, "Did the graduates of the thirty experimental high schools succeed as well in college as the graduates of the conventional high schools?" Thirty newer-type high schools were selected to carry on an experiment to gather data on the problem. An extensive study was made of the records of 2,108 graduates from the thirty schools who, under an agreement with over 300 colleges, had been freed from the necessity of meeting the usual unit or examination requirements for college admission. From the experimental group of graduates, 1,475 were matched, student for student, with graduates of conventional high schools on the basis of scholastic aptitude, interests, and socio-economic background.

A comparison of the 1,475 matched pairs revealed that the graduates of the thirty newer-type schools:

1. Earned a slightly higher total average.

2. Earned a higher grade average in all subjects except foreign language.

3. Specialized in the same academic fields as did the comparison students.

4. Did not differ from the comparison group in the number of times they were placed on probation.

5. Received slightly more academic honors each year.

[24] J. Wayne Wrightstone, *Appraisal of Experimental High School Practice* (New York, Bureau of Publications, Teachers College, Columbia University, 1936), pp. 153, 163.

[25] Dean Chamberlain and others, *Did They Succeed in College* (New York, Harper & Brothers, 1942), pp. 206-9.

6. Were more often judged to possess a high degree of intellectual curiosity and drive.

7. Were more often judged to be precise, systematic, and objective in their thinking.

8. Were more often judged to have developed clear or well-formulated ideas concerning the meaning of education—especially in the first two years of college.

9. More often demonstrated a high degree of resourcefulness in meeting new situations.

10. Did not differ from the comparison group in ability to plan their time effectively.

11. Had about the same problems of adjustment as the comparison group but approached their solutions with greater effectiveness.

12. Participated somewhat more frequently, and more often enjoyed appreciative experiences, in the arts.

13. Participated more in all organized student groups except religious and "service" activities.

14. Earned in each college year a higher percentage of non-academic honors.

15. Did not differ from the comparison group in the quality of adjustment to their contemporaries.

16. Differed only slightly from the comparison group in the kinds of judgments about their schooling.

17. Had a somewhat better orientation toward the choice of a vocation.

18. Demonstrated a more active concern for what was going on in the world.

Public Education under Fire.[26] In an article by Gray and Iverson, evidence was presented relating to the criticisms of the public school's reading program. They stated that achievement in silent reading is equal to and on the average superior to the achievement of several decades ago. The evidence is summarized in Table 3.

The Class Conducts a Local Survey of Criticisms. In the long run, the demands of the citizens will determine the program of the high school. By what procedure can a local college class become aware of the nature of the local criticisms?

A procedure that has been employed with classes in secondary education will be described. Each member of the class (enrollment 30) interviews 10 people who are known to them and which will include a professional man or woman, a parent (preferably a housewife), a business man, a college student, a high school student, a clerk, a truck driver or a representative of the transportation industry. Each interviewee is asked

[26] William S. Gray and William J. Iverson, "What Should Be the Profession's Attitude Toward Lay Criticism of the Schools?" *Elementary School Journal* 55:19-26, (September, 1952), (adaptation of Table 1, p. 22).

Table 3. Summary of Studies of Reading Achievement

INVESTIGATOR	DATES	TEST USED	GRADES	RESULTS
Tiegs	Before and after 1945	Stanford and Progressive Achievement Tests	4-11	After 1945 results superior by a slight margin
Krugman and Wrightstone	1935 and 1946	Stanford Reading Test	6-7-8	No significant difference
Worchester and Kline	1921 and 1947	Monroe Silent Reading Test	3-8	1947 group was significantly better
Finch and Gillenwater	1931 and 1948	Thorndike-McCall	6	1948 group significantly superior
Traxler	1941 and 1951	Co-operative Reading Test: Comprehension	7-12	No significant difference

to express his opinion about the high school. When the interviews are completed and summarized, there will be 300 viewpoints. And will they differ? Try it to see.

From one series of interviews, a brief abstract is presented here for different segments of the population. The two most frequently mentioned criticisms are indicated for each classification.

CLASSIFICATION	OPINIONS
1. Professionals: physicians, lawyers	a. More emphasis upon preparation for college b. A firmer discipline in high school
2. Business men	a. Greater emphasis upon the 3 R's b. Development of better work habits, skills, and attitudes
3. High school students	a. Better teachers b. Better guidance and counseling
4. High school teachers	a. Better co-ordination between the courses offered b. Better articulation between elementary and high school; between high school and college
5. Parents	a. Greater emphasis given to marriage and the family b. Better qualified teachers
6. Mothers of high school students	a. Better counseling and guidance b. More practical courses
7. College students	a. More challenging courses b. Better qualified teachers

As this summary is studied, it is obvious that some citizens look to the high school to prepare its students for family living and jobs, and that others put great emphasis upon preparation for college. All, or nearly all, put stress upon the improvement of discipline or moral and spiritual values. One fact that stands out in the summaries is that the occupation of the citizen greatly influences his opinion as to what the purposes of the high school ought to be.

A DEFENSE AGAINST CRITICISMS

In a time of crisis and criticism, the individual teacher needs to have deep convictions about the purposes and the program of the high school. A teacher must have a positive and steady faith in his work and in the institution that is aiding youth. By the nature of his services, the teacher must exert constructive leadership with students and citizens alike. He must listen with courtesy and sympathy to citizens without being swayed by critics with axes to grind and certain taxpayers who seek a way to shift their obligations onto society.

It might seem that this is the burden of the superintendent of schools and the principals of the high schools. But in the long run, it is the teachers who confirm and support or refute and destroy the appointed leaders. No school has ever been wrecked by any criticisms where the staff had accepted and practiced the tenets of a common educational platform based upon the American Way of Life and sound educational policies.

Most schools formulate an educational platform and make copies of it available to all teachers and parents. The common and conservative nature of such a platform allays the fears of some parents who have been reading about these "terrible leftist" schools. In helping parents to understand that much of the propaganda about schools originates from persons with axes to grind, a teacher helps himself to win acceptance as a dependable leader. He thereby reduces tensions within his own classroom. An educational platform would include such topics as the following:

1. New and increasing demands on the school.

2. Purposes of education: preparation for citizenship in its broadest sense.

3. Responsibilities of the school: it has primary or chief responsibility for some phases of education, partial or shared responsibility for other phases, some responsibility for educational leadership in the community.

4. How students are classified and assigned to classes and the factors that determine the teachability of a class.

5. Instructional material: the good teacher requires and uses a variety of instructional material.

6. Moral and spiritual values: these values in the curriculum are identified and attention focused upon them.

7. Controversial issues: the American heritage is taught, while controversial issues within the heritage are analyzed and studied.

Facing Criticisms Locally. Many recent articles and books are highly critical of the high school program. These accuse the school of favoring the average and below-average student while neglecting the rapid learner and the gifted. In most of these critical books and articles, the facts are distorted and the scholarship is atrocious. The authors throw "more heat than light" upon the neglect of the rapid and gifted learners. Yet, there is an underlying element of truth in the contention that the bright and gifted students are not sufficiently challenged to live up to their potential in school achievement—just as an effective case, however, might be made for the below-average and the very slow learner.

For the high school teacher, this is always a local problem, since he meets it in the high school where he teaches. Similarly, it is in the local high school that these problems must be faced by the high school principal, the teachers, and the parents. Earlier in this chapter, the major criticisms have been discussed and some evidence presented to indicate the lack of support for most of them. Here are a few suggestions on what to do about *criticisms* arising in the immediate community where you teach. Actually, your principal has the major responsibility for facing local criticisms, but the teacher can assist greatly by co-operating. In the long run, through supporting his principal, the teacher can reduce his classroom load.

What to Do About Specific Criticisms. The following outline presents common criticisms and suggests how they may be met.

1. Youth today are not as proficient in the fundamentals as were the students of former years.
   The evidence presented earlier demonstrates the falsity of this statement.
   a. Give a standard achievement test in each of the basic skills. This will measure the achievement level of students in your school against national norms.[27]
   b. Compare the results made on achievement tests (or school grades) with test results (or school grades) made by students in the same school years ago. Most comparisons of this kind favor the students of today. Such a demonstration convinces parents and boosts the morale of all concerned.
   c. In the event of apparent weaknesses in any of the skills, institute remedial programs. But study the remedial techniques carefully before attempting to use them—if at all possible, work with a teacher who has had experience in remedial techniques.
   d. Differentiate and enrich the offerings for the college preparatory group by giving them more assignments in research, composition, and formal gram-

[27] Commercial tests can be purchased from the California Test Bureau, 5916 Hollywood Boulevard, Los Angeles, California; World Book Company, 313 Park Hill Avenue, Yonkers, N. Y., and many other test and book publishers. We feel that such a testing program should not wait until critics begin the attack.

mar. The criticisms from the liberal arts colleges seem sufficiently well supported to justify more emphasis in high school upon these specific areas.

2. Those responsible for the education of the young pay little attention to the wishes of parents.

    A generation ago, many school people did take that attitude, but not today. Modern methods of teaching require the teacher to know the student and his home. The student's full potential of growth and development can be achieved only by the complete co-operation of the home and the school as partners in a common enterprise.

    a. Institute an "Open Door" policy by which parents may drop into the school to discuss their problems fully, to inspect the building, to talk to teachers, and to visit classes. Each teacher will make a parent welcome in his classroom and answer all questions as fully as possible. It is a privilege rather than a duty to do this. Teachers will be welcome in the homes of parents to discuss school problems and to establish a better partnership in the education of teen-agers.

    b. Teachers will send letters of commendation to parents whenever the occasion permits. Surely, a worthy achievement can be spoken of gladly just as frequently as a complaint can be made.

    c. Newspapers can be of tremendous value in creating this home-school relationship. Schools where an improved public-relations concept prevails make certain that newspapers are given the full story of specific youth achievements.

3. The schools are too expensive. The programs attempt too much. There is too much waste. There are too many unnecessary expenses. Teachers are overpaid.

    Education is a good financial investment. The higher the level of education, the greater the productive power of the country. The greater the productive power, the higher the income.

    a. Make the community aware of the value of education. The Chamber of Commerce of the United States has published a study presenting conclusive evidence that education does raise the standards of living. Develop charts to show this evidence to visitors. It is only right and proper that evidence indicating that education does pay off should be developed with teen-agers.

    b. Publish statements of tradesmen, businessmen, and professional persons to indicate the cash value of education.

4. The high schools have gone anti-intellectual. The practical courses have driven out the academic disciplines.

    Actually, the high school has been expanded to include all youth. Its program includes the academic disciplines, vocational courses, general education and the activities. Individuals differ greatly in their abilities and interests. While the academic disciplines are taught just as well as formerly to college-bound youth, an identical program for all who are now in school is not feasible.

    a. Enrich the academic program for college-bound students and hold them to high standards. Actually qualify them for college.

    b. Encourage bright students to compete for scholarships and publicize those who succeed. Citizens react favorably to such success and negatively to articles attacking the high school for poor scholarship.

    c. In contacts with parents and fellow teachers promote such courses as driver education, and family life and marriage. Under capable teachers such courses are of great value to many teen-agers. And the high school, through this promotion, may become an understood, constructive force in the community for assisting parents in the solution of immediately pressing problems.

    d. Keep informed about the alumni you have had in classes. Send items about them to the papers through a publicity center of the school. A teacher can rejoice over the successes of both good and poor students alike. Some poor scholars in the school become outstanding successes in life. And they, too, are the alumni of the school.

5. There is no discipline in the modern high school; kids run the schools these days. Teachers need to take a firmer hand.

    The students do not run the schools. However, they are encouraged to participate in setting the goals of instruction and even school policies. No educator asks his students, "What do you want to study today?"

    If any person is aware of the immaturity of youth, it is the modern educator, who has studied child growth and development. The belief that students run the school is a distortion of the democratic educational technique called "teacher-pupil planning." In this technique, *students* are involved in *helping to plan* programs of some phases of certain courses. Yes! the position of the teacher has changed from an explainer of subject matter to a guider of youth. A major service of teachers is the development of youth in acquiring understanding, skills, attitudes, and interests, in establishing habits, and in developing the ability to solve problems. It is the conviction of educators that this service is better adapted to our day than the previous heavy emphasis upon the memorization of textbook materials.

    a. Invite parents to visit your classes and to look around the school. Intelligent parents will see that students do not run the school.

    b. Explain to parents how discipline problems are handled through counseling and acquaint them with the punishment techniques. This is time well spent if disturbed parents are helped to see that essential procedures exist for effective discipline.

    c. Solicit parental co-operation in handling disciplinary problems. The very fact that the parent is invited to co-operate helps allay fears raised by published criticisms.

THE CRITICS AND "OPERATION STORK"

Is there a relationship between "operation stork" and the gradually increasing volume of the criticisms of the public high school? Why is so much recent criticism directed at the public high school? What is the nature of the criticism?

It is predicted that the high school population will double between 1954 and 1966. Is this because the high school will become more efficient? Not at all; this prediction is based entirely upon the assumption that the high school will remain at its present level of efficiency. This prediction is based completely upon facts already at hand; the birth rate between 1932 and 1954 doubled—there were two million births in 1932 and four million in 1954. Twelve years after 1954, or 1966, there will be twice as many teen-agers available to attend our high schools.

With the high school enrollment twice as large, a second assumption follows: the cost of supporting the high school (buildings, teachers, equipment) will be twice as much. To support this student body, the tax rate per unit of value will be twice as high. When taxes double, taxpayers' resistance stiffens. This is especially true for those who always have opposed public school education for all American youth. An elementary education for all children has been more completely accepted; hence, compulsory education for the elementary school stirs less resistance—especially since the cost for elementary education is decidedly less on a per pupil basis than for secondary school.

Is it likely that the doubling of the high school enrollment between now and 1966 will greatly increase the number and type of criticisms unleashed? How likely is it that these critics will ever say directly: attendance at high school shall be for the selected few and not for all youth? The criticisms of the high school, under stress, will probably become more overt, frequent, and spiteful.

Let us take a look at a few of the statistics on birth rates which are sure to anger some Americans when they realize that the costs of high school education are sure to be doubled in the next decade. The reported total high school enrollment as of January 1, 1955, was 8,126,000. The total projected enrollment for the high school, grades 9-12, for 1966, is estimated at 12,920,000.[28] The increase in high school enrollment from 1955 to 1966, assuming a retention of 90 per cent of the students and a somewhat more rapid acceleration of the reorganization movement, will step up the number by six million bringing the total student body to some 14 million. These are the predictions of a statistician who may not be correct. But more babies were born in 1957 than during any year from 1945 until then. In addition, with our improved medical service more of them will survive to attend the high school. Some of our fellow Americans may pour out much more pent-up wrath in stinging criticisms, and under our American Way they are privileged to do this without suppression.

SUMMARY

In this chapter, we have discussed the critics and criticisms of the American secondary schools. All youth are in high school; the mass has

---

[28] O. Oxtoby, R. Mugge, and D. Wolfe, "Enrollment and Graduation Trends from Grade School to Ph.D.," *School and Society* 76:225-231 (October 11, 1952). There are, of course, many slight variations in a number of projections, but every authority predicts greatly increased high school enrollments.

become so great, the range in individual differences so wide, the achievements so varied, and the cost so great as to disturb some people. Some
improvements in the school system are needed to make it function more
efficiently. In the next chapter on the reorganization and improvement
of the high school, we will move back to an earlier period and find there
also criticisms of the school that seem to defy correction. We will describe how these problems of an earlier period were resolved. Then there
was turmoil and commotion both within the profession and among the
people. The aims, curricula, and methods were constantly under criticism,
both friendly and antagonistic. We had an 8-4-4 system with rigid
gradation and promotion, a curriculum greatly expanded but formal and
poorly articulated, a method greatly improved but still formal and repressive. In Chapter IV we will describe the procedures by which reorganization was brought about and improvement secured.

DISCUSSION PROBLEMS

1. Do you believe that continuous criticism is good or bad for the schools? Are
   the criticisms justified?
2. Since the launching of the first Russian Sputnik, pressure groups have insisted that the schools place more emphasis upon mathematics and science.
   Is there any danger in an overemphasis of these subjects?
3. What are the purposes of the American secondary school?
4. Why should you, as a teacher, take a sincere interest in the annual "Open
   House" program? What else might you do to encourage adequate support by
   school patrons?
5. Give some examples of how educational research has changed the methods
   of instruction and the program of the secondary school.
6. Businessmen sometimes complain that high school graduates whom they hire
   are unable to write or spell. As a teacher, how would you answer this claim?
7. What implications has the continuing high birth rate for the secondary school?
8. Adult education, particularly night-school education, has been growing
   tremendously in recent years. What factors have caused so many adults to
   return to school? Does your answer support the argument that our schools
   are failing in their purpose?

RELATED REFERENCES

ALLEN, Charles M., *Combatting the Drop-Out Problem* (Chicago, Science Research Associates, 1956).

BELL, Howard, *Youth Tell Their Story* (Washington, D.C., American Council
on Education, 1939).

BESTOR, Arthur, *Educational Wastelands: Retreat from Learning in Our Public
Schools* (Urbana, University of Illinois Press, 1953).

BOAZ, G., *Our New Ways of Thinking* (New York, Harper & Brothers, 1930).

BRECKMAN, B., "Relations Between Indoctrination and the Teaching of Democracy," *Journal of Educational Sociology* 22:429-438 (March, 1947).

BURTON, William H., and BRUECKNER, Leo J., *Supervision: A Social Process,* 3rd ed. (New York, Appleton-Century-Crofts, Inc., 1955).

BUTTS, R. Freeman, and CREMIN, Lawrence A., *A History of Education in American Culture* (New York, Henry Holt & Co., Inc., 1953).

CALDWELL, Otis W., and COURTIS, Stuart A., *Then and Now in Education* (Yonkers, N.Y., World Book Co., 1924).

CHAMBERLIN, Dean, and others, *Did They Succeed in College* (New York, Harper & Brothers, 1942).

CHASE, Stuart, and CHASE, M. T., *Roads to Agreement* (New York, Harper & Brothers, 1951).

CHILDS, H. L., *The Nazi Primer* (New York, Harper & Brothers, 1938).

Citizenship Education Study (Detroit), *A Curriculum for Citizenship* (Detroit, Wayne University Press, 1953).

CONANT, James B., *The American High School Today* (New York, McGraw-Hill Book Co., 1959).

CROSBY, Otis A., "The Nation Reaches a Verdict in the Case of People versus Today's Schools," *Nation's Schools* 47:34-37 (January, 1951).

DAVIS, Allison, *Social Class Influences upon Learning* (Cambridge, Harvard University Press, 1948).

————, and HAVIGHURST, Robert J., "Measurement of Mental Systems: Can Intelligence Be Measured?" *Scientific Monthly* 67:303-314 (April, 1948).

DRUCKER, Peter F., "The Promise of Automation," *Harper's Magazine* 210:41-47 (April, 1955).

FOSTER, Emery N., and HOBSON, Carol J., "Elementary and Secondary School Enrollments in the Public School System of the United States by Grades, 1949-50 to 1959-60," *School Life* 27:26-28 (May, 1955).

FULLER, Harry J., "The Emperor's New Clothes," *Scientific Monthly* 72:32-41 (January, 1951).

GOOD, Carter V., *Dictionary of Education* (New York, McGraw-Hill Book Co., 1945).

GRAY, William S., and IVERSON, J., "What Should Be the Professional Attitude Toward Lay Criticism of the Schools?" *Elementary School Journal* 55:19-26 (September, 1952).

HAND, H. C., *What People Think about Their Schools: Value and Methods of Public Opinion Polling as Applied to School Systems* (Yonkers, N.Y., World Book Co., 1948).

HANNA, Paul R., "Three R's Have Changed," *The School Executive* 69:78 (October, 1950).

HENDERSON, Kenneth B., and HAND, Harold C., "To What Extent Is the General Public in Sympathy with the Current Attack on the Schools?" *Progressive Education* 29:110-15 (January, 1952).

HENNINGS, Senator Thomas C., "Congress Charts Quiz on Religion," *Christian Science Monitor* (August 16, 1955).

HOLBROOK, Stewart H., *Dreamers of the American Dream* (Garden City, N.Y., Doubleday & Company, Inc., 1957).

LEONARD, J. Paul, and EURICH, Alvin C., *An Evaluation of Modern Education* (New York, Appleton-Century-Crofts, Inc., 1942).

Lieberman, Myron, *Education as a Profession* (Englewood Cliffs, N.J., Prentice-Hall, Inc., 1956).

Mead, Margaret, *Coming of Age in Samoa* (New York, Blue Ribbon Books, 1932).

Melby, Ernest O., *Education of Free Men* (Pittsburgh, University of Pittsburgh Press, 1955).

Morgan, Owen W., *A Study of the Holding Power and an Analysis of Factors Related to Early School Leaving*, unpublished master's thesis, University of Omaha, Omaha, Nebr., 1951, typescript.

Oliva, Peter F., "Facing Criticism Locally," *Bulletin of The National Association of Secondary-School Principals* 204:134-145 (October, 1954).

Ortega y Gasset, José, *The Revolt of the Masses* (New York, W. W. Norton & Company, Inc., 1932).

Orwell, George, *Nineteen Eighty-Four* (New York, Harcourt, Brace & Co., 1949).

Oxtoby, O., Mugge, R., and Wolfe, D., "Enrollment and Graduation Trends from Grade School to Ph.D.," *School and Society* 76:225-231 (October 11, 1952).

Rickover, H. G., *Education and Freedom* (New York, E. P. Dutton & Co., Inc., 1959).

Rugg, Harold, *Foundations for American Education* (Yonkers, N.Y., World Book Co., 1947).

Scott, C. Winfield, and Hill, Clyde M., *Public Education Under Fire* (New York, Prentice-Hall, Inc., 1954).

Smith, Mortimer, *The Diminished Mind* (Chicago, Henry Regnery Co., 1954).

Spears, Harold, *The High School for Today* (New York, American Book Company, 1950).

Stout, Lydia, "What Strangles American Teaching," *Atlantic Monthly* 201:59-63 (April, 1958).

Strecker, E. A., *Their Mothers' Sons* (Philadelphia, J. B. Lippincott Co., 1946).

Thayer, V. T., *Public Education and Its Critics* (New York, The Macmillan Company, 1954).

Whitney, Frank P., *The Changing High School: Studies in Secondary Education* (New York, The Exposition Press, 1955).

Wilson, Sloan, "Public Schools Are Better than You Think," *Harper's Magazine* 211:29-33 (September, 1955).

——, "It's Time to Close Our Carnival," *Reader's Digest* 72:31-5 (June, 1958).

Wrightstone, J. Wayne, *Appraisal of Experimental High School Practice* (New York, Bureau of Publications, Teachers College, Columbia University, 1936).

Chapter 4

REORGANIZING THE HIGH SCHOOL
TO SERVE ALL YOUTH

The old order changeth yielding place to new.
—TENNYSON, *Idylls of the King*

A high school is established to serve all youth and, indirectly, the home, the community, and the nation. The school, through its organization, must be functional. This is measured by the way it adapts its program to the needs of those who enter as graduates from the elementary school, by the preparation of its own students for college and life (articulation), and by the adjustment made for holding students until graduation (retention). These features operate all of the time to make the relationships between student and teacher more smooth and hence more functional.

When these factors are adequately adjusted to the characteristics of youth, they tend to make the student feel that the high school is a good place to be. The teachers work with and not against the nature of the adolescent. An awareness on the part of the high school that these features operate tends to make the load lighter for everyone; teachers become happier and more successful people.

THE REORGANIZATION MOVEMENT

By 1890, the United States had come to have an 8-4-4 educational system—eight years elementary school, four years high school, and four years college—with rigid gradation and poor articulation.[1] The curriculum, while greatly expanded, was still highly formal and poorly articulated. It was greatly improved over the earlier public high school program but still formal and repressive.

Between the Kalamazoo Case of 1874 which legalized the tax-supported

---

[1] *Articulation:* the degree of relationship existing among the various parts of curriculum at a given level of instruction, such that, taken together, they have some degree of unity and coherence.

high school, and 1890, the public high school became popular and developed very rapidly. In that period hundreds of school communities throughout the United States extended the work of their schools into high schools. Yet these communities had no model or pattern in the form of constructive suggestions to go by. As a result, they followed one or two general procedures. Many communities copied from the academies while a large number of communities cut loose from tradition in setting up their high school programs. From community to community, there were wide variations in the length of a period, the years needed to complete the work of the high school, and the curricular offerings. Thus, considerable confusion existed as to the number of years the high school should include, the nature of its offerings, and what should constitute a year of credit in a given subject.[2] As expressed by many schoolmen, the American school—both elementary and secondary—"just grew up." However, the name "high school" was probably an importation from Scotland, and the description of the German secondary schools by Horace Mann in his Seventh Report to the State Board of Education in Massachusetts may have had considerable influence on fixing the pattern that became established by 1900.[3]

What Does Reorganization Mean? The problem of reorganization posed three alternatives for the secondary school. In the first place, education in other countries, preferably those across the Atlantic, could be imitated. The Latin Grammar School was an importation from Europe that was tried out by the colonists and the young republic, but it met the needs in this country only for a limited time. In the second place, the schools could develop their own pattern of culture, formal and aloof, without regard for the realities of the American Way. This would be adapted to the abilities of the most academically able students. In the past, this second alternative has been used frequently by the schools. Incidentally, this proposal is made by our contemporary critics as pointed out in Chapter 3. By the third alternative, the secondary school could develop a program of education adapted to the needs of all youth—a truly American secondary school program. If it were a program equally challenging to all students, it would have the full support of the American people. Such a program would prepare students either for life or for college or for both while orienting all toward a vocation. School reorganization in the United States has followed this third alternative.

This is primarily an internal problem of the high school which involves: (1) the administrative organization of the grades or years of work which make up secondary school education, (2) the preparation of a set of

[2] Leslie L. Chisholm, *The Work of the High School* (New York, The Macmillan Co., 1953), p. 64.

[3] Edgar W. Knight, *Education in the United States* (Boston, Ginn & Company, 1951), p. 201.

educational objectives in harmony with today's needs, (3) the rearrangement of the curriculum,—the offerings of the school, (4) a revision of teaching methods, (5) the introduction of a comprehensive guidance program, (6) the proper articulation of secondary education with elementary and college education, and (7) an appropriate program of public relations and parental co-operation. The aim is to develop an adequate program in each of these phases of the modern secondary school and to co-ordinate them into an acceptable total program of education.

Reorganization and the Secondary School. What is the place of reorganization in the development of secondary education? The coming of the high school marked an important goal in American education, for this step completed the educational ladder. Then for the first time, education, at least potentially, was made available from kindergarten through elementary school, secondary school, and on into college. However, when the gap between elementary school and college was closed, two related problems emerged. The first was to make educational opportunities at the high school level *actually* available to all youth,—new school districts had to be planned, new school buildings constructed, new teachers employed, and a host of other practical problems met. To this task, both educators and laymen gave much time and energy during the first half of the present century. The second problem dealt with the nature and scope of the education to be provided by the high school. When school people began to wrestle with this problem in terms of their community and their student body rather than to copy established school programs from other places, education was beginning to reach maturity. That was what educators began to do early in the twentieth century, that is, behave like professional people moving toward maturity.

AGITATION FOR IMPROVEMENT

Improvement of a public institution comes gradually, especially if it is a major one, and it usually comes as a result of slowly accumulating dissatisfactions over a period of years. Such is true of the *reorganization movement*. There were rumblings of protest going back into the 1870's. While many were expressed, the dominant dissatisfaction in the 1890's concerned the lack of articulation.

Early Attacks on Articulation. For the secondary level, Chart 1 summarizes some of the activities which helped to focus the attention of the public and the profession upon articulation and other needed school improvements between 1870 and 1960. All of these men, committees, and commissions had one major purpose in mind,—the improvement of the high school. Improving the high school was, is, and will continue to be one of the most important movements in American education.

As early as 1874 and at various times before 1890, the New England

Association of Colleges and Preparatory Schools met to discuss the desirability of establishing uniformity in college admission requirements. These early movements were local, centered around the private preparatory schools, and were concerned with simplifying the college entrance problem. They were not concerned with the public school, but they did indicate that articulation was a common problem for all high schools. Direct attention to college entrance requirements between levels and through the entire system came from another source.

Since it was not originally designed as a college preparatory school, the high school had to do a great deal of exploring before it established a satisfactory working relationship with the college. Early in the development of the secondary school, the National Education Association served as the organization through which the problems of articulation were debated. In 1887, the National Council of Education, which was a department of the N.E.A., called attention to the historic relations between the high school and the college. Although recognizing the original purpose of the high school as a people's college to extend general education and practical training, the committee, nevertheless, urged that education be a continuous process, extending through college. Also, it maintained that both the high school and college were partly to blame for the break in the sequence. Later, a new committee, headed by J. H. Baker, on Uniformity of Requirements for Admission to College was appointed; this committee reported in 1891. The task of articulation was re-emphasized, some general suggestions for dividing the high school studies into courses were made, and more time for study was asked.[4]

In 1892, a report of a committee of the National Council led to the formation of the Committee of Ten which was to become one of the most famous and influential bodies in the history of American education. C. W. Eliot, President of Harvard University, was made chairman of the Committee of Ten. His election was probably due to his address, "Undesirable and Desirable Uniformity in Schools,"[5] at the 1892 meeting. While the address strongly influenced the work of the Committee of Ten, activities which culminated with the report of the Committee had been started five years earlier by the secondary school men and not by the colleges.

Report of the Committee of Ten. College entrance requirements were to have been one important problem of the chief issue, *articulation* of the whole school system. However, six members of the committee were college professors, and the original purpose of the secondary school men was laid aside—something which turned out to be of enormous importance in the years ahead. At its first meeting in 1892, nine sub-committees were formed, each dealing with a field of study in the secondary school cur-

[4] Proceedings of the National Education Association, 1887, p. 282.

[5] Addresses and Proceedings of the National Education Association, 1892, p. 754.

Chart 1. Some Forces That Have Operated to Produce Reorganization and Improvement in the High School

1870 on	Ingenious attacks on various problems at elementary level: Harris of St. Louis, Parker of Chicago, and Dewey of Chicago and Columbia.
1874	New England colleges and secondary schools: conferences to improve articulation between high school and college.
1887	A Committee of the National Council of Education, a Department of the N.E.A.: reported purposes of education were to extend general education and practical training; urged that education be a continuous process extending through college.
1891	Report of the committee on Uniformity of Requirements for Admission to College: the task of articulation was re-emphasized, some suggestions for dividing high school studies into courses were made, and more time for study was asked.
1893	Report of the Committee of Ten: proposed a 6-6 plan of organization instead of the 8-4 plan.
1900 on	Enactment of compulsory attendance laws: a definite step toward making the high school a common school.
1903 on	The rise of the scientific movement in education: school surveys, investigations of the learning process, study of human growth and development, and research and study on the measuring of learning.
1907	Revolt of secondary school teachers against the rigid formal requirements of English and other subjects: led to more freedom for the individual teacher in the classroom.
1916	Attacks of Eliot and Flexner on the secondary school curriculum: urged more attention to scientific and technical materials.
1918	The Commission on Reorganization of Secondary Education: published "Cardinal Principles of Secondary Education"; this has been, perhaps, the most effective single force in the reorganization and improvement of the high school.
1918	Inglis and Alexander published the first really comprehensive textbook on the principles of secondary education.
1922	G. S. Counts' attack on the selective character of American secondary schools: although supported by all of the public, the high school serves only a select group of students.
1932	The Eight-Year Study of the Progressive Education Association: an experiment to test the assumption that there is only one pattern of preparatory studies that qualifies a student for college.
1938	Studies of the American Youth Commission: released were such studies as "How Fare American Youth?" "Youth Tell Their Story," and "Matching Youth and Jobs."
1946	Yearbook of the John Dewey Society, "The American High School": emphasis upon the steps to take in improving the high school.
1947	The Prosser Resolution: life adjustment education for that portion of the students for whom an effective program has not been provided.
1952	Educational Policies Commission, "Education for All American Youth— A Further Look": the 6-4-4 plan of organization plus an adaptation of the program to all youth.
1959	J. B. Conant, "The American High School Today": recommends the comprehensive high school, the elimination of small high schools, flexibility through individualized student programs, encouragement of above-average students to take mathematics, foreign language, and science in addition to English and social studies.

iculum. Here, too, college men were dominant—forty-seven out of ninety. The report of 1893 caused much dissension and vigorous debate among all of the leading educators of the day, but was finally accepted. These were the recommendations:

1. This was the original contention of the secondary school people. The dual purpose of the high school as preparation for life and for college was reaffirmed.

2. The doctrine of formal discipline, mind training, as the theoretical purpose of instruction was reaffirmed.

3. Four basic curricula were suggested: classical, Latin-scientific, language, and English; the last two more specifically designated as "inferior" to the first two.

4. The introduction of secondary subjects into the curriculum at the seventh grade, and graduation from the elementary school at the end of the sixth grade.

5. It was recommended that surveys of secondary fields be introduced into the upper elementary grades.

6. It was recommended that double periods be required for the laboratory subjects.

7. It was recommended that a 6-6 plan of organization replace the 8-4 plan.

Points 2 and 3 brought a vigorous minority report from J. H. Baker, who was a member of the original group initiating the reorganization movement. His foresight has been proven only too correct. Emphasis upon formal discipline and the distinction between the "worth" of courses resulted in the glorification of certain subjects which ultimately came to dominate the curriculum. Shortly thereafter, research by psychologists disproved the formal discipline theory which was to be used as the guiding principle in the selection of subject matter. By and large, the work of the Committee of Ten gave a tremendous boost to the reorganization movement. Also, it popularized the committee procedure which remains to this day the most powerful and effective procedure in American education.[6]

Forces That Gave Impetus to Reorganization. Efforts for improvement in the elementary school started earlier, were more widespread, and involved more phases than at the secondary level. Ideas for the improvement of educational practices never spring fully developed from the human brain; they require a relatively long time to germinate and grow. Also, regardless of where a good idea originates in the school system, the idea will be adapted to and gradually spread to all areas of the system. Since the secondary school in the United States developed later, mention will be made of a few ideas that originated in the elementary

[6] William H. Burton, *Introduction to Education* (New York, D. Appleton-Century Company, Inc., 1934), Ch. 9.

school at an earlier period and were later applied to the improvement of the high school.

Superintendent W. T. Harris of the St. Louis Schools, 1867-1880, introduced natural science to the elementary grades on the basis of its social and practical value instead of its value for formal discipline. He published in 1871 one of the first teachers' guides for the orderly study of the different sciences in the elementary grades. During the last half of the nineteenth century, Col. Francis W. Parker, Dean of the School of Education, University of Chicago, was probably the most influential American educator in the movement to reorganize and improve the school. He advocated and practiced flexible gradation (placing pupils in classes according to readiness), irregular promotions, and supervised study. Also, he advocated and practiced *concentration* and *correlation*, which were introduced into the high school during the 1920's as the unit plan for course organization. He put emphasis upon child growth as equal to or more important than absorption of subject matter—a common position in most modern high schools.

Harvard and Chicago Universities Press for Reorganization. Charles W. Eliot, President of Harvard University and later Chairman of the Committee of Ten, read two papers at the Department of Superintendence of the N.E.A. in 1888 and 1891. The first paper was "Can the School Program Be Shortened and Enriched?" while the second address was "Shortening and Enriching the Grammar-School Course." Eliot, being at his best, greatly aided the movement which was already under way for the reorganization and improvement of the high school. His chief points were:

1. The drill subjects can be completed in the early grades.
2. New and advanced subjects can be added in the upper grades.
3. Better trained teachers and departmental teaching are necessary.
4. The whole course of education should be shortened so that boys may begin advanced study and their life's work earlier.

In 1901, John Dewey, then Professor of Education at the University of Chicago, and in 1902, William R. Harper, President of the University of Chicago, presented papers on the same theme, "we get at the *time-saving problem by limiting* elementary education to six years." This idea startled many Americans, although France and Japan had just reorganized their elementary education on a six-year basis. In 1904, at the St. Louis expedition, it was made quite clear that the United States was the only great nation extending elementary education to eight or nine years. Within a decade, there was general acceptance of the new ideas, and cities such as Columbus, Ohio, and Berkeley, California, had made changes in the organization of their elementary schools. These new ideas had been generally accepted:

1. Drill and fundamental knowledge should be limited to six years.

2. The next eight years' work, including the old seventh and eighth grades, the four-year high school, and the first two years of college, should be organized into a single secondary institution.

3. The universities, as a group of professional schools, should follow the present sophomore year of college.[7]

In 1899, at the Los Angeles meeting of the N.E.A., the Committee on College Entrance Requirements reported that the following resolution was proposed and adopted. "Resolved, that we favor a unified six-year high school course of study beginning with the seventh grade." This one item from the committee's support of the resolution seems important:

The seventh grade, rather than the ninth, is the natural turning point in the pupil's life, as the age of adolescence demands new methods and wiser direction. Six elementary and six high school or secondary grades form a symmetrical unit. The transition from the elementary to the secondary period may be made natural and easy by changing gradually from the one-teacher regimen to the system of special teachers, thus avoiding the violent shock now commonly felt on entering high school . . . Statistics show that the number of students leaving school at the end of the sixth grade is comparatively small, while the number is very large at the end of the eighth grade. By the proposed change, the students in the seventh and eighth grades would gradually gain the inspiration of the high school life, and the desire to go farther in the languages and sciences which they have already begun under favorable conditions. The result would doubtless be a more closely articulated system with a larger percentage of high school graduates.[8]

Reorganization Indicated by Psychological Principles. In the early years of the twentieth century, five great students of psychology, through inductive research and experimentation, discovered certain principles favorable to the reorganization and the improvement of the secondary school. In this process some established assumptions with respect to the learning theory became decidedly questionable.

Formal discipline. Two men, William James and Edward L. Thorndike, tried not one but many experiments to test the theory of formal discipline. The evidence uncovered disproved this theory upon which much of the work of the elementary and the secondary school had been based prior to the twentieth century. The formal discipline theory is based upon the assumption that the mind is strengthened through exercise; hence, any mental task is desirable content for a high school curriculum. In disproving this assumption, the psychologists stated that mental exercise strengthens the mind only to the extent that what is learned increases the understandings, skills, or habits of the learner. Therefore, the curriculum must be comprised of content to achieve these ends.[9]

[7] *Ibid.*, Ch. 9.
[8] Addresses and Proceedings of the National Education Association, 1899, p. 659.
[9] S. L. Pressey, *Psychology and the New Education* (New York, Harper & Brothers, 1933), Ch. 14.

Neither of the views outlined above is in keeping with the evidence now at hand. As of now, the theory on transfer is that transfer of a behavior pattern to a new situation can occur whenever the person recognizes the new situation as similar to other situations for which the behavior has been appropriate. "When it was discovered that any problem could be taught so that the student would then be able to think through other problems for himself," it became the task for educators to discover just what are the conditions favorable to transfer. A teacher can find these methods outlined in any recent and adequate text on methods of high school teaching. Hence, to a much greater extent than was formerly believed transfer depends upon instructional methods as well as instructional materials.[10]

Individual differences. In the early years of the twentieth century, Thorndike organized several research projects on the problem of individual differences. In fact, he published a three-volume work on educational psychology in 1914, of which the third volume dealt entirely with individual differences. Over the last fifty years, psychologists have made a serious study of this problem, and they now know that in every high school there are a number of students who can do the most abstract types of academic work—their insight into the work comes quickly and is thorough. On the other hand, there are also a number of students in every high school who possess only limited ability to understand abstract relationships. Thus, the gap between what they know and what they are expected to learn must be very small. The studies of psychologists have revealed a way to identify individual differences and have shown us how to adjust our programs to students of varied abilities.[11]

A better knowledge of the psychology of youth. One of the effective forces which have operated to reorganize and improve secondary education has been the development of a psychology of youth. As early as 1904, G. Stanley Hall, a vigorous investigator and student of youth, published his *Adolescence*. Studies as to how youth learn and develop have continued to be published from then until now.

Generally, at about the age of twelve to fourteen the individual begins to take on adult biological status and to feel himself a part of the adult world. Gradually, his interests change from those characteristic of a child to those characteristic of an adult. The basis for this change is both biological and social, and an acceptable program of secondary education cannot overlook these facts. What is the type of secondary program which is best adjusted to the psychology of youth in contemporary America? Within the scope of such a program what is the specific nature of educa-

[10] Lee J. Cronbach, *Educational Psychology* (New York, Harcourt, Brace & Co., 1954), p. 253 and Ch. 9.

[11] Frank S. Freeman, *Individual Differences* (New York, Henry Holt & Co., Inc., 1934), pp. 7-32.

tional experience that will best fit each individual's needs? A persistent search for an adequate answer to these questions is a basic condition for the reorganization of American secondary education.[12]

A Brief Summary of the Agitation for Reorganization. Agitation for improvement will be persistent as long as American ways and customs are in a state of flux. When we look back over the last half-century in American education, these few brief and concise statements indicate the heart of the agitation. This is shown in Chart 2.

Chart 2. A Comparison of Old and New Educational Concepts

	THE NEW EDUCATION	THE OLD EDUCATION
Characteristics	The learner is active	The learner is passive.
	The learner is doing.	The learner is listening.
	The interest of the learner is the guide to things to do.	Textbook content alone determines what is done.
	General education stressed as content.	Academic subjects comprise the content.
Aims	Growth	Acquisition of information
	Freedom	Discipline
	Child-centered learning	Teacher-centered learning
Slogans	Self-realization	Mastery of the 3 R's
	Self-improvement	Acceptance of facts
	Co-operation	Competition

All five great students of philosophy and psychology—Dewey, Hall, James, Judd, and Thorndike—were active in promoting the reorganization and improvement of secondary education and all made significant contributions to it. However, John Dewey was the most influential in creating the new education or the new direction of both elementary and secondary education. In general, Charles Judd gave much more attention to the high school than to the elementary school. While he opposed parrot-like verbal recitation as did James and Dewey, he insisted that oral expression, memorization, imagination, and reading were all activities of importance. Also, he insisted that language, abstractions and generalizations, mathematics, and reasoning were phases of our heritage which were of such a character that they could only be transmitted from one generation to the next by the high school. Yet in the transmission of the

---

[12] G. Stanley Hall, *Adolescence* (2 volumes) (New York, D. Appleton-Century Company, Inc., 1904).

National Society for the Study of Education, *Adolescence,* Forty-third Yearbook, Part I (Chicago, University of Chicago Press, 1944).

Arnold L. Gesell, *Youth: the Years from Ten to Sixteen* (New York, Harper & Brothers, 1956).

heritage, he desired growth and understanding rather than mere memorization and the acquisition of facts; he insisted that the learner be active and not passive.

FORMS OF ORGANIZATION

All things change and we are changing with them.
—A ROMAN PROVERB

Why did the 8-4-4 plan of organization begin to change early in the twentieth century? Perhaps three decades of agitation for change had been effective. A goodly number of educators and laymen had come to believe that: (1) too much time was consumed in educating people, (2) life needs were not being met, (3) individual differences were ignored, (4) the various units in the system were articulated neither with the students nor with each other. Several national committees had advocated a six-year elementary and a six-year secondary school. By 1910, junior high schools had begun to be established and by 1922, 387 independent junior high schools were already in operation.

What Are the Common Forms of Secondary School Organization? Like the early cabins of the pioneers, the schools just sprang up with little direction from either state or national government. From that growth, secondary education has taken on many organizational forms. If the newcomer in education becomes a little confused at the way number combinations are tossed about in discussions of the organizational patterns of the secondary schools, he should not be too disturbed. After a while such expressions as 7-4, 8-4, 6-2-4, 6-6, 6-3-3, 6-3-3-2, or 6-4-4 will automatically bring a mental picture of the divisions of our secondary school as they are related to the elementary school.

Figure 1 presents the trends in reorganization of the American schools. These arithmetic symbols applied to the organizational pattern of the secondary school give the number of years devoted to each organizational unit—where 4 appears, it refers to the four-year high school course. The four-year high school is designated as the "regular" or "unreorganized" secondary school. However, when the classification "reorganized" is observed, it refers to the six-year undivided junior-senior high school or to the three-year junior high school with a separate school for grades seven to nine followed by the three-year senior high school comprised of grades ten to twelve.

The addition of the number 2 in Figure 1 to the classifications of the secondary school means that the first two years traditionally associated with the college or university are considered a part of secondary education. These two years, when set apart or associated with the regular public secondary school, are known as "the junior college." Recently, in a few

	Elementary School 8 Years Grades 1-8		High School 4 Years Grades 9-12		1890
K* 1 Year	Elementary School 8 Years Grades K1-8		High School 4 Years Grades 9-12		1900
K 1 Year	Elementary School 6 Years Grades K1-6	Junior High School 3 Years Grades 7-9	Senior High School 3 Years Grades 10-12		1910
K 1 Year	Elementary School 6 Years Grades K1-6	Junior High School 3 Years Grades 7-9	Senior High School 3 Years Grades 10-12	Junior College 2 Years Grades 13-14	1920
N† 1 Year / K 1 Year	Elementary School 6 Year Grades NK1-6	Junior High School 3 Years Grades 7-9	Senior High School 3 Years Grades 10-12	Junior College 2 Years Grades 13-14	1930
Primary School 4 Years Grades NK-2	Elementary School 4 Years Grades 3-6	High School 4 Years Grades 7-10	Community College 4 Years Grades 11-14		1940
Primary School 4 Years Grades NK-2 (separate plant)	Elementary School 4 Years Grades 3-6 (separate plant)	High School 4 Years Grades 7-10 (separate plant)	Community College 4 Years Grades 11-14 (separate plant)		1950

Figure 1. Showing the Trends in High School Reorganization from 1890 to 1950

* Kindergarten   † Nursery school

Within the same school system, old and new plans may be in use concurrently; thus, when the Junior High School is not available to all, the Elementary School might offer Grades K-8 and the High School would provide Grades 9-12.

(Adapted from Fred Engelhardt and Alfred V. Overn, *Secondary Education— Principles and Practices* (New York, D. Appleton-Century Company, Inc., 1937), p. 8, Fig. I.

communities, the secondary school has been divided into separate units of four years each known as the 4-4 plan. This organization includes grades seven through ten and eleven through fourteen.

A study of Figure 1, before and after reading these paragraphs, will make the 4-4 form of organization clearer to you. Figure 1 shows the trends in forms of organization from 1890 to 1950 and the order in which the newer forms began to be favorably received. The 4-4 plan which has gained acceptance in recent years, was originated by the Pasadena Schools in 1929.[13] As yet, its acceptance is largely on an experimental basis. Those who are experimenting with it maintain that it improves the secondary schools by: (1) improving articulation through reducing the number of transition periods within a school system, (2) a better adaptation of the

[13] *The Pasadena Plan of Organization*, Seventh Yearbook of the Department of Superintendence, 1929, pp. 227-29.

phases of human growth and development to the organizational form—the pupils within each school have similar interests and needs, and (3) making it easier to define the objectives within each school more sharply.

What Is the Present Status of Reorganization? In 1949, there were 24,020 high schools in the United States. Table 4 shows the breakdown of schools in the United States.

Table 4. Distribution of High Schools in the United States, 1949

TYPE	NUMBER OF SCHOOLS	PER CENT OF SCHOOLS	NUMBER OF PUPILS ENROLLED	PER CENT OF PUPILS ENROLLED
Public				
Regular high school	13,844	56.9	2,696,419	37.8
Public—reorganized				
Junior-senior high	6,362	26.2	1,787,837	25.0
Junior high	2,362	10.9	1,276,565	17.9
Senior high	1,319	5.4	1,160,336	16.2
Other types	133	.6	219,007	3.1
Total public schools	24,020	100.00	7,140,164	100.00

The secondary schools are predominantly small schools. Over half of the regular high schools have an enrollment of less than 100. The contrast is quite marked when this enrollment figure is compared with that of the reorganized schools where only 17 per cent of the enrollments is below 100 pupils. In fact, Conant concluded in his study that the foremost problem in many states is the elimination of the small high school by district reorganization.[14]

The size of the secondary school is steadily becoming larger, and there are good reasons why this trend should continue. Our industrialized economy attracts more and more of our people away from the farm and into the towns and cities. The typical district high school is a small high school with an enrollment of 100 or less; whereas in the towns and cities, the enrollment in a secondary school is typically 1,000 or more. Also, this typical town or city school will be a reorganized school.

THE ORGANIZATION OF THE SECONDARY SCHOOL IS BEING ADAPTED TO THE CHARACTERISTICS OF YOUTH

Have you ever said this? "I will never go to that store again. They rarely have what I want. They always want me to buy what they have to offer." Yet, on the other hand, you have located and traded with stores that study the needs of their customers. As a result, they nearly always have what you want, or will make an effort to get it.

[14] James B. Conant, *The American High School Today* (New York, McGraw-Hill Book Co., 1959), p. 38.

In this respect, high schools are like stores, and there are good and bad. Some rarely have what the student[15] needs. The student in this case must take what the high school offers or simply quit. Some schools, like many good stores, study the needs of their students and the community. Service is provided according to the needs determined. The good secondary school will formulate its program of studies as a result of investigating the needs and wants of its students. By and large, the holding power of the school is an index to the quality of instruction provided.

Youth Population. In the age group 12 through 19, what is the actual school enrollment? As revealed by attendance statistics, how well is youth being served? The evidence shown in Table 5, which follows, is developed from the *Statistical Abstracts of the Census Bureau, 1955,* since it appears to be the most reliable of the many sources. The youth population between the ages of 12 and 20 is greater than 17 million. More than 10½ million, or 62 per cent of the total, are enrolled in secondary schools, grades 7 through 14.[16] As indicated in Table 5, the secondary school retains 19 out of every 20 pupils in high school through the fifteenth birthday.

Table 5. Youth Population of the United States, 12 to 20, and
and Youth Population in High School*

AGES	YOUTH POPULATION	YOUTH POPULATION IN SCHOOL	PER CENT IN SCHOOL
12	2,301,000	2,204,840	95.8
13	2,188,745	2,099,085	95.9
14	2,135,312	2,025,730	94.8
15	2,128,873	1,954,790	91.4
16	2,079,344	1,682,200	80.9
17	2,092,272	1,426,930	68.2
18	2,180,138	867,695	39.8
19	2,158,400	533,025	24.7

* *U. S. Statistical Abstract, 1955.*

While many other factors operate, the evidence from Table 5 seems to indicate that the services provided by the American secondary school become less meaningful to youth for each passing year after the age of 15. Can it be that these same years, 16, 17, and 18, are potentially the most fruitful ones for youth? Many thoughtful citizens and educators believe so. It is only after a minimum of emotional, social, intellectual, and

[15] The *Dictionary of Education* defines a *student* as one enrolled in a high school or college. A *pupil* is defined as one enrolled in the elementary or junior high school. When speaking of the total population of a school system, the term *pupil* is employed. The term *high school* is applied to a school organized on the 8-4 plan. The term *secondary education* is employed when a school is organized on the 6-3-3 or any similar plan.

[16] The U. S. Office of Education reported the enrollments in secondary education, January 1, 1955, as 8,126,000. It is probable that part of the 10 million shown in Table 5 were enrolled in grades 7 and 8 of the elementary school.

physical maturity has been achieved that our youth can understand the complex American society and feel at home in it. For the development of citizenship, for the building of character, for vocational orientation, and for learning how to get along with people, these are the constructive years. This applies equally to the slow and rapid learners.

For more than a century, it has been the American dream of a high school to serve all youth—rich and poor, talented, average, and slow; without regard to creed, national origin, or race. All should be given an equal opportunity to develop in accordance with their potentialities— that is the American heritage. Is this being realized or is it mere fantasy? In Table 6 you will find a partial answer to this question.

As you study Table 6, you will find that one fact stands out clearly:

Table 6. Number of High School Graduates 17 Years of Age Compared with Population Peers (Continental United States, 1870 to 1950)*

YEAR	POPULATION 17 YEARS OLD	HIGH SCHOOL GRADUATES	NUMBER GRADUATED PER 1,000 PERSONS 17 YEARS OF AGE
1870	815,000	16,000	2.0
1880	946,026	23,634	2.5
1890	1,259,177	43,731	3.5
1900	1,489,146	94,883	6.4
1910	1,786,240	156,439	8.8
1920	1,885,173	311,266	16.8
1930	2,205,822	666,904	29.0
1940	2,403,074	1,221,475	50.8
1950	2,034,450	1,199,700	59.0

* U. S. Office of Education, *Statistical Summary of Education*, 1952.

the percentage of high school graduates has increased every decade from 1870 to 1950. While the total population of 17-year-old youth has increased only 2.5 times, the number of high school graduates has increased 127 times. By now, we know that better than 60 per cent of all 17-year-old youth become high school graduates. This evidence points to one conclusion, the program of the secondary school is more and more being molded to meet both students' needs and the demand of citizens. The American dream is, to a decided extent, being realized.[17]

KEEPING ALL AMERICAN YOUTH IN HIGH SCHOOL

Who are the drop-outs? What causes students to drop out of high school? What per cent of those who enter drop out before graduation? It is probable that the basic causes for early school leavers are included

[17] "Accompanying the increasing proportion of high school enrollment in Negro schools is an increase in high school graduates. In 1953-54, 61,104 pupils were graduated from Negro schools, an increase of 22.6 per cent over the number in 1951-2."—*Statistics of State School Systems: Organization, Staff, Pupils, and Finances, 1953-54*, U. S. Department of Health, Education, and Welfare, Office of Education Biennial Survey of Education in the United States, Washington, D.C., Ch. 2,

in the list shown in Table 7. All six of the studies agree on one cause—
the program of the school is unsuited to most early school leavers. Early
school leavers, when interviewed, have stated over and over again that
the school program is unsuited to them.

Table 7. A Summary of Some Factors Related to Early School Leavers
from Six Studies of the Problem

| FACTORS INVOLVED | STUDIES SUMMARIZED° | | | | | | TOTAL | COMMENTS |
	1	2	3	4	5	6		
Many possess aptitude —not motivated			x	x			2	Great overlapping between regular students and drop-outs
Social stratification (occupation)	x	x	x	x	x		5	Attitudes toward school vary widely
School program unsuited	x	x	x	x	x	x	6	All six studies accept this as a fact
Education level of parents	x		x	x	x		4	In part determines parent attitude toward school
Size of family	x						1	Affects lower income families
Race	x		x		x		3	Program not adapted to minority groups
Small high school			x				1	One program only: heavy drop-out rate
Intelligence			x	x			2	Only a minor factor
Sex	x		x		x		3	Drop-out rate for boys greater
Economic status	x			x	x		3	$125 hidden costs make friction at home
Below average marks	x		x	x	x		4	Near failure destroys morale

° The studies are listed in alphabetical order:

1. Howard M. Bell, *Youth Tell Their Story*, conducted for the American Youth Commission by American Council on Education (Washington, D.C., 1938).
2. George S. Counts, *The Selective Character of American Secondary Education* (Chicago, Chicago University Press, 1922).
3. Ruth E. Eckert and Thomas O. Marshall, *When Youth Leave School*, Regents' Inquiry (New York, McGraw-Hill Book Co., 1938).
4. William Evraiff, "How 'Different' Are Our Drop Outs?" *Bulletin of the National Association of Secondary-School Principals* 41:212-18 (February, 1957).
5. A. B. Hollingshead, *Elmtown's Youth* (New York, John Wiley and Sons, 1949).
6. Owen W. Morgan, *A Study of School Holding Power and an Analysis of Factors Related to Early School Leaving*, unpublished Master's thesis, University of Omaha, Omaha, 1951, typescript.

The drop-out problem has been a persistent one throughout the first half
of the twentieth century. When students drop out in large numbers, the

American dream of a people's college, where all may acquire both civic and vocational competence, is challenged. In *When Youth Leave School*, Ruth Eckert stated that three-fourths of the withdrawing students were woefully unprepared for either civic or vocational life. Some specialists in secondary education treat this problem quite realistically. Study this paragraph from Briggs, Leonard, and Justman.

Ideally it may be stated that a school could find profitable courses for all individuals up to the age of eighteen or twenty one; but practically it must be realized that it frequently does not do so. Small high schools are too limited in the possibilities of their offerings, and large ones by tradition or by lack of public support, for courses to which they have not been accustomed. Our campaigns to popularize secondary education have been more successful than our efforts to provide curricula appropriate to the needs and the capacities of all students who ambitiously continue their efforts. It can not be questioned that many students are now enrolled in courses that do not materially profit them and consequently can not pay dividends on the investment to society . . . Until theorists are able to propose curricula of assured value to all students . . . and society is willing to provide them . . . the inevitable conclusion is that when the law of diminishing returns is obviously operating, students should not be allowed to waste their own time and the public money.[18]

A good study of this difficult problem was done at a midwestern high school by Owen W. Morgan.[19] A freshman class in 1946 was studied throughout the four years from the date of its entrance until the time of its graduation to determine who dropped out and the apparent causes of drop-out. The class started with 424 students. Of these, 157 students graduated.

Each drop-out was interviewed by the chief counselor, who was also assistant principal, and Morgan, who was an attendance officer of the public school system. Morgan, in addition, held at least one interview with the parents of each drop-out. From these sources and the records of the school, he accumulated a vast quantity of pertinent, factual material on school leavers during 1946-1950. The conclusions of the study may be summed up in two statements:

1. Not a single one of the generally accepted causes for leaving school could be applied to more than a very few individual drop-outs.

2. These school leavers believed that the school was not preparing them for what they wanted to do as adults. Other things entered into the decision, but they were not happy with their life in the school.

For the entire United States, Table 8 shows the extent of student survival. This is, of course, an average of all schools and does not reveal

[18] Thomas H. Briggs, Paul J. Leonard, and Joseph Justman, *Secondary Education*, rev. ed. (New York, The Macmillan Co., 1950), p. 194.

[19] Owen W. Morgan, *A Study of School Holding Power and an Analysis of Factors Related to Early School Leaving*, unpublished master's thesis, University of Omaha, Omaha, 1951, typescript.

Table 8. Survival Rates, Ninth Grade Through High School Graduation, in Public and Non-Public Schools, 1948-49 Through 1951-52.*

CALENDAR YEAR	HIGH SCHOOL YEAR	NUMBER SURVIVING PER 1,000 STUDENTS THE FRESHMAN YEAR
1948-49	I	1,000
1949-50	II	869
1950-51	III	744
1951-52	IV	611

* U. S. Office of Education, 1951-52 *Biennial Survey of Education in the United States* (Washington, D.C., U.S. Government Printing Office), p. 26.

the situation for individual schools. For the class studied by Morgan, the survival rate was only 37 per cent. For the United States, 1948-52, the survival rate was 61 per cent.

Poor articulation between grades 8 and 9, a problem in earlier years, has been reduced. The holding power of the high school, grades 9 through 12, shows a steady elimination rate of approximately 13 per cent between each of the grades. The gap between the American ideal of graduation for all American youth and our achievement of 61 per cent survival is still too large.

Some Causes of Early School Leaving. Teachers are in direct contact with students. As directors of learning, they are the first persons who can detect signs of dissatisfaction with the school—the omens of a pending withdrawal. The causes of drop-outs are many, and they apply only to separate individuals and individual schools. Worthy studies, such as one by Hollingshead,[20] reveal that social stratification provides one of the best insights into the causes of withdrawals. This research points to withdrawals as coming almost entirely from the lower two classes of our society. These class stratifications can be described briefly as: Class I, people of wealth and lineage; Class II, civic leaders and those busy amassing wealth; Class III, professional and small-business people; Class IV, home owners, semi-skilled and skilled workers; and Class V, laborers and low-income families. Hollingshead indicates that the social behavior of the adolescents is related functionally to the positions their families occupy in the social structure of their communities. It should be repeated, however, that there seems to be no single factor to explain why all drop-outs occur.

Social Stratification or Socio-Economic Status. Through many interviews with withdrawees and a study of school leavers, Hollingshead attempted to answer the question, "Who are the school leavers?" He found in the Elmtown High School that school leavers are largely from the two lower social classes. One recent drop-out from a Class V family ended

[20] A. B. Hollingshead, *Elmtown's Youth* (New York, John Wiley & Sons, Inc., 1949), p. 358.

an interview by saying, "They treated me all right. They would speak to me when they saw me, but I was different from them and they were different from me." This boy wanted to play football and to date girls, but it required money to do either. For him, money was not available. It also happened that the tradition of his family considered that completing elementary school was enough schooling.

The situation, as analyzed by Hollingshead, is presented as follows:

1. The staff of the high school does not accept the kids from across the tracks. They are punished for minor offenses much more severely than the students from Classes I, II, and III.

2. The program of the Elmtown High School is poorly adapted to the needs of these students. There is a marked taboo among students and teachers against students who enroll in non-academic courses.

3. The money for good clothing and dates is not available. Hence, the kids from across the tracks feel snubbed and are made to feel that they do not belong.

4. The tradition of a high school education is not established among Class IV and V families. Many parents from these families believe that grade education is desirable but that high school education does not help.

Although Hollingshead's study was published in 1949, the data for it were gathered in 1941 and 1942. A more democratic attitude prevails in the Elmtown High School of the present decade. But much of that original tradition lingers in many other high schools. Since most of us who teach in the high schools are from the middle class, we have our own social heritage and much of the same attitude toward the lower-class children that was displayed by Elmtown teachers. For many of us this change in attitude—accepting lower-class children as having potentialities equal on the average to those of children from the middle and upper classes—is a difficult professional task.

However, studies by Davis[21] and Davis and Havighurst[22] make clear to those who can read objectively that potential intellectual power resides among "the kids from across the tracks" to a degree equal to that possessed by the children of the upper and middle classes. Here is one area of potential intellectual power which has been neglected in the past by elementary and high school teachers alike. And the school, almost the only agency that might help, can assist these neglected children in achieving and utilizing the power that is theirs.

Before we can be of much help, we must individually accept them and give them a feeling of belonging in our classrooms. We must help

[21] Allison Davis, "Poor People Have Brains, Too," *Phi Delta Kappan* 30:294-295 (April, 1949).

[22] Allison Davis and R. J. Havighurst, "Measurement of Mental Systems: Can Intelligence Be Measured?" *Scientific Monthly* 67:303-314 (April, 1948).

them to realize that attending high school is worth while. From this group, too, can come great leaders in all areas of endeavor. Somehow, the hidden costs of attending high school must be reduced, especially for those who are made ashamed and fearful. To middle- and upper-class children, these hidden costs which run frequently to more than $100 a year for each student are no more than pittances—but not so for teen-agers from "across the tracks." Our industrialized society quite naturally places the "hot rod" far higher in the scale of values than it should be. When pocket money does become available to lower income youth—often through the work-study plan of the school—they face a real crisis: Shall they meet the hidden costs of education? Or shall they start payments on a cheap car that represents immediate attainment of status and a higher class level? Girls do not have such a great conflict, although they tend to evaluate the worth of a young man in terms of whether he does or does not own a car. This factor of hidden costs and getting what seems to be the most value from a dollar is a part of the drop-out story. Teachers must help teen-agers to face it.

Intelligence. As a major factor in the elimination of certain youth from school, intelligence has been decidedly overrated. It is true that abstract intelligence is a primary element in a classical education. But the insistence of the public that all pupils can profit from an education aimed at citizenship, character, and job orientation is now established as right and proper in our democracy. Even the "kids from across the tracks"[23] as a group are shown to be as intelligent as the "kids from Nob Hill."

A program for all youth, comprised of common learnings[24] can be constructed when supplemented by elective courses for all. Of course, the larger school can offer a much greater variety of subjects and also provide more effective guidance and counseling to assist all students in the selection of a program which fits individual needs. Most studies admit that those of lower intelligence are eliminated to a greater extent than those of higher intelligence. But students of a lower or relatively lower intelligence can, by greater application, meet requirements for graduation.[25] They are less interested in the straight academic

[23] Davis, *op. cit.*, pp. 294-295.

[24] National Association of Secondary-School Principals, *Planning for American Youth* (Washington, D.C., National Education Association, 1951), pp. 20-23.

[25] Responsibility for a planned program that will not permit discrimination between students of low intelligence and those of high intelligence is encompassed in the following statement:

"Fundamentally, the school exists to provide instructional services for the boys and girls of the school community. The principal, as head of the school, is responsible for the adequacy of the instructional program . . . The principal's program of improving instruction shall be submitted as a part of the school's annual report."—*Advancing Education in Kentucky Through Improvement of Instruction*, Department of Education, Frankfort, Kentucky; Educational Bulletin, Vol. XXIV, No. 4 (April, 1956), mimeographed.

curriculum and do fail more frequently than students of average or above-average intelligence. Studies also seem to indicate that when the curriculum is revised to fit the varying needs and abilities of students, the differences in drop-out rates between the bright and dull are greatly reduced.

A Brief Summary. In developing the many factors which are related to the problem of school leavers, we have thus far found the following to be established truths:

1. Generally accepted causes for drop-outs should be examined closely since each school leaver has his individual reasons, known or unknown, for divorcing himself from his American heritage.

2. One four-year study of a large high school indicated that the drop-out almost always had a feeling of not belonging.

3. Poor articulation between grades 8 and 9 might account for a national drop-out rate of abnormal proportions between grades 9 and 10; approximately 13 per cent now drop out between each of the grades 9, 10, 11, and 12.

4. Social stratification may explain the high drop-out rate on the part of those from Classes IV and V.

5. Hidden costs of the school program must be given more consideration as we set out to reduce the drop-out rate.

6. Intelligence must not be a major factor in eliminating youth from the secondary school. Students of less than average intelligence can, by greater effort and through more adequate guidance and counseling work, meet general requirements for graduation.

THE HIGH SCHOOL—A COMMON SCHOOL

I shall try to correct errors when shown to be errors, and I shall adopt new views so fast as they shall appear to be true views.

—ABRAHAM LINCOLN

The American social order holds that every American youth is entitled to a full span of secondary education and that he will be a better citizen as a result. The errors that prevail stand out in every statistical study. Table 9 presents such evidence.

Illinois, for the school year indicated in Table 9, had 109,766 children in the kindergarten. How many will complete the twelfth grade? This failure makes it imperative that Illinois and other states with similar proportions must heed Lincoln's words and "try to correct errors when shown to be errors." Table 9 might well be framed and posted in the office of every high school counselor, guidance worker, dean, and principal for ready reference. Copies of current studies should be handed to each teacher at the annual pre-school conference. Every member of our society

Table 9. Secondary School Enrollment by Grades, 1953-4*

NORTH CENTRAL UNITED STATES	FIRST YEAR	SECOND YEAR	THIRD YEAR	FOURTH YEAR	TOTAL
Illinois	93,077	85,757	70,830	59,863	309,527
Indiana	56,711	51,121	41,408	36,311	185,551
Iowa	35,259	32,817	28,887	26,272	123,235
Kansas	26,892	25,017	21,770	19,859	93,538
Michigan	78,338	70,748	56,669	49,507	255,262
Minnesota	39,814	37,027	32,513	28,619	137,973
Missouri	48,721	40,490	35,544	30,060	154,815
Nebraska	17,559	16,033	14,499	12,925	61,016
North Dakota	8,373	7,493	6,677	6,119	28,662
Ohio	100,229	91,190	74,073	63,078	328,570
South Dakota	8,530	8,115	7,219	6,626	30,490
Wisconsin	42,181	39,956	35,153	31,654	148,944

* *Biennial Survey of Education,* 1953-54, U. S. Office of Education. Totals include post-graduate students in some states.

should know the problem, the errors in our present approach to solving it, and the nature of changes to be made if the American dream is to be attained.

Failure and Retardation. Studies concerning the causes of failure indicate that intelligence is only one of the many factors involved. Some of the elements more directly implicated are *attitudes, poor study habits, not seeing a need for the course being taken, poor reading ability,* and *lack of application.* Even such factors as illness, poor health, physical handicaps, poor vision, moving from school to school, and defective articulation are highly important. Nearly always, several of these factors are present in any case of failure.

Failure is a chief cause of retardation but not the only cause. Starting school at a later age, prolonged absences, carrying a lighter load, and working long hours at outside jobs are also factors. Much can be done to reduce failures and retardation by adjusting assignments to the varying abilities of students and emphasizing individual growth and achievement. Many good teachers are finding ways to use these procedures. Neither failure nor retardation has been found to be a helpful device for stimulating student activity other than in specific exceptions. Actually, many who fail in grade 9 will not be in attendance in grade 10. Despite assumptions to the contrary, youth are just like adults; they get little satisfaction in doing things poorly and being told that they are doing them poorly. Like adults, they will, as soon as they can, turn to something at which they feel they can be more successful.

Compulsory Attendance. All 50 states have compulsory attendance laws. However, requirements vary widely from state to state with respect to the vigor of their enforcement. In many states, especially in rural areas, compulsory attendance is enforced rather rigidly for the elementary school but very laxly for the high school. Everywhere, the laws set up the limits of compulsory attendance from a certain age to a certain age. Table 10 shows these limits for all 48 states and the territories in 1957.

States and territories vary widely as to the time and conditions for a work permit (exception to established laws). The great majority set 16 as the appropriate age for issuing a work permit provided certain other conditions prevail. Nine require graduation from high school or attainment of the age 17 or 18 before a student can legally leave school. Where attendance laws are rigidly enforced, as they frequently are in urban areas, few students can drop out of high school before the junior year. At the present time, public pressure seems to be toward a more

Table 10. Showing the Age Limits for Compulsory Attendance in the Various States and Territories of the United States, 1957

NUMBER OF STATES AND TERRITORIES	BEGINNING AGE LIMIT IN YEARS	NUMBER OF STATES AND TERRITORIES	UPPER AGE LIMIT IN YEARS
4	6	1	14
36	7	2	15
10	8	38	16
		2	17
		7	18

rigid enforcement of compulsory attendance laws; there is pressure also to make them apply to high school as well as to elementary school.

Besides, a new trend is in the offing. "In a nation-wide poll of a large number of leaders in business and industry, it was estimated that the average entry into gainful occupations will be stabilized at about the age of 20 or 21 in the foreseeable future."[26] This might well foreshadow the upping of compulsory attendance laws in many states from 16 to 18 or more.

Articulation. When the work of the elementary school is closely co-ordinated with that of the high school, articulation is smooth and the entering student is prepared or easily adapts himself to the work and activities of the new school. If the articulation is deficient, the student entering the high school feels out of place, becomes dissatisfied and unhappy, dislikes the school, and is classified as an inadequate student.

At one time, it was the custom for only a few, usually those aca-demically inclined, to seek admission to the secondary school, but the public pressed more and more for the high school to admit all elemen-tary graduates. And gradually it became the custom for all or nearly

[26] Harold C. Hand, *What People Think About Their Schools* (Yonkers, N.Y., World Book Co., 1948), p. 11.

all elementary school graduates to advance their schooling. Among many high school teachers, there was a fairly strong tradition that preparation for college was the single purpose of the high school, and they resented this influx of youth who did poorly on straight academic work. The elementary school was accused of promoting pupils who were poorly prepared in the fundamentals. But the public pays the taxes and determines what is to be taught and who is to be taught—and demands greater acceptance. This has become the basic problem between the elementary school and the high school. It is fast developing as the basic problem between high school and college.

The issue is: *Shall the high school become a common school open to all youth?* The public, by slow and indirect methods, has already decided the issue. The elementary school has always been a common school for all of the children of all of the people. The high school has now become, or is fast becoming, a common school to meet the needs of all youth. High school teachers are key people in providing smooth rather than defective articulation between the elementary and the high school. To the extent that the high school teacher adapts his instructional material and methods of teaching to the needs of these new students, as they are admitted without question to the high school, will smooth articulation be facilitated and the gap bridged.

In doing this the high school teacher needs to modify his methods of teaching, assignments, and his attitudes toward the newcomers so as to bring about a high degree of articulation with the previous experiences of the entering students. As these new entrants grow at home with their new environment, a gradual change in attitude toward the high school pattern takes place. Of course, the articulation process involves the entire staff of the school. The wise principal is the co-ordinator. Conferences between the elementary and high school staff members bring about a better understanding and improve the articulation process. Co-operation between the elementary and the high school staffs in a program of orientation for elementary school graduates helps make the entrance to high school less hazardous. The modern high school arranges visitations and tour programs for the elementary people: films are shown; conferences are held; every device is utilized to inspire a friendly feeling on the part of the newcomers.

One element in the success of the junior high school movement in the United States has been its effectiveness as a transition unit between the elementary school and the high school. The junior high school is specifically designed for and adapted to the needs and the stage of development of the pre-adolescent teen-ager; it encompasses him before he becomes a teen-ager and very naturally fosters his normal growth. But there is no magic in just any type of organization, even in that of the junior high school. Articulation between school units becomes easier when the school staff has vision and understanding. Such teachers do not force pupils to conform; they merely assist them in making the adjustments that are necessary.

Sex. America is unique in its establishment of a coeducational secondary school. Since there is a strong attraction between teen-agers of the opposite sex, this coeducational custom, in itself, has probably operated to retain many of both sexes in high school for longer periods—despite other conflicts and forces to the contrary. Until quite recently, the number of girls enrolled in the high schools exceeded the number of boys. The probable explanation for the original trend was that the economic world has had a greater attraction for boys while the school curriculum exerted a greater appeal to girls. As we know, girls mature more rapidly and, hence, appear to be more willing to pursue an academic curriculum, such as the traditional high school offered.

Since there has been recently an emphasis upon life adjustment education with a more functional curriculum, the number of boys remaining in high school until graduation has markedly increased. The addition of student activities, athletics, and the introduction of new courses plus the modification of old ones have made a stronger appeal to boys. Perhaps some of the questions an employer usually asks of a boy seeking a job have added in part to the appeal of the high school diploma. This becomes sparkling and clear when to the crucial question, "Are you a high school graduate?" the boy must reply, "No, sir!"

Early Marriage. Up to World War II marriage for any high school student was strictly taboo. A married student, especially a young woman, was immediately barred from attending high school. In general during World War II, early marriage was sanctioned as a normal outgrowth of wartime living. Since young men of 18 and 19 were called to the services, many of the young brides of 16, 17, and 18 were still in high school. These young women wanted to complete their high school education since life in our day almost requires it. As usual, the high schools responded to public demand and accepted these brides as regular students. After the end of World War II, there was no abatement in the practice of early marriage, and the custom of brides remaining to complete their education has persisted. It is probable that this practice is here to stay.

Yet the change has brought some real problems to high school teachers. The young women, faced as they were by some immediate and practical problems, desired functional courses such as homemaking, consumer buying, retail sales, income tax procedures, and even auto driving rather than the previously scheduled academic courses. Also, in their new status as wives they resented being treated as immature girls—though many were and did not know it. For other students, too, they posed the problem of establishing new relationships. Some of the high school teachers felt that the place of these young wives was in their homes rather than in the school. Some believed that the academic courses being bypassed represented the basic core of a high school education and that all other courses were so much nonsense. The easy solution, as they saw it, would be to expel the married girls.

On the other hand, the high school found that a distinct service could be rendered to these young women. Under capable teachers, the transition from high school life to family life and the responsibilities of mature citizenship can be greatly facilitated. Homemaking skills can be acquired. Many of the personal problems of the home and the community can be partially solved by discussion and sane instruction. Human relationships in family and community can be improved. Coming at a time when there is readiness for it, the knowledge which they obtain during the time they spend in high school can be highly profitable. It is a move again toward the realization of the American dream.

Teen-agers, even married teen-agers, are not proper candidates for the adult schools which have rapidly expanded since World War II. Educational TV has not yet produced evidence that it can meet the needs of teen-agers. The married teen-ager, young man or young woman, is fully entitled to the right to earn a diploma in the regular high school.

Health. Although no exact data are available concerning the extent of withdrawals from high school because of ill health, teachers and school administrators are well aware that it is considerable. Although severe illnesses and death are relatively low during adolescence, the incidence of minor illnesses and disabilities is relatively large. It is a common occurrence for teen-agers to be absent from school for several weeks and to drop out for an entire semester because they are unable to make up the work missed. These cases often lead to personal discouragement and permanent withdrawal.

You, as a practical-minded, pre-service teacher, may ask the question, "so what?" The answer will become clear if you will put yourself or someone dear to you in the place of the student who suffers illness. It makes a big difference, doesn't it? That is why high schools have set up "home teacher" programs for the homebound students. That is why, within broad limitations, high school teachers go out of their way to provide special assignments, a degree of make-up work, and course outlines that may be mastered by those who are ill. Full realization of the nature of this instructional work will not come until you have personally helped such a student to recoup classroom time lost through no choice of his own. Experienced teachers will testify that this humanitarian service provides great dividends and professional satisfaction.

WHAT PRACTICAL PROPOSALS CAN BE MADE FOR RETAINING ALL TEEN-AGERS IN HIGH SCHOOL UNTIL GRADUATION?

Some answers to this question have been suggested in the earlier chapters of this text. A few additional guideposts are as follows:

1. The program of the school must make sense to teen-agers. We cannot make the student fit the program. But we can construct a program of studies more nearly in accord with contemporary American life. Such a program will increase the holding power of the school.

2. Effective guidance and counseling will assist youth in selecting a program best suited to individual needs.

3. The introduction of more functional subjects will hold many teen-agers in school longer.

4. Making secondary education accessible to all by means of consolidation, transportation, and provision for dormitories would retain some students longer in schools where such needs occur.

5. Reduction in the number of failures would reduce retardation and elimination. As a general rule, progress at the rate of a grade each year should be permitted.

6. Improve articulation between the divisions of our school system and between the grades within a school.

7. Extend compulsory attendance laws to include secondary education and enforce the laws.

8. Try to establish a partnership between teachers and parents when parental background permits. As parents and teachers become partners, an understanding results which makes the parent a positive force in retaining the student in school.

9. Reduce the hidden costs of secondary education and the personal "school expenses" of the students. For teen-agers from poor homes, these become real burdens and cause drop-outs. The school can absorb the cost of student activities and decrease emphasis upon expensive uniforms, gowns, and jewelry; in most cases, the cost of materials and supplies can be decreased.

10. Assist worthy students in finding part-time work—but guard against exploitation of youth, i.e., long hours at low pay, especially when night-time hours rob the student of sleep or play time.

11. Give prestige-bringing activity to students of varying abilities, not just to the select few.

12. Provide opportunities for students, who are ill at home for long periods, to study under home supervision.

13. Watch for symptoms of withdrawal. Studies on withdrawal reveal that the following are the major symptoms: regression in attendance and scholarship, over-age for the grade, history of repeating grades in ele-

mentary school, failure in one or more high school subjects, little interest in school or participation in school activities.

For pre-service teachers, proposals 1 and 13 are the keys. Locating people who are likely to leave school before graduation is only a first step in retaining them in school. These students, in particular, need to be encouraged in their work and urged to participate in student activities. You will need to keep in close touch with their parents. If the teacher is tactful and understanding, intimate knowledge of parental background will frequently help to change student attitudes toward schooling. Students who are on the verge of withdrawal are often emotionally distraught; here, again, the teacher must be both tactful and understanding in order to reach them on a common ground and help retain them in school.

There is every indication that the incidence of parental failure in relation to so-called problem children is fast increasing. This caution must be noted for the beginning teacher who might count too much upon parental support in helping today's child to reach an adult decision and remain in school. Where parents are worthy—and most are—this factor could be thoroughly exploited; where they are not worthy—and many are not—the teacher must call upon personal resources, imagination, courage, and personality.

DISCUSSION PROBLEMS

1. What problems of youth helped to bring on the reorganization movement?
2. How did the Committee of Ten's report have a negative effect on the development of the secondary school?
3. What is the present form of organization in your local school system? Are there any evidences of change?
4. How does the secondary school population today differ from that of a half-century ago?
5. What class differences contribute to students leaving school before graduation?
6. How selective should our secondary schools be? Should the high school diploma be available to all youth?
7. Would you recommend that all teachers be employed until the age of 65?
8. Occasionally, a new superintendent will announce that "any boy or girl, 16 years of age, who fails in scholarship or citizenship will be banned from the school." Would it solve anything?

RELATED REFERENCES

ALEXANDER, William M., and SAYLOR, J. Galen, *Secondary Education: Basic Principles and Practices* (New York, Rinehart & Company, Inc., 1950).

Association for Supervision and Curriculum Development; *A Look at Continuity in the School Program*, 1958 Yearbook (Washington, D.C., National Education Association, 1958), Pt. II.

BELL, Howard M., *Youth Tell Their Story* (Washington, D.C., American Council on Education, 1938).

BENT, Rudyard K., and KRONENBERG, Henry H., *Principles of Secondary Education* (New York, McGraw-Hill Book Co., 1955).

BRIGGS, Thomas H., LEONARD, J. Paul, and JUSTMAN, Joseph, *Secondary Education*, rev. ed. (New York, The Macmillan Co., 1950).

BURTON, William H., *Introduction to Education* (New York, D. Appleton-Century Company, Inc., 1934).

CHISHOLM, Leslie L., *The Work of the High School* (New York, The Macmillan Co., 1953).

COLE, Luella, *Psychology of Adolescence*, 4th ed. (New York, Rinehart & Company, Inc., 1954).

Committee of Ten, *Report of the Committee of Ten on Secondary Education* (New York, American Book Company, 1894).

CONANT, James B., *The American High School Today* (New York, McGraw-Hill Book Co., 1959).

COUNTS, George S., *The Selective Character of American Secondary Education* (Chicago, University of Chicago Press, 1922).

CRONBACH, Lee J., *Educational Psychology* (New York, Harcourt, Brace & Co., 1954).

DAVIS, Allison, "Poor People Have Brains, Too," *Phi Delta Kappan* 30:294-95 (April, 1949).

———, and HAVIGHURST, Robert J., "Measurement of Mental Systems: Can Intelligence Be Measured?" *Scientific Monthly* 67:303-314 (April, 1948).

DAVIS, Jesse B., *The Saga of a Schoolmaster* (Boston, Boston University Press, 1956).

ECKERT, Ruth E., and MARSHALL, Thomas O., *When Youth Leave School*, Regents' Inquiry (New York, McGraw-Hill Book Co., 1938).

ENGELHARDT, Fred, and OVERN, Alfred V., *Secondary Education—Principles and Practices* (New York, D. Appleton-Century Company, Inc., 1937).

EVRAIFF, William, "How 'Different' Are Our Drop Outs?" *Bulletin of the National Association of Secondary-School Principals* 41:212-18 (February, 1957).

FREEMAN, Frank S., *Individual Differences* (New York, Henry Holt & Co., Inc., 1934).

GESELL, Arnold L., *Youth: the Years from Ten to Sixteen* (New York, Harper & Brothers, 1956).

GRAVES, Albert D., *American Secondary Education* (Boston, D. C. Heath & Company, 1951).

GRUHN, William T., and DOUGLASS, Harl R., *The Modern Junior High School*, rev. ed. (New York, The Ronald Press Company, 1956).

HALL, G. Stanley, *Adolescence* (2 volumes) (New York, D. Appleton-Century Company, 1904).

HAND, Harold C., *What People Think About Their Schools* (Yonkers, N.Y., World Book Co., 1948).

HOLLINGSHEAD, A. B., *Elmtown's Youth* (New York, John Wiley & Sons, Inc., 1949).

HORROCKS, John E., *The Psychology of Adolescence* (Boston, Houghton Mifflin Co., 1951).

HURLOCK, Elizabeth B., *Adolescent Development* (New York, McGraw-Hill Book Co., 1949).

JACOBSON, Paul B., *The American Secondary School* (New York, Prentice-Hall, Inc., 1952).

KNIGHT, Edgar W., *Education in the United States* (Boston, Ginn & Company, 1951).

Koos, Leonard V., *The American Secondary School* (Boston, Ginn & Company, 1927).

———, *Junior High School Trends* (New York, Harper & Brothers, 1955).

MEAD, Margaret, *Coming of Age in Samoa* (New York, Blue Ribbon Books, 1932).

MORGAN, Owen W., *A Study of Holding Power and an Analysis of Factors Related to Early School Leaving,* unpublished master's thesis, University of Omaha, Omaha, 1951, typescript.

National Association of Secondary-School Principals, *Planning for American Youth* (Washington, D.C., National Education Association, 1951).

National Society for the Study of Education, *Adolescence,* Forty-third Yearbook, Part I (Chicago, University of Chicago Press, 1944).

PRESSEY, Sidney L., *Psychology and the New Education* (New York, Harper & Brothers, 1933).

SPAULDING, Francis T., *High School and Life: Regents Inquiry* (New York, McGraw-Hill Book Co., 1938).

SPEARS, Harold, *The High School for Today* (New York, American Book Company, 1950).

U. S. Office of Education, *Biennial Survey of Education,* 1953-54 (Washington, D.C., Government Printing Office).

Chapter 5

THE TEACHER AND SOCIETY

You do solemnly swear, each man by whatever he holds most sacred,
that you will be loyal to the profession of medicine . . .
—OATH OF HIPPOCRATES

TEACHING—A HIGH PROFESSIONAL CALLING

The bearded Greek physician, Hippocrates, who treated the sick more than 1,300 years ago, is the father of modern medical ethics and practice. The immortal Hippocratic Oath begins:

I swear by Apollo, the physician, and Asklepios and all the Gods and Goddesses, making them my witness, that I will fulfill according to my ability and judgment this oath and this covenant.

There exists no similar oath or pledge to be taken by the teacher, aside from the obligations administered by some of the fraternal groups. Yet there exists within the profession of teaching just as lofty a purpose and just as sacred a trust. From one viewpoint, the physician is called upon only to heal the sick but the teacher administers to the sick and well alike. Indeed, through the quality of educational service, local, state, national, and international outcomes are established anew each generation. Everything that benefits man has been and is the result of man's own ability to rise above his base impulses, and teachers help him to achieve this control. In turn, it follows that man's failures may be traced to the inability of the schools to provide desirable educational services.

Obviously, notable gains have been made in what has been called "man's race against himself." The American economy supports a system of educational effort through taxation. This is a key factor in enabling the American people to rise above the sordid levels usually induced by sheer industrialism. Slum living and "penny wages," piece work in squalid tenements, dark filthy shops lacking even primitive sanitary conveniences, the health-destroying 70-hour week—all the attributes summed up in the malevolent "sweatshop" of industry—have been rapidly disappearing as education has become more universal in nature. The student of American society cannot but see the marked parallel between the rise of the common man and the advance of public awareness since those appalling years that followed the Civil War. The attitude of the "business mogul" has also changed—either by consent and understanding or through legislative compulsion, the result of united action on the part of workers with at least a minimum education. To be sure, a degree of exploitation is still with us, but its popularity is fading. The basic truths of our democratic heritage will never disappear if each teacher is aware of his trust. The perpetuation of freedom requires much more than mere lip service.

Ethical Concepts. To unify the teaching profession and to make it a more effective social service, there have been efforts made by a number of groups to establish a code of ethics or policies for those engaged in school work. Perhaps the best known is the code which in 1929 was officially adopted by the National Education Association. This body, the largest and best known, has instituted a Committee on Ethics for the purpose of evaluating questionable procedures.[1]

Teachers and the Trade-Union Question. Along with other white-collar workers, teachers have experienced, since the NEA Code of Ethics was adopted in 1929, severe treatment during a period of depression and inflation. In some school districts observance of ethical conduct was almost forgotten by teachers and administrators alike. Teachers often charged that ethical tenets were no more than a control device used by administrators and that the profession provided no adequate means to ensure fair play. While teachers in several instances censured those administrators who openly violated established ethical procedures, the courts almost always favored the rights and privileges of school boards and administrators as opposed to those of the teachers. A quite natural result of this critical period was for classroom teachers to give greater consideration to the trade-union movement.

The AFT Commission on Educational Reconstruction[2] has indicated that assigning the teacher to a role of respectable indigence is a universal practice. Even in the democratic United States, contempt coated with honey has always been the teacher's reward for submission to decisions that must affect him deeply. The belief that the NEA has not done enough to protect teachers' interests has led many to think that the answer to their problems is to be found by joining forces with the trade-union movement.

[1] Sarah T. Muir, "Final Report of the Committee on Ethics of the Profession," *Addresses and Proceedings of the National Education Association* (Washington, D.C., National Education Association, 1929), pp. 179-182.

[2] American Federation of Teachers, Commission on Educational Reconstruction, *Organizing the Teaching Profession* (Glencoe, Ill., The Free Press, 1955), pp. 137 and 161.

The American Federation of Teachers, AFL-CIO. With headquarters in Chicago, the AFT has sought to bring about employee-management relations for teachers just as the trade unions have been successful in doing. The AFT leans heavily upon the Education Department of the AFL-CIO and, through its affiliation with some 16 million union workers, has been able to urge the Congress and the President to give increased attention to school problems. In school communities where organized labor is not popular, school boards and administrators have violently opposed the AFT; some have dismissed teachers for their interest in affiliating with trade unions. But in the more industrialized areas, where it is now customary for management and labor to resolve their differences through legal arbitration, the AFT locals have been accepted and recognized. While the most recent federal legislation, the Taft-Hartley Act, does not provide for public employees, it does not specifically forbid teachers to negotiate with their school boards.

What of Other Professions? The issue, of course, is whether classroom teachers ultimately, through affiliation with labor, may be better able to serve youth and society. Members of the American Medical Association have never found this necessary, although it has been claimed that the AMA in a sense has "the biggest trade union" of all. Lawyers, dentists, and clergymen have also avoided trade unionism. However, the American Federation of Musicians, founded in 1896, has been closely affiliated with AFL-CIO and without question has succeeded in retaining economic status of a high order for the vocation of music. Again, a group of reporters, columnists, and editorial workers some years ago organized the American Newspaper Guild for the purpose of improving ethical and economic standards of journalism. The ANG constitution frankly states that it exists "to advance the economic interests of its members." Again, C. N. Sayen,[3] President, AFL-CIO Air Line Pilots Association, International, has written:

> While some so-called professional organizations have not reached the stage where they actively engage in collective bargaining for their members, they are nevertheless intimately concerned with rates of compensation, rules, and working conditions as well as the maintenance of standards for their particular group.

The AFT argues that ethical matters are a problem for continuing study and adjustment. Just as other professions associated with trade unions are giving attention to the rights of members, the AFT constantly evaluates such issues as tenure, rating, academic freedom, and extra assignments which concern the teacher. The general history and philosophy of the AFT, together with ethical standards, are discussed at length

[3] C. N. Sayen, "How Labor Unions Have Built Other Professions," *The American Teacher Magazine* 41:9 (February, 1957).

in *Organizing the Teaching Profession.*[4] Loyalty oaths, certification, auto-
nomy, and similar problems are examined frankly, from the AFT viewpoint, by Lieberman[5] in *Education as a Profession.*

Thus, the teacher's personal choice of a professional organization will
be determined mainly by community attitudes and economic pressures
of the moment. Joining the AFT does not necessarily exclude the classroom teacher from the excellent research program for which the NEA
is noted; more than a few members of AFT also belong to NEA and the
various local, state, and national associations that are devoted to the
cause of education.

In a comparison between NEA and AFT, Lieberman has noted that the
first, by its very size and structure, is not always capable of meeting
the individual needs of classroom teachers. For the most part it is the
administrators who reap the professional benefits provided by NEA.
A counter-argument, also noted, is that the exclusion of administrators
from NEA control might not necessarily provide the best solution to this
difficulty. Just as the labor movement is hampered by lethargy and lack of
dedicated leadership, so might NEA flounder without the guidance of experienced administrators. Probably most beginning teachers will follow
the same course of action regarding professional organizations as did
several first-year teachers who were asked: "What professional organizations have you joined?" Here are typical responses:

I was forced to save on dues since I started, like all others, at the lowest pay
level. I joined just the state organization because we draw our salary during
the two days of the annual fall convention. I belong to nothing else.

I joined NEA because I like the research and literature they provide. Of
course, my principal suggested that he wanted everyone to belong to the local,
state, and national associations—so I went along with the crowd. I might not
have done this otherwise.

I teach in a union town and have joined the AFT. We have been able to
set up collective bargaining with our school board because many of them are
union-minded. I am a delegate to the local federation, AFL-CIO, and probably
know more about union processes than most teachers.

The National Council for the Social Studies is a department of NEA, and
I find *Social Education* to be of great value in my work as a social studies
teacher.

As a math major, I like the national conferences arranged by NEA so that's
what I joined. We also have a state organization for math teachers, and I belong
to the local Schoolmasters' Club.

My vision has been broadened through my membership in the National
Council for Teachers of English. Some don't like it, but I do.

[4] American Federation of Teachers, Commission on Educational Reconstruction,
op. cit.
[5] Myron Lieberman, *Education as a Profession* (Englewood Cliffs, N. J., Prentice-
Hall, Inc., 1957), pp. 103-137.

I belong to the NEA Department of Classroom Teachers and have a part in supporting research that is of specific and general interest.

Some teachers find it beneficial to keep memberships in groups that have no direct relationship to teaching itself. A history major, for example, may elect to join his local historical society, the state association, or one of several national groups devoted to history. And there is always, for the teacher who finds himself working in an isolated area, the chance that a new organization may be started. One of your authors achieved this some years ago by writing a column of pioneer history for the local newspaper—within the year he was busy setting up markers for the Pony Express Trail in fellowship with a dozen other lonesome teachers from nearby villages. There need never be a "dull moment" in teaching if one will spur himself into organizational activity.

What Is Professional? A teacher who conforms to the stated or implied standards agreed upon by a professional organization is being a professional person. Ethical aims in rural and urban communities may vary widely, just as the personal desires and views of school administrators may be different. It is highly probable that there can never be devised a single code that would encompass all of the complex situations that do arise within every school system. Such crises are solved best through adherence to professional attitudes rather than through blind loyalty to any specific doctrine. In due time each teacher will develop a personal code of ethics or policies that will enable him to maintain self-integrity.

DESIRABLE TRAITS FOR PROFESSIONAL TEACHERS

What competencies, attitudes, and behaviors would you require if you were given the responsibility of hiring teachers? Thus far, we have hinted at those values. Certainly it is the task of teacher education institutions to screen those candidates who cannot correct or improve their emotional handicaps, since there is no place in the classroom for the bully, the tyrant, the weeper, the insecure, the drone, the coward, the pervert. Not all social and classroom situations can be anticipated by the teachers college, but it has been found helpful to set up positive "check lists" in an effort to seek out those teachers who would most likely measure up in any situation. Burton has provided such a listing to measure total personality, with qualifications, as follows:

1. The teacher's health, physical development, strength, and handicaps
2. The teacher's level of intelligence and scholarship
3. The teacher's emotional and social adjustment
4. The teacher's cultural background, interests, and appreciations
5. The teacher's social relationships in school and community
6. The teacher's attitudes toward children, social institutions, and education as a career

7. The teacher's morale.

8. The teacher's personality traits.[6]

We may borrow this listing and draw upon personal observations in citing case records. The following should not have been brought into the profession:

1. The teacher who is usually absent on a Monday, complains that the room is chilly (despite a room temperature of 80 degrees), and is "too tired" to sponsor an occasional field trip.

2. The teacher who regularly sends notes to the superintendent in which she informs him of the conduct of her principal and other co-workers; she also reports the condition of school toilets and refuses to teach in any room other than the one she has selected. She skips the unit on income taxes.

3. The teacher who rides the extreme of emotional waves, i.e., she is either prissy or base in her attitude toward the "parlor stories" and earthy incidents that often enter social contacts; she "overdresses" or "underdresses" or confines her wardrobe changes to "pink beads for the fall term and green beads for spring."

4. The teacher who takes no interest in activities outside of the school, reads no literature not related to school work, makes no attempt to cultivate an appreciation for art or music.

5. The teacher who regards all school patrons as idiots and declines their phone calls, notes, and visits.

6. The teacher who feels that the school was established for her personal convenience and that the children may have anything that remains after she is satisfied—which she seldom is.

7. The teacher who regularly sends a messenger to the office for help in managing her students; she frequently bursts into tears and runs out of her classroom; she is always the last person to submit records to the office as the school term closes.

8. The teacher who is first to leave at the end of the day—and last to arrive; she walks out of committee meetings; she refuses to take part in or lead group discussions; she is a poor driver and has been fined several times; she writes letters to the Public Pulse under a *nom de plume*.

If the aim of the educational process is to impart knowledge, social conscience, and improved attitudes, how could any of the above teachers help achieve this end?

There have now been established certain positive traits that determine the effectiveness of every teacher. Umstattd[7] provides us with a compila-

---

[6] William H. Burton and Leo J. Brueckner, *Supervision: A Social Process*, 3rd ed. (New York, Appleton-Century-Crofts, Inc., 1955), p. 533.

[7] J. G. Umstattd, *Secondary School Teaching* (Boston, Ginn & Company, 1937) (associated with Marjorie Palmer, Bureau of Recommendations, University of Minnesota), p. 437.

tion of traits, the result of 45 studies and reports. We suggest that you undertake to rate one teacher who may stand out vividly in your memory of high school days. A simple scale is indicated:

1 (Excellent)_____2 (Superior)_____3 (Average)_____4 (Fair)_____5 (Poor)

_____Personal grooming: neatness, appropriateness, good taste

_____Teaching personality: poise, judgment, mental alertness, vivacity, sense of humor, resourcefulness, tact, initiative, dependability

_____Loyalty: willingness and ability to uphold school policies and to co-operate with associates and supervisory officials

_____Vitality: general physical condition, buoyancy, ability to be on duty every day

_____Knowledge of subject matter: mastery of high school subject, breadth of interest, background

_____Selection and organization of subject matter: independence of judgment as to proper material, clearness and effectiveness of organization

_____Method: general mastery, ability to adjust method to various kinds of content and to individual differences in pupils

_____Class achievement: progress of class while in charge of this teacher

_____Management, motivation, and discipline: ability to secure good working conditions, interest and eagerness of class

_____Success as a teacher: relative standing the teacher has earned in your estimation as compared with other teachers of the same experience.

A logical result of such a rating, of course, will be a degree of self-examination. In what areas might you give added attention to the development of desirable traits?

A Word About Merit Pay Plans. Application of ratings, such as the above listed traits, has been urged by a few school administrators who feel that exceptionally superior teachers should be awarded higher salaries. A teacher, they argue, should not be placed on a salary scale merely in terms of tenure.

But, as the National Citizens Council for Better Schools said, "Did you ever try to skin a live tiger?" Feeling runs high these days in regard to the merit pay problem.[8]

Both NEA and AFT have declined to accept any merit pay plan proposed to date; the National Association of School Administrators is highly interested in several phases of the program. Here is the way it is defined by the Department of Classroom Teachers of the NEA:

. . . a subjective, qualitative judgment of a teacher, made administratively by one or more persons, with or without the participation or knowledge of the person rated, for the purpose of determining salary.[9]

[8] *Better Schools*, Vol. 3, No. 5, 9 East 40th Street, New York 16, N.Y. (May, 1957), p. 1.
[9] *Ibid.*, p. 5.

The AFT went on record first in rejecting the proposal and contended that "equal pay for equal work" was preferable. Both AFT and NEA think that graduate work coupled with years of service merit pay advances; AFT in 1957 asked that a $5,000-$10,000 salary schedule be established for all teachers and specifically voted against any merit pay plan, teacher aids, and the temporary employment of non-certified personnel. In 1959 the salary range requested was $6,000-$12,000.

Earlier, both bodies had been successful in winning a single salary scale, i.e., no differences in pay for men and women, and this is generally followed.

But merit pay? It is indeed like skinning a live tiger to venture this question, and we suggest that your class may want to give at least one period to debate and discussion of the issue. The New England School Development Council has been particularly interested in attempting to apply the plan; your college library will provide much of the literature now available regarding the pro's and con's of the proposal.

A few of the arguments for and against merit pay plans are given in Chart 3.

Others have pointed out that, in view of the present low salary schedules, this is not the proper time to install any merit pay plan that would, in a sense, place a ceiling on most teachers—since only a few find it possible to be exceptionally superior. The ethical interpretation by both NEA and AFT is that employment of such a device would not be professional.

Hidden Traits Make Good Schools. After all, the professional teacher is a human being and can hardly be driven to develop any list of traits that might be designed by an administrator. Notice, however, the traits which are suggested in the following student descriptions of "what makes a good school."[10]

1. To me, a good school does three things. It creates a respect for the truth; it cultivates good taste; it works for better understanding of mankind.

2. The high school is the end of formal teaching for almost half of the students in this country. This means that a school, if it is a good school, must provide for the student who quits after high school as conscientiously as it provides for those who will go into higher education. The good school prepares these students for the world, its problems and opportunities.

3. A good school must have an even-tempered administration which deals calmly but firmly with matters of discipline. It must have the best available teachers who not only know their subjects but know how to put them across. Teachers must take real interest in their pupils and work to gain their friendship and respect.

A good school reflects the degree of professional instruction and brotherhood that each teacher is capable of developing.

[10] "Superintendent's Bulletin," Omaha, Nebraska, May 16, 1955.

Chart 3. Some Pros and Cons of Merit Pay Plans

FOR MERIT RATING	AGAINST MERIT RATING
1. Equal pay for equal work kills initiative and encourages mediocrity. If the superior teacher is paid at the same rate as the lazy or incompetent one, excellence is penalized and poor teaching condoned. Therefore, unless salaries are based on merit, the public has no assurance that it is getting good teaching for the huge expenditures it makes for the schools.	1. The case for the single salary schedule is supported primarily by teachers and the professional organizations. They are joined, however, by many administrators and some laymen. Teachers are likely to claim that rating is impossible. The only true way to evaluate teaching effectiveness is by measuring pupil growth. Since many of the results of teaching —either good or bad—will not be evident for many years, it is impossible to draw up a neat balance sheet at the end of every year. No other objective means for evaluating teachers has been developed to date. If it is left to a single administrator, the teacher is put at the mercy of one individual's whim. If the job is turned over to a committee, evaluation of teaching tends to become a popularity contest.
2. Business and industry recognize the value of rewarding their superior employees, and teaching should do the same. There have always been ways of assessing teachers, and some of these have proved reasonably reliable even when they have been subjective. Certainly it is possible to select a committee of teachers and administrators to evaluate the worth of individual teachers on a relatively impartial, objective basis.	2. No matter how it is done, it is bound to result in lower morale and will keep young people out of the profession. At best, it destroys the co-operative relationship among teachers and that between teachers and administrators. At worst, it can be used as a club over the head of outspoken and imaginative teachers to make them conform to one individual's ideas. Finally, it is bound to be difficult to explain to some parents why their children cannot be taught by the few "superior" teachers.

TEACHER AND COMMUNITY ADJUSTMENTS

What restrictions are placed upon the teacher by the mores of a community? Is it still necessary for the teacher to live in a "goldfish bowl"? Similarly, to what extent should the teacher expect the community to adjust to his personal concepts?

Just as with any citizen, the teacher must anticipate that his privacy will be determined largely by the nature of the community which he serves. The typical American small town has been stereotyped as having inquisitive housewives, wayward husbands, and "blue-nose" school boards. Actually, most small towns have broken away from this stereotype and are eager to find and keep the best qualified teachers.

Perhaps this change was brought about by the high rate of teacher turn-over since depression days. Perhaps increased communication with the "world outside," through the growth of television and radio, may explain the break with tradition. At any rate, those who teach in small-town schools may now anticipate a degree of personal freedom comparable to that accorded any other member of the community. For example, small-town school boards more and more are providing "teacherages" for their employees who might otherwise have difficulty in finding suitable housing. Small towns need teachers.

To be sure, the community expects the teacher to conform to an accepted pattern of morality; in setting noble goals and standards, the community compliments the teacher. After all, isn't this exactly what most teachers demand of the community? The teacher encourages the community's children to be honest, sincere, courteous, and virtuous; the teacher explains the harms that come from narcotics and the excessive use of tobacco and alcohol. When the teacher urges better living for the community, it is only fair for the community to expect the teacher to "practice what he preaches."

Urban Employment and Adjustment. In terms of salary increment, the more desirable teaching positions are usually available in the larger cities. Just as other citizens may find increased cultural advantages, and perhaps increased privacy, in metropolitan areas, so may the teacher. On the other hand, there will seem to be less accomplished in larger schools since students and teachers often lose sight of each other when the school day closes. This factor in mass education somewhat explains why many teachers elect to remain in smaller communities throughout their careers; there is, indeed, more warmth and fellowship in small-town living than in city life.

While applicants for teaching positions in rural areas usually must interview personally each member of the school board, candidates who seek employment in city schools have a more intricate pattern to follow. A written request for an interview should be directed to the assistant superintendent in charge of personnel. If vacancies are anticipated, this individual will set a date and will indicate what references, certification, and degrees will be required for consideration. Following such an interview, the candidate will meet a screening committee composed of representative members of the administrative staff. In some states, the applicant will be required to take an examination. Such tests often include essential knowledge of state history and government. In times of emergency and teacher shortages, the usual requirements may be cut to a minimum. An "emergency" teacher, for example, may be hired without certification and, for that matter, without much formal schooling; such rare instances, however, carry the stipulation that the teacher will engage in academic work during his employment, that is, enroll in evening courses at a nearby college.

Upon the recommendation of the superintendent, the candidate will be formally elected by the school board and assignment to a specific school will soon follow. Where county regulations are observed, the teacher will be required to register his certificate with the county school superintendent.

Contractual Obligations. A period of probationary teaching,[11] from three to five years, is customarily followed by an "elected" status which, in time, will lead to a "permanent" type of contract. When the final level is attained, yearly contracts are discontinued, as a rule; following retirement, currently at the age of 65 years, the teacher may again receive yearly contracts that are renewable in terms of teacher ability and the needs of the schools.

Many experienced teachers do not understand that permanency and tenure legally do not prevent a school board from dismissing any employee. Insubordination, incompetence, immorality, like "cruelty" in divorce, are broad terms and not many dismissed teachers who carry their cases into the courts find sympathy. Of course, a teacher may sue for breach of contract and, prior to suit, may demand a full hearing before the board of education. The ethics of such a situation should be examined by professional organizations, and both NEA and AFT offer this support to all members. In turn, a teacher who breaks a contract should not expect professional help.

Traditionally, and in many states by law, the school system notifies the teacher in April or May that the contract will or will not be renewed for the following school year. Thus, this is the time of year that teacher candidates should make their strongest effort in seeking employment. Notice of resignation or retirement, by the way, should be given in writing to a school superintendent as soon as a decision has been made; last-minute withdrawal "for spite" is hardly professional.

If, as indicated earlier, the courts seem to favor the school board and community as opposed to the demands of the teacher, it should be remembered that public schools exist for just one purpose. That purpose is to provide adequate education for all youth in a pleasant and stimulating manner; the schools are not institutions for the employment of frustrated, incompetent, belligerent, and vicious persons who can find nothing elsewhere with which to occupy themselves. A classroom teacher throughout a normal career will be in personal and daily contact with some 20 thousand young Americans. This is a most solemn obligation to

---

[11] Certain school boards employ temporary teachers as "permanent substitutes" who are on a day-to-day basis with no contractual commitment. This procedure permits the hiring of teachers who do not meet professional qualifications or who do not desire full-time employment as teachers.

our heritage, and it calls for the most accurate system of screening and selection of personnel. Anything less is actually harmful to our nation.

The Personal Element in Teaching. Considerable attention has been given to the personal factor in teaching since it largely determines the most desirable trait in school service—the "classroom personality." Fortunate indeed is the individual who is blessed with those attributes that make him a "natural" teacher. Such persons do not have to strive for social acceptance; they practice the principles of good mental health and physical health. The many "little things" that may bring about frustrations are shunted aside; the sedentary nature of teaching is countered through an active interest in participatory sports. Of one teacher who ignored the principles of mental health and carried home each night a briefcase loaded with papers to be marked, her superintendent said, "I will not renew her contract. She just isn't a pleasant person in the classroom next day." To this superintendent it was far more important that the teen-agers should have a rested and refreshed personality in their room than to receive any number of corrected papers from a dreary grouch. Her responsibility was to organize school procedures so that evenings at home might be spent in a normal manner.

A high school principal has noted that his day is never complete unless he has received a tongue-lashing—either from a school patron or a teacher. Another has said that more than half of his school problems originate with teachers. If these opinions are valid, and many administrators will agree that they are, then the teacher must realize that continued "friction" (an administrative term used in teacher ratings) must indicate at least a degree of failure on the part of the teacher. Briefly, the teacher should not call upon the central office for assistance in solving a school problem until every other possible solution has been attempted. If we look at pupil problems objectively, we must admit that they do have a way of growing out of proportion. Constant adjustment is necessary on the part of the teacher who would be successful.

What Society Asks of Its Teachers. Historically, when common citizens wanted their children to have just as fine an education as that which was being provided for the elite, the public schools were established. This original desire is still reflected in legislative requirements that tend to make the school offerings quite uniform; social pressures demand high-quality education despite the fact that individual members of society may not always appear willing to foot the bill for such standards.

In a migratory period, when, for example, children of federal workers, including those of the military, may attend school for a time in New Orleans, then in Chicago, Seattle, or Omaha, the tradition of uniformity serves them well. Thus, we find that states generally require high school graduates to have obtained specific training in such areas as the following:

1. American history and the Constitution
2. Health and physical education
3. State history and government
4. Civics and citizenship

Those high schools that now receive federal aid under the terms of the Smith-Hughes Act, the George-Deen Act, and similar legislation, must offer courses that include agriculture, home economics, and distributive education. Here, again, uniformity is obtained. In many states, pro-collegiate forces have prevailed upon legislatures to require that high school graduates must earn credits in academic subjects—a necessary background for college entrance where formal examinations must be passed. The strong formality of the traditional college is also reflected in the various state department examinations which particularly trouble the small-town teacher. College pressures and legislative pressures may force the high school teacher to provide far more drill and memorization than would otherwise be given. Little time remains, under such demands, for practical improvement of the curriculum so that it might meet the actual needs of all American youth. The teacher who notes that few graduates ever attend college may be confronted with the problem of adjustment at this point. To what extent must uniformity and classicism prevail? The community may provide the answer.

What the Community Demands. Those who support the public schools through taxation want every youth who desires a college education to have that opportunity. At the same time, the community demands that its school give heed to local problems as well. Every state and school system within the vast area encompassed by the St. Lawrence Seaway, for example, wants its youth to be fully aware of the change that tremendous project is making in the heart of the regional economy. Larger schools, usually not so tightly bound by state department requirements, can more easily adjust to these demands. In addition, city high schools find it most reasonable to adjust to individual differences. "Academic" and "general" courses are provided for rapid and average learners in English and social studies courses. "Senior math" and "senior review" courses are offered for those who need additional training for vocational employment or college entrance. The smaller high school, with limited facilities, can not liberalize its curriculum; hence, it may fail to respond to community demands.

Professional Standards. The teaching profession, recognizing such broad needs of youth and the demands of society, has set up regional standards through several associations of schools and colleges. The North Central Association of Secondary Schools and Colleges in the Midwest, for example, constantly evaluates the nature of the school program and the community for which it is provided. When a regional association declines to approve a school, the effect is essentially psychological, but it brings increased attention to those standards which are held to be desirable.

Just as "wildcat banks" sprang up in the early days of westward expansion, so did "diploma mills" and phony correspondence courses enter education. They still operate today despite state laws, federal regulations, and efforts by the Better Business Bureau to keep them under control. Reputable newspapers do not accept advertisements of this nature in which the term "school" or "college" appears—but the "institute" seems destined to go on forever. Cheap magazines continue to circulate advertising that promises "a degree in six months," and, because they have readers who lack selectivity in the first place, the magazines get results for their advertisers.

Accreditation requires that certified teachers in sufficient number be employed, that schools and colleges support libraries that are worthy of the name, that the grounds and facilities be of a specific nature. The six regional associations blanket the nation; in addition to North Central, they are: the Middle States Association of Colleges and Secondary Schools, the Northwest Association of Secondary and Higher Schools, the Southern Association of Colleges and Secondary Schools, the Western College Association, and the New England Association of Colleges and Secondary Schools.

Just a word regarding "personal" standards as a member of the profession. How much might a beginner ask about his new job—and stay within bounds? This is a realistic problem.

It is entirely fair for a job candidate to inquire about teaching schedules, class sizes, and outside responsibilities. It is entirely proper to request and receive a copy of the salary schedule and to determine exactly what the stipend will be for the school year. There is nothing wrong in learning whether a portion of the salary will be held back until the close of the term. These are things to discover before the end of the first month of teaching—and the asking of such questions is professional.

Is it professional to ask about getting a job? Some teachers evade this question by paying teacher placement agencies as much as 10 per cent of their first year's salaries for this service.

Is it professional for a teacher to resign at the last moment? Not any more than it is for a school board to stall in the issuance of new contracts or pay schedules. But because an act is unprofessional does not mean that it will not occur.

Is it professional to carry rumors? One apprentice teacher was informed that a tenure-teacher was about to resign. He promptly asked the associate superintendent if he might have that teacher's assignment. When questioned by the associate superintendent, the tenure-teacher became furious and revoked his original recommendation of the beginner. The apprentice's action was not only unprofessional but unprofitable as well.

What professional standards, then, should the beginning teacher follow? More often than not, this question will be resolved by the wise counsel of an experienced teacher who, as a part of his own professional activity, will go out of his way to assist the first-year teacher. This may be the opening chapter of a lifelong friendship, and it will make professional "standards" seem very worthwhile.

POLICIES AND PROGRAMS CONSTANTLY CHANGE

The attitude of a high school class reflects the personality and ability of the teacher; a school reflects the qualities of leadership held by the principal; a school system reflects the needs and desires of its community as interpreted by the superintendent and the school board. Thus, everything that the child learns within the school is a direct result of community demand.

But communities change. If the school fails to keep abreast of such changes, then a merry-go-round of misunderstandings can be the only result. That is why school policies must remain as flexible as possible if they are to be practical. True, there must be written rules and regulations designed to provide a common understanding of the legal structure of a school system and its basic policies and functions. But the printed policy is seldom the final answer to questions of administration.

The following paragraph[12] illustrates a statement of policy achieved by three city superintendents over a score of years:

Functions of the School System

It is the basic purpose of the public schools to provide a set of common learnings, skills, habits, attitudes, and character traits essential in our culture. The schools shall inculcate an appreciation of the responsibilities of citizenship in our American democracy. It shall be the definite purpose of the schools to strengthen, improve, and unify American life. Schools shall aid youth in the choice and preparation for a vocation for living in an economy which encourages free enterprise and individual effort. It should be the constant aim of the public schools, as an outcome of the instructional effort, to promote staunch moral character, the appreciation of spiritual values, a love of home and country, respect for duly constituted authority, and a genuine concern for the rights of others regardless of race and creed. As a direct outcome of educational processes, the individual should be willing to act in the interest of general welfare and to assume a mature responsibility for his own acts in our democratic society.

This statement of functions will likely be valid for many years. It is far more desirable than an earlier regulation that demanded all high school boys to wear neckties throughout the day—including vocational courses where whirling machinery menaced their safety.

[12] *Rules and Regulations of the School District of Omaha* (Omaha, Nebraska, Board of Education, December, 1956).

Objectives of Secondary Education. Communities and policies may change, but there are basic objectives that seem destined to remain constant. These were given in Chapter I, and here we need only to underscore the need to keep original objectives in mind as society undergoes change.

Thus, today, a social studies class may discuss the values of "hot rods" and "drag strips"; a science class may examine the mechanics of jet propulsion and argue its future probabilities; and the English class may prepare term papers related to the study of cancer and heart diseases. Society requires that schools continue to teach basic subjects, but it does not ask that this be done in a manner that is outdated. The obligation of the teacher, then, is to instruct the children of society in a way that will not drive teen-agers into the streets before they have finished their formal education.

Policies and Curriculum. Just as a school must change to keep pace with society, so must attention be given to improving the curriculum. An advertising specialist might say, "Put some meat on the platter!" Stiles and Dorsey[13] have summarized the steps in such an activity as follows:

Participation in curriculum development or improvement involves such activities as teachers' meetings; workshops; summer study committee work with teachers, students, and parents; research projects; building resource units; planned experimentation; visits; child study; follow-up studies; and evaluative procedures.

The procedures of curriculum development are (a) agreement on a common philosophy; (b) examining the character of society; (c) studying the individual and his needs; and (d) recognizing the fundamental purposes of education.

Equally important activities are (a) determining the effectiveness of existing educational programs; (b) reconstructing curriculum design; and (c) developing teaching methods compatible with the ends in view.

Clearly, the professional teacher, with proper leadership, must contribute far more than classroom hours in serving youth and the community. Such activities, however, need not be dull chores if the teacher fully understands the purpose behind curriculum building. Reference here may be made ahead to Chapters VI, VII, VIII, and IX for purposes of discussion and agreement.

These principles or guides in curriculum work are suggested by Umstattd.[14]

1. A curriculum which would be entirely vocational in its aim would not be in accord.

2. The fact that a subject has long been in the offering is not in itself a justifiable reason for its continuance.

[13] Lindley J. Stiles, and Mattie F. Dorsey, *Democratic Teaching in Secondary Schools* (Philadelphia, J. B. Lippincott Co., 1950), p. 444.

[14] Umstattd, *op. cit.*, p. 238.

3. Content of no value in the development of the pupil should not be forced upon him.

4. The mental maturity of the student should be a factor in determining the difficulty of the content.

Umstattd reminds curriculum builders that "there should be a limited range of years in which a course may be taken. To permit seniors to attend classes predominantly, for example, for freshmen would be too wide a range and should rarely, if ever, be permitted."[15]

Let's Ask the Community. School patrons who are well informed about their teachers and curriculum problems will want to be asked for opinions regarding changes to be made.[16] "Should schools spend more time on reading, writing, and arithmetic? Are children suffering from a lack of old-time discipline? Do you like the type of report card being used in the grade schools?" These are the kind of questions which need to be asked and for which answers need to be tabulated.[17] The National Service Institute, Chicago, has provided a commercially printed folder entitled, "Just a Second," for similar surveying of opinion. Here is a sample page:

What Would You Say?

Education for these times, it seems, must be concerned with a lot more than can be found in textbooks. Here are some of the things school people seem to think are important. Your schools may already include many of them but will you check the ones you consider important anyway?

__How to get along with people
__Education for home and family living
__General understanding of religion
__Learn to drive an automobile
__Sex education
__Develop a positive personality
__Develop respect for rights of others

__Appreciation of music
__Military training
__How to be a good citizen
__Ability to speak well including use of good English
__Good health habits
__Enjoyment of sports
__Desire to vote regularly

DO CHILDREN WRITE AS WELL AS YOU DID AT THEIR AGE?

YES__; NO__

WOULD YOU LIKE TO SEE MORE WRITING TAUGHT TODAY?

YES__; NO__

---

[15] *Ibid.*, p. 239.

[16] It has been our observation that far too many schools depend almost entirely upon daily newspapers for the task of keeping school patrons informed. A more reasonable course would be to provide well-edited school newspapers which reach homes regularly through the mails.

[17] Don R. McMahill, *Public Opinion as Related to the Omaha Public Schools*, unpublished master's thesis, Omaha University, Omaha, 1944, typescript. In this study, 57 per cent of 544 patrons surveyed said that more reading, writing, and arithmetic should be taught; 53 per cent said that children were not suffering from a lack of old-time discipline; and opinion was evenly divided on the use of a new-type report card.

The attitude of the professional teacher today must reflect many studied values, some of them seemingly in conflict. The humility that is achieved only through devoutness, the scholarship that comes only through study, and the ready wit that results only through awareness must somehow be combined by the modern teacher. The wisdom of the ages must be united with the scope of television if today's teacher is to "belong" in a classroom of teen-agers. Thus, in addition to thorough preparation in subject matter and instructional procedures, the teacher must "know thy students."

1. Know all of the biological changes that are occurring within the basic being of each teen-ager. Understand that these are natural and that the teen-ager has no way to avoid his normal development.

2. Know of the battles that he must face and win or lose as moral issues catch up with him at home, on the streets, and in school.

3. Know the fears that are thrust upon him by an adult press, an adult radio-TV, an adult world of power politics, military conscription, and exploitation. Understand that abnormal acts attract teen-age attention far more than acts of common decency. Be aware that the desire to ape and to conform is strong within us.

4. Know of his struggle for balance in a day when a girl may chide him by saying, "I don't like a boy just for the kind of car that he drives —as long as he has a car."

What is the nature of modern society as the teen-ager may see it? It is the Age of Ages—automation, alcohol, broken homes, atomic energy, housing booms, slums, and jet propulsion. It is the age of fear and the hydrogen bomb. It is an age of the welfare state—an age of change from economic traditions. It is the age of conflict.

What one of us would be able to withstand the stresses that modern society places upon its teen-agers?

But what a wonderful refuge the permissive classroom affords when its leader understands himself and provides the security, the learning, and the friendship so sorely needed by all American youth.

Ideally, a school should undertake a sociological study of the community such as the classic "Madison Community."[18] Advertising agencies with products and services to sell do just that and more in these highly competitive times. In a sense, with so many public agencies striving for support, the schools do have a service and product to "sell." If public schools fail to gain knowledge of community needs and fail to go into partnership with school patrons, then it will never be possible to bring into being any objectives, no matter how noble and vital they may be.

[18] Kimball Young and others, *The Madison Community,* University of Wisconsin Studies in Social Sciences and History, No. 21 (Madison, University of Wisconsin, 1934), p. 89.

GNOTHI SEAUTON—KNOW THYSELF . . . AND THY CHILDREN

In returning to the important factor of teacher personality and its relation to professional service, it is well to recall the wisdom of Socrates who gave this key to a sound philosophy—*Gnothi seauton*—Know thyself. It was the Greek philosopher who said: "One thing only I know, and that is that I know nothing." Harold Spears[19] has been quite blunt in speaking out against "teachers who have arrived, the prima donnas, each a self-assured master in his special field with a pride in his mastery more pronounced than his feeling of the whole development of the youth he would serve." Most of us have been in classrooms commanded by such personalities, and, looking back, it is difficult to recall any warmth, pleasantness, or, for that matter, any learning. Teen-agers, particularly in our time, hold no respect for such persons; nor do communities who pay the bill.

SUMMATION

The teaching profession is one of the highest services offered by man to man.

Through affiliation with local, state, and national associations of teachers, the individual may better equip himself to meet the many demands of modern instructional service; in so doing, he assists others as well.

The ethical aims of individual superintendents may vary from community to community, but the total standard is noble and relates positively to national and world-wide purpose.

A teacher must be aware of individual differences among all teachers. He may modify those traits in himself which seem likely to make him less effective if they are permitted to continue.

Communities today regard teachers as free citizens who have privileges equal to those of any other member of the village or city.

Society asks that the schools teach essential subjects in terms of contemporary needs.

School policies and curricular offerings must keep pace with changing society.

Communities want to co-operate with schools in the development of new policies; the schools must meet the communities at least half way.

The modern teacher must know himself, his strengths, and his weaknesses; but he must also know the conflicts and struggles through which every teen-ager passes in his striving to become a worthy American citizen.

[19] Harold Spears, *The High School for Today* (New York, American Book Company, 1950), p. 261.

Such a teacher will achieve immortality in the hearts and minds of his students, his community, and his nation.

DISCUSSION PROBLEMS

1. Do you agree that man's failures may be traced to the inability of schools to provide desirable educational services?

2. Would it be proper for a social studies teacher to invite a speaker from the local labor union to address the class? Explain your answer.

3. Why do some teachers question the activities of the American Federation of Teachers?

4. Why do some teachers question the activities of the National Education Association?

5. Prepare a list of ten traits that you think would be the most desirable in a teacher. Of these, which three are the most important?

6. Let us assume that you have been employed by a small school district in which there are only two churches, neither of which is of your faith. Would you attend church services? Defend your decision.

7. Select a city other than one you are familiar with, and determine what steps should be taken in obtaining employment. What is the name of the key individual to whom you should apply?

8. Under what circumstances would you send a student to the office for help in solving a matter of discipline?

9. Why are school policies constantly changing?

RELATED REFERENCES

American Federation of Teachers, Commission on Educational Reconstruction, *Organizing the Teaching Profession* (Glencoe, Ill., Free Press, 1955).

BURTON, William H., and BRUECKNER, Leo J., *Supervision: A Social Process*, 3rd ed. (New York, Appleton-Century-Crofts, Inc., 1955).

EYE, Glen, and LANE, Willard, *The New Teacher Comes to School* (New York, Harper & Brothers, 1955).

FRANK, L. K. and Mary, *Young Adolescent at Home and at School* (New York, The Viking Press, 1956).

GILES, Herbert H., *Teacher-Pupil Planning* (New York, Harper & Brothers, 1941).

GRAMBS, Jean D., and IVERSON, William J., *Modern Methods in Secondary Education* (New York, The Dryden Press, 1952).

HUGGETT, Albert J., and STINNET, F. M., *Professional Problems of Teachers* (New York, The Macmillan Co., 1956).

KAUB, Verne P., "A Symposium on the Teacher in America," *Saturday Review of Literature* 35:16-17 (April 19, 1952).

KELLEY, Earl C., *Education for What Is Real* (New York, Harper & Brothers, 1947).

LIEBERMAN, Myron, *Education as a Profession* (Englewood Cliffs, N.J., Prentice-Hall, Inc., 1957).

McMAHILL, Don R., *Public Opinion as Related to the Omaha Public Schools*, unpublished master's thesis, Omaha University, Omaha, 1944, typescript.

MELBY, Ernest O., *The Education of Free Men* (Pittsburgh, University of Pittsburgh Press, 1955).

MUIR, Sarah T., "Final Report of the Committee on Ethics of the Profession," *Addresses and Proceedings of the National Education Association,* (Washington, D.C., National Education Association, 1929).

National Society for the Study of Education, *In-Service Education,* Fifty-sixth Yearbook, Part I, (Chicago, University of Chicago Press, 1957).

RASEY, Marie I., *It Takes Time: An Autobiography of the Teaching Profession* (New York, Harper & Brothers, 1953).

RICHMOND, Kenneth, *Education in the U.S.A.* (New York, Philosophical Library, 1957).

SAYEN, C. N., "How Labor Unions Have Built Other Professions," *The American Teacher Magazine* 41:9 (February, 1957).

SPEARS, Harold, *The High School for Today* (New York, American Book Company, 1950).

STILES, Lindley J., and DORSEY, Mattie F., *Democratic Teaching in Secondary Schools* (Chicago, J. B. Lippincott Co., 1950).

UMSTATTD, J. G., *Secondary School Teaching* (Boston, Ginn & Company, 1937).

WILES, Kimball, *Supervision for Better Schools* (Englewood Cliffs, N.J., Prentice-Hall, Inc., 1955).

YOUNG, Kimball, *The Madison Community,* University of Wisconsin Studies in Social Sciences and History, No. 21 (Madison, University of Wisconsin, 1934).

ZERAN, Franklin R., ed., *The High School Teacher and His Job* (New York, Chartwell House, Inc., 1953).

PART II

The Modern Curriculum

Chapter 6

THE HIGH SCHOOL CURRICULUM

The child does not want an easy school, he wants a challenging one.
—HAROLD SPEARS in *Some Principles of Teaching*

The actions of people can be understood only by a study of what they consider valuable. An excellent secondary school curriculum provides meaningful and purposeful experiences—valuable experiences—for boys and girls. Despite what many recent critics of the high school say, all shades of educational opinion recognize, implicitly or explicitly, the central importance of subject matter; yet for parents and most teachers the student is always more important than the subject matter. The latter is merely the means to an end—which is the wholesome development of the student being served.

The people of every society are confronted by the problem of inducting the immature members into their culture, that is, into the ways of their society. An institution such as the public school is charged with the responsibility of teaching certain things. It must create a sequence of potential experiences for the purpose of directing youth into group ways of thinking and acting. This set of experiences is referred to as the *curriculum.* Always, in every society, the curriculum is a reflection of what the people think, feel, believe, and do. This general principle is as applicable to small tribes as it is to nations.

THE CURRICULUM IN EARLY CULTURES

Puberty Rites in Tribal Life. It is customary to call the youth curriculum which has been maintained by all tribes, ancient and contemporary, *puberty rites.*[1] Usually the actual *puberty rite* ceremonial is preceded by a period of instruction that lasts from six weeks to six months in accordance with the customs of the tribe concerned. Certain tribal elders are designated as instructors; the instruction is entirely oral and in many cases on record seems to have been vivid and dramatic. It is the process

[1] *Puberty rites* are reported by anthropologists as being common, even today, among Africans and South Pacific tribes.

by which youth nearing adulthood are inducted into the adult culture. While the practices are varied, the puberty rite ceremonial has always applied to both sexes, although boys and girls are instructed separately. At different times, boys are taken into the brush some distance away from the tribal home to remain until the day of the puberty ritual. Boys are instructed by men and girls by women.[2] The areas most stressed by the tribal elders can be classified as literature, religion, science, mathematics, and civic duties.

Literature and religion. In a vivid manner, the elders retell the story of the origin of the tribe and of the heroic deeds of their ancestors. Those ancestors who pleased the gods by their acts and deeds were protected and saved; those who offended the spirit world were punished and destroyed. A classic example of such a tale from Western literature is the *Iliad*, in which the lesson is that "men of the tribe must know how to placate the gods."

Mathematics. Trade between tribes and members of the same tribe continues today. Anthropologists have established that a record of the number of sheep and cattle bought, sold, or traded was kept in earlier times just as it is now. During pubic training, boys learn trading customs and how to count and perform the simpler manipulations of numbers.

Civic duties. Historically the greatest emphasis seems to have been upon civic duties. Boys had to learn the simple rites of living together. The following two quotations (literal, as given by an elder of Torres Straits) illustrate this lesson:[3]

You no steal. You no take things belong another man, without leave; if you see a fish spear and take, s'pose you break it and you got no spear, how you pay man? S'pose you see a dugong harpoon in a canoe and take it, and man he no savvy, then you lose and break it, how you pay him? You got no dugong harpoon.

Look here! S'pose man tell you do something, you do it quick. S'pose man ask for food or water, or anything else, you give him half of what you got. If you do, you are good boy. If you no do, no one like you. You work hard to get plenty fish, and dugong and turtle. You make garden then you full up of food. S'pose you get plenty fish, you give mother and father before you give brother. You have wife, give her a little but plenty to parents for they have had hard work along you. Look after father and mother; never mind if you and your wife have to go without. Give half of all your fish to your parents. Don't be mean.

Science. Questions of how the world came to be, why crops grow, how to control the weather, and similar mysteries were raised and some

---

[2] James G. Frazer, *The Golden Bough* (New York, The Macmillan Co., 1940), p. 692.

[3] Willis L. Uhl, *Secondary School Curricula* (New York, The Macmillan Co., 1927), p. 18, from Reports of the Cambridge Anthropological Expedition to Torres Straits, Vol. 5, Sociology, Magic and Religion of the Western Islanders, Cambridge University Press, 1904, pp. 210-211.

form of answers were given. Of course, these questions were discussed by the wisest elders.

At the end of the instructional period, the tribe assembled for the puberty rite ceremonial and for the tests of courage and endurance to determine if the boys were mature enough to be accepted as men. This was often a brutal ceremony in which some mutilation of the body was inflicted. A boy had to prove that he could take cruel punishment and stand up under vigorous activity without rest or food; he had to prove that he had courage and stamina. He had to prove that he was loyal to the tribe and could defend and provide for a family. In most tribes the young woman made the proposal of marriage; such a proposal was unlikely to come to the youth who failed the pubic rite ceremonial.

The subjects of language arts, social studies, science, and mathematics had their origin in the daily activities of the people of the tribe. The instruction of the elders simply aided youth to draw generalities from their own experience. These subjects have endured and are accepted by us as the heart of the curriculum. The content is still closely related to the life activities of the American people. The American high school helps youth, as did the puberty rites of the ancient and contemporary tribes, to a better understanding of the nation and the world.

Schools for Leaders in Ancient and Modern States. In such areas as the Yangtze and Hwang Ho (China) and the Nile and Tigris river valleys, where the soil is rich, the climate favorable, and the food abundant, many tribes were combined early in history to form nations. Egypt was such a favored place. Here for the first time mathematics was developed as an abstract science. It was accomplished for a practical reason since the Nile flooded its valley annually and frequently obliterated the land boundaries of the fellahs or peasants who produced Egypt's food. These land boundaries were constantly having to be re-established by survey. The Pharoah needed priests for the temples, trained accountants for keeping records, and wise counselors for helping in the government. A school was set up at his court to educate these leaders; mathematics (especially geometry), literature, astronomy, and religion comprised the curriculum. Out of a study of the stars and the heavens came knowledge with which to design the marvelous pyramid tombs and to establish the land boundaries of the fellah. The development of mathematics was a necessity.[4] Gradually over the centuries, an abstract science evolved. All nations have since established schools for the education of learned men; in our times these are called professional persons.

The evolution of the tribal rites into a curriculum produced rigid conformity which brought security to all and destroyed the ingenuity of the individual. Any innovation was considered a heresy and a good cause

[4] Hendrik Wilhelm Van Loon, *The Arts* (New York, Simon and Schuster, Inc., 1937), Ch. 3.

for a curse by the witch doctor. Conformity in Egypt was exacted through the leaders; curiously enough, the leaders themselves had a degree of intellectual freedom.

But in Greece members of the ruling class, which comprised one-sixth of the population, spent their whole time as students and learners. Within this class, the individual who conceived a new idea was honored and respected. Out of this climate of free opinion there was laid in Greece the foundation for the entire fabric of our Western civilization. The Greeks were versatile, and had a profound faith in the dignity of the individual man. They investigated the universe around them and pondered many problems that have persisted to modern times. They showed their youth an orderly world. The man who had the best mind was the most honored. Their early mathematicians, such as Thales and Pythagoras, studied under the Egyptians, but they soon surpassed their teachers. With them, mathematics passed from a rule of procedure to a science with definitions and proofs which had universal application.[5]

The curriculum devised by the Greeks for their youth is considered by many American educators as an excellent one for the gifted youth of today. These are the subject-matter fields: literature; language arts—composition, grammar, rhetoric, and public speaking; mathematics; science; social studies; religion; fine and applied arts; physical education; and music. To all subject areas, the Greeks brought a genius for order and the establishment of basic principles. Their breakthrough to order and guiding principles is perhaps most complete (1) in the analysis of their language for the improvement of oral and written speech, especially in their oratory and their literature, (2) in mathematics as an organized science with universal principles applicable to all ages and all countries, and (3) in their study of the nature of man.[6]

The youth curriculum, developed by the Greeks over more than four centuries, has persisted in Western Civilization—in Rome, the Middle Ages, the Renaissance, contemporary Europe, and contemporary America. The culture of each era has determined the emphasis to be given to the content of each of the subject-matter fields over the intervening centuries. From 1950 to now a vigorous debate has raged in the United States as to *whether this ancient curriculum should comprise the sole content of the high school offering or remain as a special curriculum for potential leaders.* This question is a pertinent one in the remainder of this chapter.

The Apprenticeship System, Trade, and Industrial Education. Until the end of the Crusades and the Black Death, laboring with the hands was considered menial by Western Europeans. Labor was always per-

[5] Howard Eves, *An Introduction to the Problems of Mathematics* (Rinehart & Company, Inc., New York, 1953).

David E. Smith, *History of Mathematics* (Boston, Ginn & Company, 1923), Pt. I, Chs. 2-5.

[6] Uhl, *op. cit.,* Ch. 2.

formed by servants or slaves and not by the ruling classes. Trade and industrial education for teen-agers are of quite recent origin. Following the Crusades, there came a revival of trade and commerce. This, in turn, produced a class of influential, middle-status citizens; the serfs remained at the bottom of the social scale and the ruling class at the top. This new class was comprised of traders and artisans.[7]

Commercial interests and artisans alike set up guilds to restrict those who were permitted to work at a given craft to people who had acquired a high degree of skill. Commerce was expanding rapidly, and there was a greatly increased need for formal education since writing and mathematics were required for the keeping of accurate account books. The guilds established a system of education on three levels: apprenticeship, journeyman, and master workman. This system provided that the master alone could own a shop, buy raw materials, and sell the manufactured product. The apprentice spent seven years in the master's service, began usually at the age of 14, and lived in the master's house. The intention was to make the training for the trade exacting and difficult in terms of accuracy, speed, and form. The quality of the apprentice with respect to personality and intelligence may have been equally as high in the trade program as in the university program of the period.[8] Some Latin Grammar Schools enrolled students for the linguistic and mathematical skills required in the mercantile crafts.

MOTIVES FOR CURRICULUM DEVELOPMENT IN THE UNITED STATES

From the earliest colonial settlement until now, there has always been a youth curriculum in the United States. The early settlers brought with them the Latin Grammar School while all the Indian tribes had observed, with variations, the puberty rites ceremonial. What were the motives that moved our people to establish and maintain schools? Writers in education list *religious, political, and economic motives plus the motive of mass education.* Each has been operating to some extent all of the time; usually, one is dominant for several years, depending upon the climate of opinion in the era. Refusal to recognize the nature of this opinion, by the way, resulted in the elimination of the Latin Grammar School and the Academy.

The Religious Motive (1635-1770).[9] The strength of the religious motive varied among the colonies, though it was important to all. To those

[7] John S. Brubacher, *A History of the Problems of Education* (New York, McGraw-Hill Book Co., 1947), Ch. 4.

[8] Elmer Harrison Wilds, *The Foundations of Modern Education* (New York, Farrar and Rinehart, 1936), p. 159.

[9] Edgar W. Knight, *Education in the United States* (Boston, Ginn & Company, 1951), pp. 82-85.

who had found freedom to worship according to the dictates of their conscience, religion was precious. It is probable, however, that most were economically better off than they had been in their homeland. Since the great majority of the colonists were Protestant, the Latin Grammar School prepared young men to enter theology in order to maintain a constant supply of ministers.

When people are transplanted, their culture is transplanted with them. The Puritans of New England set up the Calvinist pattern of church-state. The town meetings and the state legislature provided for the Latin Grammar School whose curriculum included the catechism and study of the Bible as well as Latin, Greek, and mathematics. In Maryland and Pennsylvania, where Catholics and Protestants of many sects settled, only parochial schools were established and maintained. During the colonial period, Americans indeed used the schools to promulgate and fix their particular religious creeds.

The Political Motive (1770-1860). Shortly after 1770, the United States of America became an independent nation. The three decades that followed were dark and troubled times. The winning of independence does not of itself assure a stable state. Old loyalties must fade and new loyalties be established. The new nation, through wise statecraft, must provide channels for community, state, and national co-operation. Politics, the science and art of good government, must function. This evolution, let us note, is often by a trial-and-error process.

Conditions were unfavorable for education and would remain so until political forces could bring about a stable state. The people lived under rural conditions, isolated and shut off from interests upon which community co-operation was essential. Poor families lived in rude huts, roads were few, and stagecoaches were rare. Religion, which had monopolized colonial thought, was giving way to practical problems of statecraft.

Education was making slight progress because the energies of the people, exhausted by war, were absorbed in providing food and shelter. New conflicts within the nation added to the loss of life and property by the Revolutionary War and left many without hope and confidence. The states were deeply in debt, and commercial life was deadened. The exacting conditions of frontier life served to lower intellectual and educational standards. It was to be expected that the earlier practices of education, as an obligation of the home, the church, or sheer philanthropy, would prevail. The support of education from public funds seemed inappropriate to all but a very few persons.

But political events were taking place to knit the separate states more closely. Step by step, the wise leaders of the post-revolutionary period inaugurated political activities that gradually modified the negative attitudes toward public support of education. Slowly the climate of opinion changed until public attitudes everywhere in the United States were favorable to civil support of education as a practical and desirable procedure in a democratic nation.

The free public high school, established in 1821 at Boston, Mass., had its origin during this period. It came into existence as an extension of the elementary school. It was for children of artisans and mechanics, too young for work following graduation from the first eight grades. Labor, always indignant at the "pauper school" label, favored public support for both the elementary and the high school.

In Chart 4, some of the political forces and persons who helped to bring to a focus the movement for public support of education are indicated. It was contended that the publicly supported school was essential

Chart 4. Political Concepts, Forces, People, and Events That Created a Favorable Climate for a Public-Supported School System

1. The Constitution of the United States with the Bill of Rights was adopted, 1789-1791. Article I of the Bill of Rights provided for the separation of church and state.
2. Entail and primogeniture was abolished. The inheritance laws were modified so that all children in a family could share equally in an inheritance rather than the first-born male being the sole heir.
3. The public school is an essential institution for a democratic state. Quotations from respected leaders:
    a. George Washington—"Increase the institutions for the diffusion of knowledge among us."
    b. Thomas Jefferson—"If a nation expects to be ignorant and free in a state of civilization, it expects what never was and never will be."
    c. DeWitt Clinton—"The encouragement of education is the first duty of government: the right to vote can not be exercised without intelligence."
    d. Abraham Lincoln—"Education is the most important subject which we as a people can be engaged in."
4. There was a movement to extend suffrage to all men; the early movement simply reduced the quantity of property to be owned by a qualified voter.
5. The Lancastrian and Bell monitorial schools were plans by which a large number of children could be taught by one teacher at the same time more efficiently.
6. Labor organizations fought for the free, publicly-supported school; labor felt that the "pauper school" was an outrage in our democracy.
7. Jacksonian Democracy, by recognizing every citizen as a voter and every voter as eligible to hold office, changed many opponents of state support of education to advocates. The feeling was that office holders should have some education.
8. The newspapers and educational magazines promoted the state-supported public school.
9. Dynamic educational leaders, i.e., Horace Mann, James G. Carter, Henry Barnard, Calvin H. Wiley, and Caleb Mills, were able, vocal, and consecrated. They campaigned with vigor and conviction for the establishment of the free and state-supported public school.
10. Educational conventions held in every state promoted public education. They were quite effective in making converts for the movement.
11. The growth of commercial communication favored mass education since there was little point in printing advertisements for great masses who could not read. To this may be added the subsidization of printed matter by the postal authorities. This encouraged increased reading by all the people.

for our democratic state. In the public mind, the movement from 1770 to 1860 for civil support of a school for all the children of all the people meant just the elementary school; only a few wished to develop the high school as the people's college. As traced in the next few pages, however, it is clear that America in 1960 does have a high school for all youth.

The Utilitarian Motive (1860-1890). Though free and universal education had been accepted in principle for all children by 1860, the legality of the high school was a moot question for some citizens. These admitted that public support of the elementary school was legal, but thought that the high school was only for a select group—and not meant for all. Earlier we have noted how a suit in Kalamazoo, Michigan, in 1872 enjoined all tax funds that were to be used for support of the Kalamazoo High School. The decision, when the case reached the Michigan Supreme Court, was unqualifiedly in favor of the school board and public high school education. Chief Justice Thomas M. Cooley, in his decision, recognized the power of the board to establish a high school, as follows:

We content ourselves with the statement that neither in our state policy, in our Constitution, or in our laws, do we find the primary school restricted in the branches of knowledge which their officers may cause to be taught or the grade instruction that may be given.[10]

This decision influenced similar cases in other states and hastened the general acceptance of publicly supported high schools. As a practical people, Americans generally accept the axiom that the useful is good and that it is wiser to choose the useful than the ornamental. Hence, the high school like the early Academy usually offered, as now, the courses demanded by the public. These demands were, and are twofold: (1) that a college preparatory program be offered for college-bound students, and (2) that a program that will best prepare for life be offered for non-college-bound students.

Several leading American educators, 1800 to 1900, such as Cattell, Hall, and Judd, took their advanced degrees with Wilhelm Wundt and others in Germany where the new master science of psychology was prominent. Upon their return, they were influential in getting laboratory courses in science and foreign languages introduced into the high school curriculum. Through this master science, they were also able to introduce changes in both the content and methods of teaching in many of the subject matter fields of the high school curriculum. As shown by Tables 11 and 12, the high school curriculum was expanding rapidly by (1) the addition of new and practical courses, and (2) colleges and universities accepting many of these new courses for college entrance.

Throughout this era, 1860-1890, labor organizations favored utilitarian

---

[10] Ellwood P. Cubberly, *Readings in Public Education in the United States,* rev. ed. (Boston, Houghton Mifflin Co., 1934), p. 241.

Table 11. Developments of High School Subjects of Study[11]

BEFORE 1800	1800-1850	1860-1890
Latin, 1640	English Grammar, 1819	Modern History, 1869
Greek, 1640	Algebra, 1820	Physical Geography, 1870
Arithmetic, 1745	Geometry, 1844	English Composition, 1870
	Ancient History, 1847	Physical Science, 1872
	Geography, 1850	English Literature, 1874
		Modern Language, 1875

Table 12. New High School Subjects Accepted for College Entrance, 1860-1890[12]

SUBJECT	DATE	COLLEGE FIRST ACCEPTED
Modern (U. S.) History	1869	Michigan
Physical Geography	1870	Michigan, Harvard
English Composition	1870	Princeton
Physical Science	1872	Harvard
English Literature	1874	Harvard
Modern Language	1875	Harvard

or practical education. While labor never opposed the classical curriculum as such, its pressures in many communities provided the balance of power that led to the introduction of the laboratory sciences and the industrial and commercial arts.

The College Preparatory Motive (1890-1920). By now, the Latin Grammar School had all but disappeared, and in one community after another the Academy became a public high school supported by taxation. Both the Latin Grammar School and the Academy failed to adjust to the demands of the times. Already the enrollments in the high school were double those of the Academy, and in the years ahead the high school enrollments were to double with each decade. With the decline of the recognized college preparatory institutions, it was argued that the high school must become the major preparatory step. Hence, both the high schools and the colleges and universities sought to establish a more effective articulation between the high schools and the colleges—both desired that public education be a continuous process extending through college. Both agreed that the high school should prepare students for both life and college.

President Charles W. Eliot of Harvard was the chosen leader of the colleges and universities. His appearance before the National Education Association in 1890 showed the need, from the college point of view, for a well-defined reform of the public high school curriculum. He called for strict supervision by state inspectors and the adoption of a uniform

[11] *Ibid.*, Ch. 11.
[12] *Ibid.*, p. 315.

system of examinations in college preparatory subjects. He stated, "The schools need to be brought to common and higher standards so that the colleges may find in the school courses a firm, broad, and reasonable homogeneous foundation for their higher work."[13] In a later appearance, he presented the subjects then being taught, as shown in Chart 5, and was critical of the emphasis upon practical courses. During the 30 years that followed the work of the Committee of Ten, the NEA was to name many committees to study this problem. A report by the Committee on the Reorganization of Secondary Education[14] started the movement for mass education. It was both creative and constructive, and indicated a type of curriculum best adapted to meet the needs of the swelling enrollments of the 1920's.

The Committee of Ten recognized that the secondary schools, taken as a whole, do not exist for the purpose of preparing boys and girls for college. But its recommendations made no distinction in subject matter needs between college-bound and non-college-bound students. It set as a proper list of subjects for any high school student the following:

Latin	Geometry	Zoology
Greek	Trigonometry	Physiology
English	General History	Geology
German	Astronomy	Ethnology
Algebra	Meteorology	Physics
	Botany	Chemistry

This was what the colleges wanted—not what the people pressed for. It represents a straight, academic program which is sometimes called the classical-academic curriculum, but the committee went on to say, with tongue in cheek, "The courses that prepare best for college prepare best for life."

It was a curriculum designed for the gifted and the near-gifted, not for all youth in a common high school. It fitted the college-bound student well. But with the decided bulge in high school enrollments after 1910, this curriculum became more and more remote from the needs of most students. When the rapid industrial development of the early 1900's caused the home, the church, and the community to shift many of their responsibilities to the school, a tremendous lag developed. It was between the *actual needs* of most students and the *typical curriculum* of most high schools. Then, when secondary education became compulsory in many states, the inappropriateness of a classical curriculum for all youth

[13] Charles W. Eliot, "The Gap Between the Elementary School and the Colleges," *Addresses and Proceedings of the National Education Association* (Washington, D.C., National Education Association, 1890), p. 525.

[14] Commission on the Reorganization of Secondary Education, *Cardinal Principles of Secondary Education*, Office of Education, Bulletin No. 35 (Washington, D.C., Government Printing Office, 1918).

Chart 5. Subjects of Study in Public High Schools, 1891[15]

1. English, including both Literature and Composition and the elements of Rhetoric	15. Geology
	16. Botany
	17. Zoology
2. History, Ancient, Medieval, and Modern	18. Physiology
	19. Physics
3. Civil Government	20. Chemistry
4. French	
5. German	21. Astronomy
	22. Psychology
6. Latin	23. Moral Philosophy
7. Greek	24. International Law
8. Arithmetic	25. Political Economy
9. Algebra	
10. Plane Geometry	26. Science of Education
	27. Music
11. Solid Geometry	28. Drawing
12. Trigonometry	29. Stenography
13. Analytic Geometry	30. Bookkeeping
14. Physical Geography	

became quite evident. The public had had enough; it was ready for a change.

The Mass Education Motive, (1920-1960). In America the accepted goal of the people seems to be for every normal teen-ager to attend and, if possible, to graduate from high school. The high school has become in our American culture a common school for all youth. The high school has experienced a marvelous growth in enrollment since the Kalamazoo Case. This rapid growth reflects the faith of the American people in secondary education.

In 1918 the mood of the people was right to accept the Seven Cardinal Principles as the objectives of secondary education. Let us repeat them here: health; command of the fundamental processes; worthy home membership; vocational preparation; citizenship; worthy use of leisure time; and ethical character.[16] We have noted earlier how these proposals were welcomed as a cool breath of air in a desert land. Soon, there were many high schools offering a dual program; many of the larger schools operated as *comprehensive high schools* and provided academic, commercial, trade, and technical subjects.

The comprehensive high school aims to serve the needs of all American youth . . . It accepts without selection all the young people in the area it commands—all races, creeds, nationalities, intelligences, talents, and all levels of wealth and social status. Such a school has as its broadest objective the teaching of all varieties of skill, all kinds of knowledge to all kinds of youth bent upon

[15] Charles W. Eliot, "Undesirable and Desirable Uniformity in Schools," *Addresses and Proceedings of the National Education Association, 1892* (Washington, D.C., National Education Association), p. 93.

[16] Commission on the Reorganization of Secondary Education, *op. cit.*

living socially profitable lives. To each one it seeks to give the course for which he seems best fitted. It designs to prepare one and all for potentially successful vocations. The comprehensive high school prepares the college-oriented youth for college. It qualifies the non-college-bound youth and, as far as possible, the boy or girl who will drop out before graduation for an occupation. It is adapted to give every one a general education for the common things he will do in life and it may and should give some students of high capacity preparation for both college and occupation.[17]

But the shades of President Eliot lingered. Even now, secondary education *for all*, especially for the non-college-bound youth, is said to be too costly; graduates of the high schools are criticized by those who would eliminate all slow learners and many average students. For both the slow and the average learners, the years they spend in the contemporary high school can be the best years of their entire education. In their late teens, they have matured enough intellectually to acquire some concepts and skills for citizenship, vocations, and worthy home membership. As a result of their high school experiences, they can become better citizens, better workers, and better homemakers. Again, *if they are not in school, there is literally no place for them in our society.* The boys are too young to be drafted into military service. Labor does not want either boys or girls competing for employment, and they are not mature enough to possess the responsibility desired by employers. Indeed, the question of what to teach and whom to teach has not as yet been answered fully. But we do know that *parents do not want the high school to reject their children merely because they are non-college-bound youth.*

THE CURRICULUM AND THE PURPOSES OF THE HIGH SCHOOL

To learn is to change: the curriculum is the means by which the change is made.

In the preceding pages, the development of what to teach and whom to teach has been rapidly traced. There is a fairly common agreement that the curriculum developed by the Greeks and expanded in our Western civilization is a good curriculum for gifted youth. In the United States a curriculum for *all youth* is now created and, despite severe criticism by some laymen and educators, decided progress has been made. Like the ancient Athenians, Americans are a creative people. One phase of that creativity is being devoted to drafting a curriculum for slow and average learners and a common learnings curriculum to assist all youth in developing certain attitudes, ideals, and understandings.

The Curriculum Produces Changes in Human Behavior. It is through

[17] Franklin J. Keller, *The Comprehensive High School* (New York, Harper & Brothers, 1955), pp. 31-38.

the curriculum that desirable changes in teen-age behavior may be made. Normally, it might be said that when a young man "comes to himself" he sees the errors in his ways of behaving and means to make a change. He no longer likes himself as he was. He desires to change his behavior and become a different man. The teen-ager who finds that his behavior is harmful does so more readily in the high school than on the outside. The curriculum of the school, thus, should be so arranged as to aid the youth in seeing what changes ought to be made; it should provide the activities necessary to make these changes.

We may say that the teen-ager has had an *experience*.[18] The earlier experiences of youth are often unsatisfactory. The outcome may be unpleasant and degrading, but these experiences cause youth to want to change their ways of behaving or to learn.

While the simple story of a young man "sowing wild oats" and wasting an inheritance is well known, it is an illustration of how experiences cause changes in behavior. Modern teen-agers, as they mature, become aware that they need skills, attitudes, and understandings that they do not at the moment possess. This change from what one is to what one will be and wants to be can be hastened by the proper type of curriculum.

There is a saying that experience is a dear teacher but that fools will learn by no other. This, in light of what we know about learning, is at most a half truth. None of us learns except by his experiences. Because "fools" are slow at learning, many more experiences and some drastic ones are required. Both the wise and the foolish learn from and by experiences, but the wise perceive and understand more readily.

Ultimately society agreed that a teen-age school should be supported to create environments in which desirable changes in behavior might take place. The public wanted only desirable changes and especially those that neither the home nor any other social agency provided. Historically, a Board of Education was constituted to represent society; it was given the authority to formulate and to express the purposes of the school and to employ qualified persons to achieve them. There has been no great departure from this original concept of education in the United States, although in larger cities lay members on school boards generally accept the direction given by a specialist in school operation—the superintendent. What does *curriculum*, as such, mean to informed board members and superintendents?

The term *curriculum*[19] has come to mean the selected experiences or planned activities by which teachers achieve the purposes of the school. It is the school's job to plan worthwhile experiences that will develop

---

[18] *Experience* defined: to know or to know by trying out. When one has tried out and knows, he has had a meaningful experience.

[19] *Curriculum* defined: all of the experiences that students have under direction of the school.

the type of behavior outlined in its objectives. The curriculum, then, is what the students *do, plan, write, read, construct, talk about, react to, and think about.* It is the activities and experiences of students that cause changes in behavior. Learning takes place only when these changes in behavior occur.

Academic or Functional Subject Matter. Here is a controversial issue. But both sides of the issue are committed to the use of subject matter for the achievement of the purposes of the school. All teachers are aware of the central importance of content or subject matter. Even John Dewey, often accused of being the archcriminal on this issue, states, "Experience has no existence apart from the subject matter experienced."[20]

What subject matter or content from the vast cultural heritage of the race should the high school select? The cultural heritage is now so vast that no individual can grasp the total—there must be a selection. There are other agencies, including the home, the church, newspapers, radio, television, the movies, and clubs, which transmit part of the heritage. From the vast storehouse of the past, the school must select what it is best equipped to do.

These two questions indicate the heart of the contemporary controversy: Is the purpose of the school merely to transmit the cultural heritage of the past? Or should the school not only preserve the heritage but seek methods to put students in touch with ways to utilize it creatively in meeting present life situations?[21] The answers to these questions will depend upon the belief (philosophy) held by the individual. A teacher holding the belief that the school achieves its basic purpose when it transmits the social heritage will answer the first question in the affirmative and the second in the negative. But the teacher, or citizen, who believes that the purpose of the high school is achieved only when the social heritage has been transmitted and related to the problems of contemporary life will answer the first question negatively and the second affirmatively.

The *academic approach* systematizes each of the subject-matter fields, stressing principles and generalizations. Each subject is taught as a different entity. The *functional approach* organizes each subject as a part of the whole, and the inter-relatedness of the various subjects is clearly seen. When a situation demands, personal problems in social living can be introduced.

Where are we? Where do we want to go? No teacher can plan a semester's work without answering these two questions. And no principal can

[20] John Dewey, *Philosophy and Civilization* (New York, Minton, Balch & Co., 1931), p. 261.
[21] Arno A. Bellack, "Selection and Organization of Curriculum Content," *What Shall the High Schools Teach?* 1956 Yearbook of the Association for Supervision and Curriculum Development (Washington, D.C., National Education Association, 1956), Ch. 4.

set up an over-all program of work for a secondary school without answering them.

As an experiment to see where you stand, answer each of the questions in Chart 6. Where do you find yourself on this issue of academic versus functional subject matter? Try out these same questions on some of your friends.

The way these questions are answered brings into sharp focus what we want in education and how we get what we want. The personal attitude is revealed on problems of functional versus academic subject

---

Chart 6. An Opinionnaire on Some Issues in Public Education

Directions: Mark each item as follows—(1) strongly agree; (2) inclined to agree; (3) undecided; (4) inclined to disagree; (5) disagree strongly.
— 1. If a child has mastered reading, writing, spelling, and has learned how to study, the task of the school has been fulfilled.
— 2. In addition to learning and reciting, pupils should be taught how to secure and interpret facts.
— 3. A student should be taught to get information on all sides of a controversial question before forming his own opinions.
— 4. In school everyone should learn through experience how to share effectively in group planning and action.
— 5. All pupils should be taught to recognize and respect the rights of other races and religions.
— 6. The school should develop in every pupil a strong sense of responsibility for the welfare of the school, the community, the state, and the nation.
— 7. Schools should instill the habit of prompt, cheerful obedience in all pupils.
— 8. Hygiene and cleanliness should be taught in the school.
— 9. The teaching on morality is not a responsibility of the school.
—10. The school should lead every pupil to understand and prize for himself and all others the rights of freedom of the press, freedom of speech, freedom of religion, and other civil liberties guaranteed in the Constitution.
—11. Elementary schools, junior, and senior high schools should give all pupils experience in working with their hands in such activities as drawing, painting, clay modeling, weaving, and working with woods.
—12. The school should provide an adequate staff of counselors who are able to help pupils with personal as well as school problems.
—13. The school should be just as much concerned with the students who are not going to college as with those who are.
—14. Appropriate sex instruction should be given to all pupils in elementary schools, junior, and senior high school.
—15. The school should develop in all students an intelligent interest in world affairs.

---

matter in our schools. The research findings of the past five decades in learning, in human growth and development, and in human relations in the classroom favor the functional curriculum.

There is another difference of opinion usually present between teachers accepting the academic curriculum as desirable and those preferring the functional. The academic teacher is likely to assume that through exercise of the mind virtue is automatically achieved. The teacher who prefers the functional curriculum is more likely to assume that experience plus meditation upon the experience produces the type of behavior improvement desired by society or that the kind of activities engaged in, properly directed, may help to build attitudes and ideals.

As a student in high school and college, you have had much experience with the academic curriculum. Actually, the essential difference between that and the functional curriculum is concerned with the problem of human nature—or how student behavior is changed. The difference is brought out clearly by the pairs of comparison provided in Chart 7. The contrasts, as expressed, show the extreme range between the two beliefs. Most high school teachers will be placed somewhere on the scale between the academic at the left and the functional curriculum on the right. In their attempts to adjust their work to the individual needs of students, many contemporary teachers are moving toward the functional curriculum.

It might be observed here that there naturally exists a high degree of resentment against any immediate change; a public that has traditionalized the academic curriculum will not at once accept any other—no matter how sound. To what degree does this determine your own selections from Chart 7.

Chart 7. A Comparison Between the Academic and the Functional Curriculum Approach

Directions: Vote on each comparison for the approach which seems to be more meaningful in terms of desired objectives.

Academic Approach	*Functional Approach*
—1. Subject matter represents what is to be learned.	—1. Subject matter is a means to an end, to lead to desired outcomes in behavioral changes.
—2. The subject matter to be covered and the kinds of experiences pupils have are determined before the course begins.	—2. Content is a series of purposeful, well-planned experiences growing out of the pupils' background, needs, interests, and daily living, and out of the social and physical environment.
—3. Often subject matter has little or no bearing on youth problems and present-day social issues.	—3. Experiences are selected co-operatively by teachers and pupils, based on study and knowledge of pupils and their previous experiences.
—4. The teacher acts as the external authority and exercises full control over the learning situation.	—4. The teacher is concerned with the growth and development of each pupil rather than with the preconceived notions of what the "average pupil should know at a certain grade level."
—5. Subject matter is valuable to the extent that it exercises the mind.	—5. The development of the teen-ager, his mind, body, emotions, and social maturity are all considered equally important.
—6. Extensive memorization through drills and testing follows the concept of preparation for living in some future day of maturity.	—6. Subject matter is valued to the extent that it is functional or helps the individual to a better adjustment to his environment.

A MORE MEANINGFUL ORGANIZATION OF THE CURRICULUM

*A teacher who can change the abstract to the concrete, day after day,
becomes a master teacher.*

As a director of learning, every teacher is responsible for the selection
and organization of the subject-matter content developed in his classes.
A teacher needs some tests against which to measure the quality of the
subject matter selected from day to day. What guideposts would be most
helpful in making these distinctions? The following are four tested rules
that can be applied to any subject-matter field:

1. Is the content consistent with the maturity level and the past experience of the students?

2. Is the proposed content readily capable of adaptation to meet individual differences?

3. Does the proposed content provide sequence and continuity to
what is being learned?

4. Will the use of the content promote the development of the students
of the class?

The meaningful organization of subject matter for teen-agers with an
orderly arrangement of content according to broad general principles was
first accomplished by the creative Greeks. These gifted teachers, while
instructing gifted learners in a small world that was known to all Greeks,
were able to help learners grasp the relationships between the several
fields. Because of the rapid expansion of knowledge in recent centuries
and the high degree of specialization among our high school teachers,
the organization of a more meaningful curriculum for the American
secondary school has not been easy. George W. Henry, in *What Shall
the High Schools Teach?* explains why.[22]

There is the vast accumulation of knowledge that will not fall into any
"accepted" disciplines of the nineteenth century. This store of knowledge seems
to defy a sorting of any formerly known kind: and yet it is still being spun
off at such a rate that no matter how long or how intensive the schooling, each
generation will know relatively less per individual of the total cultural heritage
than the previous generation.

Procedures for Improving the Curriculum. By what procedures can a
meaningful organization of the curriculum be achieved? Or how can the
subject-matter content be made more meaningful to students? Does the
pattern of curriculum organization help rather than hinder the students
in getting meaning from what is taught?

[22] George W. Henry, "Foundations of General Education in the High School,"
What Shall the High Schools Teach? 1956 Yearbook, Association for Supervision
and Curriculum Development (Washington, D.C., National Education Association),
p. 138.

The trend since 1918 in curriculum reorganization is shown in Chart 8. It reveals in graphic form the search being made by educators in the selection and organization of instructional material. The aim is to bring out the rich relationships between separate subjects and to assist teachers in the development of their own courses so as to make greater sense to teen-agers. The most traditional and least helpful pattern for the achievement of broad understandings is that of the separate subjects. The most recent and the most helpful pattern for the socialization of students is the core. Each step away from the separate subjects has been a move toward a curriculum organization more favorable to effective classroom instruction in the common learnings or general education.

Chart 8. Patterns of Curriculum Organization in Our Contemporary Secondary Schools—Arranged According to Effectiveness

LEAST EFFECTIVE				MOST EFFECTIVE
I	II	III	IV	V
				Core
Separate				General Education
subjects	Correlation	Fusion	Broad fields	Common learnings

The Broad Field Pattern. Research, as well as school practice, supports the proposition that a set and rigid curriculum for all is unsuited to a public high school where all must attend and be retained through the eighteenth birthday. The broad fields pattern of curriculum organization is found in a large number of our contemporary *elementary schools.* This is comprised of the language arts, social studies, science, mathematics, fine and industrial arts, and physical education and health. The high school probably has reorganized its curriculum much less rapidly because of its traditional relationship to the American college as a preparatory school. Most of our four-year high schools are still organized on the traditional or separate subject basis.

The Fusion Pattern. However, most of the separate subject offerings[23] of 1891 have now been fused into a much smaller number of subject-matter fields, and in many ways resemble the broad fields pattern of subject organization. For example, the subject-matter field of English formerly comprised a long list of separate subjects such as American literature, composition, debate, declamation, dramatics, English literature, grammar, language, penmanship, reading, spelling, and similar studies. The fusion of many separate subjects to form the subject-matter field of English has been a very gradual process which is not yet complete. But the broader field which now comprises English has given the teacher greater freedom to adapt classroom activities to the needs of a class.

[23] See Chart 5, Ch. VI, p. 139.

The broad fields of science where many subjects have been fused into one is another good illustration. Some of the subjects that were formerly taught separately are astronomy, botany, geology, natural history, physics, geography, and zoology. Thus, scientific content has been assembled into a single broad field which permits the science teacher to draw subject content from all related fields—general science is the outcome. The teacher is also free, under this pattern, to bring out relationships between and among all areas so that he can select and organize instructional material which has meaning to teen-agers. The content can even be varied to meet the needs of a single class. Although subject content needs to be quite flexible for the *common learnings,* all of the separate subject-matter fields are retained in the curriculum under *special education* to serve the special needs of all students.

Although fusion is not complete, as has been stated, most of the separate subjects formerly offered are now concentrated into a few subject-matter fields. The subject-matter areas as now found in most high schools are: English, social studies, mathematics, science, foreign languages, homemaking, industrial arts, fine arts, commercial arts, and physical education and health.

Correlation. As indicated in Chart 8, correlation is an attempt to use related materials from two or more separate subjects to add breadth to the development of a single topic. For example, the development of power by the motor of an automobile is a topic suitable for science, but the use of the motor in an automobile to change the mores of the people is a topic best treated in social studies. These relationships, the science of the motor and the impact of the motor on society, need to be developed together for real understanding; either alone is a half truth. As the power phase is developed its counterpart, the moral phase, should be developed, too.

Common Learnings. Probably, the pattern of curriculum organization which best meets the needs common to all youth is that of the common learnings.[24] The content is so selected and organized that teen-agers learn how to be good citizens by practicing citizenship and how to solve problems by solving problems. To illustrate how content is selected and organized, a contemporary social problem can be chosen that affects both adults and adolescents. A transportation strike in the city would be such a social problem. Some students and some adults would be very much annoyed by the inconvenience while others would believe that the strikers had a just grievance. All elevators, as well as street transportation, would be affected, and a few students living in apartments would have to walk up several flights of stairs to reach their homes.

In common learnings as much time can be and is given to a topic as is necessary. In one class the teacher and the students stated the prob-

[24] Uhl, op. cit., pp. 210-211.

lem. Then subtopics to be studied were listed on the blackboard, and for each subtopic a committee volunteered to collect and organize all facts available. The chairman of each committee presented a summary of the committee's findings to the class. A discussion followed which was led by a student chairman on the question, "Do labor unions have a right to disrupt a city's transportation?" The discussion was lively and the interest high. The conflicts involved were understood and new attitudes and ideals were acquired.

Selection of Subject Matter. During the period of transition from the old curriculum to the new, the procedure for the selection of curricular content has been shifting. The old and the new are paired in Chart 9—the old on the left and the new on the right. The conservatives in education

Chart 9. Old and New Methods of Selecting Curriculum Content

THE OLD METHODS OF SELECTING CURRICULUM CONTENT	THE NEW METHODS OF SELECTING CURRICULUM CONTENT
1. Select content to discipline the mind or the acceptance of the belief that rigorous exercise of the mind creates virtue.	1. Society determines the purposes of the high school: the high school selects the content to achieve them.
2. Implant moral training through didactics or stories with morals.	2. Social efficiency and moral growth are acquired through personal and social experience in the home, at school and in the community. Curricular content is selected to achieve social efficiency and moral growth.
3. Select content to prepare students for college or university only.	3. Select content to transmit the best of the cultural heritage as well as to develop habits, skills, and understandings most useful for now and tomorrow.
4. Select content on the basis that the old is good and should be retained.	4. Select content to meet the basic needs of teen-agers.
5. Select content for intellectual development only.	5. Select content for intellectual, vocational, personal, and social development.

advocate the old while the liberals advocate the new. The conservatives are against any change in the curriculum while the liberals seek to alter or adapt it to the innovations in our culture.

Getting the Meaning from What Is Taught. "The curriculum consists of all the experiences that students have under the direction of the school." This is the usual definition given by curriculum specialists, with some minor variations. Hence, it is assumed by the high school staff that only subject matter which causes learning is suitable for the curriculum. It might be asked: What kind of activities produce or cause learning that is desirable? The following guideposts are proposed as indicators of appropriate subject matter.

1. Students need to know and understand, to achieve status, and to

achieve partial acceptance of their right to independence. When they discover that subject matter aids them in the achievement of all of these needs, they become active, and through their activity comes experience and a change in behavior. Subject matter that meets the needs of teen-agers may also meet their desires, wants, and inadequacies. In this inter-action within the classroom, the individual expresses his needs and desires, and, to the extent that he is constructively active, he achieves real experience.

2. Making content meaningful helps the student learn to organize facts and principles into meaningful units. Since a learner has experience only when the content studied makes sense, gear the content to the vocabulary level of the class; relate the content to the background of the class; provide activities in context, as they will be used; show relation-ships among the various subjects and concepts; and provide a variety of experiences in accordance with the individual differences in the class.

3. Adequate mental and educational readiness as well as physical maturation is necessary before effective learning is possible. This is true at all grade levels. In any course on the high school level, it is important that activities and materials be prepared which will provide for a decided range in maturity levels—there will be such a range in readiness for curricular content in every class. To be meaningful, the curricular content must be adapted to the readiness and previous experiences of the learners.

4. Learning efficiency varies with the length of study or practice periods and with the spacing of such periods. Also, it varies with the *rapidity with which content material is presented.* Content to be learned should occur at properly spaced intervals. When too much is crowded into too short a time, the individual is unable to relate it to his experience. The learner, then, becomes confused or frustrated.[25]

5. Content material should be presented so that the learner will have *correct and successful responses.* Unless these are experienced, the type of learning that is desired will not continue to occur. Effective learning is an active process. Only the learner can learn; no one can do it for him.

These five guideposts, which show how learning and subject matter are related, put the major emphasis upon experiencing as the core rela-tionship. Educational psychologists also stress experiencing as a superior factor in all learning. The following story well illustrates the fine differ-ence between real experience in a class as opposed to an effort to learn only subject matter.

The story relates the visit of two job applicants to the personnel director of a telephone company in a metropolitan city. His office, on the eleventh floor, overlooked many large industries in the valley below.

---

[25] Psychiatric research in time may explain the strong correlation between this lack of teaching skill and the phenomenon of a high degree of mental illness in our young adult population.

When the business at hand was completed, the director said, "Now I want to ask a question." But first the story:

My company is carrying on research in sound. We recently announced this in the local newspaper, described our hopes, and indicated our desires to employ a few promising graduates from the high schools who might like to participate in the experiment. Yesterday, there came two boys to my office. Both were from the same school. My secretary immediately sent one of them to me for an interview.

As I chatted with him to put him at his ease, I saw a train moving north along the river bank in the valley below. As it rolled along, I saw a puff of steam spurt out from the engine. Immediately, I directed the boy's attention to this; and, when shortly thereafter we heard the sound of the whistle, I asked why there was such a difference. Why did we see the steam before we heard the whistle? He replied at once, 'Sir, the speed of light is faster than the speed of sound. Sound travels 1,087 feet per second and light travels 186,-000 miles per second.' It was a perfect explanation, and I was pleased.

I took him for a tour of the sound laboratory. And, as we moved about, I raised a number of practical questions that had to do with sound, all of which he answered immediately and correctly. I then carried on a conversation with him that had nothing to do with sound, or science—he upheld his part adequately. I was pleased with him—he was a good prospect.

The secretary then sent me the second boy. I followed the same procedure with him as I had with the first boy. I chatted with him to put him at his ease and, when the opportunity offered, posed the question of why we saw the steam before we heard the sound of the whistle. He looked at me blankly and without reply. I then took him to visit our laboratory. And again I raised the same practical questions with him as I had with the first boy. To none of these did he have an answer. He listened but made no response.

I was puzzled. Both of these boys came from the same school. Both had just recently completed a unit course in physics under the same teacher with the same grade. Both had similar scores on an intelligence test and the grade average for the four years of high school was close.

Then I remembered that I had a copy of the high school physics textbook in my office. I took the second boy back to my desk, located the book, and opening it to the section on sound I asked several questions. The boy gave correct answers immediately. He did not hesitate on a one. The answers were perfect.

Now, this is my question: *Why could the first boy answer practical questions about sound, freely and easily, while the second boy, with seemingly an identical academic record, could answer questions on sound only from a text-book?*

Here is a *crucial* question. How would you answer it?

Specialists in both curriculum and learning agree that subject matter will continue to be employed to produce learning or changes in behavior. They identify four stages in the process of utilizing subject matter to achieve the purposes of the high school. These are illustrated in Chart 10.

Chart 10. Stages in the Process of Getting Meaning from What Is Taught

TOTAL SITUA-TION (I)	DIFFERENTIA-TION (II)	INTEGRATION (III)	APPLICATION (IV)
New field	A distinct element becomes separated from the total	The new element becomes associated with the previous experience of the learner; there is meaning	As a part of one's actual experience, the learning can be applied to every-day activities

One starts as a stranger in a specialized elective field such as physics. In the beginning the content is confusing, and one feels disturbed. Gradually, a few phases of the subject stand out and become differentiated from the total field. Many students who get good marks in a course such as physics have simply memorized the statements in the textbook. They get bogged down at Stage II in the process of getting meaning from what is taught. Other students, through reading the textbook, class discussions, laboratory experiments, their own experience with physical things, and meditation upon these experiences are able to integrate and relate the course activities into their lives to that point. At Stage III, in Chart 10, what is being learned becomes meaningful and makes sense. A few students, under efficient teaching, so co-ordinate their in-school and out-of-school experiences with their own backgrounds that the concept is made their very own. They can employ the principle to either their in-school or out-of-school activities. The subject matter plus the activities within the class become an integral part of the experiences of the learner; hence, in using subject matter to produce meaningful results, the teacher needs to guide the process beyond Stage III.

The traditional subject approach to the curriculum has been such that a goodly number of classes never get beyond Stage II. This consists of identifying and memorizing textbook material to be given back to the teacher through tests and examinations. This type of learning never has meaning for students since it never becomes a part of their own experiences. A textbook can be a fine tool when properly used, but rote learning from a textbook remains outside of matters which are important to teen-agers. In the illustration that is given later (pp. 161-162), Helen Keller tells the real differences, the contrast between learning the Braille system by rote and the actual realization that symbols have meaning.

A BRIEF SUMMARY

Our rapid survey of the development of youth education from ancient times to now reveals four major developmental steps.

1. Youth were given intensive education by the tribal elders just

previous to being inducted into the tribe as accepted adults. When the content of this tribal education is analyzed, it bears a decided resemblance to the content of such modern subject areas as literature, religion, civic duties, science, and mathematics.

2. The Greeks took these subject-matter areas, expanded the content of each, and added language (English for us), fine and applied arts, physical education, and music. They brought order and the establishment of basic principles to each of these subject fields. Most of them are now included in the classical-academic curriculum of the modern high school.

3. The rise of the middle class in Europe concurrent with the decline of the feudal system brought a need for vocational education. As a result, education of youth for industry, trade, and industrial arts has now become an integral part of the curriculum.

4. The United States has been original in creating the mass education movement. Education for all youth through high school is a *novel* idea. The basic concept, *education for all youth,* is implied as a phase of our American heritage, but a realization of the idea has occurred largely since 1920.

An original idea, that of mass education, has been made to work. To Europeans and to many Americans, it was a violation of tested customs. The classical-academic curriculum had been a sacred cow; any changes made in it were considered a breach of established tradition. Yet the idea also had an appeal. It gripped the imagination of the American people. Since 1920, Americans have been engaged in making the dream of mass education work. It has been sufficiently successful to cause Canada, England, and the U.S.S.R to adapt it to their secondary schools in whole or in part.

The adoption of a functional curriculum to achieve the purpose of the modern high school has proven satisfactory for the below average and average students where teachers have had an understanding of how to make and keep contact with their classes, and also, where classroom activities were such that the teacher could assist the students in relating these activities to their previous experiences. A careful analysis will indicate that the basic principle applies to all students; however, the curriculum activities and the rate at which concepts are developed must vary in accordance with the abilities and backgrounds of the students.

DISCUSSION PROBLEMS

1. On occasion, the comprehensive high school is derided as "the unrealistic dream of educators, just as futile as the school within a school." What are the arguments for and against this combination of educational purposes?

2. Basing your premise upon available information that is reliable, in what respects would you say that the educational system of Soviet Russia is superior to that of the United States? How is it inferior? Would the United States have more or less class distinction without public education?

3. Is memorization strictly a matter for academic courses? Compare the items that must be remembered by a "parts mechanic" with those that a physician must recall; what is the difference in values here? Then indicate what must be memorized by: a railway mail clerk, a milkman, a bus driver, a carpenter, a chemist, a ditch digger, a dish washer. Are the schools right in differentiating between academic and functional courses? What does society do to mark this difference?

4. It has been said that environment outside the school will provide sufficient common learnings. What can the school offer that will not be given by agencies off the campus?

5. Is it true that some drivers are "accident prone" and that nothing much can ever be done about it? Discuss driver education in light of its present status and determine whether it is a course that should be amplified or withdrawn.

6. What youth agencies should receive fullest co-operation from the schools?

RELATED REFERENCES

American Association of School Administrators, *American School Curriculum*, Thirty-first Yearbook (Washington, D. C., National Education Association, 1950).

BELLACK, Arno A., "Selection and Organization of Curriculum Content," *What Shall the High Schools Teach?* 1956 Yearbook of the Association for Supervision and Curriculum Development (Washington, D. C., National Education Association, 1956).

BRUBACHER, John S., *A History of the Problems of Education* (New York, McGraw-Hill Book Co., 1947).

BUTTS, R. Freeman, *A Cultural History of Western Education* (New York, McGraw-Hill Book Co., 1955).

Commission on the Reorganization of Secondary Education, *Cardinal Principles of Secondary Education*, Office of Education, Bulletin No. 35 (Washington, D. C., Government Printing Office, 1918).

CUBBERLY, Ellwood P., *Readings in Public Education in the United States*, rev. ed. (Boston, Houghton Mifflin Co., 1934).

DEWEY, John, *Philosophy and Civilization* (New York, Minton, Balch & Co., 1931).

DOUGLASS, Harl R., ed., *The High School Curriculum*, rev. ed. (New York, The Ronald Press Company, 1956).

ELIOT, Charles W., "The Gap Between the Elementary School and the Colleges," *Addresses and Proceedings of the National Education Association* (Washington, D. C., National Education Association, 1890).

"Undesirable and Desirable Uniformity in Schools," *Addresses and Proceedings of the National Education Association* (Washington, D. C., National Education Association, 1892).

EVES, Howard, *An Introduction to the Problems of Mathematics* (New York, Rinehart & Company, Inc., 1953).

FRAZER, James G., *The Golden Bough* (New York, The Macmillan Co., 1940).

FRENCH, William M., *American Secondary Education* (New York, The Odyssey Press, 1957).

GRAVES, Albert D., *American Secondary Education* (Boston, D. C. Heath & Company, 1951).

GWYNN, J. Minor, *Curriculum Principles and Social Trends* (New York, The Macmillan Co., 1948).

HAIG, George C., *The High School for Tomorrow* (New York, Harper & Brothers, 1936).

HENRY, George W., "Foundations of General Education in the High School," *What Shall the High Schools Teach?* 1956 Yearbook, Association for Supervision and Curriculum Development (Washington, D. C., National Education Association, 1956).

JACOBSON, Paul B., *The American Secondary School* (New York, Prentice-Hall, Inc., 1952).

INGLIS, Alexander, *Principles of Secondary Education* (Boston, Houghton Mifflin Co., 1918).

KELLER, Franklin J., *The Comprehensive High School* (New York, Harper & Brothers, 1955).

KNIGHT, Edgar W., *Education in the United States* (Boston, Ginn & Company, 1951).

SMITH, David E., *History of Mathematics*, Pt. I (Boston, Ginn & Company, 1923).

UHL, Willis L., *Secondary School Curricula* (New York, The Macmillan Co., 1927).

VAN LOON, Hendrik W., *The Arts* (New York, Simon and Schuster, Inc., 1937).

WILDS, Elmer H., *The Foundations of Modern Education* (New York, Farrar and Rinehart, 1936).

Chapter 7

COMMON LEARNINGS

OR GENERAL EDUCATION

We think that for a landlady considering a lodger it is important to know his income, but still more important to know his philosophy.
—G. K. CHESTERTON

HOW EDUCATION FOR ALL CAME TO THE HIGH SCHOOL

Moral character in a lodger, as Chesterton infers, is probably a greater security for a landlady than the amount of money a lodger possesses. Likewise, the development of moral character in a student is a highly important measure of security for a state and a community. The common learnings have for their purpose: (1) to assist students to grow in understanding and in competent performance of their obligations as members of the community, state, and nation; (2) to assist students to grow in the skills and knowledge of social and ethical principles involved in their relations with other people, particularly in family-life relations; (3) to assist students to grow in understanding of democratic principles, in their application of the scientific method, and in their acceptance of the values basic to our civilization; and (4) to develop skills in the 3 R's, improve communication in reading and in oral and written communication, and establish and maintain physical fitness. The common learnings are the means by which students acquire character-developing experiences.[1]

As education for all youth was extended upward to the secondary school, the common learnings, after a lag of some years, were also extended upward to the secondary school. Education for all youth, or the mass education motive, is probably here to stay. Why has this happened? What brought it about? One answer frequently given is that the changes in our American culture, which were caused by our rapid industrialization, have brought it about.

[1] James G. Frazer, *The Golden Bough* (New York, The Macmillan Co., 1940).
Franklin J. Keller, *The Comprehensive High School* (New York, Harper & Brothers, 1955), pp. 31-38.

Another factor is easy to see. In 1890 the employable age was *10*; but since then the employable age has moved to 12, then to 14, and then to 16. As the employable age moved upward, the common learnings moved upward through the intermediate grades and then through the junior high school. The movement now is to extend the employable age to 18, and recommendations by labor and management have been made in a joint agreement for certain industries to set the minimum employable age for youth at *20*. Both labor and management maintain that our youth are too irresponsible before this minimum age to handle the complicated machinery of today. In the past, after a lapse of time, such recommendations have been enacted into law, and the age of employability, as recommended, became the legal age.

The early secondary school did not distinguish between general and special education. One curriculum composed of many separate subjects was used to achieve both purposes. Every subject was taught to every student in the same way and to the same extent. Students who couldn't learn that way dropped out. Spitnas describes a typical high school, 1907-1911, which had a freshman class of 63, of whom 13 graduated four years later.[2] The mass education motive had not yet come to the high school. There was simply no attempt being made to relate what was being taught to the background and experience of high school students. But in the elementary school, where the mass education motive already had been established, the teachers were aware of the realities of the situation. They knew of the great differences in the rate and extent of maturation, mentally, emotionally, physically, and socially, among children of the same age, and were adapting the curriculum to the needs of the children.

Our culture has accepted education for all youth and has supported the principle by laws which compel attendance up to 16 or 18, varying with different states. That changes must be made in the high school curriculum to adapt it to the mass education motive is the general recommendation of secondary-school specialists who have studied this problem. The specialists recommend that there be two curriculums for the high school: (1) a common learnings curriculum for socialization and (2) a special learnings curriculum for specialization. Individualization and socialization, the special and the general in a democratic society, are two essential phases of the mass education motive.

The common learnings, or general education, are intended to teach students how to co-operate with others and to help them acquire the common attitudes or ideals which bind our society together and which establish loyalties to the community, the state, and the nation. It should

[2] James E. Spitnas, "General, Special, and Vocational Education: An Exploration of Distinctive Differences," *What Shall the High Schools Teach?* 1956 Yearbook, Association for Supervision and Curriculum Development (Washington, D.C., National Education Association, 1956), p. 177.

build the habit of co-operation for a common cause which is so essential to a great state. On the other hand, the special learnings program is intended to provide a variety of offerings to young people who are preparing for college or who are not planning to attend college. Every student must be given the opportunity to develop himself as an individual; for each needs to develop his potentialities to the fullest. Likewise, each must be a social being as well as an individualist.

THE NEED FOR A PROGRAM TO PROVIDE FOR DIFFERENT MENTALITIES

The curriculum of the modern secondary school places great stress upon contemporary problems as well as those common to all youth. Because of changes in our mores or our customs and manners which have resulted from technology and the urbanization of our culture, youth need help in selecting the enduring values from the old ways and relating them to the new ways. Some of the horse-and-buggy-day morals apply equally well to the age of stream-lined autos and jet airplanes. Our teen-agers need to recognize, accept, and practice the moral values of modern times. Ours is a dynamic society, and we are proud of it. Yet, in a time of too-rapid change, adults, also, lose their sense of what is right and what is wrong; they, likewise, become confused and uncertain.

The public has always turned to the school for those services which parents feel inadequate to provide.[3] The enduring values from our social heritage and the emerging new values of our time need to be fused. The school is the only agency that deals with all of the children of all the people. Since it is also an institution supported by taxation, it is the agency that is empowered to provide these new services as needed. As revealed in Chapter III, the most damaging current criticism of the high school resides in its apparent failure to develop moral values. This is one of the specific outcomes which the common learnings are designed to correct. It is in the common learnings section of the modern high school curriculum, which includes the development of moral values that the problem of youth may be resolved. It is here that the abiding values of our social heritage and the emerging new values can be fused.

What are some of the questions about the education of their children that parents are now less able to answer? Here are a few of them:

1. Getting prepared to earn a living has become much more complex. The advent of automation will make it more so.

2. Citizenship education, involving as it does in the modern state the understanding of many complex political, economic, and social relation-

---

[3] The Commission on Reorganization of Secondary Education, *Cardinal Principles of Secondary Education*, U. S. Bureau of Education, Bulletin 35, 1918 (Washington, D.C., Government Printing Office, 1919), p. 7.

ships, requires the extension of teen-age education to the eighteenth birth-day. Rightly used, the classroom can provide some direct experiences that are essential to sound citizenship education.

3. Orientation to the emerging moral and social customs and to the demands of our time can best be done by an emotionally mature and professional individual. Class discussion of controversial, moral, and social issues under the competent guidance of a capable leader can lead to the acceptance of real moral values. Teen-agers are idealistic enough to accept a good conduct code, especially when they have helped to develop it and understand why it is important.

Purposes and Content of the Common Learnings. The general purposes of the common learnings are determined in advance, but the teachers have latitude to plan the details of the course and to fix the order of the problems to be considered. Just as for the academic and vocational programs, subject matter will be the means of achieving the purposes of the common learnings program, but it is selected when and as it is needed. Although there are many exceptions, the course of study for the common learnings is formulated as a series of problems. Usually, the students assist in determining the order in which the problems will be presented.

Again, this question is often asked: Just what is taught in the common learnings program, grades 7 to 12? Here are some of the most common themes that are being developed in the modern high school:

1. The students learn about themselves and other teen-agers.

2. The students learn the way people serve the community in which they live.

3. The students learn the way in which goods are distributed.

4. The students learn the common heritage of America.

5. The students learn the way in which science has changed the world.

6. When and as they are needed, the students develop essential skills in reading, expression, and study.

7. The students check their own aptitudes and qualifications for more than a single occupation.

8. The students take tests in reading, basic mathematics, English, and study skills.

9. The students in senior high school study problems of family life, unions and management, sanitation and community health, consumer spending, and personal problems.

Some Proposed Advantages. What are some of the proposed advantages of the common-learnings program? Where this program has been developed, these are the most commonly mentioned advantages:

1. All activities—things we think about and do—are bound together. The subject matter can be selected from any field and, therefore, is not restricted to one particular field. Important social problems are studied

in their entirety. There is a time and opportunity to carry the study of a problem beyond the classroom.

2. Students can learn to handle big problems as a whole. For example, such a timely problem as the guaranteed full-year wage for labor can be thoroughly explored. By such an approach, the relations between all the different factors in a problem can be evaluated.

3. Classes can begin work in any year with the problems and purposes that are at hand.

4. Intensive work to improve study skills, reading habits, and other desirable traits of scholarship can be inserted wherever and whenever the need is felt.

5. The common-learnings program allows time and flexibility for changing activities to fit the maturity and socio-economic background of the class.

6. Each teacher in the program has fewer different students than the special learnings teachers and more time to observe them; hence, the teacher can serve as a counselor for his students.

7. The common-learnings program is in harmony with the best we know about the nature of learning. The best principles of experience-learning are utilized.

8. The common learnings serve also as a means through which other experiences and subjects, not a part of the course itself, may be inter-related and unified.[4]

9. The common-learnings program provides for a natural integration of school, home, and community living. It is recognized that experience learning cannot be restricted to the schoolroom or the school itself. This requires closer co-operation of school, home, and community to insure consistency in the learning experiences of the pupils.

10. In the common-learnings program, teachers take on a new status. In this program, just as a matter of course, the teacher is expected to be a more careful student of the nature of pupils and the learning process, more adept in human relations, and more able to stimulate and guide the pupils in the development of problem-solving skills, and in the acquiring of personal-social skills so essential for the social development and the participation in co-ordinated group activity.[5]

THE NATURE OF THE COMMON-LEARNINGS PROGRAM

What is the nature of a common-learnings program? It is apparent that an examination of several such programs would provide a sound basis for discovering the attributes of the common-learnings program. Since most

[4] Stephen A. Romine, *Building the High School Curriculum* (New York, The Ronald Press Company, 1954), p. 339.
[5] Ronald C. Faunce and Nelson L. Bossing, *Developing the Core Curriculum* (Englewood Cliffs, N. J., Prentice Hall, Inc., 1958), pp. 61-64.

pre-teachers will not have had this experience, it is desirable to outline in more detail the important attributes that such an examination would reveal.

Important Characteristics. Some characteristics are absolutely essential to a true common-learnings program, while others are the usual attributes, although they too are necessary to an effective and sound curriculum. In the list which follows, those characteristics which are accepted by the authors as essential will be designated by an asterisk (*).

* 1. The common learnings include experiences which are important to the growth and development of all pupils. (See the Helen Keller illustration presented later in this chapter.)

2. Guidance and instruction are more closely related in the common-learnings program. Usually the common-learnings teacher is responsible for the guidance and counseling of all pupils in his classes; that is, the common-learnings class supplants the homeroom entirely.

3. There is a great deal of student-teacher planning. When students are involved in the planning of their work, they see more clearly what is to be done and why it is important. Hence, they put more effort and time into it—it has more meaning for them and greater growth occurs. Likewise, when all common learnings teachers within a high school become involved in the planning of a common-learnings course of study, they grow in an understanding of the program and are more effective in giving direction to the program within the classroom.

* 4. A longer block of time is provided for the common-learnings program. Normally, these time blocks vary from 1½ to 3 hours in length and meet every day of the school week. While the length of the time block varies greatly from school to school, the length of the period given to a common-learnings class is always greater than that for classes in the regular program.

5. Learning experiences are organized in broad, comprehensive units based upon and organized in terms of challenges, needs, interests, and problems of the learner and his community (illustration later in this chapter of a class's attack on mental health).

* 6. The common-learnings program deals largely with general education, that is, those problems or needs common to all students.

7. Problem-solving techniques find more frequent use in the common-learnings program and incidentally usually involve the student to a greater extent in his own learning. This is especially true if the teacher is highly competent.

* 8. Common learnings and experiences are organized and taught without much regard for subject matter lines or departmental boundaries. Any content pertinent to the topic is employed. Rather than being an end in itself, subject matter is employed as a means to an end.

9. There seems to be more experimentation and greater effort aimed

at the improvement of instruction in the common-learnings program. By and large, the program results in a more meaningful experience to the student and greater satisfaction to the teacher.

10. Learning experiences tend to be more functional, to involve more activity, and to put greater responsibility on the learner.

ILLUSTRATIONS

An important purpose of the common learnings is to involve students in their own learning. The two illustrations that follow indicate how this might be done. In one, a renowned private teacher found a way to involve a pupil in meeting a common and an urgent need. In the other, a teacher of a regular class (Problems of Democracy, grade 12) utilized a community situation to involve the whole class in meeting a common adolescent need. Both illustrations reveal how items 1, 3, 5, 6, 8, 9, and 10 of the important characteristics of the common learnings might operate in the classroom.

Relating Specific Content to a Need. Why does the relating of specific content to a problem or a need cause student growth or development? An incident in the life of Helen Keller[6] shows why.

Helen Keller was a healthy and sensitive child at birth. Between her first and second birthdays an attack by a virus disease left her blind and deaf. Her famous teacher, Miss Anne Sullivan, came to her a few months previous to Helen's seventh birthday. The immediate problem of Miss Sullivan, as she saw it, was to assist Helen in communicating with people and her immediate environment. Her next problem was to assist the little girl to communicate with her cultural heritage through books.

She began to teach Helen the names of familiar objects. The word "doll" was the first which was taught by Braille symbols spelled into the girl's hand. A month after coming to the Keller home, Miss Sullivan wrote:

Helen has taken the second great step in her education. She has learned that everything has a name, and that the manual alphabet is the key to everything she wants to know.

This morning as she was washing she wanted to know the name for water . . . I spelled w-a-t-e-r in her hand and thought no more about it until after breakfast. Then it occurred to me that this new word might help to clear up a confusion between "mug" and "drink". We went to the pump house, and I made Helen hold her mug under the spout while I pumped. As the cold water gushed forth filling the mug, I spelled w-a-t-e-r in Helen's hand. The word coming so close upon the sensation of cold water rushing over her hand seemed to startle her. She dropped the mug and stood as one transfixed. A new light came

[6] Helen A. Keller, *The Story of My Life* (New York, Grosset & Dunlap, Inc., 1902), p. 23.

into her face. She spelled "water" into my hand several times. Then she dropped to the ground and asked for its name and pointed to the pump and the trellis and suddenly turned around and asked for my name.

(Next morning) Helen got up this morning like a radiant fairy. She flitted from object to object, asking the name of everything.

In her autobiography, Helen Keller tells of the same incident in these words.

We walked down the path to the well-house, attracted by the fragrance of the honeysuckle with which it was covered. Someone was drawing water and my teacher placed my hand under the spout. As the cool stream gushed over one hand she spelled into the other the word w-a-t-e-r, first slowly, then rapidly. I stood still, my whole attention fixed upon the motion of her fingers. Suddenly, I felt the misty consciousness of something forgotten—a thrill of returning thought; and somehow the mystery of language was revealed to me. I knew that w-a-t-e-r meant the wonderful cool flowing over my hand. The living world awakened my soul, gave it light, set it free! There were barriers still, it is true, but barriers that could in time be swept away.

In her notes, Miss Sullivan comments, a few days before the incident took place:

It occurred to me the other day that it is absurd to require a child to come to a certain place at a certain time and recite a certain lesson.

And again, a few days after the incident at the pump house, she wrote in her notes:

The scheme works splendidly . . . I am beginning to suspect all elaborate schemes of education . . . if the child is left to himself, he thinks more and better.

A Unit Is Developed. This high school, open to all youth in a city of 300,000, quite naturally reflects the social patterns or mores of the entire populace. Several industrial and professional surveys reveal certain trends each year in age groups, jobs, number of persons in the home, home ownership, banking habits, and other pertinent data. These collected data indicate to the teaching staff what the needs of youth actually are. Examination of the students in a single class gives evidence of personal needs as follows:

1. All but three of this class of 30 are working at outside jobs.
2. Eight of the girls are married, one is a mother; all husbands are serving military time.
3. Five students hope to attend college.
4. Two are making their own way without parent or guardian.
5. Six are in families receiving aid to dependent children. (These are colored).
6. Five live in federal housing projects.

Cumulative records compiled as completely as possible, since the first day each student entered kindergarten, reveal a range of interests, abilities, and experiences. In general there are no borderline cases with extremely low I.Q.'s and neither are there any extremely high I.Q.'s. One boy has succeeded in earning only the highest mark throughout his entire school career. Reading levels range from grade 8 to above grade 13.

This will suggest the nature of the teen-agers with whom we are about to embark upon a combined subject-matter and common-learnings unit. The students, with whom this unit was developed, were typically American children.

Not all units will receive the strong send-off here illustrated. There had been a series of sex slayings within the state, and to meet this social problem a new State Psychiatric Institute had been established in connection with the State Medical College. Both were located near the high school, and the following script grew out of natural interests:

PETE: I heard something good on the radio this morning.
INSTRUCTOR: What was that? Is the cold war over?
PETE: Naw, they think they've caught the guy that killed that girl.
INSTRUCTOR: Sure it was "a guy"?
MARY: Never trust a man, I always say.
PETE: You should talk—you're married aren't you?
MARY: What makes people go crazy?
PETE: Why don't you ask the experts in psychiatry? They've just moved to town. Maybe we ought to get them over here.
INSTRUCTOR: Maybe you didn't know it, Pete, but there are four women on that psychiatric staff. Thought you didn't like women?
PETE: Well, I am like Mary, here. Maybe there is some reason for all these sex slayings. Calling the cops doesn't do any good—after it's happened. Why not bring the psychiatric people to school? We're ready for that unit on public health. I've been reading ahead—did you know that one out of every twelve Americans will have mental health trouble?
MARY: If this is a democratic class, like you say, I call for a vote. How many would like to hear from the psychiatric staff?
INSTRUCTOR: Do we want them here just for entertainment? Or should we know what they are talking about first?
MARY: Probably, we should get into the mental health unit first. But, meanwhile, someone should invite them here.

At the proper time—after considerable study of the mounting incidence of mental disease—the senior class met as a group in the school auditorium for a Mental Health Institute. Pete, as student chairman, introduced the psychiatrist, who explored the need for mental health and marriage counseling services his department hoped to meet. Mary, with some feeling of being hostess, presented a number of written questions that had been compiled earlier. The following are just 12 of them, but they gave the emphasis for the day-long Institute.

1. Should a girl of 18 have to ask her parents if she can go out whenever a boy asks for a date?

2. When school is out I plan to be married. My father is an invalid, and now I have to assist in making the living for the family. Should I go ahead and get married and let them shift for themselves or should I stay home, not get married, and continue my assistance?

3. Do you think we should marry right after we are out of high school?

4. What should a person do when one's boy friend and mother do not always see eye-to-eye?

5. What can we do to help support the mentally ill?

6. Do all teen-agers, popular, average, or unpopular, have the same problems with friends, teachers, parents, and emotions?

7. How can young persons control their emotions when with the opposite sex?

8. I have a girl, and I am going steady with her. There is a boy trying to get a date with her. What should I do?

9. How can two people find happiness if they both belong to different religions?

10. I am an epileptic; is it possible to overcome this?

11. I have gone steady for three years with this boy. He graduated last year and now I have met someone else whom I like much better and is better to be my companion in the years to come. How can I tell the first boy that he is not the one?

12. What makes a man who owns his own carpenter's business say that he hates his children? And always hollers at them? Every time they do something or ask him for something he always goes back to when he was a kid and had nothing. He was married on five dollars and thinks his daughter can do the same now.

Several sections of this same course had been invited to join in the Institute, and, as the day progressed, several other classes—English, Latin, mathematics—moved quietly into the auditorium. Not only did this show the intensity of teen-ager problems here, but it made manifest the prevailing air of permissiveness within the school. Before the day's session closed, several of the administrative staff had somehow found time to sit in and to listen to the professional treatment of specific teen-age problems.

An evaluation followed. New questions arose and quite naturally research continued. Scarcely a book on mental health went untouched during the two-week unit; the *Reader's Guide to Periodical Literature* was well thumbed through. Chapters in reference textbooks such as *Making the Most of Marriage, The Family Standard of Living,* and *Promoting the Nation's Health* were read again and again. Even the standardized tests which accompanied the textbook were taken and scored with a high degree of personal interest.

The Common Learnings in the Modern High School Curriculum.
Perhaps, the best high school curriculum yet devised is shown in Chart 11.
It was developed by the Educational Policies Commission as a curriculum
for *all* youth with an equal emphasis upon a broad general and a specific
individual education. As you study Chart 11, note the five major areas
into which the curriculum is divided: personal interests, individual interests, vocational preparation, common learnings, and health and physical
fitness. The important feature of this curriculum is the use of subject
matter materials as a means for the development of youth. Education, or
the development of youth, is the central theme.

Its structure. What is the structure or framework of the modern high
school curriculum? What form will it take as it is put into operation in a

Chart 11. The Curriculum of a Modern High School*

PERIODS PER DAY	GRADES							
	7	8	9	10	11	12	13	14
1	**Personal interests** Exploration of personal abilities and individual interests in art, music, science, language, sports, crafts, home and family problems and leisure activities.			** Individual interests Election by pupil, under guidance of teacher, in fields of avocational, cultural, or intellectual interests.				
2				Vocational preparation Includes the study of sciences, mathematics, social studies, literature, and foreign languages in preparation for advance study in Community Institute,				
3					commercial, homemaking service and other occupations leading to employment, apprenticeship, or homemaking at end of Grades 12, 13, or 14 and work experience.			
4								
5	Common learnings A continuous course in social living to foster growth in personal living and in civic competence. Guidance.							
6	Health and physical fitness Includes games, sports, and other activities to promote physical fitness together with the study of individual and community health.							

* Educational Policies Commission, *Education for All American Youth—a Further
Look,* 1952; National Association of Secondary School Principals, "Planning for American Youth," 1951, p. 48. (Adapted, with modifications).

** Broken lines indicate flexibility of scheduling for youth who need to spend more
time in either of these areas, depending upon their occupational or further educational plans.

high school? Actually, there are four curriculum strands woven together to produce the modern high school curriculum—each strand stresses a definite phase of youth education. One strand puts the emphasis upon common learnings or on meeting the needs common to all youth. A second strand stresses special learnings or differentiated courses which meet the specific needs of individual youth, both academically and vocationally. A third strand accents student activities or providing a laboratory where youth learn how to lead, how to plan wisely, how to share honors with others: that is, how to grow toward becoming a stable and competent adult. Student activities provide a type of student development for bridging the chasm that separates youth from the adult he can become. A fourth strand accentuates physical fitness or sound mental and physical health. This is truly one of the common needs of all youth, but since it requires specialized personnel as well as gymnasiums and playing fields, it has been accepted as a distinct curriculum strand.

In a time of rapid change, there is always a battle between those who desire to change the curriculum to provide better services for *all* youth and those who like the curriculum as it was. The exact form the curriculum will take will vary from high school to high school. But most American high schools, under the pressure of the mass education motive, have made decided changes in the old academic curriculum. Under the modern high school curriculum, with its four interwoven strands, a much better synthesis for the high school program has been established.

A Course of Study. The course of study in the common learnings presented in Chart 12 illustrates the first steps in introducing the common learnings to a four-year high school by its staff.[7] As is usually done, the common learnings faculty of the school formulated the course of study. Such pre-planning of the content contributes to the essential continuity and sequence of the subject matter, and insures a more carefully selected and a broader series of problems than any one teacher would produce by himself. Such a plan gives order to the program and much freedom of choice to the individual teacher. The high school for which this program was planned provides a common-learnings class for every student each day of the week for all four years.

The above outline of the common-learnings course of study is shown as it came from the hands of the instructional staff. It was developed by the staff through a workshop and other inservice procedures. This is a first and a necessary step in a transition period between the old and the modern high school curriculum. As teachers work with the common-learnings course of study in the classroom, it is gradually improved and adapted. Each unit (topic) is usually presented as a problem. A class is organized as a study group by dividing it into subgroups, each of which will collect

[7] Sam R. Hill, "How Adequate Are Today's Secondary Schools?" *Bulletin of the National Association of Secondary-School Principals* 34:154-60, April, 1950.

Chart 12. The Common Learnings Course of Study

I. 9B—Common learnings
    A. Orientation to the building, the personnel, and the rules
    B. School citizenship and the school organization
    C. How to get the most out of school
        1. How to study
        2. Library information and skills
        3. Planning a four-year program
    D. Vocational orientation
    E. Personality development
    F. Contributory units (certain contributory units which are essential are shifted within half grades, students new to the school do not miss essentials)
        1. World geography
        2. Graphic language
        3. Math fundamentals
        4. Choral music

II. 9A—Common learnings
    A. History and government of city and state
    B. Contributory units
        1. Math fundamentals
        2. Graphic language
        3. Choral music
        4. Science

III. 10B—Common learnings
    A. Citizenship—school, city, state, nation, world
    B. Contributions of past ages to modern civilization
    C. Orientation (for students new to the school)
    D. Library information and skill (if not studied in 9B)
    E. Contributory units
        1. Personal health
        2. Vocational analysis
        3. Auto driving
        4. World geography
        5. Medieval culture

IV. 10A—Common learnings
    A. The work of the world
        1. Surveying the fields of work
        2. Investigation of specific vocations
        3. Basic economics
    B. Replanning the high school program
    C. Library information and skills (if not received in 9B or 10B)
    D. Wise use of leisure time
    E. Contributory units (same as 10B)

V. 11B and 11A—Common learnings
    A. American history
    B. Contributory units
        1. 11B
           a. World problems
           b. American problems
        2. 11A
           a. World problems
           b. Word study

Chart 12. The Common Learnings Course of Study—Continued

VI. 12B and 12A—Common learnings
- A. Student evaluation of the school program to the present, based upon the ten educational needs of all American youth
  1. To develop saleable skills
  2. To maintain good health and physical fitness
  3. To understand the rights and duties of a citizen
  4. To understand the significance of the family
  5. To purchase goods and services intelligently
  6. To understand the influence of science on human life
  7. To appreciate the beauty in art, music, theater
  8. To use leisure time wisely
  9. To think rationally, to express thought clearly, and to read and listen with understanding
  10. To develop the ability to live and work successfully
- B. Development of a plan of living in a democracy and a code of ethics through
  1. Family relationships
  2. Marriage
  3. Personal and family finance
     a. Everyday law
     b. Program of insurance
     c. Installment buying
  4. Consumer education
  5. Religious values
  6. Strategy of job finding

VII. 12B—Physical education: senior boys' problems and senior girls' problems, each two days per week

and organize data on a subtopic which will be presented to the total class. The class as a group participates actively in the summarizing discussion of the problem. Incidentally, a discussion procedure within a permissive atmosphere has been found to be highly effective in the establishment of desirable attitudes.

However, not all parts of the program, as set up by the school staff, are equally appealing to all students. An analysis of the above courses of study will reveal two types of units: (1) those arising from the demands of teen-age nature and (2) those arising from the demands of society. Of course, the units that originate out of the demands of society will have less appeal to teen-agers and will require considerably more pre-planning by teachers.

SUMMARY

The heart of our democratic culture is its universals, those cultural values common to all. The heart of the universals is their value in creating an orderly and stable society, that is, the establishment of rules according to which each citizen governs his relations with others. The high school as the only institution common to all youth clarifies and tranmits this social heritage, especially through the common learnings or general education. Because of the rapid social, economic, and technological changes of recent decades which have left both adolescents and adults confused, greater emphasis is now being given to the common learnings in order to meet a special need. Teen-agers now need help to find, accept, and practice the rules that will give direction and order to our democratic society.

The last three decades have broadened the curriculum of the modern high school so that it now includes more than the preparation of students for college. When custom and law extended compulsory education and the employable age to 18, the high school became a common school for all youth. Therefore, the modern curriculum had to be expanded to serve a wider range of purposes. Parents of teen-agers have demanded a program that has expanded the curriculum to include three definite parts: (1) common learnings or general education, (2) vocational education, and (3) special education, which includes all of the academic subjects, for meeting the special needs of all students. This is our American way for attaining the realization of an American dream—an equal opportunity for all.

DISCUSSION PROBLEMS

1. What arguments might be given for starting a child to school, as is done in England, at age 4? Similarly, should age limits be raised to 18?

2. Educators deny the claim of some critics that the Three R's are no longer being taught adequately. What practical evidence can you produce to answer this criticism?

3. Under what circumstances should such subjects as Latin, algebra, geometry, and physics be required for graduation from high school?

4. One historian related the attitude of an experienced teacher who, in early times, was applying for a school position. When asked, "Do you teach that the world is flat or round?" he responded, "I teach it either way you say." How would you reply if the question concerned racial integration in the schools?

5. Briefly list the points that favor the inclusion of vocational training in all high schools.

6. Review a high school work-study program with which you are familiar, that is, a curriculum that permits qualified students to receive credit and pay for on-the-job training during school hours. Consider the need for income, but also note the time lost from traditional school activities. Would you vote in favor or against such work experience as a common learning?

RELATED REFERENCES

AIKIN, Wilford M., *The Story of the Eight Year Study* (New York, Harper & Brothers, 1942).

ALBERTY, Harold, *Reorganizing the High School Curriculum*, rev. ed. (New York, The Macmillan Co., 1953).

The American Council on Education, *Helping Teachers Understand Children* (Washington, D.C., The American Council on Education, 1945).

The Association for Supervision and Curriculum Development, *Toward a New*

Curriculum, 1944 Yearbook (Washington, D.C., National Education Association, 1944).

———, *Fostering Mental Health,* 1950 Yearbook (Washington, D.C., National Education Association, 1950).

The Commission on Reorganization of Secondary Education, *Cardinal Principles of Secondary Education,* U. S. Bureau of Education, Bulletin 35, 1918 (Washington, D.C., Government Printing Office, 1919).

DEWEY, John, *Experience and Education,* The Kappa Delta Pi Lecture (New York, The Macmillan Co., 1938).

Educational Policies Commission, *The Purposes of Education in American Democracy* (Washington, D.C., National Education Association, 1938).

Education for All American Youth—A Further Look, rev. ed. (Washington, D.C., National Education Association, 1952).

FAUNCE, Roland C., and BOSSING, Nelson L., *Developing the Core Curriculum* (Englewood Cliffs, N.J., Prentice-Hall, Inc., 1958).

FRAZER, James G., *The Golden Bough* (New York, The Macmillan Co., 1940).

GRAVES, Albert D., *American Secondary School* (Boston, D. C. Heath & Company, 1951).

GRUHN, William T., and DOUGLASS, Harl R., *The Modern Junior High School* (New York, The Ronald Press Company, 1956).

HENRY, George W., "Foundations of General Education in the High School," *What Shall the High Schools Teach?* 1956 Yearbook, Association for Supervision and Curriculum Development (Washington, D.C., National Education Association, 1956).

HILL, Sam R., "How Adequate Are Today's Secondary Schools?" *Bulletin of the National Association of Secondary-School Principals* 34:154-60 (April, 1950).

JENKINS, G. G., SHACTER, H., and BAUER, W. A., *These Are Your Children* (Chicago, Scott, Foresman & Company, 1953).

KELLER, Franklin J., *The Comprehensive High School* (New York, Harper & Brothers, 1955).

KELLER, Helen A., *The Story of My Life* (New York, Grosset & Dunlap, Inc., 1902).

The National Association of Secondary-School Principals, *Planning for American Youth* (Washington, D.C., National Education Association, 1951).

OLSON, C. M., and FLETCHER, N. D., *Learn and Live* (New York, Sloan Foundation, Inc., 1940).

QUINN, James A., and RIPKE, Arthur, *Living in the Social World* (Philadelphia, J. B. Lippincott Co., 1956).

ROMINE, Stephen A., *Building the High School Curriculum* (New York, The Ronald Press Company, 1954).

ROSENBERGER, Homer T., "What Should We Expect of Education?" *Bulletin of the National Association of Secondary-School Principals* 40:13-348 (February, 1956).

SPITZNAS, James E., "General, Special, and Vocational Education: An Exploration of Distinctive Differences," *What Shall the High Schools Teach?* 1956 Yearbook of the Association for Supervision and Curriculum Development (Washington, D.C., National Education Association, 1956).

SPECIAL LEARNINGS

A task incumbent on modern education is to combine respect for future vocational life with a liberal education which prepares man to enrich himself through contact with the cultural values of human life: another task is to find a more constructive relationship between the school and the future vocation of the student.
——Robert Ulich, *History of Educational Thought*

THE CLASSICAL CURRICULUM—AMERICAN VERSION

An accurate description of academic and vocational education in the United States is a hazardous task. Since we do not have a national system of schools, the variations from state to state are great, and the variations within a single state are as great as they are in the nation because we do not have a state system of schools anywhere. Although each state is the sovereign power in education, the tradition of local responsibility is deeply rooted, and the power has been largely delegated to the locally elected board of education. The peculiar needs of each community plus the rivalry between communities have led to much experimentation and great diversity among high schools. As a result, many outstanding as well as many inferior high schools exist.

The Academic and Vocational Subjects Are Electives. Due to the situation described above, the curriculum in many high schools in the United States is a traditional one. In fact, in some of the more traditional high schools especially where the college preparatory motive is still dominant, the graduates are well prepared neither for college nor for life. But the mass education motive has penetrated nearly everywhere in America because our people believe in equality of opportunity for all. The wide range of individual differences among high school students is becoming more and more a reality and not a theory to high school teachers. Experimentation with programs better adapted to all youth has been a fairly common practice for many high schools. Out of this experimentation there has emerged a movement to set up *academic* and *vocational* education as special learnings.[1]

The American high school has shown genius in the organization of educational programs tailored to the talents of every student. On the other hand, the Europeans have set up only one high school program and have deliberately eliminated all students lacking in talents for this one program. At all grade levels from junior high school through junior college in the United States, general and special education operate concurrently. To the junior high school there is allocated general education and exploration (special education) where pupils are encouraged to explore and to specialize in accordance with their own ability and maturity. To the senior high school is assigned general education and special learnings (specialization) where students relate their own individual experience to their own purposes. To the junior college is assigned general education (limited) and special education (academic and vocational). Individualization and specialization, the special and the general, comprise the two major programs of the modern high school curriculum. The general program is required of all students while each student in the special program elects all courses according to his needs, purposes, and abilities.

This is true only in the United States. In general, it can be said, with some exceptions, that in all other countries of the world the students of the secondary school take the same subjects in the same order and with exactly the same type of instruction.[2] Many European children must choose, at the age of 11, on the basis of a state-administered achievement test, the classical academic curriculum or the vocational curriculum, which are provided in separate schools. Once the choice is made, it is difficult to change. Their expectations in life have been fixed for them at 11.

The academic and vocational programs are both elective in the United States, while general education is required of all. The high school counselors assist students in the selection of academic and vocational courses in accordance with the purpose and abilities of the students. Academic courses give students an insight into the laws which govern the universe. They come to understand that ours is a world governed by natural law, not man-made, which must be obeyed and accepted by all of us if we are to live full and complete lives. These basic understandings are essential to all youth and should not be reserved for the college-bound only.

While the academic and vocational programs are elective—no one course will be required of all students—every high school student prior

[1] Any school that provides such a program is classified as a comprehensive high school provided that vocational, academic, and general education are held in equal esteem; the homeroom is made to function; democratic thinking and living are promoted; and special opportunities for both gifted and slow learners are made a reality.

[2] James B. Conant, *Education and Liberty* (Cambridge, Mass., Harvard University Press, 1953), Ch. 1.

to graduation will elect several of them. College-bound students will elect the academic courses required by the college or by the profession to which they aspire. Vocation-bound students or those who plan to go to work or to the junior college upon graduation from high school will choose the academic or vocational courses that best prepare them for their vocation. As indicated earlier, the common-learnings program meets the basic requirements for citizenship and communication. The counseling program, as revealed above, is an essential feature of the modern high school curriculum. The counselors aid students to make correct choices according to their needs and abilities. Through this procedure, choices remain flexible to the junior or senior year and are not fixed at the early age of 11 as is true in European practice. Hence, the modern high school curriculum is sometimes called the classical curriculum, American version.

Individual Differences. Ours is a democratic culture. By and large, other cultures operate their secondary schools on the basis of a class system. For these cultures, the elementary school with continuation education is their common school. The ruling class operates the secondary schools to prepare their children and select rapid learners from the middle and lower classes for the university and the professions. In the United States, the high school is not only a common school open to all youth; it is also compulsory for all youth. Our culture has both supported and enforced this principle.

Gradually high school teachers have become aware of a fact that has long been recognized in the elementary school—the great range of individual differences among students. The elementary school teachers have been developing ways for adapting instruction to the wide range of individual differences in the same class. This procedure is just as necessary for a high school where all youth attend.

Extent of Individual Differences. It is generally known that students do differ one from another—no two are exactly alike. What is not so readily apparent is the number, range, and complexity of individual differences represented among secondary-school students.[3] Students differ with respect to race, sex, religion, health and physical constitution, intelligence, socio-economic status, cultural background, educational attainments, emotional make-up, specific traits of character, personal values, special aptitudes and interests, habits of work and study, and in many other ways. These differences are to a greater or lesser degree educationally significant and decidedly complicate the work of the school.

Figure 2 represents not only how traits are distributed in general but also how mental ability is distributed in a comprehensive high school. The range of I.Q. scores from 55 to 180 reveals that this high school is a truly

---

[3] Thomas H. Briggs, J. Paul Leonard, and Joseph Justman, *Secondary Education* (New York, The Macmillan Co.,), Ch. III.

comprehensive one which is serving all youth. A line graph plotted for the distribution of any one of the traits listed above would probably produce a normal frequency curve. Mental ability is only one of the many individual differences operating in a classroom. Specific aptitudes is another factor which is always operating in a classroom and which must be kept in mind. Students differ widely with respect to their specific aptitudes for music, mathematics, languages, and other fields. Class grouping based largely upon mental ability, which is a combination of many mental abilities, may destroy entirely the homogeneity sought because of the wide variations in special aptitudes.

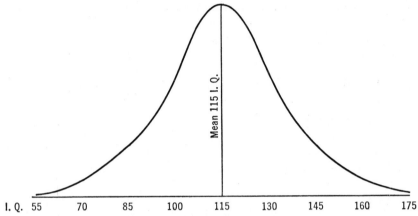

Figure 2.   The Probable Distribution of Intelligence Quotients in a Comprehensive High School.

All graduates of the Elementary or Junior High School are eligible to attend the Comprehensive High School. The program of study is adjusted to the needs of students of all types of intellectual ability.

Adapting instruction to individual differences. First, the total school program must be adapted to the actual situation. Each of the millions of boys and girls now in the secondary school is a unique individual. Each has his own unique heredity, and each has been subjected to a unique environment in his formative years. The high school program of common learnings assists all students in acquiring common loyalties and common understandings; vigorous individuality is the outcome sought through special learnings by developing special aptitudes and strong desirable traits to their fullest. Hence, all special learnings are elective in accordance with student purposes and plans. The program must be sufficiently flexible to permit each student to utilize his special aptitudes.

Second, the teacher must know his subject matter and also must be concerned about the interests, capacities, and weaknesses of his students. In fact, the real difference between the mediocre teacher and the good teacher resides at this point; the good teacher adapts his instruction to his students. A teacher can no more say that he has taught until his students have learned than a merchant can say that he has sold until someone has bought.[4] A mathematics teacher, drawn into World War II and assigned to teach mathematics to young men who were being trained as pilots, explains this point. Said the former mathematics teacher to the officer in charge, "I cannot teach mathematics to these men," naming certain ones, "they have not had the requisite background." The officer in charge replied, "Those men can fly; you *will* teach them the mathematics they need." The teacher-soldier states, "I did teach those men the mathematics they needed." With all youth in high school, the stereotyped teaching of the early academic era must give way to adapting subject matter to the varying needs of individual students.

On methods of teaching. First, how to assign students to classes has been a controversial issue for a long time. Various practices have been followed in order to achieve homogeneous groups or to group students together in a class with like abilities, interests, and backgrounds. The great majority of our high schools, especially the larger ones in the academic and vocational areas, practice homogeneous grouping. But since students are assigned to classes by the high school principal, the problem of grouping is usually decided by the administration and not by the teacher. As all courses in the academic and vocational areas are elective, the usual teacher prefers a homogeneous group, one in which all the members of his classes have similar interests, backgrounds, and abilities.

Yet, there are a number of problems in homogeneous grouping.[5] By what procedures can students of like abilities, interests, and backgrounds be selected and assigned to a class group? Is the practice of ability grouping educationally wise? Does ability grouping promote academic, vocational, and social development?

By and large, the intelligence test has been the major instrument employed for the selection and assignment of students to homogeneous groups. The use of intelligence test scores for such grouping assumes that intelligence is a single variable. As a matter of fact, a glance at any intelligence test reveals clearly that intelligence as measured by the test is made up of such different factors as verbal, spatial, problem-solving, manipulative, and imaginative aptitudes. Hence, the score earned on an intelligence test is not an accurate index of a student's ability to succeed in any one subject matter field such as English, mathematics, or history. For example, let us assume that two students earn an identical score on an intelligence test. When analyzed for the two subjects of English and mathematics, the scores for one on verbal and quantitative (spatial and

[4] John Dewey, *How We Think*, rev. ed. (Boston, D. C. Heath & Company, 1933), p. 35.

[5] *Homogeneous:* from the Greek *homos* (the same) plus *genos* (race or kind).

mathematical) aptitudes are 60 and 20, respectively, while the scores for the other are 20 and 60, respectively. Although the two students have an identical score on the intelligence test, their aptitudes for English and mathematics are in an inverse ratio. From the above discussion, one very pertinent fact stands out—a group that is homogeneous for one subject, English, for example, will not be homogeneous for any other subject. There is also some evidence to indicate that the vocabulary of the usual intelligence test is geared to the vocabulary of upper-class children and does not always measure accurately the innate aptitude of children from the lower classes. Likewise, such factors as interest, reading deficiencies, health, and social background are not revealed by intelligence tests. These additional factors are often not considered by principals in the assignment of students to homogeneous class groups. In reality, as indicated above, there can never be such a thing as true homogeneous grouping: there can only be groups that are more homogeneous than others. In any homogeneous group, there will always be found a wide range of differences in all human characteristics.

Also, there are courses for which homogeneous grouping is unsuited. For example, the common learnings or general education course by its very nature requires that the class be comprised of a heterogeneous group. "Common learnings are intended to teach students how to cooperate with others and to help all to acquire the common attitudes and ideals which bind our society together and which establish loyalties to the community, the state, and the nation."[6] American ideals have been derived from the aspirations and desires of all classes of American society. The course in common learnings has been deliberately designed to help all students, not a selected group of students. To the teacher of common learnings, in our present confusion, has fallen the task of clarifying for our youth our American ideals. Hence, in selecting and assigning students to the common-learnings classes, students from all types of homes and with quite varied backgrounds in ideals and attitudes are deliberately placed in the common-learnings classes, that is, each class is a cross-section of and representative of the entire community. The teacher of such a class will seek deliberately to take a definite stand on all questions of moral values. He will attempt through discussion and problem-solving approaches to gear his instruction to the clarification of the democratic value system and to assist all students in achieving common values and ideals in accord with contemporary values now emerging in American society.

According to the American plan, the student elects courses through a conference with a counselor; no course is blindly chosen. Since the counselor will know the ability of the student, only courses that a student will be able to pass will be approved. Likewise, a student elects a course because it fits in his program and purposes. In the election of a course,

[6] Chapter VII, pp. 165-168.

the student puts himself into competition with other students in a class for grades; in an elective course he must compete for and earn all grades just as he will compete and earn in life after graduation.

Second, the method of teaching employed should be adapted to the maturity of the learner. When students pass to the senior high school, they should mature enough to acquire and use methods that lead as rapidly as possible to independent progress. All too frequently, methods employed on the lower level are continued on the senior high school level. Even slow learners do not like an easy school; they want a challenging one. The methods employed, in part at least, should demand independent thought, that is, the type of activity demanded in the adult world. Some drill, of course, is a "must" for the mastery of skills, concepts, and principles, but students are capable of much more independent study than is now required of them.

Third, it is never the class that learns; it is always the individual. Hence, instruction must always be adapted to the individual. Some cartoonists employ the symbol of a Mr. Milquetoast as a representative of the average citizen. Such a symbol of the average student might help a teacher make a more adequate adaptation of instructional materials. Teaching only goes on when students are learning. A teacher needs to have several procedures for adapting instruction to students. Frequent variation of the procedures usually helps since variety in itself causes an increased interest and will often catch the attention of the inattentive student. One is adapting his instruction to a class only when the adaptation is such that every student is learning. Under some conditions, it may even be better to break a class down into three or four groups and present material in a different way to each of them while the other groups are working on an assignment.

The Academic Program. The curriculum of the high school is in a period of gradual transition. It is no longer exclusively a college preparatory curriculum. It has gradually taken on the additional services of preparation for citizenship, physical fitness and health, vocational preparation, and the development of the student's personal and avocational interests. The trend is toward a somewhat more functional curriculum and a somewhat less academic one. The factors which have operated to change the high school curriculum have been experimentation with new combinations of subject matter and pressure from the public to retain and educate all youth. The experimenting agency has been the relatively independent school system.

A period of transition. Since the curriculum is interwoven with the whole cultural pattern, it follows as a matter of course that a rapid change in the cultural pattern, as is happening in the United States, will be accompanied by rapid changes in the curriculum. What are some of the cultural changes which have been and are operating to produce curricular changes? In the comparisons that follow, two periods are being contrasted. On the left are a series of statements describing the American culture prior to 1900; while on the right the series of statements describe the American culture since 1950. The contrast between the two reveals the extent of cultural change.

FROM (BEFORE 1900)	TO (SINCE 1950)
1. The community was a closely knit unit based upon face-to-face relations, affection, and friendship: most men were dependent upon themselves for food and shelter.	In the present industrialized culture, the old community has been largely replaced by an urbanized community. Now the individual is less and less shaped by the total community and more and more shaped by his occupation and other specialized activities; most citizens are now employed by industry. In time, the value patterns of these employees, in part at least, are so shaped that with an absence of a common social faith in the community to keep citizens working together in harmony, there is a constant struggle between occupational groups over power and prestige.
2. The free enterprise economy prevailed, and the profit motive and individual initiative were given free rein to stimulate the individual to produce as fully as possible to compete in an open market. The ownership of property was almost entirely individual. There was little interference by the government.	There has been a perversion of the free market under corporate control, a decline of the free enterprise system, and a marked trend toward regulation of the market by the government. Although the older, classic free-enterprise economy has all but disappeared, the public still retains faith in it.
3. The American value system, borrowed from earlier civilizations, came into full focus and fused into a series of universal values, that is, rules of conduct by which people determine their behaviors and from which they derive their hopes. A fairly clear set of purposes had been established with a fixed sense of right and wrong.	Science and technology have multiplied; mechanized industry and increased knowledge have uprooted habitual modes of action and are destroying old rules of conduct. Yet, a core of the old system remains in our beliefs with respect to the maximum development of the individual, educationally and personally; free speech; the right of common men to rule themselves; to solve the problems that face them as a people; and to know when those who represent them are serving their interests. However, on economic, social, and political issues, there is much confusion and conflict.

From (before 1900)	To (since 1950)
4. This was a period of transition from laissez faire to an interdependent society.	This has been a time for the reconstruction of our values so that each can attain the material development of which he is capable. Interdependence is increasing and spreading into more aspects of human activity. A lack of universals, that is, accepted and established conduct patterns, is gradually being reduced. Tensions among us are gradually being lessened.

What changes in the curriculum are indicated by these cultural changes? The immense number of intricate machines created by science and technology for the production of goods requires trained operators. To become competent workmen, these machine operators must have a broad understanding of the science and technology involved in the construction and operation of these machines and of the guiding rules and regulations that apply in acquiring and processing the raw products and in the distribution of the finished product. If prior to employment these operators of machines have been oriented for common industrial skills, they adjust to a job more quickly and in general become more competent employees. The high school curriculum must be planned to provide for the attainment of these basic understandings, habits, and skills, especially for those students who plan to immediately go to work upon graduation from the high school. Hence, in our time of confusion, the task of the high school is to instruct so that the cultural elements, both old and new, will be mutually adjusted and a new cultural synthesis will be achieved. There must be an integration of all curriculum elements—the vital new with the vital old.

In our urban communities and larger metropolitan areas which have largely supplanted the old rural community, there has come a transformation in the basic patterns of American society. A new type of common sense must be built into the curriculum of the modern high school. This will aid students in attaining the essential impersonal and remote associations which have developed from the interdependent character of our society. The curriculum must stress these relationships in both general and special education. Competency on the job requires an understanding of the interdependent relationships among all of one's fellow workers. Also, the worker must acquire the personal habits and skills which will make his social contacts on the job more rewarding and effective.

Our economic structure is now interdependent, requiring the co-operative effort of thousands of individuals, that is, the great majority of our producers are now interdependent workers rather than owners and managers of property. Since all phases of our American life are now interdependent, it is no longer possible to separate economic questions from political and social issues. Economic policies permeate all areas of the entire society. All subject-matter fields are involved in any comprehensive grasp of our economic structure. Hence, all high school teachers are involved in transmitting the contemporary pattern of our culture to youth. The teacher who is competent must have a general education, as well as a thorough education in a special field. All areas of the high school curriculum must be so articulated that each area supports and enriches all other areas.

Smith, Stanley, and Shores[7] have made some predictions as to the shape of America's future culture pattern. These predictions have implications for the future of the high school curriculum. In summarized form, these are their predictions:

1. Interdependence is increasing and spreading into most human activity.

2. It is less and less possible for uneducated individuals to perceive the entire pattern of human relationship activities.

3. The basic social processes are being increasingly regulated and integrated by deliberate human effort based upon social knowledge and insight.

4. Since all must prosper if all are to attain the material development of which they are capable, democratization with respect to material welfare is becoming a matter of public concern.

5. The suppressed races and social classes are increasingly asserting their rights to the equalities and freedoms promised by the democratic process.

6. The assimilation of national rights into a world state, strong enough to supersede anarchic states' rights, is already under way.

7. The value system of the democratic state is undergoing a thorough reconstruction.

8. Habits of thinking and social skills, retained from earlier cultural periods, are undergoing transformation in order to enable men to deal effectively with social and psychological realities.

What should be the character of the curriculum in the current stage of social transition? The educational program should be both conservative and progressive. Conservative in that it includes and gives appropriate emphasis to persistent elements of the past and the present; progressive in that recognition is given to those elements of the culture that are new and must be understood if men are to adjust to the mergent state of affairs and to create the kind of human relationships they desire. Basically, the

---

[7] B. Othaniel Smith, William O. Stanley, and J. Harlan Shores, *Fundamentals of Curriculum Development* (Yonkers, N. Y., World Book Co., 1950), Chs. 1-5.

task is to design an educational program that will produce the following outcomes:

1. Provide common social goals, which lend meaning to individual efforts and achievement.

2. Build a new frame of acceptance—an adequate social and moral orientation.

3. Develop a new conception of human nature which is based upon psychological and sociological descriptions and which embraces new insights into personal and social actions and achievements.

4. Establish new patterns of thinking, wherein a number of social variables in politics, economics, and the like, are kept in the picture in the process of reaching conclusions about social policies and actions, instead of the prevailing and now obsolete habit of thinking in a linear and compartmentalized fashion, that is, keeping economic and political thought in separate spheres.

5. Create new methods and techniques of dealing with social conflicts —methods and techniques that will release creative energy rather than give rise to repressive measures.

What proof is there to show that the high school curriculum is changing? What evidence indicates that there has been a gradual transition from the college preparatory curriculum to a high school curriculum better adapted to all youth? Table 13 compares the old and the new. The left-hand column of the table presents the college preparatory curriculum as recommended by the Committee of Ten (1893), which was the program found in most high schools from 1893 to 1910. In the right-hand column which is based on a survey by the U. S. Office of Education (1948-49) of the modern high school curriculum, all of the courses offered in 14 subject-matter areas are enumerated. The offerings of approximately 40 courses in 1893 in five subject-matter areas have expanded to more than 500 courses in 14 subject-matter areas in 1949. It seems almost incredible, and yet it is true. Although the high schools of today recognize that the college preparatory curriculum of the past is no longer adequate for all students, there are many, many exceptions. It requires greatly extended and much more varied curricular offerings to meet the diversity of needs of today's high school students. High school leaders, who are working for the adjustment of the modern curriculum to all youth, recognize that we have been, now are, and will continue to be in a period of transition from the curriculum *that was* to the curriculum *that is to be.*

The addition of new subject matter. What new courses have been added to the modern high school curriculum during the last two decades? A few of the most common titles are listed below:

Common learnings: duties and responsibilities of citizenship; social and ethical principles in relation to people and family life relationships; democratic principles, the scientific method, and values basic to our civilization;

Table 13. Comparing the Subject Areas of the College Preparatory (1893) with the Subject Areas of the Modern High School Curriculum (1949)

	COLLEGE PREPARATORY CURRICULUM COMMITTEE OF TEN (1893)*		SUBJECT AREAS OF THE MODERN HIGH SCHOOL CURRICULUM (1949)**	
SUBJECTS		COURSE OFFER- INGS†	SUBJECTS	COURSE OFFER- INGS†
1. Grammar, rhetoric, composition, English literature		10	English	37
2. History, ethnology, geography		6	Social studies	66
3. Astronomy, botany, chemistry, geology, meterology, physics, physiology, zoology		7	Science	48
4. French, German, Greek, Latin		11	Foreign languages	35
5. Algebra, geometry, trigonometry		6	Mathematics	25
6. Industrial arts		0	Industrial arts	78
7. Trade and industrial education		0	Trade and industrial education	59
8. Business education		0	Business education	58
9. Home economics		0	Home economics	39
10. Agriculture		0	Agriculture	5
11. Health, safety and physical education		0	Health, safety and physical education	9
12. Music		0	Music	18
13. Art		0	Art	33
14. Other courses		0	Other courses	13
Total		40		523

* Report of the Committee of Ten, (New York, American Book Company, 1894).
** ASCD and NEA, Yearbook 1956, *What Shall the High Schools Teach?* Chapter 3 (Hovet, Kenneth).
† List of distinct course offerings (subject titles).

acquiring skills in the 3 R's, communication and establishing and maintaining physical fitness

Unified studies: teachers of separate classes in English and social studies cooperate to relate the contents of the two fields

English: radio speaking and broadcasting, debate, remedial English, creative writing

Social studies: Latin American history, consumer education

Orientation: home living, social living, problems in living, group guidance

Science: conservation, fundamentals of electricity, advanced general science, advanced biology, advanced chemistry, aeronautics, earth science

Mathematics: mathematics reviews

Foreign language: Russian, Portuguese[8]

The academic program as basic education. The academic program, although not the whole of the secondary-school curriculum, is an essential part of the whole. Our cultural heritage has been systematized and made

[8] Association for Supervision and Curriculum Development, *What Shall the High Schools Teach?* 1956 Yearbook (Washington, D.C., National Education Association, 1956), Ch. 3.

orderly by the logical organization of the content in the academic subjects of English, social studies, mathematics, and foreign languages. As
so systematized and arranged, the cultural heritage can be transmitted
to teen-agers through the specific courses in each subject area, provided
the teacher adapts the contents of each course to the age and maturity of
the students in his classes. When so developed, the academic subjects can
increase the intellectual grasp of teen-agers. They see more distinctly and
understand more fully; for each student the world becomes more orderly
and more systematic. Each feels at home and at ease in his world. These
subject areas are basic to the intellectual development of youth. They
comprise a vital part of our basic education, but by no means all of it.

Both vocational education and common learnings draw heavily from
the content of the academic subjects. In general, what students take
from the academic subjects to these other two curricular areas are as
follows:

From English—the structure and form of the language, certain highly important
language skills, and a favorable attitude toward acceptable English usage
From mathematics—principles governing number systems, a symbolic language,
number skills, and insight into number relationships
From science—accumulated knowledge, systematized and formulated to aid in
the discovery of general truths or laws that govern physical or biological
phenomena: in short to give teen-agers a better understanding of the
physical and biological world in which they live
From social studies—an understanding of the interrelationships that bind men
together into states and nations and an insight into how our modern
civilization has come to be for a teen-ager must have some comprehension
of the past to obtain a clear insight into the present.

When adequately mastered, any academic course closely related to
preparation for college, a vocation, common learnings, or an avocation
can increase a student's ability to succeed; however, he must perceive
clearly what outcomes selected from the academic subjects can give help.
Which of these outcomes should make success for a student more likely:
graphic symbols, general laws, numerical symbols and systems, a percep-
tion of language structure and form, or insight into human relationships?
What academic course or courses provide such outcomes? With a particular student clearly in mind, any academic teacher should be able to
answer both of these questions distinctly and without a quibble. When
wisely selected, academic courses are of vital importance to students,
but an educational diet needs balance.

The status of the academic subjects. What is the status of the academic
subjects in the modern high school curriculum? Are the academic subjects
equal to, greater than, or inferior to common learnings or vocational education? Is the college-bound youth any less interested in a vocational future
than a work-bound student? These are to some extent controversial ques-

tions, but the answers given by the regulations of boards of education strongly support the position that the academic program is merely a co-ordinate of the total curriculum—all parts of the curriculum are of equal importance. To the staff of the modern high school, every student is an individual of supreme worth; complete development of every student to his fullest potential is the operative purpose of the staff and the school. Common learnings, the vocational program, the academic program, and the avocational program are of equal standing; there are no subordinate programs. All are equally important for the development of youth.

By tradition, the academic is an older program; for up to very recent times, it has comprised the total curriculum of the high school. As the high school expanded to include all youth, the personnel of the academic staff maintained an attitude of superiority and at times disdain toward the newer programs. There were occasions when the situation resembled that of a new boy coming into a neighborhood. A new boy always has a bad time of it until by a series of fights he establishes his position with the other boys. By name-calling, innuendo, and propaganda, this type of struggle has been going on for some years between the personnel of the old and the new programs. From ancient times until now, groups have used propaganda to retain a superior position, but the time has come, as it does among neighborhood boys, to accept the status quo or a co-ordinate relationship which will give all programs an equal rank.

What are some of the difficulties still blocking co-ordination or the giving of an equal status to all areas of the curriculum? This is a difficult question to answer for the satisfaction of all concerned. Many deep biases still exist, for the mores of a culture change slowly. Certainly, all of us see clearly that prejudices still remain to be removed. A few of these difficulties will be discussed briefly.

Expansion of knowledge. We are privileged to live in one of the great creative periods of all time. The expansion of knowledge during the past three decades has been phenomenal, but the expansion during the next three decades may exceed the progress of the recent past. The combining of new and old knowledge into an orderly and systematic program has exceeded the creative ability of many academic teachers. At the same time, these same teachers have been pressed to be creative at adapting instruction to a wide range of student capacities and needs. Some of the new content seems to defy classification under the old. Indeed, the new content in certain areas seems to contradict the truths previously set forth by the old. Students of this problem assert that because of the conflict between the new and the old, considerable disagreement exists in all academic areas today.

All students can profit. Intellectual development is highly important to all students. The academic program by its very nature stresses this vital phase of teen-age development. Undoubtedly, the depth of understanding will vary from student to student; all students can gain essential insights into many truths, laws, and principles through the study of selected academic courses. Slow learners with I.Q.'s as low as 80 will have a mental age sufficiently advanced to grasp and to utilize many of the truths and principles developed by an academic program. However, the slow and the average learner require a less abstract presentation with more specific assignments as well as special help on many topics. The academic program for these students must be selected with care both for the teacher and the course involved; however, to the extent that an academic program is adapted to their abilities, all students can profit. All of us are somewhat intolerant on this issue. Academic courses are difficult to teach to *all* students. We need to know more than subject matter to do it well, but it both can be and needs to be done.

The assumed superiority of academic teachers. Any teacher is proud of teaching in an academic area, for the transmission of the cultural heritage is an old and respected service. But all high school teachers are engaged in the all-around development of youth. They are members of a single team, co-operating to achieve a common purpose—the work of the team must be co-ordinated. Competent instruction requires of all members of the team high academic scholarship and, in addition, demands that each shall be a specialist in a definite curriculum area. Perhaps, if any teacher could be named as superior on the basis of academic standards, it would be the common learnings teacher. This teacher must be highly competent in all academic areas as well as in counseling, the vocations, all areas of communications, and superior in the ability to teach. The strength of a state and of a community depends as much upon loyalty and co-operation as it does upon developed intellectual power. Physical fitness and vocational efficiency are both essential qualities of the good citizen. Even good habits in recreation and leisure make for security and peace. For our time and our place in the modern world, each of these outcomes is highly important.

THE VOCATIONAL PROGRAM

The basic resource . . . is the reserve of talents and aptitudes in the young.
—GEORGE S. COUNTS in *Education and American Civilization*

Vocational Education Becomes a Necessity. Our American ancestors hewed a civilization out of the wilderness and the prairies by hard work. To produce food and shelter, toil was essential. At an early age children learned to work in the fields and in the home. Their food and shelter was so clearly related to the toil of their hands that even small children saw this relationship early in life—food and shelter resulted from the work one did. "He who works can eat" was more than a copybook maxim to the children of the pioneers. This tradition of the necessity for all to work is an attitude deeply entrenched in our culture. Under pioneer conditions, all youth learned to farm, to hunt, to build houses, and to manufacture equip- ment under the tutelage of their parents. The responsibility for vocational education was taken for granted by the pioneer family, but to the school was assigned the responsibility of teaching the children how to read, write, and do sums.

Between then and now, America has become a great industrial nation because of an ingenuity engendered, in part, by the pioneer's complete dependence upon himself for the manufacture of tools—the reproducing of worn-out tools and the inventing and making of new tools. By now, even farming requires an understanding of science and has become a highly competitive occupation where only the vocationally fit can survive. Formerly, all food was grown on the farm and processed by pickling, drying, or other procedures. Wool and flax were produced and completely processed at home to become the clothing for the family. Nearly all of these former industries of the home and of the small shops are now incorporated into a few large industries. In these large plants, the work of the employees has been specialized or classified into many specific occupations. The *Dictionary of Occupations* now lists more than 20,000 occupations. Even the apprenticeship system, by which youth could learn a specific vocation under realistic conditions, has all but disappeared.

As occupational specialization became more and more common and the number of occupations spiralled into the thousands, parents began to feel more and more inadequate. Since most of them were employed by facto- ries, businesses, transportation industries, and other occupations outside of the home, the conditions under which they worked did not permit them to teach their skills to their children. Besides, many hoped that their children might have a better income and an easier life in a different occupation.

As a rule, parents are aware that children vary widely in talents and aptitudes, but they lack the specific understandings and the skills to determine what aptitudes children possess. Hence, parents are no longer willing to assume the responsibility for the vocational education of their children. Since parents are stockholders in the public school corporation, they can and have delegated that responsibility to the public high school. Even the farmer, who originally opposed vocational education for the high school, has become a strong advocate of it. The mechanized farm on which there are several children needs only one to handle the farm work at maturity while the others must receive a vocational education com- mensurate with their talents and aptitudes. Most parents understand that they need the assistance of the high school in determining the talents and aptitudes of their children and for orienting them to a vocation. Voca- tional education by the high school has become an essential. The old plan under which the parents assumed the full responsibility for their children's vocational education has faded away, giving place to a new order wherein the high school is held partly responsible for it.

The Objectives of Vocational Education. Vocational education has been a latecomer to the high school curriculum. With some exceptions, it has been accorded the welcome of the stepchild or the ugly duckling of myth and fable. The Cardinal Principles of Secondary Education (1918) listed "vocational efficiency" as one of the objectives of secondary education. There have been no criticisms of this objective then or since. However, the statement of the objective did not answer these questions: (1) At what age should vocational education be offered? (2) How much vocational education should be offered? (3) Should vocational education emphasize specific skills or general vocational education?

Neither educators nor parents, even now, agree on the answers to these questions. Yet, certain trends seem clearly evident. A few of these trends are discussed below.

One trend is that vocational education has a place in the modern high school curriculum equal to that of any other curriculum area. There are still some high school principals and teachers who look upon vocational courses as a dumping ground for students lacking ability in the academic and classical courses. But gradually a basic fact has been accepted by all except the badly biased—with some exceptions, students lacking ability for academic and classical subjects also lack ability for vocational courses. The absence of a specific academic ability is no assurance of talent or aptitude for mechanical skills. In the hands of a competent teacher, there is order and systematization to a vocational course. These courses are challenging, not easy, and require study and work.

Vocational education is an inseparable part of all education. The conflict between vocational and academic education exists only in the fevered brains of the badly biased. There must be a co-ordination among common learnings, academic subjects, and vocational subjects because many understandings, attitudes, and skills essential to success in a variety of occupations are usually taught only in general and academic courses. Research indicates that the loss of their jobs by workers is due not to lack of specific vocational skills but to emotional instability or an inability to get along with other workmen. What are some of the outcomes essential to vocational success that are developed through the common learnings and the academic courses? A few of these are included in the list that follows:

1. The ability to read, write, and speak effectively

2. An understanding of the number concept and the ability to manipulate numbers with accuracy and ease

3. The ability to understand and use the laws and principles of elementary science

4. A healthy mind within a healthy body

5. An understanding of industry, business, and personal services as related to our total social and economic life

6. Habits of industry, thrift, promptness, and resourcefulness

7. A respect for honest labor regardless of its social and economic level.

An objective is that vocational education comprises any experiences or activities in which students engage that aids them in becoming more efficient at any type of vocational work. The present trend is to defer specific vocational skills to the junior and senior years of high school, to junior college, or to learning them on the job.[9] Automation is outmoding many specific skills previously required for handwork in wood, metals, clay, and other materials. Now, machines fashion the product as a piece. The men work on an assembly line where only a few skills are required for each worker. These skills can be acquired in a very few hours on the job. The present trend is definitely in favor of general vocational education and unfavorable to stress upon specific vocational skills.

Another trend is that the school should provide exploration and guidance for youth. For every youth, an answer to the question—What are my talents and aptitudes?—is always meaningful. Even a partial answer to this question will assist a student to find a more appropriate place in the workaday world, and it is a service that a teacher-counselor is qualified to render. He does this through the administration and interpretation of selected commercial tests and a study of the student's cumulative file. The teacher-counselor also studies the behavior of the student in the classroom, about the school, and at home. Through interviews and conferences, the teacher-counselor tries to help the student answer several questions such as: What are my strengths and weaknesses? What am I best qualified to do? In what occupation am I likely to be the most successful and the happiest? What vocational and academic courses will help me most to discover my strengths and weaknesses?

The counselor helps the student to understand himself, to form judgments on sound evidence, and to reach out toward maturity. Through interviews, test scores, and a careful analysis of performance in courses taken, the counselor and the student set up occupational goals and a plan to achieve those goals. From time to time the student needs to take stock of the progress being made toward the goals and to raise a question as to whether these goals or this plan need to be modified or changed. During his high school career, every student should give some time to a serious study of his proposed lifetime occupation.

One more trend is that the school should develop vocational flexibility. In a time of little or no change when the methods and techniques of

[9] James E. Spitznas, "General, Special, and Vocations Education: An Exploration of Distinctive Differences," *What Shall the High Schools Teach?* 1956 Yearbook of the Association for Supervision and Curriculum Development (Washington, D. C., National Education Association, 1956).

technology, occupational skills, and understandings have remained nearly static generation after generation, the school may teach specific crafts and skills. But with us now, changes are so rapid that specific skills and understandings acquired in high school may be out-of-date before the student graduates or finds employment. For example, automation is making many skills which were of recent value obsolete, and it is demanding new skills and understandings.

This situation has caused vocational teachers to stress general vocational skills. From the work of the secondary school, they believe that a student profits most who has a broad vocational education in one occupational family rather than in a specific division of that family, that is, in business education rather than in bookkeeping only. If general skills and understandings are well established for an occupational family, essential skills and understandings can be acquired for a specific division of that family after graduation either in junior college or on the job. Writers in the field of vocational education, such as Charles A. Prosser, point out that today from 75 to 95 per cent of the jobs require little or no preliminary training and that 95 per cent of those workers requiring skilled training are trained on the job by the foreman.[10] Students of secondary vocational education strongly recommend broad, general vocational education or vocational flexibility rather than emphasis upon specific vocational skills.

Vocational Education. "Go to school and learn or spend your life digging in a ditch" was a maxim of an earlier time, and one occasionally heard even now. The implication is clear—physical work requires no preparation and is for the illiterate. The work of the literate, which is honored and respected, requires study and time. Today, ditch-digging has been upgraded. The work is done by a machine which is operated by a man who is trained and better paid than most scholars. He has learned many specific skills and possesses an aptitude for operating a complicated machine. The ditch-digging machine is only one of many complicated machines found in modern industry. The men who operate these machines need to understand the basic principles that make the machine function, such as physics and its application to industry; to understand the role of such machines in our economic life; and to acquire the specific technical skills needed to operate a particular machine. This is vocational education or the new basic education. This vocational education is vital to industrialization—the men who control industry as well as parents in industrialized areas demand it. Under pressure the high schools have accepted this new basic education as a co-ordinate part of the modern high school curriculum.

In recent years, there has arisen a new concept in vocational education —fitting the boy to the job. Vocational talent and aptitude are just as

[10] Charles A. Prosser and Thomas A. Quiggley, *Vocational Education in a Democracy* (Chicago, American Technical Society, 1950), pp. 387-388.

important in industry as intellectual ability for academic subjects; in fact, many laboring occupations require intellectual capacity on a par with the most demanding of the academic subjects. In the past, guidance personnel and vocational teachers have often lacked the essential understandings and skills needed for the exacting task of fitting the student to the job; however, considerable progress is now being made on this problem.

Vocational education is new to the high school as a co-ordinate part of the modern high school curriculum. Teachers of the academic subjects have been somewhat slow in changing their attitudes and in planning their courses with a dual emphasis—academic education for the professions and basic education for the occupations. Originally, as industry pressed the high school for service, some teachers of academic courses set up two types of courses—one for the professional and the other for the vocational student, such as shop mathematics. Later, it became obvious that the same truths, laws, and principles were applicable to both groups; consequently a good academic teacher was needed rather than two separate classes for each subject. Both vocational and academic students need a broad understanding of basic principles because these truths and principles are as important to one group as to the other.

There has been much experimentation with the vocational program. The learning of specific skills was emphasized at first; however, it is now realized that specific skills can be more readily acquired on the job. The worker makes the best adjustment to the job if he has been oriented to the occupational family. Also, he needs to understand how the occupation is related to our economic life. Stability on the job will usually be improved if the worker has an understanding of the free enterprise system and of its modification in our contemporary life. Adding to the ideal of *free enterprise* is a second and complementary idea, *"those who work are entitled to eat,"* which really makes the ideal of free enterprise more complete. This second ideal seems to be accepted by both labor and management.

The vocational subjects and the BIG FOUR. The occupational subjects are comprised of the *Big Four* and of a large number of separate vocational courses offered in the comprehensive high school and in public and private trade schools.

Industrial arts, homemaking, agriculture, and business education comprise the Big Four. With a few exceptions, one or more of these courses are offered in all high schools of the United States. They are the oldest, most popular, and probably the best organized of all vocational subjects. Industrial arts and homemaking are offered in both junior and senior high school and at every grade level. Although classified as general education by many principals, the vocational skills and understandings which are transferrable to on-the-job work are recognized as highly important. Newkirk,[11] a specialist in the industrial arts, states:

The industrial arts is the interpreter of the machine age in the secondary-school curriculum. Its development has parallelled the machine age, and its content has been selected from industry and the use of the products of industry. Industrial arts education prepares for living in our modern technological society by providing developmental experiences which deal with the materials, processes, products, and occupations of the modern industrial world.

The enrollments in homemaking have exceeded those in industrial arts by a considerable margin, and, in recent years, many boys have enrolled in certain homemaking courses and some girls in industrial arts courses. Some topics treated in homemaking, such as the operation and maintenance of electrical equipment for the home, appeal equally to boys and girls. On the other hand, some topics treated in industrial arts, such as the repair and maintenance of furniture, can be as important to girls as to boys. A wife with some developed mechanical fluency can mend many little things around a home more competently than a butter-fingered husband. If the present trend continues, industrial arts and homemaking may become coeducational courses.

Industrial arts. This course is taught in all grades from 7 to 12. Its content includes woodwork, metal work, mechanical drawing, handcrafts, plastics, electricity, and many other topics. Industrial arts instruction is primarily shopwork with little stress upon formalized projects or tool exercises. Approximately 80 per cent of the time is devoted to work with tools, machines, and construction materials while 20 per cent of the time is devoted to demonstration, reference reading, planning, visual instruction, lectures, field trips, and class discussion.

Although the objectives of the industrial arts differ somewhat as between the junior and senior high school, the following four could be selected as the major ones for the over-all program.

1. To provide general industrial experience of wide value to all
2. To offer exploratory activities to aid in revealing interests, aptitudes, and vocational possibilities for all concerned
3. To develop an appreciation of design and quality in manufactured goods
4. To offer opportunities for beginning specialized preparation for entrance into industrialized pursuits.[12]

Industrial arts is a good example of a course that develops general skills and understandings. These skills and understandings are readily transferable to the job for students going into industry upon graduation.

[11] Louis V. Newkirk, in *Secondary Education* by Harl Douglass (New York, The Ronald Press Company, 1952), Ch. 15.

[12] A. H. Edgerton, "Industrial Arts Education," in *Objectives and Problems of Vocational Education,* edited by Edwin Lee (New York, McGraw-Hill Book Co., 1938), p. 300.

Investigators in this area assert that a broad understanding of modern industry and the general skills acquired are more advantageous than specific skills. Three reasons are given for this assertion: (1) specific skills are acquired more quickly in a realistic situation, (2) too few students who have acquired specific skills in high school get an opportunity to use them, and (3) few high schools can justify the huge cost of the machines common to industry.

Homemaking. Homemaking is probably the most popular and successful subject of the Big Four. The teachers of this program have been selected largely from the federally subsidized program of the big state universities. On the whole, the homemaking teachers in the high schools have been alert to the economic and social changes in our culture. They have made adjustments in their courses to keep them modern. Homemaking courses are available through grades 7 to 12. Course titles and topics include foods, nutrition, textiles, consumer education, child development, and personal and family living. It is a program to prepare girls and some boys for more effective home life. As a rule, homemaking teachers have to be sensitive to improving human relations within the family group. To some extent, the nature of the program is determined by the nature of the community in which the school is located. A community survey by the homemaking teacher is itself a worthy project for raising important questions and especially for aiding her in the selection of the most pertinent topics to include in the program.

Homemaking goals vary somewhat from high school to high school and from grade to grade within the same school. The three goals listed below seem to be the most common to homemaking programs:

1. To contribute to general education of the individual in relation to everyday living

2. To increase the vocational competency of the individual in homemaking and special occupations

3. To promote the enrichment of the individual's special interests.

Agriculture and business education are the two additional subjects of the Big Four. All four of these subjects are semi-vocational in character and are offered in a majority of the American high schools. General understandings and skills are acquired in every one of these subjects, and they carry over as preparation either for college or for the job. The laboratory or the shop approach is the major teaching method employed in all four. Some of the courses in agriculture and homemaking are subsidized by the federal government under the Smith-Hughes Act (1918). The George-Barden Act of 1946 partially subsidizes certain courses in agriculture, homemaking, industrial arts, and business education.

Trade and industrial education. Trade and industrial education are primarily restricted to secondary education in cities and towns located in industrial areas and to cities and towns in distributive centers. Most of the programs operate under a state co-operative plan through which reimbursements are received from the federal government (Smith-Hughes and George-Barden Acts). These reimbursements are available to a secondary school only when students are being *trained* in an industrial pursuit, skilled or semi-skilled craft, or occupation which functions in the designing, producing, processing, assembling, maintaining, servicing, or repairing of any manufactured product.

The above definition of vocational education describes specific vocational education with emphasis upon *training* or the teaching of specific skills under conditions similar to those prevailing in industry—this is training for a specific job. Trade and industrial education are partially restricted to the public and private trade school. Ordinarily, trade and industrial education are restricted to the junior and senior years of the high school or grades 13 and 14 of the junior college. Both public and private trade and industrial schools have had to compete in the open market with industry for highly skilled and qualified teachers in each of the specific occupations being taught. Since industry can usually offer a larger annual income to such men and women, industry frequently attracts the best qualified, while the vocational teachers found in trade and industrial schools are sometimes not the best.

What are the goals of trade and industrial education? Of the many proposed goals, the three listed below seem to indicate the particular emphasis usually evident.

1. All instruction must be directly related to the needs of the individual.

2. All manipulative skills must be taught in conformity with the operations and processes of the particular trade or industrial occupation.

3. Students selected for training must be interested in and qualified to enter the selected occupation after training.

The total offering in trade and industrial education is quite extensive. A typical trade preparatory program is indicated below:

Machine shop	Welding	Refrigeration
Auto mechanics	Electricity	Baking
Carpentry	Radio repair	General maintenance
Cabinet making	Shoe repair	Aircraft engines
Pattern making	Painting and	Dressmaking
Printing	decorating	Saddle making
Sheet metal	Bricklaying	Watch repair

The Contribution of Work Experience. Work experience was originally a function of the family through chores and participation in the economic life of the family, but now in urban and suburban areas, there are no longer chores to do. In addition, work by young people is closely regulated by state law and municipal ordinance. Because work promotes development toward maturity, especially in meeting moral and social responsibilities, a work experience program is educationally sound. Since many parents can no longer meet this responsibility, the high school seems to be the logical institution to assume it. Parents, as taxpayers, are pressing the high school to provide direct work experience in realistic situations.

Due to the fact that real work usually sobers youth and causes them to mature, high school staffs have been well aware of the need. Parental demands have caused many high school staffs to study this problem and to conclude that it could be solved if industry were willing to co-operate. Gradually, a co-operative plan has emerged which has been fairly successful. According to the plan, an industry accepts a student or students, usually a junior or senior, for one half-day at standard pay while the student's schedule is arranged at school for the other half of the day. Thus, a student assigned to work experience earns a minimum of two credits at school and a maximum of two additional credits for work experience.

A teacher-co-ordinator supervises all students assigned to work experience so as to provide a constructive program. He sees to it that every student gets experience on different types of machines. The students' vocational courses at the high school plus the supervision of the co-ordinator so complement the work experience of the student that the inter-relationships of the different types of jobs to the over-all product are made clear, that the processes in this one plant are related to the total industrial process, and that the class work in school is so arranged as to implement the skills and understandings learned on the job. A real educational process must be set up, not just some additional activity.

Work experience adequately co-ordinated with the vocational program at school is real education, but there are pitfalls in it. Some employers in industry participate to exploit each student as fully as possible. A student will be put at a routine job, taught a few simple skills, and driven to produce at greater than capacity. Such a student only gets experience on a single machine, acquires just a few routine skills, and fails to get a basic understanding of the workings of industry or the inter-relationships of the various industrial processes. Also, the teacher-co-ordinator may not be a skilled workman or have an understanding of the place of the industry in the over-all industrial pattern. And although he is given the title of co-ordinator, he may be unable to co-ordinate the work experience of the student and the vocational experience provided by the school.

Work experience can make a substantial contribution to both the common learnings and vocational education. Actual money is earned by genuine labor. Youth learns the habit of working steadily at a job for a definite number of hours and comes to realize the relationship between the skills acquired to the work done. This in turn is related to dollars received. There are decided potentialities in work experience, but until better co-ordination between the high school and industry can be attained, the possibilities of work experience becoming an integral part of vocational education will remain half a hope and only in part a reality.

DISCUSSION PROBLEMS

1. You have been assigned to a senior high school class in which reading abilities, according to reliable tests, range from grade three to college. Assuming that instructional materials are readily available, how would you meet such a wide range in, let us say, a "Modern Problems" course?

2. As a high school teacher, you will be expected to teach not only average learners, but slow and rapid learners as well. For the gifted, a course may be enriched; goals may be set that are only remotely related. In English and social studies, you should be familiar with such as the following: (Check those you do not readily know and select at least one for outside reading.) ( ) Thouless, *How to Think Straight;* ( ) Flesch, *The Art of Clear Thinking;* ( ) Plato, *The Republic;* ( ) Aristotle, *Politics;* ( ) Machiavelli, *The Prince;* ( ) Bellamy, *Looking Backward;* ( ) Smith, *The Wealth of Nations;* ( ) Veblen, *Theory of the Leisure Class;* ( ) Hamilton, Madison, Jay, *The Federalist Papers;* ( ) Jefferson, *Selected Writings.*

3. In a mathematics class, what resource material would you provide for the rapid and gifted learners who are interested in the following: Prisms? Cylinders? Pyramids? Cones? Pentagons? Hexagons? Octagons?

4. There are several encyclopedias now on the market, and they are of particular value in special learnings. If your school budget is not large enough for the purchase of all references, which encyclopedia would you prefer for class use?

5. High schools traditionally present talent shows for the general public. To what extent are special learnings encouraged by such affairs? As a sponsor, what limitations would you make in the nature of such a presentation?

RELATED REFERENCES

Association for Supervision and Curriculum Development, *Creating a Good Environment for Learning,* 1954 Yearbook (Washington, D.C., National Education Association, 1954).

——, *What Shall the High Schools Teach?* 1956 Yearbook (Washington, D.C., National Education Association, 1956).

BRIGGS, Thomas H., LEONARD, J. Paul, and JUSTMAN, Joseph, *Secondary Education* (New York, The Macmillan Co., 1950).

CONANT, James B., *Education and Liberty* (Cambridge, Mass., Harvard University Press, 1953).

DEWEY, John, *How We Think,* rev. ed. (Boston, D. C. Heath & Company, 1933).

DOUGLASS, Harl R., *Secondary Education* (New York, The Ronald Press Company, 1952).

EDGERTON, A. H., "Industrial Arts Education," in *Objectives and Problems of Vocational Education,* edited by Edwin Lee (New York, McGraw-Hill Book Co., 1938).

Educational Policies Commission, *Education and Manpower* (Washington, D.C., National Education Association, 1956).

GRAVES, Albert D., *American Secondary Education* (Boston, D. C. Heath & Company, 1951).

GRUHN, William T., and DOUGLASS, Harl R., *The Modern Junior High School* (New York, The Ronald Press Company, 1956).

HOYT, E. E., REID, M. G., and McCONNELL, J. M., *American Income and Its Uses* (New York, Harper & Brothers, 1954).

HOVET, Kenneth, "What Are the High Schools Teaching?" in *What Shall the High Schools Teach?* 1956 Yearbook of the Association for Supervision and Curriculum Development (Washington, D.C., National Education Association, 1956).

GIFFORD, Dorothy W., "Trends in Teaching High School Chemistry," *The Education Digest* 21:40-43 (November, 1955).

KELLER, Franklin J., *The Comprehensive High School* (New York, Harper & Brothers, 1947).

KELLEY, Earl C., *Education for What Is Real* (New York, Harper & Brothers, 1947).

National Society for the Study of Education, *Adapting the Secondary School to the Needs of Youth*, 52nd Yearbook (Chicago, University of Chicago Press, 1953), Pt. II.

NEWKIRK, Louis V., in *Secondary Education* by Harl Douglass (New York, The Ronald Press Company, 1952).

PIERCE, Paul R., *Developing the High School Curriculum* (New York, American Book Company, 1942).

PROSSER, Charles A., and QUIGGLEY, Thomas A., *Vocational Education in a Democracy* (Chicago, American Technical Society, 1950).

Report of the Committee of Ten on Secondary Education (New York, American Book Company, 1894).

SHOEMAKER, Francis, and BELLOCK, Arno A., "Curriculum for Youth," *Teachers College Record* 56:371-76 (April, 1955).

SMITH, B. Othaniel, STANLEY, William O., and SHORES, J. Harlan, *Fundamentals of Curriculum Development* (Yonkers, N.Y., World Book Co., 1950).

SPITZNAS, James E., "General, Special, and Vocations Education: an Exploration of Distinctive Differences," in *What Shall the High Schools Teach?* 1956 Yearbook of the Association for Supervision and Curriculum Development, (Washington, D.C., National Education Association, 1956).

ULICH, Robert, *History of Educational Thought* (New York, American Book Company, 1945).

DEVELOPING THE CURRICULUM
IN THE CLASSROOM

School days, school days,
Dear old golden rule days,
Read'n and 'Rit'n and 'Rithmetic
Taught to the tune of a hickory stick.

With what gusto and zeal middle-aged men and women sing this ditty at community gatherings. One sometimes asks himself, "Why?" Does it bring back memories of accomplishments in science, drama, or music? Certainly, there are many parents who were thrilled with performances in athletics, and even in mathematics, foreign language, and social studies which brought recognition and a feeling of importance. There have always been teachers who could help their students get meaning from their teaching. There have always been teachers who could develop the curriculum in the classroom so as to make the lives of their students richer —there have always been creative teachers. What must a teacher do to be creative? In the next several pages, suggestions about creative teacher behavior in the classroom will be given.

Education is unique in that it is the only profession in which the individual being trained has already experienced, since five or six, the methods to be employed in his profession. Hence, when the pre-service teacher enters his first course in education, he is likely to have fixed ideas about how to teach. He has absorbed ways to teach from a score of teachers in elementary school, high school, and college. The student comes to such professions as engineering and medicine untainted by previous experiences. Because of this, he is ready and willing to learn the new and better ways resulting from research and experimentation; but not so in education! He must be helped to understand the basic research upon which modern school procedures are based. During the last five decades, research and experimentation in education have discovered more effective procedures just as is true for the fields of medicine

197

and engineering. The imitator of another professional does not thereby become himself a professional.

When exploring his subject in the classroom, the new teacher meets this issue directly. If he heeds and explores, he can be the unusual teacher about whom parents and students speak enthusiastically; or he can, without having learned the art of teaching, ape his former teachers and become the drab and routine person who has chosen the hard way to earn a living. Each of us is a unique individual. It is a rare person who can imitate the procedure of another and still be creative.

OLD WAYS VERSUS NEW WAYS

Content and Procedure Are Tied to Purpose. A new and an excellent curriculum can be and often is made ineffective by the way it is developed in the classroom. Content and method can never be sharply separated because they are both directly related to the same purpose. Hence, a teacher must determine *why* he is teaching a unit, topic, or lesson *before material* and *method* take on real meaning. The teacher must answer satisfactorily to himself these three questions: (1) Why am I teaching this? (2) What method will achieve this purpose best? (3) What subject matter is most appropriate for accomplishing the end sought?

Old or new. Which is best—the old ways or the new ways? In the United States, this question is answered by each local community in its own way. The economic and social situation in America is such that parents desire their teen-age children retained in high school. If their sons and daughters seem unable to learn classical subjects, parents insist that there are practical subjects that can be learned. Also, there is an underlying belief with most parents that their children can learn if teachers will teach. By and large, they accept the *new ways* for a broader curriculum and a more competent instructional staff. Chart 13 is an attempt to state briefly and compactly the *old* and the *new* in contrast.

Chart 13. The Old versus the New

In method:	*The old*—the daily recitation is dominant with emphasis upon memorization
	The new—the unit or laboratory method puts emphasis on problem solving and understanding
In principle:	*The old*—mental discipline; routine; *compel the student*
	The new—student activity; experiencing; *guide the student*
In purpose:	*The old*—retain only the best; eliminate all others
	The new—high school education for *all* youth; adapt the curriculum to the needs of *all*

Introducing a Subject-Matter Unit or Topic to a Class. The introduction of a unit to a class needs to be planned with care. The attitude of the class toward the whole unit is set by the way it is introduced. How do superior teachers present a topic or a unit to a class? An excellent source for good illustrations can be the students of a class. In a secondary education class, the following five selected descriptions came from that source.

Teacher A. I well remember my introduction to trigonometry. The teacher had on her desk numerous ads from the newspapers and magazines. We read these over and put the crux of the situation on the blackboard . . . "She never had a date until she started using such-and-such toothpaste . . . and now she is the most popular girl in school." The faulty logic in such advertising was at once apparent. We then discussed the merits of reasoning things out and why it was important. By this introduction the teacher aroused our interest and helped us to see the importance of clear thinking every day of our lives.

Teacher B. This happened in a physics class. The teacher displayed apparatus applicable to the principle to be learned in the unit. For example, to illustrate the principle of the vacuum, a sphere cut in half, with handles attached, was used. The teacher pumped the air out of the steel sphere and asked two boys to pull it apart. Of course, they couldn't do it. There followed a discussion of why the boys could not separate the two pieces. Finally, there was an explanation by the instructor, a discussion of atmospheric pressure, and other apparatus was introduced.

Teacher C. In my junior year in high school, I was taking a course in American history. The teacher was an elderly woman who commanded the respect of all her students. The unit was the role of the United States in World War II. The unit was opened by playing several records from the album, "You Can Hear It Now." On the record was a capsule history of the Twentieth Century, narrated by Edward R. Murrow. The class listened to Neville Chamberlain, Hitler, Roosevelt, and others. The teacher also had a collection of German and Japanese war relics which she displayed. One boy in the class put on the uniform of a German officer for a further display. One would not have thought that this teacher could be so familiar with the relics and know such interesting facts about each one. She later divided the world into two war areas and had the students report on each. I feel that the students in this class were so stimulated by this opening that they naturally became interested and receptive to learning.

Teacher D. One experience that I remember vividly was in the service. We were being trained in the use of infantry weapons, and there was a demonstration of the tremendous fire power of an infantry unit. We were seated on a hillside and part of the company took up positions on our front with rifles, BAR's, light and heavy machine guns, mortars, flame throwers, recoilless rifles, and grenades. At a given signal, the entire unit opened up and continued firing rapidly for one minute. The noise was deafening and the unbelievable fire power developed by this relatively small unit was positively overwhelming. After this strong demonstration, the idea of an infantryman as just a man with a rifle was completely changed. We saw the rifleman in his true role as a part of a tremendous power unit.

Teacher E. "Not worth a continental." This saying has been used in the United States for a long period of time. In fact, many have forgotten that it refers to the Continental currency and the breakdown in our economic system at the end of the Revolutionary War. I have a collection of Colonial currency and coins. I take these to my class when this problem is being studied. Some of the bills were for five hundred dollars, but most of the coins were one-cent pieces. Through this exhibit, students suddenly realize what it means to have a five-hundred-dollar bill go bad. They understand the value of the two-dollar and fifty-cent gold pieces because of the gold content. They also become aware of the following:

   a. This money represents a loss to someone
   b. The desire of early settlers for specie money
   c. The opposition to paper money
   d. The need for a federal form of government
   e. The need for a national bank
   f. Foreign economic conditions

An analysis. All teachers are directors of learning though good teachers are more efficient at it. Superior teachers raise real problems with students and lead them step-by-step to a solution.

Why did the above introductions to a unit or a topic stand out so sharply for certain students? What conditions are most favorable for learning? For all teachers, these are lifelong problems, but the creative teacher through research and experimentation finds better solutions.

Each of the five teachers above introduced a unit or a topic to a class in a manner which made clear the purpose of the unit. Students sensed the importance of the problem presented, and they appreciated the skill and understanding of the teacher in making the clear presentation. One can predict that the presentation was followed up on successive days, step by step, until a basic truth or principle was firmly established and understood.

These students learned because they were motivated. The classroom activities were related to the readiness and previous experiences of the students. They were ready to achieve the purpose proposed. They learned because they saw clearly what it was that they were to achieve. They learned because they were being helped to apply what was being taught.

Inadequate planning of introductions. Some teachers, when introducing a unit or a topic to a class, are quite inadequate. Since the introduction sets the tone for the several days that follow, a faulty beginning usually results in what students call dull and boring teaching. A few descriptions of inadequate introductions to a unit are given below. Study these carefully. Wherein do they differ from the ones given above?

Teacher A. This teacher lectured for a full period while introducing the topic, "The development of France during the Renaissance." It was a good lecture on the college level. A few students understood and showed interest; the teacher made contact with four students but not with the other 26. To the latter, it was a dull and tiresome class period.

The purpose of the unit was not made clear. There had been no opportunity for class participation. The activities of the hour were not related to the readiness or the previous experience of the students. They failed to see the importance of the topic to them. Throughout the remainder of the time given to this topic, the teacher had a difficult time of it.

Teacher B. The topic to be considered was, "Parts of Speech." The teacher assigned pages 60 to 70 of the text to be studied carefully. When the class assembled on the following day, the teacher asked factual questions from the assigned pages of the text—one question directed in turn to every student in the class. Occasionally there was a comment by the teacher on the correctness of an answer—nothing more. However, the questioning was so timed that it ended just before the bell rang to end the period.

The teacher made no attempt to explain through vivid verbal examples, blackboard illustrations, language charts, or other visual aids in what ways "Parts of Speech" were important or why students should give time to their study. There were no hints even of basic principles that might be an outcome. The teacher seemed as bored with the chore as were the students.

Teacher C. A style book written by another teacher was used as a text. For introduction, the teacher turned to the first section of the text and assigned it to be memorized for the next class. On the next day the students were asked to close their texts and write the memorized section verbatim. The second section of the style book was assigned to be memorized for a test on the next day. This was a standard procedure day after day, with the exception that once each week a theme was to be written by each student. The teacher corrected the themes by checking errors in red ink and inserting the number of the section violated in the style book.

A few students in this class received considerable help in writing compositions free from violations of the style book. But to most students it was a deadly monotony devoid of meaning. The teacher did not vary her procedure or adjust her instructions to the needs of the individual students. Yet in the hands of the author of the style book, in other classes, the procedure took on meaning. The purpose was clearly understood by all students and all acquired permanent skills in the writing of the English language. In the introduction the teacher-author helped students see the purpose of the course. From day to day the difficulties of individual students were cleared up so that each had a feeling of achievement. As needed the teacher-author took time for conferences with students having specific difficulties. In helping a student with a specific difficulty the teacher-author moved slowly step by step until the student could see the basic principle and apply it.

Teacher D. For the introductory unit in an industrial arts course, the teacher put the class to squaring blocks, using a plane to smooth the rough surfaces of the wood, and the chisel to make smooth joints. It was routine work. There was no attempt made to set up broad purposes or to interpret the machine age. There were no field trips to see the kind of work being done in industry and no films to explain industrial arts activities and no projects. To teen-agers squaring blocks of wood, sawing a straight line and making smooth joints day after day seemed pointless. Teen-agers are like all other Americans. When they see a purpose in what they are doing and feel it is important, they like to do it and put forth effort to learn to do it well.

Teacher E. The course was algebra and the topic to be introduced was *equations.* The teacher merely said, "On tomorrow we will start with equations." The teacher then assigned as homework certain exercises from the text, after which he spent a few minutes demonstrating how to solve the assigned problems. There were no explanations then or later of the role of this important mathematical principle in industry, research and science, or in the everyday life of all of us. A student asked the question, "Why do we have to study algebra?" The teacher replied, "It is a required course at this school: you know that." What a way to answer an honest question!

A summation—the presentation of a unit.

1. Help students to see what the purpose is and why the topic or unit is important. Once the purpose and the importance of the topic are clear and are accepted, students are willing to study and work to learn.

2. Use all of the old procedures that have been developed over the past several decades, but adapt them to modern youth. With all youth in high school, there is a need to vary the procedures. One must search for new ways to present old materials. Also, one must search for and experiment with both new materials and new procedures.

3. Help students apply what is being learned. Once the purpose is clearly evident, students want to know how what is being learned can be used. Any content material that is worth a teacher's time to present is important. However, a teacher's real worth lies partly in his ability to explain how what is being taught can be used.

THE UNIT OR LABORATORY METHOD

"We are gradually developing a new view of the world to replace the philosophy which we have used for three centuries . . . and which no longer fits either the science or the society of our time."
—Peter F. Drucker in *Harper's Magazine* 215:36-40 (August, 1957).

By and large, each teacher will employ a procedure in accordance with his understanding of how students learn. There are two competing points of view about the teaching of a subject. (1) The subject comprises a fixed body of content material to be developed in a logical order, bit by bit, based upon the atomistic psychology of learning or the daily recitation plan. (2) The subject is conceived as a body of experiences employed to cause students to grow and develop. The teacher conceives of each student as a growing and developing organism. Through the understanding of essential course principles, the student attains more mature intellectual insights. Through guided social contact with fellow students and teachers and through discussion of social problems, the student attains more mature social and emotional behavior. The growth process tends to maintain a balance between all types of development. The subject matter is the means to an end. When properly selected, it provides for activities and experiences that will lead to the all-around development of a student. The procedure now replacing the daily recitation plan is the laboratory method or unit plan. Why is this so? These are some reasons why:

1. Teaching by units represents a revolt against the daily assignment and its assign-study-recite counterpart.

2. In teaching by units, the learning experiences are organized into larger blocks of work.

3. The idea of teaching by units has a psychological foundation in the organismic view of learning as contrasted with the atomistic psychology that conceives of growth as a piece-by-piece additive process.[1]

About types of units. In all instructional procedures four factors are involved—subject matter, experience, interest, and logical thinking. To be sure, the extent to which each factor is associated with others will depend largely upon the individual learner, the competency of the teacher, the type of organization of instructional content, and the instructional outcomes sought. Since the beginning of the twentieth century, educators have been seeking ways to blend all of these factors together through unit instruction. Gradually, over the decade since 1900, such practices as the project, the problem, the center of interest, the experience curriculum, and the socialized recitation have faded and have been replaced by the unit concept. The wide acceptance of the unit concept has come, at least in part, as a protest against treating each day's lesson as an unrelated and isolated segment of learning. Unity and continuity improve instruction and make learning more meaningful and more permanent. Previous to 1950, two types of units had evolved—(1) the experience unit with subunits based on pupil interests and problems and (2) the subject-matter unit with subunits organized on topics, themes, surveys, and problems. In regard to subject-matter and experience units; Smith, Stanley, and Shores state that:

This classification does not go to the heart of the difference among units. According to the prevailing educational opinion, the chief difference between the subject-matter and the child-interest schools of thought is that the first minimizes interest and the second maximizes it. Interest has, of course, always been a prominent feature in the child-interest school of thought, but it is not an exclusive consideration. It is well to bear in mind that the revolt against formalism and over-emphasis upon subject matter in education stems from the instrumental theory of logic no less than from educational theory and studies of child behavior.[2]

[1] Harold Spears, *The High School for Today* (New York, American Book Company, 1950), Ch. 10.

[2] B. Othaniel Smith, William O. Stanley, and J. Harlan Shores, *Fundamentals of Curriculum Development* (Yonkers, N. Y., World Book Co., 1950), p. 556.

What do Smith, Stanley, and Shores suggest to sharpen the differences among units or to make differences more clearly perceived? They recommend two types of units—(1) the subject-matter unit with subunits of topical, theme, survey, and problem and (2) the process unit with subunits of discovery and verification, normative, and criticism. The process unit is suggested as one that is different in purpose from the subject-matter unit and one that has been accepted by leading educators as differentiating more sharply between subject-matter units and others. The purpose of the subject-matter unit is defined as a process by which certain materials are assimilated so as to produce learning products in the form of attitudes, knowledge, skills, personal adaptations and the like. Under the subject-matter unit, students *assimilate* the subject-matter materials as a body of ready-made knowledge. Instruction may also be approached from the standpoint of the processes of thinking, in which materials of instruction are used in overcoming a difficulty. Of course, such a view of instruction would emphasize the processes of thinking which involve appraising what someone says or does and reaching conclusions about factual and moral problems. Skills and understandings may result from the process unit as well as the subject-matter unit, and in addition special learnings in the form of effective habits of thinking may also result. The last mentioned outcome does not result from assimilation except as an accident.

Developing a Unit in Science. By the unit procedure, students are challenged to solve problems rather than asked to memorize isolated or unrelated lessons. A unit competently taught becomes a real experience. The description that follows is, in part, an account of how an actual unit was developed in the classroom. The course was General Science and the unit "The Interdependence of Plant and Animal Life." Mr. M, the teacher, handled the unit with a high degree of competency.

Ten days before he planned to introduce the unit to the class, Mr. M filled a large glass bottle with distilled water. Some clean sand was dropped into the bottle. Then three goldfish, several strands of seaweed and three small snails were added. He inserted a cork into the wide mouth of the bottle and covered the top of the cork and the bottle mouth with melted paraffin to seal out all air. He put the bottle on the corner of his desk where it could be seen by all, yet made no comment about it. Within a day or so, many students had noticed the bottle and their curiosity bubbled over. "Don't fish breathe?" they asked each other. The answer is, "Of course fish breathe." Then how can they continue to breathe in a sealed bottle?

The little cosmos[3] had been purposely set up by Mr. M. to arouse just such curiosity. The problem to be resolved by the unit had already been raised by members of the class. In planning and timing the actual presentation of the "Little Cosmos," Mr. M. demonstrated a very high type of professional skill.

[3] *Cosmos*—a small model of the universe. By definition, any self-inclusive system characterized by order and harmony.

The expertness of a creative artist at work in the classroom was made evident.

Animals and plants so sealed in a large glass bottle could go on living until the end of their normal lives in a *little cosmos,* if a complete balance between plant and animal life were established. Several questions arise that need an answer. If fish breathe, how can they obtain the needed oxygen in the cosmos? From what source comes their food? From what source will the seaweed get plant food needed to replace the leaves nibbled away by the gold fish? What contribution do the three snails make to the cosmos? Why have they been introduced?

On the following Monday, the unit was introduced to the class. The class already had been challenged. The questions came tumbling. The first half of the period was used in helping students think through the answers to their own questions.

In the development of the unit, as in any effective instruction, order and organization must prevail. Observe that the procedure in this unit is arranged in a series of four steps. This is the pattern widely employed by teachers who use the unit procedure.

I. *Introduction and attack.*[4] Once the questions mentioned above had been raised and partially answered, the problem was to relate the demonstration in the little cosmos, the glass bottle and the life within it, to the world in which the students lived. To broaden and extend the discussion, these questions were raised. Is what we have just discussed about fish and seaweed also true of life in the real world about us? Is animal life, which includes man, dependent upon plant life? And conversely is the plant life on our planet dependent upon the continuation of animal life? These and other questions broadened the discussion and the outlook to include the earth and all animal and plant life upon it. The students were thoughtful as Mr. M led them into this broadened phase of the problem—the interdependence of plant and animal life. Three days had been devoted to the introductory phase of the problem. The problem had come to have meaning to the students. They wanted to know the answers to the questions raised. There had been no wavering of attention up to now. The class was ready for the next step.

II. *Study and work.* This is literally a work period. The classroom becomes a laboratory where students attack the problem by reading, experimenting, making field trips, and doing any type of acceptable research bearing upon the problem that has been raised. Normally, this period will continue for several days. The work may be planned by the teacher and class together, or the teacher may plan the work entirely in advance. The teacher acts as a director and supervisor of study. Some teachers participate with the students in collecting data.

Students work as individuals or in groups under the direction of a student leader or the teacher. Much of the teacher's time will be given

[4] J. G. Umstattd, *Secondary School Teaching* (Boston, Ginn & Company, 1944), Ch. 9.

to individual students who need specific help. In the modern high school, the study and work phase of the unit is the time and place where students gradually acquire the ability to work on their own. The competent teacher, as a director of learning, assists students in acquiring work and study habits that will make them more and more independent of the teacher's direction.

Mr. M outlined the schedule for the work and study phase of the unit in advance. He also developed a worksheet which was mimeographed and was ready for the Tuesday meeting. This worksheet included the following items:

1. A series of questions to guide the work of the students in their study of the problem, "Interdependence of Plant and Animal Life," during the study and work phase.

2. Instructions on how to use the textbook and other books in the search for basic facts which might bear upon the problem.

3. An extended variety of references related to this problem such as:

Books (help was given to the whole group and to specific individuals on use of the index and table of contents)

Magazines (titles, dates of issue, specific articles)

Newspapers (titles, dates, issues, articles, news items)

Names of encyclopedias, dictionaries, guides to periodicals

New references discovered by students during research

4. The laboratory experiments were introduced on a partially elective basis. Mr. M planned for laboratory demonstrations during the work and study periods.

5. Field trips were outlined, but only one would be made.

6. Interviews were suggested, and several resource people were listed with the potential contribution of each noted.

Mr. M realized that more work was indicated than could be done by any one student. Hence, he aided students in the selection of problems according to their interests and capacities. Some students worked better in groups than as individuals, Mr. M had prepared for this.

Additional procedures often employed in the study and work phase of unit teaching are listed below:

1. Demonstrations are given by teachers and students. A superior demonstration with competent showmanship is an excellent device for clearing up moot phases of a principle. Considerable practice should precede the demonstration itself. Poor readers may profit more from a spectacular demonstration than from any amount of reading.

2. Radio material can be excellent. Building up a file of tape recordings can be valuable to a teacher of a subject-matter field. Stations often will supply transcripts.

3. Frequent use of slides and filmstrips in addition to sound films can be helpful if selected with care.

4. Student leaders may be assigned to help others having difficulty. This should not be done indiscriminately but only after careful planning by the teacher.

5. The bulletin board is used for special reports of contemporary happenings related to the unit. Some teachers employ student committees for this purpose. On certain occasions, this can be an excellent way to recognize certain students.

6. Student interviews are conducted with adults known to be interested or highly competent in the area being studied. Here, names of professional organizations and service clubs are used as sources.

A mastery of a problem never comes without study and work. Learning requires that one be active and put forth effort. Even the memorization of assigned material requires that one give time and effort to it. The discovery of relationships and the deriving of generalizations exact much effort and activity, but they bring to the learning process the feeling of well-being and of achievement that is permanent. To achieve a new insight or a new understanding is to integrate the new experience with the old. With this integration comes a change in behavior which is a product of development or growth. But these changes are always preceded by a period of study and work. The time it takes to make the adjustment may vary with individuals, but no individual can escape the study and work that precedes.

A controversy enters here. Must the subject-matter content for all members of a class be identical in order to achieve a specific outcome? Can the same generalization be derived by different students through the use of different reference material covering similar content? Must every student in a class read exactly the same assignments and do exactly the same experiments to achieve the same basic understandings? The controversy concerns the use of the textbook as the only reference source for students. The daily recitation plan emphasizes the use of one reference book only—the textbook. The unit or laboratory plan proposes that a study of several references on the same topic not only permits students to derive the same generalizations but due to the breadth of the approach makes the concepts more real to the learners. Because of this, many modern high school teachers prefer to have their students work on a variety of content material during the work and study period. Such a variety of study material makes the integration period, which is to follow, more alive and zestful.

A problem challenges and gives direction to mental activity; hence, the problem-solving approach is the natural way to achieve integration. There is a natural feeling of tension and/or frustration which accompanies problem-solving. Many students need help and guidance to understand and accept it as such. Certainly teachers with insight will guide slow-learing students in the selection of types of problems at which they can succeed. Indeed, all students need to be guided to select work difficult enough to require them to learn the essential habit of persistence in the face of discouragement. All must learn to take the essential step of learning to work and study; man has not yet discovered a satisfactory substitute for study and work.

III. *Integration and application.* When what is being learned has meaning, integration is taking place. The new learning becomes an integral part of one's past experience. The integration and application phase of the unit is designed to make the basic principles of the unit usable. With a unit such as the inter-dependence of plant and animal life, students should come to understand clearly that a balance between all life has been established and must be maintained. During this phase, the teacher will employ those techniques that focus the learnings of the study and work period upon formulating generalizations. Once these generalizations are formulated, the class will attempt to apply them to their own out-of-school life.

For guiding the activities of the students during the integration and application phase of the plant-and-animal-life unit, Mr. M proposed the following questions:

How are the lives of plants and animals related?
How does man profit by cultivating plants and animals?
How can farm pests be controlled?
How can we control household pests?

The class was organized as a discussion group. The above questions were written on the blackboard. Having spent the past five days studying and working on this problem as individuals and as groups, the class was anxious to talk. Mr. M's major task was to be a good discussion leader.

Since all of the members of this class had participated in the study of the problem, all had ideas on it. Incomplete and even erroneous ideas came to the surface. But the give-and-take of action and reaction within the group is the best procedure for bringing out clearly the core ideas of the unit. The teacher's work is to keep the discussion moving and to formulate the basic concepts governing the relationships about plant and animal life. Mr. M asked questions that called for alternative answers; he gave the students time to think as he asked for illustrations of points made. Defenses of conclusions were welcomed. He listed on the blackboard the points that were made by the class on plant and animal relationships, and, finally, with the help of the group, he formulated a statement of the basic relationships.

But there are many other procedures that can be employed with the integration and application phase of the unit. Here are a few of them.

1. Demonstration by a student or a group of students of the processes that have been ascertained

2. Exhibition of products made by students to illustrate the unit

3. Dramatization of episodes studied

4. Debates, pro and con

5. Defense by students of their own solutions to the problem

6. Preparation of articles based on the unit for the local school and community newspaper

7. Planning for the full use of information in out-of-school life.

8. Panel presentations in the style of television-radio shows.

In the actual development of the unit in the classroom, there is no such sharp distinction between the different steps or phases as have been made so obvious in the descriptions above. Each phase merges into the next, gradually and smoothly. An example of the same smoothness is seen as childhood merges into adolescence. No one can tell at just what point the change occurs. The class itself is unlikely to be aware of the four phases of the unit. This is true in part because the next phase begins before the final step of the preceding phase is completed. The phases so overlap that they become merged, but the teacher must constantly be aware of these four definite steps.

As the class moves through the integration and application phase, the teacher is concerned as to how complete the integration actually is. Such questions as these persist: Have the students understood that the life cycles of plants and animals are interacting? Have they understood that all of the waste products cast out of the animal body are vital for plant growth and development? Have they understood that plants are a food product for animals, and, in part, the wastes cast off by plants are vital to the growth of the animal? They should see clearly that both plants and animals have an appointed place in maintaining system and order in the universe.

IV. *Appraisal of outcomes.* While still on the integration and application phases, Mr. M began working on the problem of constructing a valid and reliable test for the unit. From his observation of the class at work, he had acquired some tentative opinions about the understandings achieved by most students in the class. The outcome sought was an understanding that plant and animal life are interdependent, and he decided that an objective test could be used to get a wide sampling of their new knowledge and understanding. He formulated several multiple-choice items which would require the students to make the one best choice out of five statements listed. The insight of each student would be revealed by his ability to choose the one best statement from each of the questions. He also set up five problems, each of which required an understanding of certain relationships between plant and animal life.

The principal outcomes sought from this general science course by Mr. M were *concepts, understandings,* and *information.* Had he been teaching a course in woodworking, the principal outcomes would probably have been *skills* and *habits*. If it had been a course in English literature, the principle outcomes would probably have been *appreciation* and *new interests,* while in an American history course, the principal outcomes would have been *attitudes, ideals,* and *concepts.* All of this means that the outcome or outcomes sought must determine the type of examination to be employed for the appraisal. For example, in everyday life, if distance is to be measured, the instrument selected will be in inches, feet, or miles; but if we desire to measure time, a watch or clock calibrated in hours will be used. For measuring the outcomes of instruction, the quiz and written examination are only two of many instruments available to teachers. Always, the outcome to be appraised will determine the instrument selected for the appraisal.

In addition, here are three general principles related to appraisal that are practical and serve to make the outcomes of appraisal valuable to students and the appraisal itself more accurate.

1. *Appraisal is a continuous process.* The teacher who is alert will utilize every opportunity to evaluate or appraise the progress being made from the day the unit is initiated until the final day when it is completed. This continual awareness on the part of the teacher as to what progress each individual within the class is making tends to keep the class alert and to cause the teacher to be more effective in his instructional guidance. Most of us as individuals put forth greater efforts when standards are maintained day after day: continuous appraisal is one procedure for the maintenance of these standards.

2. *Student participation in appraisal can be highly effective.* The unit approach provides a permissive atmosphere in which students and teacher can co-operate in appraisal. Such student participation in evaluation strengthens confidence in the teacher and provides him with an opportunity to gain a better insight into the understandings of students as to tests and their purposes. Incidentally, discussion led by the teacher-leader may bring out many helpful ideas from students on types of test items and test construction that can be utilized in adapting appraisal devices to students. A frequent outcome of such sessions is the establishment of more favorable attitudes toward appraisal by students and a better understanding of the purpose and place of appraisal in unit teaching. Another outcome of these sessions with students is that the teacher becomes more and more competent in appraisal.

3. *Evaluation is an essential phase of the instructional process.* One purpose of education is to change behavior. Unless the changes sought by society have occurred, in part at least, the cost to society in time and effort of teacher and learners has been to no avail. Evaluation is a device by which to determine whether there have been changes and to what degree they have occurred. Of course, observation can determine, in part, that changes in behavior are occurring. Yet, because the specific

evaluative device is more accurate, the evaluative device is a vital phase of the instructional program. The evaluative device is an essential phase of the learning cycle.

Other techniques are available for appraising outcomes. A few of them are listed below. These are not to be employed indiscriminately, but with caution. Select only the instrument suitable for appraising the outcome or outcomes sought. If this is not done, the results will be neither valid nor reliable.

1. Oral questions should be asked by the teacher on confused points. Competent questioning is a remarkably effective procedure for focusing the attention of the learner on the specific detail that needs to be corrected. These questions will need to be asked slowly. The reaction of the student will determine the timing and the nature of each succeeding question.

2. Anecdotal records are a record of significant bits of behavior for each student. As these records accumulate, they help the teacher understand each student better.

3. Teacher evaluation of student behavior is helpful, for an unbiased and mature observer can make observations that will supplement all other types of appraisal.

4. A brief presentation of the final summary by an individual or chairman is valuable.

5. Performance tests can be used to appraise acquired skills.

6. Achievement may be tested by standardized tests and informal objective tests.

7. Review and remedial teaching can be based upon test findings.

8. A discussion of general errors and misunderstandings can be carried out with the students.

Teaching by Units *versus* Learning by Units. The unit plan of teaching is not a fixed pattern for common adoption and identical use on the part of all who would do unit teaching. It is a promising instructional concept that must be carefully studied by the teacher. One cannot take over the practice of others who use it, without a careful study of the idea to make it his very own. Also, it lends itself to some purposes better than to others, and it lends itself to some subject matter better than to others.

As the teacher explores the possibilities of the unit, it is quite natural for him to think in terms of teaching by units, that is, to make the teaching emphasis dominant in the planning. But as he studies the psychological aspect of the idea, he moves over to the student position in the process and begins to think of the possibilities of learning by units. Unless he goes beyond the teaching-by-units process, he is likely to think of planning his course into larger blocks of work, that is, breaking the course down into several smaller parts under comprehensive headings, each labelled a unit. If the teacher goes beyond this teaching-by-units and if he plans according to how students learn, he will be thinking of helping his students plan experiences that are meaningful to them and in keeping with the particular subject matter concerned. The first approach puts the stress upon subject matter *per se;* it does not recognize individual differences. The second emphasizes the selection and organization of subject matter as a means of student growth and development.

It is natural that the more a planner gives consideration to a unit area, the more there will be developed some kind of guides on paper. But good instructional preparation requires a compromise. A more flexible outline that permits adaptation to each particular class taught is required. This is a major difference between the professional person and a routine worker. Even an engineer constructing a bridge adapts his design to the material being used.

Three Methods for Developing the Curriculum in the Classroom. The three methods most widely used for developing the curriculum in the classroom are: (1) the daily recitation, (2) the subject-matter unit, and (3) the process unit. In Chart 14 the three methods are presented, and the steps or phases employed in each of the processes are indicated. The daily recitation is an old method that can be adapted to recent developments in education. The subject-matter unit is especially suited as an instructional procedure for *special learnings.* A relatively new method, called the process unit method, is being developed to use with the common-learnings course of study. It is employed for teaching teen-agers ideals, attitudes, and understandings essential to the development of loyalty to a common nation and a common community. All three methods can render an indispensable instructional service for developing the high school curriculum in the classroom. Each has a time and place in the work of the teacher. The one-method teacher behaves like the physician who, regardless of the malady, prescribes the same remedy for every patient who consults him.

When and where should each of these methods be employed? The content being taught, the purpose to be achieved, and the students being taught are three determining factors, although there are many other factors that must be considered. Yet content and method are always closely related to purpose. "Why is this content being taught?" will always remain a crucial factor in the selection of a method.

PLANNING AND DEVELOPING A SUBJECT

Usually the beginning teacher is employed to teach in a single subject. This should be the same field in which the teacher majored as a student in college. In its recommendations, the college does indicate the strength possessed by each pre-service teacher in his major field. It

Chart 14. Three Methods for Developing the Secondary School Curriculum in the Classroom

I *Daily recitation*	II *Subject-Matter Unit**	III *Process Unit**[†] (Normative, Criticism, Discovery, and Verification)
The textbook is the curriculum.	The curriculum comprises all of the subjects offered, which are subdivided into courses that are further subdivided into units.	The high school staff formulates the course of study for each year. Teacher and class co-operatively select and plan the development of each problem.
(Development of the course)	(Steps in the development of the unit)	
Daily recitation pattern	Unit pattern	Unit pattern
The assignment	Introduction and attack phase	A problem which is important to class, on social conflict, is selected, defined, and stated.
The study of the lesson	Study and work phase	Research is carried out by class on problem—usually by small committees
The recitation	Integration and application phase	Research committees report to class, followed by discussion
The quiz or the examination	Appraisal and outcome phase	Summation: class discussion to achieve a consensus or a true norm
The curriculum is the separate subjects being taught in the school with a textbook for each.	The curriculum is the series of separate subjects with a course of study developed for each subject-matter field. The textbook is used as a tool only.	A general course of study is developed by the high school staff. But each teacher feels free to modify it to meet needs of students.

* B. Othaniel Smith, William O. Stanley, and J. Harlan Shores, *Fundamentals of Curriculum Development* (Yonkers, N. Y., World Book Co., 1950), p. 558.

† Unit pattern for normative unit only. (Normative units are concerned with situations in which action is impeded by differences of social views, interests, and values. See Chapter VII of text, students study mental health, pp. 163-164.

is a responsibility of each beginning teacher, as a trained specialist in a given area, to guide the development of the curriculum in the classroom. To do this will require some original planning on his part. In addition, he must interweave the plan of the principal into his own plan. How well this is done will be a major gauge of his success as a teacher.

The Teacher's Guide. Many city school systems and all states in the United States have available for the beginning teacher teacher's guides for each of the subjects. In most of the cities and states, each subject is bound in a separate volume. However, there are some exceptions, as some cities and states include all subjects in one course of study bound in a large volume. The subject content presented in these teacher's guides represents what the public feels is important. The beginning teacher should study them with care.

Every teacher, as well as the beginning teacher, will keep a copy of the course of study for his subject in his desk. It will explain to the teacher *what to teach, why it is being taught,* and *the available aids to be employed.* Each course of study also outlines the sequence of courses in each subject, that is, the courses to be offered in each of the freshman, sophomore, junior, and senior years of the high school or by grades 9, 10, 11, and 12. Many of the courses of study suggest the units to be developed in each course, year by year. Such courses of study have obvious value, especially for the beginning teacher, in offering specific suggestions for teaching the subject.

A particular illustration of one course of study, English, is shown below. Here is presented a course outline in an abbreviated form. It shows the nature of the content in the typical but good course of study. The state course of study explains in simple language what the beginning teacher wants to know, that is, what should be taught in an English course. For pre-service teachers other than English, the outline will indicate the nature of the content generally found in any course of study for any subject-matter field.

The Course of Study for English[5]

Section I.   The Nature of a High School English Program
(Purpose, functions of, a continuing developmental program; the basic program in English, English usage.)

Section II.   Determining Student and Community Needs
(Understanding the student: diagnosis, testing, general information, personal interviews, informal contacts and anecdotal records. Understanding the community.)

Section III. Instructional Material and Equipment and Library Resources
(Classroom equipment and facilities: libraries and the English program; major purposes of the library; co-operating agencies; audio-visual aids; list of and types of audio-visual aids.)

Section IV. Suggested Procedures in English Instruction
(Suggestions for effective English instruction; articulation with the elementary school program; correlating English with other high school subjects; the developmental reading program; a finding list for free reading.)

Section V.   Outline of the Essential English Program
(Important aspects of the major areas of language usage; basic English for the ninth grade; and suggested tentative list for class reading; essential English for the tenth grade and suggested tenta-

[5] Nebraska Department of Public Instruction, 1949.

tive list for class reading: essential English for the eleventh grade and tentative lists for class reading; essential English for the twelfth grade and suggested tentative list for class reading.)

Section VI. Aids in Organizing the Basic English Program
(Suggested four-year pattern for basic units in English; sample units of study: (1) a sample library unit for the ninth grade, (2) a sample unit on book discussion, (3) a sample newspaper unit for the ninth grade.)

Appendix

A partial list of general textbooks, anthologies, and workbooks
Suggestions for English teachers' library
Chart of useful standardized tests

In any state the beginning teacher will always be able to get a copy of the course of study for any subject. The detail with which each course of study is developed makes it very helpful for the inexperienced teacher, and busy teachers may rely upon it, too. However, a course of study can become a "crutch" for the indolent teacher. As a teacher gains the confidence that comes with experience, he should depend less and less upon a detailed course of study and more and more upon himself, that is, upon his own ingenuity in developing the course. To do otherwise will make the teacher a slave to the printed course of study.

The Textbook. To many experienced teachers, the textbook is too restrictive. They feel that much reference material and more than one textbook broadens a course and widens the perspective of students. A few creative teachers develop their courses, year after year, without the use of any regular textbook. For a beginning teacher, a textbook can be decidedly helpful in outlining the subject matter of the course being taught, but as experience and confidence are gained, the teacher should free himself from dependence upon the textbook and use it merely as a valuable tool. A textbook for each course taught is still prescribed in several states though the laws dealing with textbooks now permit adoption of several textbooks for each course. Where this is done, the teacher is free to choose one or more texts from the list.

If the teacher is free to choose a textbook, he should consider whether the scope or range of the book covers the topics he believes to be significant; whether it is written in an interesting style; whether the vocabulary and study helps are suited to the students; and whether there is a teacher's manual for the text. Some teachers like to use two or three books of varying difficulty and points of view in the same class; some students may use one text while others use another text. However, there must be sufficient similarity between the different texts so that the same topics are discussed in each textbook; such a procedure encourages students to discuss different points of view and provides for differences in ability and interests.

Manuals to accompany textbooks are now prepared by many publishing companies. Suggestions for teaching each unit or topic, as well as general ideas for developing the entire subject, are made in these manuals. If a manual is available, the teacher, especially the beginning teacher, should secure it; for the effective use of the textbook is thereby increased.

Student Participation in Planning. Students learn much more readily if they are aware of their goals. An excellent way to make students aware of their goals is to encourage student participation in planning the course or unit. In such planning, students can and frequently do make highly pertinent suggestions. Besides, one of the ultimate purposes of education is to develop in each teen-ager the ability to plan co-operatively with others and for himself. All need *guided* planning experience to develop this ability.

The teacher, who can raise pertinent questions and keep a discussion rolling, may well devote the first few days of a semester to planning activities in which members of the class participate. For example, the teacher of tenth-grade English may raise the issue that most students have already spent nine years learning to read, write, speak, and listen; that some have had more success than others; that most could use some skills better than other skills; and that the students know or could determine more accurately than he what they needed to concentrate on during the coming year. This could easily lead to a discussion of the major plans for the year ahead.

What are the advantages to such planning? The teacher has a chance to get acquainted with his students quickly, and they learn something about each other. The students get a feeling of *belonging* to the group. They know where they are planning to go, and they work with enthusiasm because they have chosen the road. Also, the resulting purposes and plans will probably not vary greatly from those of the teacher. In fact, they may be better.

MODERNIZING STUDY

Study and work as an essential phase of developing the curriculum in the classroom has been presented earlier in the chapter. However, additional attention needs to be given to the development of study habits and skills. Until such habits and skills are acquired, study is a chore; after they have been acquired, students learn to work with facility and ease and study often becomes fun. Although there is more to study than habits and skills; yet, when habits and skills have been acquired, increased achievement in school is a very apparent outcome. Once the lazy and loafing student acquires such habits and skills, his attitude toward study changes—there has been a behavior change. Study then becomes for even the lazy and the loafer a rewarding rather than a frustrating experience.

All pupils who have completed the elementary school are admitted to the high school, and all students are classified for aptitude established by their achievement in the elementary school and by administered aptitude tests, usually tests of intellectual aptitude. Students are distributed to classes where the teachers assign them the tasks to be done. However, only a few of the teachers instruct students in the requisite skills needed for the performance of academic work. Burton[6] explains this situation:

Be sensitive to and diagnose cases of insufficient study or actual ignorance of study procedures. Ample evidence shows that difficulty is not confined to the dull, lazy, and uninterested. Many bright, willing, and interested students need much specific, detailed help with study skills, habits, and attitudes.

The usual teacher is more likely to tell students how to study than to demonstrate how-to-study skills, provide practice at acquiring these skills, and briefly explain to individual students how to overcome their own deficiences.

General study skills can be taught. The illustration which follows explains how a social-studies teacher taught one such skill. He wished to trace the emergence of the United States as a world power and to help students realize that the Spanish-American War was a part of the movement that has become increasingly important in recent years. The assignment was to read a chapter in the text during a supervised study period. To one student, study meant *READ*. He read the material as if it were a novel. During the discussion next day, he was shocked to discover how little he had retained. A second student read the assignment word-by-word and had little comprehension of the main idea of the chapter. A third student supplemented this reading of the chapter by memorizing all of the details. No member of the class was able to discuss the main idea of the chapter on the following day.

The teacher stopped the discussion and asked the class to turn to a particular paragraph in the chapter. He then proposed this question: "What is the main idea in this paragraph?" He guided the class in discovering the main idea in the paragraph. The next day, he asked the same question about a section of the chapter, "What is the one big idea in this section?" and guided the class in locating it. On the third day, he proposed another question, "What is the central idea of the whole chapter?" and helped the class determine what it was. It took a little time, but the students learned how to attack a chapter to get real meaning from it. He was demonstrating, giving practice in, and explaining one specific study skill.

Business, whose very existence is dependent upon a profit, discovered early that demonstration, practice, and limited explanation helped new

[6] William H. Burton, *The Guidance of Learning Activities*, 2nd ed. (New York, Appleton-Century-Crofts, Inc., 1952), p. 356.

employees learn essential skills quickly. Study skills can be taught to high school students, in general, by a principle similar to that employed in industry. Skilled performance, whether it be in industry or in the classroom, makes it possible for civilization to function, and whether one is a workman in industry or a student in high school, skilled performance is learned by acquiring through practice certain prerequisite skills.

What are the study skills that many students lack? A few such skills are listed below:

1. A goodly number of high school students are unable to read comprehensively the textbooks which are required reading for high school courses. They must have help with key words (the vocabulary) in which key concepts are stated.

2. They are unable to find reference material in the library.

3. They are unable to take brief notes that comprise the pith of a lecture or of a reference read.

4. They try to memorize formulae, concepts, dates rather than establish meaningful relationships that fix formulae, concepts, and dates as the core of the course or unit.

5. Many seem entirely unable to phrase a question that requires a reply which will reveal relationships. For example, why does an application of nitrogen fertilizer tend to cause a lawn to become green?

6. Most are unable to write and document a short research paper.

7. Many cannot state a basic concept in their own words. Surely, if an idea is understood, a student should be able to state it.

The establishment of a desirable habit pattern is necessary for adequate study. Habits keep one at study, while skills make the time spent profitable. When the student becomes aware of some difficulty or a lack of skill or knowledge and when he engages in appropriate activities in order to fill his need, he really studies. Study can be defined as the concentration of attention upon a series of activities for the purpose of satisfying a felt need.[7] Gradually, under the competent direction of a teacher, the student develops favorable attitudes toward study, that is, he establishes study habits which are defined by the psychologist as tendencies to act in certain ways under certain conditions. Study habits, as well as study skills, can be developed only in connection with study activities. One develops favorable attitudes toward study by acquiring the type of study skills that make study a pleasure and bring some measure of recognition to the student.

With respect to the practice of study skills, note this comment from Cronbach[8] on the role of the teacher in guiding the acquisition of study habits and skills:

---

[7] William G. Brink, *Directing Study Activities in Secondary Schools* (Garden City, N. Y., Doubleday, Doran and Co., Inc., 1937), p. 11.

[8] Lee J. Cronbach, *Educational Psychology* (New York, Harcourt, Brace & Co., 1954), p. 365.

Practice does not guarantee expertness. One can practice and make no progress, or one can fix an awkward and undesirable response pattern. Practice is only an opportunity for learning. Whether that opportunity is used effectively depends upon many things. Among the determining factors are the proper amounts and spacing of practice, proper demonstration and interpretation of the task, monitoring or evaluation, and the use of suitable practice materials. In addition, of course, practice is influenced by such matters as motivation and readiness.

Guided practice of study can prevent the fixing of undesirable study skills.

Productive Study. Research on child development and the learning process points to a new emphasis in study. Formerly, the emphasis was upon memorization while now it is upon experimenting, understanding, and using what is learned. Memorization still has a place, though a much more minor place, in all learning. In general, we accept today the idea that what is being learned must have meaning for the learner. Hence, the modern teacher needs to guide students in the modification of their study procedures at both home and school. The drudgery type of routine that was formerly associated with study must give way to the modern type of problem solving or "of getting meaning" from what is being studied. Certainly, in assigning work to be done or in devoloping the assignment co-operatively, more challenging study procedures can be introduced. Study must be modernized—a fact that few parents see clearly. This introduces a new public-relations problem for teachers and principals.

DISCUSSION PROBLEMS

1. Adult education has grown tremendously during the last few years. Does this seem to indicate a need for amplification of the experience unit in high schools? Explain why so many young adults are returning to the classroom.
2. What outside sources might be utilized in obtaining additional literature for the following: Personal health? Vocational training? Occupations? Mixed marriages? Job finding?
3. Diagram the curriculum of a typical high school. Then invent a second diagram that would permit a floating activity period. Why hasn't such a change been more universal?
4. Parents do not generally understand the term *core*. What might be done so that parents would know that their child is studying English and Social Studies—Mathematics and Science—instead of simply "core" subjects? Why has the core been so slow in obtaining general acceptance on the high school level?
5. List six sources outside the school of guest speakers who might be employed in your major field (science, mathematics, English, social studies).
6. What activities of the teacher serve best to aid students in acquiring essential study habits and skills?
7. Should the classroom teacher ever be held responsible for helping students acquire essential library skills?

8. A visitor, who accompanied a high school principal in observing several classes, turned to the principal as they arrived at the office and said, "Why the difference between the last two classes observed?" The principal replied, "You noted that those were sophomore classes in the same subject and comprised of students from the same socio-economic area and taught by teachers with almost identical background in experience and training. In both classes the last twenty minutes were given to supervised study—one class employed the full twenty minutes in serious study; the other class loafed most of the period." With this information, explain why one class spent the supervised study period in serious study while the other class loafed.

9. The long assignment (unit plan) for many high school subjects has gained wide acceptance in recent years. Its advocates insist that superior work and study habits and skills are encouraged by it. Why? What features of the plan promote more adequate study?

10. Assumption: where libraries are available in high school or the community, instruction of students in how to use library facilities is incumbent upon the school (teacher). Is this a valid assumption? Why? In what library skills and habits should students be instructed?

RELATED REFERENCES

Association for Supervision and Curriculum Development, *Creating a Good Environment for Learning*, 1954 Yearbook (Washington, D. C., National Education Association, 1954).

BRINK, William G., *Directing Study Activities in Secondary Schools* (Garden City, N. Y., Doubleday, Doran and Co., Inc., 1937).

BURTON, William H., *The Guidance of Learning Activities*, 2nd ed. (New York, Appleton-Century-Crofts, Inc., 1952).

CRONBACH, Lee J., *Educational Psychology* (New York, Harcourt, Brace & Co., Inc., 1954).

DRUCKER, Peter F., "The New Philosophy Comes to Life," *Harper's Magazine* 215:36-40 (August, 1957).

GRUHN, William T., and DOUGLASS, Harl R., *The Modern Junior High School* (New York, The Ronald Press Company, 1956).

KELLEY, Earl C., and RASEY, Marie I., *Education and the Nature of Man* (New York, Harper & Brothers, 1952).

LEONARD, J. Paul, *Developing the Secondary-School Curriculum* (New York, Rinehart & Company, Inc., 1950).

RIVLIN, Harry N., *Teaching Adolescents in Secondary Schools* (New York, Appleton-Century-Crofts, Inc., 1948).

ROBINSON, Francis P., *Effective Study* (New York, Harper & Brothers, 1946).

ROMINE, Stephen A., *Building the High School Curriculum* (New York, The Ronald Press Company, 1954).

ROSSOFF, Martin, *Using Your High School Library* (New York, H. W. Wilson Co., 1952).

SMITH, B. Othaniel, STANLEY, William O., and SHORES, J. Harlan, *Fundamentals of Curriculum Development* (Yonkers, N. Y., World Book Co., 1950).

SPEARS, Harold, *The High School for Today* (New York, American Book Company, 1950).

STRANG, Ruth, *Study Types of Reading Exercises* (New York, Bureau of Publications, Teachers' College, Columbia University, 1955).

STRICKLAND, Ruth G., *How to Build a Unit of Work*, Office of Education Bulletin 15 (Washington, D. C., 1956).

THUT, I. N., and GERBERICH, J. Raymond, *Foundations of Method for Secondary School* (New York, McGraw-Hill Book Co., 1949).

UMSTATTD, J. G., *Secondary School Teaching* (Boston, Ginn & Company, 1944).

LEARNING THROUGH STUDENT

ACTIVITIES

"I have but one lamp by which my feet are guided, and that is the lamp of experience."—Patrick Henry

We live in one of the great creative periods of history. Due to rapid industrialization and many new scientific discoveries, American customs are in a period of flux or a fusing of old and new beliefs. Peter Drucker describes our position when he says, "But what matters most for us—the first 'post-modern' generation—is the change in fundamentals. We still profess and teach the world view of the past three hundred years, but we no longer see it. We have as yet no name for our new way of looking at things—no tools, no method."[1]

New discoveries, new knowledge, and new insights into the nature of man and the universe have come so fast in the last fifty years that we have been unable to incorporate them into our old disciplines. One reason is that the old is based upon a system with which the new is in conflict. For example, in the study of speech, the old puts emphasis upon grammar and parts of speech while the new puts emphasis upon communication. It is the whole of speech, including not only the words left unsaid but the atmosphere in which the words are said and heard, which communicates. The old was static and mechanical; the new is purposive and expanding. There are too many things to learn and too little time in which to learn them unless we devise a system by which the learning can be more quickly done. While there were six or seven disciplines in 1900, there are perhaps fifty today; each has become a full-blown science which takes a lifetime to master. The disciplines (subject-matter areas) of both high school and college are still organized as static bundles of knowledge; neither high school nor college teachers seem to be able to interrelate the new knowledge with the old.

[1] Peter F. Drucker, "The New Philosophy Comes to Life," *Harper's Magazine* 215:36-40 (August, 1957).

In their emphasis upon purpose and the all-around development of youth, student activities are entirely in accord with the attitudes being developed by the first "post-modern" generation. A new emphasis and a new program have been added to the contemporary high school; an emphasis and a program quite foreign to the high school of a generation ago. The purpose of this new program of student activities is to promote the all-around development of youth by providing rich experiences through a variety of activities.

THE ACTIVITY MOVEMENT

If teen-agers are not active, they are asleep or sick. High school teachers have always known this to be true. Up to about 1900, a common belief was held that no red-blooded student would work at school tasks of his own accord. A student had to be made to work at mental tasks in order to discipline his mind (mental discipline). Some believed that the greater the dislike for a mental task, the greater was the mental discipline achieved.

Just prior to 1900, several psychologists began to be skeptical of the mental discipline theory, and set up a number of experiments to test it. Two men, William James and Edward L. Thorndike, demonstrated the falsity of the theory. Educators, as well as psychologists, continued through detailed and broadened experiments to confirm what James and Thorndike had found, that is, an activity must have meaning for the student if he is to profit from it. Somewhat later Thorndike stated three laws of learning that very decidedly advanced our insight into how learning takes place. These three laws were: (1) the law of readiness or the willingness—the desire and ability to engage in a given activity depends upon the learner's level of maturation, previous experience, and mental and emotional set; (2) the law of exercise—the more often a connection is used, the more firmly it will become fixed, and if it is not used, it gradually fades away; (3) the law of effect—connections are strengthened or weakened according to the degree of satisfaction or annoyance that accompanies their use.

The activity movement was on its way. New insights into the nature of man and the universe have continued to be made evident. We know that active experience is an essential for intellectual, social, and emotional development or that a student with a definite goal or purpose in mind is likely to seek this active experience more vigorously. The patriot, Patrick Henry, was right in asserting that one's behavior is guided by the lamp of experience. Guided learning is indispensable, but compelled learning, except under unusual circumstances, is never wise.

The Student Activities Movement. The conditions which brought about the activity movement, at the same time and in about the same way, operated to launch the student activities movement. In Chapters I and IV of this book, it was explained that by 1900 the American high school had become a college preparatory school with only a single curriculum, the college preparatory curriculum. Most students, who attended, planned to go to college, but between 1910 and 1940 large numbers of students, not college-bound, crowded into the high school. The traditional high school teachers of the period saw student activities as only fads and frills. The real function of the high school, as they saw it, was to prepare students for college; in fact most of them believed that the best training for non-college-bound students was also mental discipline, mind-training.

Neither parents nor students were satisfied by the situation, and there were many teachers who saw a need for more activities. Shortly, a suggestion was made that a curriculum outside the "traditional" secondary school program be instituted. It seemed to be a way out of a dilemma, and many traditional high school teachers reluctantly agreed. This new program was given the name of "the extracurricular program." Thus music, athletics, and health education entered the curriculum, indirectly, from the extracurricular program, and the door was opened for the direct entrance of shop, home economics, commerce, and other non-academic subjects.[2]

As teachers were introduced to the activity concept through college courses, they began to try out in their own classes some of the practices which were found successful in the extracurricular program. Many teachers began to organize extracurricular clubs and to experiment with new and untried ideas. If the ideas were generally found to be successful in an extracurricular club, they were generally incorporated into regular courses such as general science, physics, problems of democracy, and others. Thus the extracurriculum became a means of testing new practices before they were incorporated into the regular curriculum.

This two-way flow of activities from the extracurriculum to the regular curriculum and from the regular curriculum to the extracurriculum is particularly valuable in keeping the curriculum flexible and adequate for our time. A recognition of this function of extracurricular activities is implied in the recent wide use of the terms *cocurricular activities* and *student activities* to replace *extracurricular activities*. Student activities are probably with us permanently, because there is a long list of activities in themselves worthy of the student's time that can not be incorporated into the regular classroom program due to lack of time, and because in our time of rapid expansion of new knowledge it is imperative that this knowledge either replace the static subject-matter fields or be merged with them. Many teen-agers are eager to know and understand this new

[2] Franklin A. Miller, James H. Moyer, and Robert B. Patrick, *Planning Student Activities* (Englewood Cliffs, N. J., Prentice-Hall, Inc., 1956), p. 39.

knowledge. Through clubs, the academic teacher can experiment with this new content and, as effective ways are found, combine the new with the old. Incidentally, it might happen that the old static material might be somewhat modified to make it more consistent with the new insights of our time.

The Needs of Youth. What are the needs of youth, that is, their wants, their lacks, and their deficiences? Teen-agers rarely recognize just what their needs are. A good teacher who studies his pupils usually can see what some of the wants, lacks, and deficiences are.

Take Frank, for example. He is 16 years old and large for his age. "Unco-operative," says his English teacher; "Surly," says his history teacher; "Defiant of authority," says the librarian. His grades are mediocre, and he is sent periodically to the principal for getting into fights with other boys in the corridors and to and from school. He tested 118 and 134 on two paper-and-pencil intelligence tests.

The homeroom teacher and the coach persuaded Frank to come out for the basketball team last fall. Because of his height and his aggressiveness, he will probably be the varsity center next year. Frank's homeroom teacher reports that Frank is certainly easier to live with. No anecdotal records of a derogatory nature have reached the homeroom for several months now, and a few good reports have filtered through. Frank's grades have improved, he dresses better, and he even brought a girl to the "scruff" dance a few weeks ago.

What was Frank's need? Why didn't Frank recognize his need? Yes! whether it's Frank, Joe, Henry, or Jim, they all have needs. The needs they have are all shown clearly by the way they behave. While some students recognize their needs, most do not, but an adult, who knows teen-agers, can analyze the unmet needs and make suggestions. Ann, Mary, Wilma, and Sophia also have needs and reveal these needs through their behavior. Here, too, an adult who has studied youth problems can make suggestions.

Always, in the well-organized high school, there is a student activity to match nearly every need. The regular academic program of the high school is too narrow and rigid to satisfy the multitudinous needs of all youth. But the student activities program can be made as broad and as wide as the creative genius of teachers and students permit. Such a program is vital to a high school where all youth attend. Teen-agers are active when they are awake and well, and it is through these activities that they gain experience and learn to live.

However, student activities can be as dry as the sands of the desert and as barren. Creating the form only does not necessarily provide the kinds of activities that meet the needs of youth. Guidance, with a core of hard common sense and good leadership, is required to produce an appropriate group climate in which student activities can nurture the unmet needs of youth. The purposes must be clear and evident, and the program must be derived from the purposes. Frank's need was met because he was given an opportunity to compete with peers who could hold their own and to work with a coach who could teach a neophyte how to play basketball effectively. The guidance and leadership of the coach was a probable key to Frank's changed behavior.

HOW STUDENT ACTIVITIES DEVELOP

"Young fellows will be young fellows."—Isaac Bickerstaff

Some Factors in their Development. In Chart 15, consider the many social affairs listed and try to determine the needs being met by the students who participated. These were outcomes of student desire and teacher-student planning. It represents social activities, aside from athletic events and other normal group functions, that occur during any high school year. Some element of tradition is found in such a listing—the "Recognition Dinner," for example, is held annually for the purpose of honoring all students who have made outstanding contributions through service in activities. This was originally an exclusive event for award winners on athletic teams; by extending the honors to all activities, a fine integration was brought about. In some schools, this event now receives more faculty support than any other social event of the year.

Solicitation. Membership in the debate club, as in choral groups, instrumental organizations, the Hi-Y, and Y-teens, is constantly built through teacher encouragement. For that matter, every high school coach finds it necessary to urge hesitant youth to sign up and participate in the various sports. Many youth, while feeling the need to join others in activities, somehow fall into a "come and get me" attitude. Students who are in activities will urge outstanding newcomers to join; it is the teacher's role to identify those who need encouragement before they will sign up. In this connection, many people of the community are quite ready to assist in school activities and will respond to invitations. Some will merely chaperon at affairs that require such assistance; others will take part in programs and provide needed materials. Here is an opportunity for furthering school-community relationships that should not be overlooked.

It should be apparent from Chart 15 that social activities tend to originate with the student and are guided by teacher-sponsors. A major task or a major need of youth is to learn to work and play with others at ease and in harmony. Readiness for social activity is already present with most teen-agers. It is the function of the high school to provide the opportunities and to encourage certain students who feel the need but are hesitant to participate. Since social skills come slowly for some, there is a definite need for adult guidance.

Chart 15. Social Activities in a Typical High School

DATE	SOCIAL ACTIVITY	SPONSORING GROUP	NUMBER PARTICI- PATING	TYPE OF ACTIVITY	NUMBER OF SPONSORS
Oct. 13	Movie (Audit.)	Stage crew	1,000	Money making	3
Oct. 18	Club party	Y-Teens	40	Afternoon party	1
Oct. 18	Splash party	G.A.A.	50	Swimming	1
Oct. 22	Halloween dance	Freshmen	600	Dance	18
Oct. 27	Halloween dance	12B Class	250	Fun and money	12
Oct. 29	Bus trip	School newspaper	130	Support team	11
Oct. 30	Picnic	12B class	150	Afternoon	3
Oct. 30	Party	10B class	32	Halloween	1
Nov. 3	Movie (Audit.)	12B class	650	Money making	3
Nov. 5	Sports dance	T-Club	300	King and queen	13
Nov. 15	Tea	Y-Teens	40	Afternoon	1
Nov. 19	Carnival	12A class	350	Money making	17
Nov. 24	Dance	School newspaper	450	All school	9
Dec. 1	Swim party	G.A.A.	50	Swimming	1
Dec. 3	Dance	Band	300	Informal	10
Dec. 17	Choir party	Senior choir	60	Private home	4
Dec. 17	Dance	Student council	500	Christmas	13
Dec. 18	Student council	Student council	250	Recognition	90
Jan. 15	Hotel dance	Grades 11-12	500	Jr.-Sr. Prom	19
Jan. 18	Senior banquet	12B Class	280	Dinner dance	12
Feb. 14	Talent show	Student council	1,800	Student show	3
Feb. 14	Choir program	Senior choir	50	Sunday supper	4
Feb. 18	"Heart Hop"	Y-Teens	350	Gym dance	17
Mar. 11	"Most and Best"	12B class	275	Senior dance	13
Apr. 1	April dance	Grade 10	225	Gym dance	17
Apr. 13	T-Club dance	T-Club	400	City (Audit.)	18
May 6	Mothers' tea	G.A.A.	85	Tea and program	16
May 10	Picnic	Friendship club	16	City park	1
May 13	Choir dance	Jr.-Sr. choirs	175	Gym dance	3
May 17	Sales picnic	Sales club	30	City park	1
May 23	Choir picnic	Junior choir	35	City park	4
May 23	Instrumental	Orchestra picnic	30	City park	5
May 25	Band picnic	Marching group	55	City park	8
May 27	Lilac time	G.A.A.	275	Gym dance	17
May 28	Sr. choir	Picnic	50	City park	5
June 2	Dinner	Friendship club	15	Sponsor's home	3
June 3	Banquet	Council & PTA	75	Cafeteria	18
June 7	Banquet	Senior class	378	City hotel	23
June 8	Senior picnic	Senior class	390	City park	20

Recognition versus tolerance. With some school boards, school officials, and teachers, the attitude prevails that "young fellows will be young fellows" or we will let the students play a little in order to get them to work harder the rest of the time. Schools need to recognize that student activities are just as important as any other part of the curriculum; they should not be tacked on to the program at the end of the day. They should be a part of the regular day's program. Many districts feel that it is necessary to choose between new buildings and broadening student activities—with the usual result that the activities are limited.

Why are schools having difficulty in keeping qualified teachers capable of directing student activities? Either extra services must be paid for or the student activity program must be assigned a regular place in the daily schedule of the school. Our present teacher shortage is caused by many things, one of which is a natural refusal by teachers to become associated with travesty, such as a school policy that declines to accept and provide for student activities which are necessary to the all-around development of youth. No teacher desires to join the faculty of a school that ignores student activities which are such a vital factor in the education of students. This general refusal on the part of many qualified teachers will undoubtedly hasten the incorporation of student activities into the regular school schedule, the provision in the school budget for support of student activities, and the adjustment of class load and increment for teachers who participate in student activities.

All Activities Have Purposes. Some prevailing conditions in regard to student activities need to be recognized and corrected or else eliminated. Edgar G. Johnston[3] summarizes these as follows:

1. Many schools have adopted the form of activity programs without any real understanding by teachers and students of the function it should perform.

2. We have been afraid of democracy. We have lacked faith in the ability of students to plan, to make intelligent decisions, and to accept responsibility.

3. Participation in the activities program has been limited to too few students, both through regulations denying opportunities to students scholastically unsuccessful and through failure to provide for appropriate distribution.

4. The competitive aspects of the program have been over-emphasized. The winning of contests has been allowed to overshadow more important outcomes.

5. In some instances, national organizations developed to encourage a particular phase of the activity program have devoted energy to promoting the organization and have lost sight of more inclusive objectives.

6. Organizations representative of special groups in the community or engaged in promoting one point of view on controversial issues on which public opinion is divided are permitted in some instances to function as school organizations.

7. The activity program has not been vitally related to the curriculum.

8. There has been no consistent effort to evaluate activities in terms of fundamental objectives.

9. Teacher training institutions have failed to provide appropriate experiences for prospective teachers to prepare them for responsibilities in relation to student activities.

[3] Edgar G. Johnston, "Critical Problems in the Administration of Student Activities," *Bulletin of the National Association of Secondary-School Principals* 36:1-12 (February, 1952).

10. Duties in relation to the activity program have not received adequate recognition in considering the teacher's load.

An effective student activities program will have goals; students need to know exactly what the purposes of a particular activity are. Why is the activity being offered? How will it help me? What are the objectives of the activity? A qualified sponsor will be able to answer all of these questions immediately and in language concise and clear. Even the name of the activity should indicate the values to be received.

Learning Is Informal, Not Formal. From one viewpoint, the school sometimes stands in the way of natural learning processes. This occurs when the school lags far behind in providing opportunities for social growth; in such instances the community may look upon the school as little more than a "baby-sitting" mechanism where the three R's should be taught "between feedings."

When lethargy permeates the school atmosphere and when opportunities for the full education of all youth are not provided, then the school is not much more than a holding device with legal support that keeps some teen-agers off the streets for a few hours each day. What a dismal process this is when we realize what really might be done in terms of democratic concepts and freedom to learn. How many studies must be made, such as by Dr. Sheldon Glueck and his wife, Eleanor,[4] and by Albert Deutsch,[5] before our school communities understand their failure to fulfill their obligation to all youth? Besides, in the long run, the fully implemented school program is actually cheaper in dollars and cents.

Do all activities have purposes? This is answered affirmatively when we consider John Dewey's analysis of "a complete act of thought." It is amazing how activities provide a means for the natural development of the student. The five steps outlined by Dewey are as follows:

1. A felt difficulty
2. Its location and definition
3. Suggestion of a possible solution
4. Development by reasoning from the bearings of the suggestions
5. Further observations and experiments leading to its acceptance or rejection; that is, of the conclusion of belief or disbelief.[6]

Thus, Thorndike's Law of Readiness explains the annoyance or felt difficulty that occurs when the lack of action does not not permit a bond to function. The teen-ager, doing what seems most natural, cries out: "Let's have a school party! May we have a picnic? Why is there nothing in this town for teen-agers to do?" He feels the difficulty, defines it in

[4] Sheldon and Eleanor T. Glueck, "The Family, the School, and Crime," *Harvard Teachers Record* 15:71-81 (April, 1935).

[5] Albert Deutsch, *Our Rejected Children* (Boston, Little, Brown & Co., 1950).

[6] John Dewey, *How We Think* (Boston, D. C. Heath & Company, 1910), pp. 72-78.

terms of need, and suggests action that may remove his annoyance. If the party is arranged, as a result of his plea, he will "observe and experiment" further in order to bring about acceptance or rejection of the school activity as a means of satisfying a felt difficulty.

Other formulae have been proposed by educators and psychologists. The following is a popular psychiatric view:

And what occurs to the growing child if desires and annoyances are not given some reasonable outlet through social activities? Let us here follow through an objective analysis based upon the psychiatry of Sigmund Freud. The child will *suppress* unpleasant experiences ("Young man, we are here to study arithmetic, not to talk about any school parties!") and *repress* drives ("You are never again to put your arm around a girl!"). His failure to achieve some sort of harmony between his natural desires, which apparently are anti-social, and his mild interests, which are said to be all-important, produces a *neurosis*. Then anything can happen.

He may respond to his neurosis in a mild way, by carving a desk, being truant or tardy, pretending to be lazy or shiftless, and being openly defiant of authority, dominating his classmates, attempting to dominate his parents. Or his outbreak may be not mild at all. We may read in newspaper headlines: "Youth Invades School—Shoots Principal and Teacher."

Now the curious part about such negative behavior is that it follows the "activity" pattern right down the line. The teen-ager's purpose is a desire to "get even with somebody." He plans his course of action and puts it into execution. And then, only then, does the adult world rush to help him judge the wisdom of his activity.[7]

The purpose in providing a variety of activities is apparent when we note: that all students are not equally mature; that in the cosmopolitan high school, students have fewer interests in common; and that students acquiring work experience are less interested in student activities. School morale can be highly developed through many school activities, such as the all-school assembly, the newspaper, the student council, and the planned homeroom, which tend to inculcate common ideals, attitudes, and beliefs.

The Role of the Sponsor. Since learning is best done through friendly teachers who qualify scholastically and professionally, students quickly determine whether the adult is in sympathy with the activities program. Permissive atmospheres are built most easily when the teacher actively participates in sponsorship of one or more activities. Through work with a debate club, the teacher will come to know intimately the boys and girls who provide school leadership. Sponsorship of the student council gives the teacher an opportunity to interpret and foster an ideal school policy. The teacher, for example, who will help

---

[7] For additional reading related to possible harm done to youth by schools that fail to provide activities outside the traditional classroom courses, backgrounds have been outlined by Alfred Adler, Carl Gustav Jung, Otto Rank, Karen Horney, Harry Stack Sullivan, Erich Fromm, and others.

in the promotion of a "splash party" in the school swimming pool has far more insight than the teacher who meets students at the door of the classroom—and bids them farewell at the door when the class ends.

Some sponsor guideposts. Here are some major factors that will help the sponsor of any activity to determine the worthiness of such work:

1. Is the activity developed and carried on in terms of clearly defined purposes and goals? (Or is it a makeshift matter that is conducted merely because the teacher was assigned to it?)

2. Is it integrated with other aspects of the school's instructional program? (Or does it create friction?)

3. Is it broad and varied enough to provide for the needs, interests, and abilities of all students?

4. Are the programs carefully planned? (This would include the use of a master calendar to avoid conflicts.)

5. Is it carried on largely through regular school hours? (Many students have personal obligations after school closes.)

6. Is it continuously evaluated?

7. Is it provided at little or no cost to the student? (In a democracy, the teen-ager is entitled to a well-rounded educational program without regard to his ability to pay for it.)

When sponsorship of an activity is an added duty, the teacher may develop a tendency to under-evaluate its worth and ask that he be relieved. When sponsorship is a regular duty, a more factual evaluation may be forthcoming.

An Activity Is Born. Perhaps the newest activity to thrust itself into the school scene has been the dance band or orchestra. This is usually a musical organization formed of, by, and for students who manifest an intense desire to perform instrumentally and vocally. While it is not accepted in all regions of the United States, it does stand as a recently approved but somewhat novel activity in many schools. It represents, where it has been established, a sharp change in community mores over as brief a period as the last two decades. While there have always been students who, as amateur musicians, were eager to play popular ballads in the privacy of their rooms, or beneath a shade tree on the school grounds, the official "school dance band" has only recently been recognized. There are many arguments that favor its acceptance:

1. Since teen-age dances without open supervision invite violations of liquor and drug laws, schools must sponsor such affairs and provide adult leadership.

2. Youthful musicians should not be forced to rehearse in back rooms of taverns or pool halls. Schools provide a wholesome environment.

3. Since the musician's profession is both worthy and desirable and since society approves of modern music as well as classical, youth need encouragement and training in this vocation by trained musicians.

4. It is the obligation of the school to prevent the exploitation of young

theme" are proposed, they will be tried out as extra activities until they find a place in the physical education program.

While it is questionable whether competitive sports activities among schools that are located hundreds of miles apart should be fostered, there can be slight argument against intermural sports as such. In the teen-ager, the basic desires for recognition and response run high; some pupils, who may seldom attain satisfaction within the classroom, may find greater opportunity in the gym program. The youth who establishes himself as a worthy player in the gym may develop new attitudes toward leadership in certain courses other than physical education. This carry-over occurs in high school year after year, and it explains, in part, how new scholar-ship is sometimes developed through gym activities.

The sporting spirit may be extended to include not only the familiar competitive tournaments among the homerooms and clubs, but also many non-sport rivalries such as those in debating, journalistic contests, and choral enterprises. Later in this chapter, the activity hour is discussed to show how such a program may be carried on within regular school time with a minimum of interruption or interference.

The School Newspaper. These student publications are the product of junior and senior students who, in the larger high schools, receive one year of credit for their work. This credit may be substituted for one year of English. On occasion, credit in "Advanced Journalism" may be given as an elective.

A lively student newspaper can serve as a "spark plug" in the stimulation of all school matters and serve to bind together the entire student body in a common enterprise. Under qualified sponsorship, the paper can be self-supporting; an integrated course, such as advertising or retail sales, can provide actual experience in the promotion and sale of advertising that will support the publishing costs. Where there is clearly a need for im-proved community relations, the paper can reach homes, the major businesses, other schools—every part of the area served by the school. An "Information Bureau" can provide adult newspapers and radio-television outlets with important stories about the school. Actual surveys may be staged, and skill in creative writing may be gained.

Every student of journalism soon realizes that the widest possible back-ground in political science and related academic areas is essential to success. Field trips, interviews, writing editorials, discerning between opinion and fact, compiling statistical data—all, under a tradition of free activity, provide the most natural opportunities for learning.

Too often, journalism classes are limited to those students who have already attained a high degree of ability in the formalized English courses; thus, what the newspaper experience might bring about in growth for the average student is prohibited by school regulations. It is a rule that was devised, probably, by teachers, inexperienced in journalism, who sought to lighten their responsibilities by having only the "bright" scholars in their courses. From a vocational viewpoint, let us note that the newspaper industry hires workers who may not be from the "bright" group. While staff membership on the school newspaper or annual does carry honor with it, this group experience should not exclude those who would benefit the most. It is not the purpose of the school to establish a policy of *exclusion* from any learning experience.[11]

The Student Council. One of the greatest opportunities for citizenship training and school service is provided by the student council. Membership in this organization is determined, almost entirely throughout America, by the democratic process of proportionate election of representatives from the various classes. Where there is a minimum of interference with the normal functions of democracy, there can be a maximum of benefit to the school and the students—both those who take part actively as members and those whose affairs are guided by the council.

Two cautions are given here to further indicate the role of the teacher in this activity:

1. A tendency on the part of the faculty to select students for council membership, and to direct all functions of the council, must be sublimated. We must have faith in the democratic process.

2. A non-professional desire to exploit a single talented student—so that it might appear that the entire school bulges with genius—must be kept under control. Certainly, the president of the student council is entitled to a basic education in common learnings, and he will receive this best through regular class attendance. He will not long remain a leader if he is constantly called out of class to be a guide for school visitors or an errand boy for the school principal.

There are, of course, hundreds of promotional affairs in which the student council might engage. The sponsor will remind council members early in the year of the dangers in "mounting a horse and riding off madly in all directions at once." The sponsor will also determine, as the group is organized, what the exact limitations to student enterprise may be—this must be done before programs are outlined, not after.

In larger schools, the student council may delegate authority to lesser bodies, that is, a student court may judge disciplinary cases and recommend action to the council and to school officers. A school store may function under council direction; a publications board, responsible to the council, may assist with the school newspaper, the yearbook, and the "Welcome Freshmen" booklets. Patrols, operating as a part of the student council, may be of great assistance to the faculty; however, as with the safety patrol and fire patrol groups on the elementary level, we must

[11] Consult several high school journalism texts, if you are curious here about sponsoring such an activity; one of the most popular is *High School Journalism*, Harold Spears and C. H. Lawshe, Jr. (New York, The Macmillan Co., 1947).

never ask the student to do the work of an adult. In no case should adult responsibility for the welfare of every child be released entirely to other children. When this happens, teachers ultimately lose sight of professional goals and find themselves "blaming the council" for every turn of events. And then the first evil arises; the teachers decide to select students for council membership, hoping that somehow this will correct things.

The role of the student council sponsor is above indicated. He must insist upon democratic processes, point out the limitations of council action, provide guidance in the development of a growth program, foster friendly relations within and outside the school, and remind himself constantly of the goals that are within reach of his membership. Rewards for successful sponsorship often include administrative promotion, and it is not unusual to find assistant principals who still carry the student council responsibility.

Dramatics. What a wealth of ability that might otherwise be lost is afforded development through the lure of the stage! As in the case of journalism, options are ordinarily possible at the third-year level, and "Advanced Dramatics" may be an added elective in English during the senior year, with emphasis upon the senior play. Dramatics in the smaller schools, like music, is often nothing more than a separate activity or an elective subject that may not be substituted for English credit.

Despite the strong impact of professional perfection that has been brought about by television and established theatrical presentations, youth continue to respond to plays and pageants in which their peers take part. It seems that there is an abundance of work to be done in preparing for and presenting a stage show—so much that no student need be excluded from doing what he greatly desires to do. Stage crews, while vocational in nature only in the large cities, provide human experiences that no classroom might duplicate. For that matter, what classroom could offer any reasonable substitute for the actual promotion, advertising, ticket sale, ushering, make-up, costume rental, and similar details that are so real in dramatic work?

Vocal and Instrumental Music. While most metropolitan high schools have for many years incorporated music with the basic curriculum, it is ordinarily considered an activity, or, at best, an elective subject in the small high schools. Singing and playing instruments alone or in groups, as a student activity, journeyed from the community and the private teacher to the school and the public teacher. There are several viewpoints with respect to the merits of public school music as opposed to private instruction, but the single issue with which we must be concerned is: Does youth attain improved stature through music? With an affirmative answer, then the only problem remaining is to broaden the school curriculum so that no teen-ager is excluded from the opportunity to develop musically.

The teacher who carries on the music sponsorship must know the nature of this responsibility. Since private instruction is expensive, communities look to their public instructor or music sponsor for help and leadership. In small towns, this may bring about conflicts between the teacher and the status quo, that is, those instructors who have been earning their livings through fees from churches and individuals. This problem is intensified when the school teacher, also seeking income, may accept private students. School boards often stipulate that this must not be done by the school employee. The problem is easily resolved, of course, when there are no private teachers in the community. Here the school instructor or sponsor may develop town bands and orchestras, and undertake the leadership of church choirs, adult choruses, and spectacular pageants.

Debate Club. It would be interesting to interview many of today's Congressional leaders and political chairmen to discover where they first found pleasure in the development of their oratorical talents. Any law work was probably prefaced by early teen-age experiences as a member of the school debate squad or club. Membership in such groups, as with other activities, need not be exclusive; such matters as time-keeping, delivering ballots to judges, and general errand work may be handled by the teen-ager who, while not fully capable of actual debate participation, will take pride in being associated with the activity.

Parliamentary knowledge is today an essential in any common-learnings program. It may be achieved through classroom drill, or it may be learned much more naturally and thoroughly in actual forensic work. When the National Forensic League selects such a topic as "Federal Aid to Education," the correlation with social studies courses becomes quite challenging. When invitational tournaments are arranged, informed speakers from other schools present their best; rivalries intensify the need for learning, so everyone experiences added growth.

When the curriculum does not provide a place for debate, then the negative "before-school, after-school, after-dinner," routine slowly and surely reduces the activity to its lowest level. Few are served and few profit if it is not a part of the curriculum.

An Endless List of Activities. Every activity, upon examination, provides evidence that justifies including it in the student activity program. The Junior Red Cross, the Girls' Athletic Association, the Hi-Y, the Astronomers' Club, the Biology Club, the Pan-American Club, the Hobby Club, and all the others reveal two factors: (1) a prime interest that may bring about desired growth and development of attitudes leading to worthy citizenship, and (2) the enrichment of the regular classroom curriculum by adding new content and procedures after an experimental tryout with selected activities. The activities provide a worthy outlet for the natural abundance of energy that teen-agers possess—a tormenting desire that will make itself felt somehow.[12] When teachers understand that they must strive to be expert in the fine art of human engineering,

[12] Arnold Gesell, Frances L. Ilg, and Louise B. Ames, *Youth: The Years from Ten to Sixteen* (New York, Harper & Brothers, 1956), p. 453.

they will channel teen-age desires into activities that bring about desirable growth and behavior. With such an understanding, there can be no end to the many activities that teen-agers themselves will initiate. Language arts classes may decide to hold a Latin breakfast, complete with togas and wreaths; Spanish students may form Pan-American Friendship Clubs and carry on extensive correspondence in a foreign language. Pre-engineering students may form an Edison Club and tour nearby electrical plants or atomic installations if permitted. Science Clubs may devise improved ways to build telescopes. Is there any sound reason why these activities should not be fostered? If they are educational, is there any reasonable argument against incorporating such activities within the curriculum? Certainly, from the viewpoint of the preservice teacher, acceptance of an activity sponsorship is as essential as any classroom assignment.[13]

AN INTEGRAL PART OF THE INSTRUCTIONAL PROGRAM

"The battle of Waterloo was won on the playing fields of Eton."
—DUKE OF WELLINGTON

Student activities are coming to be an integral part of the instructional program of the high school rather than an extra or independent program. The practice is widespread; more than half (63 per cent) of all high schools schedule an activity period during the regular school day.[14] What are the advantages to students and teachers of scheduling student activities within the daily schedule of the high school?

Advantages to Students. As the playing fields of Eton were given credit for winning the battle of Waterloo, so many school boards and school officials have come to accept student activities as an essential type of education to prepare students for winning industrial, political, and professional battles in the United States. Student activities seem to be moving from the position of stepchildren into a full status as members of the instructional family.

Student activities are electives and have proven to be of great value to students; hence, they must be scheduled at a time when they do not conflict with other programs. The practice is to set aside one period in the school day as a student activity period. Local conditions will decide the most desirable period of the day to be used as a student activity period; however, the two most popular periods are the first and last periods of

[13] Schools often hire teachers primarily on a basis of coaching, music, or dramatics experiences and aptitude—with classroom assignments being secondary in importance. (Some years ago, when town bands were quite popular, the local firms might advertise as follows: "Wanted—Barber who can play cornet.") The qualified teacher today, from the school board's viewpoint, at least, must "double in brass."

[14] Miller, Moyer, and Patrick, *op. cit.*, p. 101.

the day. Such an established period permits all students to participate since nothing is scheduled at this time but student activities.

Nevertheless, there are activities that require out-of-school experience or that cannot be adapted to the length of a period or the facilities available. A dancing club, for example, might find the activity period too short or the essential facilities not available. Also, this would be true for a baseball game between two intramural groups. The "before-school, after-school, or after-dinner" hours are still available to these groups.

Some of the advantages to be gained through a regular student activities period are:

1. All students may participate in activities if they elect to do so, without infringement upon other duties during out-of-school hours.

2. Transported students will have the same advantage as the students who live near the school.

3. The faculty members who sponsor an activity can usually do so within the regular school day.

4. Since regular academic classes are not in session, the students of lower scholastic achievement can participate in the activities without sacrificing time from other schoolwork.

5. Since the activity period falls within the regular school day, faculty members, having released time from academic classes, will participate more freely, for it will require less personal sacrifice of time and energy than would be the case if it were in addition to the full day of teaching.

6. It will become possible for the school to control the number of activities in which a student can engage. In general, the activities will be limited to three. Ordinarily, only two or three of the five periods of the week are set aside for clubs and group organizations. The other two periods of the week will be held in reserve as special periods for assemblies, homerooms, student council, and other special programs.

Advantages to Teachers. The standard work day of the teacher, by common agreement of the public and school officials, has been set as 8:00 A.M. to 4 P.M. In practice teachers spend several additional hours each day reading and correcting homework, marking tests and examinations, planning the class activities for the next day, organizing and revising instructional units, looking up and checking references, attending teachers' meetings, and doing other professional jobs. When the student activities are assigned to a regular schedule, sponsoring student activities becomes a part of the work for which the teacher is paid, hence, these activities are recognized as being an important part of the work of the school. Teachers are like all human beings; they plan their work more carefully when an employer is willing to pay for the service rendered.

Previously, sponsoring student activities had to be done outside of the regular program and in addition to a full instructional load. Because many teachers sensed student activities as being so vital in meeting the needs of youth, they planned for the activity period with the same care and thoroughness given to their regular work. But other teachers did this work grudgingly and without careful planning as an extra duty exacted by a mean employer.

In a goodly number of the high schools of the United States, student activities are still a "before-school, after-school, and after-dinner" routine where the sponsoring of student activities is an extra service beyond the regular instructional load. There are many essential needs of youth not being met in these communities by the regular academic program. The teacher is a human engineer with a broader vision than that exhibited by the community, and he will not let youth down.

DISCUSSION PROBLEMS

1. Publication of the student newspaper encompasses many excellent learning situations—real interest, recognition, regularity . . . the work requires knowledge of grammar, expression, punctuation, spelling, proofreading . . . it has a business side . . . yet journalism, as such, is often considered nothing more than a student activity. Can you explain why this important public-relations element has not been more fully developed in most schools?

2. Present the arguments for and against fund-raising enterprises.

3. The National PTA Congress has tended to discourage playing of such games as Bingo as a means of fund-raising. Some schools have promoted the giving of expensive door prizes as a substitute. Discuss the ethical implications of these enterprises.

4. To what extent should a professional teacher accept the assignment of more than a few duties outside the classroom?

5. Explore the medical arguments, pro and con, relative to the participation of youth in such contact sports as football and basketball. Do you favor post-season games for charity?

6. Examine insurance programs which cover the transportation of students on field trips, injuries in sports, and accidents that may occur in school gyms. What has been the attitude of courts when suits against the school are brought to trial?

7. Select a student club or activity and make a list of suggestions for organizing and managing the activity so that it will contribute to the growth of the students participating.

8. Identify the arguments for and against integrating student activities with the curriculum.

RELATED REFERENCES

BRAMMEL, P. Roy, *Guiding Home-Room and Club Activities* (New York, McGraw-Hill Book Co., 1953).

BROWN, Willis C., *Extraclass Activities in Aviation, Photography, and Radio for Secondary School Pupils* (Washington, D.C., Superintendent of Documents, 1956).

Commission on Teacher Education, *Helping Teachers Understand Children* (Washington, D.C., American Council on Education, 1946).

CUNNINGHAM, Ruth, and others, *Understanding Group Behavior of Boys and Girls* (New York, Bureau of Publications, Teachers College, Columbia University, 1951).

DEUTSCH, Albert, *Our Rejected Children* (Boston, Little, Brown & Co., 1950).

DEWEY, John, *How We Think* (Boston, D. C. Health & Company, 1910).

DRUCKER, Peter F., "The New Philosophy Comes to Life," *Harper's Magazine* 215:36-40 (August, 1957).

DULLES, Foster R., *America Learns to Play* (New York, D. Appleton-Century Company, Inc., 1940).

Educational Policies Commission, *School Athletics* (Washington, D. C., National Education Association, 1954).

FEDDER, Ruth, *Guiding Home-Room and Club Activities* (New York, McGraw-Hill Book Co., 1949).

GESELL, Arnold, ILG, Frances L., and AMES, Louise B., *Youth: The Years from Ten to Sixteen* (New York, Harper & Brothers, 1956).

GLUECK, Sheldon and Eleanor T., "The Family, the School and Crime," *Harvard Teachers Record* 15:71-81 (April, 1935).

GRUBER, Frederick C., and THOMAS, B. B., *Secondary School Activities* (New York, McGraw-Hill Book Co., 1954).

JACOBSON, Paul B., *The American Secondary School* (Englewood Cliffs, N.J., Prentice-Hall, Inc., 1952).

JOHNSTON, Edgar G., "Critical Problems in the Administration of Student Activities," *Bulletin of the National Association of Secondary-School Principals* 36:1-12 (February, 1952).

―――, "Democracy and the Student Council," *School Activities* 19:7-15 (September, 1947).

―――, and FAUNCE, Roland C., *Student Activities* (New York, The Ronald Press Company, 1952).

KILZBERG, L. R., STEPHENSON, H. H., and NORDBERG, H. O., *Allied Activities in the Secondary School* (New York, Harper & Brothers, 1956).

KIRKENDALL, Lester A., and ZERAN, Franklin R., *Student Councils in Action* (New York, Chartwell House, Inc., 1953).

KVRACEUS, W. C., *The Community and the Delinquent* (Yonkers, N.Y., World Book Co., 1954).

LEAVITT, J. E., "Latent Abilities," *Clearing House* 30:242-3, December, 1955.

McKOWN, Harry C., *Extra-Curricular Activities* (New York, The Macmillan Co., 1952).

―――, *The Student Council* (New York, McGraw-Hill Book Co., 1944).

McMAHILL, Don R., "He Who Throws Stones," *The School Executive* 75:418 (August, 1956).

MILLER, Franklin A., MOYER, James H., and PATRICK, Robert B., *Planning Student Activities* (Englewood Cliffs, N.J., Prentice-Hall, Inc., 1956).

OBERTEUFFER, Delbert, *Physical Education* (New York, Harper & Brothers, 1951).

SHANNON, J. R., and KETTLE, M. A., "Economic Discrimination in School Activities," *Clearing House* 22:71-73 (October, 1947).

STRANG, Ruth, *Group Activities in the Secondary School* (New York, Harper & Brothers, 1946).

TRUMP, J. Lloyd, *Extra-Curricular Activities* (Chicago, University of Chicago Press, 1950).

TUTTLE, Harold S., *Dynamic Psychology and Conduct* (New York, Harper & Brothers, 1949).

Chapter 11

UTILIZING INSTRUCTIONAL MATERIALS

It is not enough to know a recipe; one must be able to bake the cake.

Variety is the spice of life. Words alone are sheer verbalisms unless given reality through meaningful experiences. Students like teachers who are sympathetic and can explain things well; explaining is an essential service expected of teachers.

During recent decades, a wide variety of instructional materials such as audio-visual aids, resource people and materials, field trips, and surveys have become available to teachers. All are effective, when correctly selected and used, for helping teachers make clearer explanations. But even sympathetic teachers do not necessarily use a wide variety of instructional materials effectively without practice. It is not enough to know the recipe; one must be able to bake the cake.

Instructional materials efficiently utilized help students form concepts which are clear and exact and which are an integral part of the future thought process. Words only memorized are without meaning; hence, they are of no service in giving direction to thought or action. For example, there is this "blooper" by a pupil given in answer to a question about the Chinese religion; the pupil wrote, "The Chinese worship their aunts' sisters," instead of, "The Chinese worship their ancestors." This is a good illustration of verbalism in the use of words which had no clear meaning to the student. Instructional materials, capably employed, avoid such "boners." They make what is being learned more concrete and less abstract; hence, it is more meaningful and important to the student.

School work can be dull and boring unless there is considerable variety in the classroom. Varying the procedure, if properly timed, can bring little thrills or a rich experience to classroom instruction. Of what is a rich experience comprised? If an idea being taught is understood, has meaning, and is perfectly clear to a student, he is having an experience. One may have a rich experience when: (1) he is perceiving through the senses, (2) a marked emotional tone is present, (3) he is exploring something new, (4) there is a culmination or fulfillment from other

243

experiences, and (5) he is recognized or has an increase in status. Varying instructional materials and adapting them to a specific situation may give, to what would have been a dull routine, an element of interest and even of mild excitement.

There must be surprises and variety in the classroom or school becomes dull and tiresome. Even the most fascinating material can be killed by routine, but if instructional materials are selected, adapted, and varied so that there are surprises, interest and excitement can be present. There is a wide variety of instructional material available to help make a class stimulating and exciting.

INSTRUCTIONAL RESOURCES, AIDS, AND MATERIALS

Based upon types of experiences, there are three kinds of instructional experiences available.[1] These are aids that stress doing, observing, and the use of abstract symbols. If employed selectively, all three are valuable. When and how each kind can be utilized will depend upon the maturity and the previous experiences of the class. For example, in an agriculture class of a metropolitan high school, the farm boys in the class may quickly and easily be led into the discussion of broad, general principles (verbal symbols) while the city boys, without any previous experience, will not perceive or understand—the discussion will be meaningless to them. The city boys will need to acquire some experience through doing and observing before they can profit by a discussion of broad general principles in agriculture.

Experience Through Doing. What are some of the aids, instructional resources, and instructional materials for providing experience through doing, observing, and the use of symbols?

Semi-direct experiences. The laboratory and the shop have been an integral part of instruction in science, industrial arts, home economics, and business education for more than a half century. The quality of the instructional aids and materials has varied widely from classroom to classroom and from time to time, but chemicals, physical apparatus, machines, tools, typewriters, and other essential materials have usually been available. In these laboratories and shops, the experiences provided have been much more direct and purposeful than those found in other academic classrooms.

Laboratory and shop procedures are now being introduced into all of the academic subjects to make the instructional materials more real and lifelike. The most useful aids seem to be recorders, wire tapes, motion pictures, and slide films. In physical education much direct experience is being provided through intermural and intramural sports and games.

[1] Edgar Dale, *Audio-Visual Methods in Teaching* (New York, The Dryden Press, 1947), Ch. 4.

Contrived experiences. In contrived experiences, the direct experience is modified to make it fit our purposes. The earth cannot be brought into a classroom while a model to represent the earth can, and such a model can be made as simple or as complicated as the readiness of the class permits. We cannot study the lighting system of a huge modern airplane, but a simplified mock-up can be made by using the switch board and selected portions of the complicated system. A huge factory where automation is dominant cannot be studied directly, but a simplified mock-up can be made to help students understand automation in industry. We cannot observe the bottom of the ocean, but specimens from the bottom of the ocean can be brought into the classroom. We only faintly can see the heavens with our naked eyes, but we can build an observatory on the school grounds or take our students to visit a planetarium where the heavens can be studied in some detail, and stars and clusters of stars can be identified and named. What otherwise would be obscure can be viewed by all.

Experiences Through Observation. Often it is not possible to give the individual student an actual experience; however, the basis for much meaningful learning may be laid by observation.

Dramatic participation. Any situation where a student puts himself into the role of another by playing a part could be called dramatic participation. Dramatic plays are frequently written and produced by classes in English, the core, social studies, and the homeroom. Through portraying a role in a play, a student may acquire insight into other people, other groups, and even foreign cultures. Drama provides socializing experiences. A Latin Breakfast, planned and carried through by a Latin class, which features the food, the clothing worn, the manner of serving the food, and the way of living of the Roman people, can help a class become quite sensitive to the culture of the Romans and much more interested in the Latin language. Many teachers have found sociodrama with its role-playing and related techniques especially helpful in improving social relations in the classroom.

The demonstration. This can make a concept or a skill vivid and real, but a beneficial demonstration must be practiced until it can be performed with ease, without errors, and in correct form. Either a student or the instructor can serve as the demonstrator. Frequently, a resource person with a hobby is quite willing to put on a vivid demonstration for a class. Many different types of materials can be used in a demonstration. Some of these are scientific equipment, maps, charts, globes, cartoons, posters, stereographs, photographs, radio transcriptions, phonograph records, various types of exhibits, motion pictures, and slide films.

Field trips. These provide a first-hand acquaintance with varied natural and social phenomena outside the classroom. Any organized excursion, which is taken by students as an integral part of their academic work, is a field trip. By their use, the entire community may become an extension of the school curriculum. The field trip can include museums, farms, industries, unusual natural phenomena, and public buildings. Careful pre-planning, good organization for the trip, and a thorough follow-up are essential for securing results justified by the time given. If the field trip is to be defended, it must be planned in detail in advance.

Exhibits. Literally thousands of material objects, specimens, and models are available and can enrich and amplify the curriculum. Exhibits of fauna and flora and models of farm machinery and famous places are much more vivid than wordy descriptions or even pictures. In such subjects as home economics, industrial arts, and general science, exhibits of the students' work in downtown stores or at the school quicken the interest of students, the parents, and the public. Other students are stimulated to attain an even better exhibit for next year.

Motion pictures. Movies literally bring the world into the classroom. By using different types of photography such as the time lapse, slow motion, animated cartoon, microphotography, and miniature photography, practically every form of physical activity may be realistically reproduced. In every subject-matter field, there are many concepts, skills, and appreciations that can be made more real and vivid through motion picture films. No other aid is as valuable as motion pictures for developing attitudes or studying motion so reduced in speed that the observer can see just how a ball is thrown or a bird flies.

The slide film. A 35 mm. continuous filmstrip carrying a number of photographs called frames or pictures is a valuable aid. Slide films can be made by the teacher or purchased commercially. They usually are shown with accompanying oral explanations. If the timing of the presentation in relation to the topic is correct and if the presentation is done with ease and poise, the interest of students is aroused, and their attention is focused upon the topic being taught. Slide films are adaptable to every one of the subject-matter fields.

Slides. These can be made at very small cost to the teacher. The procedure is to use a camera for the snapshots and print them on 2 x 2 slides. With a suitable camera and some care, pictures from books and many other sources can be copied and projected from 2 x 2 slides in a classroom.[2] Slides are highly flexible aids and can be used for many purposes. Some teachers put their often-repeated blackboard illustrations onto slides for projection on a screen and thus save the time and effort of repeated blackboard drawings. Slides are excellent devices for varying classroom procedure. In reviews of material that will be repeated several times, varying the procedure each time keeps interest and attention higher and makes for better retention of the material reviewed.

Stereographs. Details are vividly brought out by the third dimension;

[2] Bob L. Taylor, "Make Your Own Slides," *Educational Screen* 33:418 (December, 1954).

however, they are adapted only to individual use and require careful planning if students are to profit fully. Unless helped to see the details made evident by the third dimension, students are apt to glance at them as they do at a photograph. Use of mimeographed questions on each stereograph is one way to cause students to study each more carefully.

Radio recordings. Either tape or disc recordings add much to a topic under discussion, especially if it is a respected authority who is being heard. "You Can Hear It Now," edited by Edward R. Murrow, is a good example. Since radio or television programs rarely coincide with a high-school class schedule, the teacher will need to make the recordings or obtain them from the local station. Selected radio recordings which bear directly upon a topic under discussion add zest and freshness to the discussion. Incidentally, selected recordings from radio and television programs will, from time to time, fit into any subject-matter field.

Experiences Through Word Symbols. For a long time, textbooks were the only available teaching material for all high school instruction. Very slowly the blackboard and a few additional materials and aids were added. Only since 1900 have the laboratory and the shop been added as instructional aids. Formerly, students who were unable to read and understand the textbook or the teacher's lecture were quickly eliminated from the high school.

To say, as some extremists have, that everything worthwhile can be learned through reading and listening is at best a half-truth. We know that some of our most respected leaders in industry and commerce found the bookish high school of two generations ago meaningless. We also know that thousands of teen-agers have been eliminated from the high school because they did not learn from books. Certain types of teen-agers do learn much this way while others learn very little. Some learning cannot be acquired in this manner at all.

Burton,[3] a highly respected educator, has summarized the issue as follows:

Direct experience . . . is the best method of learning. Most persons do not learn solely by direct experience; nor do they learn some of the most important things that they know by that route.

The contemporary high school is designed to retain all teen-agers until graduation, or until they are 18 years of age. We know that all, or nearly all, teen-agers can learn and profit by high school attendance. For some, learning verbal symbols through the textbook is difficult. Many instructional resources, aids, and materials have been made available to the high school in recent years and are being used extensively by high school teachers.

[3] William H. Burton, *The Guidance of Learning Activities,* 2nd ed. (New York, Appleton-Century-Crofts, Inc., 1952), p. 42.

Textbooks for such high school courses as chemistry, physics, and trigonometry are replete with technical symbols where others are heavily laden with verbal symbols. But textbooks are now being produced for the high school with less emphasis upon difficult technical and verbal symbols and with greater emphasis upon effective illustrations and explanations. Yet, there will be in every high school those students who must have specific help from the classroom teacher and from supplementary aids. By and large, every course in the high school, with a few exceptions, will use a textbook which provides an outline for the course.

The textbook is only one instructional aid, and there are sound reasons to depart from the textbook as a single source of information. The printed word is no longer held sacred, for too many changes have occurred in scientific principles, too many maps have been revised overnight by violence or negotiation, and too many forces are constantly changing all subject-matter areas. We can no longer depend upon any textbook with full confidence. Respect for the teen-ager and for the truth demands that a teacher utilize additional resource material so that instruction may point toward truth and strength rather than toward bias and weakness.

In many classes, the textbook is being supplemented by several additional textbooks beacuse each text treats a topic in a slightly different way, that is, it provides an opportunity for students to meditate, compare, and discuss the topic both among themselves and in class. A problem situation is set up for students to reach a conclusion on their own. Students need to keep up with changes in fact and principle, and this can be done by setting up library and classroom reference lists such as the following: (1) reference books related to course materials, (2) periodicals, (3) bulletins, (4) pamphlets, and (5) newspapers.

THE SELECTION OF INSTRUCTIONAL MATERIALS

The prevailing economy of any community will determine largely the nature of the instructional resources. In rural areas, where dairying may be the principal industry, natural interests will center around the husbandry of a cow that will yield six to seven thousand pounds of milk a year on one and one-half acres for total feed. The nature of this economy will be far removed from that of a highly urbanized community where natural interests might rather center around, perhaps, Western Electric's one-billion-dollar interest in radar or radio-telephone and teletype systems. Somewhere else, management and labor arbitration and the guaranteed annual wage program might be important. In the comprehensive high school, unique combinations of varied natural interests provide the summit of all challenges in the problem of selecting suitable instructional materials. Such a school normally draws together the children of all neighborhoods, all classes, and nationalities—a cross-section of the melting pot that is America. The instructional resources, then, will depend upon the economy of the high school community.

For the purposes of illustration, let us assume that you are to teach in a comprehensive high school since it represents, for the most part, all communities and even offers courses in vocational agriculture. You hold sacred your obligation to every child. There must be no waste in this process because it is expensive. The high school must be effective or the stockholders, the taxpayers, will not continue to support it. What should be the first step?

Analysis of Need. Cumulative records will indicate the students' home backgrounds and experiences, reading levels attained, complete records of achievement in elementary school, and vocational and avoca-tional abilities and aspirations. Highly subjective evaluations will have been made by successive teachers, some of whom were more skilled than others. There will be several intelligence quotient scores. All of this material may be valid, but, on the other hand, it may not. Just as a physician or surgeon who, when examining a patient for the first time, must undertake a complete analysis and diagnosis—regardless of findings by others on the case—so must each teacher re-evaluate the child and his needs.

Someone has recommended that every teen-ager should have at least one adult friend among his teachers during his entire high school life. How might you set about to build and establish such a friendship in terms of obvious need? Such friendships can be built only to a degree. Certainly, in the mass educative process, no teacher can have intimate, person-to-person friendships with hundreds of teen-agers, but an effort to this end will result in at least a few warm, personal relationships that are sincere.

The analysis may reveal many things. Your impressions of one boy may be as follows:

Larry has an extremely low reading comprehension. His median is fourth grade although he is in the eleventh grade of high school. This 18-year-old boy is a victim of retarded maturity, and nothing much can be done about it. Earlier teachers have pressed him too far and then ridiculed him. He has many failures in the record. Shop teachers would not let him operate any power machinery since he would endanger himself and others. Larry's parents operate a neigh-borhood grocery that is not very productive. They keep him at the store at least two days each week and then give him notes that state he was ill. He is on the point of dropping out of high school.

Friendship is a two-way street. As a result of your active interest in Larry, his impressions of you might be as follows:

This teacher taught me how to play checkers during the home room recrea-tional period. One day when it snowed hard, I went out and put the tire chains on his car. I am not as smart as other students, but I will have to study if I want to learn how to operate the store.

What resources will be best to meet Larry at his level and spur him on? Does he like to create models of Conestoga wagons or clipper ships? Would he go into the art museum near his store and bring back an account of what he saw there? Does he ever go hunting, and is he interested in gun collections? Any one of these might be the means to arousing his interest in the study of history.

The analysis of a class will be the result of person-to-person interviews and the administration of diagnostic tests. Over the years, teachers have discovered that in group work it is well to single out the three or four extremes for added attention—the rapid learners who easily achieve the objectives of the class unit and the slow learners who have great difficulty in doing the same work. The least able and the talented students do receive a greater share of attention from the teacher; some have argued that the bulk of attention should be centered upon the so-called average students since they constitute the majority of our society. Other viewpoints are that students in the lower quartile need added help so that they may be self-supporting and less of a social problem as adults. Leadership for tomorrow, it is felt on the other hand, will come from those in the upper quartile, and they must be challenged by higher goals and more varied experiences. The philosophy of the school, plus your own attitudes as to the responsibility of the teacher, will determine where the emphasis, if any, will be placed. This, in itself, will help in the selection of resource material.

Method of Attack. After the first departure from the textbook as the only instructional device, a teacher will begin to explore possibilities that may create more natural learning situations. The range is great, but a few examples given here will illustrate the attack.

Appeal to humor. It has been written that humor is a still, small voice that, on occasion, cries out, "Fiddlesticks!" The strong pull of humor, for teen-agers in particular, is seen in their search for comic books that are genuinely funny, for filmed comedies that are more than slapstick, and for television shows that provide lasting enjoyment. A teacher who lacks a sense of humor will have difficulty in avoiding sarcasm, especially at the expense of a fellow teacher or one of the students. Sarcasm and ridicule do not constitute humor. Both are unfair, for the student who may be singled out for punishment cannot fight back on even terms. The only result of sarcasm within a classroom is a generally uneasy attitude on the part of each student, who may wonder, "Am I next in line?"

On the other hand, tremendous good fellowship can be established when teacher and class together enjoy real humor. The trite treatment by certain historians of the career of Davy Crockett, for example, and of the American Indian or the early pioneer often reaches a point of sheer fantasy. Mountain men had far more to think about than getting up at daybreak to shoot a few more Indians on the run, and this may rightly be observed by teacher and class. Critical thinking may be a pleasant result of an occasional humorous attack. On the other side of the coin, there is no need to turn each section of a course into a "stage show," complete with dancing girls and clowns.

Appeal to ego. Personal illustrations by the teacher tend to make each student want to thrust his own experiences into the scene. In a discussion of personalities who dominate the world of sports, it is likely that the athletes in the class will demand to be heard. They may even undertake outside of class to establish a point—perhaps one that all true athletes have developed the technique of being liked by their public. Again, a project unit that invites the construction of model clipper ships or Conestoga wagons may appeal to the sense of craftsmanship in many students. While certain girls will prefer to build Indian villages or create dress designs for Colonial dolls, the boys will set out to correlate their shop activities with the academic classroom. Each will want to produce the very best—an obvious result of the ego incentive—and the wise teacher will arrange public displays of such enterprise.

Appeal to practicality. It would be a sorry day in the comprehensive high school if a majority of the freshmen boys did not demand to take the auto mechanics course. Almost every normal boy wants to know more about the automobile. Primarily, shop teachers tell us, he wants to take it apart—maybe he will get it together again and maybe not. Ultimately, he will want to improve upon existing models. The strong drive to be practical in such matters is part of a public demand; parents prefer to have their children take specific courses that seem to lead to worthy vocations. Not all boys can be handled in the auto mechanics course at the same time, and they soon understand that related, exploratory courses can be just as practical.

The teacher who will emphasize that an understanding of mathematics is important to engineering an automobile does youth a prime service. There is just as much practicality in the study of English literature, but it must be brought to the attention of all youth—together with tons of evidence in support of the statement. All cultural and background subjects have sufficient practicality for such support.

Readiness for material. As pointed out earlier in the text, there must exist, in the teen-ager and within the teen-age group, an actual desire for learning before any material can be presented with any degree of success. In the example given in a previous chapter, teen-agers, through their written questions, disclosed a real interest in mental health and in marriage problems. It remained for competent psychiatrists to carry out the program which answered their expressed need.

Such readiness need not be delayed until it develops of its own accord. An illustration of the development of a unit was given in Chapter IX, the interdependence of plant and animal life, where Mr. M utilized the curiosity of teen-agers by placing the "little cosmos" within a bottle and sealing it. By this procedure, the readiness of the class was decidedly heightened by a real professional artist.

The arousal of a desire for learning is so essential that still another illustration of how it has been done will be given. This is a brief acccount of a series of actual observations by the authors of the text.

On the first day of this observation, Miss Marjorie Hardy was starting a group of children in the first stages of learning to read. There were just eight children of ages five and six. Miss Hardy was seated on a small chair and the children were seated in a semi-circle about her. She very cleverly managed to get each child in the group to tell a story. The stage had been set for the following day. On the bulletin board in front of the room next day there were eight charts. Each contained in neatly printed form one of the stories that had been told the day before. Since the children already knew their names when printed, each child was invited to find the chart with his name on it. Miss Hardy explained simply and in very few words that this was another way to tell a story. Then she had each child tell his story to her and to the other children by using the chart. She helped them to associate key words they used with the printed words on the chart. Thus, on the second day, each child retold his story to the group and learned that the chart told the same story in writing. Toward the end of the period, Miss Hardy helped the class to understand that in this way one could tell the story to mother even though mother might be in another city.

Separate charts by the third day had been combined into a chart roll on a stand. On this day each child "read" his story again and then was to "read" Billy's (another child's story) from the chart. By the end of the first week, a primer had been introduced. By the end of another three weeks, one primer had been completed and another started. In a short time thereafter, a first reader was introduced and completed. By the end of the semester, the children were ready for more advanced reading.

This approach to learning to read was adjusted to the nature and need of young children. This group quickly made the adaptation to reading because (1) they were ready to learn to read, (2) their first efforts at reading brought them success rather than failure, and (3) Miss Hardy, their teacher, was a highly competent person, especially able in guiding young children in learning to read. This illustration also indicates how to kindle the readiness already present and make it glow.

Availability of material. It would be an excellent instructional procedure to either take a class to the North Pole or to bring the polar cap to the classroom for a learning unit. But the nature of things does not always permit first-hand experiences, and man's life is too short for him to acquire all of his learning that way. A secondary type of learning, which is almost as valuable, can be obtained through presentation of sound films taken by those who have flown over the North Pole and who know some things of interest about the polar cap. Such films must be available for showing as close to the precious "moment of learning" as is possible. A fine sense of timing will enable the teacher to schedule materials far in advance so that the right film, film strip, or recording will be ready for use.

Once the "moment of learning" has passed, any return to it at a later date, say when the delayed materials or resources have arrived, tends to be discounted heavily by the teen-ager. It is "old stuff" that has lost its importance somewhat through the passage of time. Even the unit on mental health and marriage, we suspect, would have suffered if speaker talent from the psychiatric institute had been long delayed.

AIDS AND RESOURCES FOR GROWTH

In the departure from the rigid use of the textbook, there may be seen a tendency on the part of inexperienced teachers to become so interested in a single phase that all other resources are slighted. In the project method, there is a pitfall that may be indicated here. The teacher may enter into such a unit so enthusiastically that he loses sight of the learning outcome desired. We remember two teachers, during World War II, who undertook to have their classes collect copper and tin as a patriotic measure that would help to win the war. Such a highly competitive spirit soon developed between the two that their entire time was ultimately given to the collection of vital war materials, and the basic purposes of their courses were forgotten. There is no place for the whimsical approach in the modern high school. Employment of additional instructional resources is not intended to be, as some critics have said, "a sugar-coating process." Nor should the need for strong application of research and study habits be discouraged. Any variety that is added by the teacher must be a worthy addition and supplement to the learning outcome that is desired.

The Conservatives Object. Those who argue against all projects and other deviations from textbook instruction point out that the nature of high school organization—the physical needs such as opening the school at a given hour, checking the roll, seating a large student body, and transporting and directing many groups and individuals—makes any sort of deviation impractical. A simple question might be asked: Is it worth the effort? Will these students gain more basic skills and attitudes, more knowledge, and more appreciations through departure from the textbook? Or will any change from established routine result in chaos?

Joseph Wood Krutch[4] has reflected the views of those who oppose utilization of devices and materials beyond the textbook and the teacher, and tends to support the traditional method of instruction by writing as follows:

Are what our school principals grandly call "audio-visual aids" usually anything more than concessions to the pupils' unwillingness to make that effort of attention necessary to read a text or listen to a teacher's exposition? Can anything be said in favor of most of them except that they are, at best, a surrender to the delusion shared by children and adults alike that the mechanical techniques of communication are interesting in themselves, no matter what . . . is being communicated? Are they not, at worst, merely devices for "catching" an attention which can never be given freely or held for long?

Thus, at the outset, whether projects, institutes, audiovisual aids, or similar devices and materials are to be utilized, the teacher must be aware of the challenges and the nature of the dangers to worthy scholarship. There may be more than one highway which leads to desired scholarship. To insist upon following but a single trail, merely because it is the traditional approach, would be to admit to other weaknesses. Foremost would be the inability to adjust to changing times which now require the teacher to attract and hold, through positive means, all youth until the eighteenth birthday. Since the lecture-textbook method does not serve all youth, and we suspect it never did, then it follows that some intelligent application of other established devices and materials must be made by the modern high school teacher.

Growth Experiences. Perhaps, the only restrictions to be placed upon any of the following growth experiences would be to determine the type of learning outcome desired, to evaluate the need of the students, and to estimate the readiness of the class for the selected resource material. When these simple steps have been taken, the variety of possible growth experiences includes the following:

Field trips—packing houses, banks, telephone company, railroads, nearby universities, disposal plants, water pumping stations, power plants, military installations, transportation firms, hotels, art centers, museums, school headquarters, power dams, courts and district courts, reformatories, police headquarters.

Experimenting—an outgrowth of the science laboratory—Y-enterprises in stock selling, teen drivers, hobby shows, innovations in student activities (ticket sale promotions, traffic control methods), student courts, hall patrol systems.

Community surveys—door-to-door interviews with housewives on matters related to school welfare, business interviews, labor interviews, housing problems, recreational needs, public health.

[4] Joseph W. Krutch, "If You Don't Mind My Saying So," *American Scholar*, Summer Quarterly 24:348-51, 1955.

Community resources—bringing community problems into the school for hearing: if the transit firm wishes to increase student fares, let spokesmen for all sides state their views.

Utilization of professional and industrial leadership within the classroom.

Drawing upon eyewitnesses of historical events to relate their experiences to the class.

Visiting institutions and firms that provide research data pertinent to the problem at hand.

Obtaining the views of those who need the services of youth, either in business, industry, or in the military.

Listening, speaking, thinking—hearing fine recordings of music, drama, history; delivering oral interpretations; developing new concepts of the nature of the universe and man's place in it.

Playing games—There is more to game activity than afforded by the gym or athletic field. Learning to lose gracefully and to win with dignity can be provided through thousands of established games that are available.

A game of baseball can be played with the spelling of words determining "strikes," "balls," "outs," "runs," etc.

Simple graphs can be made of test scores, points for being on time, or merits for participating in class and school activities.

Reading, study, research, reports, homework—rapid learners need not be given additional work in the same subject-matter area: they may be supplied with reading lists in related areas.

Study can be an honest endeavor participated in by students who earnestly want to achieve knowledge.

Research once begun by a student, with the possible help of a trained librarian, can be a fascinating, life-long endeavor.

Reports, given easily and frankly in a discussion group or before an entire class, serve to develop (1) a personal desire to be intellectually informed, (2) the ability to "think on one's feet," and (3) impart new knowledge to listeners.

Homework is not intended to be "busy work" that will keep the teen-agers off the streets at night. It is a logical extension of school interests which carries into the student's own time; if part-time work is necessary to many students in a class, the proper place of homework should be re-evaluated.

The legal responsibility and liability of the school and teacher is a matter that varies in many states. A desirable course to follow, in any departure from normal school routine, would be to obtain "Parental Permission Slips," a brief permissive note, signed by parents, which authorizes the teen-ager to participate in a properly guided visit to research points outside the school. This note not only informs the home of the whereabouts of the student, but also serves as a measure of good public relations—it lets the public know that the school is attempting to provide realistic learning experiences.

The above are a few of the variations from textbook procedure which may be employed by the teacher who desires to bring about desirable learning outcomes. There are no limits to the possibilities that might be contrived and presented by a teacher who is highly imaginative and competent.

Building Readiness for Resource Materials. It is not always necessary for the teacher to provide a formalized reason for the introduction of any variation from the textbook method. Agricultural communities, for example, work at animal husbandry and soil conservation for reasons that are obvious to all who depend directly upon the land for survival. Teenagers in such areas will accept an animal or soil project without question since it ties up directly with their major interests outside the school. A project in vocational agriculture to build an improved farm trailer would be accepted as a natural outgrowth of the course. However, when projects are not directly related to apparent goals, then some introduction may be necessary.

In the following situation, note how this introduction is achieved, and how the teaching aids and devices discussed in this chapter are used in a natural manner. This incident actually occurred in a rural Nebraska high school.

TEACHER: I didn't have much luck shooting ducks yesterday. Somebody else must have gotten to the Platte River before I did.

KEITH: There's a good backwater you ought to try, just above our farm. I spotted it when we did some contour work there last summer. Great place for ducks. Saw some geese in there, too.

TEACHER: When I can't bring in the ducks, I always manage to get something else that I prize just as much. Have a look at these. (*Shows class a dozen arrowheads*)

KEITH: I know where you got them, all right. There's an old trail up where you were. Dad says the pioneers made it. It's loaded with arrowheads, especially after a rain.

GEORGE: You ought to see the collection we've got. I'll bet there are over a hundred. Good ones, too. Flint rock for sure.

TEACHER: I'll bet, Keith, that you're talking about the Oregon Trail—the same pioneer trail we've been reading about in history.

KEITH: You mean that thing is right here—in Nebraska?

TEACHER: Sure it is. Here, (*lowers map*) let's have a look at the state. Not much here about the Oregon Trail, is there? Wait. I'll find my Pioneer Trail maps. (*Searching in resource file*) Here we are. There's the Oregon Trail, and, Keith, you must live somewhere along about here.

KEITH: Is this the best map we can get? Isn't there a county map?

GEORGE: No, there's no county map because we tried to get one. At least, there wasn't one we could have. Let me tell you about my arrowheads . . .

TEACHER: Later, George. Suppose you get permission to bring the whole collection to school this week—not a hundred or so, as you said, but just a few good ones. Then find out what's in our library on arrowheads. Care to work out a report?

GEORGE: I'll help. Suppose I can have some help?

TEACHER: You are hereby made chairman of the arrowhead committee. Go right on, select your group, and start to work.

KEITH: Why can't I be chairman of a county map committee? We can make a honey—I know all the section lines and the townships.

MARY: We have a history scrapbook. It tells all about the Indian raids.

TEACHER: And raids on the Indians.

MARY: And the Mormon cow, the Ash Hollow massacre, and the burning of Julesburg. Can I be on the committee?

TEACHER: Quiet, all. It now appears that we are ready to bring in added resource material, as it says here in the book. We will take several field trips.

CLASS: Hurrah!

TEACHER: We will prepare maps, exhibits, reports, scrapbooks, and—by the time that is done—we'll even bring in a sound film that shows the pioneers fighting their way along the Oregon Trail. All in favor, say aye.

CLASS: Aye!

TEACHER: And there will even be a test or so, just to see if we learn as much this way as we might with just the textbook.

SUGGESTED SOURCES OF RESOURCES AND MATERIALS

In closing this chapter, it must be indicated that modern society provides a never-ending stream of resource material for the teacher who is alert to this enrichment procedure. Directions for obtaining, evaluating, and selecting such materials follow, together with certain cautions.

Periodicals. Almost every magazine that is at all related to school problems carries a feature similar to "Free for the Asking" in which lists of pamphlets, films, slides, and similar aids are published. Many businesses, through their advertising and public relations departments, will use direct mail to keep you informed as to material that may be of value to you and to your students.

Road Maps. For many years, the Conference Board, 460 Park Avenue, New York 22, N.Y., has supplied teachers with weekly graphs that assist in visualizing economic, social, and political trends. The colored charts are called "Road Maps of Industry," and there is no charge for them.

Funds. From the fund for the Advancement of Education, established by the Ford Foundation, reference data of the highest order is available upon request. Address: 655 Madison Avenue, New York 21, N.Y. Small fees are usually charged for research materials published by the National Education Association, 1201 16th St., N.W., Washington, D.C. So much has been prepared by various Federal Agencies that a special bulletin is regularly issued by the Superintendent of Documents, United States Printing Office, Washington, D.C. From this list, you may select the bulletins that meet your particular need.

Agencies. Local agencies of the Federal government are anxious to serve you and make available needed quantities of pamplets and bulletins upon request. The U. S. Department of Health, Education, and Welfare and the U. S. Department of Agriculture have been particularly active in this service through the Social Security Administration, the Bureau of Old-Age and Survivors Insurance, and the various County Agents. The Treasury Department and the Federal Bureau of Investigation have always been particularly co-operative with the teaching profession.

Catalogs. When the teacher must personally select and place orders for films, film strips, slides, and similar visual materials, it is best to consult complete catalogs which are available in school and public libraries. Or individual catalogs may be obtained from the lending agencies as well as the firms engaged in sale of films. Most universities issue film catalogs and provide films from their own libraries at cost. The United States Chamber of Commerce and the National Association of Manufacturers, together with the rival AFL-CIO, offer up-to-date audio-visual aids.

Displays. Through co-operation with local dentists, physicians, and pharmaceutical representatives, displays that pertain to physical and mental health are available.

News Magazines. In addition to publishers who specialize in school newspapers and magazines, such as Scholastic Magazines and the Civic Education Service (*American Observer, Weekly News Review*) the major news magazines will provide special student rates for school. Wall maps and colored charts are supplied gratis with quantity orders.

Books. The annual editions of the *World Almanac* and the *Information Please Almanac* are most suitable as classroom references.

Bureaus. Through local social service agencies, the teacher may obtain names of co-operating groups who maintain a speaker's bureau for the schools. Aside from periods of wartime emergencies, every firm will welcome student visitations through field trips. An excellent source of such host firms is the list of co-operating businesses supplied at the time of Business-Industry-Education Day, now a nationwide event in most states. In a few instances it is known simply as B-E Day.

Hints. Here are some additional procedures to help you in this area.

1. Build a calendar and schedule materials, speakers, and field trips with a sense of timing.

2. Specify exact materials that will be needed when you write for pamphlets, bulletins, graphs, and charts.

3. Strive for balance in areas where political or business competition may be keen, that is, a film from the NAM might well be balanced by a second film from the labor groups, AFL-CIO.

4. When in doubt as to policy, consult your principal, supervisor, or superintendent. Great harm may be done to worthy planning by school authorities should a teacher inadvertently schedule controversial resources without informing his superiors.

5. Not all firms offer free materials merely in the interest of helping youth; some will intend to exploit teachers and youth, or to capitalize upon natural desires to join "book clubs," "organizations," "thrift banks," and such enterprises. Good judgment and common sense must prevail in determining the differences between worthy services and dishonest enterprises.

Parents. Among the resources sometimes overlooked are the teachers and parents themselves. Look for the veteran on your faculty who was at Pearl Harbor, Dec. 7, 1941; the second veteran who still carries shrapnel scars from World War I; or the teacher who has patented a successful invention, established a record in mountain climbing, or once published a newspaper. It was mentioned in this chapter how pioneer stock is anxious to help teen-agers in school; there will be other parents who can relate stories of personal experiences in the vital areas of Europe, the Middle East, and the Orient. Presentations by parents known to students make the activities of the classroom seem more important to students. Our schools also have parents who are outstanding authors, artists, composers, industrial chemists, athletes—there is no end to this precious resource if the teacher will be aware of it and utilize it fully.

SUMMARY

To bake the cake, one must know the recipe. Once the teacher has added greater variety and wider use of instructional resources to sincere respect for each student as an individual who is just as important as any other individual, plus professional competency, there can be no question of success. To assume that learning for the good life and for vocational efficiency may occur through instruction by an adult who has little regard for individual differences and who feels that the single device of the textbook affords sufficient resource materials would be to remain in the dark ages in education. It is not a question of ease, for the employment of variety and rich resources is a most difficult task; it is rather a question of which is better for the youth of this democracy.

DISCUSSION PROBLEMS

1. Are you sufficiently familiar with library science to set up at least a minimum service in a school that has no library at all?

2. Give the current addresses of the following: National Education Asso-

ciation, National Association of Manufacturers, United States Chamber of Commerce, AFL-CIO, United Nations, National Conference of Christians and Jews, American Red Cross. Such organizations supply specific data and literature of interest to all schools.

3. From current catalogs available in your school library, select six films that would be helpful in the high school course you prefer to teach. Indicate how these might be ordered and list any costs—including postage.

4. To what degree would you utilize television, radio, and recordings in classroom work? What are the necessary steps to be taken so that these devices may be meaningful and worthwhile?

5. What newspapers and magazines should be readily available in the science classroom? Social studies? Mathematics? English?

6. Assuming that psychiatric services are easily available, how would you prepare a public health institute that would be of greatest benefit to the entire school? In drawing up this program, remember that regular classes have been scheduled throughout the week—to what extent might these be interrupted?

7. Check out from your college library copies of several high school textbooks used in one of the courses you plan to teach. Make up a list of criteria for comparing the books based on how you plan to use a textbook in the course.

8. Do you think you will teach as you are being taught to teach or will you teach as you were taught? What bearing does this have on your use of instructional materials in the classroom?

RELATED REFERENCES

Association for Supervision and Curriculum Development, *Toward Better Teaching*, 1949 Yearbook (Washington, D.C., National Education Association, 1949).

———, *Group Planning in Education*, 1945 Yearbook (Washington, D.C., National Education Association, 1945).

ALEXANDER, William M., and HALVERSON, Paul M., *Effective Teaching in Secondary Schools* (New York, Rinehart & Company, Inc., 1956).

ALCORN, M. D., HOUSEMAN, R. A., and SCHUNERT, J. R., *Better Teaching in Secondary Schools* (New York, Henry Holt & Co., Inc., 1954).

BACHMAN, J. W., *How to Use Audio-Visual Material* (New York, Association Press, 1956).

BURTON, William H., *The Guidance of Learning Activities*, 2nd ed. (New York, Appleton-Century-Crofts, Inc., 1952).

Citizenship Education Study (Detroit), *A Curriculum for Citizenship* (Detroit, Wayne University Press, 1953).

CUMMING, W. K., *This Is Educational Television* (Lansing, Mich., Communication Series, 1955).

DALE, Edgar, *Audio-Visual Methods in Teaching* (New York, The Dryden Press, 1947).

DEBERNADIS, Amo, "Tools of Learning," *National Education Association Journal* 40:552-54 (November, 1951).

DEWEY, John, *Experience and Education* (New York, The Macmillan Co., 1938).

Douglass, Harl R., and Mills, Hubert H., *Teaching in High School* (New York, The Ronald Press Company, 1948).

Grambs, J. D., and Iverson, William J., *Modern Methods in Secondary Education* (New York, The Dryden Press, 1952).

Koskey, Thomas A., *Baited Bulletin Boards—A Handbook for Teachers* (San Jose, Calif., Globe Printing Co., 1954).

Krutch, Joseph W., "If You Don't Mind My Saying So," *American Scholar,* *Summer Quarterly* 24:348-51 (1955).

Miller, Neal, *Graphic Communication and the Crisis in Education* (Washington, D.C., National Education Association, 1957).

Mort, Paul R., and Vincent, William S., *Modern Educational Practice* (New York, McGraw-Hill Book Co., Inc., 1950).

Olsen, Edward G., *School and Community* (Englewood Cliffs, N.J., Prentice-Hall, Inc., 1946).

————, *School Community Programs* (Englewood Cliffs, N.J., Prentice-Hall, Inc., 1949).

Olson, Clara A., and Fletcher, Norman D., *Learn and Live* (New York, Sloan Foundation, Inc., 1946).

Rasey, Marie I., *This Is Teaching* (New York, Harper & Brothers, 1950).

Taylor, Bob L., "Make Your Own Slides," *Educational Screen* 33:418 (December, 1954).

University High School, Class of 1938, *Were We Guinea Pigs* (New York, Henry Holt & Company, Inc., 1938).

Wittich, Walter A., and Hanson, G. L., eds., *Educator's Guide to Free Tapes, Scripts, Transcriptions,* 2nd ed. (Randolph, Wis., Educator's Progress Service, 1956).

Wiles, Kimball, *Teaching for Better Schools* (Englewood Cliffs, N.J., Prentice-Hall, Inc., 1952).

PART III

*Some Significant Problems
in Secondary Education*

Chapter 12

REPORTING STUDENT PROGRESS

There was a girl at McMaster
Whose head was alfalfa and plaster;
But she looked like a queen
And she smiled at the dean,
And he marked her paper and passed her!
—C. C. Ross, *Measurement in Today's Schools*

As indicated in the above jingle, marks are a sore point with students and a headache for teachers. Certainly, it would seem that a clearly stated and well-circulated policy on marking practices should clear up any difficulties. However, what clearly stated and well-circulated policy can provide for this problem in the modern American high school where the individual differences of a highly diverse student body must be considered by the teachers? Most youth of high school age are in school. These youth vary widely with respect to their talents. Should teachers set minimum standards in all areas which students must meet in order to pass? Should teachers mark students on the basis of their standing within a class? Or should teachers mark students on the basis of the individual's growth in light of his talents?

This is a problem with which every secondary teacher eventually finds himself confronted. If the American secondary school had a single purpose, such as the preparation of youth for college, it would be far easier to ignore individual differences and adhere to an established standard of achievement or class standing. In the comprehensive high school, individual differences must be considered, and the secondary teacher must think through a marking rationale which does not ignore the wide range of talents and capabilities of his students.

RECOGNITION OF AND ADJUSTMENT TO INDIVIDUAL DIFFERENCES

Human progress depends in part upon the improvement of the tools of evaluation. In our experiment to provide equal educational opportunity for all, we have discovered that a single educational program for all does not provide a common education for all. Teachers in the early part of the twentieth century believed, with some exceptions, that students could by developing their minds become equally competent. These teachers did not believe that individuals differed widely in their ability to learn. By and large, they were unaware of the experimentation even then under way that would make the theory of mental discipline, which they accepted, a questionable one. They were also unaware of such investigations as the one by Judd[1] which indicated that as early man developed number concepts his standard of living improved—number concepts were social tools through which man became more civilized.

Arthur Compton[2] expressed the same idea when he stated:

In 1912, at the University of Chicago, we thought that all of the basic discoveries in physical science had been made. We agreed to spend our time in refining our tools of evaluation. And to our surprise, as soon as we did, we began to make new discoveries.

This refinement of evaluation has been continuous from then until now. The decade of the 1950's has experienced an enormous expansion in the refinement of evaluation, especially in the physical science—the decade of the 1960's holds a promise of a still greater extension of this refinement. More recently these continued refinements of evaluation have been extended to the study of individual differences. And what has been revealed has astounded even the most astute of American educators.

Recognition of Individual Differences. Slowly educators became aware that a class does not learn as a group; it is the individual student within the class who learns. Edward L. Thorndike,[3] in the early part of the twentieth century, made an extensive study of individual differences. Since then individual differences have been under almost continuous examination. For adequate investigation, many tests had to be devised and then refined to achieve a more accurate differentiation. In the world of the engineer, there has been a similar inquiry—the engineers had to reduce the tolerance in measurement from one hundredth to one millionth of an inch before the jet propulsion engine became practical. Also, in education there has been innovation after innovation to reduce the tolerance in our evaluation so that our instructional services might be improved. Everyone recognizes the fact that individual students differ one from another. What has not been so apparent is the number, range, and complexity of individual differences represented in the student body of the American secondary school—almost all youth are in high school. Here are some of the

---

[1] Charles H. Judd, *The Psychology of Social Institutions* (New York, The Macmillan Co., 1926), Ch. 5.

[2] In a lecture, Omaha, Nebraska, 1938.

[3] Edward L. Thorndike, *Individual Differences and Their Causes* (New York, Teachers College, Columbia University, 1926), Vol. III.

ways in which they differ: race, sex, religion, health and physical condition, socio-economic status, emotional make-up, specific traits of character, personal values, special aptitudes and interests, and habits of work and study. Please note that each of the differences mentioned above can be broken down into many separate categories.

The range and depth of individual differences among high school students indicated by the investigations awed the educators—in every classroom the range was wide and deep. They saw that new ways needed to be found for appraising the readiness of every student in each class so that the instruction in all subjects might be adapted to the different strengths and weaknesses of individual students. Gradually, originators began to devise tests to serve the pressing demands. The recognition of individual differences, as a key problem in the solution of many difficult instructional problems, came very slowly to educators. The innovators had to devise the instruments for the identification of the differences. Ultimately, tests were so improved as to reveal both what students can do and the extent to which they have profited by their high school experience.

Maskelyne, who in 1786 was Astronomer Royal at the Greenwich Observatory, noticed his young assistant, Kinnebrook, reported observations of stellar transits that differed from his own by over half a second. When they continued to differ, even after the young man had been told of the discrepancy, Maskelyne felt it necessary to dismiss him. About twenty years later, the German Astronomer, Bessel, took note of the incident. Suspecting its significance, he compared the observations of a number of astronomers of established reputation and found that slight variances or discrepancies were the rule. In other words, there are individual differences among observers in reaction time required for the highly complex process of noting and estimating the instant a star crosses a hairline in the field of telescope.[4]

That we are not alike was completely established by the Greenwich Observatory discovery. During the long interval between then and now, research and experimentation in psychology and education have conclusively verified the basic principle that individual differences among students are normal, extensive, and applicable to all humans. No two human beings are ever exactly alike. Yet teachers in their everyday activities have barely begun to recognize the wide range of individual differences existing in their own classrooms. Especially is this true for the process of marks and marking.

The Modern High School Adjusts Its Program to Individual Differences. The premise of *EDUCATION FOR ALL YOUTH*[5] proposes that edu-

[4] Edna Heidbreder, *Seven Psychologies* (New York, Appleton-Century-Crofts, Inc·, 1933), p. 7.
[5] Educational Policies Commission, *Education for All American Youth—A Further Look*, revised (Washington, D.C., National Education Association, 1952), p. 30.

cational opportunity be provided for all. It has been established as true that youth differ widely in such competencies as verbal communication, computation, mechanical manipulation, memorization and retention of facts, symbols, and images, and arriving at generalizations.[6] The *modern high school* will recognize and adapt its instruction to a wide range of individual differences.

Table 14 shows the wide range of individual differences in intellectual aptitude for one comprehensive high school; it is probable that an equally wide range of individual differences for this group of students would be found for all of the ways in which students might differ. However, the range of individual differences in this school will not be much greater, perhaps even less than in the high school where you will be employed as a teacher. In general, it is true that a wide range of individual differences will be found in any high school, whether it be public, private, or parochial. Indeed, the range will be wide regardless of whether the students come from either upper- or lower-class homes.[7]

Because there are certain difficulties in the usual high school, try to answer the five questions below so as to adjust the program of the school to the individual differences among the students. What will be best for each student?

1. Should a student with low achievement that is the result of low ability ever receive the same mark as a student of high achievement that is the result of high ability?

2. To what extent should a school differentiate between a high mark in a common learnings course and a high mark in a special or academic course?

3. Should a student be made aware of his actual standing with respect to a skill such as reading?

4. Should the school formulate a policy that would eliminate certain students from certain classes?

5. How might we explain the apparent paradox seen when a student who fails in general and special courses becomes a leader and a good citizen as an adult?

If we desire to adjust our instruction according to the needs of individual students, what should be our decision in each of the following cases?

A victim of polio who is badly crippled obviously will have difficulty in meeting the standard requirements in physical education that have been set up for normal students. And yet, when the course is modified by

---

[6] George K. Bennett, Harold G. Seashore, and Alexander Wesman, *Differential Aptitude Tests* (New York, Psychological Corporation, 1947).
L. L. Thurstone, and Thelma G. Thurstone, *Primary Mental Abilities* (for ages 11 to 17) (Chicago, Science Research Associates, Inc., 1947).
[7] Social Implications of the 1947 Scottish Mental Survey, London, England, University of London, Ross, 1953, reported in Segel, David; Wellman, Frank E.; and Hamilton, Allen T., *An Approach to Individual Analysis in Educational and Vocational Guidance* (Washington, D.C., U. S. Department of Health, Education, and Welfare, 1958), pp. 15-16.

Table 14. A Study of Intellectual Aptitude in a Comprehensive High School*

A tabulation of intelligence quotients for all students in one high school is provided in the table which follows. This distribution was based on the Terman-McNemar Test of Mental Ability. The median intelligence quotient is 112.3. As a result of this distribution there were 199 students in eight class groups registered in General English.

RANGE	NINTH GRADE		TENTH GRADE		ELEVENTH GRADE		TWELFTH GRADE		TOTAL
	BOYS	GIRLS	BOYS	GIRLS	BOYS	GIRLS	BOYS	GIRLS	
150 and up	2	1	2	–	–	2	–	–	7
145–149	–	–	3	–	–	2	2	2	9
140–144	2	3	3	3	3	3	4	1	22
135–139	2	2	2	6	2	9	2	4	29
130–134	3	10	12	4	10	4	7	12	62
125–129	13	18	12	19	11	20	14	12	119
120–124	24	27	17	33	18	10	13	17	159
115–119	28	31	25	34	30	24	23	21	216
110–114	20	28	33	17	25	22	13	14	172
105–109	33	27	26	21	27	16	13	26	189
100–104	21	22	20	10	13	17	17	18	138
95– 99	25	15	21	15	12	12	12	12	124
90– 94	15	6	12	9	14	7	12	5	80
85– 89	2	6	12	3	13	8	5	3	52
80– 84	9	3	1	3	–	1	2	3	22
75– 79	4	1	1	3	2	–	1	1	13
70– 74	1	2	1	2	3	2	2	3	16
65– 69	1	–	1	1	–	1	–	–	4
60– 64	–	–	1	–	–	–	–	–	1
55– 59	–	–	1	–	–	–	1	–	2
Total									1,436

* A near-by academic high school, which students may elect to attend, attracts many above-average and high-ability students from this community.

devising specific objectives to meet special needs, physical education can be of great value to a polio victim. If the teacher does make this modification and if the student works hard and profits, should the polio student be required to take the standard test administered to other students in the course? Or should it be a test that is based upon the modified objectives set up for him? If a special test is built in accord with special objectives for polio victims and if the student receives a good score, should he be given a very high mark for superior achievement or a near-failing mark because of his inability to achieve the standard set for the class? Should there be a recognition of individual differences in all tests employed in a class, just as there is recognition in teaching and instruction?

A study of the intelligence test scores from such a test as the Terman-McNemar Test of Mental Ability, given in Table 14, reveals to a decided extent the aptitude for general education of the students in all classes. In a twelfth-grade American Government class we may find a girl with an intelligence quotient in the 55-59 range and two boys and two girls with intelligence quotients in the 145-149 range. The range between the lowest and the highest intelligence quotients in the class is 90 points. Since a course geared to the all-school average of 112.3 I.Q. would hardly serve these extremes in intellectual ability, what should a teacher do to adjust his course outline to the abilities of all students in the class?

America is on the move. The American people are rapidly recognizing and adjusting to automation, missiles, jet-propelled planes, and other recent inventions. Education for youth must reflect this national adjustment to modern discoveries. The high school, too, must make changes. Through research, it has been discovered that we are not alike—each is a unique individual. In secondary education we recognize and adjust the program of the high school to the varying needs and abilities of individual students. Mass education for all can be provided only by the maintenance of a good education for each. Hence, we must know the peculiar needs of each. A student can no longer be assigned to a shop course arbitrarily because he is failing in Algebra I. Success in a shop course, where definite standards prevail, also requires specific aptitudes on the part of the student failing in Algebra I. Such a reassignment requires a careful study by the director of guidance of all records to discover the areas where the student has potential strengths.

To the modern high school teacher, the purpose of high school education is to change the behavior of youth. Such behaviors as the following are sought: (1) the student can and does co-operate with others; (2) he supports before others the right of each person to freedom of speech and expression, freedom to worship God in his own way, freedom from want, and freedom from fear; (3) he is prepared to earn a living; (4) he is competent and active in civic affairs; and (5) he is physically fit.

Behavior changes such as those mentioned above can be attained only when instruction is directed toward such outcomes. Because the modern teacher has an increasingly better insight into the nature of the learning process, outcomes sought, and individual differences, he has come to insist that students must be able to use what they have learned. Also, because the development of personality is so highly prized by both parents and employers, some modern high schools require that teachers must specifically provide for its development and make an appraisal of how well they succeed. In Chart 16 a few of the most common procedures for the evaluation of personality are listed and briefly explained.

MODERNIZING MARKS AND MARKING

Progress, man's distinctive mark alone.—Browning

The perpetual desire for recognition or to know "How well I am doing" is universal. It is just as dominant among the politically powerful as among the lowly. The major professions—medicine, engineering, the military,

Chart 16. A Few Procedures for the Evaluation of Personality

ANECDOTAL RECORDS

The teacher keeps a folder for each student where records of significant behavior such as co-operation, verbal expressions, attitudes, participation in classrooms, and other activities are kept.

A review of these records at the end of the year or the semester reveals changes in attitudes and interests. For example, the James Jones file:

10/31 Strongly supported the right of the KKK to organize.

11/16 Questioned the right of any citizens to take the law into their own hands.

THE INTERVIEW

Person-to-person interviews, teacher-to-teacher interviews, teachers-to-student interviews, teacher-to-parents interviews. All interviews to be about students for improved understanding.

Two or three interviews for each student during the year provides evidence of changes in attitudes and interests. Notes on each interview are filed in the student's folder and keep the vividness of each interview alive. A comparison of the interviews at the end of the year will provide evidence of changes in areas of personality not touched by tests.

OBSERVATIONS

Observations by the teacher of the attitudes and actions of students in classroom and hallways and on the street.

A record of such observations about behavioral changes placed in the cumulative folder becomes of great value for rating personality development and growth in citizenship of all students.

A SIX-STEP RATING SCALE FOR THE APPRAISAL OF STUDENT PARTICIPATION

1	2 Partici-	3	4 Passively	5	6
Participates in all activities	pates in most activities	Passively carries out most activities	carries out a few activities	Actively resists participating in a few activities	Actively resists most activities

Used by a coach or teacher to help a team or a class to become aware of its behavior

The scale can be applied to a class, a small group, or an individual. A student can be rated by both himself and his teacher: then any difference between the ratings can be discussed. A student is helped to see himself as others see him. This is a superior instrument for evaluating objectives that slip by other rating devices.

THE SOCIOGRAM

A device to help a teacher discover the social relationships within a class: it can reveal the cliques, the isolates, and those with the greatest influence. A repeat administration of the sociogram later reveals changes in social development—attitudes, interests, skills.

Students are asked to reply to a question such as: You are now seated alphabetically. Some of you have said that you would like to change seats to be near your friends. List in order of preference whom you would like to sit with or near.*

* Commission on Teacher Education, *Helping Teachers Understand Children* (Washington, D.C., American Council on Education [NEA], 1945).

law, the ministry, and teaching—all have their specific symbols by which differences in performance are recognized. For the high school, marks are the symbols by which differences in performance are recognized. Parents and students alike demand ratings that clearly indicate the status of each student in every class.

Yet, for the teacher, marking is the least liked of all professional duties.[8] Why is this true? It is true because both the students and their parents tend to hold the teacher accountable for any low marks received, while assuming that high marks are earned entirely through the industry of the students. Also, marking differs from most of the teacher's other duties, in that, while he is free to determine when to administer tests or in selecting and constructing tests, he must conform to practices within the school in reporting grades to parents.

A goodly number of high schools are experimenting with marks and marking with the avowed purpose of improving their marking systems. However, the improvement or modernization of the high school curriculum, classroom instruction, measurement, and other features of the high school program should precede or accompany the improvement of the marking system.[9] The problem of determining the student's marks or an index of achievement brings into contrast two theories of learning: (1) The older approach to education is the mastery of assigned segments of a subject arranged in a series of steps. Marks are assigned largely on the basis of teacher judgment as to how well the materials have been retained (2) The modern approach to education is the progressive development of personal-social-moral traits, understanding, attitudes, and appreciations of the learner. Marks are usually accompanied by a description of the student's actual achievement of functional learning outcomes.[10]

What are the purposes of marks? Every modern teacher must answer this question for himself honestly and frankly. There are some purposes about which most agree:

1. To inform parents and students of the quality of work being done and the progress being made. The mark must convey to parents and students an accurate and complete view of growth. (Common agreement by all on this purpose)

2. To enable the home and school to work together more effectively on the common problem of encouraging learning. (The purpose of marks is co-operation between home and school.)

3. To motivate or stimulate students to continued or greater effort. (A purpose emphasized by the conservative school—the mark is payment for

<hr />

[8] Dorothy DeZouche, "The Wound Is Mortal: Marks, Honors, and Unsound Activities," *Clearing House* 19:339-44 (February, 1945).

[9] *Marks* and *marking* are synonymous terms for *grades* and *grading*—either usage is acceptable. A teacher will follow the usage of the community where employed.

[10] William H. Burton, *The Guidance of Learning Activities*, 2nd ed. (New York, Appleton-Century-Crofts, Inc., 1952), p. 657.

effort. To the modern school, the mark indicates the growth or improvement made.)

4. To provide the administration with a simple system for classification, promotion, and certification to higher institutions of learning. (This purpose is less prominent today. The modern college accepts a student on the recommendation of the principal or the composite recommendations of the school staff—not on the basis of grades.)

The Common Marking Practices. What are the most commonly employed marking practices? There are three main marking practices: (1) the letter grade, (2) the numerical system, and (3) a combination of the first two plus a subjective evaluation of the more intangible objectives of the course or courses being taught.[11]

The letter-marking system. The most widely used marking system in the United States employs five letters: A for excellent, B for above average, C for average, D for below average, and F for failure. A modification of the letter-marking system, used in many schools, substitutes numbers for letters. Such schools use 1 for A, 2 for B, 3 for C, 4 for D, and 5 for F. It is estimated that 75 per cent of the American high schools employ the letter-marking system or some modification of it.

Some high schools designate finer gradation by additional letters, such as a seven- or nine-letter scale rather than a five. Others obtain the same results with a plus or minus after each of the five letters or numbers. Again only three letters may be used, an H for honors, an S for satisfactory, and a U for unsatisfactory. However, many teachers and more than a few parents object to the three-letter system because it tends to include too large a percentage of students in the average gradation. Although a two-letter system seems sufficient for nursery schools and kindergarten, it has not been accepted by the upper elementary and secondary schools. The five-letter system has the advantage of wide acceptance; yet it has the disadvantage of attempting to classify a wide range of achievement under a single mark.

The numerical system. The four common numerical systems are the percentage, rank order, percentile rank, and standard scores. The systems are described in Chart 17.

Normalized standard scores give statistically more meaningful marks and statistically fairer marks than other common numerical marking systems, such as percentages and percentiles. Standard scores indicate the student's standing within a group, and when averaged they are not unrealistically affected by extreme scores in distributions with large standard deviations. However, the usual classroom teacher has neither the mathematical ability nor the time to work out normalized standard scores for every set of papers which he grades.

On the other hand, it is usually not difficult to arrive at the rank position

[11] All of these systems are gradually being modernized.

Chart 17. The Common Numerical Systems

THE PERCENTAGE MARKING SYSTEM

This system has been long in use and is popular with parents. It is flexible enough so that percentages may be adjusted somewhat to the difficulty of the tests.

A theoretically perfect paper is given the mark of 100. The marks are based upon an absolute standard and not upon growth or achievement. It is employed with the essay-type examination where it is assumed that a student can write a perfect paper.

THE PERCENTILE RANK SYSTEM OF MARKING

This system of marking is an innovation of recent years. It is easily explained. The percentile rank score does not reveal what the person earning the score can do.

A percentile rank mark indicates the percentage of the class excelled by any one student: thus, if there are 98 students in a class, the fiftieth percentile is the point below which 49 of the students will fall. It does show an individual's standing within a specified group.

THE RANK ORDER SYSTEM OF MARKING

This system is employed by such schools as the U. S. Military Academy at West Point. Since classes in our American high schools vary greatly in size, this system is not a popular one in our high schools.

Students are ranked in the order of achievement: thus, in a class of 30 students, the student with highest achievement earns a rank of "1," while the one with the lowest achievement earns a rank of "30."

THE STANDARD SCORES SYSTEM OF MARKING

In general the standard scores system of marking tends to correct the defects found in all other systems; it is probably the most reliable of all. If the class distribution is approximately normal, standard scores are easy to interpret. Otherwise, a mastery of phases of statistics is necessary.

Each mark is determined by its position in standard steps or deviations from the class average. One practice is to establish the mark of "50" as the mean or average grade with three standard deviations of ten above and below the mean. Thus, the range of marks in a large class would be as follows: 20, 30, 40, 50 (average), 60, 70, 80. The mark of any one student could fall at any point between 20 and 80

of a test paper within a set of test papers. Raw scores or a simple grouping of papers will give this. Having established the rank position of each paper within the set, the assumption may be made that the variable ranked is normally distributed. A rank-order table of T-scores can be used to convert the rank of the paper in the set of papers to a normalized standard score. While the normalized standard scores taken from a rank-order table are not quite as accurate as those actually computed, the error is neglible, and by using a rank-order table, any teacher can use T-scores in his grading.

The Merging Marking Systems. There is an urgent demand by the public that cannot be denied for an appraisal of the social and emotional development, as well as for an evaluation of intellectual development.

Letter marks are now popular; probably because this system is, outwardly at least, a practical short cut for overloaded teachers. The percentage system, previously popular, is fading away; it now has status only in a few high schools. The percentile and standard scores systems are still largely on an experimental basis. The principle of distributing grades according to the normal frequency curve is still followed in some classrooms, even though the principle of the curve is not applicable to small class groups. Forget the curve where possible, and distribute grades according to the progress and achievement of individual students.

Characteristics of a Sound Marking System. What are the attributes of a sound marking system? One requisite is that misleading, unessential factors be excluded from the determination of the *mark*. Studies show that girls get higher marks or grades than boys, though boys have similar, if not higher, I.Q. scores than girls. The chance that boys will fail is 2¼ times that of girls; girls, because of this bias in grading by teachers, are consequently better able to get into the honor society than boys. At the same age, girls are socially, emotionally, and physically, but not intellectually, more mature than boys. Also, they are more apt to be clean in personal habits and appearance.[12] A similar study revealed that discrimination often operates against students from minority groups and from lower socio-economic status groups.[13] The implication is clear: evaluation of growth and learning must be a measure of what the individual himself has accomplished and not distorted by the teacher's feelings about the group to which the individual belongs.

A second requisite of a sound marking system is defining the symbols. Actually, the mark is a symbol that informs the student and the parent of the growth that has been made in a specific course. Assuming that the symbols to be employed are A, B, C, D, and F, then the A symbol might carry this description: (1) The student shows an intelligent comprehension of the subject content. (2) The student can apply the subject content learned to new problems. (3) The student organizes his work well. (4) The student performs required skills with a high degree of precision. Likewise, the descriptive marking scale would provide a description for each of the other symbols of B, C, D, and F. If for each course handled the teacher were to develop a descriptive marking scale, the teacher, students, and parents all would know what the symbols in the marking system meant.[14]

[12] George Johnson, "Girls Lead in Progress Through School," *American School Board Journal* 95:23-26 (October, 1937).

[13] A. B. Hollingshead, *Elmtown's Youth* (New York, John Wiley & Sons, Inc., 1949), pp. 172-73.

[14] Burton, *op. cit.*, pp. 658-663.

Grambs and Iverson state the situation clearly as follows:

The whole process of grading is a deep dark mystery and the teacher is the only person who has the clue . . . Where such a situation exists, obviously the student can not learn a major lesson for competency, that is, to appraise accurately his own achievement.[15]

Describing the mark is but one step in the improvement of marking. Ultimately, the symbols now employed as marks will, in all probability, be replaced by descriptive statements about the individual student. These statements will show the student's progress, strengths, shortcomings, and difficulties. Better communication between the parent and teacher concerning the progress of the student should be the purpose of any change in marking practice.

There are many additional competencies, beyond those mentioned above, that will be required from the teacher by a modern marking system. Certainly, the teacher will give much more attention to gathering and compiling data as a basis for the mark. The evidence upon which the mark is based must go beyond the daily recitation, homework papers, tests, and mid-semester and final examinations averaged. Additional evidence such as the reliability and validity of tests and examinations as well as evidence as to what the tests and examinations measured is needed. Did the tests and examinations measure only memorized details and facts or did they also measure understandings derived and the ability of students to apply what has been learned to problems? Do these tests determine real changes in behavior or just verbal manifestations of change?

A modern marking system requires an understanding of educational measurement by teachers, as well as the application of its principles to the marks given. Ultimately, marks as symbols, whether letters, numbers, or other types, should be replaced by a brief and concise description of the student's achievements. These descriptive scales can be developed over a period of years by teachers in any school system. If statements of the educational product can be simply and briefly stated, there will be no mystery about what a mark means.

Over the years, many teachers have added to or subtracted from a mark in accordance with whether a student was co-operative, put forth effort, persisted in his attack upon assignments, or paid attention to the explanations. There are many desirable attitudes and traits that a student should be encouraged to develop. However, a mark in Algebra I or in any academic course must reveal achievement in the course for which the mark is given. Any mark given in Algebra I must evaluate achievement in Algebra I only; progress in Algebra II is dependent upon the skills and understandings acquired in Algebra I—a mark must reveal what these understandings were.

[15] Jean D. Grambs, and William J. Iverson, *Modern Methods in Secondary Education* (New York, The Dryden Press, 1952), p. 380.

Many high schools have found a solution to the problem of the recognition of desirable attitudes and traits by providing extra spaces on report cards for supplementary ratings on attitudes and traits. Growth and development in desirable personal traits and attitudes are legitimate learning outcomes; the student should be evaluated on his growth and development in these as well as in the formal subject outcomes.

MODERNIZING REPORTS TO PARENTS

There is one very happy aspect involved in attempting to bring about improvement in marking practices—whatever you may do has little likelihood of being more objectionable than the practice it replaces.
—WILLIAM L. WRINKLE

The Need to Inform Parents of Student Progress. Parents are the employers of teachers; they provide the school buildings and all instructional facilities, and through the school board determine what they want taught. Yet many of these parents did not fare too well in school. They were burned and hurt by teachers in earlier and more rugged decades. These feelings about their teachers, in part, still guide their relations with their children's teachers. Also, teen-agers are in a period of development where they are breaking the ties of dependence upon parents. In many homes this causes considerable tension between teen-agers and parents. Teen-agers are likely to be evasive about their work at school, and when pressed behave as mother and father do when a neighbor is prying into the private affairs of the family. Also, during the last decade, the high school has been excoriated by hundreds of articles and books; some well intended and others meant only to bring a quick profit to the author. This, too, has made parents anxious to know more about what the high school is teaching.

When all of the above factors are operating, a few parents get the jitters, many feel anxious, and most desire to know what the high school is teaching—in areas of the intangibles as well as in the subjects being studied. Every report to parents should provide this information. Does a mark of 90 in English or a B in algebra tell the parent what John is learning?[16] While most high schools have outlined the objectives of the high school and each course offered, few parents take the time to understand them. Frequently, these objectives are written in professional language. Teachers think of these objectives or of the outcomes sought as changes in student behavior. Brief descriptive statements on each report to parents in language which the parent comprehends would indicate what the student can do and is doing in every scheduled course.

[16] The use of such symbols as A, B, C, D, and F are legitimate for the permanent record of the high school—the principal can interpret them. But do they give the parent the accurate information needed?

Some random illustrations of descriptive statements are outlined:

1. Extent of student's achievement of the general objectives
   a. Works with others easily and effectively
   b. Plans work, gets to work promptly, and concentrates on the job at hand
   c. Reads with ease and understanding
   d. Is self-reliant and requires a minimum of supervision
   e. Needs to complete work and turn it in on time
2. Extent of student's achievement of subject-matter objectives
   a. Social studies: can explain the essential differences in theories of social-economic-political organization or the differences between democracy, fascism, and communism
   b. Mathematics (algebra): can select and apply principles to new situations
   c. Business education: effectively files materials and finds materials which have been filed
   d. Music: uses correct rhythm in singing and playing
   e. Science: constructs and interprets graphs, tables, charts, and diagrams

Improvement of Reports. Every high school in the United States is unique in that it serves a unique community and is controlled by an elected community board of education. So the improvement of reports to parents can never be a standardized procedure, it must always be in accord with the prejudices of parents and teachers and the peculiar needs of students and the community.

What is the key to improving reports to parents? We know that the end product of all educative experience is the modification of student behavior; therefore, to improve the reports to parents, we need to establish educational objectives as the desired behavior.[17] In Chart 18 several illustrations are given that demonstrate how earlier educational objectives are modified to fit this modern concept.

The problem of improving reports to parents involves two issues: (1) the complete elimination of letter and number symbols from the report card—only the brief statements of educational objectives achieved will be placed upon the report—or the letter and number symbols can be retained and supplemented by statements of educational objectives, and (2) the formulation of modern statements of educational objectives so that they make sense to students, parents, and teachers—based on the peculiar needs of students and community. The improvement of the high school curriculum, the quality of educational and community leadership, and the quality of the instruction in the high school should be linked with the improvement of reports to parents.

[17] William L. Wrinkle, *Improving Marking and Reporting Practices* (New York, Rinehart & Company, Inc., 1947), pp. 93-99.

Chart 18. Pre-Modern Versus the Modern Statements of Educational Objectives

PRE-MODERN STATEMENTS OF OBJECTIVES—USUALLY PHRASED TO INDICATE WHAT STUDENTS KNOW OR HAVE LEARNED	MODERN STATEMENTS OF OBJECTIVES—USUALLY PHRASED TO INDICATE WHAT STUDENTS CAN DO AND WILL DO
1. He knows how to spell.	1. He spells correctly.
2. He knows the relationship between past and present history.	2. He participates actively in the discussion of local political and social problems because he understands past and present history.
3. He learns good work habits in the food laboratory.	3. He practices good work habits in the food laboratory.

An essential factor for the improvement of reports to parents is to set up educational objectives in terms of behavior changes—the end product of all educative experience is the modification of behavior.[18] Can objectives be set up this way? Yes, it can be done. The statement, "He spells correctly," is clearly a statement of an objective that discloses a behavior change. Now, look at this statement, "He knows the relationship between past and present history." The statement of a course objective indicates clearly what a student can do after he has achieved an objective. Does the verb *know* in the above sentence indicate clearly what the student can and does do with his knowledge of the relationship between past and present history? However, if the statement were changed to read, "The student participates actively in the discussion of political and social problems because he understands the relationship between past and present history," it would indicate clearly what he can and does do. Here is another attempt to state an objective indicating a behavior change, "He learns good work habits in the food laboratory." But does this objective clearly state what the student can and does do? As a parent or a teacher, would you be satisfied with a student merely learning good work habits? Certainly, it would be a more understandable and clearly stated objective if it were to read, "He practices good work habits in the food laboratory."

To state an adequate educational objective, a teacher must be aware that the purpose of every educational objective is to change or modify student behavior. When behavior changes, the activities of students change or are modified. Then, because the teacher is stating educational objectives that indicate behavioral changes, action words such as *spell, practice,* or *participate* supplant such passive words as *know* and *learn.* For the most part, the verbs employed in the statement of adequate educational objectives will be transitive (action) verbs, while those employed in stating the inadequate educational objectives will usually be intransitive verbs. Educational objectives are formulated to indicate clearly what the student can and will do. If for any objective set up, a teacher can give

[18] *Ibid.,* pp. 93-99.

a positive answer to each of the following questions, he can feel confident that the objective is valid and will be understood by parents. These are the questions:

1. Will this objective be understandable to all of the parents of your students?
2. Is the objective stated as an acquired behavior?
3. Is the objective based upon the needs of the learner?
4. Can the objective really be achieved?
5. Is the objective socially desirable?
6. Can the achievement of this objective actually be appraised?[19]

Every teacher should set up a list of objectives which are important to the subject-matter area in which he teaches. His efforts will achieve greater reward if he works co-operatively with those other teachers who are also teaching in his subject-matter area. Usually, though not always, there will be fewer "bugs" in a list of objectives so formulated. The teacher should encourage other teachers and parents to criticize such lists of objectives in order that these criticisms may give better insight into official and community desires. Once these lists of objectives are formulated and clearly understood by all concerned, the teacher is in a position to answer more effectively the questions of parents, and he is in even a better position to find answers to some of his own disturbing questions.

CHARACTERISTICS OF GOOD REPORTING

Students of this problem suggest the following tips with respect to the preparation of the report. Reports to parents need to do more than give a concise statement of the student's progress in academic subjects. Most parents want to know why the student is not making the expected progress and what they can do to help. Reports are poor when (1) teachers have failed to observe the social and emotional changes in individual students and (2) teachers are unaware that the report has decided communicative value to parents. The wrong kind of a report can do much harm to an over-conscientious student by the inclusion of minor unfavorable details or by details that are inaccurate. A teacher must be able to support by facts any statements which are included.

What, then, are some of the characteristics of adequate reports to parents? The following questions are proposed as standards for appraising reports to parents.

1. Have your methods of reporting to parents been developed co-operatively? An old adage among democratic people maintains that if a plan affects several people, all of them should co-operate in reaching a decision on it. The report to parents does affect the parents, the students, and the school. Hence, this general principle does apply to the preparation

[19] *Ibid.*, p. 97.

of the report. Unless parents, teachers, and students help to formulate a plan for the report, they will not fully understand it. If they do not understand why each item is important and how it will be used, they will not give it the attention it deserves. The co-operative report utilizes parents, teachers, and students in the formulation of a report card that will answer this question, "What is the school trying to do for the student and what kinds of growth are most important?" They also need to answer this question, "Which of these developments is best for the student (1) to see how the student compares with other students or (2) to see how the student is growing up?"

Teachers and parents on committees can become deeply involved in this problem concerning the improvement of reports to parents. What is more, they educate each other and develop a reporting form that both can understand. Therefore, it is better for a high school to develop its own report forms than to copy the form used by other schools. Incidentally, if teachers discuss the report with students, explain what the school is trying to do, and how the report can be helpful, students understand and accept them. This is especially true if teachers draw students into a discussion over improving the reports to parents. Students then make constructive suggestions, some of which may be incorporated into the report. There is considerable evidence to show that the modern diagnostic report, properly developed, is acceptable to students because it gives them information about themselves that they need.[20]

2. Does your report to parents show progress in the kinds of behavior important for persons in our American society? Does it show whether the student is growing healthier, more co-operative, more able to express ideas, and more capable in acquiring ideas to express?

3. Is your report to parents accurate? Are the statements made objective? Attendance has not been satisfactory when a student has had several absences. Avoid making any statements that cannot be supported by substantial evidence. A teacher holds a responsible position and is a responsible person; accurate reports support this public ideal, while inaccurate reports destroy it.

4. Are your reports to parents constructive? Do they help to build rather than tear down? Do they suggest how progress can be made? Constructive comments take the sting out of low marks. If a mark is accompanied by specific suggestions as to how the student may do better next time with a maximum of encouragement, it is less likely to cause a feeling of inferiority. But what is suggested must be in the realm of the possible.

5. Is your report easily understood by different parents in your community? Does it speak their language? In some communities there is a wide range of educational backgrounds among parents—all of the way

[20] Ruth Strang, *Reporting to Parents* (New York, Bureau of Publications, Teachers College, Columbia University, 1947), pp. 3-7 and 52-53.

from being illiterates to being professional people. In such situations, the simple report must be supplemented by letters in some instances and by conferences in others. Yet most parents like the simple reports. And it is likely that they will do something constructive about a relatively few points where improvement is possible.

6. Do your students share in the writing of their own reports? For the high school teacher, who meets 100 to 150 students daily, individual conferences to discuss reports to parents will be too time-consuming. But, for the homeroom or core teacher, a discussion of reports to parents is easily possible. Of course, every teacher will find time to have conferences with a few students with learning difficulties—this is an intrinsic part of the teaching process.

Yet, if the teacher will set up objectives as behavior changes with a class, it will be natural for students to try to determine how successful they have been in the attainment of the objective. A part of a class period can be set up for having each student evaluate himself on a form report to parents and, when completed, he can submit it to the teacher. On the whole, students are surprisingly accurate in the estimation of their marks —their estimates are nearly identical to those of the teacher. Do not force students to evaluate themselves. They will ask to do this, or agree to help only as they grow and become more mature. In cases where their ratings of themselves are highly inaccurate, the teacher must find time to discuss the rating with the individual student. To the extent that a student can become more objective in his ratings, he better understands both the goals sought and his progress toward the goals. Such an understanding is the first step in growing up or maturing.

Methods of Reporting. Reports to parents can be one of the most useful instruments for the personalization of education and the guidance of students. What procedures do the schools follow in making these reports? The three most widely employed are: (1) report cards mailed or carried to the home by the students, (2) conferences with parents, and (3) letters to parents.

The method of reporting most extensively employed and the *least* helpful is the report card. Most parents make very ineffective use of the report card. Some are indifferent to it, sign it, and return it without knowing or caring about what was recorded on the card. Others blame the teacher for their son's or daughter's lack of progress. A few parents take a laissez-faire attitude or one of amused tolerance toward it. Still others are primarily interested in comparing their child's report with those of the neighbor's children. However, a goodly number are appreciative and co-operative.

As a result of these parental attitudes, there has been extensive research by school people to find ways for improving the report card. Reports have been written in teacher rather than parent language. A mark of *A* can not easily be interpreted by a parent; it may mean that his boy who received an *A* is superior to his neighbor's boy who received a *B*. But, if progress is expressed in simple statements of behavior changes according to the goals of the school, the emphasis is placed upon specific growth or the development of the student which is the real purpose of the school.

Although the report card can be greatly improved by modernizing it, a dynamic teacher in conference with the parent can interpret the work of the school more adequately than any report card. A teacher with warmth and charm can answer parental questions with a clarity that a report card always lacks. In such a conference, the parent comes to perceive that the work of the school is to bring about behavior changes in the students as they achieve the goals of the school. Hence, the parent-teacher conference is by far the best method of explaining the goals of the school to the parent.

However, a teacher must make specific preparation for the parent-teacher conference. It requires a reflective study of the student's cumulative records and a consolidation of all the information about a particular student. As a representative of the school who wants to create favorable home-school relations, the teacher must possess personality and interviewing skill. He must be able to answer questions about what the school is trying to do and how the parent can help the school. In this face-to-face relationship, the teacher will help the parent understand that the school places a major emphasis upon the guidance of student growth. The school does not pass judgment upon the student; it helps him set up goals and assists him in achieving these goals. The report to parents is a progress report which indicates the advance made, as well as some difficulties that parents and teachers working in co-operation can reduce or eliminate. The parents and the school comprise a team whose purpose is to support students in their attempt to achieve goals that students, as well as parents, and teachers deem desirable. Through the parent-teacher conference, the parent gains a better understanding of what the school is trying to do, and the teacher gains a better insight into the home, both its strengths and its weaknesses, as an institution that serves to produce effective adolescent growth toward maturity.

Yet, reports to parents via the parent-teacher conference are a near impossibility for high school teachers. With an instructional load of five to eight classes, with inadequate student records, and with little opportunity to acquire the essential guidance techniques, the usual high school teacher has neither the time nor the essential information to adequately report by conference to 100 to 150 parents twice each semester. A few high schools, usually those in suburban areas, have experimented with the parent-teacher report and recommend it. In such experiments, the time required for these conferences is included as a part of the instructional load.

In some high schools the report card has been replaced by written reports in the form of letters to parents that describe student progress in all phases of achievement. At their best these letters provide vivid descriptions of student progress. They are written in an informal style and are very interesting. They usually call attention to: (1) the outstanding features of the student's work, (2) phases of the school program in which the student is making satisfactory progress, and (3) phases in which the student needs special help and can make improvement. Besides such statements, these letters contain specific suggestions to the parent about the student and an analysis of the student's problems. The parents are also invited to visit the school, to express freely their thoughts and feelings, and to discuss the progress of their children.

These letters have some decided advantages over other methods. They can easily be adapted to the individual differences of either the parent or student. The teacher can also emphasize essential factors in student growth and development, especially as it applies to one particular student. There can even be a central theme to the letter around which all of the details are organized.

Despite the obvious advantages, letter reports to parents have some decided disadvantages. It takes time to assemble the information about a particular student and to write a superior letter to the parents about him. To write such a letter, a teacher must be highly articulate and possess a flair for vivid expression. The usual high school teacher just does not have enough free time to write from 400 to 600 such letter reports to parents during each school year. Where this plan has been tried, the letter reports shortly become stereotyped and formalized. They are no longer individual letters about individual students.

As of now, the report to parents remains the only regular channel of communication between the school and the parent. Of course, teacher-parent conferences and letters to parents are still employed as supplementary reports. Many parents still continue to visit the classroom and confer with teachers about individual students. Although progress has been made, the need to improve the report card so that the language of the card will be intelligible to parents remains one of the unsolved problems in education. Americans are noted for their ability in solving technical problems. As a practical person, each high school teacher needs to translate the goals of the school into the language of the man of the street. When this has been done, the reports to parents will be improved and made more understandable.

DISCUSSION PROBLEMS

1. One teacher, desiring to make real certain viewpoints with respect to types of government, told the class, "This time there will be no differences in the grades; everyone will receive the same thing." Everyone was happy

until a class leader asked, "What grade will that be?" The teacher explained, "Our average mark—a C." The class protested and demanded an immediate return to the traditional system. Explain why you would or would not be willing to accept such a proposal.

2. Despite the fact that public schools are not geared for individual instruction, many superintendents and leaders in education favor automatic promotion, that is, no failures. Discuss this problem in terms of school morale. Does it markedly remove a form of incentive that teachers should have at hand? If so, what does this reveal about the nature of today's classroom teacher?

3. On occasion, the frustrated parent will demand that her child be placed with some other teacher since the one at present gives low grades. If you were a school counselor, how might you attempt to solve this difficulty?

4. As chairman of the school scholarship committee, you have the deciding vote in granting three awards as follows: $2,400; $1,200; and $250. You must decide among these three candidates: Mary has the highest scholastic average of the school. She has not been active in co-curricular affairs and has held no class offices. She wants to become a medical missionary. In one election, she was a "write-in" candidate and was called "the biggest sap." John ranks tenth scholastically in a class of 400. He has been president of his class and was chosen all-state quarterback on the football team. In a similar election, he was named "the boy most likely to succeed." He was sent to his counselor once, as a freshman, for having smoked in a school rest room. His behavior since that time has been good. Pete, the third candidate, ranks at midpoint scholastically but has ranked in the 99th percentile whenever all-school tests were given. He won a National Merit Award scholarship but turned it down because he wanted to enter military service. He was a drum major in the marching band; he had no record of disciplinary trouble. To what extent will you rely upon marks and averages in making your selection? Is this a valid way in which to solve the problem?

5. It's the end of the year and the final marks are being entered into the record. In one class Mary received an *A*, Henry a *B*, Arthur a *C*, Madeline a *D*, and Jack an *F*. Each letter mark is based upon valid evidence of learning outcomes achieved. Also, each letter mark represents a performance that varies in quality from every other letter mark. Think of yourself as being the above teacher assigning these grades to a class in your teaching field. Describe concisely what each letter mark represents in learning outcomes.

6. In some high schools, marks in courses in general education are dependent upon improvement in learning to work with other members of the class as well as mastery of subject-matter content. Is this a wise or an unwise policy? Make a list of arguments for and against.

7. In some high schools any student who is co-operative and has handed in all assignments will receive a passing grade in all general education courses, while for such special courses as science, mathematics, foreign languages, and industrial arts, all students must demonstrate a mastery of the concepts or skills by meeting a relatively high standard on all tests and examinations, especially the final examination, to receive a passing grade. Is this

fair to all students? How do these high schools justify this difference in standards?

8. In tests and examinations some teachers place much emphasis upon memory by taking all test and examination questions directly from the textbook, while others place the emphasis upon understandings by phrasing test problems. Is the memory-type, the thought-type, or a combination of the memory- and thought-type questions most apt to evaluate accurately the degree of attainment of course objectives?

9. In a high school where students are sectioned into three distinct groups—slow, average, and rapid on the basis of ability—and where the course content and the instruction are adapted to each of these separate sections, should separate final examinations be formulated in accordance with course content presented or should one final examination be constructed by all teachers in each field (for example, chemistry)? Which is the wisest procedure? Why?

10. Present arguments for or against each of the following methods of grading: (a) Percentages—100, 99, 98, etc. (b) Letters—A, B, C, D, F. (c) Plus and minus—A plus as opposed to 100 plus; A minus as opposed to B plus, etc. (d) Points—3.2, 2.1, 4.5, etc. (e) Pass or fail.

11. Under what circumstances might a personal visit with parents or a friendly note mailed to the home supplant all report cards?

12. Educators are about evenly divided on the issue of whether a student and his parents should be informed as to scores on I.Q. tests. What is your opinion?

13. In a senior class in social studies, a non-reader submits only one prepared assignment, which is a very poor review of *Thirty Seconds Over Tokyo*. In the same class a rapid learner and an outstanding reader submits five book reviews, which include *The Mature Mind, The Mind That Found Itself*, and *Plato's Republic*. On the basis of achievement as related to ability, has each of these students earned a grade of *A*?

14. Student A was present on every day of the semester, while student B was absent on 40 of the 90 days. On tests, on the final examination, and on class work when present, the academic performance of student B was equal to student A. Should students A and B receive an identical final grade for the semester? Should absenteeism *per se* influence the final grade?

15. Ability to get along with others and academic proficiency are two objectives often stressed by high schools. Where this is a policy, to what extent should the ability to get along with others be reflected in the final mark for a course in algebra?

RELATED REFERENCES

BURTON, William H., *The Guidancee of Learning Activities*, 2nd ed. (New York, Appleton-Century-Crofts, Inc., 1952).

CAMPBELL, Roald F., and RAMSEYER, John A., *School-Community Relationships* (Boston, Allyn and Bacon, Inc., 1955).

Commission on Teacher Education, *Helping Teachers Understand Children*, American Council on Education (Washington, D.C., National Education Association, 1945).

CONANT, James B., *The American High School Today* (New York, McGraw-Hill Book Co., 1959).

———, "A Hard Look at Our High Schools," *Look Magazine* 23:27-28 (February 3, 1959).

DEZOUCHE, Dorothy, "The Wound Is Mortal: Marks, Honors, and Unsound Activities," *Clearing House* 19:339-44 (February, 1945).

Educational Policies Commission, *Education for All American Youth—A Further Look, revised* (Washington, D.C., National Education Association, 1952).

GRAMBS, Jean, and IVERSON, William J., *Modern Methods in Secondary Education* (New York, The Dryden Press, 1952).

GRUHN, William T., and DOUGLASS, Harl R., *The Modern Junior High School*, 2nd ed. (New York, The Ronald Press Company, 1956).

HAND, Harold C., *Principles of Public Secondary Education* (New York, Harcourt, Brace & Co., 1958).

HEIDBREDER, Edna, *Seven Psychologies* (New York, Appleton-Century-Crofts, Inc., 1933).

HOLLINGSHEAD, A. B., *Elmtown's Youth* (New York, John Wiley & Sons, Inc., 1949).

HYMES, James L., *Effective Home-School Relations* (Englewood Cliffs, N.J., Prentice-Hall, Inc., 1953).

JOHNSON, EARL A., and MICHAEL, R. Eldon, *Principles of Teaching* (Boston, Allyn and Bacon, Inc., 1958).

JOHNSON, George, "Girls Lead in Progress Through School," *American School Board Journal* 95:23-26 (October, 1937).

JUDD, Charles H., *The Psychology of Social Institutions* (New York, The Macmillan Co., 1926).

SEGEL, David, WELLMAN, Frank E., and HAMILTON, Allen T., *An Approach to Individual Analysis in Educational and Vocational Guidance* (Washington, D.C., U. S. Department of Health, Education, and Welfare, 1958).

STILES, Lindley J., and DORSEY, Mattie F., *Democratic Teaching in Secondary Schools* (Chicago, J. B. Lippincott Co., 1950).

STRANG, Ruth, *Reporting to Parents* (New York, Bureau of Publications, Teachers College, Columbia University, 1947).

THORNDIKE, Edward L., *Individual Differences and Their Causes* (New York, Teachers College, Columbia University, 1926), Vol. III.

WRINKLE, William L., *Improving Marking and Reporting Practices* (New York, Rinehart & Company, 1947).

YEAGER, William A., *School-Community Relations* (New York, The Dryden Press, 1951).

Chapter 13 ══════════════════════════════

THE SLOW AND THE RAPID LEARNER

A debate coach said this to a fellow teacher, "I'm having a tough time with my debate squad this year."

"Why? Aren't they catching on? Do you mean they aren't very bright?"

"Quite the contrary—there isn't a one of them with an I.Q. of less than 130!"

Here was a coach's dream indeed, but the young teacher had assumed that his worries would be all over, once he had attracted such a group. Like many teachers, he had thought that almost all difficulties came from slow learners and poorly adjusted youth. His problem, as the year went on, was to make drastic improvements in his goals for the debate course. Hurdles and challenges had to be increased, research tripled, and enrichments intensified. Once he succeeded in doing this, every member of the team responded eagerly, and the school team went on to win several championship ratings.

In contrast, consider this statement:

The dismal school records of delinquents, reflecting their generally frustrated reactions to the school situation, are further borne out in chronically poor levels of school performance.[1]

And compare it, in turn, with this one:

The intellectually gifted child thinks differently from other children in that he displays more intellectual curiosity, develops concepts more rapidly, and displays more agility with symbols and other abstractions. He becomes quickly dissatisfied with the routine of the usual classroom work and must find other means of satisfying his needs. Often he becomes impatient and intolerant of the less capable, and frequently seeks the companionship of older children because their thinking and interests are more mature.[2]

THE PROBLEM

Why do the problems of the slow and rapid learner plague us now? Is the old order changing? Are we actually beginning to practice some

[1] Herbert A. Bloch, and Frank T. Flynn, *Delinquency* (New York, Random House, 1956), p. 201.
[2] Roy DeVerl Willey, and Dean C. Andrews, *Modern Methods and Techniques in Guidance* (New York, Harper & Brothers, 1955), p. 439.

of the ideals of a generation long past? How is this related to the problem of developmental reading? (This phase is more fully developed in Chapter XVI).

Up to very recent years, our high schools have been operated as selective institutions. A single assignment was made to each class, and every student was accountable for its achievement. It was a basic assumption that if a student was unwilling or unable to do the assignment, he had no right to be in the high school. It was proper to eliminate those who could not or would not do the assignment, and only those who could and would do the assignment were permitted to graduate. Neither the teachers nor parents of that generation knew about the causes of individual differences. They believed that students who failed were lazy or deliberately loafing and deserved to be eliminated.

The United States has been a land of great natural resources—soil, timber, ores, coal, climate, and always its youth. Our abundance has been so great that, at times, we have been wanton in the wasteful use of our substance. But with the great increase in population, there has come a need to conserve our resources more fully, especially our youth.

We have always recognized the dignity and worth of the individual. During the past decade, the expression "Education for ALL American Youth" has represented the American attitude toward youth education. We believe that all youth can learn and can profit by attending the secondary school. But can all youth profit by an identical education? Or to get maximum benefits must education be adapted to individual differences and needs? Will the quality of education provided by the state make a difference in the quality of its citizens? Although education is provided for all, it may not be equally adapted to all.

There are certain professional truths, well known to teachers, that are only dimly understood by many laymen. The following are a few of them:

1. An identical education for all youth is a good education for only a part of all youth.

2. There is a vast difference between the mentally retarded and the gifted in ability to learn, though both can learn and profit greatly by what they learn.

3. The learning readiness of the student will determine the type of activities he can learn best.

4. If the developmental pace of classroom activities is too fast, the mentally retarded are unable to learn; ultimately they lose all contact with classroom activities.

5. If the pace of the development of classroom activities is too slow, the gifted become bored and disgusted by being forced to learn what they already know; gradually they lose all interest in the class and the course.

Attitudes within a professional group develop slowly. After we see, understand, and even accept, it takes months and sometimes years before a new practice is adopted and perfected.

Facts About the Problem. High school teachers of today are quite aware of individual differences, and this helps in the retention of school-age youth. As a result of this change in teacher understanding, more adolescents enter the high school and remain to graduate. A high per cent of all American teen-agers are now in high school. From 20 to 25 per cent of these are slow learners, 54 to 55 per cent are average learners, and 20 to 25 per cent are rapid learners. The situation is complicated somewhat in that 1 to 3 per cent of the slow learners are mentally retarded students with I.Q.'s of 75 and below. They can learn and profit greatly from high school attendance if given individual attention by the teacher. On the other hand, 1 to 3 per cent of the rapid learners are gifted and/or talented. Some are intellectually gifted with I.Q.'s above 130; others have special talents such as leadership ability, artistic ability, creative writing ability, musical talent, dancing talent, mechanical skills, and physical skills, either with or without unusually high intellectual ability. The gifted and talented learn very rapidly. The intellectually gifted learn in all academic areas while the talented may be rapid learners only in special fields or areas. Nevertheless, it is from this 1 to 3 per cent that the innovations and inventions of tomorrow, with some exceptions, will come. They are our hope for finding the solutions to the great problems of our world.

Although teachers are aware of individual differences, the practice, with minor exceptions, is to use a single textbook and to make an identical assignment to the class as a group. This assignment is usually well adapted to the average learners but poorly adapted to the slow and rapid learners. *Yet high school teachers seem to realize that such an assignment is really suited to only half the class.* Where a teacher is not conscious of this fact, the poor work of the slow learners and the bored attitudes of the rapid learners soon force him to recognize that something is wrong.

Why Do These Conditions Persist? Under such conditions, both the slow and rapid learners are doomed to complacency even though they may receive high or low marks. It is right to ask the question, "Why should this situation exist?" Some parents are irked, although they rarely see the problem clearly. Often the teacher, as the person most closely related to the problem, is criticized, and teen-agers, who are unable to make adjustments to the situation, remain in school only because by law or custom they are forced to comply until enough birthdays have gone by. Parents still insist that a son or daughter be kept in the high school, although a satisfactory quality of learning is rarely achieved. Parents have faith that such children, by remaining in school, will learn something.

Teachers who continue this travesty of not adjusting their assignments to the individual differences among teen-agers in their classes give four reasons for their action. (1) The teachers need to meet too many classes each day which require several preparations. (2) The classes are large and average from 35 to 45 students. (3) Every teacher carries other assignments in addition to regular classes, such as sponsorship of student activities, hall duty, toilet supervision, committee meetings, faculty meetings, supervision at athletic events, P.T.A. service, and many others. (4) Short class periods prevent effective work with three groups of students—this would entail three sub-classes in addition to the single assigned class. The core curriculum, where an entire morning or afternoon may be available for recognition of individual differences, is an attempt to meet the fourth problem. To summarize, the work load of the teacher is far too heavy for him to adjust his instructional procedures effectively to the varying needs of the class. Many more teachers are needed if individual differences are to be cared for in the instruction. Although most communities desire this additional service, boards of education, as representatives of the community, seem unwilling to recognize the problem and provide a solution for it.

Our Slow and Rapid Learners May Be Cheated. Our schools are set up to help the teen-ager acquire: (1) understandings about our physical world, our physical bodies, our society and culture, our industry and technology; (2) attitudes and interests toward our country, our own communities, our way of life; (3) skills of reading, arithmetic, and writing, games and recreation, orientation to a vocation; and (4) habits of work, industry, daily routine, co-operation.

Under our present plan of one assignment directed toward the average learners, are we cheating our slow and rapid learners out of their birthright? A single assignment set up for the average learners tends to discriminate against the slow and rapid learners. The class moves at too fast a pace for the slow learners to acquire the understandings, attitudes, habits, and skills as they are developed. Since nothing comes through clear and concise, there is little meaning to what is being taught. They are so confused that they never grasp or understand it. The slow learners learn just as all of us do, but they learn more slowly. In many cases, they are unable to learn what they could achieve because they learn slowly— the class moves on before they learn what is being taught.

For the rapid learners, the pace is as much too slow as it was too fast for the slow learners. They are never forced to extend their reach beyond their grasp; they are never challenged to wrestle with problems and big ideas somewhat beyond their immediate understanding. Hence, they never develop study habits and skills that are essential for moving toward their true potentialities. They never experience the thrills that come from the mastery of a difficult intellectual task. They fail to live up to their potential because school is dull and boring. They frequently fail to achieve the deep understandings and insights that are the birthright of highly capable students. Too often, they are satisfied with the mediocre when they are capable of making creative and constructive contributions. To a certain extent, the high school may stunt rapid learners rather than stimulate them to live up to their real potentialities.[3]

Probable contribution to delinquency. How big is this problem? What difficulties operate to prevent its solution? By nature, it is similar to the issue of segregation; but it is not unique for any section since it is common in all parts of the United States. The problem represents the key to juvenile delinquency as such; it also brings into full focus the question of whether we are serious when we talk about America's heritage. Researchers into the matter of delinquency are uncovering the urgency for action and are no longer so soft-spoken. Bloch and Flynn[4] declare that the schools are actually *promoting delinquency* through refusal to recognize individual differences and in not taking appropriate professional action. The school's primary contribution to delinquency arises from its presenting a series of frustrating situations to the child who already gives evidence of basic delinquent traits or a possible tendency toward maladjustment. Wickman[5] has shown that teachers are often woefully deficient in understanding the dangerous behavioral symptoms manifesting themselves in the classroom. In rating their pupils, teachers tend to condemn outgoing or overt behavior as undesirable and to consider introverted and docile behavior as the desired type of classroom deportment. In either event the reaction may be dangerous. In the first place, it intensifies what may be a malignant situation, and in the second, it fails to recognize a sinister latent tendency.

In subsequent studies, it was found that teachers can be quickly trained to note more dangerous symptoms; however, school boards must be made to believe in it and accept it before they will pay the cost of this specialized service. More than teacher awareness is necessary if the needs of rapid and slow learners are to be met. Curiously enough, boards of education have been somewhat liberal in providing for the education of those children who differ markedly in physical, mental, emotional, and social traits.

Some teachers find it "less exhausting" to broaden and enrich the offerings for those who learn easily, and to bring in simple materials for the slow learners. Only through much individual experimentation with administrative approval can teachers achieve this goal.

Bloch and Flynn point directly to recent studies by Sheldon and Eleanor Glueck, *Unraveling Juvenile Delinquency,* in which it was

---

[3] The above statements are true for some classrooms but not for all. There are many high school teachers who do differentiate their assignments and keep all students working up to or near to their potentialities.

[4] Bloch and Flynn, *op. cit.,* p. 199.

[5] E. K. Wickman, *Children's Behavior and Teachers' Attitudes* (New York, Commonwealth Fund, 1928), pp. 89-90,

determined that 88.5 per cent of the many delinquents surveyed showed *a marked dislike or indifference to school* as compared with 34.4 per cent of the nondelinquents. The reasons for such strong antipathy are highly revealing. Inability to learn, resentment of restriction and routine, and lack of interest were offered in that order.

How serious are we about the American heritage? We are willing to admit that all citizens of the United States should be of equal status before the law. All should have the right to develop their potentialities fully, but as our high schools are now operated, the slow and the rapid learners are discriminated against. Neither is getting a fair break in the development of his potentialities or his talents. As with segregation, contrary customs and practices are widespread. To change these will take time and the mutual assistance of all forces. When we Americans see that solving the problems of the slow and rapid learners can be done through equalizing the educational opportunities, we will be more likely to accept such a movement as just and right.

It will not be easy. The traditional organization of our high schools cannot be changed overnight. We are a people of good will. As we see our way clearly, changes will come in school organization, instructional practices, and work loads for teachers. It may take several decades. In the meantime, those who are planning to teach in the high schools will seek better methods for differentiating class assignments as between the slow, average, and rapid learners.

HETEROGENEOUS AND HOMOGENEOUS GROUPING

Arguments that favor placement of students of similar abilities in separate classes seem to be based upon this philosophy: All adults ultimately place themselves in such groups, occupationally and socially. When they find their work too difficult or too easy, they make changes, not in themselves but in the job itself. Schools, on the other hand, traditionally have asked the individual to change, while the work to be done has remained constant. This adult phenomenon extends into churches, neighborhoods, fraternal orders, and amusement centers. If the schools find that the traditional assignment of students of varying abilities to a single class does not work, why shouldn't changes be made?

Some of the counter-arguments, those against grouping, are these. (1) Without the sparkle of leadership furnished by rapid learners, all classes and homerooms would be very dull. (2) It would be too expensive to operate a class on three or more levels with three or more teachers. (3) Students in a slow-learning class might develop social inferiorities and students in a rapid-learning class might think they were superior to everyone else.

Heterogeneous grouping, the assignment of students at random to classes, has been in effect since education began. School administrators find that it is statistically most functional when a student may be sent to any room at any hour of the day. Homogeneous grouping, placement of the student in a class geared to his learning ability, creates endless problems in class loads and the availability of classes and teachers. It is fair, however, to ask the administrator who favors heterogeneous grouping for statistical reasons: Would you like to do something to improve your retention record? Would you prefer to serve youth or to keep administrative cost theoretically low?

An excellent compromise is currently being attempted in many of our larger high schools. Proponents of the homogeneous grouping theory have discovered that a slow learner in one area may not be slow in another. And proponents of the heterogeneous group, including those who must make out class schedules, have admitted that it is often best, as well as possible, to set up experimental classes for rapid learners and others for slow learners. As a result, such schools offer English, history, science, and mathematics on two or more levels. It has been found that generally a group with nearly identical intelligence quotients may vary widely in specific abilities.

Grouping individuals of like interests and abilities into classes is desirable if and when it can be done. Such research workers as Baker,[6] Featherstone,[7] and Hildreth,[8] in seeking ways to improve our practice in guiding the slow and rapid learner, agree that segregation or grouping is a minor, unimportant factor. To them, the adaptation of the curriculum and methods of teaching to the personal characteristics of slow and rapid learners is the all-important element. Featherstone presents the gist of the problem of grouping in one short sentence, "The often rather tedious process of leading slow learners through even two or three steps of reasoning takes time and makes the rapid learner impatient."[9] Yet this is a procedure that must be employed with slow learners.

Most high school teachers handle regular classes that are composed of slow, average, and rapid learners. The extremes of mentally retarded with I.Q.'s below 75 and gifted with I.Q.'s above 135 occur rarely. Hence, the practical problem in the usual classroom is to adjust the curriculum to the known abilities of the slow, average, and rapid learners *in that class*. If all three types of students are to be equally stimulated, some differentiation in assignments and procedures must be made. Remember

[6] Harry J. Baker, *Introduction to Exceptional Children* (New York, The Macmillan Co., 1953).

[7] W. B. Featherstone, *Teaching the Slow Learner* (New York, Bureau of Publications, Teachers College, Columbia University, 1951).

[8] Gertrude H. Hildreth, *Educating Gifted Children at Hunter College Elementary School* (New York, Harper & Brothers, 1952).

[9] Featherstone, *op. cit.*, p. 116.

that all classes are individually different and that a single "rapid learner" assignment will not necessarily apply to all sections of a given subject. Likewise, one "slow learner" assignment will not meet the needs of all slow learners in all classes, although the subject is the same. Even the ordinary class can be divided into three sections, slow, average, and fast, and can be handled as a group for some activities or as separate sections for others. Before this is done, the teacher needs to face two questions and answer them affirmatively: (1) Am I emotionally and intellectually prepared to meet this challenge of providing for the slow, average, and rapid learners? (2) Are there other prejudices within me that may operate against successful grouping, and do I have the power to recognize them and subordinate them?

Before assignments can be differentiated, of course, the teacher must identify the slow and the rapid learners.

THE SLOW LEARNER

Identifying the Slow Learner. Are there behaviors by which the slow learners in a class can be identified? The slow-learning student can learn if the pace is not too fast and if the methods of teaching fit his needs. In general, the slow learner can be characterized as follows:

1. He is below average in school achievement. He has had to repeat one or more grades in the elementary school. He is likely to be older than his peers.

2. On the average his general strength and stamina are slightly below par, but this will vary within a group of slow learners.

3. There may appear to be some lack of desirable personal qualities, but this also will vary within the group.[10]

4. Few slow learners enter high school and fewer remain to graduate.

5. Slow learners may sometimes be classed as lazy. Usually, this is the result of a lack of interest or a lack of adjustment in the program to needs; experienced teachers term it nothing more than a defensive attitude brought about by continued failure to achieve anything within the classroom.

6. Slow learners may also lack mechanical skills; the slow learner is not necessarily manual-minded.[11]

7. Slow learners seem to come from low social and economic backgrounds, but percentage-wise there are about the same proportion

[10] Wickman, quoted earlier in this chapter, has underscored the tremendous importance of differentiating between personal qualities that are essential in society as opposed to those which the teacher may subjectively prefer. Whether a teacher likes or dislikes the teen-ager should not enter into this appraisal.

[11] The assumption that a slow learner will possess mechanical skills sends too many teen-agers into vocational courses, where additional frustrations are quickly developed.

originating from well-to-do families as from impoverished families in our society.

8. Specifically, the slow learner almost always is deficient in reading skills.[12]

The slow learner will achieve mature status, hold a job, and vote. It is well to remember that in voting he will help to determine the outcome of elections directly related to school problems. By and large, at 14 he begins to achieve an intellectual development that permits an elementary understanding of the economic, social, and political problems that he will face in maturity. When the instruction is adapted to his readiness and geared to his needs, the high school years are the most functional part of his school life. The conventional subjects of the high school, as formerly taught, have little meaning for the slow learner. Hence, the question arises, "What adaptation in method and the curriculum must be made after the slow learner has been identified?"

Teaching the Slow Learner. Should the slow learner be taught in the regular high school class? Let us remember that the regular class of the conventional high school is not the best place for the education of a slow learner. *Some subject matter cannot be taught* to slow learners, although it may be readily learnable and functional for average and rapid learners. Some change in the curriculum must be made, even though the standard curriculum is maintained for the other students. The achievement standards for marking, grading, promotions, and graduation can not be maintained for the slow learners; yet, these slow learners can profit by the time spent in high school. These are outstanding years for them, but they, by nature, cannot learn as average and rapid learners do. The regular teacher as a specialist in subject-matter education, who must meet and guide several large classes, will find it difficult to come to know these slow learners well enough to adapt his method to them.

These slow learners are in your classes. You desire to serve them as best you can. Naturally, you ask, "What are some ways in which to guide and instruct them more effectively?" The few suggestions which follow will be of value:

1. Accept the slow learner for what he is—a human being. He has a right to guidance and instruction. He has a right to feel the thrill of a teacher's joy over his little successes and his small achievements. Fractional growth and achievement may be as significant for him in his mature years as is the much greater growth and achievement of the rapid learner.[13]

2. Make the assignments explicit and precise. When at all compre-

[12] Jack Kough and R. F. DeHaan, *Identifying Children with Needs* (vol. I in *Teacher's Guidance Handbook*, Elementary School Edition), (Chicago, Science Research Associates, 1955), pp. 17-57.

[13] See: Marion E. Smith, and Arthur J. Burks, *Teaching the Slow Learning Child* (New York, Harper & Brothers, 1954), pp. 3, 4.

hensive, they must be written. Write them on the blackboard as you speak, and insist that they be copied into notebooks. Avoid all abstract statements in assignments. Make them as concrete and as vivid as possible.

3. Avoid homework for slow-learning students. If homework assignments are made, they should be specific and require no original work by students. The school day should be arranged so that needed periods of study can be held under supervision in the classroom. Avoid study halls; for slow learners they serve no useful purpose.

4. Thought questions put to the slow learner are likely to elicit no response at all or a hodgepodge of irrelevant ideas. A slow learner can not jump from a known or given fact to a conclusion or inference some two or three steps removed. He must be guided slowly and gradually from the question to the conclusion. It is a tedious process, but it must be done. One learns to reason by being given practice in reasoning. Questions need not be limited to the simple recall variety of who, what, where, when, and why. Slow learners can think through problems, but it takes much time and real teaching. Impatience and ridicule simply frustrate the slow learner; he withdraws into a shell from which it is quite difficult to extract him and establish rapport again.[14]

5. Words are not enough for slow learners; they need to be supplemented by visual and other sensory aids. Use pictures, diagrams, objects, maps, models, posters, and demonstrations wherever they can help to give greater concreteness and reality to an idea. While such aids are also valuable for average and rapid learners, they put spirit and meaning into the skeleton of words for the slow learners. Many concrete, vivid details help the slow student to make an idea his very own. A few topics fully developed, and without too much variety, help to give the slow learner that rich feeling of achievement so rewarding to all of us—and so seldom experienced by slow learners.

6. For rapid learners in the conventional high school course, once over the subject matter may be adequate—but not so for the slow learner. With him a daily, cumulative review as a build-up for the unit or topic is an essential. Then an over-all review of the unit must follow, plus an over-all review of the course at the end of the term. While this means repeating the material as originally covered, it is necessary for the slow learner. Continuous review here is inseparable from good teaching.

What has been suggested in the preceding paragraphs, if skillfully employed, will increase the likelihood that slow learners will gain something from a conventional curriculum. However, no one should assume that the improvement of teaching methods alone is sufficient. This con-

[14] *Ibid.*, Smith and Burks give excellent descriptions of how a teacher may assist the slow learner in taking several short steps to an end product. To see clearly how it is done, visit a school for the feeble-minded and observe an experienced teacher working with the best pupils. See pp. 1-6; 22-25; 29-32.

ventional curriculum is not at all suited to the needs of the slow learner, and ultimately modifications must be made. In the decades just ahead, slow learners will, in all probability, crowd into the high schools in increasing numbers. Their presence there must be recognized by curricular adjustments tailored to their needs.

THE RAPID LEARNER

Thomas Gray was thinking of the rapid learners and the gifted when he wrote, in his "Elegy Written in a Country Churchyard":

> Full many a gem of purest ray serene
> The dark unfathomed caves of ocean bear
> Full many a flower is born to blush unseen
> And waste its sweetness on the desert air.

Gray was bemoaning the waste of human talent in that isolated rural village. Well may we join him as we view the waste that occurs through neglect of our outstanding teen-agers in the high schools. As Americans, we are a peculiar people. We are quick to recognize superiority in athletics, in business, and in industry; but we disparage it in scholarship and statesmanship. And yet, for the years just ahead, superiority in scholarship and statesmanship are the two types of leadership most needed. From our rapid learners and our gifted young people, that leadership must come. The leadership in our professions, in our businesses and industries, and in all walks of life must be filled from the ranks of today's teen-agers. The gifted have contributed to our civilization those ideas, processes, and inventions that have made us wealthier, wiser, and happier. In our day, Einstein, a gifted man, created a new concept, $E = mc^2$, that brought to us atomic power and is ushering in a new era for mankind.

At birth, the rapid learners and the gifted are only potentialities. These potentialities become abilities and realities as they are developed or permitted to develop. Giftedness remains largely a dormant power unless it is developed in a favorable environment. Our schools and our gifted teachers are the most fertile sources for such development. Currently, our schools are under intense criticism for failure to provide a stimulating program for the rapid learners.

One cause lies in the weaknesses pointed out in the preceding section on slow learners: the inability of teachers to provide several assignments tailored to the needs of the slow, average, and rapid learners; the reluctance of our school boards to attack this problem by providing more teachers and smaller classes; and the heavy hand of tradition which burdens the conventional school program. As we must remember, just a generation ago only the rapid learners attended high school. Then, a single assignment more nearly suited their needs. Even today a single assignment is within the grasp of the average, but falls far short of meeting the potentialities of the rapid and slow learners. Hildreth[15] speaks of the rapid and gifted learners as "high-powered dynamos without established outlets for the generated power." She chides the high schools for not adapting their program (establishing outlets) to use this power. Dr. D. A. Worcester, an educational psychologist at the University of Nebraska, expresses the same idea when he says, "We fail to challenge the rapid and gifted learner. It is as if a citizen were to buy a high-powered automobile and then throttle it down to a speed of twenty miles per hour."

Identifying the Rapid Learner. What are the characteristics of rapid learners? Such a student does well in high school if challenged by superior teaching. Unless he is urged to work at top or nearly top capacity, his growth and development will be somewhat dwarfed. Many such learners slip through the high school with slight effort, limited growth, and without their teachers being aware that they are capable of superior achievement; hence, a teacher must identify students who are in reality rapid learners.

As a group, rapid learners have several characteristics that will assist a teacher in identifying them. While not every rapid learner will have all of the characteristics listed below, they are common to most. The basic assumption here is that the greater the number of these characteristics possessed by a learner, the greater is the likelihood of his being a potentially rapid learner.

1. They enjoy better health, have better physical stamina, and attend school more regularly than do slow and average learners.

2. They have excellent personalities and get along well with teachers and classmates.

3. The typical rapid learner with a chronological age of 12 will have a mental age of 16.5.

4. A marked number of rapid learners have specific aptitudes for art, music, commerce, journalism, debate, and similar activities.

5. Rapid learners can be identified by achievement, mental, and aptitude tests.

6. Rapid learners have usually skipped one grade and have earned better than average marks throughout their school careers. The cumulative records in the school office will show this.

7. Rapid learners have many extra interests inside and outside the school.

8. Rapid learners have the respect of their fellow students.

9. Most rapid learners are interested in going to college. On the whole, they are worthy college material.

[15] Hildreth, *op. cit.*, p. 9.

10. They are capable of abstract reasoning; it is important that they be taught careful methods of abstract reasoning and to avoid incorrect and illogical deductions.

11. They have the ability to emphasize the abstract rather than the concrete. They need help in constantly relating the abstract to the concrete, that is, to keep their feet on the ground.

13. They are versatile in the use of their mental processes. When one mental process does not get results, they turn to another and another until the correct answer is found. They like school much better if encouraged to use these methods. Since it is a practical procedure in everyday life, it is wise for the teacher to aid in its development, within reason.

14. They prefer long-time units of work with large returns to small, specific units with small returns.

15. They tend to be creative, even to the point of teacher frustration.

16. They will "be on their toes" socially, academically, and morally.[16]

Teaching the Rapid Learner. Are you a versatile person? You will need to be versatile as a teacher of a regular class that is comprised of slow, average, and rapid learners. An occasional class will include a retarded or a gifted student, and your need for versatility will be expanded. To illustrate, it may be assumed that every student in a class may have a chronological age of 14 while the range of mental ages could be from 8 to 20 (a retarded 60 I.Q. and a gifted 150 I.Q.). A teacher must be decidedly versatile to do the obvious task well. All members of the class must be effectively taught and measurable achievement must be a result of the teaching. In Chart 19, a contrast is made between methods of teaching the slow and rapid learners. The contrast reveals in part some of the problems involved in professional instruction.

Teaching problems with rapid learners. These students like going to high school. Manipulating words and ideas is stimulating and congenial for them. They do not like routine tasks or to be held at a snail's pace when they might be learning a great deal more than is offered.

For the teacher, the two most difficult problems are the adjustment of the curriculum and his methods of teaching to three distinct groups of learners. However, as we have said, the curriculum is largely a carry-over from that developed for rapid learners of an earlier period, and its adjustment to rapid learners is much less difficult than its modification for slow learners. In the regular classroom, two additional problems with rapid learners are concerned with enrichment and acceleration. For the most part, the present practice is to enrich the curriculum for the rapid learner rather than to accelerate him. Plans for enrichment include: (1) the addition of several more somewhat difficult problems on each unit or topic, designed especially to challenge the rapid learner or (2) an extension of the maximum work load from four to five or six units per year for rapid

[16] Kough and DeHaan, *op. cit.,* pp. 17-57.

Chart 19. Contrast in Methods of Teaching Slow and Rapid Learners

METHODS OF TEACHING SLOW LEARNERS	METHODS OF TEACHING RAPID LEARNERS
Make the assignment explicit and precise—insist that assignments be written down exactly as given.	Plan the assignments with rapid learners —control the conditions under which they work but do not insist upon routine.
Work with objects and direct experience —abstract words carry slight meaning.	Use abstract words for they are meaningful and important—a teacher must sometimes guide toward the concrete.
In using the thought question, guide the group by slow steps from the given facts to the logical outcome.	Use broad guidance in the problem-solving approach. Rapid learners revel in the thrill of moving from the given facts to the conclusion rapidly and with ease.
Maintain a permissive atmosphere with well-established routine—slow learners feel insecure without definite routine and direction.	Maintain a permissive atmosphere largely free from routine restrictions—rapid learners delight in innovations.
Avoid assigning homework. Slow learners do best under close and continuous supervision.	Assign homework. Homework originated when rapid learners alone attended high school. They like homework, especially when given freedom to explore and think through a problem.
For slow learners, use constant review.	Use review to bring out new relationships and new insights.

learners who meet certain qualifications—the additional units to be chosen from electives rather than required courses. In acceleration, the work program of the student is so planned that a rapid learner at 16 or 17 carries through a maximum work load per year or meets certain requirements by passing a comprehensive standardized achievement test. Thus, the student is ready for college and entrance into a profession one or two years earlier. Some high schools follow both the acceleration and the enrichment practices by formulating a policy of enrichment and by studying the records of individual students who make a request for early graduation.

Teaching methods. Acceptable teaching methods for any situation apply to the problem of the rapid learner, but there are some special characteristics of methodology that can be identified. Among these are the following:

1. The teacher should share with rapid learners his reasons for using the method he does. When they understand, they co-operate more fully. It is difficult to do this with slow learners.

2. Rapid learners should have more opportunities to select their own activities. They will have some unusual ideas that are educationally sound.

3. Assignments should be so phrased as to invite original and creative responses. Assignments can be given in far less detail to rapid learners.

4. The teaching of skills should involve repeated practice until a reasonable degree of mastery has been attained. For rapid learners, higher degrees of attainment can be required; but less time will be needed. Avoid unnecessary drill beyond the actual attainment of mastery.

5. Teaching for understanding should focus on explanations of the reason for things. The understanding achieved by all learners will be increased by the teacher's skilled use of "why" and "how" questions—such questions are especially suited for guiding the thinking of rapid learners.

6. Rapid learners should have access to a wide variety of books, pictures, and other instructional materials. A greater variety is needed though the rapid learners will require less guidance in the selection and use of such materials.

7. Rapid learners should have direct and guided contact with the out-of-school community.

8. The rapid learners should be given a large measure of responsibility for the evaluation of their own work.[17]

RETARDED, GIFTED, AND TALENTED LEARNERS

The Mentally Retarded Learner. Mentally retarded teen-agers now are attending our American high schools. By law and custom, they are required to attend up to 16 or 18, and since there is no other place for them in our society, they will, in all probability, continue to attend in increasing numbers during the decades ahead.

By intelligence-test classification, the mentally retarded fall into the I.Q. range of 75 and below, and they comprise from 1 to 3 per cent of the population. Their minds can be described as perfectly good dynamos or engines—they just have less power. In *Teaching the Slow Learning Child,* Marion F. Smith[18] describes how several of her mentally retarded graduates were holding good jobs—their incomes were somewhat above what she earned as a teacher. These mentally retarded can learn even involved concepts and skills, but they learn very slowly.

These teen-agers learn more slowly than the average learners. The pace, even when set for the slow learner (I.Q. 75-90), is so fast they are confused, get lost, and become frustrated. They need help, especially, in reading, number relations, elementary science, social studies, and social adjustment. For the most part, parents have been entirely unable to teach these retarded students elementary social skills which are essential for getting along with others. Why is this so? These children, unlike average

---

[17] A highly interesting process permits such students to estimate their own final grade in terms of established facts about themselves. Several high school teachers who have been successful in teaching rapid learners do this each semester; invariably, the students under-grade themselves.

[18] Smith and Burks, *op. cit.,* p. 133.

children, do not learn the simple social skills by watching other children. They must be taught these skills by short simple steps with much repetition and parental guidance. Parents, not being good teachers, look upon these children as being hopeless. The home has failed these children. The school must not fail them, too.

They can learn, though they learn slowly. They can fit into American society and become taxpayers. They can produce much-needed goods and services rather than becoming criminal or indigent. They are not hopeless; they are educable; and they need not spend their lives on relief. For them the high school years are promising ones; the high school can make the difference.

Under present conditions, and especially in the small high school, these students will be found in the regular classroom. Yet much of the work with the mentally retarded must be individualized instruction.[19] These students need help in learning how to improve their reading, to express ideas more concisely and clearly, to get along with their peers, and especially to acquire and use the most important rules for playing the game of life. If the student can acquire a confidence and a belief in himself and if he can become a respectable and self-supporting citizen rather than criminal or indigent, our society becomes more stable, and the individual lives a happier and a more rewarding life.

There is a movement in the United States to provide for the education of mentally retarded teen-agers in special rooms with trained teachers for this service. Such methods make for improved instruction, though the teachers recognize that the danger of stigma runs high. It is quite possible to have such students segregated for some things and taking part in general activities in other phases of the regular school program. The mentally retarded teen-agers may be slow in learning certain intellectual tasks, yet they are emotionally sensitive and perhaps "bruise more easily." Specially trained teachers know this, while others may not. This is why schools sometimes err when they assign any available teacher to such work.

The Gifted Learner. "If it is possible to teach genius instead of merely hoping it will come along, the future will belong to the society which discovers how."[20]

A University of Nebraska educational psychologist, D. A. Worcester, has stated:

There is no evidence that genius will out in spite of environmental deprivations. All of which is to say that wise guidance—helping the individual to understand his abilities and to choose intelligently and informedly his goals and

[19] Smith and Burks, *op. cit.* Under unit method procedure, time can be found to work with the mentally retarded. See Ch. IX and pp. 1-6, 55, 112.

[20] Eugene Ayers, "Social Attitudes Toward Inventions," *The American Scientist* 43:521-540 (October, 1955).

ways to achieve them—is as much the right of the gifted as of all other children.[21]

The gifted do not automatically develop of and by themselves. A program adapted to their capacities and needs is as necessary for them as for the mentally retarded teen-agers. Gifted teen-agers comprise approximately 1 to 3 per cent of our teen-age population. A program well adapted to the rapid learner is a very spare diet for the intellectually gifted youth. To develop fully, the gifted learner must be challenged to reach beyond his present grasp. If this challenge leads to the thrill of a worthy achievement, good study habits and skills can be developed. These good study habits and skills are prerequisite to the persistent work that precedes new inventions and new discoveries. It is usually the gifted person who makes the new steps into the previously unknown. Frequently, the gifted fail to develop these necessary study habits and skills because too easy a program is being provided.

These gifted teen-agers must be identified before they can be guided wisely. Gifted children have to learn. Their potentialities may be largely inherent, but the degree and manner in which they develop are in terms of their opportunities. As with the mentally retarded so it is with the gifted: the regular teacher must guide the gifted students in the usual class along with the very slow, the slow, the average, and the rapid learners. He must provide the extra problems and projects to challenge teen-agers at the summit of their intellectual ability

However, there is a movement, which seems now to be gathering momentum in the larger communities of the United States, to provide special teachers and special rooms for the gifted. In Cleveland, where such a movement has been in progress for more than two decades, these special rooms are called Major Work Classrooms.

Identification of the gifted. Mental tests are nearly always employed in the identification of the gifted; however, mental tests alone are not enough. They should be supplemented by teachers' judgments and especially by demonstrated exhibitions of talent. What are the clues by which a gifted teen-ager can be identified? A few of the identifying characteristics of the gifted teen-ager are: (1) he retains what has been read or heard without much rote drill, (2) he knows about many things of which other teen-agers are unaware, (3) he uses a large number of words easily and accurately, (4) he performs difficult mental tasks, (5) he does some academic work one or two years in advance of the class, (6) he is original and uses good but unusual methods or ideas, and (7) he is alert, keenly observant, and responds quickly.

In an experiment watched closely by the writer, teachers were invited to select two or three rapid learners from the 18 sections of a high school

---

[21] D. A. Worcester, *The Education of Children Above Average Mentality* (Lincoln, The University of Nebraska Press, 1956), p. 65.

American History course. From the 50 students who were identified, a special class of 30 was established. Work ordinarily done in five days was advanced to four days and special consideration was given for good achievement. Remarkably, it was found that this selected group soon produced its own kind of rapid and slow learners. Research on identification of the gifted, this experiment indicated, is not entirely realistic. Neither do teachers of the gifted, as yet, know precisely how to go about it. Enrichment, it has been found, does not mean the addition of subject matter. Some teachers report unusual success in suggesting that individual students might profit from and enjoy specific selections from *Great Books of the Western World* published by the Encyclopedia Britannica in collaboration with the University of Chicago. The whole problem of identifying the gifted has been a matter for continuous study by Science Research Associates. Meantime, there is nothing to prevent the imaginative teacher from attempting experimentation. For the gifted, who grow restless, almost any change would be for the better.

The Talented Learner. A talented teen-ager may or may not be intellectually gifted. Nevertheless, all or nearly all talented students will be rapid learners and many of the talented will range above 120 I.Q. Students who possess special aptitudes or potentialities that permit the development of unusual understandings, skills, and attitudes can be classified as talented. For example, all of us have known athletes who possessed a muscular co-ordination decidedly above that found in the typical teenager. In the area of physical skills, such an athlete is a talented individual. Likewise, there are a goodly number of students in every large high school with talents—either developed or undeveloped—for science, leadership, art, creative writing, dramatics, music, dancing, or mechanics.

Many students possess talents without being aware that they do. Surely, it is a sound assumption that the personnel of the high school, especially the guidance personnel, will assist every student in all possible ways to identify his special aptitude or talent. Also, where there are clues to indicate that a student may possess a latent or hidden talent, the school staff will "go all out" to cause the latent talent to unfold. A student whose latent talent is cultivated or developed becomes in maturity both a more valuable individual to his community and a happier person.

There are nine of these talents listed above. What are the clues by which a latent or undeveloped talent can be identified? Certain characteristics or behaviors reveal these latent talents. A few rare teachers have been cognizant of this for centuries, but recent research carried on in the area of talents makes it possible for all teachers to detect them through known clues. Not only can the student with talent be identified but also the specific talent possessed. To illustrate, four of the nine talents are listed in Chart 20 with three or four clues indicated for each.

Chart 20. Illustrative List of Talents with Clues

TALENTS	CHARACTERISTICS
Scientific ability	1. Likes and is highly efficient in mathematics 2. Has good motor co-ordination, especially eye-hand co-ordination; can do fine, precise manipulation 3. Wants to know the causes and reasons for things 4. Spends much of his time on special projects of his own, such as constructing a radio, making a telescope, or learning a language
Leadership ability	1. Enters into things with contagious enthusiasm 2. Can take charge of a group 3. Can judge the ability of other teen-agers and find a place for them in group activity 4. Is able to figure out what is wrong with an activity and to show others how to make it better
Dramatic art	1. Readily shifts into the role of another character, animal, or object 2. Uses voice to reflect change of idea and mood 3. Understands and portrays the conflict in the situation, when given the opportunity to act out a dramatic part 4. Communicates feelings by means of facial expressions, gestures, and bodily movements
Mechanical skills	1. Has limber fingers, can manipulate tools easily 2. Is interested in mechanical gadgets and machines 3. Has a hobby involving mechanical devices such as radios, automobiles, household electric devices 4. Can repair gadgets and put together mechanical devices

DISCUSSION PROBLEMS

1. Are the critics of the high school correct in reproaching high school teachers for coddling students when they adapt their class assignments to the abilities and needs of their students? Contrast the *for* and *against* arguments. Which is based upon the sounder principles?
2. Are classes in English, mathematics, science, social studies, and foreign language really made homogeneous when students are assigned to classes in these subjects on the basis of scores earned on intelligence tests? List the facts to support your answer.
3. Slow learners who are in trouble in such academic subjects as English, science, and mathematics are automatically transferred to industrial arts by some high school principals. Can such a policy be justified? Will students who lack aptitude for English, science, or mathematics necessarily have an aptitude for industrial arts?
4. Retarded students are now attending high school. Should these retarded students be placed in regular classes, in special classes for the retarded, or in some regular classes and in some classes for the retarded only? By what evidence can you justify your answer?
5. In what ways, other than by intelligence tests, can the various types of students such as the retarded, the slow, the average, the rapid, the talented, and the gifted be identified?
6. An ideal in every high school is to keep all students learning at or near their

maximum capacity. In what ways should the procedures (methods) differ among the following groups—the retarded, the slow, the average, the rapid, the talented, and the gifted—to achieve this goal?

7. When extensive grouping occurs within a school, what becomes of the traditional "normal" spread of ability within a class?

8. Indicate the probable fate of a slow-learning teen-ager in 1920 as opposed to a similar youth today. What evidence is there that it is best for young people to remain in school?

9. Discuss the tendency of American schools, in times of emergency, to place increased emphasis upon the education of rapid learners and the gifted. Should this be a regular policy?

10. In several regions, including Washington, D.C., and California, it has been found that the inclusion of minority groups has tended to lower the median I.Q. of certain high schools. Is this evidence that minority groups generally provide slow learners and marginal students? Discuss fully.

11. It has been said that a gifted person will acquire much learning under any circumstance—that the gifted poet will produce just as fine poetry whether he lives in an attic or palace. This is an interesting problem that should be understood by all who teach. To what degree must true genius be helped?

RELATED REFERENCES

AYERS, Eugene, "Social Attitudes Toward Inventions," *The American Scientist* 43:521-540 (October, 1955).

BAKER, Harry J., *Introduction to Exceptional Children* (New York, The Macmillan Co., 1953).

BLOCH, Herbert A., and FLYNN, Frank T., *Delinquency* (New York, Random House, 1956).

BOND, G. L., and BOND, Eva, *Adapting Instruction in Reading to Individual Differences*, Series on Individual Instruction No. 5 (Minneapolis, University of Minnesota Press, 1948).

Bureau of Special Education, *Suggested Activities for Mentally Retarded Children* (Sacramento, California State Department of Education, 1952).

BURR, Emily, "Prime Factors in the Placement of the Below Normal," *American Journal of Mental Deficiency* 40:429-34 (January, 1947).

CRUICKSHANK, William M., ed., *Psychology of Exceptional Children and Youth* (Englewood Cliffs, N.J., Prentice-Hall, Inc., 1955).

DeHAAN, R. F., "Identifying Gifted Children," *School Review* 65:41-48 (March, 1957).

ELICKER, P. E., "Our Brightest High School Seniors," *Journal of the National Education Association* 45:225 (April, 1956).

FEATHERSTONE, W. B., *Teaching the Slow Learner* (New York, Bureau of Publications, Teachers College, Columbia University, 1951).

FIDONE, W., "Above-Average Class Studies Hamlet," *English Journal* 45:470-76 (November, 1956).

GARRISON, Karl C., *The Psychology of Exceptional Children* (New York, The Ronald Press Company, 1950).

GLUECK, Sheldon and Eleanor, *Unraveling Juvenile Delinquency* (New York, The Commonwealth Fund, 1950).

HALL, Theodore, *Gifted Children: The Cleveland Story* (Cleveland, The World Publishing Company, 1956).

HAVIGHURST, R. J., STOVERS, Eugene, and DEHAAN, R. F., *A Survey of the Education of the Gifted* (Chicago, The University of Chicago Press, 1955).

HILDRETH, Gertrude, *Educating Gifted Children at Hunter College Elementary School* (New York, Harper & Brothers, 1952).

HILL, Arthur S., "Special Education in the Secondary School," *Journal of Exceptional Children* 13:93-97 (April, 1947).

INGRAM, Christine P., *Education of the Slow-Learning Child* (New York, The Ronald Press, 1953).

JACOB, Walter, *New Hope for the Retarded Child* (New York, Public Affairs Committee, 1954).

JEWETT, Arno, and others, *Teaching Slow and Rapid Learners in High School,* United States Office of Education Bulletin No. 5 (Washington, D.C., 1954).

KIRK, Samuel A., and JOHNSON, G. Orville, *Education of the Retarded Child* (Boston, Houghton Mifflin Co., 1950).

KOUGH, Jack, and DEHAAN, R. F., *Identifying Children with Needs,* (vol. I in *Teacher's Guidance Handbook,* Elementary School Edition) (Chicago, Science Research Associates, 1955).

LATINE, J. J., "Algebra Program for the Bright Ninth Graders," *Mathematics Teacher* 49:179-84 (March, 1956).

LEAVITT, J. E., "Latent Abilities," *Clearing House* 30:242-43 (December, 1955).

LOVELL, Catherine, and INGRAM, Christine P., "A High School Program for Mentally Retarded Girls," *Journal of Educational Research* 11:74-82 (April, 1945).

MALLIS, J., "Seminar for Superior Students," *Clearing House* 31:175-78 (November, 1956).

MARTENS, Elise H., *Curriculum Adjustments for the Mentally Retarded,* United States Office of Education Bulletin No. 2 (Washington, D.C., 1950).

Modesto Program for Gifted Students (Modesto, Calif., Public Schools, 1954).

MONES, Leon, "What Program for the Slow Learner?" *Bulletin of the National Association Secondary-School Principals* 33:47-58 (May, 1949).

NORTON, M. S., "What Are Some of the Important Factors to Consider in a Program of Identifying Gifted Pupils in Mathematics and Science?" *School Science and Mathematics* 57:103-8 (February, 1957).

PASSOW, Aaron H., and TANNENBAUM, Abraham, "How Fare the Talented in Our High Schools?" *Bulletin of the National Association of Secondary-School Principals* 39:10-15 (May, 1955).

PRESSEY, Sidney L., "Concerning the Nature and Nurture of Genius," *Scientific Monthly* 81:123-130 (September, 1955).

ROBERTS, Helen E., *Current Trends in the Education of the Gifted* (Sacramento, California State Department of Education, 1954).

ROSS, S., and others, "Development of High Level Science Talent," *Science Teacher* 23:279-81 (October, 1956).

SMITH, Marion E., and BURKS, Arthur J., *Teaching the Slow Learning Child* (New York, Harper & Brothers, 1954).

STRANG, Ruth M., "Gifted Adolescents' Views of Growing Up," *Exceptional Children* 23:10-15 (October, 1956).

Superior Pupils in Junior High School Mathematics, United States Office of Education, Bulletin No. 4 (Washington, D.C., 1955).

WICKMAN, E. K., *Children's Behavior and Teachers' Attitudes* (New York, Commonwealth Fund, 1928).

WILLEY, Roy DeVerl, and ANDREWS, Dean C., *Modern Methods and Techniques in Guidance* (New York, Harper & Brothers, 1955).

WORCESTER, D. A., *The Education of Children Above Average Mentality* (Lincoln, The University of Nebraska Press, 1956).

Chapter 14 ══════════════════════════════

THE IMPROVEMENT OF READING

What should we expect of education? H. T. Rosenberger has said:

The world's storehouse of knowledge is available to those who read well. To them the written word is a means of increased usefulness and a source of companionship. Persons who read very slowly or with poor comprehension need assistance. Those who believe all they read are a potential danger.[1]

This is a relatively new problem for the secondary school; in earlier years, students who had difficulty in reading were not admitted to the high school. But with the eight-fold increase in high school enrollments during recent decades, one-third of the high school students today are unable to read ninth-grade textbooks quickly and with understanding. Yet, there is evidence to show that teen-agers as a group read better today than at any previous time. This is true of the contemporary student population despite the large influx of students who are poor readers.

Schools must be practical and face up to the increasing complexity of material that the American citizen is expected to read today. The AFL-CIO publications—*Economic Trends, Economic Review, Collective Bargaining*, as examples—are not all geared to the slow reader. Reference is made to "cost-of-living adjustments provided automatically under agreement escalator provisions" as though such a phrase were a part of basic English. Daily newspapers disclose that the "foreign aid program and its military component" are urged to "modernize and improve friendly forces." And even the news magazines do not hestitate to brighten an account of a foreign minister's latest visit to Moscow with such foreign phrases as *Dobry Dien* ("Good day") and *Vsievo Haroshevo* ("All the best").

THE NATURE OF THE READING PROBLEM

What is the nature of the reading problem in the high school? Classroom teachers, school administrators, and other educational experts are

[1] Homer T. Rosenberger, "What Should We Expect of Education?" *Bulletin of the National Association of Secondary-School Principals* 40:196 (February, 1956).

310

unanimous in their observations that a distressingly large number of high school students are poor readers. Many hundreds of American youth who enter high school expecting to go to college find that cherished ambition impossible because they do not read well enough to succeed either in high school or in college. Numerous studies show that the vast majority of failing high school students rank low in performance on standardized reading tests. In fact, it has been found that a large number of secondary school students read with a comprehension of only the fourth-, fifth-, or sixth-grade level. There are girls and boys in grade 11 who read with an understanding of less than 150 words per minute—the speed of a normal grade 3 pupil. Such students, even though they may understand what they read, are doomed to failure because they cannot keep up with their assignments.

Two Factors in the Problem. Bulging enrollments and the need for a greater amount of reading in the school program have increased the problem of the poor reader. The same factors that have made the slow learner a difficult problem in our contemporary high school operate to cause poor readers. As revealed earlier in Chapter IV, enrollments in the secondary school have increased by leaps and bounds. Thirty teen-agers go to high school today for every one who attended in 1890. Nothing in the whole contemporary scene is more dramatic than the growth of enrollment in the public high school. As millions of teen-agers have crowded into our high schools, the number of poor readers has multiplied again and again. Our mores and our laws have brought students into the schools from all kinds of homes and with a wide range in their capacities for achievement. Yes! the high school has become less and less selective.

Furthermore, our modern emphasis upon student participation in learning has made it necessary for them to do more reading and to do it in more fields. Books provide vicarious experiences. Thousands of books in every area of knowledge contain the wisdom of the ages. In a comparatively short time, through reading, we can take full advantage of the earlier experiences of others. The number of books is rapidly growing with the advance of knowledge. In order to keep up with recent developments, teachers are compelled to revise their procedures to include wider ranges of reading. The student with more to do in a fixed amount of time, which is often less than that of a generation ago, is faced with the necessity of increasing his reading efficiency.

HOW TO IMPROVE READING

How can reading in high school be improved? There is ample cause for posing such a question. Some students read with high speed and easy comprehension. Some high school freshmen read as competently as the average university graduate student, but there are other teen-agers in high school who need help and need it badly. The reading level of more than a few is deplorably low.

A Modern Approach. For more than a decade, educators have given serious attention to the improvement of reading in the high school. Even now, there is only partial agreement as to how this might be done, but the problem has been defined more clearly through discussion and experimentation. Today, educators chatter less and talk more common sense on this problem than was previously true. The resulting differences in emphasis are briefly outlined in Chart 21.

Chart 21. Differences in Emphasis with Respect to the Improvement of Reading

OPINIONS OF PARENTS AND MANY TEACHERS	OPINIONS OF READING SPECIALISTS AND SOME TEACHERS
1. It is not necessary to teach reading at the high school level. This is the task of the elementary school. Learn to read in elementary school in order to read well in high school.	1. Skill in reading is not acquired all at once. New skills in reading continue to be acquired and perfected throughout elementary school, secondary school, and college.
2. The reading problem can most easily be remedied by increasing the speed of the reader.	2. While speed is important, comprehension is the real essential. Besides comprehension, there are many other skills that an acceptable reader will acquire.
3. The establishment of remedial classes for those students who read too inefficiently for success is sufficient to solve the problem.	3. Remedial reading classes are only for those who have decided reading disabilities. For others who have failed to adjust the speed to the difficulty of reading as they have moved along in school, assistance from the regular teacher in the regular classroom for each course carried is a much more direct approach. The reader simply needs help in developing reading skills that have not as yet been acquired.
4. Regular instruction in reading is an integral part of the English curriculum.	4. This is right and proper for the improvement of reading in literature. It is also right and proper for mathematics, science, homemaking, and all other teachers; all teachers need to work on the problem of reading improvement for the students in their classes.
	5. Every high school teacher is a teacher of reading. Each course in the high school curriculum poses certain special problems in speed, comprehension, vocabulary, and other reading skills. Only the teacher of the course can know of the particular reading difficulties that his course involves.

The Development of Reading Ability in High School. Should a continuous program of developmental reading for high school students be established? Reading specialists urge this since they believe that no child will have learned to read by the end of the fourth, the sixth, or any other grade in the elementary school. By grade four the average pupil will have done slightly more than to master the mere fundamentals of reading. The fact is that reading is not at all a simple skill. It is a composite of many abilities. Pupils get a start in reading in the elementary school, but they need years of practice in the higher forms of reading and interpretation in order to become fluent and able readers. The high school can no longer assume that students should be complete masters of reading when they enter. Habits and skills partially developed in the elementary school must be further refined. In addition, there are specific skills which should be learned at the high school level. There is no such thing as a general reading ability. Successful reading of such subjects as history, science, and mathematics requires a variety of abilities too complicated and too varied to have been achieved through a general elementary reading course.

Three Specific Proposals. Currently, the thinking of educators and especially students of reading supports three proposals:

1. A student rarely, if ever, achieves perfection in this complicated process. Regardless of his age or his capacity, *a reader is always able to improve his performance.* The development of reading ability can go on as long as he lives or desires to read more effectively. High school students are more likely to extend their reading capacity and establish more effective reading habits and skills if the high school teacher plans to assist them in making these improvements.

2. Every high school teacher is a teacher of reading in his subject area. As the American high school operates, reading is a predominant factor in nearly every subject in the curriculum. No other teacher can know the problems involved in a subject, such as mathematics, as well as the mathematics teacher knows them. Hence, only mathematics teachers can adequately assist students in learning the vocabulary of this subject and the other reading problems involved. This is equally true for most of the other subject-matter areas.

3. A high school student who has high reading ability in English may have low reading ability in mathematics, and vice versa. Many students are superior readers in some subject areas and very inadequate readers in others. This can be interpreted to mean that *a student may possess essential reading skills for one subject but not for another.*

In view of the mounting number of required subjects in the modern high school, it may appear that there remains no place for our recommendation of reading as a necessary course. Ideally, however, this should be done, with much emphasis upon specialized vocabularies rather than upon reading skill alone. The vocational areas of some comprehensive high schools have approached this by offering, for example, Printer's English and Technical Knowledge (TK) courses.

Here is a most troublesome question: How valid is any form of written examination, any I.Q. test, any measurement of educational development, when the vital factor of the ability to read may be missing? It is probable that in more than a few cases nothing beyond reading itself gets measured, although the school office files may bulge with "scores" and "percentiles." Obviously, until the reading problem is better understood, no other measurement should be fully accepted.

The qualified teacher must identify the students in his classes who lack essential reading habits and skills for the subject area. If at all possible, this should be done during the first week of a semester. He will then plan to assist them in acquiring the habits and skills that are essential to functional reading in the subject area. What are these skills and abilities needed for the improvement of reading on the high school level?

SOME ESSENTIAL READING SKILLS AND ABILITIES

Nearly all of us are aware that students who read very slowly or with low comprehension need assistance. But are speed and comprehension the only reading skills and abilities? Is it true that even slow reading in some types of study may be desirable rather than undesirable? Or might the individual read so slowly that he would fail to grasp the intent of the author? Many questions could be raised on this problem of reading improvement. A long list could be compiled on the problems of skills and abilities in reading. The following list is relatively short and is restricted to those stressed by reading specialists:

1. Speed, comprehension, and vocabulary
2. Skimming and other speed-reading techniques
3. Following directions
4. Organizing and outlining material
5. Using reference aids and the library
6. Interpreting tables, charts, and diagrams
7. Forecasting results and drawing conclusions
8. Challenging and evaluating what is read

As stated earlier, a student who reads well in one subject area may do badly in another because he lacks the particular reading skills required throughout. This raises several questions. What reading skills and abilities are most prominent in each of the separate subject-matter areas? What are the reading problems peculiar to each of the separate subjects? It is important that a teacher be aware of the type of reading skills and abilities essential to good progress in his field. In the subjects discussed below, each presentation is brief but developed to assist the preservice teacher in seeing the reading problems for his area of instruction.

English. Fiction requires rapid reading for full enjoyment of the story. Students who specialize in mathematics, science, industrial arts, and similar subjects develop the habit of reading for detail. In English they read too slowly to get the story and complain bitterly about having to read novels. They need assistance in adjusting their speed to the type of material to be read. In reading drama, it is highly necessary that one use his imagination; and this type of reading is least familiar to the average student. It is common with English teachers to select plays for class study that are more suitable for the rapid and gifted learners than for the average high school student. These plays may be beyond the maturity of the typical class. Plays should be selected on the reading level of the teen-agers in a specific class. Recordings and films will help them to see imaginatively through the words of the play.

Reading poetry with a class runs into a negative cultural attitude held by a majority of the typical secondary class. Poetry should be read aloud if rhythm and lilt are to be appreciated fully. If you as a teacher can read poetry well, try reading selected poems to a class—but on the maturity level of the class rather than your own. Then experiment with choral reading and the singing of ballads and lyrics by the class. Attitudes toward poetry can be changed very quickly when teen-agers come to appreciate rather than detest it. The skill or ability by which this is done is learned through reading aloud.

Mathematics. This subject, unlike much of the material in English, requires slow and intensive reading. There is a new and technical vocabulary that must be understood for success. The teacher should develop the technical phases slowly and fully. In meeting these responsibilities, the mathematics teacher is merely helping teen-agers to learn how to read in the field of mathematics. The skill or ability to be acquired here is the adjustment of mathematics students to a new type of reading. Some students fail in mathematics because they never learn how to read mathematics material. Another reading skill that needs to be emphasized in mathematics is the interpretation of tables, charts, and formulae.

Science. Teachers of science are faced with the following problems: (1) getting teen-agers to understand and use a technical vocabulary, (2) using effective symbolic language, especially in chemistry and physics, (3) helping students to see the cause and effect relationships and distinguishing between relevant and irrelevant material, (4) aiding them in understanding and employing formulae and equations, and (5) encouraging students to read widely in the field of science. Note that reading in science can include every one of the eight reading skills and abilities listed above. The comments of observers indicate that science teachers, as a group, are not very effective in getting students to read widely in science and in adjusting their speed to the type of material read.

Social Science. The literature in social science courses requires the most comprehensive and complex forms of reading—more than any other subject. Actually, a major problem for teachers in the social sciences is the guiding of reading. Every skill and ability in the above list must be possessed by a teen-ager who hopes to meet the reading requirements in social science. Five of the problems most frequently mentioned are as follows: (1) assisting students to understand the large vocabulary load—many of the words are old words with new meanings and are difficult to define, (2) helping students to develop critical thinking, particularly on controversial issues, (3) instructing students in the interpretation of maps, charts, and graphs, (4) assisting students in the analysis of propaganda or in learning not to believe all they read, and (5) guiding students through the research steps that lead to wide reading in the social sciences.

Industrial Arts. Mental short cuts, which reading provides, increase the hand-speed of teen-agers; superior readers learn more and do more in a fixed period of time. The four reading problems of the industrial arts include: (1) instruction of students in accurate detail—they must carry cryptic instructions and visual images in their minds after reading the instructions since a mistake at a machine can be costly; (2) reading charts, blueprints, diagrams, and maps requires special attention to detail—the students learn a new set of symbols and develop a new concept of spatial and symbolic relations; (3) the teacher aids the student in developing the ability to translate written instructions into mental understanding; and (4) the teacher must save time by spending time on these reading processes and aiding students with unfamiliar material. Note that the specific reading skills and abilities, which are essential for industrial arts students, differ markedly from those in other subjects. The specific nature of the reading in industrial arts makes reading in this field as difficult as in any academic subject. Some vocational schools, as has been stated, recognize this by providing special classes devoted to "TK"—technical knowledge. But a common complaint by industrial arts teachers is, "They just can't read!" We suggest that if the students could read and do manipulative tasks, there would be no justification for the existence of these courses.

Business. The material used in business courses is essentially adult in nature. The business forms—contracts, insurance policies, invoices, and governmental material—are all couched in adult language; they require a special vocabulary and a formalized grammar. Students need help in adjusting to a new type of reading material and a heavy vocabulary that may seem quite unreal. By demonstrating how to read this adult material and by giving some attention to speed and comprehension through orderly routine, the teacher may be of value.

DIAGNOSTIC AND REMEDIAL PROCEDURES

Reading is a highly essential tool in the American high school; it is the key to the world's knowledge. To be a successful student, one must be a competent reader in general, as well as in several special subject-matter fields.

Diagnosis of Reading Ability. Retardation in reading has two implications: (1) the retarded student's reading capacity will be two or more grades below his actual grade status or (2) his reading capacity will be inadequate for a subject such as mathematics, science, English, or social studies. The procedure for determining the reading status, in general, of a student or a class is through the application of a standardized reading test. To find what specific reading skills and abilities a class or a student has or lacks, administer a diagnostic reading test such as the *Iowa Silent Reading Test*.[2]

Thus, when a diagnostic test is being employed, the teacher is attempting to discover the nature of the learning difficulties and deficiencies of students in his classes.[3] The study of scores earned in such a test will reveal the students who have deficiencies, and it will indicate the specific reading difficulties for every student. A teacher, through such testing, gains important clues as to what needs attention.

Diagnosis by teacher test. In addition to a standardized diagnostic test, the teacher may want to devise a simple reading test of his own. To administer a simple reading test for determining reading speed and comprehension, follow these steps:

1. Select a representative section from the class textbook.

2. Count and indicate the cumulative number of words for each line up to 1,000 words.

3. Set the time limit for the test at ten minutes.

4. Duplicate and administer the test. As the test is being administered, say, "stop, and check the line being read"—at the end of three minutes and again at the end of six minutes.

5. Provide for exact timing, good motivation, and no interruptions during the administration of the test.

6. Prepare an objective test over the 1,000 words. Administer it promptly after the reading is finished. (Reading speed is determined by Step 4, comprehension by Step 6.)

[2] Harry A. Greene, A. N. Jorgensen, and V. H. Kelley, *The Iowa Silent Reading Test* (Advanced Form, Grades 9-13) (Yonkers, N. Y., World Book Co., 1939), pp. 173-74. For a detailed description and reviews of this and other like tests, see: O. K. Buros, *Mental Measurement Yearbook* (New Brunswick, N. J., Rutgers University Press, 1953).

[3] School superintendents on occasion do this for an entire school system, but for another purpose—to quiet critics of the schools. Positive gains are greatly emphasized to advantage.

Such a test will not be standardized. It will not necessarily be based upon established vocabularies, and its outcome will depend much upon the graded reading level of the textbook. Nevertheless, it will serve to identify, rather accurately, those students who are retarded, slow learners, average learners, rapid learners, and gifted.

Gifted readers and rapid learners. Diagnosis is not entirely a matter of seeking out retarded students or slow learners. When gifted readers and rapid learners are revealed through this process, two steps may be taken: (1) enriching and implementing subject-matter reading, and (2) providing exploratory reading that is apart from the course at hand. The procedures outlined in Chapter XIII must be developed for the student who obviously has tremendous reading ability and skill.

The Retarded Reader. Approximately one-third of all high school students today are retarded readers; hence, we must emphasize here the need to help them. Not all of these are slow learners; a number of average, rapid, and gifted learners will be retarded readers. Even though a gifted learner may be reading at or somewhat above his grade level, his reading rate and comprehension may be decidedly below his capacity to achieve. Retardation in reading is usually due to several causes—mental, physical, and emotional factors, as well as overcrowded classrooms, may all be involved.

How to identify. The following guideposts offer clues for identifying the retarded readers.

1. The student neglects to do necessary reading.

2. He is dissatisfied with his reading; he complains and objects to any assignments that require reading.

3. His reading test scores are low, usually in the lowest fourth.

4. He uses words when speaking that he does not comprehend when reading.

5. He displays personal attitudes that are negative, such as an extreme hostility toward teachers, poor family attitudes toward school, unusual nervousness, undue belligerence, and general discomfort.

Visual difficulties may be apparent: holding the book very close to the eyes or very far away; severe squinting when reading; the reversing of words; using a bad headache as a reason for not studying. It is the teacher's job to follow through and arrange for correction of such physical defects as can be repaired.

Help for the Retarded Reader. Who is responsible for helping the retarded reader? Practices vary widely. High school enrollments have grown so rapidly in recent years that principals have been kept in a state of indecision regarding this problem. However, it is agreed that the regular teacher is responsible for assisting all students in acquiring the reading skills and abilities needed to understand the content material of his subject. Also, the responsibility of the teacher extends to locating retarded readers.

Types of remedial classes. What may be done to help is a matter of divided opinion. A fairly strong trend is emerging to provide special classes for those who need further diagnostic and remedial help beyond what the classroom teacher may be able to provide. It has been found that according to their mental age the reading capacity of many slow learners is perfectly normal. A study by Blair[4] indicated that three types of remedial classes are developing in the United States.

1. Special classes in English and remedial reading are being established. In high schools following this practice, students who have been identified as retarded readers are assigned to classes in English, usually without any indication that their classes differ from regular English classes. In some schools only those who are average in mental ability but below average in reading achievement are assigned to these classes. In other schools such classes are primarily for students of general inferior ability. Some schools attempt to group these students homogeneously by arranging classes with students of similar capacity together. Easy textbooks are selected, and students earn a standard credit for the course.

2. Specialists are being employed to coach individuals or small groups. For the most part, high schools following this plan employ teachers especially trained for diagnostic and remedial procedures in reading. Students are sent to the reading laboratory in groups of ten or less. Approximately thirty minutes each day is given to each group. Every student is given a series of reading tests to determine the cause of retardation. The teacher-clinician then studies the test results and arranges a remedial program in accordance with the findings. No credit is earned by this plan, although it has been recommended.

3. The core-program plan includes provisions for problem readers. Remedial reading is taught in connection with social living classes. These are organized according to I.Q. and reading ability. Special emphasis is given in those sections which contain poor readers, and standard credit is provided. There is great variation in the methods employed from school to school in the core plan.

The role of the regular teacher. Classes for the seriously retarded are not too numerous in the regular high school, and teachers, specifically trained for remedial teaching, are rare. Of course, the regular teacher is responsible for all reading related to his subject-matter area; and some aid can be provided by him in even extreme cases. The classroom teacher can: (1) develop personal rapport with those who need remedial assistance, (2) help the student gain insight into the basis of his own difficulty, (3) find a problem important to the student which requires

[4] Glenn M. Blair, *Diagnostic and Remedial Teaching in the Secondary School* (New York, The Macmillan Co., 1956), pp. 151-163.

him to use some reading skill in order to obtain a solution, (4) use the diagnostic devices that are available, and (5) discuss the student with his other teachers.[5]

On occasion, an entire school may embark upon a reading program. It may be voluntary, such as those sponsored frequently by public libraries; it may be emphasized within the English curriculum; it may be an outgrowth of school guidance workers; or it may center in homeroom activities. In any event, the classroom teacher will find himself enthusiastically developing reading skills and abilities related to his own course content. Running throughout the process will be a philosophy similar to that of Alexander Meiklejohn, who wrote:

A book, I think, is in its best meaning an offer of friendship from him who writes to him who reads.

AN OUTLINE OF THE READING PROGRAM

Our secondary schools, under pressure, are slowly recognizing the need to improve the reading skills of *all* high school students. While all students can profit by such a program, a few are in desperate need of it. Up to the present, there are very few qualified teachers available for this specialized work; furthermore, there has been a tendency for principals and teachers to ignore the problem by laying the blame on the elementary school or the parent. As yet, very few high schools have instituted a satisfactory reading program though some experimentation has shown promise. However, if the parents and the public really want the service and are willing to pay for it, specialized teachers will be trained and the high school teachers and principals will face the problem involved realistically.

The reading program described below is somewhat more extensive than the programs now being tried out in our high schools, but it is the type of program recommended by reading specialists. Enough is known now about the reading deficiencies of high school students to indicate that greatly expanded reading programs will become more common in the high schools of the next decade.

Who should be responsible for instituting and supervising the high school reading program? What should be the pattern of organization for this program? What facilities are necessary for an adequate program? The answers to these three questions will probably indicate most distinctly the nature of the high school reading program of the next decade.

Who Should Be Responsible for the Program? The high school principal, by law and custom, is responsible for the over-all program of the

---

[5] J. D. Grambs and W. J. Iverson, *Modern Methods in Secondary Education* (New York, The Dryden Press, 1952), pp. 293-94.

high school. By and large, the high school principal is a realist. Even if capable, he could not find time to supervise the kind of reading program required in the contemporary high school; hence, he will delegate this responsibility to a qualified reading specialist, a Director of Reading. What are the duties of such a specialist? In general, the Director of Reading will: (1) supervise all activities related to reading, (2) administer and interpret all diagnostic reading tests, (3) serve as consultant on all reading problems, (4) direct all of the activities of the reading laboratory, (5) supervise and advise on the reading phase of the reading program with all teachers of general English, the core-curriculum teachers, the special-room teachers for non-readers, and the regular classroom teachers, and (6) offer in-service training on the teaching of reading to all teachers.

The Director of Reading is the key person in the high school program for the improvement of reading. There are four phases to such a program: (1) increase in speed and comprehension in reading for all students; (2) improvement of essential reading skills, other than speed and comprehension, for poor readers, (3) special classes for non-readers, and (4) orienting students to the type of reading required in each of the separate subject areas. The Director of Reading co-ordinates the reading program so as to give each student the amount and type of reading instruction needed. As a reading specialist, he will understand how to identify the reading deficiencies of students and to prescribe the correct reading program for removing the identified deficiencies. Much that has been done up to now for remedying deficiencies has lacked this understanding of how to identify and prescribe a program for eliminating the deficiencies.

The Organization of the Reading Program. Reading is a complicated process, for there is a wide range of reading needs among high school students. No one type of program will meet all of these varying needs. As a matter of fact, five distinct types of reading programs to meet the varying needs of students have been developed. These are: (1) the reading laboratory, (2) general English classes, (3) special classes in reading, (4) core classes, and (5) reading in regular classes. In general, a high school staff creates a program to meet a need that has become evident to the staff. As the staff becomes aware of other reading needs, the program is extended.

The Reading Laboratory. The reading laboratory is organized to provide three types of services: (1) increase the speed of reading, (2) increase reading comprehension, and (3) administer diagnostic reading tests to all students to identify reading deficiencies.

With some exceptions, all students can increase their speed of reading by subjecting themselves to short reading periods under pressure if there is supervision to guide, stimulate, and interpret. This program must be sufficiently flexible to serve slow, average, rapid, and gifted learners. It can be especially helpful to the gifted student who has the capacity to learn to read very rapidly; however, he often requires a specific environment to achieve the speed and comprehension for which he has the potential. Likewise, all students, for whom the program is suited, need this special environment. This is an elective program open to all students; however, it is not a program appropriate for the mentally retarded or the non-reader.

In many school systems, a general reading test will have been administered to all students in grades five or eight. However, in cases where this has not been done, a general reading test will be administered to all students in the reading laboratory. From the scores on the general reading test, students who earn very low scores can be identified for further testing. Later, other students will be discovered who read much below their indicated capacity, and they, too, will be invited to take diagnostic tests in order to identify their specific difficulties.

The director of the laboratory will want to identify the reading deficiencies of all students who need help. Once the specific deficiencies are known, individual instruction for a few extremely poor cases will be initiated and carried on until these particular students can be assigned to a reading group. On the basis of the diagnosis, students who are non-readers, ineffective readers, or mentally retarded will be assigned to either general English or special reading classes.

General English classes. Perhaps, the most widespread practice, as of now, for the improvement of reading in the high school is through the general English class. This program operates for grades 7 to 12 and is designed for students whose proficiency in the mechanics of language and spelling, as well as in reading, is from one to four years below their grade level.

The student is assigned to general English primarily because he is an ineffective reader. He may be a student with ability who has learned how to read but who has used his reading skills too little to get satisfaction from his reading, or he may be one who has never learned how to read due to ineffective teaching, lack of opportunity, or other causes. There are certainly many other students in general English classes who are very slow learners. They are retarded because they learn slowly and have not had the kind of teaching that slow learners must have.

The general English student is not fundamentally different from other students of his own age. He feels the same needs and has the same interests and drives; and he even has the same struggle to communicate through reading and language. But there are some differences. He reads poorly and doesn't enjoy reading. His vocabulary is meager, and his use of language is poor. Socially he is insecure. His needs and drives are normal for his age, but his social consciousness and competence are below par. He is irresponsible. He does not feel responsible for a classroom group. He assumes no responsibility for such necessary materials as his books, notebook, paper, and pencils.

The general English course puts much emphasis upon developmental reading, that is, helping students improve essential reading skills to meet the reading needs at the high school level, but general English also includes writing, spelling, listening, speaking, and English essentials.[6]

Because these students have spent their elementary school life in crowded classrooms and with reading materials adapted to the average learner, they now need reading materials adapted to the slow learner. Also, they need the necessary time to learn, and they need step-by-step instruction. The materials in their textbooks must be easy-to-read literature, expressed in simple language, and have an appeal to slow-learning students. The materials selected from literature should tell a story with continuity and sequence. Pictures and various visual aids with brief notes to the reader in short and easy sentences will also help these readers. Furthermore, they need help with words; it is essential to make a simple explanation of words that are beyond a minimal vocabulary.[7] Any of the students in general English can choose to improve their reading speed and comprehension through the reading laboratory. It is an elective program, and some students from general English would surely find it an excellent supplement to the work in general English.

Some help should be given to students in general English on basic reading skills, such as word meaning, phonetics, structural analysis, use of the dictionary, and promoting thoughtful interpretation. They have good though not powerful minds; they can be taught these skills, though it must be done slowly and step by step. Many manuals on basic reading skills are available and are excellent as supplementary references for use with a class in general English.[8]

Core classes. In high schools where the core curriculum has been initiated, reading improvement with the exception of the special subject class is delegated to the core teachers. With a class period of from two to three hours in length, they can provide for all of the common needs of their students. Reading has been accepted by them as a common need, and under the core program, the usual practice has been to set up short instructional units on reading improvement for those who need help in reading. Since, under the core program, the same students may continue with the same teacher for as long as three years, the core teacher is in a position to determine reading deficiencies and remedy them.

---

[6] A student, once assigned to general English, will in all probability continue with it throughout his secondary-school career.

[7] A great deal of suitable material for slow learners in general English is now available. See William Schramm, and others, *Adventures for Americans* (New York, Harcourt, Brace & Co., 1956).

[8] See Marion Monroe, Gwen Horsman, and William S. Gray, *Basic Reading Skills for High School Use* (Chicago, Scott, Foresman & Company, 1948).

Special classes for non-readers. In every group of teen-agers that enters the high school, with some exceptions, there will be a small number of severely retarded readers who are literally non-readers. Some of them will be mentally retarded teen-agers who have been promoted to high school because of age and physical and social development and who are entirely out of place in the elementary school. Others will be mentally capable teen-agers who are non-readers due to maladjustments, crowded classrooms, home conditions, illnesses, absence, or other causes.[9]

Being a non-reader marks a student as different in a society where the mores take learning to read as a matter of course. Not being able to read in our high schools, where success is dependent upon reading, is a distinct indication of maladjustment. Both students and teachers look upon such a student as odd. In his neighborhood, eyebrows are raised with the question, "Is there something wrong with that Jones boy?" It poses for the teacher of a special class not only very difficult educational problems but social and psychological problems as well. He must study the cumulative records of each non-reader, and study each non-reader as an individual to determine the specific reading difficulties which have blocked his reading progress. Non-readers are usually discouraged and are negative toward all reading activities. These students who have accepted failure in reading as their fate in life can be taught to read by a special teacher qualified to work with them. Furthermore, these students must be made to feel that reading is important to them, and the attitude of the teacher should be that these non-readers can be taught to read.

These non-readers have been identified by diagnostic and other reading tests which are administered to all entering freshmen. When identified, they are placed in special classes for non-readers. These classes are usually listed in the high school class schedule as English. Normally, the class size of the special classes for non-readers is held below 25. The instruction is mostly individual though small groups may be formed for non-readers with similar deficiencies. A wide variety of instructional material will be accumulated and used. Situations will be created where reading is needed, and the student will be helped to learn to read in order to meet this need. A rigid conformity must be avoided in these special classes, and ordinarily the instructional load of teachers for special classes of non-readers is limited to five classes per day.

Reading in the regular classroom. It has been pointed out already that reading is a complicated process which is never complete and which is ever subject to improvement. No individual has learned to read adequately at grades 4, 8, or 12. Developmental reading means that as one is promoted in a school system, he must acquire or add new reading skills to

---

[9] *Non-reader*: one who is unable to read even after more or less extended instruction.

those previously developed, just as he must learn new ways of behaving as he grows older in years.

Each subject-matter area of the high school offers a new vocabulary and requires a somewhat different type of reading ability. Hence, every academic teacher must be a teacher of reading because the student must develop new reading skills and abilities for each of the several academic subject areas. The academic teacher must: (1) teach the vocabulary of his subject to each and all of his students, (2) assist the student to identify and practice the type of reading required by the subject, and (3) help the student understand all parts of the textbook being used as well as how to use reference material.

Teaching the vocabulary of a subject-matter area to a class is a crucial matter. There are a large number of technical words in every subject-matter field, and each of these words is an essential symbol, the understanding of which leads to a grasp or mastery of the course. A student cannot express certain ideas without using certain word symbols.

The competent teacher will formulate a definite program for developing the needed vocabulary with his classes. There are several elements in such a program. Three of these are: (1) formulate a definite program for developing the special vocabulary of each course with the class, (2) identify the indispensable words in this vocabulary and have an alphabetical list of them mimeographed, and (3) take every opportunity to bring these words before the class and to cause students to use them.

Many students make the adaptation to reading science, mathematics, or social studies easily and quickly. However, others go on reading literature just as they did science, entirely unaware that the two are different types of reading. Many students will not make this adjustment at all unless the teacher guides them in the adaptation of their reading to the new type of content. They need definite instruction in the reading of science. Of course, one can do as many teachers have—fail them in the course and explain that they were not interested or lacked scientific aptitude. But it is more professional to teach them how to read science and thus to gain the necessary insights into this important area which are needed by all citizens.

The textbook is a tool and a very vital tool if used competently. Textbooks differ markedly for the different subject-matter fields. With many students, a little time spent in helping them understand how to use the textbook and reference materials can make a considerable difference in their progess in and attitude toward their school work.

The ability to read well is one key to success in the secondary school. This has been true for the past several centuries. In spite of the many new devices to aid the student, reading remains as an essential key for opening the world's storehouse of knowledge. Because we live in a time when technological learning is rapidly expanding, reading has become more necessary than ever before. A student who fails to learn to read rapidly and with understanding will not achieve his life expectations.

DISCUSSION PROBLEMS

1. Mrs. Brown relates that her older children learned to read much sooner than her small daughter who is now in grade school. She feels that the schools must have changed. How might you discuss this with other teachers? What would you say to Mrs. Brown?

2. Experienced teachers often feel that improved reading methods have hampered spelling and punctuation. In your own experience would you estimate whether this is true or not? If spelling and punctuation have suffered, what must be done? Should teachers return to early methods in the teaching of reading—or should spelling and punctuation receive additional attention?

3. From current resources determine whether there is any acceptable evidence that television has reduced reading time for high school students. What other factors should also be considered?

4. One high school student exclaimed, "After I graduate, I intend to get *Silas Marner* at the library and read it for pleasure . . . all this classroom analysis has spoiled my real enjoyment." What factors have influenced this attitude? Do we assume too much when we assign an "English major" to teaching literature?

5. Enrichment does not necessarily mean the assignment of additional lessons in the same subject matter. List 10 books that might be suggested for enrichment reading in history, mathematics, or science courses. Have you read them yourself?

6. It is stated that regardless of age or capacity a reader is always able to improve his performance. Is this a true statement? Why or why not? What suggestions might you make to a student who desired to improve his reading?

7. Would you favor the establishment of a reading laboratory in every high school? Why would you favor such a proposal? Why would you oppose such a proposal?

8. There are two students in your class who are handicapped by deficient reading skills. How could you verify this? Through what activities could these students begin to improve their reading skills?

9. Specialists in reading have coined the following descriptive words to classify types of readers: retarded readers, slow readers, average readers, rapid readers, and gifted readers. A precise concept of each of these types is helpful to the teacher. Through library research determine exactly what each of these words connotes.

10. Reading performance can always be improved: this applies to every college student as well as to every high school teacher. Visit the reading specialist on the college campus for a diagnosis of your reading strengths and weaknesses.

11. Of the three proposals that follow which one is the best for the improvement of reading on the high school level: (1) provide a reading laboratory

for the students that need help, (2) require the classroom teacher to work with students deficient in reading skills, (3) agree on a partnership between teacher and laboratory so that each is responsible for certain phases of the reading service.

RELATED REFERENCES

BETTS, E. A., *Foundations of Reading Instruction* (New York, American Book Company, 1954).

BISH, Charles E., "An Experiment in Reading Improvement," *Bulletin of the National Association of Secondary-School Principals* 36:89-96 (January, 1952).

BLAIR, Glenn M., "Remedial Reading in Senior High Schools," *School Review* 49:32-41 (January, 1941).

———, *Diagnostic and Remedial Teaching in the Secondary School* (New York, The Macmillan Co., 1956).

BOND, George W., "A Program for Improving Reading in the Secondary School," *School Review* 60:338-342 (September, 1952).

BOND, Guy L., and BOND, Eva. *Developmental Reading in High School* (New York, The Macmillan Co., 1941).

BOND, Guy L., and HANDLAN, Bertha, *Adapting Instruction in Reading to Individual Differences,* Series on Individual Instruction No. 5 (Minneapolis, University of Minnesota Press, 1948).

BURG, Ruth M., "Book Happy: Raising Reading Levels 2 to 4 Grades," *Clearing House* 25:34-44 (February, 1951).

BURR, Emily, "Prime Factors in the Placement of the Below Normal," *American Journal of Mental Deficiency* 40:429-434 (January, 1947).

CENTER, Stella S., and PERSONS, Gladys L., *Teaching High School Students to Read* (New York, Appleton-Century-Crofts, Inc., 1937).

DAVIS, Nelda "Extended Reading for the Gifted," *Bulletin of the National Association of Secondary-School Principals* 39:123-26 (November, 1955).

DURRELL, Donald D., *Improvement of Basic Reading Abilities* (Yonkers, N.Y., World Book Co., 1940).

FAY, Leo C., *Reading in High School* (Washington, D.C., Department of Classroom Teachers and National Education Association, 1956).

GRAMBS, J. D., and IVERSON, W. J., *Modern Methods in Secondary Education* (New York, The Dryden Press, 1952).

GRAY, William S., "Provisions for Poor Readers in High School and College," *Recent Trends in Reading: Supplementary Educational Monograph,* No. 49 (Chicago, University of Chicago Press, November, 1939).

———, *On Their Own in Reading* (Chicago, Scott, Foresman & Co., 1952).

GREENE, Harry A., JORGENSEN, A. N., and KELLEY, V. H., *The Iowa Silent Reading Test* (Advanced Form, Grades 9-13) (Yonkers, N.Y., World Book Co., 1939).

HAVIGHURST, R. J., STOVERS, Eugene, and DeHAAN, R. F., *A Survey of the Education of the Gifted* (Chicago, The University of Chicago Press, 1955).

HOVIOUS, Carol, *New Trails in Reading* (Boston, D. C. Heath & Company, 1956).

————, *Suggestions for Teachers of Reading for Grades 7 to 12* (Boston, D. C. Heath & Company, 1939).

Improving Reading Instruction, Bulletin of the California State Department of Education, Vol. 16, No. 1 (Sacramento, May, 1947).

KIRK, Samuel A., *Teaching Reading to Slow-Learning Children* (Boston, Houghton Mifflin Co., 1940).

KOTTMEYER, William, *Handbook for Remedial Reading* (St. Louis, Mo., Webster Publishing Co., 1947).

MARTENS, Elise H., *Curriculum Adjustment for the Mentally Retarded,* United States Office of Education Bulletin No. 2 (Washington, D.C., 1950).

McCALLISTER, J. M., *Remedial and Corrective Instruction in Reading* (New York, Appleton-Century-Crofts, Inc., 1936).

MONROE, Marion, HORSMAN, Gwen, and GRAY, William S., *Basic Reading Skills for High School Use* (Chicago, Scott, Foresman & Co., 1948).

National Society for Study of Education, *Reading in the High School and College,* 47th Yearbook, Part II (Chicago, University of Chicago Press, 1949).

PENTY, R. C., *Reading Ability and High School Drop Outs* (New York, Bureau of Publications, Teachers College, Columbia University, 1956).

ROSENBERGER, Homer T., "What Should We Expect of Education?" *Bulletin of the National Association of Secondary-School Principals* 40:13-348 (February, 1956).

San Francisco Unified School District, *The Teaching of Reading in the San Francisco Junior and Senior High Schools,* 93 Grover St., San Francisco, 1944.

SCHRAMM, William, and others, *Adventures for Americans* (New York, Harcourt, Brace & Co., 1956).

SHORES, J. Harlan, "Skills Related to the Ability to Read History and Science," *Journal of Educational Research* 36:584-593 (April, 1943).

SIMPSON, Ray H., "A Basic Approach to Remedial Reading," *The English Journal* 31:219-226 (March, 1942).

STRANG, Ruth, *Problems in the Improvement of Reading in High School and College,* rev. ed. (Lancaster, Pa., The Science Press Printing Co., 1940).

"Teaching Reading for the Gifted in Secondary Schools," *Bulletin of the National Association of Secondary-School Principals* 38:5-72 (October, 1955).

TRIGGS, Frances O., *We All Teach Reading—A Guide for Subject Matter Teachers in Schools and Colleges,* The Author, 419 W. 119 St., New York 27, 1954.

WITTY, Paul, *Reading in Modern Education* (Boston, D. C. Heath & Company, 1947).

————, *How to Become a Better Reader* (Chicago, Science Research Associates, 1947).

WORCESTER, D. A., *The Education of Children of Above Average Mentality* (Lincoln, The University of Nebraska Press, 1956).

GUIDANCE AND THE TEACHER

Thou wert my guide, philosopher, and friend.—POPE

Every teacher, whether he is aware of it or not, has an important role to play in guidance. Teachers for years have been contributing to guidance, but they must become more conscious of their specific functions and the relationships of their duties to the total guidance program.

Instruction and guidance cannot be separated, nor can experience and development. As mentioned several times previously, developmental experiences provide for the continuous adjustment of normal youth. This does not imply that guidance is not involved, but rather it implies that the developmental experiences should be carefully selected and directed by a skillful teacher. This is the best form of guidance and also the most desirable. From a functional viewpoint, the classroom teacher is and always has been the important person in the guidance program.

On the other hand, this does not mean that the teacher can function of and by himself, but rather it emphasizes that he is in continuous contact with the student and in a favorable position to change the student's behavior. The writers suggest, even in the absence of complete consensus, that the responsibilities of the classroom teacher for guidance fall into the following areas: (1) understanding the student, (2) developing the student's personality, and (3) providing occupational information and counseling.

GUIDANCE IN THE HIGH SCHOOL

A Point of View. What is guidance? Why provide it? How is it provided? These are three pertinent questions. They can be answered much more readily in terms of a specific school than for all of the high schools of the United States. In part, the truth is that principals and school staffs rarely see eye to eye on any of the three questions, and also that principals are not in general agreement on the answer to any of these three questions.

The guidance services have always been performed by some teachers in our high schools and neglected by others. The rapid changes in American society, during the last three or four decades, have created a demand for an expansion of all guidance services. For example, the great increase in juvenile delinquency during the decade of the 1950's indicated a neglect of guidance services by both home and school. The time is at hand when all high school teachers must be aware of and alert to guidance and the services provided by guidance.

What is guidance? One high school has expressed it this way. Its purpose is to help the students see beyond their own needs to their responsibility for others, to help them see that only as they are able to live co-operatively and democratically are they able to realize their own personal destiny, and to help them to see that only as they contribute to the best of their ability to other individuals do they achieve happiness and success themselves.

The definition of guidance developed by the staff of this same school is, "Guidance is defined as the process of assisting the individual to determine, analyze, and understand his interests, aptitudes, abilities, limitations, and opportunities, problems and needs, and, in terms of knowledge, to make wise choices and adjustments in order that he may serve society and live happily." Guidance is a functioning part of the total school program rather than a separate service divorced from the curriculum.

A point of view. This is the viewpoint of only one high school. It was developed by the faculty as a group and represents, as nearly as they could put it into words, the consensus or common belief of the staff about the purpose of guidance services. A guidance program is not imposed upon a staff; it must evolve and be representative of a common point of view which is held by the staff as a group. Guidance services cannot be provided by specialists alone, by teachers alone, nor by the principal alone. These services must reach each student in such a way that he is influenced. Unless the guidance service concept permeates the consciousness of all staff members, a common guidance point of view cannot prevail.

Specifically, guidance services are always provided by individuals. From person-to-person relationships or through counseling is where the individual is helped to make decisions. But in a school system, especially the large high school, the guidance services are inadequate for most students unless they are co-ordinated or organized. This is the specific duty of the high school principal; hence, the over-all guidance program of a high school can never rise above the vision of the principal of the school.

The Plan of Organization. The plan of organization for guidance services will vary greatly from high school to high school. By and large, these guidance services are rendered by three specific groups: (1) guidance specialists, (2) counselors, and (3) regular classroom teachers.

Guidance specialists. In large high schools, the Director of Guidance is made responsible, under the high school principal, for the guidance program. Normally, the duties of the Director of Guidance are: (1) to set up the testing program for entering freshmen and to direct all other testing outside of the regular instructional program, (2) to interpret test scores, (3) to name the counselors, and (4) to conduct in-service classes in guidance for all members of the staff (to establish a common point of view on guidance for the school). In addition, difficult cases in mental hygiene or counseling in special vocational fields are referred to the guidance specialist.

The counselors. The counselors are named by the Director of Guidance with the confirmation of the principal. They are ordinarily selected from the regular teaching staff and are teachers who have been rated superior and who find it easy to establish rapport with students. Their teaching load is lightened to give them free time for counseling.[1] These teachers counsel each student assigned to them in the selection and registration for courses which are best adapted to the potentialities of the student and which are of the greatest assistance in the achievement of the student's specific goals. The counselor studies the student's cumulative folder and the test data about each of his counselees to determine their interests, aptitudes, and potentialities. Also, they hold with each counselee during a semester from one to three interviews in addition to the registration interview.

What does a counselor do? The following is an abbreviated example of a counselor's work. In grade 8 of an elementary school, each member of the class was asked, after careful preparation, to write a theme on "My Future Plans." This short sentence comprised all of John's theme: "I plan to lean on my father's everlasting arms and eat three square meals a day." John's friends thought this was a great joke, but John meant every word of it.

When John's cumulative record with this statement in it fell into the hands of his high school counselor, the counselor studied it carefully for implications. Entrance test records, especially the intelligence test, indicated that John had potentialities for superior academic achievement. But John's record for the first year of high school implied that he meant to get through high school on a gentleman's grade of "C."

John came from a good family. Both his mother and father were sociable, well-liked, easy-going, and unambitious. The father owned and operated a small grocery store. The income from it had been sufficient to meet his obligations on a modest scale. It was evident to the counselor that John and his father had not thought through his future plans. The father was then forty, and it was clear that the store could not sup-

---

[1] *Counseling:* the procedure by which the counselee comes to understand himself so that he can solve his own problems.

port two families in comfort. Besides, the trend in the grocery business was definitely toward the chain grocery which was eliminating many small groceries such as that of Mr. Adams.

Through a series of conferences with the family and John, the situation was analyzed at length. The father knew about competition and had seen a number of small groceries fold up because of it, but it had not occurred to him that he, too, might be pinched. The outcome was that John and his father ultimately decided to drop the old goal and to meet during high school the college entrance requirements for medicine.

Fortunately, John's cumulative record, as well as his test scores on admission to high school, indicated that John was strong in science and mathematics plus being intellectually competent for the medical profession. With a clear-cut goal in mind, John went to work on a much stiffer series of courses and finished his school with all "A's" during the last three years.

Note please that John's counselor did not tell John what to do. Nevertheless, he helped John to interpret the facts and reach his own decision.

The classroom teacher. What services can the classroom teacher render in counseling and guidance? Classroom teachers are in contact with students every day of the week and every week of the year; hence, they are at hand to answer questions when personal and vocational problems are urgent, that is, when students feel the greatest need for help. Usually, the guidance specialist or the regular counselor can be seen only by appointment. If the teacher is a friendly, trusted, and wise person, the student will seek him out, or the teacher may sense the pupil's need for an interview. The teacher will have many of the essential facts at hand and can assist the student in stating the problem and arriving at a decision. Besides, the regular teacher knows the student as an individual in a way that the specialist or counselor may not.

However, when the interview reveals a complex problem of mental hygiene or a special vocational problem, the wise teacher will refer the student to the counselor or guidance specialist. The teacher must be aware of his specific functions as a counselor, for some students he can serve quite adequately while others will need to be referred to the specialists.

The classroom teacher is a specialist in a particular subject-matter area. He sees clearly how his subject-matter material is related to the work of the world and should indicate to students in what ways and how it can be practical. For example, with what jobs is chemistry most closely allied and what chemical skills and understandings are specifically related to industry and commerce?

Classroom teachers, as a group, have a better understanding of individual students than most other members of the high school staff. In fact, a goodly number of classroom teachers have a more complete understanding of their students than the parents of the students have. Because they understand students so well and are competent teachers, their students grow in responsibility, ability to get along with others, and in integrity. Also, classroom teachers guide student development by being sponsors of student activities.

However, not all academic teachers understand their students or plan to guide them in personality development. Some academic teachers are more interested in their subject matter than in their students. They have little time for or interest in the fine art of counseling students. They can tell students what to do, but they lack the essential insights or skills for helping them arrive at decisions. They are unable to help a student change an emotionally charged situation into a concisely stated problem which is an essential step toward reaching a correct decision. Such teachers lack the qualifications for guidance or counseling service except on dealing with questions in their subject-matter fields.

Guidance Is a Newcomer. Guidance, as an organized program, is of very recent development in the high school, but, as an activity of high school teachers, it is as old as the puberty rites of ancient tribes. Why has guidance and counseling become so prominent in recent years? Here are some of the situations which have brought about this change.

Modern life is complex. Full-time employment of youth is now delayed until the late teens. Each teen-ager needs to choose a vocation from hundreds of occupations and to make some preparation to qualify for his chosen field. Until recently a teen-ager simply found a job and learned his needed skills on the job. Or if he was dissatisfied with the job, he quit and tried another job until one was found that suited him. This trial-and-error process was a wasteful one; hence, today a choice is made from many occupations while in high school. This makes for a richer and a happier life.

All youth are in high school. The old academic curriculum was not adapted to all youth; thus, a greatly expanded curriculum had to be developed for all. As counselors plan the four-year schedule of courses in accordance with the needs of each entering freshman, the demand for courses not provided in the curriculum is made evident. Guidance and counseling, properly planned, serve to indicate the new courses that should be added to the curriculum. Thus, counseling is a procedure by which the contemporary curriculum of the high school is kept up-to-date.

Each individual is unique. A recognition of individual differences requires that the courses scheduled for each individual be tailored to fit, that is, be selected in accordance with the abilities and the goals of each student. Again, counseling is the procedure by which this is done.

Guidance had its origin in vocational need. It was an early practice in school guidance work for the director of guidance to announce, "We have a call for twenty boys to work at the telephone company," and then to seek out not the six or eight boys who wanted such work but rather a full quota of twenty. Today's worker in student personnel will say, "We have six or eight boys who are qualified. They will call at your office for an interview." John Dewey was not alone in leading education into a more democratic program, but his experimentalism, or the idea that experience is a basic element in insight and understanding, has probably done more to improve guidance concepts than the methods suggested by other educators. The obligation of the American schools, Dewey stressed, was to enable the individual to integrate his culture and his vocation effectively.

Today, warmth and sympathy are basic ingredients of guidance and counseling, as opposed to the "printer's devil" concept of an earlier generation. When the public was permitted to look upon guidance as a form of placement service provided by the schools, it seemed reasonable for business men to say, "Send us twenty boys for telephone work." Business alone is served when the school directs rather than counsels. Today, the school serves both business and youth by counseling in terms of the individual's aptitudes and goals. When the student makes the decision, he serves both himself and industry more efficiently, and the worth and dignity of youth are recognized. Every youth is an individual worthy of respect. If our touch is chilly and our tone self-righteous, we fail in our obligation to youth and the nation. Warmth and sympathy are desired in our relationships.

GUIDEPOSTS TO GUIDANCE AND COUNSELING

Guidance and counseling are more and more becoming accepted as fundamental services for every high school, and more and more every professional teacher is expected to serve in some capacity as a counselor. The competent teacher, as a matter of course, will function as a counselor within his own classroom, especially in the development of student personality and in helping students answer many personal and vocational questions. Organized guidance merely makes these services of the regular classroom teacher more obvious. Hence, a few guideposts to guidance and counseling will point the way to appropriate action. In Chart 22 these are purposely phrased as questions so that the reader will search for some answers.

The answers to this even dozen of "why questions" give insight into the needs for and the effective application of guidance techniques. Besides, these guides to action probably will remain as such throughout the professional life of the teacher.

Chart 22. Guideposts to Guidance and Counseling

GUIDEPOSTS	COMMENTS
1. Why should guidance and counseling be integrated with all aspects of the educational program of the school?	It is through guidance and counseling that ability to get along with others and other like outcomes are achieved.
2. Why should guidance and counseling draw on all the resources of the school and community which contribute to guidance services?	Helping youth make wise choices is a problem of the whole community and not of the school only.
3. Why are adequate information and records essential as a basis for individual counseling?	Decisions are reached on the basis of information and facts.
4. Why should provisions for guidance activities be made in all areas where teen-agers need to make decisions and adjustments?	Guidance and counseling is concerned with any decision or adjustment that a teen-ager makes.
5. Why should adequate information be available in the school concerning vocational and educational opportunities beyond the secondary school?	This information bears directly upon the decisions that teen-agers must make.
6. Why is it important that time for both group and individual activities be provided in the school program?	It is essential to have a time and a place for any organized service.
7. Why should an effective placement or follow-up service for students leaving school or graduating be a part of any well-rounded guidance service?	The transition period is difficult for many students; the school has the know-how for this service. It provides a check on the quality of the program of the school.
8. Why should specialists be available to assist with planning and organizing guidance activities and with difficult guidance problems?	Specialists help to co-ordinate guidance activities and to improve counseling services.
9. Why should there be competent leadership for the guidance program of the secondary school?	Without it the program lacks co-ordination and is ineffective.
10. Why is the teacher the key person in the guidance and counseling program of the secondary school?	The teacher more than any other person is in continuous contact with students.
11. Why should the teacher have some preparation in the psychology of adolescence, mental hygiene, and the theory and practice of guidance and counseling?	Content materials which are included in these courses help a teacher organize his experiences and achieve a better understanding of what makes a teen-ager tick.
12. Why should the teacher be assisted in improving his effectiveness for guidance and counseling through a continuous program of in-service training?	A common point of view for the whole staff is thus developed. Without this the guidance program lacks co-ordination.

GUIDANCE TECHNIQUES

Instruction and guidance are inseparable functions in the classroom; subject-matter mastery should never be the sole objective. How students learn and how they feel are just as important as how much they learn. The way students feel largely determines their attitudes toward life and other people. It is in the field of learning that guidance is most closely integrated with good or poor social adjustment. And it is the classroom teacher who is the key to how the student feels and how he learns.

Students need to feel that they belong and are approved. With belonging and approval, there comes a feeling of being secure or of knowing where one stands. Teachers vary greatly in their ability to create a social climate where this feeling of security exists, but in doing so, they come to know students as individuals and bring about constructive changes in the personality of the individual. These are two essentials to the complete process of guidance and counseling.

Guidance Techniques in the Regular Classroom. One experienced teacher developed a list of 24 statements which was entitled "Good Teaching Is Going On If." The following statements were taken from this list. Good teaching is going on:[2]

1. If the students seem devoid of tension and are free in speaking, expressing opinion, and movement;

2. If the students regard the teacher as a friend rather than a task-master;

3. If there is some humor and some laughter when appropriate;

4. If courtesy is the accepted mode of behavior;

5. If the students, as evidenced by their eyes, are interested and eager;

6. If every opportunity for emphasis on good character is seized.

This has been characterized as good teaching. What are the implications from the above statements as to the relations between the teacher and students? Are they not similar to those that need to be established between the counselor and the counselee? If the statements were accepted and practiced by a teacher, would he not know his students as individuals and also be interested in the development of teen-age personality? Couldn't these statements also be labeled, "Good Group Guidance Is Going On If?" To the authors, it seems clear that the social climate described above makes the statement, "Instruction and guidance are inseparable functions in the classroom," obvious and true.

Discussion. Why may discussion be an effective guidance technique when in the hands of a good discussion leader? It is a give-and-take technique that provides for action and interaction within the group. There

[2] Edgar M. Finck, "What Do We Mean by Good Teaching?," *Nation's Schools* 48:49 (December, 1951).

is vigorous student participation in discussion under a proper leader. In the discussion of a controversial issue, all phases of the controversy are presented. A newspaper may be biased, but a bias or a prejudice has no place to hide in a healthy discussion.

In a discussion where all points of view are brought out and all factual and supporting evidence is presented, student attitudes usually change. As the discussion proceeds, a competent discussion leader keeps the discussion organized and summarized on the blackboard. Courtesy, or giving each student an opportunity to express his ideas, is maintained. In such a permissive atmosphere, decisions, representative of the class consensus, can be reached; decisions are reached in guidance and counseling by a nearly identical procedure.

To teen-agers, the truths accepted by peers in a permissive atmosphere go unchallenged. Thus, a decision reached through discussion may be truly significant; especially if the controversial issue is concerned with a moral or social problem, it may become an accepted decision to every member of the group. This is group guidance of a high order.

Sociodrama. Frequently, children play "Let's pretend" and forthwith produce alluring versions of school, family, and cowboys. An observer to such play-acting can often gain a child's insight into the world by hearing four-year-olds play house. The "mother" will discipline the "children" much as the children are actually disciplined. This technique, when applied to a high school class, is also a useful technique to safely disclose the feelings of teen-agers.

In real life, there is no chance to retreat after making a statement or revealing one's true feelings, but in the drama, individuals are able to express their feelings without danger of reprisal. In fact, if the role is played worthily, even though it is an expression of true feelings, it may win approval and even high praise.

To illustrate, an actual sociodrama will be presented. The teacher prepared for the event by saying, "Today, we are ready for a deeper look at child-parent relations. Let's imagine our family as father, mother, and teen-age girl of twelve or thirteen. What might be a typical problem of this size family?"

STUDENT: Her parents think the girl is too young to wear make-up.
TEACHER: What kind of family might this be?
STUDENT: Middle-class, middle-aged, owners of a shoe shore in a small town. The girl is a crybaby and tells fibs. The father has a soft mustache, and smokes a pipe; he has suspenders; he is a Deacon of the church; and he is worried about the behavior of his kids.

Three students are selected to play the role of the family and are sent from the room to plan their individual roles. Then, the teacher instructs the class. "We will give the players two minutes to rough out their plans.

During the act let's keep notes on aspects of effective or ineffective parenthood. When the players return, they will act as they themselves would in such a situation." Here is how the dramatization went:

MOTHER: (*enters the room*) Mmmm, that is nice music. Going to be home all evening?

FATHER: Uh huh! What is Mary getting ready for?

MOTHER: She is going skating with Sammy Morse.

FATHER: Be sure to tell her to get home early. Kids aren't like when we were kids. They are on the street at all hours.

MOTHER: (*nods as though it were an old story*)

MARY: (*enters*) Good night, Mom. Good night, Pop.

MOTHER: Have a good time. Your father says he wants you to be home promptly at nine.

FATHER: And we mean nine! What's on your face, rouge?

MARY: No, it isn't. I washed my face in cold water and rubbed hard with a towel.

FATHER: It is paint! You look like a painted woman.

MARY: Oh, Daddy! All the kids wear it. They will laugh at me.

FATHER: So it's more important what they think than what your mother and father say? I want you to wash your face!

MARY: Never mind, I'm not going (*on the verge of tears*)

MOTHER: I agree with you about the paint, but I don't think that makes Mary any less trustworthy.

FATHER: Why? She denied she had the stuff on, a few minutes ago! That was a lie, wasn't it?

MARY: (*Begins to sob*)

MOTHER: Father was too harsh. Never mind, Mary. Stop crying. There, there—

FATHER: (*Begins to retreat*) I didn't mean that you could never wear it. Maybe, when you are old enough you can wear it. Now stop crying. Well, maybe it won't bother to wear a little bit.

MARY: (*Rises and goes out of the room*)

A discussion by the whole class follows. The sociodrama had made it acceptable to talk about parent-child relations. The sociodrama had released the feelings of the participants and made a certain conflict between parents and teen-agers clear. By the end of the class period, the interaction within the ·class had led to three specific generalizations which were written on the blackboard. These were:

1. An important conflict between today's parents and children is a cultural lag, that is, a disagreement between past and present standards.

2. Parents can push so hard that their children are forced to lie.

3. Attempts to change behavior in a family setting are complicated by the expectations that the rest of the family puts upon you to behave the way you have done in the past.[3]

[3] Charles E. Hendry, Ronald Lippitt, and Alvin Zander, "Reality Practice as Educational Method," *Psychodrama Monographs* No. 9 (New York, Beacon House, Inc., 1947), pp. 9-24.

Where intense feelings are involved, sociodrama is an excellent technique for starting a discussion. One can talk about an imaginary family that has been portrayed quite objectively and still draw inferences from the play that one applies to himself. Incidentally, such a free discussion of the sociodrama helps to reduce tensions within each student in respect to a relationship that is not freely talked about in public. The student's insights into the causes of family conflict move him a step toward maturity, that is, in the development of his personality.

Organized Guidance Techniques. The feelings of strangeness, loneliness, fear, and even helplessness are known to everyone when placed in a new environment. Orientation services assist the individual in developing a "sense of belonging" in the new environment. By providing assistance with minor problems, major problems may be prevented from arising.

Orientation. Normally, orientation starts during the latter part of the year previous to high school entrance. An elementary teacher with a keen understanding of high school life and with a little flair for the dramatic can make eighth-graders eager to attend high school. Usually, an outstanding student is sent to the elementary school to explain the program of the high school and to answer questions. Sometimes a former pupil of the elementary school, now attending high school, will represent the high school and explain the many good features of the school he is now attending. Since each high school has its own peculiar orientation practices, a brief description of orientation in a regular, four-year, comprehensive high school is outlined here. Although practices may vary, the purpose of orientation is identical—to assist incoming freshmen in developing a sense of belonging in the new environment.

Understanding the physical plant of a school can best be achieved from a diagram of its floor plan and actual visitation. Conducted tours of the building provide ninth-graders with their first glimpse of the school shops, swimming pool, gymnasiums, boiler room, key room, book room, libraries, and secondary teachers. Witnessing the musician at work, the printer feeding a press, or a sheet-metal student welding may provide the spark of interest and curiosity desired. Again, review of the many courses the school offers, the identity of teachers in subject areas, and the success of graduates may bring about added zest for a particular course of study.

Students in the ninth grade need help in locating rest rooms, the athletic field, the greenhouse, the cafeteria, and the stairways. They must have a working knowledge of the numbering system for classrooms and lockers. They need to understand the plan for a fire drill or an emergency evacuation. They want to become a part of the student body and follow traffic regulations and other school rules.

The guidance classes[4] serve as a place for the implementation of

[4] In this school freshmen are grouped into orientation classes where a series of guidance tests are administered and interpreted. Much help is given in selecting the academic or vocational field to which each will give his major attention.

"Freshman Day" activities, the many class assemblies, and the social affairs planned by and for the ninth-graders. Through it, the freshman counselors may develop personal friendships that will endure for a life-time. An established routine, where guidance programs exist, is to hold at least one personal interview with each student each semester. This may be for the purpose of selecting a desirable course of study, checking on continued absence or tardiness, or solving personal problems inside or outside the school. Of late, the counselor of the freshman class is auto-matically promoted with the class, and following graduation, he returns to a new freshman group and becomes their friend and leader for a new four-year period.

Obviously, in the large high school, counselors, guidance specialists, and teachers must meet frequently to insure a unified program and common objectives. At such meetings, individual cases may be discussed freely and confidentially so that all teachers are aware of unique personalities and any specific programs planned for them. All counselors, of course, will not be familiar with the highly technical aspects of vocational courses, and an exchange of views and experiences make for improved guidance. Here, too, the school principal or guidance specialist may develop aims or goals that seem desirable. Basic core programs, life-adjustment classes, and the techniques of "selling" the classic courses are subjects often crystallized through meetings with counselors.

Homeroom guidance. After the freshman year, where in the high school program might guidance be continued? What inroads are made to dis-courage such a continuation?

As outlined earlier, the modern high school provides for a counselor to continue with his class throughout the four years until graduation. He will interview each member at least once each term—more frequently, if time permits. But the heart of the guidance program, after the initial semester, is now assumed to be in the homeroom. Here, another teacher may build friendships through assisting students in solving personal, school, and home problems. Class officers may be elected, and formal business meetings may be held to stimulate interests in parliamentary procedures. Homeroom parties help to encourage leadership, participation, and self-awareness. Social courtesies may be discussed. The homeroom may enter teams in intramural athletic competitions; spelling bees are sometimes profitable; chess and checker tournaments negate any desire to be tardy. The active homeroom will have a low number of discipline problems as opposed to the inactive homeroom. The high school home-room may foster friendships and understanding, or it may discourage the student in many ways. Chart 23 presents some homeroom guideposts.

Perhaps the greatest evil that may beset the homeroom program is the administrative attitude which has grown out of the need to (1) assemble a large number of students for a preliminary roll call before regular classes

Chart 23. Homeroom Guideposts

GOALS CAN BE ACHIEVED	GOALS CAN NOT BE ACHIEVED
When teacher and students have ample time to know each other	When the teacher gives full time to processing excuses for absence
When the teacher understands each student as an individual	When the teacher must rely entirely upon cumulative records
When permissiveness includes classroom activities, games, and other departures from routine	When the homeroom "curriculum" is prescribed by higher authority and closely supervised
When the student is a member of the homeroom for a long time	When the homeroom membership is changed each semester
When students and teacher may plan programs together	When the homeroom is regarded as nothing more than an assembly room
When the teacher is free to discuss school rules and to interpret them in terms of social needs	When the teacher is directed to "lay down the law" of the school and to administer punishments for non-compliance
When the teacher may know the parents and home backgrounds through personal contacts	When the teacher lives "socially above" or "socially beneath" the students and parents
When students and teacher may develop mutual likes and dislikes	When teachers retreat into an exclusive "ivory tower"
When the teacher's personality is consistent and students may come to anticipate limitations	When the teacher is "love and sunshine" one day and "mean and stormy" the next
When the school regards the homeroom as an essential factor in the guidance program	When the school fails to establish the homeroom as an instructional period

begin, (2) obtain many clerical records for school and city files, and (3) provide teacher supervision of lockers, sale of school supplies, activity association memberships, school rings, annuals, P-TA memberships, Red Cross enrollments, and similar activities that might otherwise invade the established classroom curriculum. Inroads are made upon the guidance program when such homeroom activities are not held to a minimum.

Also, we should point out that teachers, who were paid according to the number of instructional periods in earlier days, now may feel that the homeroom is an added burden for which no stipend is given. Recognition of this period as an instructional assignment may, in time, remove that obstacle. In order to meet the objections of teachers to an extra assignment, some high schools have incorporated the homeroom with the first period of the day. Teachers point out that over the years the addition of the homeroom has moved the traditional starting hour of the day from nine to eight A.M. This situation needs recognition because it bears directly upon teacher attitudes toward the homeroom responsibility.

Homeroom activities. Friendship is a two-way street. Each student will come to rely upon and have faith in the adult leader who manifests a personal interest in his welfare and the outcomes of his school experience. This is the spirit which must prevail in any program undertaken by the homeroom.

Group dynamics. Through homeroom activities, students may be helped to see themselves as others see them; in turn, they may be helped to adjust attitudes that tend to be harmful to themselves as well as to the group. Willey and Andrew[5] have provided a rather complete listing of roles that members of a group play—whether or not they are aware of it—under any type of autocratic or permissive leadership.

1. Facilitate the group task by defining the problem, co-ordinating group effort, or making suggestions in solving problems

    a. initiator-contributor
    b. information seeker
    c. opinion seeker
    d. information giver
    e. opinion giver
    f. elaborator
    g. co-ordinator
    h. orientor
    i. evaluator-critic
    j. energizer
    k. procedural technician
    l. recorder

2. Strengthen, regulate, or maintain group efficiency

    a. encourager
    b. harmonizer
    c. compromiser
    d. gatekeeper and expediter
    e. standard setter
    f. group-observer
    g. commentator
    h. follower

3. Promote individual interest which is not relevant to the group

    a. aggressor
    b. blocker
    c. recognition seeker
    d. self confessor
    e. playboy
    f. dominator
    g. help seeker
    h. special interest pleader

A sampling of self-evaluation in role-playing. To this list of roles played by group members were added: non-participant, escape seeker, morally uncertain, parent hater, and skill lacker. Students in one section of a twelfth-grade social-studies course were invited to rate themselves during a day in which panel discussions were held. Results, tabulated in order of frequency, are given in Table 15.

To illustrate what may be learned through follow up of each declaral —the single boy who admitted that he hated his parents was found to be on probation for auto theft, an extremely important item unknown by the teacher until this exercise in group dynamics was given. Again, the course of action by the teacher in helping the three who said that they were "morally uncertain" called for the highest sort of strong, positive, and regular techniques in guidance. Basically, this study was intended

---

[5] Roy D. Willey, and Dean C. Andrew, *Modern Methods and Techniques in Guidance* (New York, Harper & Brothers, 1955), pp. 563-564.

Table 15. **Student Identification of Their Class Roles**

FREQUENCY OF MENTION	ADMITTED ROLE	FREQUENCY OF MENTION	ADMITTED ROLE
14	Group observer	2	Self confessor
13	Opinion giver	2	Follower
8	Information seeker	1	Opinion giver
7	Initiator-contributor	1	Information giver
5	Non-participant	1	Co-ordinator
3	Compromiser	1	Procedural technician
3	Escape seeker	1	Playboy
3	Morally uncertain	1	Dominator
2	Evaluator-critic	1	Special interest pleader
2	Harmonizer	1	Parent hater
2	Gatekeeper and expediter	1	Energizer
2	Commentator		

to be of value to the group in arriving at solutions to problems, but the process also yielded information that the teacher might have missed entirely. In this instance, it was well that the teacher did not confine guidance to the homeroom only.

Students of psychology, anthropology, and sociology by now are agreed that effective learning takes place best when there is active participation. The following homeroom activities indicate a variety of approaches that lend themselves to the enterprise centered around group dynamics.

1. Some modification of accepted parliamentary procedures can be very practical for the student who is to be a participant in school elections; he will later find this of use in union and lodge meetings, as well as in political assemblies and PTA gatherings. The homeroom can be quite realistic in the election of officers and the appointment of chairmen who will have specific responsibilities. Committees may be selected for courtesy (when someone is ill), housekeeping, projects, entertainment, publicity, and a host of teen-age matters. On occasion, sheer parliamentary drill continues to be a source of pleasure and learning, but this should not be forced upon any homeroom.

2. Common charities include interest in and support of Junior Red Cross, United Community Fund, the Polio Foundation, the Heart Fund, and the Cancer Fund—when approved by the school administration. Letters may be written to hospitalized youth, and toy collections may be held for such groups as the Salvation Army. (Charity exploiters too often turn first to schools as a source of easy revenue; hence, school policy should be strictly followed.)

3. Games and athletics within the homeroom are limited for space and time; however, some orientation is possible here. Teachers are often amazed to discover that teen-agers who cheer wildly at school athletic contests generally do not know what they are shouting about. Hence, a

most natural approach would be to invite athletes to visit the homeroom and discuss in detail the rules of the various sports. Again, students will display a remarkable interest in mathematical processes—if batting averages of local and national baseball stars are computed on the homeroom blackboard.

4. When a majority of the homeroom show interest in oral activities, opportunity is provided for development of improved attitudes through simple discussion of contemporary topics, panels, and extemporaneous speeches. Once this ability has been advanced, a homeroom may become a speakers' bureau for the promotion of all school activities—members may tour the building to speak to other homerooms. Clubs may also be formed and debate tournaments may be held during homeroom time.

5. Guest speakers from the community find that they invariably express themselves best before a small group, such as the homeroom. They may talk on health, personal grooming, how to apply for work, how to file an income tax form, Hi-Y organization, summer camp activities, first aid, hobbies, crafts, and sundry topics of interest to the homeroom. Many schools utilize the homeroom period for an annual Occupations Day during which outstanding business leaders deliver short talks and answer questions pertinent to their work. (Here it may be necessary to combine homerooms, that is, let the girls who are interested in nursing meet together, and boys who want to know more about engineering gather in a special place.)

6. Films that do not conflict with established audio-visual aids in use by other classes have a place in the homeroom. Titles should be selected by a homeroom committee and the teacher.

7. Radio broadcasts often are made to coincide with homeroom time. When these are sponsored by the public schools, there should be no questions regarding participation. Certain news broadcasts add to the day for students in social studies.

8. Recordings, which do not interfere with programs provided in other classes, may be a special feature presented by the entertainment committee with teacher approval. Public libraries now make available a number of recordings that may not be available in school libraries.

9. Political campaigns directly related to school functions can provide an interesting activity. Participation in the American Legion program for Boys' State and Girls' State and County days may include backing a homeroom candidate for office.

10. Unusual events might include the nature of work done in various school communities. In agricultural areas of the Midwest, where corn is king, center attention upon detasseling operations done by teen-agers. Citrus crops of Southern areas provide employment for youth, and also recreational jobs hold an attraction for youth.

The professional library will be of value to the homeroom teacher in exploring other suitable areas.

Guidance and the common learnings. In schools having the common-learnings course of study, sometimes called the core curriculum, guidance and counseling are included as a responsibility of the common-learnings teachers.[6] The common-learnings course of study is based upon the assumption that there are certain common learning experiences which everyone needs in order to live happily and usefully. The common learnings can be described by the following characteristics.[7]

1. Common learnings are free from subject-matter patterns.

2. Common learnings emphasize problem-solving and teacher-pupil planning. This is in contrast to predetermination of group goals and procedures by teachers or textbook writers.

3. Common learnings provide for a daily block of time longer than the conventional forty-five to sixty-minute period—usually two to three hours. Common-learnings classes often work together with the same teacher or a team of teachers for two to three years.

4. Common learnings place emphasis upon improved guidance and counseling at the classroom level.

In high schools adopting the common-learnings pattern, the homeroom of the traditional high school is merged with the common-learnings course of study. Since the teachers of the common learnings are also counselors, they administer, score, and interpret all of the various guidance tests given. Under these conditions, needs become clear, and, with direction by the guidance specialist, the teacher will attack personal-social-moral learnings in such a way that individual students will be helped. Current interest in guidance, on the part of the federal government, will undoubtedly disclose that the area of personal-social-moral learnings is most neglected by schools through the limitations of trained personnel and of lack of time. Perhaps "getting a job" is a typically American trait, and the emphasis upon occupational counseling merely reflects the demands of our society.

One or more units on vocational guidance, such as "Choosing a Vocation," are always included in the common-learnings course of study. Homeroom, common-learnings, and other teachers use the *Occupational Outlook Handbook*, revised in 1957, so much that an official of the Labor Department is quoted as saying, "The school kids use this book so much that they really wear it out."[8]

Copies of the cumulative files from the elementary school, all test facts, and all other information on each student in the common-learnings class

---

[6] See Chapter VII, pp. 61-64 of this text for the discussion of this topic.

[7] R. C. Faunce and N. L. Bossing, *Developing the Core Curriculum* (Englewood Cliffs, N. J., Prentice-Hall, Inc., 1951), pp. 7-8.

[8] Cited in *The Omaha World-Herald,* Sunday edition, September 22, 1957,

are kept in the teacher's classroom files. Usually, the teacher holds three or more counseling conferences with each student during a semester. By being with the same group of students from two to three hours per day for five days a week and for two to three years, the common-learnings teacher comes to know each student intimately as an individual. This is especially true since sixty students is his maximum load. In a common-learnings program, the high school student has one durable adult friend on the high school staff, and the problem of a close adult friend and advisor for the high school student is thus permanently resolved.

Work experience and qualified co-ordinators. Those who link the school with business and industry through work-experience programs are, in a sense, counselors and guidance workers. We may briefly refer to the need for maintaining a balance between the employers' demands on students to produce and students' needs to acquire progressively more difficult work skills. The problem is so persistent that co-ordinators have found it expedient to set up regulations which are uniformly observed. The following paragraphs illustrate the principle involved:[9]

Work experience must be supervised by a member of the teaching or administrative staff of the school in which the student is enrolled, as well as by the employer. Unless care is exercised to insure proper working conditions, the student may gain little from the experience. Credit for work experience should, therefore, be contingent upon supervision which will insure continued learning.

Work experience must be so organized as to reproduce continuous growth in specific skills and knowledge. Repetition of a few simple processes which may be learned quickly must not be long continued if credit is to be granted. While the student should learn to report to work on time, to continue to work at one job even though he may prefer to be elsewhere, and to continue to give an honest day's work for a day's pay, he should not be left for long on a job after he has learned all the skills and knowledge which the job requires.

When exploitation is attempted, the co-ordinator must be alert to the situation early and withdraw all students. No high school can tolerate for long the exploitation of students for private gain under the guise of teaching them basic work skills. Society has formulated laws against such practices.

SCRIPT FOR A GUIDANCE PROGRAM

If a film were being prepared for public relations purposes which featured a warm and friendly narrative to show the modern high school at an advantage, where should it open? A logical beginning would be the

[9] Educational Policies Commission, *Education for All American Youth: A Further Look* revised (Washington, D. C., National Education Association, 1952), p. 347.

day when the new freshman crosses the school threshold for the first time. The new student receives an information sheet from a member of the student council who is stationed at the door, and he is directed to an assembly room. Here, he meets his new principal and his class counselor. In a brief program, the curriculum for the freshman year is explained. The student is encouraged to elect courses in addition to those required by state law and the local school system. His interests are directed to those activities which will help him to orient himself to the school and to gain new friends. Here is where guidance begins.

As our film continues, the teen-ager is given a battery of tests to further determine his qualifications and interests. These scores are recorded in the cumulative folder which has been forwarded from his grade school. Usually, in a private conference with his class counselor, the student is informed as to his previous school record—it may come as a pleasant surprise when he learns that he is not such a poor scholar after all. Such knowledge is necessary if he is to make a reasonably wise choice in the program which he is to follow during the next four years in high school.

Vocational aptitude tests will be of value to him and to his counselor. Exploratory courses in the comprehensive or vocational high school will help him in the selection of a possible lifetime occupation. During that first year, he and others in his class will study occupations in guidance classes and take the exploratory courses included in the curriculum.

The camera records his experiences as the student comes to know more about himself and his capabilities. He may, as growth continues, elect to change his course of studies—perhaps several times. As his reading ability improves, he may feel that the general course lacks sufficient challenge. He may elect to enter engineering if he likes mathematics. Again, he may concentrate upon journalism if the written word captures his interest. Or, he may think highly of teaching if he catches the spirit from an outstanding instructor. As scholarships materialize and as family finances permit, he may elect a college preparatory course and postpone any final decision as to his occupation or profession. Again, he may point directly toward law, medicine, dentistry, or a kindred profession. *He will seldom do this alone.* Rather, it will be the result of of day-to-day guidance supplied indirectly, for the most part, by teachers who are well aware of the several obligations of their profession—and who are encouraged by a permissive curriculum to meet such obligations fully and well.

A flashback in our public relations film shows our student taking an active interest in school activities. Like all youth who are activity-minded, he will attempt to enter and become a vital part of too many organizations and too many activities. Again, guidance will be the means of channeling him, by his own choice, into a selected and limited number of activities.

There he will learn to avoid many frustrations through the achievement of a limited set of goals and to thus gain a sense of accomplishment.

Guidance prevents the youth from exploiting himself at the cost of the adult he is going to be. Basic subject matter and essential drill will not be neglected in favor of countless activities. His graduation will be an honorable event, and he will have learned to share the responsibilities and glories of teen-age offices with others. His parents, having been in close touch with his school life, will attend the commencement and baccalaureate services with an intense liking for the school and its guidance program.

SCHOOL AND TEACHER FOLLOW THROUGH

It is probable that in some schools a follow-up program, to determine the actual outcomes of the school's program, might be as embarrassing as a search for a family tree sometimes proves to be. From the thousands who enter our high schools each year, how many drop out? Of these drop-outs, how many soon become an actual menace and an expense to society? It is obvious that the high school of tomorrow will accept, practically and culturally, such a challenge and do more to provide for those who now drop out.

In conclusion, we present a survey which has been conducted each year for several years by a Midwestern comprehensive high school. This is a follow-up survey of what the most recent graduates are doing. Table 16 discloses how the graduates of a recent class are employed. This information is made available to all counselors, as well as to all teachers. From it each counselor can appraise his competency as a counselor. He can partially answer these questions: Wherein can my services as a counselor be deemed effective and wherein ineffective? What changes need to be made in myself or my procedures to improve my counseling? Teachers, who have counseled students, need to test their predictions against the facts disclosed by the survey. The teachers of this school now know much more about the actual outcome and the effectiveness of their guidance program. The follow-up survey represents a necessary final step in any guidance effort.

After graduation from high school, students move about. The girls marry and change their names, and it is only through a general notice in the press that class reunions are possible. Wouldn't it be interesting to learn to what degree the school guidance program has been effective? How many actually hold jobs for which they were trained? How many are happily married and good citizens of the community? You will know this only as your graduates return on occasion to shake your hand and thank you for your guidance efforts. It happens frequently in the modern high school—may you have a part in it.

Table 16. Follow-up Survey of the Graduates of a Midwestern Comprehensive High School

	BOYS		GIRLS		TOTAL	
	NUM-BER	PER CENT	NUM-BER	PER CENT	NUM-BER	PER CENT
Total number of graduates	205	100.0	138	100.0	343	100.0
COLLEGE ATTENDANCE						
Number attending college or university	57	27.8	24	17.4	81	23.6
Number attending University of Nebraska	4	1.9			4	1.1
Number attending other Nebraska colleges	49	23.9	21	15.2	70	20.4
Number attending college outside Nebraska	4	1.9	3	2.2	7	2.0
OCCUPATIONAL ANALYSIS						
Number having full-time employment at time of survey	93	45.4	85	61.6	178	51.9
Number not having full-time employment at time of survey*	11	5.4	24	17.4	35	10.2
Number of full-time employees in one of the trades	78	38.0	2	1.5	80	23.3
Number of full-time employees in commercial or retail activities	15	7.4	83	60.1	98	28.6
MILITARY SERVICE						
Number in the military services	36	17.5	4	2.9	40	11.7
OTHER						
Moved from city—no forwarding address	8	3.9	1	.7	9	2.6

* 10 unemployed: 18 married and doing no work: 7 part-time jobs.

DISCUSSION PROBLEMS

1. That guidance services become more essential when all youth are in high school is a general assumption among guidance personnel. What proof can be offered to support this assumption? By what arguments can the assumption be opposed?
2. That educationally sound guidance programs lead to a curriculum better adapted to the needs and abilities of students is an assumption accepted by high school principals. As a spokesman for a principal, indicate how a sound guidance program would serve to produce a curriculum better adapted to the needs and abilities of students.
3. The question, "What do you mean by guidance?" is asked by a parent in a conference. Formulate a short answer to this question that will be sufficiently concise and brief to satisfy the parent.
4. What guidance services were most helpful to you in high school? Make a list of some of the competencies of the high school personnel that you respected. Were these people providing guidance services?
5. What evidence exists to prove that guidance is, or is not, of value in the

learning processes? (You may be able to obtain recent research studies in your school library.)

6. A Midwestern high school employs a full-time dean of girls and a full-time dean of boys; guidance counselors are assigned just two periods daily for this work. Can you estimate any change that might occur in this school if these assignments were all full time?

7. While the homeroom is ideal for guidance purposes, some schools have abandoned this period. How else might effective guidance be achieved?

8. Discuss the relationships between valid testing and good guidance procedures.

9. Federal legislation has been created to broaden guidance understanding and to train additional teachers for this specific service. How might you explain this comparatively new interest in guidance as such?

10. Formulate a brief definition of guidance that would help a parent or community leader comprehend the basic service of guidance to youth.

11. What are some of the guidance services that only a classroom teacher can provide?

12. In what types of guidance services is the classroom teacher usually superior? The counselor? The guidance specialist?

RELATED REFERENCES

ANDERSON, Vernon E., GRIM, Paul R., and GRUHN, William T., *Principles and Practices of Secondary Education* (New York, The Ronald Press Company, 1951).

APPY, Nellie, *Pupils Are People,* by a Committee of the National Council of Teachers of English (New York, D. Appleton-Century Company, Inc., 1941).

Association for Supervision and Curriculum Development, *Guidance in the Curriculum* (Washington, D.C., National Education Association, 1955).

BACHER, Otto R., and BERKOWITZ, George J., *School Courses and Related Careers* (Chicago, Science Research Associates, 1945).

BEAR, Max F., and ROCHER, Edward C., *Occupational Information* (Chicago, Science Research Associates, Inc., 1951).

CHISHOLM, Leslie L., *Guiding Youth in Secondary Schools* (New York, American Book Company, 1945).

Citizens Education Study (Detroit), *A Curriculum for Citizenship* (Detroit, Wayne University Press, 1953).

Cox, W. L. Phillip, DUFF, John C., and McNAMARA, Marie, *Basic Principles of Guidance* (Englewood Cliffs, N.J., Prentice-Hall, Inc., 1949).

CUNNINGHAM, Ruth, and associates, *Understanding Group Behavior* (New York, Bureau of Publications, Teachers College, Columbia University, 1951).

DAVIS, Jesse B., *The Saga of a Schoolmaster* (Boston, Boston University Press, 1955).

DAVIS, Frank G., *Guidance Handbook for Teachers* (New York, McGraw-Hill Book Co., 1949).

DUGAN, Lucille, "How to Plan a Social Program in Large High Schools," *Bulletin of the National Association of Secondary-School Principals* 214:104-6 (November, 1955).

Dunsmoor, C. C., and Miller, Leonard M., *Principles and Methods of Guidance for Teachers* (Scranton, Pa., International Textbook Co., 1949).

Educational Policies Commission, *Education for All American Youth—A Further Look*, rev. ed. (Washington, D.C., National Education Association, 1952).

Erickson, Clifford E., *The Counseling Interview* (Englewood Cliffs, N.J., Prentice-Hall, Inc., 1950).

Faunce, R. C., and Bossing, N. L., *Developing the Core Curriculum*, 2nd ed. (Englewood Cliffs, N.J., Prentice-Hall, Inc., 1958).

Fedder, Ruth, *Guiding Home Room and Club Activities* (New York, McGraw-Hill Book Co., 1949).

Finck, Edgar M., "What Do We Mean by Good Teaching?" *Nation's Schools* 48:49 (December, 1951).

Gesell, Arnold, Ilg, Frances L., and Ames, Louise B., *Youth: The Years From Ten to Sixteen* (New York, Harper & Brothers, 1956).

Gordon, I. J., *The Teacher as a Guidance Worker* (New York, Harper & Brothers, 1956).

Gruhn, William T., and Douglass, Harl R., *The Modern Junior High School*, 2nd ed. (New York, The Ronald Press Company, 1956).

Hendry, Charles E., Lippitt, Ronald, and Zander, Alvin, "Reality Practice as Educational Method," *Psychodrama Monographs* No. 9 (New York, Beacon House, Inc., 1947).

Jacobson, Paul B., ed., *The American Secondary School* (Englewood Cliffs, N.J., Prentice-Hall, Inc., 1952).

Johnson, Earl S., "An Experience in Getting Meaning," *Educational Leadership* 10:229-33 (January, 1953).

Kirkendall, Lester A., and Zeran, Franklin R., *Student Councils in Action* (New York, Chartwell House, Inc., 1953).

Little, Wilson, and Chapman, A. L., *Developmental Guidance in Secondary School* (New York, McGraw-Hill Book Co., 1953).

Miller, Franklin A., Moyer, James H., and Patrick, Robert B., *Planning Student Activities* (Englewood Cliffs, N.J., Prentice-Hall, Inc., 1956).

Rothney, John W. M., and Roens, Bert A., *Counseling the Individual Student* (New York, William Sloane Associates, Inc., 1949).

Strang, Ruth, *The Role of the Teacher in Personnel Work* (New York, Bureau of Publications, Teachers College, Columbia University, 1946).

Van Pool, Gerald M., "The Home Room," *Bulletin of the National Association of Secondary-School Principals* 36:150-56 (February, 1952).

Wallace, Whilden, Cheretzburg, James, and Sims, Verner M., *The Story of Holtsville* (Nashville, Tenn., Cullom and Cherlnen Co., 1944).

Warner, W. L., Havighurst, Robert S., and Loeb, M., *Who Shall Be Educated?* (Chicago, Science Research Associates, 1948).

Waters, Jane, *Techniques of Counseling* (New York, McGraw-Hill Book Co., 1954).

Willey, Roy D., and Andrew, Dean C., *Modern Methods and Techniques in Guidance* (New York, Harper & Brothers, 1955).

Williamson, E. G., *Counseling Adolescents* (New York, McGraw-Hill Book Co., 1950).

Chapter 16

DISCIPLINE AND ADJUSTMENT
TO SCHOOL LIFE

The childhood shows the man, as morning shows the day.
—MILTON, *Paradise Regained*

WHAT IS THE PROBLEM?

Discipline is a word to conjure with in our day. It means many things to many people. In early civilization, it meant to instruct, to teach, or to assist the convert to grow or adjust. Later, during the Middle Ages, it came to mean to conform, to ask no questions, or to do as one is told.

Guided Growth *Versus* Enforced Conformity. As a matter of fact, our concept of discipline reveals our views on the nature of man and, incidentally, ourselves. When we think of children as small, petty, and mean-spirited creatures, we are likely to think of discipline as enforced conformity. We feel, by this view, impelled to force students to fit into a preconceived behavior mold. On the other hand, when we think of students and ourselves as human beings capable through guidance of becoming nobler, more self-disciplined, and more co-operative, we view discipline as guided growth in self-control and self-discipline. Hence, the beginning teacher must choose between enforced conformity and guided growth toward self-discipline and self-control.

But the question is asked, "Can good working conditions be maintained without enforced conformity?" The answer can be found in your own school experiences. Among the teachers whom you encountered as a pupil, there was at least one, maybe more, who maintained good discipline in the classroom without resorting to enforced conformity or who seldom resorted to it. Classroom behavior is caused. Good behavior is acquired or learned. Pupils respond to teaching that reveals faith and trust in human beings. By and large, discipline in the classroom is a product of good leadership. Through good leadership, the teacher guides the development of the pupil toward self-discipline and self-control.

Parents, teachers, and citizens may not agree on how to achieve discipline; nevertheless, all recognize that discipline is needed. There cannot be a decent family or a decent business or a decent school or a decent town without discipline.[1]

As an effective adjustment to school life, discipline is dependent upon the achievement of certain developmental tasks of the teen-age period. To acquire them leads to happiness and success with later tasks, while failure to acquire them leads to individual unhappiness, disapproval by society, and difficulty with later tasks. For the teen-ager, these tasks are: (1) achieving new and more mature relations with age mates of both sexes, (2) achieving emotional independence of parents and other adults, (3) desiring and achieving socially responsible behavior, and (4) acquiring a set of values and an ethical system as a guide to behavior. As the individual teen-ager achieves these tasks, he acquires self-control and self-discipline.

Other factors, such as community mores, community attitudes toward the school, teacher background, and school morale, are highly important. Also, discipline includes the individual's adjustment to those injustices which adults heap upon youth, such as color barriers, religious disputes, and nationality conflicts; the acceptance of or ignoring of obvious adult violations to civil law and moral codes; and the patient forbearance of teachers who should not be teachers and textbooks that should not be textbooks. All too often, adults pretend that they represent the epitome of perfection and that any challenge by youth presents nothing more than a problem of discipline. These are realistic issues and should not be glossed over by the adult who sincerely wishes to assist the youth and thereby correct, in time, world-wide evils.

Anyone who helps teen-agers acquire self-control is a friend to them. They need and desire discipline as much as the adult desires it for them. Since such behaviors are acquired or learned, they can be taught. Effective guidance by a teacher who can help a group or an individual to find the right way to behave—and there is a right way, as opposed to a wrong way—is performing a teaching function for the group or individual. For a teen-ager to be accepted, to belong, and to become a part of the group is for him to achieve the necessary control and discipline.

However, the American teen-ager is an individualist in addition to being a member of a family, a school, and a social group, and a citizen of a state and the nation. He is somewhat of a rebel. In this sense, George Washington was a rebel and so was Abraham Lincoln. The successful business man is a rebel. Our way of life encourages each teen-ager to think for himself and to be constructive and creative. Slave

---

[1] James L. Hymes, *Behavior and Misbehavior* (Englewood Cliffs, N. J., Prentice-Hall, Inc., 1955), p. 2.

states such as Nazi Germany and communist Russia train citizens to conform to the political system. Methods of enforced conformity are used that make conformity stick. In the slave states, the leaders only are encouraged to do independent thinking. Americans are rebels; all are encouraged to think and to find ways to make a better life. If rebellion is stamped out to make a place for enforced conformity, there is nothing left but a dry, lifeless rot that can generate no force, no power, and no service.[2]

Discipline is the whole basis of society. Human beings cannot exist together if people lie, if they cheat, if they steal, or if they think only of themselves. Americans are rebels, but they are also a disciplined people. It is discipline and control by the self. The task of the high school is to assist teen-agers in acquiring this type of discipline. It requires quality teaching, and perhaps this is the reason why some beginning teachers in America are afraid of the discipline problem.

Everyone is in favor of discipline. Parents, teachers, and students are fine judges of whether desirable discipline has been achieved, that is, whether the guided development of teen-agers in the classroom has brought about personal control. American teen-agers, however, are restive under enforced conformity or the slave-state pattern of discipline. They sense immediately that this approach to solving the problem is a direct violation of the American way of life. Stable teen-agers want the real feeling of security that comes when guided behavior development leads toward becoming mature citizens; they do not want the false feeling of security that comes through enforced conformity.

How does one teach discipline? It can best be taught as an experience, just as one teaches science, football, or English. The teacher may discuss, explain, and interpret, but some way must be found through which to provide living situations that require the actual doing. In a sense, this might be called one of the prime services of modern education: the provision of lifelike situations plus the warm guidance of those who are interested in the development of acceptable behavior patterns. Every moment of their lives teen-agers are working toward the above-mentioned developmental tasks; they desire to acquire behavior that is acceptable to other teen-agers in their community. With maturity they desire acceptance by community adults as equals.

THE CAUSES OF DISCIPLINE PROBLEMS

What are the causes and why should there be discipline problems? Behavior, be it good or bad, is man-made. The present behavior of the American teen-ager results from his past and present experiences. As a people, our faith in education is so deep that we provide high schools and

[2] *Ibid.,* p. 10.

compel attendance. In many of our American states, the teen-ager has no choice in the matter; neither do his parents who might, through a low sense of values, prefer that he stay out of high school and work to add to the support of the family. In this light, attendance is an obligation and not a privilege. This is but one of many factors which make discipline an ever-present problem in the American high school. Yet, there are certain critics who would solve the teen-ager's problem by releasing him from high school attendance. It is highly questionable whether this is an approach that would resolve the difficulty. If we consider the future of America without an organized high school, the outcome from such an approach becomes crystal clear.

Within the classroom itself, such factors as the following operate:

1. *Alien subject matter.* It has little meaning for students, and they have no readiness for it.

2. *Enforced inactivity.* Sitting still for long periods of time is physically difficult and nearly impossible for normal teen-agers. Sitting still and listening is almost as impossible. Teen-agers like to move around, exchange ideas, establish themselves in relationships to others.

3. *Tasks that are too difficult or too easy.* If individual differences are not met within the classroom and if there is no challenge to do the tasks assigned, there will be little desirable activity. Some of the students face failure day after day which in turn brings about smoldering rebellion. Others, who easily achieve the tasks assigned, will by nature seek new activities. These are not always approved by the school society.

The above factors are operating in nearly every classroom all of the time. They challenge every teacher, including the best. Alert and successful teachers who are aware of these factors will set out to counteract them before they become established patterns.

Who Causes the Discipline Problems? The emphasis above was upon what causes difficulties in discipline; a second pertinent question now arises. Who causes discipline situations? Teachers are frequently mentioned as prime instigators of many classroom emergencies. A few are guilty all of the time, and all are occasionally guilty of acting so as to cause a degree of overt resentment in students. Many of the classroom discipline problems may be traced to teacher failure, just as much of the juvenile delinquency outside of the school may be traced to parental delinquency.

Social and instructional skills. What skills do teachers lack? What deficiencies of teachers lead to or cause discipline problems? Two teacher deficiencies are easily identified. These are: (1) lack of essential social skills, and (2) lack of essential instructional skills. In Chart 24 a few of these deficiencies are identified.

There are many other shortcomings of teachers in social and instructional skills; some of these include personal tastes in dress, mannerisms,

Chart 24. Teachers' Deficiencies Which Cause Discipline Problems

TEACHERS LACK SOCIAL SKILLS	TEACHERS LACK INSTRUCTIONAL SKILLS
1. Use sarcasm	1. Conduct classes in a monotonous manner
2. Fail to answer reasonable questions	2. Speak in a rasping voice
3. Are insensitive to certain physical problems of students such as farsightedness, hard of hearing, stammering, or stuttering	3. Give indefinite assignments
4. Are inconsistent; may accept a tardy excuse one day but at a later time may denounce a student for tardiness	4. Give assignments that are either too difficult or too easy; lack awareness of readiness on the part of the students
5. Are rude with students	5. Do not give attention to the heating and lighting of the classroom
6. Openly show favoritism to certain students	6. Fail to plan classroom routines in advance
7. Gossip about students in public places	7. Fail to make clear the steps in learning

lack of intellectual curiosity, and a poor sense of humor. Few teachers possess the wide range of essential skills needed to reduce teacher-caused discipline problems to a zero. Any pre-service teacher can recall former teachers who obviously lacked such skills. Of course, the teacher is remembered who "bawled out" the class for not paying attention to a boring lecture, who never knew students' names, or who did not recognize anyone outside of the classroom.

An analysis of former teachers within your own experiences could afford quite a list of teacher deficiencies—those who lacked social and instructional skills and who were themselves the cause of their difficulty with disciplinary problems. Even outstanding teachers, when objectively examined, will display such shortcomings. It may help you to recall and make a list of such deficiencies and to compare them with the above lists.

Then, in fairness, it may help you to determine which of these skills you have or do not have. If you face the matter honestly, it will help you in facing the discipline problems that lie ahead.

From what services provided by your college can you receive help in changing weaknesses to strengths? If the deficiencies which produce teacher-caused discipline problems are corrected now, many of your potential heartaches may be prevented.

A behavior code. There are, of course, degrees of maladjustment and bad behavior. Our premise is that the truly dangerous teen-ager is usually the product of inept handling of his earlier acts which were normal deviations from acceptable behavior. While there can be no case made for continued retention in school of the "bad actor," there are many arguments which support better understanding of why teen-agers behave as they do in the beginning.

The need to talk, to be active, to participate, and to interact may be utilized for providing both instructional development and social growth. This is constantly done by those successful teachers who know how to create a warm social climate in the classroom. The organization aids students in achieving more mature relations with their age mates and in acquiring socially responsible behavior. Teachers who create a permissive atmosphere, where students feel free to raise questions, can establish a feeling of belonging and of being an accepted member of a cohesive group.

For certain adolescents, the most important thing in the world is to work at establishing new and more mature relations with age mates. The need to converse is urgent. This desire, plus the task of gaining emotional emancipation from adults, naturally creates a resentment of teachers and other symbols of authority. Some of the disturbing acts in which they engage are: (1) continued and disturbing conversation, (2) the passing of notes or comic books, (3) one teen-ager doing the work for another, and (4) student-contrived accidents. When the teacher has established himself with the group, the class as a group restrains the few who would disturb the class. The teacher needs to ask himself, "Why shouldn't these teen-agers be permitted to converse and work together on many tasks?"

Short discussion periods about acceptable behavior—*before disturbances occur*—can lead to a clear understanding of the type of behavior which is essential to good working conditions. This should be an exploration of what rules are necessary and an explanation of why they must be enforced. This should not be a process of "laying down the law." (We have observed that many young teachers with a background of military experience quite naturally confuse military discipline with classroom guidance; similarly, young teachers with college backgrounds too often confuse the college lecture with an approach more suited to high school instruction.) To talk it through with all members of a class leads to a consensus of what is best. The prevalent attitude becomes one of freedom under restraint. This is a procedure in accord with the American way of life. A warm, friendly feeling pervades the classroom. Since the group has been consulted, the mores of the group or the manner of living within the classroom seems right to all members. They feel secure. Rude students are ignored by the class as a whole, and disturbances quickly subside when not recognized. The teacher as an understanding adult is accepted as the proper person to enforce the standards of conduct established by the group. The good teacher works with, rather than against, adolescent nature.

Students with personality problems. Creating a friendly social climate in the classroom minimizes student misbehavior which interferes with desirable working conditions in the school, but this does not entirely eliminate it. Nevertheless, this procedure does aid most teen-agers greatly in their march to maturity, and it is a highly constructive approach for achieving self-discipline.

On the other hand, some students come from disorganized and unhappy home situations. Their out-of-school lives, often the result of poor home conditions, lead to many acts of aggression. They present such problems to the teacher as: (1) failure to do homework and assignments, (2) refusal to obey requests, (3) being impudent, and (4) deliberately provoking student accidents—spilled ink, stumbling, and knocking books off desks. These acts arise because of irritations or annoyances that temporarily upset or disturb them. Some of the "bad actors" are very emotionally immature.

For the most part, these acts of aggression are merely an expression of the usual adolescent reaction to adult authority. These young people, let us remember, are amenable to discipline. They can be dealt with by a firm tone of voice. Usually, they have not acquired productive work habits, and a wise teacher will plan a program to instruct them in study skills just as effective instruction in algebra and American history are planned. An important step, sometimes overlooked by the teacher, is the making of an assignment. An acceptable assignment has the four characteristics of (1) being challenging, (2) being clear, (3) being neither too easy nor too difficult, and (4) being in accordance with the facilities available to the student and his readiness to learn. The teacher must perform this service in helping the student acquire proper study habits and skills, keeping order, and presenting suitable assignments. Discipline problems sometimes result when an assignment is not workable —either the students did not know how to do it or it was impossible for anyone to do it.

The work of the high school teacher goes beyond instructing a given subject-matter field. To adjust to group mores, to build good work and study habits, and to make adjustments in terms of needs and abilities are tasks expected of students and teachers alike. If there are conflicts, it may comfort the teacher to remember that he has every advantage in the situation: (1) he is mature and experienced, (2) he has been trained in understanding adolescent behavior, (3) he is more prepared for any challenge, mentally and physically, and (4) he constitutes the final authority in any classroom difficulty. There is no need to control any student through brute force.

Parents look to the high school as a state-supported institution for assisting youth in the process of growing up. They expect their children to grow toward becoming responsible adults through their school experiences. The obligation of the teacher is to guide youth toward acceptable maturity—socially, emotionally, intellectually, and physically. The public holds discipline in high esteem, and teachers who are successful in the area of discipline will achieve respect and recognition from students and parents alike.

Here are some guideposts to the development of effective classroom control. These are neither mutually exclusive nor exhaustive, but they are good points of reference.

1. These teen-agers are still immature. Their disruptive acts are not attacks against the teacher as a person. They need to be understood. A study of the individual's cumulated records and background will give an understanding for the cause of poor behavior and certain clues as to how best to correct it.

2. Treat individuals as capable of a right response to a right request. Teen-agers want to be liked and accepted. They are struggling to find ways to achieve this end. Develop with them the idea that normal adjustment to the world is harmed by misbehavior, then a motive for the right behavior will become established.

3. When the teacher meets an emotionally charged situation by becoming emotionally upset, then the teacher is showing immaturity. Hence, it is a good procedure to underact rather than overact in meeting any type of irritating situation.

4. Remember that students are very much alive. Activity is essential to them. Some discrimination must be shown in dealing with behavior problems. Not every breach of a classroom regulation is worthy of teacher attention.

5. Some individuals are sufficiently immature that a form of punishment is necessary to restrain them. But it should be used with care. Adjust the punishment to the nature of the offense and to the known out-of-school situation of the student.

6. Students will always "try out" a teacher who is new to them. This is a common experience for substitute teachers. By some means, the fact must be established that the teacher is in charge and does have control of the situation; this is best done through handling a single case of poor behavior, rather than attempting to challenge the entire class or study hall group.

Students not amenable to discipline. As a beginning teacher, you may come early into contact with students who are behavior problems. These students have faced frustration for a long time and are badly disturbed. They have struggled so long that they are now maladjusted or are in poor mental health. To their classmates, they are "peculiar" because they do not react as normal students do.

Some of them are quiet, far too quiet. They will not participate in class activities; sometimes they only sit and stare at nothing. Others are overactive and aggressive. They may be extremely hostile to other teen-agers and to the teacher. They are nearly always anti-social. Such offenses as destruction of books and property, fighting, lying, and stealing are committed by them.

A teacher who handles such students as though they were normal, poorly behaved teen-agers, rather than as mentally ill individuals, intensifies their abnormalities. Their behavior has been caused by the problems they face. The psychiatrist is the specialist who is most qualified to help them achieve normality.

Naturally, the question is asked, "What can a teacher do to help them?" As suggested earlier in this chapter, it is sometimes helpful to build a warm social climate. In a permissive atmosphere, where there is a give-and-take among teen-agers of the class, the problem student may come to feel that other students have problems, too. A friendly situation may aid the abnormal student to change gradually to normal behavior patterns. If the teacher is a warm and friendly person, this in itself will be of value. Making a case study of the student is suggested, and it certainly helps a teacher to better understand the basic causes of his maladjustment and to assist in his improvement. The teacher, of course, will need to be alert in order to prevent such a problem student from harming others in the class. Limits must be set and enforced for these students as for all students.

GROWTH TOWARD MATURITY

Adult Recognition and Respect. When Father Edward J. Flanagan founded Boys' Town, he said simply, "There is no such thing as a bad boy." This is the faith in humanity that successful teachers cling to whenever the problem boy or girl can be kept in school. All teen-agers need adult friends, they need affection, and they need someone in whom to confide. However, students who are not amenable to discipline, sometimes called the maladjusted, need adult friends most of all. They need to be wanted, to be accepted, and to be a part of the group.

Usually, they have been rejected by parents and are not acceptable to other teen-agers. They have been hurt so often and so badly that they have built hard, defensive shells about them. A teacher can understand and befriend them. A teacher who is a friend can help such students break through the defensive shell.

Only too often, the teacher also repels them. The teacher may be too directly concerned with teaching the subject—English, algebra, or general science—to be concerned with building youth.

After all, there are not a large number of these youth who are in poor mental health. Their need is for someone who cares, and the teacher can fulfill that need. Opportunities can be found to talk with them and to explore their interests. As friendly relations are established, the student will come to feel that he is accepted and will come to recognize the teacher as a sincere friend. A feeling of security begins to develop.

Yet, this is only the first step. These students need to be accepted by their peers, the class as a whole. As the teacher explores the interests of these students, types of activities may be found that will impress the class as a whole. A demonstration of skills or achievements by the student before the class may bring about recognition and can be a thrilling experience as initial acceptance of peers is granted.[3] With the isolated student, the taking of the second step and being accepted by his fellow classmates is most essential. Acceptance by a peer group requires conformity and self-discipline of a higher order. There are several additional steps to be taken by the isolate before even a semblance of moderate security or growth toward maturity is achieved. With each forward step, the discipline required becomes more and more of a personal type; for it becomes self-control and not enforced discipline.

Establishment of Limits. Such teen-agers will not long disturb a class if the teacher sets limits or bounds. Being stopped by the friendly hand of an understanding person is a different matter to an affection-starved teen-ager than encountering the enforced discipline of an angry teacher.

Feelings betray the teacher. If one is angry, youngsters sense it. But if the teacher understands the "hunger" which causes them to strike out, they will sense that, too. They are supersensitive. How you feel about teen-agers is the basic factor in reaching them. It is so important that without it self-control for troubled teen-agers is not possible, but by coming to know them as individuals and by understanding their troubles, the teacher can establish a form of kinship that provides the basis upon which self-discipline can be established.

How One Teacher Served Youth. Here is a true story of a high school teacher who also served as Dean of Boys. Mr. M taught in a Midwestern high school and lived in the area where the high school was located. He was active in civic and professional affairs, and knew the parents of many of the high school students intimately. Two years after he joined the staff of the school as a teacher, a boy from one of his classes was brought before the juvenile court. Mr. M appeared in court and asked that the boy be paroled to him. Under his guidance, the boy became a normal student, participated in many school activities, and caused no further trouble either in the school or the community.

Following this first incident, the judge of the juvenile court proceeded to notify Mr. M whenever a boy was brought before the court. Ultimately, Mr. M left a written request with the police to notify him at any time, day or night, when a boy attending his high school was brought to the police station, and the police force did just that. Over the years, every

---

[3] See the film, *Learning to Understand Children* (New York, McGraw-Hill Book Co., 1947).

boy arrested by the police was checked for school attended, and those from Mr. M's school were paroled to him immediately. The record shows that every boy paroled to him made a change in behavior and was never arrested a second time. Mr. M was honored by both the parents and the students of that school.

What made this teacher so successful with boys who had strayed so far from acceptable behavior? First of all, he cared. To him, a boy in trouble was a boy in need of a friend. He felt that the boy was not a bad boy but a misguided boy. In his work with such boys, he could be firm, but never angry. He thought of the boys paroled to him as boys with problems. Hence, he never attacked the boy but rather helped the boy to attack the problem that got him in trouble.

He was also successful because:

1. He had respect for and faith in boys. And through his faith and respect, they learned to believe in and respect themselves.

2. He studied the home records and home life of every boy in his school. He knew the boys by name and as individuals.

3. He knew the parents of the boys and had their respect. They believed that their sons were more secure because he was a member of the school staff.

4. He understood boys. They knew that he was for them rather than against them.

5. He found ways to get the boys accepted by peers, in some cases through sports and athletics or in other cases through drama and music. He placed them with teachers who knew how to adapt classroom instruction to their needs and to help them acquire self-control.

Development of Self-Discipline and Self-Control. What is self-discipline and self-control? Students of adolescence tell us that these outcomes result as teen-agers achieve: (1) more mature relations with age mates—move away from self-centered behavior, (2) more acceptable social behavior—a desire for it that makes them seek to conform to the adult-approved way of living, (3) a set of standards to live by as they seek to accept and use the rules for playing the game of life. The veritable core of self-discipline and self-control is growth toward behaving in an expedient manner. The adult takes responsibility for his own acts. Teen-agers, as they mature in behavior, move toward this adult pattern.

The above answer to the question is supported by the researches of psychologists, sociologists, and anthropologists. A teacher who accepts it will believe that a child at birth is amoral, that is, neither good nor bad, and that the values accepted by the child as he grows toward maturity are a product of the home, the school, the community, and the church. Although the quality of the organism may limit it, the environment is the determining factor as to how the individual behaves or how behavior is learned. Teen-agers want to belong to the group, but to achieve this they must conform or acquire the behavior sanctioned by the group. To belong to any group, a teen-ager must acquire a measure of self-control. Teachers who are most efficient in developing self-discipline assist fringe teen-agers at being accepted by peer groups.

Yet, there are teachers who hold another belief. To them a child is sinful by nature, and to them it is only by force or compulsion that any teen-ager can be induced to accept a common set of values. In their beliefs about children, they resemble such totalitarian outlooks on life as those commonly held by communists, Nazis, or fascists.

However, all of us who teach hold certain beliefs in common. One of these is that being firm at times is an essential quality in all discipline. Most of us believe that firmness, mixed at times with some punishment, is a requisite for causing students to stop and think. To do this is certainly one factor in producing self-control. Growth toward responsible adult behavior is an outcome held in high esteem by teachers and the public. Our American way of life puts great emphasis upon respect for the dignity of the human being, and respect for every youth is a sound basis for self-respect because self-control is founded upon that attitude. Our aim is to help the teen-ager solve the personal problem which is harming his behavior.

FAVORABLE CONDITIONS FOR GOOD WORK IN THE CLASSROOM

What conditions need to prevail in a classroom for it to be an adequate environment for good work? An answer might be: There must be order in the classroom. Yet order may exist where very little is being accomplished. Cemeteries are very orderly places. In the discussion which follows, several other factors will be discussed.

Building Morale. Are you from a middle-class family? It is probable that you are. Most high school teachers are, and being from the middle-class group, they try to impose their middle-class values and standards upon all of the students in their classes. Yet, the students come from all levels— the upper, the middle, and the lower. Teen-agers from upper- and lower-class families have had much more freedom in their homes than those from the middle class. Classroom morale will depend in part upon reaching a common understanding as to what comprises acceptable behavior.

Time must be taken at the beginning of the school year to formulate with the group a policy on class behavior. Classes desire the kind of conduct that induces proper conditions for effective work. If a permissive atmosphere exists and if a class is invited to discuss the conditions making for the right working conditions, the teacher will be in a position to sense quite clearly the kind of behavior which is the most offensive to the group. A consensus of what is right and wrong soon emerges. There is a clear understanding as to what is desirable behavior. As a matter of course, there is delegated to the teacher the responsibility for maintaining this type of classroom behavior. What is acceptable is agreed to by all. Because there is agreement, the class members help to bring the violators into line with the rules. Of course, where necessary, the teacher imposes penalties on violators, but there are fewer violators.

The Role of Routine. What is the role of routine? In creating conditions for good classroom work, appropriate organization is essential. Sheer routine can be tiring, but if all the needed materials are at hand and if details are cared for, the teacher will have much more free time in which to actually instruct. When instruction moves forward in an orderly fashion, learning can be accomplished, the students feel secure, and the classroom seems a good place in which to be. A classroom without an orderly routine will cause students to become bored and restless.

In Chart 25 a few of the essential routines are listed. For each, a comment is given about its relationship to effective working conditions:

Yet, a word of caution is in order. Routine is essential for a feeling of security and will help a class to operate smoothly. However, too much emphasis upon routine can be deadly, even as too much security can end in revolt. Adventure is also a need of youth; hence, while retaining the routine for yourself, provide some variety for the class. Plan for the continuous renewal of the bulletin board, and change the pictures on the classroom walls. Vary the pattern of procedures from day to day in the classroom. It will brighten your own tasks and help to eliminate boredom from your own life in the classroom. You will be a better teacher.

Some Suggested Techniques. Creating conditions for effective work in the classroom helps to produce improved study habits and skills. As this is done, teacher-student relationships are also improved. What are some of the techniques for creating effective working conditions in the classroom? A few which have been frequently mentioned by experienced and successful teachers are indicated in the list that follows. By and large, these techniques apply to teachers in all subject-matter fields.[4]

1. Take time in class for some of the common difficulties and make yourself available out of class for assisting individual students. (This is only common courtesy for students who fail to understand.)

2. Prepare and distribute mimeographed statements of assignments previous to the time you make them orally. (A joint oral and written assignment is much clearer. There is less opportunity for not understanding the assignment.)

3. Correct short quiz papers in class. (It saves time for the teacher

---

[4] Raleigh Schorling and Howard T. Batchelder, *Student Teaching in Secondary Schools*, 3rd ed. (New York, McGraw-Hill Book Co., 1956), p. 115 (paraphrase).

Chart 25. List of Essential Routines

ESSENTIAL ROUTINES	RELATIONSHIP TO EFFECTIVE WORKING CONDITIONS IN CLASSROOM
1. Check physical conditions of the room: light, temperature, and ventilation.	1. It makes the room a pleasant place in which to live.
2. Maintain tidiness of the room: waste, blackboard appearance, the neatness of the bulletin board, selection and care of pictures, storage and care of equipment.	2. It makes for orderliness and produces a sense of pride in belonging to the class—a sense of oneness is engendered.
3. Organize student seating so as to provide for activities, seeing, and hearing.	3. If possible, provide movable seats. These permit formation of discussion groups, panels, and round tables. Less formal arrangements permit increased social development and active participation in course work.
4. Establish systematic procedures: learning names of students, prompt beginning and dismissal of classes, and keeping everyone busy all of the time. Provide for student participation at every meeting of the class.	4. These represent keys to building a good social climate in a class. Students feel secure all of the time because they are members of an organized group.
5. Supply instructional materials: distributing, collecting, filing, and displaying.	5. Orderliness prevails. Materials are available as needed, and all students are busy.
6. Make records and reports: keeping the attendance record, recording marks, filling out official forms, and making periodic reports.	6. Most of these are legal forms. You establish good relations with the principal and superintendent when you get them in on time, neatly and accurately done. To neglect them gives you the reputation of being irresponsible and incompetent.
7. Maintain courtesy in the classroom: follow the customs of the community in the way you address your students and in meeting the local people. Learn quickly to call your students by name and to recognize them wherever met.	7. If the community accepts you, so will your students. Knowing them as individuals is an excellent basis for essential interviews. Sound classroom courtesy will establish a sound basis for building a good social climate.

and is more effective for the class. Errors are corrected while the quiz is still fresh in mind.)

4. Either have the library reserve reference materials in advance or bring them to the class. (References assigned must be made available or students lose respect for you as a teacher.)

5. Use class committees to summarize contributions from all members of the class. (The committee members profit greatly, and the class will give complete attention to the report.)

6. Give students definite instructions as to the best way to report outside readings or to prepare outside reports. (Many students need this help. It is an essential step in teaching students how to study.)

7. Set definite office hours for consultation with students. (This is the best way to establish rapport with individual students. When so established it becomes more evident in the classroom.)

8. Make sure that all students hear you clearly. (Not to hear clearly is a boring experience—especially when one is compelled to attend. Simple courtesy requires that a teacher makes himself heard distinctly.)

9. Teach with an outline of objectives in the hands of all students. (Help students see how your teaching adds up to these objectives. To do so gives meaning to your classroom activities.)

10. Use a pre-test with each unit of work as you come to it. (An analysis of the results of the test indicates what areas of the unit need emphasis.)

Some Curbs to Thoughtlessness. By what means can thoughtless students be caused to stop and think? What are some of the ways open to the teacher for checking impulsive acts that interfere with conditions for effective work in the classroom? In nearly all classrooms, there are impulsive students who tend to disrupt the work of the class. The problem of keeping the attention of the class focused upon schoolwork is a common one to all teachers. With some teachers and some classes, it is a more serious problem than with others. Students are acting normally when they engage in lengthy conversations, pass notes, and do the work for another student. However, these acts are disruptive, even though they usually come from those who are immature and uninterested. How can a teacher cause such talkative teen-agers to remember that there is a time to work and a time to play?

In one study of teacher-student relationships, it was shown that in no case was a teacher liked by every student or disliked by every student. Nevertheless, teachers who are able to establish a good social climate in a class have fewer disciplinary problems.[5] A tentative list to curb disruptive acts is proposed in Chart 26 which follows. Select the methods which seem best to use, and add others to the list as they occur to you.

It is suggested that you rate each of the methods on a five-point scale. Place in the blank at the left the number which indicates your own feelings—(1) best, (2) good, (3) helpful, (4) probably harmful, and (5) usually harmful. Compare your ratings with other members of the class. If a rating on certain methods varies greatly, it will be a point for class discussion. However, such differences are found among experienced teachers and are to be expected.

[5] N. S. Bush, *The Teacher-Pupil Relationship* (Englewood Cliffs, N.J., Prentice-Hall, Inc., 1954), p. 85.

Chart 26. Methods for Checking Disruptive Behavior in a Classroom

_____ 1. Request a private conference.
_____ 2. Use sarcasm to bring the student to attention.
_____ 3. Send the offender from the room.
_____ 4. Demand that the offending student be transferred to another teacher.
_____ 5. If the disruption is general, detain the whole class after school.
_____ 6. Direct a question at the inattentive student.
_____ 7. Differentiate the assignments in accordance with individual differences in ability.
_____ 8. Assign extra work to the offending student.
_____ 9. If a student is caught cheating, fail him in the course.
_____10. If a class is inattentive, stop and administer a test.
_____11. Isolate the offending student on a seat away from the class.
_____12. If a class is becoming inattentive, introduce humor to bring it back to attention.
_____13. If a class is inattentive or misbehaving, deliver a lecture on the duties and responsibilities of students.
_____14. When a student is inattentive, stop and look directly at the inattentive student.
_____15. Assign students who are disrupting the class to an hour after school.
_____16. Send unruly students to the office of the principal.
_____17. Plan some of the work of the class around committee reports.
_____18. Set up a system of demerits to reduce the student's grade unless the demerits are canceled by prescribed study.
_____19. Cancel student privileges for disruptive behavior.
_____20. For offensive behavior to a teacher, administer a vigorous slap in the face to cause the student to stop and think.
_____21. Stop and remain perfectly quiet.
_____22. Have a class discussion on the disruptive behavior.
_____23. Speak to the inattentive or misbehaving student in a firm tone of voice.
_____24. Talk your discipline problem or problems over with the principal.
_____25. Talk your discipline problem over with other teachers or take it to the discipline committee.
_____26. Help the students in your classes develop good work and study habits and skills.
_____27. Frequently reorganize the courses you teach.
_____28. Set aside each day some play time for yourself.
_____29. Listen to students' good times and problems.
_____30. Visit the student's home and discuss the matter with parents.

FACTORS AFFECTING ADJUSTMENT TO SCHOOL LIFE

What are the factors that affect student adjustment to school life? Of the many possible factors, only five will be discussed here. Awareness of these factors has a distinct advantage, for the teacher can use them to achieve a better student adjustment to school life. He can work with and through students rather than against or contrary to them.

The Community. The community where you teach definitely influences the character of classroom discipline. Is there a strong "we" feeling in the community? Does the community in general feel that the teen-ager is an important asset? Or is there discord and strife in the community? Are teen-agers looked upon as "pests" and "liabilities?" Certainly the community attitude toward its youth is a highly important factor in the adjustment of the teen-ager to school and to life. Communities do differ in their over-all attitudes toward their youth.

In transitional neighborhoods, the middle-class-teacher standards frequently clash with the lower-class-pupil standards. In order for the teacher to work effectively, he must come to know and understand the pupils and parents of the school as individuals. The teachers need to take the initiative in coming to grips with another set of class mores, for they are not going to be able to force the students to accept their standards. In attacking this problem, teachers may: (1) set up study groups, (2) hold faculty meetings, (3) conduct field trips, (4) set up a testing program, (5) organize weekend conferences, and (6) organize a Parent-Teachers' Association.

To establish the best of discipline, the teacher must understand the community and its ways. Failure to do this will cause conflicts that give rise to tensions which create additional discipline problems. The first efforts of any teacher new to a community should be to determine how the values and beliefs of the community differ from his own and to accept their values in establishing human relations in the classroom.

Empathic Communication. Can you communicate empathically? Can you sense the mood of an audience or a class? Good public speakers can; they are said to possess *empathy*. The outstanding orator is highly sensitive to the cultural background of his audience. This is equally vital for the classroom teacher who desires to establish fine working conditions in his classroom.

By what signs can a teacher become aware that empathy exists? One proof is a sense of humor that adjusts automatically to the varying moods of the class. While there is a time and a place for seriousness, the addition of an occasional chuckle can give spice and variety to the teaching process. Another proof is seen when a teacher will pause and help a class to acquire an essential meaning, perhaps by analysis of the structure of a word and the use of it in context. One communicates most empathically when a class is giving complete attention—a class gives complete attention when one communicates empathically. It is the process that makes a teacher a respected individual with teen-agers, and it does much to improve human relationships and discipline within a classroom.

School Morale. The staff of the high school is a team working toward common goals. When all members of the team work in unison, the morale of the school is good and the school spirit superb. However, if the school faculty has too many stars who are seeking to run the school their way, the morale of the school will be low, and the outcomes will be less desirable. When morale is high, students and teachers feel secure and know what is expected of them. Discipline is not a great problem; classrooms and hallways are friendly places; and beginning teachers soon feel at home.

The key figure in the high school is the principal. It is his obligation to co-ordinate all of the activities of the school; hence, he needs to discuss with his staff the major school problems. Through teacher committees and staff discussions, a general opinion of what is right may be derived. The problems of student adjustment, the over-all instructional program of the school, and school and community relations are made clear. Under such situations, the answers to questions are usually the same regardless of who gives the answer. With a strong principal, the co-ordination of school staff and school program will result. However, if the principal lacks the essential understandings and insights for developing fine co-ordination, the staff may not become a team, and school morale will be low.

Teacher Personality. Teacher personality is a factor and an important one. Personality is often defined as the way a person influences others. Some personality characteristics are inherited while others are acquired. Only three of these personality characteristics will be discussed here, and they are the ones which may be improved—voice, personal life, and grooming.

As an instrument for effective discipline, a teacher's voice can be an important asset or a decided liability. A light, silver-toned voice soothes while a gravel-toned voice irritates. Such little things influence student behavior. Find out about your voice—soon. If there is no speech specialist in your school, arrange to make a recording of your voice. Play it back, note the imperfections, and then record it again. Practice perfecting your voice and your speech, because you will be a better teacher as a result. As a teacher, you will use your voice every working hour of your life; hence, it is important that you care enough about the quality of your work to make your voice as fine as possible.

In general, teen-agers are moody, gay, and jovial one day and dour and unhappy the next. As a transition between childhood and adulthood, adolescence is a time of heightened emotion. Many teen-agers are perfectionists. To them, the grooming of the teacher is of paramount importance. They are affected negatively by drabness in dress, slovenly habits, and untidiness. In the world of the teen-ager, good grooming is a part of the price a teacher must pay for potential respect. When the teacher is well groomed, he is troubled with fewer discipline problems.

For parents, the personal life of the teacher must approach the prevailing idea of what is right and proper. Parents insist that a teacher's life be free of all the vices they themselves possess. The teacher must serve *in loco parentis* as a model of what is right and proper; hence, in many communities the new teacher is under constant observation. In some small rural communities, even such a minor act as smoking a cigarette may cause comment and gossip. Habit patterns which parents wish to prevent their teen-agers from adopting may be prohibited to a teacher.

Discipline and the Group Process. How is the group process related to discipline? What advantages accrue from the employment of the group process to produce a cohesive class group? Welding an aggregation of individual students into a cohesive classroom group is a means for helping students make a good adjustment to school life. A basic problem for teen-agers is to learn how to become accepted and how to become members of a gang or crowd. As the teacher arranges for this in the classroom, he is helping teen-agers achieve a developmental task that is proper and right. This is especially true because the class will take on the characteristics of a teen-age crowd. As a member of a cohesive group, self-control is a natural outcome for the teen-ager.

This is the democratic process in action. Where the group accepts responsibility for maintaining good working conditions in the classroom, the group itself curbs behavior contrary to this purpose. The teacher's function is to know each student, and the teacher will utilize his understanding of students, especially the isolates and the fringe group, by helping them become acceptable to the group as a whole. To do this, he must understand the group process.[6] For the teen-age student, the group and the group process is normal and natural; independent action is irregular. It is as a member of a group that the individual becomes a social being.

To the extent that a teacher helps the lone wolf to co-operate with the class group, he leads the individual to conform, to become more moral, or to become more social. As the group becomes more cohesive— identifies group's common purposes—it can be led to attack course content as a group. Working as a member of a group on the achievement of the class purposes can socialize an individual or teach him how to work with others. Of course, the effectiveness of the teaching will depend as much upon the teacher's social skills as upon his instructional skills. As students learn how to work together, they will like being in the group, as well as the course being studied.

However, the teacher must utilize all of the social and instructional skills that he possesses in order to guide the group (1) in the formation of course and unit goals, (2) in the achievement of these goals, and (3) in helping students to see clearly what goals have been accomplished. In doing this, the teacher must differentiate assignments in accordance with the varying abilities of the group. As a class becomes cohesive or more nearly of one mind, students, to a greater extent, accept the responsibility for their own learning. Certainly, the achievement of a completely cohesive group is only an ideal, but only partial achievement of cohesiveness will reduce discipline problems decidedly and bring to pass improved student attention to teacher instruction.

[6] Lindley J. Stiles and Mattie F. Dorsey, *Democratic Teaching in Secondary Schools* (Chicago, J. B. Lippincott Co., 1950), Chs. 12-15, especially pp. 270-275.

DISCUSSION PROBLEMS

1. A beginning teacher relates that his junior high students show little respect for discipline and that he "has tried everything in the book" to bring about some semblance of order. List the steps you would take in attempting to solve such a problem.

2. Smoking is now accepted as a social function on the adult level in almost every situation. A few high schools have established special rooms where senior students are permitted to smoke. Discuss this problem in terms of what the community might expect to find in the schools.

3. Formulate a plan for reducing tardiness and absenteeism in your high school. In your opinion, are these failings receiving too much or not enough attention? What real difference does it make whether a student is tardy or absent?

4. Minority groups tend to segregate themselves before school and during lunch hours. Occasionally, through playful scuffling, tempers flare and fights result. What might you suggest here in the way of "human engineering" to prevent disorders of a serious nature?

5. A boy who has admitted "hanging the coach in effigy" because the school's team lost many games during the season is asked to leave the school. He refuses. What direct action, if any, should be taken?

6. If as a beginning teacher you find that your convictions about discipline conflict with those held by the community, do you persist in your beliefs about discipline or adjust to the customs and ways of the community? You could make that decision now: seek out several experienced teachers and ask them to help you answer this question now.

7. Are self-discipline and self-control always basic factors in either intellectual development or citizenship? Can one maintain even self-respect without self-discipline or self-control? What are the constituent elements of the concepts, self-discipline and self-control?

8. For superior class control, which is more important to a teacher, effective social skills or effective instructional skills? Are they each equally important or is one type of skill more important than another? With which type of skill are you most competent?

9. Is our practice of compulsory attendance of youth through the 18th birthday merely an ideal or a custom highly essential to the maintenance of our civilization? What are the pros and cons on this issue?

10. To what extent are self-discipline and self-control basic factors in either superior scholarship or superior citizenship? Are self-discipline and self-control always factors in either of these outcomes?

11. What are some of the common causes of malicious and persistent misbehavior among high school students? Start your list by recalling some of your own malicious acts in school: then for each try to discover through introspection why you misbehaved.

RELATED REFERENCES

American Council on Education, *Helping Teachers Understand Children,* (Washington, D.C., National Education Association, 1945).

BAKER, Harry J., *Introduction to Exceptional Children* (New York, The Macmillan Co., 1953).

BARTELS, M. H. "Participation in Classroom Management," *American School Board Journal* 125:23-24 (July, 1952).

BARUCH, Dorothy, *New Ways in Discipline* (New York, Whittlesey House, 1949).

BAXTER, Bernice, and CASSIDY, Rosaline, *Group Experience, the Democratic Way* (New York, Harper & Brothers, 1943).

BLOCH, Herbert A., and FLYNN, Frank T., *Delinquency* (New York, Random House, 1956).

BUSH, N. S., *The Teacher-Pupil Relationship* (Englewood Cliffs, N.J., Prentice-Hall, Inc., 1954).

BUTTERWORTH, Ivan, "Discipline," *Bulletin of the National Association of Secondary-School Principals* 38:70-76 (November, 1954).

Citizenship Education Study (Detroit), *A Curriculum for Citizenship* (Detroit, Wayne University Press, 1952).

CLARK, Robert W., "A High School Principal Looks at Juvenile Delinquency," *The Clearing House* 32:89-92 (October, 1957).

CRUICKSHANK, William M., *Psychology of Exceptional Children* (Englewood Cliffs, N.J., Prentice-Hall, Inc., 1955).

CUTTS, N. E., and MOSELY, Nicholas, *Teaching the Disorderly Pupil in Elementary and Secondary School* (New York, Longmans, Green & Co., Inc., 1957).

————, (Discipline section), *The National Education Association Journal* 45:339-49 (September, 1956).

FINE, Benjamin, *1,000,000 Delinquents* (New York, Signet Books, 1957).

GLUECK, Sheldon and Eleanor, *Unraveling Juvenile Delinquency* (New York, Commonwealth Fund, 1950).

GRAMBS, J. D., and IVERSON, W. J., *Modern Methods in Secondary Education* (New York, The Dryden Press, 1952).

HART, Frank, *Teachers and Teaching* (New York, The Macmillan Co., 1934).

"High School Discipline in American Society," *Bulletin of the National Association of Secondary-School Principals* 40:1-103 (January, 1956).

HOLLINGSHEAD, A. B., *Elmtown's Youth* (New York, John Wiley & Sons, Inc., 1949).

HYMES, James L., *Behavior and Misbehavior* (Englewood Cliffs, N.J., Prentice-Hall, Inc., 1955).

JONES, E. L., BARRY, Ruth, and WOLF, Beverly, eds., *Case Studies in Human Relations* (New York, Bureau of Publications, Teachers College, Columbia University, 1956).

JENKINS, Gladys, and others, *These Are Your Children* (Chicago, Scott, Foresman & Company, 1953).

LEWIN, Kurt, and others, "Patterns of Aggressive Behavior in Experimentally Created Social Climates," *Journal of Social Psychology* 10:271-299 (1939).

POLIER, J. W., *Back to the Woodshed* (New York, Public Affairs Pamphlets, 1956).

ROSENBERGER, Homer T., "What Should We Expect of Education," *Bulletin* of the National Association of Secondary-School Principals 40:13-348 (February, 1956).

SCHORLING, Raleigh, and BATCHELDER, Howard T., *Student Teaching in Secondary Schools,* 3rd ed. (New York, McGraw-Hill Book Co., 1956).

SHEVIAKOV, George V., and REDL, Fritz, *Discipline for Today's Children and Youth* (Washington, D.C. National Education Association, 1944).

STILES, Lindley J., and DORSEY, Mattie F., *Democratic Teaching in Secondary Schools* (Philadelphia, J. B. Lippincott Co., 1950).

TABA, Hilda, *School Culture* (Washington, D.C., American Council on Education, 1955).

"Teacher Opinion on Pupil Behavior," *Research Bulletin 1955-56,* Vol. 35, No. 2 (Washington, D.C., National Education Association, 1956).

WICKMAN, E. K., *Children's Behavior and Teachers' Attitudes* (New York, Commonwealth Fund, 1928).

Films:

Learning to Understand Children, Part I (New York, McGraw-Hill Book Co., 1947), black and white, sound, 23 minutes.

Maintaining Classroom Discipline (New York, McGraw-Hill Book Co., 1947), 16 mm. black and white, sound, 14 minutes.

PART IV

Better Service for Youth

Chapter 17

IMPROVING SCHOOL
AND COMMUNITY RELATIONS

He that plants thorns must never expect to gather roses.
—PILPAY. (Brahmin Gymnosophist)

Writing in the N.E.A. Journal, Chester Swanson[1] pointed out:

When the chairman calls the school board to order, only the members and the superintendent are at the table. But what an invisible crowd stand behind each chair!

Dr. Swanson, a recognized authority in school-community relations, made a point which is often overlooked by classroom teachers as well as superintendents and school board members: the public, which supports the school system, is entitled to full information at all times regarding the problems, the needs, and the operational procedures of the public schools. This basic concept is known to every successful business person as "good public relations." The schools have long failed to practice it.

PUBLIC RELATIONS—A BUSINESS PRINCIPLE
FOR SCHOOLS

There is a marked parallel which runs between school affairs and modern business methods. Adoption of businesslike procedures in public relations would enable the school to serve youth and society much better than it is now doing. It is quite evident that, if schools are to achieve the lofty goals which are so often voiced, school persons in general must become aware of this business principle and put it into action.

Comparisons Between the School and Business. Every business man insists that his workers, particularly those who meet the public as representatives of the firm, be worthy exponents of the fine art of salesmanship. The teacher, in this sense, not only should arouse interest and desire

[1] J. Chester Swanson, "Community, Schoolboard, Superintendent, Staff: What Are Their Relationships?" *National Education Association Journal* 45:76-7 (February, 1956).

for learning among his students, but he is obliged to stimulate, in a positive way, public interest in matters which are related to the proper conduct of the schools.

Some businesses, sadly enough, have learned what can happen when inadequate attention is given to public relations and advertising. When America was going through the economic strain of World War I, certain men in business elected to forget their public relations responsibilities, and when the emergency was over, they found that the public had joined them in forgetting. They never opened their business doors again. Advertising men make the most of this classic example, and they urge businessmen today to keep well abreast of the tide of favorable public opinion. It is done either through institutional advertising or direct sales methods.

Now the schools, too, should know that neglect of public relations matters—including legislative lobbying—can result in emergencies that border upon catastrophe. While it might seem that the public does want the best of educational opportunities for all youth, these things do not automatically come to pass. Indeed, the rapid pace of our economy will tend to shunt aside school matters if educationalists do not constantly practice good public relations with increasing intensity.

The White House Conference on Education in 1955 came about only because school leadership in America had *failed* to keep the public informed. Faulty estimates of population growth, continued neglect in establishing high standards for the teaching profession, and ignorance of the techniques of "political fence building" resulted in an emergency that astounded the Congress, the public at large, and the President of the United States. Every informed person is now familiar with the political stalemates that prevented the President and the Congress from meeting the emergency through a strong program of Federal Aid to Education. This state of affairs never would have developed had it been anticipated through school leadership and treated in a businesslike manner. Unless a quickened awareness of public relations techniques can be developed among those who represent a fresh generation of school workers, additional crises will undoubtedly continue to harm the cause of public education in America.

A Word About Advertising. Professional workers tend to regard advertising as a technique to be employed only by quacks and frauds who peddle "snake oil" as a cure for all illnesses. While the finest leaders in modern advertising will readily admit that there is a degree of dishonesty in some advertising, they also will emphasize the tremendous part that valid advertising plays in the American economy. Government agencies, media outlets, and the Better Business Bureaus are constantly on the alert to insure that dishonest promoters will not violate accepted codes. This policy of self-policing, coupled with professional and legal controls, should be understood by the teacher who has the stereotyped attitude that all advertising is evil. Legitimate advertising methods in business, as has been demonstrated often, represent the backbone of modern America. It has been determined by the specialists in economics that our economy, as now structured, would collapse if advertising were removed from the scene.

To clarify how important advertising has become in the American economy, here are some statistics on how much has been spent annually for advertising.

General Motors[2]

Newspapers and Supplements	$37,391,415
General and Farm Magazines	20,560,238
Network Radio	3,780,932
Network TV	10,304,242

Proctor and Gamble

Newspapers and Supplements	7,251,400
General and Farm Magazines	6,543,905
Network Radio	12,339,668
Network TV	23,701,228

These expenditures do not include the costly additional advertising carried on in booklets, handbills, billboards, contests, and similar devices. Probably the amounts have increased with the inflation of recent years.

Now, there are no comparable figures given by schools. You may say that schools are not intended to yield dollar profits directly to stockholders and need not advertise. But the parallel is quite apparent. If good practice in America requires commercial advertising to this extent, the schools may capitalize upon this and through it provide a higher quality of education. Or, conversely, the schools may avoid falling into decline if the public is told again and again what the goals are and what the needs are. We need to note that every social agency now recognizes this procedure and that many utilize it to advantage.

The owner of one of the largest advertising and public relations firms in the nation, called in by school leaders to discuss certain problems related to a campaign for school bonds, spoke frankly as follows:

From a practical viewpoint, you have the greatest advertising media of all —right in the classroom. There isn't a businessman in the country who wouldn't spend his last dollar to utilize this contact with students and their parents to sell more merchandise. I think the school should use this regular contact to tell the public what the goals are, how it can best be done, and what it will cost. There is nothing unprofessional about it. You need to take off the blinders and get busy.

At this meeting it was explained that the purposes of advertising are to bring about increased consumption of goods and services. School people

[2] These are expenditures for 1954, as listed in *Advertising Age,* June 6, 1955.

should understand that advertising is: (1) a study in the psychology of human interests, (2) a means of directing public opinion, and (3) anything that focuses attention favorably upon a product or service.

Some Professional Limitations. There is a dividing margin, of course, which separates legitimate advertising procedures for schools from the daily advertising practices of business. In a community, for example, where voters must register in advance of a general election, youth may be urged by teachers to influence their parents and other adults to exercise the American voting privilege. Other means may be used to stimulate active participation in political matters, but the school should recognize the dividing line. While schools may inform youth of the issues in elections, the schools must not exploit youth in determining the outcome of such elections.

We feel strongly that it would not be professional to arouse youth emotionally about any outcome—even when school bond issues, a proposed athletic field, or teachers' salaries hang in the balance. While some communities have "gone all out" and have won such elections in this manner, it is questionable whether the public accepts this utter lack of objectivity. Certainly, the public would protest if the school were to use students in getting votes for a political party. There is, on the other hand, no reason why a teacher should not join other adults in the promotion of school and political interests outside the classroom.

While General Motors, Proctor and Gamble, and other major firms are concerned with increasing mass consumption, schools are attempting to gain local interest and support. The schools will not spend millions of dollars for advertising via national media because the problem is local in nature. The school can, however, utilize an exclusive privilege and reach all of the members of a community through its youth.

ADVERTISING—A BUSINESS PRINCIPLE FOR SCHOOLS

The Printed Word. There are a number of printed devices which may be used legitimately by the schools to promote added interest in education.

Report cards. These periodic messages to the home are so traditional and so much a part of the educative process that any alteration produces loud cries of objection from parents and students alike. The real purpose of the report card is to inform parents of their children's rate of progress and to indicate areas where additional effort is needed. Unfortunately, the negative aspect of the report card tends to outweigh the brighter side —only a few students will receive the highest marks, while the majority will carry home grades that are somewhat less than perfect. Parents, products of the traditional school, inevitably make comparisons between current grading systems and the time-honored percentage marks they received. The marks received by the children in the neighborhood will be compared. This will lead to other comparisons—of teachers in yesterday's schools, teachers in other cities, and teachers in private schools. The specialist in public relations would suggest that this invites controversy.

The traditional report card is not diplomatic; however, this element can be balanced by a personal note from the teacher. Every child must grow and develop in some area, and it should not be too difficult for the teacher to note progress in, say, athletic ability, art, music, social behavior, personal cleanliness, or mere friendliness. The simple essence of this process, the public relations expert would say, is "to let parents know what you know" about certain gains being made. It is so apparent to many teachers that it is taken for granted; parents do not want their children to be taken for granted—the wise course is to tell parents in writing, if personal visits are not possible, that the child's growth in skills or attitudes has been entered into the record. This, in a sense, "makes it official" and everyone is happier about it.

Special reports. The "danger notice" is also a product of tradition. The negative aspects of the "down card" can be brightened if the teacher and school have followed through the positive steps outlined above. A high school principal, who usually receives carbon copies of all failure notices, can balance each hundred that tend to arouse hatred for his school by sending another hundred personal notes of praise to other parents. These complimentary letters may pertain to perfect attendance, outstanding recitations, or other individual achievements. It is a good public relations practice to ask each teacher to prepare a note of praise for every note that does not praise. The same parents, of course, will not receive the notes, but the general result will be a school that is not sincerely hated by the patrons. A glance at school routine shows that many parents never hear from their children's teachers until something has gone wrong. How easy it would be to anticipate this and create a spirit of friendship *before* the report cards and danger cards are sent out.

News notes of good cheer. A number of other written messages which should be sent regularly to parents have been suggested. Notes of good cheer and other types are discussed here. Schools that are sensitive to good parent relations have hit upon a simple scheme. The teacher writes a very brief note home. "Johnny made an excellent report today on butterflies. He really knows his hobby."[3]

Newsletters. In addition to whatever spot-news notes are sent, the teacher sends home a weekly or biweekly newsletter to inform the parents of what is being done each week—the stories the youngsters heard; the trips they took; the people who came into their classroom; the films the children saw; and the problems they worked on.

[3] James L. Hymes, Jr., *Effective Home-School Relations* (Englewood Cliffs, N.J., Prentice Hall, Inc., 1953), pp. 184-201.

On the high school level, some parents might rejoice to learn that their teen-ager was actually interested in the hundredth birthday of George Bernard Shaw; that the student's reading rate had increased; or that a review of Poe's "Raven" had been remarkably well done. Parents who do not understand the mysteries of adolescent behavior need constant assurance from school authorities that development is, despite appearances, actually occurring.

Start-to-school booklets. The child who enters school for the first time must have full emotional support from his parents, and a friendly booklet does help parents to do this. But what of youngsters who are moving into the junior high school for the first time? They, too, have new wonders and new fears. They may have been told that the freshmen are tormented, teased, and perhaps beaten by upperclassmen. It is highly important to help them establish a degree of faith in their new teachers. A school orientation booklet will help, just as it helps children of kindergarten age. Where this need is sensed, the high school student councils have done most of the work in preparing orientation booklets. Inside the booklet is a brief history of the school, its honors, its activities, and other material that will deeply concern the newcomer. While members of the student council on occasion distribute these booklets at the school, it would be better to mail them directly to homes of new students prior to the first day of school.

Personal notes. If other ways are sought to improve school relations with the home, birthday cards should not be overlooked. In small schools, this can be done as a matter of routine with a minimum of effort. It can be made, in large schools, a project for students in office practice classes or similar commercial courses. Again, journalism students might do it as an exercise in public relations—a relatively new unit that is a necessary part of modern journalism. When birthday cards are sent, care must be taken not to miss a single student; otherwise isolates may be created.

Sympathy notes. While they are also personal in nature, they constitute an area so sensitive that perhaps only teachers should send them. How cold a school must seem to those who have been absent because of severe illness or the death of a loved one! Yet, how warm a school would be if a sincere note of sympathy were received from the teacher or principal! The school presumably does know why students are absent. Why, then, is the sympathy note so often neglected by adults who are said to be skilled in the understanding of human behavior?

Commercial printing. Since not all parents will be active members of school-parent groups such as the Parent-Teacher Association, the school should not rely entirely upon these organizations in reaching the home. Direct-mailing of pamphlets which are pertinent to student needs may be a part of the school's obligation. Community attitudes, as has been noted, will vary. In some school districts, it is an acceptable procedure to mail out such material as "How to Tell Your Child About Sex."[4] If the school budget does not provide for purchase and delivery of such booklets, then a mimeographed list of recommended studies may be sent home by the students.

School newspapers. Many school administrators rank the regular and frequent publication of a worthy school newspaper as the strongest link between school and community. The problems related to this project are manifold. Where may qualified instructors be found? Should the newspaper be a curricular offering? How should it be financed? How much of the material should be written by the faculty? What are the limitations to the freedom of the press in terms of immaturity? We cannot take the space to suggest the solutions to these problems, but we do recommend that the school newspaper be published in a professional manner if it is expected to achieve professional goals. The tendency has been to neglect this vital link, and thus many communities are not adequately informed about their school.

Other printed media. The school yearbook or annual can have a tremendous impact in the promotion of school-community unity, but the increasing expense of publication has tended to eliminate this project. It is questionable whether a yearbook fee, ranging from five to twenty-five dollars, is within reason. Certainly, the annual should be placed in the hands of all members of the school society if it is produced. If only a few are able to purchase it because of high costs, then it should be discontinued.

A formal newsletter, apart from personal on-the-spot notes, is being utilized to advantage by high school principals and college heads. Such a mailing piece may be called "That You May Know," "Your School Speaks," or simply "Notes." It places the recipient on a level with the school leader, and can effectively promote fine public relations.

Schools with silk-screening equipment, fully developed art areas, and printing departments have excellent devices at hand for publicity purposes. Ribbons and certificates may be produced in quantities, and no activity may be overlooked in the process of recognizing worthiness and achievement. Special days may be set aside for "Perfect Attendance" or "Good English" badges and ribbons. School elections may be stimulated by printed stickers, posters, and billboards. Book covers may carry the motto or slogan of the school to promote unity of purpose. This "production" service may be utilized by community groups in the preparation of handbills and tickets for events which benefit the school.[5]

[4] Public Affairs Committee, 22 East 38th Street, New York City. The principal and teacher should examine every booklet personally before placing it on any recommended list or sending it to a student's home.

[5] Adult activities that are not directly related to the school should not necessarily be permitted to take advantage of the school facilities in obtaining printed materials. Here, again, we note the dividing line between worthy school projects and exploita-

Face-to-Face Relations. In advertising and salesmanship, the person-to-person meeting is considered the most productive approach to success. Such relations may be fostered by schools in a number of ways.

Parent-Teacher Association. The National Congress of Parents and Teachers was founded in 1897 for the purpose of distributing literature and promoting discussion groups. It grew out of the Child Study Association, 1888, and reached a new level of unification as a part of the United Parents Association of New York City. The PTA is remarkable. While its membership is ever changing, its goals remain constant; and the participation by schools has provided this steadying influence. Yet the schools have, in most instances, remained in the background as counselors and guides—rather than self-seeking promoters. On occasion, teacher attitude toward the local PTA has been that attendance at meetings and participation in activities added too many hours at the end of the day. If school leadership brings the teaching staff to an understanding that the work with the PTA is as essential as any class, teachers will welcome the frequent meetings with parents. Better outcomes will be achieved in the classroom if teachers know the parents and the home environment more intimately.

Home visitation. Again, the teacher may say that there is little time for visiting student homes after the school day closes. However, schedules may be lightened for this purpose, and classes may be combined on occasion to permit teachers to meet parents at home. Phone calls are reasonable substitutions for a personal visit, and, in a day of working mothers and fathers, who may be on night shifts, some notification should be made in advance of the actual visit.

Teacher membership in local organizations. Instructors in vocational areas ordinarily are members of their local trade unions; and all teachers belong to churches and service clubs. School administrators have learned that participation in the Chamber of Commerce, Rotary Club, Kiwanis International, and similar adult activities does much to foster favorable attitudes toward school problems. From a practical viewpoint, teachers are able to bring about positive relationships in a more natural way when such person-to-person meetings are encouraged.

It should be underscored here that all of these personal meetings with the supporting public are directly opposed to the traditional routine wherein parents and teachers met only on the occasion of marked discord. These infrequent meetings in the dean's or the principal's office will continue, but they need not provide the only occasion for parent-teacher meetings.

---

tion of youth service. The adult who uses school facilities merely to save the cost of a commercial printing job will have this called to his attention by members of the International Typographical Union. The school will also be challenged by unionized workers whenever legitimate, commercial production is attempted.

Demonstrations. As every sales person knows, showing the prospective customer how a device or service actually performs is vital. Schools, also, should show their wares.

Radio and TV. As early as the 1920's, radio contacts with the community were being established by schools. Although listeners were limited to crystal sets and headphones, some schools presented regularly programs of vocal and instrumental music, plus occasional weather forecasts. Schools generally may utilize the facilities of commercial radio-TV stations, as a part of the public service phase in broadcasting, to establish better community relationships. The current TV Schools of the Air represent a practical outgrowth of the radio-TV utilization by schools. When school bond issues hang in the balance, school boards may capitalize upon established communication channels, such as are provided by radio-TV.

School program. While attendance at school plays, class demonstrations, exhibits, operas, and concerts is often the result of intensive ticket sales, parents do appreciate having an opportunity to witness their youth in action. Proposals have been made to finance all school events, including sport activities, through the general budget and, thereby, to encourage the attendance of parents and school patrons. While this has been done in a few school districts, the general trend is to continue the sale of tickets. Publicity chairmen who are alert to their responsibilities always provide complimentary passes for key persons in the community news agencies, such as press and radio-TV workers.

Student talent. Many service clubs, churches, and fraternal organizations will welcome the addition of student talent to their regular programs. An outstanding vocal or instrumental trio can do much to change negative opinions about a school. Public speakers, particularly those who are skilled in presenting contemporary problems, are often invited to appear before adult groups. Also, service clubs like to honor athletes at public affairs dinners. The task of the school, in such instances, will be to let the adult organization know what student talent is available.

Faculty talent. Communities often require leadership in matters of city charter revision, library improvement, and city planning. Those of the teaching force who are particularly skilled in such matters may be urged to join the various committees, and the service provided here can be of great help to the school. When teachers comprehend the nature of such activity, there will be cordial acceptance and participation.

SCHOOL PUBLICITY SHOULD NOT BE SPASMODIC

Teachers, who have noted with some amusement the tendency of teenagers to attempt to do far too many things in too short a time with great interludes of absolute inactivity, should note, also, how this phenomenon occurs on the adult level. Weeks may pass when parents hear nothing from the school. Then, failure notices are sent home. Suddenly, with no prefacing, there will come an avalanche of printed material that demands the parent to send fifty cents for P-TA membership, attend National Education Week programs, vote for school bonds, buy a season ticket for athletic events, sew a costume for a city-wide spectacular, send old newspapers for a paper drive, bake a cake for a school sale, and similar events. The schools, when this occurs, are as guilty of immaturity as are teenagers. It need not occur on the adult level if teachers organize and plan the school year with some degree of professional skill.

Schools Survive Through Public Support. The parallelism between schools and business must be remembered. Schools depend upon public support for survival. If the public is not aware of school problems and objectives, the degree of support will be slight. It will be less than that if forces that are anti-school come into the area. When schools reach a crisis, such as that indicated during the White House Conference on Education, it becomes apparent that public relations have been permitted to lag.

This need for a good relationship between the school and the society has been fully explored in educational literature. As far back as 1921, Theisen and Carter had this to say:

> Under present conditions in most school systems, publicity campaigns are advisable in connection with all efforts to secure any increased school support . . . Avenues of approach are meetings and speakers; the press; advertising; objective demonstrations of school work; personal campaigning; school surveys; visits to the school by prominent people; endorsements of school work or policy; letters and postcards; petitions; advance polling; active workers; instructions to voters.[6]

The authors offered a psychological basis for the campaign that is still valid in public relations practice: build all on the proposition that the people of the community wish to do the right thing by their children and that they will make any necessary sacrifice to this end if needs are clearly and convincingly shown. *Make the good of the children the paramount issue.*

Such an approach in developing an attack for a single effort, winning a school bond election, is much simplified if the public relations concept is not spasmodic. A regular, routine matter for the public relations director would be to determine from time to time what the public really wants from the school. Attitudes to illustrate this point may be similar to those developed by the National Education Association Research Division as follows:

[6] W. W. Theisen, and Alexander Carter, *Publicity Campaigns for Better School Support* (Yonkers, N. Y., World Book Co., 1921), p. 5.

Proportionately more of the better-educated people favor much freedom of discussion.

On questions involving need, the benefits that may be expected apparently exert a special influence on opinions. Although a majority of groups favor educational aid for the poorer families, the lower economic groups show marked approval; the highest economic groups show relatively more opposition to the proposal.

When it comes to the questions of fact, the educational level of groups again exerts special influences upon responses.

Where respondents have no definite opinions, they are likely to state opinions colored by their attitudes toward education in general.[7]

We may accept the fact, then, that public desire will be greatly influenced by socio-economic backgrounds. Urban or rural locale, religions, economic status, age, sex, color, national origins, political or union affiliations, and similar factors will indicate the nature of the public mind. In business, all advertising must take these elements into account, that is, the type of media will be determined by the nature of the customer to be won. The school man, similarly, must check constantly the nature of his public, if he is to avoid educational bankruptcy.

Current school-public relations, we contend, are nothing more than a flurry of appeals and apologies on special occasions. How might a business-like approach be employed in solving a school issue? It might be as follows:

The Problem: What is the status of our schools in terms of public opinion and public support?

The Survey: What are the attitudes of the people in this community? How does it determine what they want from their schools?

The Needs: If the American heritage of free education for all youth is to be fostered, what essentials are needed for the attainment of democratic objectives?

The Methods: What techniques of American business may be employed in a professional manner by the schools?

Surveys to Determine Public Demand. Established survey methods may be adapted for solving school-community problems. Elmo Roper, George Gallup, William G. Carr, Hadley Cantril, Paul T. David, and the University of Denver National Opinion Research Center all used techniques which will work for school surveys. Like the Bureau of Advertising, so famous in publishing surveys, each used a sampling technique which gave adequate cross sections for indicating trends of opinion.

Population maps. If coded pins, indicating each student's home, are placed upon an area map, certain areas of population concentration become apparent. The code may be established in terms of desired out-

[7] "What People Think About Youth and Education," *National Education Association Research Bulletin XVIII*, No. 5, November, 1940, p. 208.

come. How many students hope to attend college as opposed to those who plan to work after graduation? How many live in rental homes as opposed to those whose parents own their home? This may be a student project. Other details, more intimate, should be carried out privately by the school staff. How many Negro youth are in the school, as opposed to others? How many are from homes broken by death, divorce, or separation? How many live in multiple dwellings that are not approved by the city or community codes? Population maps, also, will show clearly the transportation problems of school youth, and transit companies will need to know such facts in setting up fare rates and schedules.

As has been suggested, no single factor determines the nature of the public mind and what it wants from the schools. The factor of occupation, however, stands out as a strong determinant. A person's occupation determines not only his income, economic status, and prestige, but his personal interests and behavior as well: such things as political participation, religious participation, activity in general community organizations and contributions toward their support, reading habits, and recreational activities.

Census cards. Schools are taking part in the process of helping to determine population trends. The taking of the school census involves many hours of difficult clerical work, but the results obtained can give the school many details as to the nature of its public. Those who live in public housing projects and those who are employed in certain federal occupations become identified through the census. Their needs are somewhat different from the traditional needs of the American family. The military employee, subject to frequent transfers, has a good reason for not entering into the mores of the community. The transient laborer, who follows the course of the seasons, likewise, has reasons for not identifying himself with community goals. Such factors will be disclosed by the census and may be entered on the census map. We must not overlook the invasion of trailer homes, for in areas where housing shortages exist they are the only means for providing shelter. The remarkable quirk in the law which exempts most trailer-home families from paying taxes to support the schools has a strong bearing upon school problems. Again, the intensity of integration problems in the South has forced many Negro families to move into the North with the consequent upsetting of school population predictions. The census will reveal all such impacts to a degree.

Questionnaires. When it becomes necessary to learn what the trends in public opinion might be, the school may capitalize upon existing knowledge and devise questionnaires. Questions should not be devised upon the spur of the moment, but developed carefully before general circulation. Replies from an adequate sampling of parents need skillful interpretation in terms of parental backgrounds.

WHAT IS MEANT BY GOOD PUBLIC RELATIONS?

How Attitudes Are Formed. There are many viewpoints that help us to formulate a clear-cut definition of good public relations. Walter Lippmann[8] contended that men living in a complicated world cannot have an accurate picture of reality; consequently, they construct a picture of that world which pleases them. (School patrons may want their children to achieve the impossible.) Again, Doob[9] has suggested that men follow a stereotype which men imagine they possess as knowledge. This stereotype is formed through certain suggestions as follows:

Suggestion results from the manipulation of stimulus situations in such a way, through the consequent arousal of pre-existing related attitudes, there occurs within the mental field a new integration which would not have occurred under different stimulus situations.

Some of us will remember from childhood the dishonesty of certain adults and how we still go out of our way to avoid any further contact with them. It is not difficult to visualize a schoolboy in conflict with a member of the school staff, and the unfortunate attitude that may linger after the boy has grown into manhood and has become a key citizen in affairs related to the school. While we accept a thousand kindnesses in school, as a matter of course, we never forget the teacher who slapped us, the dean who sneered at our request to be excused to attend a grandmother's funeral, or the janitor who falsely accused us of throwing paper towels in the toilets. Psychiatry contends that such incidents will never be erased from memory; the only reasonable stand for the schools is to make certain that they never occur.

A Practical Application. It has been suggested that a positive attitude in all school matters will bring about more desirable results. How might you manage such situations as the following?

Public relations problems. (1) A parent accuses you of teaching communism in the classroom. (2) A rumor is circulated that you are planning to be married. (3) Two Negro boys start a fight during study period. (4) The school's best athlete is failing in your course. (5) Several members of the class refuse to recite or study during the last fifteen minutes of the day. (6) A student who wants a passing grade has been absent 18 days of an 18-week semester. (7) Members of your class drive recklessly around the school. (8) The local newspaper refers to all teachers as crackpots. (9) A church group requests that your principal not allow you to discuss the fluoridation of drinking water. (10) One girl in your class dis-

[8] Walter Lippmann, *Public Opinion* (New York, The Macmillan Co., 1957).
[9] Leonard W. Doob, *Propaganda: Its Psychology and Technique* (New York, Henry Holt & Co., Inc., 1937), p. 7.

plays her wedding ring and announces that married life is simply wonderful.

Before you read the discussions that follow, examine each of the above problems in terms of school and community relations. While the teacher can never hope to manage every conflict successfully, the assistance of a good public relations spirit can be most helpful.

Possible solutions. Here is one solution for each of the above problems.

1. When it had been determined that stories carried home by the student were not factual and that the teacher had been teaching about communism rather than teaching communism as such, the issue was resolved.[10]

2. Informally, the teacher admitted that there was no truth to the rumor and that he actually was planning to buy a home. Did the students know of any reasonably priced homes for sale in their communities? (His problem thus became their problem.)

3. An experienced teacher, substituting in this study hall, had no class roll, no seating chart, and no acquaintance with any of the students. Rather than force the fighting boys apart, he noted that small damage was being inflicted and merely stood quietly and watched the scuffle. Soon, both boys were panting, stopped fighting, and simply glared at each other. Then the teacher announced, "You're both out of condition. Shame on you. Now sit down at your desks and go to work, or meet me in the dean's office." Given a choice, the boys sat down; both came to the teacher, later in the period, and apologized. While a report was given to the dean, no further action was taken, at the request of the teacher. (The teacher had wisely avoided any personal contact since Negro youth sometimes capitalize upon this social problem when a white teacher is in conflict with Negro boys or girls. The teacher was merely a part of the group, but a firm leader with a sense of humor.)

4. The question of athletic eligibility has always been troublesome. In this instance, the teacher assigned several classmates to assist the athlete in finding his way through a series of open-book tests. He learned more this way than he might have through mere failure and inability to participate in his major interest.

5. "Those who are loafing on company time will have to serve extra hours with me after school—and I, personally, do not care to stay." Note that the entire class was not penalized by this teacher and that choice was offered. This occurred in a vocational school where all were familiar with the term, "company time." There was no further "loafing."

6. Absences must be limited at some point if a school is to retain its professional dignity and worth. The teacher explained that the Carnegie Plan requires attendance in class during at least four hours of each week of the school term; thus, the teacher suggested someone might question any credit given when the attendance was below standard. (Teacher and class bowed to a mysterious "someone" and attendance improved. A reasonable

[10] See the film, "Freedom to Learn" (Washington, D. C., National Education Association, 1955).

amount of make-up work was provided, just in case "someone" might ask embarrassing questions.)

7. Personal conferences with student drivers, meetings with instructors of driver training, reference to traffic officers, and home visits brought about some improvement. The point was established that the school holds authority over every youth from the time he leaves home until he returns home. Perhaps, the most effective treatment was when the class agreed that such offenders, including drag racers and tire squealers, are hopelessly immature. (Youthful drivers, through safe driving, may attempt to prove that they are mature.)

8. Newspapers live on controversy. It has been well established that teachers, like other professional persons, must ignore such open challenges to controversy. There is no practical opportunity to win such a debate since the newspaper has every advantage in the way "Public Pulse Items" are treated. (Another trick in the editor's bag is to pit school against school; students need to be cautioned not to fall into this trap.) A teacher's daily conduct will best determine whether he is a crackpot or not. (Severe instances, of course, may be brought to the attention of professional organizations.)

9. You and your principal have a right to academic freedom, and will be staunchly supported by every American citizen, as well as the labor and education associations. It is not the obligation of the teacher to take sides in the classroom, where controversial issues are debated; it is the duty of the school to demonstrate the functions of many chemical substances and to indicate possible uses. This was made clear to the group of patrons, and no further objection was offered. (In small schools, actual representation of the community must be determined in such cases; if the objectors have sufficient strength, they will ignore academic rights and will set out to find teacher replacements who will conform to their views.)

10. Since World War II, teen-age marriages have entered the high school with resultant problems. This girl was reminded privately by the teacher that, while marriage is a natural matter, it is also a personal thing—not a state to be violated through discussion. After the first day, no other reference was made to this marriage.

A PROGRAM FOR PUBLIC RELATIONS ACTION

One recommendation for schools would be to establish a central authority for all public relations matters. It is a task that businessmen might assign to a vice president; in schools, it should be delegated to an assistant principal or an assistant superintendent. The duty should not be given to a classroom teacher or a committee on public relations, since it calls for more attention than they can give it. The phrase, "every teacher is a public relations worker," holds true, but it does not relieve the school from the need for central authority and management.

Activities Calendar. So far as possible, every school activity, including all sports events, should be indicated on a master calendar that is available to every member of the staff and every patron. The reason for this seems clear; a senior play should not occur on the same day that athletic championships are being determined. A music festival should not conflict with a debate tournament and, for that matter, several neighboring schools should not offer senior plays at the same time, since patrons may want to attend more than a single event. An organized school, like an organized classroom, minimizes conflicts and gives participants a feeling that they are a part of a well-planned program.

Communication Channels. If all publicity is planned by a central authority, schools need not compete with each other for space in the local newspaper or for time on radio-TV outlets. The school public relations office will regulate the use of newspapers, periodicals, handbills, billboards, posters, circulars, cartoons, contests, displays, museum exhibits, field trips, and similar activities which help to shape public opinion about the school. Also, it might well supervise the production of radio scripts, recorded transcripts, and TV shows. The outcome can be determined by the nature of the public relations program. The communication channels are usually open to schools, but they may become clogged when, through failure to plan an outcome, all schools want the same facilities at the same time.

Reaching the Community. The Board of Education, the superintendent, and the business manager may discover that a central public relations office can provide easy and direct access to the entire community. Such a public relations department might well emphasize the following:

1. Good community-school relations start in the classroom.

2. Schools and parents, as partners, must work together.

3. Assignments, homework, reports, and home visits must be tempered by the nature of the community.

4. A planned program, which will include every phase of the educational offerings, will enable teachers, students, parents, and school administrators to achieve wholesome understandings, mutual support, and rich fulfillment of the American heritage.

The public relations responsibility of the school thus becomes a task for each school employee; it promises a direct solution to many difficulties that now stand as roadblocks between youth and education. The problem will be resolved only in terms of the understanding and vigor brought to the arena by each fresh generation of new teachers. You, through your positive action, can do much to help schools in determining the outcome.

DISCUSSION PROBLEMS

1. Public relations experts refer to "avenues of approach" and "channels of communication" that may be utilized in keeping the public informed. Prepare a list of these in your community and indicate which might be used regularly by your high school.

2. In a few school systems, parents are admitted to all outside activities such

as athletic contests, plays, and band concerts free of charge. Should this be encouraged? Explain why.

3. It has been recommended that a carefully edited school newspaper should be mailed to student homes regularly. If you agree with this recommendation, can you outline a procedure for getting it done? In your opinion, do many teachers and principals actually understand journalistic processes?

4. You have been appointed chairman of the Open House Committee and will be in charge of a special program during National Education Week. Outline the work to be managed by your committee—including the publicity.

5. How might a high school co-operate with businessmen of the community in establishing friendlier relations?

6. Compare the similarities between "selling a school" and "selling a product." What are the differences? Is good education a tangible thing? To what degree?

RELATED REFERENCES

BEGGS, Walter K., and others, *Community Schools for Nebraska* (Lincoln, University of Nebraska Press, 1944).

BENJAMIN, Harold, *The Saber-Tooth Curriculum* (New York, McGraw-Hill Book Co., 1939).

CAMPBELL, Bernard, *Sixty-three Tested Practices in School-Community Relations* (New York, Metropolitan Study Council, 1954).

CAMPBELL, Roald F., and RAMESEYER, John A., *The Dynamics of School-Community Relationships* (New York, Allyn and Bacon, Inc., 1955).

CHATTO, C. I., and HALLIGAN, A. L., *The Story of the Springfield Plan* (New York, Barnes & Noble, Inc., 1945).

Citizenship Study (Detroit), *A Curriculum for Citizenship* (Detroit, Wayne University Press, 1953).

Committee on Research and Publications, *Your Public Relations* (Washington, D.C., American Vocational Association, 1954).

DAVIES, Daniel R., and HELLER, Kenneth F., *Citizens Committees* (New London, Conn., Arthur C. Crofts Publications, 1954).

DOOB, Leonard W., *Propaganda: Its Psychology and Technique* (New York, Henry Holt & Co., Inc., 1935).

Educational Policies Commission, *Strengthening Community Life* (Washington, D.C., National Education Association, 1954).

GRINNELL, J. E., and YOUNG, Raymond J., *The School and the Community* (New York, The Ronald Press Company, 1955).

HYMES, James L., Jr., *Effective Home-School Relations* (Englewood Cliffs, N.J., Prentice-Hall, Inc., 1953).

JUNKER, H. H., and LOEB, M. B. "The School and Social Structure in a Midwestern Community," *School Review* 50:686-695 (December, 1942).

LIPPMANN, Walter, *Public Opinion* (New York, The Macmillan Co., 1957).

McCHAREN, William K., *Selected Community School Programs in the South* (Nashville, Tenn., George Peabody College for Teachers, 1948).

MOEHLMANN, Arthur B., and VAN ZWOLL, James A., *School and Public Relations* (New York, Appleton-Century-Crofts, Inc., 1957).

National Citizens Commission for the Public Schools, *How Can We Help Get Better Schools?* (New York, The Commission).

National School Public Relations Association, *It Starts in the Classroom: A Public Relations Handbook for the Classroom Teacher* (Washington, D.C., 1951).

National Society for the Study of Education, *Citizen Cooperation for Better Public Schools: Part I*, 53rd Yearbook, (Chicago, University of Chicago Press, 1954).

OLSEN, Edward G., ed. *School and Community Programs* (Englewood Cliffs, N.J., Prentice-Hall, Inc., 1949).

——, and others, *School and Community* (Englewood Cliffs, N.J., Prentice-Hall, Inc., 1945).

PUIS, Maria, *How to Work with Parents* (Chicago, Science Research Associates, 1956).

REEDER, Ward G., *An Introduction to Public-School Relations* (New York, The Macmillan Co., 1953).

STEARNS, Harry L., *Community Relations and the Public Schools* (Englewood Cliffs, N.J., Prentice-Hall, Inc., 1955).

SWANSON, J. Chester, "Community, Schoolboard, Superintendent, Staff: What Are Their Relationships?" *National Education Association Journal* 45:76-77 (February, 1956).

THEISEN, W. W., and CARTER, Alexander, *Publicity Campaigns for Better School Support* (Yonkers, N.Y., World Book Co., 1921).

TOY, Henry, Jr., "How to Organize Local Citizen Committees," *Nation's Schools* 46:26-29 (July, 1950).

WERNER, William G., "One Business Man to Another," *The Education Digest* 23:4-8 (March, 1958).

"What the People Think About Youth and Education," *National Education Association Research Bulletin* 18:187-218 (1940).

WHITELAW, John B., *The School and Its Community* (Baltimore, Johns Hopkins Press, 1951).

YEAGER, William A., *School-Community Relations* (New York, The Dryden Press, 1951).

Films:

Broader Concept of Method, Parts I and II (Teacher Education Text Film Series) (New York, McGraw-Hill Book Co., 1947), 16 mm., black and white, sound, Part I—13 minutes, Part II—19 minutes.

Education Is Good Business (Des Moines, Ia., General Pictures Productions, 1947), 16 mm., color, sound, 10 minutes.

Freedom to Learn (Washington, D.C., National Education Association, 1945), 16 mm., black and white, sound, 17 minutes.

Learning to Understand Children, Parts I and II (Teacher Education Text Film Series) (New York, McGraw-Hill Book Co., 1947), 16 mm., black and white, sound, Part I—21 minutes, Part II—23 minutes.

Sixth Chair (Chicago, National School Service Institute, 1949), 16 mm., black and white, sound, 18 minutes.

Skippy and the Three R's (Washington, D.C., National Education Association, 1953), 16 mm., color, sound, 30 minutes.

Chapter 18

MORE THAN A STUDENT AND A LOG

Give me a log hut, with only a single bench, Mark Hopkins on one end and I on the other, and you may have all the buildings, apparatus, and libraries without him.
　　　　　—JAMES A. GARFIELD,
　　　　　　　Address to Williams College Alumni, December, 1871

This classic reference to Mark Hopkins, a great teacher who specialized in moral philosophy and rhetoric, has been somewhat changed through the years. Speakers now declare that the "perfect school is a log in the forest, with me on one end and Mark Hopkins on the other." Conservative members of school boards refer to this when they lack any other arguments for continuing to restrict the development of school plants and facilities in the light of modern concepts. We need only to consider how much more effective Mark Hopkins might have been if he had taught in a properly designed building with contemporary instructional facilities.

Dreary institutions and mediocre teachers can combine to break the free spirit of the American teen-ager. One teen-ager expressed his views of such a school as follows:

> No freedom in the classroom
> No freedom in the hallways
> Herded and hounded the day throughout
> From 8 to 4 this school is a gaol,
> No doubt.

He gave voice to a felt sentiment on the part of many youth who react in a stereotyped way to school buildings and school teachers. When the plant lacks the elements of a design that might foster a feeling of freedom and adventure, resentment becomes the seed of rebellion. Rigid, regimented, routinized programs, coupled with dreary and obsolete buildings, do not personify the American dream of education for all youth. Superior teachers, who are teaching in school plants suffering from decay, might be far more successful with nothing more than a log in the forest. Nature alone would provide a fresh environment with each change of the seasons.

Contemporary secondary schools seek moral, social, and physical development in addition to intellectual growth for each student. We know that student activity and participation is a prerequisite to an adequate educational program. This is dependent upon a permissive atmosphere that provides space, facilities, and resources that are not in conflict with the characteristics of teen-agers. Thus, the clarion call of our day is sounded, "Let the characteristics of youth determine the type of school program provided." The extent to which this can be done is determined by (1) the design of the high school building, (2) the care given to the selection of teachers, (3) the outdoor space available, (4) the extent of related professional services, and (5) the instructional facilities at hand.

THE NEEDS OF YOUTH SHOULD DETERMINE THE NATURE OF THE PROGRAM PROVIDED

Teen-age traits are merely the outward manifestations of normal behavorial growth which is dictated by our American culture. It is axiomatic that democratic teachers must work with, rather than against, teen-age nature. Yet only recently has the concept been accepted to "let teen-age characteristics determine the type of program that is to be provided."

Teen-Age Characteristics. What are the characteristics of teen-agers? At least eight of them are common to the early teen-ager who is a junior high school pupil. These are:

1. A teen-ager desires and needs to acquire knowledge and skills to permit him to proceed on his own. He is eager for knowledge and for new skills. Observe a boy learning to use a saw or hammer in the basement of his home. Or observe a girl learning a dance step or learning to swim. They want to acquire the skills that make them accepted both at home and among their pals. They desire and strive to acquire the knowledge and skills that can be used right now. Once on their way, all that the school need do is guide with a steady hand. Students of the early teen-age period maintain that a free rein is more stimulating to them than the use of the whip.

2. A teen-ager desires many outlets for expressing his ideas and feelings. Our old school buildings, as well as our ways of teaching, have said to them instead, "You listen. We will do the talking. You will talk in response to the questions we ask." But the design of our new school buildings and our more recently devised instructional facilities open up many opportunities for this drive to express ideas and feelings.

3. A teen-ager is concerned about his relationships with other people. He needs opportunities to talk with peers of both sexes and in small groups, and he needs free time for meeting and talking with others. Several nooks in the hallways and in the cafeteria plus seats along paths between buildings should be arranged to serve this purpose. The program must also encourage and provide for talks with adults.

4. A teen-ager shows increased curiosity about himself and his environment. Book corners can be planned for displaying a small collection of books on this problem. At appropriate times, films presenting certain phases of adolescent growth can be shown with the invitation to raise questions either in the group or with the teacher. The program of the school will deliberately face this need because assisting the individual now leads to a steadier maturity.

5. A teen-ager has to adjust to profound body changes. For some, these changes are so rapid as to be emotionally disturbing. For others, the changes are relatively slow, permitting time for adjustment. Many parents seem unable to help. For many, if help comes, it will be through the school. Teen-agers need to understand that what is happening is perfectly normal. Talks with teachers, other adults, or older adolescents allay fear and fright. For some, a selected movie can help make the explanation, while for others a selected book is better.

6. A teen-ager tries to achieve independence and at the same time maintain security. In his immaturity, he finds it difficult to keep a balance between the two. Parents are often quite unaware that the time has come when this child can be trusted with more independence. Junior high school teachers, who are students of this problem, should sense the situation and provide opportunities for practicing independence—camping trips sponsored by the school, community surveys, or developing and presenting an independent report to the class. Wherever new skills are being established, the opportunity to practice them under guidance is essential.

7. Teen-agers strive for personal values in their social setting. They want to do the right thing. They want to gain the recognition of parents, teachers, and peers. They need help in choosing and living by the rules that will become second nature to them. Many junior high schools have planned a homeroom program that gives great assistance here. For other junior high schools, the core curriculum has been found to be the best source for needed help.

8. A teen-ager wants to participate as a responsible person in large social groups. The phrase *large social group* is being interpreted by many school architects as a maximum of 200; hence, junior high school auditoriums are now designed to this size. In a larger room than this, the teen-ager cannot make himself heard. But this drive exists; the change in the size of auditoriums is a recognition of it. Principals with insight are finding ways for much wider use of these auditoriums for just this purpose. Because of this characteristic of teen-agers, many junior high school teachers set up a formal organization in their classes with president and secretary to let the students participate in running the class.[1]

What are the characteristics of the late teen-agers, that is, senior high

[1] Hollis A. Moore and William W. Caudill, "Designed for the Early Teen-Ager," *Nation's Schools* 55:55-76 (January, 1956).

school and junior college students? Because there has been growth and change in youth and because their characteristics change with increasing age, the nature of the program must also change. Although there are several distinctive characteristics of senior high school and junior college youth, the following six are the most common:

1. These youth desire economic independence and need assurance of how to achieve it.

2. These youth desire an opportunity to select and prepare for an occupation.

3. These youth want and need to acquire the understanding, the attitudes, and the preparation for successful marriage and family life.

4. These youth need to strive for the development of intellectual skills and concepts essential for civic competence; they sense a void.

5. These youth desire and should have an opportunity to achieve socially responsible behavior.

6. These youth desire and need an opportunity to acquire a set of values and an ethical system as a guide to behavior.

A close analysis of the two descriptions of teen-age characteristics indicates that a modern educational program requires much more than a teacher and a log. It requires more than a worn-out school house. In many subtle ways, the environment in which the teen-ager lives each day from 8 to 4 is sensed as a constructive or a restrictive factor in the healthy development of his personality. As all school people will testify, cleanliness begets cleanliness, and a certain way to reduce vandalism within a school is to apply fresh paint. And a sure way to increase it is to ignore the elements of housekeeping. Upon this basis, changes have taken place in the design of high school buildings during this era, when new construction is replacing the old. Have the characteristics of teen-agers been recognized as these changes were made? In the next few pages an examination of this issue will be made.

Design the School Plant to Serve Youth. By 1955, the great increase in birth rate that accompanied World War II began to affect our high schools, especially the junior high schools, in numbers that caused buildings to bulge. As cartoonists began to dwell upon this theme time and again, school boards looked at census reports and formulated building programs. Should recent changes in home and industry be reflected in these new structures? Or, should the vision of school communities continue to be conservative? They gave heed to a truism among architects: make the design of the building fit the purpose it is to serve.[2] School designers ask two basic questions: (1) Who is to be served by this building? (2) What is the nature of the activities that are to be carried on in it? Educators, who specialize in school building construction, replied, "Let the characteristics of the pupils determine the design of the building." With glar-

[2] John Reid, "Architectural Design of School Buildings," *School Executive* 74:92-95 (January, 1955).

ing exceptions, our new school buildings for high school students are being custom-fitted to the teen-agers who are to occupy them.

A contemporary design provides for more than a single building on the school site. Some high school buildings, particularly junior high school buildings, are constructed with detached wings for each grade. Thus, each grade has its own immediate neighborhood and may follow through its own program without undue interference from others. This is called a *humanization of space arrangement* and keeps the same group in close relationship with the same staff for a large part of the daily program throughout a three-or four-year period. In one sense, these are citizenship laboratories, as students in each group learn how to work together for the common welfare. The phrase sometimes employed by advocates of this plan is *decentralized education for early teen-agers.* Still other high schools provide small, isolated units for special activities such as shop, music, drama, journalism, and student council. Note how these measures provide for the teen-ager characteristics and needs described earlier.

Decentralizing the dining service. Another innovation has been called *individualizing the cafeteria* or *decentralizing the dining service.* There is a general recognition that teen-agers have been unhappy with mass feeding, cafeteria style, and the adult supervision that seems to cast a wet blanket over the entire process. The new plan provides many small nooks in the cafeteria where congenial friends may dine together, just as they do at the corner drugstore. One high school principal, emphasizing that this arrangement is important and valuable to teen-agers, commented, "Our cafeteria with its semi-private booths competes successfully with the neighborhood drug stores." With this same view, new high schools provide loges and nooks in the corridors and along the walks between buildings. Corridors are thus made educationally useful, as are the travel-ways between the buildings.

Classrooms become laboratories. A number of high schools are transforming classrooms into laboratories. The same subjects, such as English, mathematics, foreign languages, and social studies are taught; but the activities within the classroom are not the same. In many more class periods, individual students are working on their own as responsible persons. Teachers and principals have discovered that every subject, in fact, can be approached on a problem basis—a method that has been utilized by science for a long time. They have found that a laboratory approach, along with conventional teaching, is more likely to result in the acquisition of basic concepts, skills, and appreciations which are more practical and permanent. Of course, in the laboratory classroom there is a greater abundance of materials with which students can work.[3]

This transformation of classrooms into laboratories is being made less

[3] There is an excellent reference to this in the film, *Drop Outs and Stay Ins* (New York, McGraw-Hill Book Co., 1950). See also, *Design for Learning* (San Francisco, Photo and Sound Productions, 1952).

rapidly for the academic subjects than for speech, drama, foreign language (appreciation), and journalism. There is less traditional drag for these subjects because they are relatively new. In such a transformation, it is very clearly seen that modern education must transcend the concept of Mark Hopkins on the log.

Laboratories in the outdoors. Building plans held by school designers reject the practice of locating the high school building on a cramped land site with only a few feet of ground on either side of stark walls. The new high schools are rarely located on campuses of less than ten acres. Some high school sites exceed one hundred acres, and others have acquired large camping areas in nearby mountains. Lincoln-Way Community High School,[4] located just 20 miles southeast of Chicago, illustrates this trend with a campus of 70 acres. Principal Chapman, of that school, stated, "Throughout its discussion the board kept in mind one question, 'What is best for the young people of our district?'" To this, he added his own philosophy—the school of the future will be more of an outdoor school than the school of the past. At Lincoln-Way, this feeling is implemented by the design of the outside campus to include playing fields, a nature study laboratory for biological science, a vocational agricultural laboratory, a laboratory for outdoor sketching by art students, and many other open areas. A large campus such as this gives flexibility to a program for youth which is not possible on the older, cramped sites.

Some new features. New features make modern classrooms seem neat and friendly to our modern boys and girls. Asphalt tiling on the floor and sound-proof ceilings eliminate much noise. Ventilation approaches natural-ness, and pastel colors for the walls take away some of the stuffiness and drabness of the earlier classrooms. A flexible placement of bulletin boards and chalk boards lends an informal air to the room. Some teachers have been able to establish the same friendly informality that prevails in many homes. Lightweight chairs and tables aid in transforming the room into a workroom or laboratory, and, to the relief of all teachers, storage space exists for instructional facilities. In some of these new classrooms, modern needs have been fully recognized, and a film projector has been provided as a permanent fixture—along with a tape recorder, television set, radio, and two-way communication system. Compact classroom libraries, in addition to books and newspapers, provide films and recordings pertinent to the subject. Screens and dark shades, of course, are also supplied.

PROVISIONS FOR SPECIAL SERVICES

It takes more than teachers for the operation of a modern secondary school. There are tasks to be done in the modern high school that require

[4] A. Hunter Chapman, "New High School Puts Its 70-Acre Site to Work," *School Executive* 75:69-72 (September, 1955).

special and complex skills not closely associated with actual classroom teaching. Custodial services, for example, were originally performed by the teacher, but now have become so technical that school engineers must be licensed by the state for safety. Regular custodial schools are held for training custodians in the use of cleaning equipment and building maintenance, and the management of a school swimming pool requires a working knowledge of chemistry and human behavior. Care and operation of athletic fields are now specialized tasks.

Another responsibility of the modern high school is the provision for detection and correction of physical and emotional defects. When 40 per cent of the recruits of World War II were rejected for service because of such weaknesses, it was determined that *most of the cases could have been corrected* had they been detected five to ten years earlier. Although the teacher may note such defects, actual detection and correction call for specialists who are adequately trained and licensed by the state for this work. If physical and mental troubles are to be corrected in early years, as thoughtful citizens urge, then the high school is the place. The acceptance of school dental clinics demonstrates this public interest in the well-being and health of our teenagers. Some of the other special services are described below.

The High School Library. Why this emphasis upon library service? A generation ago not many high schools had libraries, and those that did offered a meager service. What has caused this change in emphasis? The following four causes have been mentioned previously in this text.

1. The high school has become a common school—nearly all teen-agers now attend.

2. The entering students, ninth-graders, have a range of reading capacities from grade 4 to grade 14. Too many of these students read the required textbook with little comprehension. Others find the adopted text too easy and are offered little challenge.

3. There is a great need for a diversity of instructional material for more effective teaching. There is a broad variation in student readiness and interest. A diversity of materials must be made available.

4. The textbook no longer comprises the course of study. Teachers now build courses of study that make the textbook little more than a reference book, although an important one.

No one textbook can span the range of individual differences found in a high school; however, special texts prepared for unusual class situations do provide for individual differences. Although the usual textbook will continue as a highly valuable tool, other resources are needed. The problem of storing these materials and locating them so that they can be found and used with ease can best be solved by a trained person, the librarian. This new type of library contains more than books, magazines, newspapers, pamphlets, and sets of references; it is a storage place for films, projectors, filmstrips, maps, globes, radios, television sets, records, and record players. What the classroom cannot provide can be found in the school library.

What specific skills does the librarian possess that are not ordinarily found among teachers? The librarian, trained in library science, classifies and catalogs all materials. Proficiency in the details of the Dewey Decimal system or the Library of Congress system and classification procedures common to our high schools is obtained neither easily nor quickly. Building a card catalog file requires meticulous care, and no errors can be tolerated. Teaching students how to locate library materials is also a difficult and highly technical service. While the subject-matter teacher assists in this, the over-all service is definitely the responsibility of the librarian.

The capable librarian will establish stable work patterns and maintain order for the convenience of all who use the library. Books and instructional materials returned to the library must be checked and re-shelved at once. Adults and teen-agers, alike, are prone to be careless with library materials. This, coupled with the tendency to forget the rights of others (through loud talking, scuffling, or book slamming), creates a need for the librarian to be a specialist in what might be called human engineering. Library patrons must not be discouraged from wholehearted use of facilities and services, but at the same time, they must be guided into understanding that others too have a right to study and do research in comparative quiet. This fine distinction is often lost when libraries are turned into study halls comprised of retarded students, slow learners, average students, rapid learners, and the gifted. With so much to be done, librarians have slight opportunity to perform the services for which they are trained; as custodians of a mass of 200 to 400 students of divergent maturities, their specialized training goes for nought. This situation is deftly avoided in the modern high school.

Libraries are seldom turned into study halls in modern schools. Instead, classrooms are utilized as work centers and laboratories; through the use of a double set of card catalogs, library materials may be checked out to teachers who, in turn, set up a circulation system within the individual classrooms. The library itself, in appearance, is quite similar to the modern adult libraries. There are book stacks to be sure, but they are arranged in small units with a compactness which places most references for a particular subject within easy reach. In such high schools, no students are compelled to sit for hour after hour in a stuffy library as a result of poor administrative planning. Each student who uses the library has a functional knowledge of the reference system, and he wants to be there for a known purpose. Thus, every improvement in the school is reflected in the library; the nature and characteristics of the teen-ager determines the service offered.

The Physical Fitness Program. A remarkable change is taking place in public attitude, as indicated by the increased emphasis upon nursing services in our high schools. Only now are we, as civilized people living in an industrialized state, beginning to understand that prevention of illness is far better than detection and correction. And it is much cheaper in terms of human suffering, as well as dollars and cents. This holds true whether we deal with social problems, maladjustment, delinquency, and crime, or with known viruses. An earlier attitude caused us to push aside the lame, the deaf, and the blind—with some sympathy but meager support. The deformed and mentally disturbed were incarcerated in dungeons as unfit to associate with human kind. Now, through nursing service and a physical fitness program, we can save this human waste of a former age for a happy and productive life.

The school nurse. Not only did teachers of yesterday do their own janitorial work, but they practiced medicine within the limitations of home remedies. The child who was apparently ill, who scratched himself constantly, or who walked with a limp was not isolated from others. Chickenpox, a highly infectious disease of children, was usually mild in nature, and, although it was characterized by a vesicular eruption, it was generally held that if the boy were "able to navigate" and get to school, he could do slight harm to others or himself.

By slow stages, on the advice of family physicians, schools began to isolate such cases by sending them home. Quarantine became the rage, and many a home was posted with large yellow or red signs that warned passersby to beware. As vocational schools became more popular, a real need grew for regular school nurses and first-aid service. Today, the modern high school has a full-time nurse, who not only is active in preventing the spread of infectious diseases but also carries on a regular testing program, such as eye, ear, nose, throat, with referral to family physicians or public clinics as necessary. Her task includes individual conferences on matters related to personal health, and many schools, with parental approval, call upon the nurse for guidance in sex education classes. Thus, the school nurse personifies modern attitudes in our society, such as prevention in addition to detection and correction.

Physical Fitness for Self and Country. Let us list here the recommendations of the President's Conference on the Fitness of American Youth which was held at Annapolis, Maryland, in 1956.

1. Total fitness means mental, spiritual, and physical fitness.

2. The public must be made aware of the problem of establishing and maintaining fitness.

3. Fitness must be popularized and promoted among children.

4. Research on fitness is needed to decide what kind and how much.

5. Out-of-school programs should include such agencies already in the field as Boy Scouts and YMCA.

6. Funds should come from private industry, foundations, community chests, and a greater share of the tax dollar.

7. Schools should have more time, equipment, and personnel for physical education and should focus more attention on the athletically untalented child, rather than on the star.

8. The standards and prestige of the physical education profession must be raised.[5]

Some rather startling statistics were revealed at this conference. Of 150,000 elementary schools, 91 per cent of them had no gymnasiums; and less than 50 per cent of our high school boys and girls had the opportunity to take physical education. While Selective Service Director Lewis B. Hershey defined fitness as "the ability to do your work without tension," medical experts rejected 40 per cent of the recruits in World War II. It has been pointed out that fitness is a debatable matter, for sailors, who were fit for their shipboard jobs during World War II and knew how to swim, were not fit enough to keep from drowning because they lacked sufficient strength to push off and keep free of sinking craft.

One standard test for physical fitness, based upon muscular flexibility and co-ordination, is the Kraus-Weber test. It was administered in 1956 to 1,087 youth in Omaha, Nebraska, under supervision of the YMCA. Of those examined, 57.3 per cent passed and 42.7 per cent failed; however, all the youths tested had an active interest in physical education.[6] The Kraus-Weber test was also administered to about 13,000 children and youth in the Omaha Schools, grades 4 to 8, in September, 1956; the percentage of failure in the public school was considerably greater than at the YMCA. In a different test, 1958-9, school youth had improved.

Preparing for Military Service. Why is military service a problem? How does it concern the high school? Does youth have an option in this matter?

Since World War II, the peacetime draft has come to America. Although avoided and legislated against until World War II, it now presents youth with a problem never faced by their parents. Parental adjustment to the peacetime draft, experts say, has often been more difficult than teen-age adjustment. The resulting tensions, although aroused quite normally, have brought negative attitudes toward the new custom. Whether we accept the peacetime draft or not, we must observe that negative attitudes are often the result of a lack of understanding of just what is required of an American citizen. While neither supporting nor defending conscription, we are concerned with its impact on high school youth. Compulsory military service is a tremendous school problem and must be accepted as such.

[5] *Fitness of American Youth: A Report to the President of the United States on the President's Conference on Fitness of American Youth* (Washington, D. C., Superintendent of Documents, 1956).

[6] Omaha World-Herald, August 26, 1956, p. 12B. Statistical data for this test was compiled by Don R. McMahill, Jr., Omaha YMCA staff.

As students near their eighteenth birthday, they become more concerned and disturbed. They have heard many rumors, and they become confused. They may ask a respected teacher or counselor, "What should I do about military service?" It is an honest question, and it deserves an honest answer. At the same time, however, it does not lend itself to the usual routine of adding up advantages and disadvantages, since there is actually limited free choice. The adult may point out the opportunities provided by the military service, and they are many and varied. A wide range of technical and professional skills is covered. Rightly guided, the time in the service can be helpful; wrongly guided, it can be wasteful and harmful. For adequate guidance, the teacher must have all the facts about the various military branches and know the aptitudes and potentialities of the student who asks the question. The reply must be based upon facts and sound judgment.

What are the issues involved? This is a new service. The need for it arises from the United States having become a dominant world power. Certain conflicts in ideology, as between this nation and other strong world powers, make it essential for us to maintain a strong peacetime military establishment. The extent of this strength, of course, has become a political issue, as well as a moral one. Our adults, through the United Nations and several peace organizations, are striving for a return to the older order where large armies were disbanded at the conclusion of each war. Yet, the military leadership insists that the only security lies in continued strengthening of our services. Is it any wonder that teen-agers are confused?

Another basic issue concerns the program through which the schools must recognize the facts and produce changes in the attitudes of teen-agers. Whether of great strength or minimal in size, the practice of maintaining a fighting force undoubtedly will persist so long as the conflict between East and West continues. The high school must include the preparation of young men, and incidentally of young women, for military purposes. What should be the nature of such a program?

Being new, it must be experimental to a degree. Such topics as the following help formulate a program that deals frankly with the facts of our present way of life.

1. A survey of student and parent opinion to determine the need for such a program. Interviews with military personnel will help to clarify basic misunderstandings.

2. Why must there be a peacetime draft?

3. Who should be subject to call? Why does the military prefer to have the assistance of young, unmarried men and women? Is this the best for America?

4. An examination should be made of the five branches of military

service and of the several types of occupational experiences offered by each.

5. Help for each student in answering the question: "In what specific activity in the service will I contribute most and, also, receive the most help in vocational preparation for civilian life?"

6. The problem of whether to volunteer or wait for the draft should be discussed.

The location of instruction on preparation for military service in the schedule of a school will depend upon several factors. It may be included in the common-learnings curriculum; where an ROTC unit exists, many principals expect the information to be presented by the course instructor. In other schools, it may be handled by the Modern Problems teachers.

Student quandary. Desire for adventure, to get out from under parental or social pressures, or to somehow gain the status that apparently can not be had within the high school may cause the teenager to drop out and join up. In a few instances, enlistment before graduation may be desirable for certain young fellows. However, the military has teamed well with the high school and generally insists upon graduation, if at all possible, prior to enlistment. This is a major issue to be mastered by the skilled teacher or counselor in meeting questions youth will ask. One instructor writes:

I handle it this way. Whenever the boys in service come home on leave, all prettied up in their uniforms, I ask them to appear before my seniors. The question always is asked, "Should I quit school and join up?" I have never found a former student who would encourage dropping out of school for any reason. That seems to be good enough for the students, and we forget much of the problem altogether until graduation time rolls around.

Summary. We have come a long way from the time when the lone teacher attempted to provide all of the services that are now specialties in the modern high school. In addition to custodial services, medical services, physical education programs, and preparation for military duty, the school provides: (1) an attendance organization that keeps strict accounting of the whereabouts of teen-agers, who are largely a school responsibility from the minute they leave home until they return, (2) supervision of transportation services, including the actual ownership and operation of bus facilities, (3) a school treasurer who is bonded to handle large sums of money in the school activity fund, from the treasuries of various classes and student organizations, and in accounts of all school departments— the gymnasium, the library, and the cafeteria, plus (4) scholarship assistance, proctoring of special examinations, and preparation for college entrance.

There are many other services including the guidance and counseling work which have been fully developed in earlier chapters. All of this, let us remember, is a direct result of public attitude and demand; if there are any *frills* in modern education, as has been suggested by some critics, they may be removed by the will of the public.

BETTER INSTRUCTIONAL TOOLS FOR BETTER TEACHING

According to Confucius, all implements of civilization are spiritual in origin.—Hu Shih in *Whither Mankind*

Creative imagination is an important factor in the invention of new instructional tools. Since teachers are constantly devising better instructional tools, it is evident that teachers have creative imagination to a decided degree. Such additions to the teacher's kit of tools increase the variety of classroom activities and may greatly expand the learning outcome per instructional hour. New channels of activity—to see, hear, and do—are opened up by these devices. This abundance of instructional aids makes the adage of the teacher and the log as outmoded as would be "the man with a hoe" in a Midwestern cornfield. It is, in part, because of these new aids that the modern high school is able to help students keep pace with the rapidly expanding knowledge of our times. These new aids are not frills, as the uninformed sometimes state; with each passing decade, they become more and more essential to our national survival.

Instructional Tools for the Classroom. The decade 1945-55 was a highly creative period in the production of new instructional materials. A part of it was an inheritance from World War II where, under pressure to change millions of raw recruits into fighting personnel, the military sought, without regard for cost, the best creative talent in education and directed that more effective devices be utilized in the military classrooms. It was found, through this intensive drive, that superior tools exact from teachers more careful attention in adapting them to productive purposes.

For example, such a simple device as a bulletin board is now a part of every modern high school classroom because the military services and industry demonstrated how effective it can be. It is not a place for the display of unrelated data, but rather must make a single idea stand out.[7] The bulletin board can be a superb instructional tool, when the teacher learns how to make it so through a study of how to fashion the display to express clearly and pointedly a single wordless message. Like the felt boards, chalk boards, maps, charts, films, texts, and reference books, the bulletin board will increase the power of the teacher. However, it takes time and effort to acquire speed, accuracy, and form in the use of such instructional tools. Superior teaching has become more complicated in our complex culture.

[7] Thomas A. Koskey, *Baited Bulletin Boards—A Handbook for Teachers* (San Jose, Calif., Globe Printing Co., 1954).

Building and Site, Also, Are Instructional Tools. In the days of James Garfield and Mark Hopkins, the school buildings and sites were regarded as unimportant teaching tools. But now we know that they are highly valuable factors in molding character and determining the quality of learning that occurs. As we have said, the modern school building is designed to achieve the purposes for which the school exists. As with the classroom and the laboratory, however, the function of the school site must be to invite greater student participation and interest. Nooks, loges, playing fields, outdoor laboratories, camp sites, libraries, small auditoriums, little theaters, and similar innovations mean nothing unless there is teacher vision. This, after all, is the real difference between the professional and the unprofessional teacher, that is, the ability to use the instructional tools with ease and efficacy. A major step here is to encourage students to explore and experiment, something that an imaginative teacher can do without difficulty.

The Community as a Laboratory. Carlton Washburne[8] has written:

Children who come into the schoolhouse to learn must leave the schoolhouse to learn—they must find in the outside world the stuff that makes education real. Book learning—even learning from pictures and talks—is detached, ungrounded, unless it grows out of substantial experience with the real world.

The community that supports the high school is real. People work, worship, wed, quarrel, and settle their differences in a democratic way. If the teen-agers can gain this view of their community, they will acquire a direct experience that helps them to know vicariously how other communities live. Surveys of the ways they earn their living, of racial and national backgrounds, or of the number of youth who are attending schools of higher learning are examples of what might be done.

A plan for making a community survey, assuming that parental permission and encouragement have been gained, includes the following: (1) clear understanding of what is to be done, (2) accurate recording of all replies, (3) keeping information confidential, and (4) organizing and interpreting facts collected. Teen-agers who have participated in surveys achieve a feeling of belonging. When they talk about results, it is news to adults, and they are listened to with deep respect. The experience gained in these surveys, even to the surprise of their teachers, often sends students back to their textbooks with a new degree of interest. Perhaps, you will be able to explain why this occurs.

The professional teacher leads each group to formulate its own plan for the survey. There are just a few rules to be established. But the unprofessional teacher completes the whole organization by himself. He tells teams what to do and how to do it. He checks frequently to find whether the

[8] Carlton A. Washburne, *Living Philosophy of Education* (New York, The John Day Company, Inc., 1940), p. 395.

rules are being followed, and he scolds those who need help. Again, you may be able to explain why the outcomes differ.

The field trip and student project are two other devices for use in the community laboratory. The first can be employed by any subject-matter teacher to supplement the text and other facilities. Each community has resources, such as the waterworks system, transportation centers, units of local government, industrial and business establishments, and hospitals or other institutions that fully illustrate the principles being studied in the subject-matter course. A visit to such a community resource can make principles real and worth learning, particularly when adults on the job explain the procedures involved.

The student or class project often grows out of class discussion. Physics or advanced mathematics students may actually use a transit and measure the angles of the school yard or playground. In social studies, someone may ask, "Why can't we clean up that vacant lot and turn it into a community playground?" Such a project, when carefully planned, may provide first-hand experience in group planning, as well as the work required to change a vacant lot into a playground. It should be repeated that, in any venture away from the school, care must be taken to secure parental consent in advance of the activity.[9]

BETTER SERVICE TO OLDER ADOLESCENTS WHO ARE LOW IN ACADEMIC ABILITY AND SOCIAL STATUS

A common tenet of our American faith is that the public high school should serve equally well all of the educable youth. This has been clearly expressed by the Educational Policies Commission in *Education for All American Youth*. As of now, however, more than one-third of our educable youth leave school before graduation. Wherein have we fallen short in the achievement of an avowed purpose? What needs to be done to fulfill a sacred obligation? Is high school education vital for the upper years of adolescence and for America as well?

Wherein have we fallen short in the achievement of an avowed purpose? Studies, in the years from 1900 to now, clearly indicate that the high school is not suited to older adolescents with low academic aptitudes.[10] By and large, it has been demonstrated time and again by intelligence tests and school marks that students who withdraw from high school have low academic aptitudes.[10a] Because both boys and girls with low academic apti-

[9] See: *Broader Concepts of Method* (New York, McGraw-Hill Book Co., 1947), an outstanding film that reveals how such projects may be developed.
[10] Harold J. Dillon, *Early School Leavers—A Major Educational Problem* (New York, National Child Labor Committee, 1949), p. 14.
[10a] R. E. Eckert and T. O. Marshall, *When Youth Leave School* (New York, McGraw-Hill Book Co., 1938), pp. 50, 51, 59 and 60.

tudes tend to drop out everywhere, it is an obvious conclusion that persistence in school and success at academic tasks are closely related.

Yet, there are factors other than intelligence which seem to operate in the elimination from high school of students in the older adolescent years. Perhaps the high school is not suited to youth from homes of low socio-economic status. Bell, in a study of youth in Maryland, found that eight out of ten adolescents from higher-income groups graduated from high school while only one out of ten graduated who came from the under-privileged families. Bell stated that the strongest single factor in determining how far a youth goes in school is the occupation of his father.[11] Additional studies in New York, North Carolina, Illinois, Ohio, Kentucky, and Indiana indicated (1) that the socio-economic status of the family determines how far up the educational ladder its children will go, (2) that the grade in school attained by the individual child determines, in no small part, the type of work he will pursue as an adult, (3) that the type of work he does will determine the socio-economic status of the family he establishes, and (4) that this in turn will determine how far his children will progress in school, the kinds of jobs they will secure, the socio-economic status of the families they will establish, and the length of time their children will remain in school.[12] To an extent greater than many educators like to admit, studies indicate that the poorer a student is, the sooner he leaves school. Those who desperately need what the school might offer because of their limited home background and their lack of ability to learn directly from experience are least likely to receive help from the school. Even though decided progress has been made in our high schools with respect to the retention of students, two classes of students (those of low academic aptitude and/or social status) have found the program of the high school entirely inadequate for their needs. Indeed, there are many other ways by which the high school discriminates against students of low academic aptitude and low socio-economic status. A few of these are listed and briefly discussed here.

1. Very few high schools have adapted their curriculum and their instructional procedures to the wide range of intellectual aptitudes in nearly every class. Originally, high school education was set up for the select few and even today is oriented toward a more select group of students. The tendency is to emphasize the academic and the abstract; whereas, the real need of students of low academic aptitude is to stress the practical and the functional. The instructional procedures best suited for students from low socio-economic backgrounds are to stress the practical and to recognize every student as a human being who is worthy of respect.

2. Most Americans assume that high school education is free. Yet, re-

---

[11] H. M. Bell, *Youth Tell Their Story* (Washington, D. C., American Council on Education, 1938), p. 63.

[12] Harold C. Hand, *Principles of Public Secondary Education* (New York, Harcourt, Brace & Co., 1958), p. 87.

search on the problem has indicated that the average cost for high school attendance, aside from costs of food, clothing, shelter, and transportation, is $125 per year. To the student from the upper-class home, this sum is a mere trifle. But $125 is not pittance for the student from the low-income home, where no excess income exists after the costs of food, shelter, clothing, and transportation have been met. Students who come from these homes have the pride and the independence characteristic of all Americans. Being humiliated by costs that the family cannot meet, plus the many other factors that operate against them, causes them to quit school and go to work. Many families in the low socio-economic group are not chagrined by such behavior—they have been relieved of a financial burden too heavy to bear.

3. Students from the low socio-economic home, with many exceptions, lack the social poise and ease possessed by students from the upper-middle and the upper-class homes. The conditions in the home and the way of life of the low socio-economic group are not such as to develop ease and grace in social situations. Pogue's study[13] of participation in extracurricular activities found that nothing had any noticeable bearing upon participation in extracurricular activities except the socio-economic status of the student's family. The student from a family in the upper third of the socio-economic scale was far more likely to engage in extra-curricular activites than were most of his schoolmates from the less-favored homes. The truth is that students from homes near or on the verge of poverty participate in far fewer extraclass activities, though they could profit greatly from them, than do students from more-favored homes, who have much less need of them. They feel excluded. They are unable to become identified with the school society—escape from this frustration is inviting and they drop out of school. Of course, these are not the only causes for quitting school. There are still others.

4. Remember, also, that the parents of students with the low socio-economic status were not happy in high school. They see little advantage in school beyond the elementary grades. In fact, in many cases these parents much prefer that their teen-age children bring home a paycheck —they are encouraged to drop out of high school.

5. For the most part, teachers come from the middle class. They do not understand the students from the lower socio-economic classes and unconsciously are somewhat antagonistic to them. Some of the attitudes and morals of students from the low-status group are quite contrary to those of the middle class. Real teachers, however, learn to understand the culture of students from such homes and learn to adjust the class program to their needs.

6. A full-time job is really alluring to these students from low-income

[13] Harold C. Hand, *Principal Findings of the 1947-48 Basic Studies of the Illinois Secondary School Curriculum Program* (Office of the Superintendent of Public Instruction, Springfield, Ill., 1949), pp. 23-27.

homes, especially for students attending schools where no effort is made to adjust the curriculum of the high school to meet their specific needs. To most of them, the academic curriculum makes little sense—they have no desire to attend college and parents do not encourage it. What substitute program do you think might appeal and have meaning to these students?

What needs to be done to fulfill a sacred obligation to serve equally well all educable youth? As one faces squarely the difficulties confronting the adolescent from across the tracks who attends high school, he is led to exclaim, "Oh! that the benign spirit which guided the American Indians could descend upon the teacher with his middle class ideals and lead him to perceive that all men are brothers and equals." Surely, this idea of brother includes the older adolescents with soiled clothing and crude manners from across the tracks. To treat these youth as equals should mean to recognize and accept them as fellow human beings. Hand states it this way, "The faculty of the high school must be dedicated to the principle of universal public education."[14]

To fulfill our sacred obligation to these adolescents who live in dire poverty and come from barren homes, deficient in order and culture, the high school should provide a program adapted to the needs of this specific group. This problem has already been presented earlier in Chapters 7 and 8. We are now facing a specific phase of this problem, that is, the development of educational programs better suited to the older adolescent from underprivileged homes.

The following are suggested as the distinguishing characteristics of a program to achieve the proposed goals: (1) remove the stigma of low status; of ignorance, superstition, credulity, ugly speech, slovenly appearance, boorish manners; and of the distorted views of life, (2) help these prospective workers to prepare for better levels of work, that is, to rise on the occupational scale, and (3) assist them at all levels to discover the finer values in their social heritage and to qualify for some measure of social leadership. (Number 3 can best be provided through the core or common-learnings curriculum—see Chapter 7.)

There are two additional suggestions concerning the retention of older adolescents that must be considered:

1. The single marking standard must be altered. Individual growth must be taken into consideration when marking in courses other than the academic and the vocational. Those handicapped youth, who lack economic status as well as intellectual aptitude, must be given a chance to taste success.

2. The high school should help these older youth with practical problems related to earning a living, developing their personalities, spending personal income wisely, living healthily, and taking an active part in civic

[14] *Ibid.,* p. 106.

affairs. Spot these older students who are likely to drop out before it is too late.

Is a high school education vital to the older adolescents with low academic ability? As with other students, the years 17 and 18 may be the most rewarding years of their school life for individuals of low academic ability. Or, they can be wasted years unless the instruction and the program of the high school are adapted to the needs of these youth who are nearing adult status. Although, when both the program and the instruction are adapted to the peculiar needs of these older adolescents who are handicapped by poverty and/or limited intellectual aptitude, they can and do blossom out when a suitable educational program is provided. Some researchers in this field believe that the juvenile delinquency of the late 1950's and early 1960's may be a result of school programs poorly adapted to these youth.

Studies concerned with the formulation of a suitable program for the older youth of low economic status and below-average intellectual aptitude indicate that the high school must take three essential steps. First, a guidance and counseling service of merit must be organized. To each of these youth a series of vocational, intelligence, and personality tests should be administered and carefully interpreted. To a skilled specialist, the test should reveal the type of general, special, and academic education most suitable to each youth. Second, each youth will be assigned to classes in accordance with his ability to achieve. Where no suitable courses are available, the principal of the high school will add such needed courses as facilities and staff permit. Such a program must have meaning and pertinence to the background, interests, and aptitudes of these students. Third, teachers assigned to courses for these students should understand older youth, learn to know them as individuals, and be especially vivid and articulate in the presentation of course material. Actually, the teacher selected for the presentation and development of the course material is the key to the success of the program.

Studies indicate clearly that the high school graduate enjoys a somewhat higher economic status. To the extent that the school can help these older adolescents mature emotionally and acquire general vocational skills, they will improve their economic status and gain the respect essential for law-abiding Americans.

Summary. Our high schools have become common schools that admit and strive to retain all teen-agers. We still have the problem of adjusting the modern secondary school so as to provide an adequate education for both the slow and the rapid learner. The student-and-the-log tradition, designed for the rapid learner, has by now become outmoded—even for the rapid learner. The problem is to design buildings, services, and instructional tools for all youth. To the teacher of tomorrow is bequeathed the problem of planning an educational program that will permit every student in the high school to work up to his capacity and, thereby, become a better person and a better citizen. No more should be asked.

DISCUSSION PROBLEMS

1. A high school counselor relates that many of the boys in his school feel that there is nothing ahead of them since military service is compulsory. What acceptable arguments might you give to such a boy?
2. Discuss the problem of whether school gymnasiums, playgrounds, and auditoriums should be made more available to youth after regular school hours. Would it be more costly to keep them open or closed?
3. How are textbooks selected in your high school? Should this be done by (a) the classroom teachers who will use them, (b) a committee selected from the general faculty, or (c) by the school superintendent and his staff? Justify your answer.
4. Present the arguments for and against the "open library," that is, a program that permits students to come and go from the school library as opposed to one in which students are assigned to seats in the library for a period each day.
5. In some areas student surveys of the community have revealed valuable information. What reasons might be given against community surveys by students?

RELATED REFERENCES

AHL, F. N., *Audio-Visual Material in the High School, with Special Application to the Social Studies* (Boston, The Christopher Publishing House, 1946).

American Association of School Administrators, *The Expanding Role of Education,* Twenty-sixth Yearbook (Washington, D.C., National Education Association, 1948).

BEGLEY, J. L., (Captain), *So You Are Going to the Army* (Harrisburg, Pa., The Military Service Publishing Co., 1956).

BELL, H. M., *Youth Tell Their Story* (Washington, D.C., American Council on Education, 1938).

BOOKWALTER, Karl W., and BOOKWALTER, Carolyn W., *Fitness for Secondary School Youth* (Washington, D.C., American Association for Health, Physical Education and Recreation, 1956).

CAUDILL, William W., "Housing the Secondary School of Tomorrow," *Teachers College Record* 56:393-403 (April, 1955).

CHAPMAN, A. Hunter, "New High School Puts Its 70-Acre Site to Work," *School Executive* 75:69-72 (September, 1955).

DALE, Edgar, *Audio-Visual Methods in Teaching,* rev. ed. (New York, The Dryden Press, 1954).

DILLON, Harold J., *Early School Leavers—A Major Educational Problem* (New York, National Child Labor Committee, 1949).

DULLES, Foster R., *America Learns to Play* (New York, Appleton-Century-Crofts, Inc., 1940).

ECKERT, R. E., and MARSHALL, T. O., *When Youth Leave School* (New York, McGraw-Hill Book Co., 1938).

ENGELHARDT, N. L., Jr., "Laboratories for Learning," *School Executive* 74:63-66 (November, 1954).

Fitness of American Youth: A Report to the President of the United States on the President's Conference on Fitness of American Youth (Washington, D.C., Superintendent of Documents, 1956).

GRAMBS, Jean D., "Human Relations and Audio-Visual Materials," (New York, Conference of Christians and Jews, 1955).

HAND, Harold C., *Principles of Public Secondary Education* (New York, Harcourt, Brace & Co., 1958).

————, *Principal Findings of the 1947-48 Basic Studies of the Illinois Secondary School Curriculum Program* (Springfield, Ill., Office of the Superintendent of Public Instruction, 1949).

KOSKEY, Thomas A., *Baited Bulletin Boards: A Handbook for Teachers* (San Jose, Calif., Globe Printing Co., 1954).

MEEKS, M. F., *Models for Teaching* (Austin, University of Texas, The Extension Division, 1956).

LOPEZ, Frank G., ed., *Schools for the New Needs: Educational, Social, Economic,* Editors of Architectural Record (New York, F. W. Dodge Corporation, 1956).

Military Guidance in Secondary Schools (Washington, D.C., Department of the Army, 1956).

MOORE, Hollis A., and CAUDILL, William W., "Designed for the Early Teen-Ager," *Nation's Schools* 55:55-76 (January, 1956).

MULTON, Lucy, "A Classroom for Living," *Educational Leadership* 11:291-95 (February, 1954).

REID, John L., "Architectural Design of Schools," *School Executive* 74:92-95 (January, 1955).

ROSENBERGER, Homer T., "A Proper Setting for Learning," *Bulletin of the National Association of Secondary-School Principals* 38:23-56 (October, 1954).

United States Navy Recruiting Service, *Stay in School* (Washington, D.C., Government Printing Office, 1956).

WASHBURN, Carlton A., *Living Philosophy of Education* (New York, The John Day Company, Inc., 1940).

"What to Do About the Draft: A Guide to Young Men Facing Military Life," *Life,* May 14, 1956.

WITTICH, W. A., and HANSON, G. L., eds., *Educators' Guide to Free Tapes, Scripts, Transcriptions,* 2nd ed. (Randolph, Wis., Educators' Progress Service, 1956).

WERNER, William G., "One Business Man to Another," *Education Digest* 23:4-8 (March, 1958).

Films:

Broader Concept of Method (Parts I and II, Teacher Education Text-Film Series) (New York, McGraw-Hill Book Co., 1947), 16 mm., black and white, sound, Part I—13 minutes, Part II—19 minutes.

Problems of Pupil Adjustment: Part I—Drop Outs and Stay Ins (Teacher Education Text-Film Series) (New York, McGraw-Hill Book Co., 1950), 16 mm., black and white, sound, 20 minutes.

Design for Learning (San Francisco, Photo and Sound Production, 1952), 16 mm., black and white, sound, 25 minutes.

Chapter 19

LEADERSHIP FOR LEARNING

A leader is best when people scarcely know that he exists.
—From A Way of Life According to Lao-tzu

WHAT IS LEADERSHIP FOR LEARNING?

Leadership means various things to different people. To some it means, "Do as you are told. Ask no questions. Rewards come only to the loyal." To others it means, "Seek the advice of followers before coming to a decision. Formulate policies through compromise. Discuss all issues with those who are affected by them. Attempt to eliminate the sources of real grievance so far as situations permit."

Castillo, in his delightful book on Mexico,[1] reveals over and over again some of the fundamentals of leadership without referring to it by name.

Hernando Cortes constantly consulted with his followers when planning the recurring battles and hardships of the campaign—and his followers shared in the rewards. Cortes ferreted out the grievances of the natives against their rulers and exploited them. The natives ultimately made up the greater part of the army corps that defeated the Mexicans.

By maintaining a friendly and conciliatory attitude toward his own followers, Cortes quickly learned of grievances among them. Outwardly, at least, he was a warm friend of follower and foe alike; differences were resolved by battle only when friendship failed. It is probable that these traits of leaderships were the prime factor that brought victory rather than defeat to the campaign to conquer Mexico.

Competing Concepts of Leadership. The three most common concepts of leadership are: (1) a belief that leadership is closely related to status, (2) a belief that only the intellectually elite are capable of leadership, and (3) a belief that all, or nearly all, of the people have leadership qualities. These concepts are so contradictory that a choice must be made—all cannot be true. In the reference above, Hernando Cortes was

[1] Bernal Diaz del Castillo, *The Discovery and Conquest of Mexico* (New York, Farrar, Straus and Cudahy, Inc., 1956), p. 36. See: Book 2, "The Conquest," starting p. 31.

not a status leader. He was chosen by his followers because they believed he was best suited to bring order and security to the expedition. It was recognized by those men that different situations require different leadership qualities.[2]

In recent years, educators have given much attention to the problem of educational leadership. Research in this area supports the concept that nearly all people have leadership qualities, though most practices follow the beliefs that status and intelligence are prerequisites for leadership. Research indicates that:

1. Effective leaders have an intelligence level only slightly above the average of the group.

2. Academic success in school does not correlate with leadership ability in out-of-school situations.

3. The characteristics which correlate with leadership most highly are: originality, ambition, persistence, emotional stability, judgment, popularity, communication skills, insight, co-operation, and knowledge. These skills and characteristics are not necessary to leadership in all situations, for different situations require different characteristics to varying degrees.[3]

Earlier research by Kurt Lewin and his students[4] has had decided implications for leader-group relations. They found that the relationships (social climate) established between the leader and the group markedly influenced the character of behavior of the group and the extent of its achievement. The three leader-group relationship structures used in the experiment were: autocratic, democratic, and laissez faire.

Greater Achievements under the Democratic Leader. The group with the autocratic leader, who dictates the policy, the techniques, and the activities, as well as the work tasks and work companions, will usually develop nothing more than hostile attitudes within the group plus an apathetic attitude. Under a democratic leader, who assists the group at arriving at policies and decisions through discussion, activities and policies may be expected to grow out of a common goal. Where technical advice is needed, the leader suggests two or three alternatives from which a choice is made. Under the democratic structure, there is, as Lewin's experiments revealed, a minimum of hostility within the group—individuals are more alert and interested. The *laissez faire* group, which attempts to function with little or no leadership, tends to develop hostilities and become apathetic. It achieves almost nothing. In the experiment, the students who took part were enthusiastic about the democratic structure

---

[2] See also: Patrick J. Bratton, and others, "Status and Student Leadership in the Secondary School," *Educational Leadership* 13:209-215 (January, 1956).

[3] Robert M. Myers, "The Development and Implications of a Conception of Leadership for Leadership Education," unpublished doctoral dissertation, College of Education, University of Florida, Gainesville, Fla., 1954, typed.

[4] Kurt Lewin, and others, "Patterns of Aggressive Behavior in Experimentally Created Social Climates," *Journal of Social Psychology* 10:271-299 (1939).

and disliked both the autocratic and the laissez faire patterns. However, the autocratic was liked the least of all.

Everywhere in our land, these three patterns of relationships, as between administrators and teachers and as between students and teachers, can be observed. Those who study this problem believe that the same weaknesses and strengths, as revealed in Lewin's research, exist in our school systems. Tensions are high when either the autocratic or the laissez faire pattern prevails; tensions are low when democracy is observed. Teachers and students are alert and active in the democratic school— they are proud to be a part of it. But under the autocratic and the laissez faire patterns, the school is disliked. Any procedure that produces apathy and hatred hardly has a place in the American school.

What Controls Are Best? Of these three control patterns or social climates, which is best for administrators, for teachers, and for students? If we truly believe that teaching is a profession, this question must be faced and answered. Most desired is that type of control which will make the teacher most effective. But how much control should a teacher impose on a class? Will the outcomes sought or the beliefs of the school patrons in any way determine the type of control imposed?

Such questions point directly at the problem of control, that is, the control of the teacher by the administrator and of students by teachers. To get at the specific problem, we may take an illustration from management and labor experiences:

In an effort to increase output at the Hawthorne Plant of the Western Electric Company, research was designed to measure various control patterns. Conditions of labor as related to output of workers was the subject of study over an eighteen-year period. With the inauguration of research efforts, production began to increase at once for both the experimental and the control groups. Illumination was improved, rest periods were introduced, the length of the work period and the work day was shortened, free lunches were served during the rest periods, and similar innovations were introduced. With each of these changes the output per worker per group was increased. But when, in the course of the experiment, former work conditions were restored, that is, longer hours, no rest periods, etc., the quality and quantity of the output was *not* reduced to its former level.[5]

Why had production increased regardless of the manipulation of working conditions? A careful analysis of the problem pointed to one factor. In order to conduct this research, management had to secure the co-operation of the workers. To do this, (1) foremen and workers met together as equals, (2) workers were asked their opinions about plant conditions,

[5] F. J. Roethlisberger and W. J. Dickson, *Management and the Worker* (Cambridge, Mass., Harvard University Press, 1940), p. 615; quoted with added commentary by Lindley J. Stiles and Mattie F. Dorsey, *Democratic Teaching in Secondary Schools* (Philadelphia, J. B. Lippincott Co., 1950), pp. 272-294.

and (3) some of the meetings were held in the plant superintendent's office where the problems of the workers were handled sympathetically. Doesn't this clearly indicate a shift from the former autocratic control to democratic control? Formerly, the boss had told the workers when and how to do their jobs. But under the experimental conditions, democracy slipped in—the problem of output was discussed with workers, suggested changes were made to improve production, and the pro's and con's of each proposed change were threshed out. The latter control is very similar to that which may be employed by any democratic-minded teacher.

This Hawthorne research was one of the sources that have brought about improved management-labor relations. Make the enterprise a co-operative one, recognize the worker, call him by his first name, and production goes up—or so management has learned. Whether one is a student, a teacher, or a worker in business or industry, the pattern of control is a big factor in the output of the individual. It may be that the situation is an element in determining the pattern of control; perhaps, in the transmission of straight academic subject matter, there may be less significance in autocratic control. But for the achievement of socially centered objectives, the democratic pattern is highly significant as indicated by the Hawthorne study.

This is not new in the history of education. In 1853, an Indiana judge observed that "the public seems to cling to a despotism in the government of schools which has been discarded everywhere else." He gave this philosophy which needs repeating, for teachers have often failed to heed it over the last hundred years.

One thing seems obvious, the very act of resorting to the rod demonstrates the incapacity of the teacher for one of the most important parts of his vocation, namely, school government.

For such a teacher the nurseries of the republic are not the proper element. They are above him.

It can hardly be doubted that the public opinion will, in time, strike the ferule from the hands of the teacher, leaving him as the true basis of government, only the resources of his intellect and heart.[6]

Thus, leadership for learning must, by nature and law, recognize the spirit of democracy that has made America strong.

CHARACTERISTICS OF LEADERSHIP OF THE SECONDARY SCHOOL

Present Leadership Is Largely Autocratic. Who is the leader of the high school staff and the student body? Who specifically provides leader-

[6] Cooper vs. McJunkin (1853), 4 Ind., in J. F., Weltzin, *The Legal Authority of the American Public School*, The Mid-West Book Concern, pp. 240-41; quoted by Willard S. Elsbree in *The American Teacher* (New York, American Book Company, 1939), pp. 236-37.

ship for learning? The principal of the high school is the leader of the staff and the student body. He is specifically charged with the responsibility of leadership for learning. In general, what is the pattern of control that may be found in the American high school? Is it autocratic, laissez faire, or democratic? A statement by Kenneth L. Pederson, Hibbing High School, at Hibbing, Minnesota, indicates the current answer to this question.

In many respects the administration of American schools has been undemocratic and at times autocratic. The tradition of line-and-staff responsibilities provided that plans and policies be handed down from the superintendent, to the principal, to the supervisor, to the department head, and to the teacher. No doubt this procedure will continue, but it can become democratic. A study of administrative techniques in the United States indicates that there is a definite tendency to substitute democratic practices for traditional authoritarian directives.[7]

The pattern of control for our American high school is generally autocratic. It is a part of our European heritage. It was that way in Europe, and we have tended to keep it that way in America. This is so despite the fact that we have changed very largely the curricular content of the educational program. Change is taking place, and control patterns are becoming more and more democratic. However, a look at contemporary court rulings provides evidence that teachers still have a long way to go. Here is what courts have regarded as reasonable rules, and they have upheld schools for suspending students who violated these rules:

a rule prohibiting pupils from leaving the school grounds during noon recess without permission
a rule prohibiting pupils from taking lunch during recess except at the school cafeteria
a rule requiring pupils to prepare for a rhetorical exercise
a rule prohibiting pupils from attending moving picture shows except on Friday night and on Saturday
a rule requiring all pupils to study music
a rule prohibiting the use of face paint and cosmetics
a rule requiring all pupils to write compositions and enter into debates
a rule requiring all pupils to read the Bible in the school.[8]

It is difficult at times to remember that we are citizens of a democracy. But we do believe in it, despite our actions. Since 1900, the pattern of family life has changed from one largely autocratic to one largely democratic. Can one learn to live democratically by reading about democracy under autocratic directions? Should teachers and principals demonstrate

[7] Kenneth L. Pederson, "How Is Democratic Administration Achieved?" *Bulletin of the National Association of Secondary-School Principals* 38:34-36 (April, 1954).
[8] Newton Edwards, *The Courts and the Public Schools* (Chicago, University of Chicago Press, 1955), pp. 601-602. (court cases cited).

their faith in our way of life by following a democratic type of control in class and in school? There can be but one answer.

Some objectors will say that discipline, as such, is impossible under a democratic control pattern—the teen-agers get too noisy and learn too little. The democratic pattern is not the lax pattern. Beginning teachers are sometimes taken to a classroom, given a class roll, and then deserted by the school principal. This is no more democratic than would be the autocratic process.

What are some relationships that make home and school more democratic? A simple illustration of desirable human relations in the home is found in *These Are Your Children.*[9]

> Children grow best in a home in which they participate. Taking part increases their feeling of belonging, of being valued, of being wanted and accepted . . . Work in a home rarely goes smoothly when children are "told" to do jobs. It is better to talk over the work to be done and let the family decide how it will be distributed. It is not the specific job which is important but the fact that the child has a valued contribution to make . . . In some homes there is a regular family council where everyone sits down together. Even the littlest child can take part. Chores are discussed and chosen, problems are talked over, "gripes" against each other are aired, and plans are made.
>
> In all families there will be decisions which must ultimately be made by Mother and Father but the children's ideas will be welcomed, considered and talked over before a decision is reached. Children follow decisions more readily and with greater understanding when they have had a part in making them.

In the home, the mother and father are the leaders; in the school, the superintendent and principal hold these leadership posts. However, the most effective control patterns are very similar. As Americans, most of us are followers, but like to be respected for our true worth. We want to be accepted, and we desire to help recognized leaders who make final decisions that concern us personally.

Guideposts to Leadership for Learning. To a degree, all men have leadership characteristics. Emphasis here is placed upon those unique characteristics that help teachers in working with students. The following guideposts indicate how favorable human relations within the classroom can be produced by the principal.

The democratic leader is most effective when he frees the creative talents of all who work with him. To be creative, the teacher must be free to experiment, to discuss problems with his principal, and to feel accepted. When the principal gives orders and demands that they be obeyed, the the teacher is no longer a member of an honored profession—he is an underling and the principal has become nothing more than the autocratic boss so common in an earlier era.

---

[9] Gladys G. Jenkins, and others, *These Are Your Children* (Chicago, Scott, Foresman & Co., 1953), pp. 232-3, extended edition.

When, through give-and-take discussion with the principal, the objectives to be achieved in a subject or problem are perfectly understood by both—and the teacher feels free to find ways to achieve them—he is challenged. As a free and accepted person, he enters creative activity with a zest for life and work.

Leadership is more effective when it is shared among the group. Legally, staff-and-line organization, as borrowed from the military, still persists in school administration. The school principal is appointed by the superintendent with the approval of the school board. It follows, as a matter of course, that the principal has direct authority over the teachers within his school. In practice, this rule by the elite is becoming outmoded in many high schools, and administration through shared leadership is becoming more and more common. This is in accord with a democratic society.

The principal cannot delegate his basic responsibility for the administration of the school, but he can do much to improve human relations. There are many teachers with leadership qualities in every school. In such areas as dramatics, music, athletics, public relations, industrial arts, and similar positions, the teacher may have better leadership qualities than the school principal. Just as the wise principal will distribute the leadership among his students, so will he capitalize upon the rich experience and training of his faculty. This may also be done in community relations—the talents of the parental group must not be overlooked.

All individuals affected by practices and policies should have a share in their determination. Lex majoris partis is the fundamental law of every society of equal rights. In our political democracy, the vote of the majority decides the policies and the practices. But the legal status of the principal permits him to make changes in the curriculum, the daily schedule, the assemblies, and the various schedules without consultation with his staff. But are such changes conducive to leadership for learning? Would teachers and principal co-operating on a curriculum problem, for example, produce changes more suitable for the classroom? Will teachers and principal, working co-operatively, increase mutual respect through shared power? Teachers as professional persons, are respectable and dependable. When all understand why changes are made and have a voice in making them, the work which follows change will be competently done.

Once the policy has been determined co-operatively, the status leader is the one to administer it to the best of his ability. However, if what has been created is not workable, he has an obligation to bring it before the group again for rethinking.

The democratic leader employs the group process. The heart of the democratic process is the group itself. It is the way by which it is made to function. Goals are reached through discussion, and the decision provides a motive for action. Under the autocratic way, the group soon splits into cliques and achieves less. Trained and qualified teachers, who as a group can do better with a superior leader, usually become irritated when told or commanded what to do. One loses heart under such conditions.

Leadership must define problems, draw upon talents available, and help the group to identify possible solutions. The unity of the group process can produce high morale within the school. Such a social climate is highly conducive to learning.

The primary function of educational administration is the improvement of the learning process. Many principals are so busy with details such as building maintenance, attendance, textbooks, and schedules that they may lose sight of the primary function of the school. The promotion of student growth and learning should come first; details may be delegated to others if the faculty is well balanced. The leader plans and devotes much of his time to improving the curriculum and the instructional program. He sets a definite time schedule for consultation with teachers in order to help them resolve some of their problems. By talking through such matters with individuals and by following the give-and-take process of group action, he helps the faculty to make decisions that result in improved learnings.[10]

Leaders must be constantly aware that the public determines what the school is to do and how well the school renders this service. This guidepost applies not only to professional educators but to all public servants. The board of education, representing the public, formulates a policy statement as a guide for the secondary administrator. Since the specialists, the high school staff, have the know-how, they are left relatively free to execute the program by which to achieve the goals presented. Through evaluation, the public determines whether sons and daughters develop the traits and characteristics desired.

This poses the questions of how the school may keep constantly informed as to what the public wants and wherein the service may be deficient. For teachers, it explains why all classroom activity must be challenging and meaningful, why it is necessary to help parents understand the program of the school, and what is being attempted.

Principal and teachers must listen to all grievances as courteously as possible, but when individuals or groups not representative of the community challenge the school, a firm stand must be taken. The public will support an adequate program wholeheartedly if kept well informed.

Attaining Democratic Administration. By what means can democratic administration be attained? For the answer to this question, let us turn to a successful principal, Raymond Moore, a proponent of democratic secondary-school administration. Principal Moore[11] admits that there are no pat answers to this issue. However, he does offer the following sugges-

[10] Much potential value may be lost when faculty meetings are scheduled late in the school day; but we have come far from the practice of holding these meetings late into the night. The before-school meetings are greatly to be desired.

[11] Raymond Moore, "How Is Democratic Administration Achieved?" *Bulletin of the National Association of Secondary-School Principals* 38:36-39 (April, 1954).

tions as possible solutions. His three-fold approach is to establish better public relations with the community, the faculty, and the student body.

Moore believes that favorable attitudes toward school administration can be attained by these methods:

1. The faculty will serve as a sounding board of community sentiment. The students will communicate prevailing community attitudes through classroom projects, themes, debates, panel discussions, and regular activities.

2. The high school will provide opportunities to bring parents into the school through the presentation of plays, concerts, special nights for visitation, personal conferences, and the support of such groups as the Parent-Teacher Association.

3. The administrator will respect the fact that the board of education represents community interests, and the board, in turn, will respect the fact that the administrator should have freedom as a trained educator to exercise his best judgment in matters dealing with educational policies.

Better relations can be established with the high school faculty if the administration will: (1) recognize that teachers differ in personality and ideas, (2) maintain equality in school duties, (3) keep a sound balance between duties and privileges, (4) permit free choice of teaching methods with the understanding that objectives must be reasonably attained, (5) give constructive criticism to all teachers, especially to those new to the system, and (6) provide an opportunity for teachers to express freely, in an informal atmosphere, their ideas and attitudes with regard to grading, book selection, and student conduct. Here, the informality of atmosphere is in a direct relation to the attitude of friendliness and confidence displayed by the administrator.

Some additional steps in establishing better relations with the high school faculty might be: (1) providing faculty meetings for general discussion of certain problems, (2) appointing special committees to study problems before a report is made to the faculty, and (3) abiding by faculty decisions. When the principal is aware of gains made, recognition of the fact should be acknowledged and credit given; or, if the problem or problems studied are not solved, further study should be encouraged. A committee should know at all times when its work is finished or when further study is expected.

How can better relations be established with the student body? Principal Moore suggests the following steps: (1) impartiality toward race, nationality, religious creed, and social standing, and (2) friendliness of the sort that rejects familiarity but assures the student access to an interested audience. He also suggests encouragement of self-expression and responsibility with (1) a student council representing each homeroom, (2) a student publication program, (3) student activities that, while representing many special interests, contribute because they instill a sense of proprietorship, (4) homerooms where officers are elected by popular vote, and (5) a suggestion box which provides a means of gleaning student sentiment.

Qualifications Peculiar to Leadership. The role of a leader in our democracy is far more complex than his role is under other forms of government, such as a monarch or dictator. Free Americans recognize the need for some type of leadership in government and business, as well as in education. But woe unto the school administrator who arbitrarily assumes monarchial or dictatorial powers! When this occurs, as it does on rare occasions, such planned confusion results that the community soon seeks an administrative replacement.

By some means, the worthy administrator achieves a balance among the several extreme views that are at work in every American community. He must resolve political differences between reactionaries and progressives; economic differences between savers and investors; religious differences between and among faiths; patriotic differences between nationalists and those who seek world government; and social differences between social classes. Above all, he must recognize his own views and strive for impersonal decisions.

Campbell[12] has suggested that people expect and sometimes demand that superintendents lead and teachers follow, and that, when this occurs, there are inevitable implications. Three of the results are listed as follows:

1. Many administrators are embarrassed if staff members display superior knowledge in a field, especially when this occurs in the presence of laymen or members of the board of education.

2. Many administrators are tempted to employ those who know less than they do, or at best, those who agree with their fundamental point of view.

3. Many titular leaders carefully refrain from training a logical successor. In a few instances, they hope that a poor leader will follow them.

A good leader, on the contrary, will (*a*) be proud to have on his staff a number of persons who have special skills and knowledge and are adding to them so that they are recognized as experts, (*b*) welcome differing points of view as a wholesome part of our check-and-balance system, and (*c*) encourage others to "learn the ropes" since, for the school itself, trained replacements are better than strangers.

Need for leadership analysis. As a pre-service teacher, you may wonder why there is a need for any classroom worker to examine briefly the qualifications of leadership. There are several. Beginning teachers who are not aware of the peculiar tasks of leadership may feel that the administrator is charting a pointless course of action. Again, the leader may indeed be at fault, and this may explain why the teacher's efforts apparently fail.

[12] Clyde M. Campbell, *Practical Applications of Democratic Administration* (New York, Harper & Brothers, 1952), pp. 290-291.

Every facet of leadership in school administration is applicable within the classroom. And, finally, the classroom teacher is a logical candidate for advancement to school administrative work. Thus, as a pre-service teacher, it is to your advantage to understand the characteristics of a democratic leader. Burton and Brueckner[13] suggest that quack volumes in the field of personality and the art of influencing others should be avoided. Instead, the reading of competent authorities in the psychology and practice of leadership, carried out in conjunction with the study of actual situations, is of definite assistance. Highlights of a rather complete analysis by Burton and Brueckner include the following:

1. A leader is selected for a given special ability or fitness to lead a specified co-operative project . . . This is the opposite of selection of a leader on the basis of seniority, political power, religious or social affiliations. Any member of the group may become a leader at a given time.
2. A leader has the willingness and ability to create a truly co-operative spirit and procedure . . .
3. A leader has better than average intelligence and emotional balance.
4. A leader has confidence in self, ability, aims, but also at times a profound feeling of humility, sometimes even distrust of self.
5. A leader has confidence in human nature, its improvability, the creativity of all individuals . . .
6. A leader recognizes critical points in the democratic development of policy, recognizes when issues must be brought into the open, thoroughly discussed and decisions secured . . .

An interesting specific analysis of two types of leadership made by a classroom teacher is cited[14] in Chart 27.

Leadership and Group Dynamics. The teacher who permits the group dynamics technique to prevail within the classroom can bring about a vast improvement over the old-fashioned lecture or question-and-answer approach to learning. Where this relatively new method has failed, it has been because the leader did not understand that this technique is not suited to autocratic principles. It, indeed, is not a method to be used by any leader in an effort to reach a personal goal.

It would be correct to say that the good leader will *permit* group dynamics to function. It would not be correct to suggest that group dynamics can be *used*.[15] The degree of activity within each group will vary widely since there are talented members in some and not in others. Since a group of teachers will consist of those who, in some measure at least,

[13] William H. Burton, and Leo J. Brueckner, *Supervision: A Social Process,* 3rd ed. (New York, Appleton-Century-Crofts, Inc., 1955), pp. 190-191.

[14] Robert G. Koopman, Alice Miel, and Paul J. Misner, *Democracy in School Administration* (New York, Appleton-Century-Crofts, 1943), pp. 15-16.

[15] Daniel E. Griffiths, *Human Relations in School Administration* (New York, Appleton-Century-Crofts, Inc., 1956), p. 187.

Chart 27. An Analysis of Two Types of Leadership

THE AUTOCRATIC ADMINISTRATOR	THE DEMOCRATIC ADMINISTRATOR
1. Thinks he can sit by himself and see all angles of a problem.	1. Realizes the potential power in thirty or fifty brains.
2. Does not know how to use the experience of others.	2. Knows how to utilize that power.
3. Cannot bear to let any of the strings of management slip from his fingers.	3. Knows how to delegate duties.
4. Is so tied to routine details that he seldom tackles his larger job.	4. Frees himself from routine details in order to turn his energy to creative leadership.
5. Is jealous of ideas. Reacts in one of several ways when someone else makes a proposal . . .	5. Is quick to recognize and praise an idea that comes from someone else.
6. Makes decisions that should have been made by the group.	6. Refers to the group all matters that concern the group.
7. Adopts a paternalistic attitude toward the group: "I know best."	7. Maintains the position of friendly, helpful adviser . . .
8. Expects hero worship, giggles of delight at his attempts at humor . . .	8. Wishes to be respected as a fair and just individual as he respects others.
9. Does not admit even to himself that he is autocratic.	9. Consciously practices democratic techniques.
10. Sacrifices everything, teachers, students, progress, to the end of a smooth-running system.	10. Is more concerned with the growth of individuals . . . than with freedom from annoyances.
11. Is greedy for publicity.	11. Pushes others into the foreground so that they may taste success.
12. Gives to others as few opportunities for leadership as possible. Makes committee assignments, then outlines all duties and performs many of them himself.	12. Believes that as many individuals as possible should have opportunities to take responsibility and exercise leadership.

have demonstrated many individual abilities and talents, it remains only for the alert leader to permit these values to operate.

Just as this permissive attitude on the part of the leader will improve the amount of learning within a classroom, so will it help adult groups to approach a desirable goal. Faculty meetings, for example, might well follow the pace that has been set by competent leadership in the modern classroom. In such a case, what are the techniques that might be permitted to function?

Superior Leadership Seeks to Achieve Our Basic Goals. The usual principal is not a Sir Galahad who crusades for impossible ideals. He is an employee of a community which has its own notion of what youth should gain through schooling. For one thing, the people want all or nearly all of their youth to attend high school, and they are proud of any report which shows this to be achieved. But there are other goals which are best known to the principal, who is a specialist in educational trends. The principal displays leadership in his own school and community. The result is that all citizens become quite enthusiastic in their support. Common goals include the following:

1. Secondary education is for all American youth.
2. The facilities of the school are equally available to all youth.
3. Student differences are met through adjustments in the curriculum.
4. Public high school education is free; instructional materials must be provided at no cost to students.
5. Each student progresses at his own rate of growth.
6. The objectives of the school are realized through a functional curriculum.
7. Every high school serves equally well youth from all walks of life.

There is a difference between goals and actual achievements. The struggle of high school principals and teachers to increase the retention of youth until graduation has been highly successful, although the goal of 100 per cent retention is yet to be attained. A summary[16] of such goals and the degree of success attained indicates the task ahead.

Only fifty per cent of ninth-graders are retained until graduation. The goal here is half met. All teen-agers need to be retained; the more able need to be helped to meet the requirements for the professions and skilled occupations. For the slow learners, these should be the most profitable years of life for a better understanding of our culture and for acquiring the more difficult vocational skills of a highly industrialized society. To retain them longer should increase their earning power and establish deeper loyalties to the common values of this age. Many principals now emphasize the principle of service to youth combined with service by youth.

Youth from well-to-do families participate in student activities to a much greater extent than those from underprivileged homes. Too little attention has been given this problem by principals, who would never place students who read Latin well with others who are just beginning to read Latin. Students from homes that are underprivileged should not be expected to be socially mature. They lack the self-assurance of the sophisticated group and need special help in attaining social skills.

The average I.Q. of grade 12 students is quite a few points higher than that of grade 9 students. What problem does this present for the principal to solve? There are at least three factors involved—the dead hand of meaningless tradition, the curriculum of the school, and the teachers on

[16] Edgar G. Johnston and Roland C. Faunce, *Student Activities in Secondary Schools* (New York, The Ronald Press Company, 1952), p. 316.

the staff. What would be your solution? Is it in accord with that of other members of your class? Why is this problem more serious in some high schools than in others?

It costs the typical high school student $125 per year to attend the free public high school; and these costs do not include such essentials as shelter, food, clothing, and transportation. With home income too limited to meet such extra costs, tension in the home increases and unhappiness at home can cause numerous drop-outs. Some principals meet this situation by cutting extra costs to a bare minimum. Others offer needy students certain school jobs and give them priority on outside requests for student help. Some principals ignore the problem entirely. How would you solve it?

Teachers mark against a single class standard despite the fact that any normal class of teen-agers has a range of six or seven grades in reading ability. Are we playing fair when we do this? On the one hand, we say that the high school is for everyone, yet we make it impossible for all but a select few to gain satisfaction. In the academic high school, such a procedure was acceptable; the students who were unable to make good marks soon dropped out of school and went to work.[17] But a concept of democracy has developed that provides common learnings for every student despite his lack of ability, with feeblemindedness being the only exception. Some have termed the borderline teen-agers as "uneducable," whatever that may mean. But the principal must act as a referee and decide whether a single standard is enough. What is your opinion? When all teen-agers have an opportunity to attend high school, should there be a chance that even the poorest in ability might have some degree of success?

Principals and teachers continue to state the objectives of secondary education in terms of what people do in the world, yet they persist in following an academic curriculum as a logical and scholastic division of the cultural heritage. A program that reflects preparation for world activity makes sense. But the high school, because it is part of the mores of our culture, changes slowly; the old seems right and proper while the new seems out of place. Yet, leadership for learning requires that change be made and that everyone must accept new concepts intellectually even while rejecting them emotionally.

The lower the position of the father on the economic ladder, the sooner his son or daughter will drop out of school. This has been true since Plato and before. In America, the belief has been deep-seated that elementary education is desirable for the child from an impoverished home but not high school education. However, a change in our economy has

[17] This attitude makes newspaper headlines whenever an educator proposes it; we wonder what would be the public feeling if high schools today actually reverted to the practices of the 1800's.

come about, and work for such children is more difficult to find. Opportunities for these teen-agers are reduced more and more each year.[18]

Evidence shows that their potential capacity to learn in school and to do creative work in the world is as fine as that of other children. The heart of this problem will be found when we learn how to change beliefs long held by teachers and the public at large. In some communities, it has been done by superior leaders. What do you believe and how would you do it?

The above goals may be studied in terms of mores that block action. When the principal becomes aware of a specific difficulty, he studies a strategy to improve attitudes of specific persons. If the tactics he employs are effective, the desired goal may be approached. The superior leader for learning moves toward his goals in terms of his ability to change attitudes for the better.

LEADERSHIP FOR LEARNING IN THE CLASSROOM

Teachers, too, are leaders. Many adults testify to the way that competent teachers have influenced them. It may be through words alone that life is made more full; sometimes punishment, justly administered, will bring this about; and sometimes kindly interest in a shy boy or girl will help. But in every instance, the influence comes from an adult who understands youth. Teachers, more than other school workers, have person-to-person contact with teen-agers. Because of this, such matters as grooming, friendliness, cheerfulness, sincerity, pleasant voice, and humor are of great importance to the teacher-leader.

Teachers Study People. The classroom leader studies the students, their parents, and the community where he teaches. All behavior is caused; some of it is desirable and some of it is not. The leader-teacher deliberately seeks to change that which is undesirable and to develop new attitudes.

To know the names of all students is important, and that all students know your name is also important. A first step, usually overlooked by pre-teachers, is to write your name on the blackboard, pronounce it clearly, and then add any comment that might reveal a desire to know every student more personally. In calling student names for the first roll, be especially careful to ask for pronunciation of difficult names; excuse yourself, if any errors occur, and mark in the classbook certain clues to unusual names and pronunciation. Association with established names should be made carefully; a teen-ager whose father is also a teacher will not necessarily want this called to the attention of his peers at that moment. A seating plan will be of value in recalling names and faces, and it should be prepared early.

[18] See Allison Davis and R. J. Havighurst, "Measurement of Mental Systems: Can Intelligence Be Measured?" *Scientific Monthly* 67:303-314 (April, 1948).

The better a teacher knows parents, the better will he know his students. Ideally, home visits should be arranged, but, practically, the teacher will meet most parents during school functions. Respect by the parents will engender respect by the students for the teacher.

If the teacher becomes a part of his community, he will find many things to praise. The principal will tell new teachers about important community customs that must be observed, and participating in community affairs will provide a firm steppingstone to leadership in the school and classroom. Factions exist in every community, to be sure, and the wise teacher will avoid alliances.

The Teacher-Leader Understands Human Nature. The master teacher is a real specialist in human behavior. He is able to explain the concepts in his subject-matter field and to relate them to other disciplines in language that is easily understood. The ability to make complex ideas clear is a professional skill of the highest order. The teacher who can meet this rigid test day after day receives the respect of his students and his community.

Discipline, or classroom control, is a much-used word by school personnel. To some, it means conformance; to others, it means inducing self-control. The exact pattern of discipline differs among teachers, but the goal is the same—respect for the rights of others. It is best achieved when the teacher is an emotionally mature person who has learned to live at peace with himself and others. Teen-agers admire him because he is consistently good-natured though firm as the occasion demands. Since he has no complexes, he can laugh heartily at a joke on himself. Because most teen-agers live with much inner turmoil and a deep feeling of inferiority, they respect the teacher who is self-assured but not cocksure in his behavior. They honor him because he respects each of them as an individual American. They like him because he knows what he is doing.

The Teacher-Leader Influences Fellow Teachers. All education associations and federations in America had their start through teacher-leaders. Educational policy has been guided along constructive lines through sound strategy developed by outstanding educators. The excellent research studies by the National Educational Association would never have been developed if teachers had not seen the need and set up the proper machinery to bring them about. State associations have done much to provide legislation which has improved educational opportunities. The various local groups, both those of the National Education Association and the American Federation of Teachers, have contributed tremendously to the cause of free education for every youth. Without the teacher-leader, this work might not have been started. The individual who senses a need and who discusses it with other teachers may not realize that he is going through the same germination process that brought about every gain that the profession has made. The teacher-leader strives to improve the teaching profession.

What is needed to make the educational profession more respected and more efficient? There must be a greater testing and refining of educational theory in the classroom. This is a service that the teacher-leader can do. For example, the core curriculum is more than something to be read about and discussed briefly. As yet, it has been incorporated into actual practice in only a relatively small number of high schools. However, two teachers easily might set up an experiment with an English and a social studies core combination by: (1) carefully defining the purposes or the goals of the venture, (2) planning a course of study to achieve the goals, and (3) evaluating the outcome. Such an enterprise would bring to the school a factual test of the core theory and acquaint all teachers on the staff with the process. It might even do more. When such theories are actually tested through experimentation before they are promoted by colleges of education, they assure less classroom failure and a greater respect for the educational profession.

Pride in the teaching profession is a prime essential if greater respect is to be fostered. The worker who says, "I am just a teacher," in the sense of an apology, should either change his viewpoint and attitude or resign from the profession. If he lacks pride in his work, he will never be successful at it. Few people respect those who fail to respect themselves.

Researches on learning, on human growth and development, and on intergroup relations have been numerous during the last two decades. Many of them are closely related to the classroom work of the teacher. When our more astute teachers, as they read and meditate on these studies, see in them certain applications to their own classroom needs, then an effort to improve their instruction is born. As these creators talk with fellow teachers, new ways of teaching are suggested and often tried out. This is leadership. It is only as professional people have challenging ideas that the work of the teacher comes alive and commands public respect.

DISCUSSION PROBLEMS

1. Great pressures are placed upon school superintendents to provide educational services without adding to school costs. At the same time, teachers often regard the superintendent as the one person standing between them and salary increases. As a teacher, how would you present the need for improved salaries to such a superintendent?
2. A militant group in your community has charged that the schools are teaching communism. What acceptable defense might be offered by a superintendent and his teachers?
3. Public schools are often criticized for "not teaching the Three R's." How might a superintendent refute this charge?
4. Under what circumstances may students be excluded from a public school?

(See: Punke, Harold H., "What the Courts Have Said About Exclusion of Pupils from Public Schools," *The Bulletin of the National Association of Secondary-School Principals* 42:41-59 [September, 1958]; reviewed in *The Education Digest* [December, 1958], pp. 22-25).

5. Under what circumstances do conflicts arise between the administration of public and parochial schools? How might these be resolved?

6. What co-operation is necessary between school administrators and civil authorities? Real estate promoters? Community newspapers and radio-TV stations? Local businessmen? To what extent might school difficulties be traced to this lack of co-operation?

7. Among your high school teachers recall five or six of the best. After each name on your list place the label *democratic* or *autocratic* and state concisely why each was so labelled.

RELATED REFERENCES

ANDERSON, Vernon E., GRIM, Paul R., and GRUHN, William T., *Principles and Practices of Secondary Education* (New York, The Ronald Press Company, 1951).

The Association for Supervision and Curriculum Development, *What the High Schools Teach*, 1956 Yearbook, (Washington, D.C., National Education Association, 1956).

BARTHKY, A. John, *Administration as Educational Leadership* (Stanford, Calif., Stanford University Press, 1956).

BESTOR, Arthur, *The Restoration of Learning* (New York, Alfred A. Knopf, Inc., 1955).

BRATTON, Patrick J., and others, "Status and Student Leadership in the Secondary School," *Educational Leadership* 13:209-215 (January, 1956).

BURTON, William H., and BRUECKNER, Leo J., *Supervision: A Social Process*, 3rd ed. (New York, Appleton-Century-Crofts, Inc., 1955).

CAMPBELL, Clyde M., *Practical Application of Democratic Administration* (New York, Harper & Brothers, 1952).

CASTILLO, Bernal Diaz del, *The Discovery and Conquest of Mexico* (New York, Farrar, Straus, and Cudahy, Inc., 1956).

Citizen Education Study (Detroit), *A Curriculum for Citizenship* (Detroit, Wayne University Press, 1953).

COMMAGER, Henry S., "Our Schools Have Kept Us Free," *Life*, October 16, 1950.

DAVIS, Allison, and HAVIGHURST, R. J., "Measurement of Mental Systems: Can Intelligence Be Measured?" *Scientific Monthly* 67:303-314 (April, 1948).

DEWEY, John, *Experience and Education* (New York, The Macmillan Co., 1938).

Educational Policies Commission, *Education for All American Youth—A Further Look* (Washington, D.C., The National Education Association, 1952).

Educational Policies Commission, *Education of Free Men in American Democracy* (Washington, D.C., The National Education Association, 1941).

EDWARDS, Newton, *The Courts and the Public Schools* (Chicago, The University of Chicago Press, 1955).

ELSBREE, Willard S., *The American Teacher* (New York, American Book Company, 1939).

GRIFFITHS, Daniel E., *Human Relations in School Administration* (New York, Appleton-Century-Crofts, Inc., 1956).

HOOK, Sidney, *Education for Modern Man* (New York, The Dial Press, 1949).

HOPKINS, L. T., *Interaction: The Democratic Process* (Boston, D. C. Heath & Company, 1941).

JENKINS, Gladys G., and others, *These Are Your Children* (Chicago, Scott, Foresman & Co., 1953) extended edition.

JOHNSTON, Edgar G., and FAUNCE, Roland C., *Student Activities in Secondary Schools* (New York, The Ronald Press, 1952).

KOOPMAN, Robert G., MIEL, Alice, and MISNER, Paul J., *Democracy in School Administration* (New York, Appleton-Century-Crofts, Inc., 1943).

LEWIN, Kurt, and others, "Patterns of Aggressive Behavior in Experimentally Created Social Climates," *Journal of Social Psychology* 10:271-299 (1939).

MACKENZIE, Gordon N., and COREY, Stephen M., *Instructional Leadership* (New York, Bureau of Publications, Teachers College, Columbia University, 1954).

MOORE, Raymond, "How Is Democratic Administration Achieved?" *Bulletin of the National Association of Secondary-School Principals* 38:36-39 (April, 1954).

MYERS, Robert M., *The Development and Implication of a Conception of Leadership for Leadership Education,* The University of Florida, Gainesville, Fla., unpublished doctor's dissertation, College of Education, 1954, typed.

PEDERSON, Kenneth L., "How Is Democratic Administration Achieved?" *The Bulletin of the National Association of Secondary-School Principals* 38:34-36 (April, 1954).

ROETHLISBERGER, F. J., and DICKSON, W. J., *Management and the Worker* (Cambridge, Mass., Harvard University Press, 1940).

SHANE, Harold G., and YAUCH, Wilbur A., *Creative School Administration* (New York, Henry Holt, 1954).

STILES, Lindley J., and DORSEY, Mattie F., *Democratic Teaching in Secondary Schools* (Philadelphia, J. B. Lippincott Co., 1950).

WELTZIN, Joachim F., *The Legal Authority of the American Public School as Developed by a Study of Liabilities to Damages* (Grand Forks, N. Dak., The Mid-West Book Concern, 1931).

WILES, Kimball, *Teaching for Better Schools* (Englewood Cliffs, N.J., Prentice-Hall, Inc., 1952).

Chapter 20

EQUALIZATION OF EDUCATIONAL

OPPORTUNITIES

Only an education specifically designed to support and advance free-dom, equality, and self-government will equip the American people to meet the challenges of our day.
— "Public Education and the Future of America,"
Educational Policies Commission, NEA, 1955

OLD WAYS VERSUS NEW WAYS

What is preventing or what prevents the United States of America *from designing its educational program to best meet the challenges of our day?* Customs or ways of life uniquely suited to a nation in its early develop-ment may be quite inadequate for a later period of its history. As new inventions and technology change our political, economic, and social ways, our earlier customs, ways of thinking, and behavior must also change. A nation may treat these new demands as problems to be faced and solved, rather than as stumbling blocks. It may move away from its old ways of behaving and explore the possibilities of the present and the future. If a nation fails to discard those techniques and skills that are antiquated, it may not long survive. This does not mean that everything old is of slight value. It does mean that we must evaluate the elements of our American heritage in terms of modern needs. Constitutional democ-racy is based upon far more than mere tradition; indeed, it has served as well through its flexibility and readiness to meet change.

When our forefathers came to this new continent, they brought with them the European pattern for their schools. The Latin Grammar School, our first attempt at secondary education, was an importation from the Old World, as later was the academy. It took a half-century, after the American Revolution, for an elementary and a secondary school, adapted to our way of life, to evolve and become known as the common school. This school, supported locally by a self-imposed tax upon all citizens, was entirely under home rule and was ideally suited to the sparsely settled areas of that time. A school board or a board of trustees, elected at a community meeting, employed the teacher and decided what would be taught. In its origin, the common school was created, supported, and controlled by the initiative of the local people.

How good were these early common schools? Some were superior, some were fair, and some were inferior. But they all maintained a common curriculum of reading, writing, and arithmetic. These were skills which could not be acquired adequately through home instruction, especially when more than half of the people in some communities were illiterates. The schools did provide a common program adapted to the needs of the period. The children who remained in school did learn to read, to write, and to use numbers in practical situations. Schools were valuable enough to establish a belief among the people that an institution served best when it was controlled locally. Although these schools were established under state authority, which is the origin of today's legal authority, neither the state nor the federal government had a part in designing the pattern of their organization and policies.

Seemingly, the people were satisfied with the private and parochial schools until 1800. What were some of the changes in the United States during the first half of the nineteenth century which led to the establishment of the common elementary and secondary school? The following four changes have been identified as among the most significant:

1. Suffrage was extended to all freemen. At the first election of George Washington, only one out of seven freemen were eligible to vote. The ideal of shared leadership among the populace was so pronounced that gradually the right to vote was extended to all freemen in the seaboard states. As each frontier state was admitted to the Union, there was provided a constitutional basis for universal suffrage, that is, suffrage for white male citizens who met certain requirements. Soon, the idea became generally accepted that any eligible voter might also be eligible to hold office if a majority so willed. This brought about the belief that our political system could endure only if voters and office holders had at least a basic or common education.

2. Trade and industry, as we know, developed very rapidly after 1800. Great numbers of workers were needed, both in the offices and in the factories. Business leaders soon realized that employees who could read, write, and compute were essential.

3. After 1800, immigrants began to flock to America in large numbers. They came as they were, ignorant of our language and customs. Many citizens saw the common school as a means whereby new Americans and their children might be taught the elements of learning as well as our customs. This premise still operates.

4. Men of the frontier, facing hardships and building for a future in

which individual worth would rate high, took the initiative in establishing common schools. They saw education as an equalizer between their children and the children of the aristocracy and privileged.

This common-school movement of the 1830-50's is summarized by Hales[1] as follows:

An inevitable result of the doctrine of equality, of industrial development, and of the extension of suffrage, however, was the attempt to extend and equalize educational opportunities. Not only was it believed that public education was a safeguard for republican government; it was further argued that the school would eliminate corruption, elevate the standards of public officials, and increase the ability of the citizen to judge well and wisely . . . Aided by the widespread belief that education would insure protection of property, assimilation of aliens, success of democracy, achievement of prosperity, and produce an intelligent and moral citizenry, the founders of the public school won success for their enterprise.

Despite the strenuous efforts of certain educational and political leaders to bring about a greater measure of federal participation in education, the centrifugal forces of a pioneer agrarian society . . . nullified such a possibility. Distance . . . family, and community rights, belief in human perfectibility through freedom from law—all these paralyzed not only the federal government but state government as well and made schooling a local function.

The District System. Even though the conditions that brought about the district system, especially local control and support, no longer exist, loyalty to the means rather than to the end results continues. This is true in rural areas, as well as in our metropolitan cities; school people and citizens everywhere cling to the pioneer concept. The two symbols, local control and local support, have become associated with liberty, freedom, and democracy. Those in politics, of course, make the most of this stereotype.[2]

Under the district system, where schools are close to the people, the initiative for change resides in the immediate community. Schools, accordingly, are good, fair, or inferior in terms of the vision and desire of the people. The school is what the people make it. Such a plan does stimulate creativity, and some highly superior schools are the result. Where vision is lacking, some highly inferior schools exist. Under the system of local control, the responsibility for the quality of education is specifically that of the local community.

What are some of the defects found in the district system? The basic weakness of the district system resides in its inability to provide for *equal*

[1] Dawson W. Hales, *Federal Control of Public Education* (New York, Bureau of Publications, Teachers College, Columbia University, 1954), p. 21.

[2] Reference should be made to the number of counties that exist in every state: there are far too many for efficiency in government, though by now they are a fixed part of our customs. County seats originally could be reached only after a day's drive with horse and buggy.

educational opportunity for all youth. One integral strand of our American heritage, and this is no sentimental reference to means, is equality of opportunity for all. Each individual is worthy of respect; each must have an opportunity to develop as fully as the laws of heredity permit; and each youth, given life by the Creator, is entitled to an even chance. The district, or home rule system, does not meet this obligation.

Soon, after the battle for support of the public school by a general tax had been won, new conditions arose to alter the equalities that had been established. Cyr, Burke, and Mort[3] summarize:

> In general, we can say that the beginning of today's inequalities in education date back to the beginning of industrialization in our country; to the building of the first factory and the first railroad, the opening of the first mine, the first move from the farm to the cities, the establishment of the first mechanical farm, the creation of the first corporation, the development of the first wealthy suburb, and all of the other changes accompanying the industrial revolution.

As industrialization has advanced, educational inequalities between areas within a state have become greater. Districts 30 and 59 in Nebraska well illustrate this fact. For many years, the schools in these adjoining districts comprised of productive farmland were rated high. Then industrialization came to one—a railroad was pushed through, and later a power plant was constructed. With the added wealth, the industrialized district was able to provide a complete twelve-grade school plant and site. Abundant instructional materials and a superior instructional staff were provided on a levy of six mills for each dollar of assessed valuation. In the other district, where there remained only farms which were subject to the rise and fall of economic conditions, the tax levy was set at nine mills. But this provided only a drafty, one-room schoolhouse, a single teacher who was poorly qualified, and no instructional material beyond the textbook. Standards had changed over the years, and industrialization spelled the difference for the favored district. Thus, even though the creative spirit might have been equally strong in each district, the financial means were not the same.

Equalization of Educational Opportunities. Frederick Solomon[4] indicates why industry brings about educational inequality within a state.

> Most of the wealth is concentrated in a few centers. It is entirely beyond the reach of most other states, not to mention the local government . . . . Modern wealth is relatively immune to state and local taxation.

Industry is located in very few of the many school-tax areas of a state. Hence, in the specific areas where industry is established, superior schools

---

[3] Frank W. Cyr, Arvid J. Burke, and Paul M. Mort, *Paying for Our Schools* (Scranton, Pa., International Textbook Co., 1938), p. 26.
[4] Frederick Solomon, "Federal Aid to Education," in *University Debaters' Annual*, (New York, H. W. Wilson Co., 1949), p. 37.

can be provided because added taxable wealth can procure the best teachers, equipment, and buildings. As a matter of course, the most capable teachers move into areas where the salaries are highest. Schools in nearby districts soon fall far behind the needs of the time and are rated as inferior. Wherever industry intrudes, it distorts the principle of equal educational opportunity, which has been and remains dear to the hearts of most Americans. Ultimately, they are forced to choose between *old ways* and *new ways* and make modifications which are suitable to modern living.

In nearly every chapter of this textbook, the problem of providing for equality of educational opportunity for youth has been presented. We know, for example, that the problem of educating the slow or the rapid learner can be met through the reduction of class size to 20, as opposed to the present practice of 35, 40, or more. Increasing the salaries and improving conditions of employment will attract a greater number of gifted people to the classroom. Larger buildings and more attractive sites are needed, as opposed to single-room schools that are not far removed from log cabin days. Industrialization has brought great wealth, power, and prestige to America, but under our system of district support, this has not been tapped efficiently for the support of all public schools.

Many able citizens and educators, after study of this problem, have come to believe that it is time to seriously consider some practical modifications in the old ways of supporting public education. Several states, especially the heavily industrialized ones, have experimented with new types of taxation to supplement the older property tax plan. The strong impact of emergency conditions, which began during World War II, has caused the Federal Government to give outright aid to areas that suffered most through military programs. During the 1954-55 school year,[5] the Federal Government contributed more than one and one-half billion dollars to 81 educational programs. Expenditures included aid to local school districts crowded with children because of new Federal activities, to veteran education, to school lunches, to agricultural extension work, and to the education of Indians. Nearly twice this amount was given in 1948-49 when veterans' payments were at their highest level. Thus, though citizens and educators hesitate to urge a complete change to Federal support and are about evenly divided on the issue, the Federal Government is extending the use of its tax dollars to education, and the states do everything they can to qualify for the grants.[6]

But the problem of inequalities of educational opportunity is not restricted to areas within states; there are interstate as well as intrastate

[5] United States Office of Education News Bulletin, November 1, 1956.

[6] An informal debate on this moot question will do much to bring the pro's and con's into the open. When this is done, the student will be in a much better position to make a personal decision. All evidence on both sides should be obtained and presented.

inequalities. On a per capita basis, some states are much wealthier than others. In general, the wealthy states have more industry or are developing resources such as mining. In 1955, Delaware was the wealthiest state[7] with a per capita income of $2,513, and Mississippi ranked lowest with a per capita income of $946. Thus, the ratio between the two extremes is 2.6 to 1. The U.S. *Biennial Survey of Education* for 1950-52 indicates that the top state, Delaware, spent $495.54 per child in average daily attendance while the bottom state, Mississippi, spent $125.90. The expenditures for each Delaware child were 4.1 dollars to each 1 dollar expended by Mississippi. With four times as much money to invest in each child, Delaware can attract superior teachers, construct superior buildings, and purchase superior instructional materials. If differences in living costs exist between these two states, they are not that great.

What is the true result of this wide variation in the ability of states to support education? Do the states having the least wealth put forth as much effort as the wealthiest states in support of education? Certainly, full credit must be given to the states that, despite their poverty level, make tremendous efforts to keep the public schools in operation; but the "widow's mite," blessed though it may be, cannot equal the demands of modern living. The youth who happens to be born in a poor state, or a poor region within a state, is clearly discriminated against from the moment he enters his substandard school. Here is not the educational equality implied in our American way of life.

The facts given in Table 17 contain the basic argument for Federal aid to education. There can be no question but that the quality of education in the various states and in the local districts will determine the welfare of the nation. Democracy requires that our citizens be capable of discharging their responsibilities. Only the high school, as stated early in this textbook, provides for youth a suitable program for acquiring understandings, skills, and drives that are so essential for civic competence.

In 1947, Benjamin Fine, Education Editor for the *New York Times*, made a survey of school problems and published his conclusions. His study of Federal aid is a superior summary of this controversial issue, and the pro's and con's are presented in Chart 28.

"On the basis of evidence I have been able to gather," Mr. Fine states, "I believe that some form of Federal aid bill is essential." In reference to the points against Federal aid, he says, "These issues are important and have stood in the way of Federal aid for many years. Sometimes, they are raised honestly, at other times merely as a smoke screen."[8]

---

[7] Road Maps of Industry, Conference Board, 460 Park Ave., New York 22, N. Y., September 21, 1956.

[8] Benjamin Fine, *Our Children Are Cheated* (New York, Henry Holt & Co., Inc., 1947), p. 210.

Table 17. A Comparison of Income and Educational Investments by Five States Making the Greatest and Five States Making the Least Educational Investments

STATES	AMOUNT IN-VESTED PER CHILD IN AV-ERAGE DAILY ATTEND-ANCE*	AMOUNT IN-VESTED PER CHILD, AGES 5-17*	PER CAPITA PER-SONAL INCOME** 1950	1955	PER CENT OF PERSONAL INCOME DEVOTED TO EDUCATION
(Least)					
South					
Carolina	$173.46	$128.69	$ 881	$1,108	19.6
Alabama	163.23	121.57	867	1,181	18.8
Arkansas	157.52	115.14	805	1,062	19.1
Kentucky	162.55	112.27	958	1,175	16.9
Mississippi	125.90	102.35	729	946	17.3
(Greatest)					
Delaware	494.54	343.55	2,153	2,513	23.0
Oregon	417.40	327.33	1,602	1,834	26.1
New York	471.03	326.38	1,883	2,263	25.0
Washington	365.83	298.23	1,671	1,987	21.2
Wyoming	373.26	289.62	1,629	1,753	22.2

* U.S. Biennial Survey of Education, 1950-52, Ch. 2, p. 80.
** Road Maps of Industry, Conference Board, New York, September 21, 1956.

Chart 28. Pros and Cons of Federal Aid to Education

PRO'S	CON'S
1. Denial of educational opportunity and gross inequality of educational opportunity are far too prevalent in the United States.	1. Federal aid would mean federal control.
2. The social ills which result from denying decent schooling to millions endanger the whole of education.	2. Federal aid should go to private schools as well as to public schools.
3. The gross inequalities in educational opportunity which exist today are primarily due to similar inequalities in the financial structure of education.	3. Federal aid would cause regimentation and destroy local initiative.
	4. Federal aid is unnecessary as the states are financially solvent.
	5. Federal aid would upset our democratic way of life by centralizing control over education.
	6. The wealthier states should not be called upon to support the poorer states.*

* Benjamin Fine, *Our Children Are Cheated* (New York, Henry Holt & Co., Inc., 1947), pp. 206 and 209-10.

HOW TO PROVIDE EQUAL EDUCATIONAL
OPPORTUNITY FOR ALL YOUTH

Basic Elements of the Program. What must be done to permit indus-trialization "to serve rather than to cheat youth?" Each state could modify its tax laws for the support of our schools so as to permit industry and business to carry its appropriate share of the cost of a program that would give every young American an equal chance to win life's prizes in accord-ance with his latent talents. If we play fair with youth, a key to a more adequate high school education can be found in the programs being offered by our superior high schools. Such programs include, at least, three essential areas: (1) a minimum foundation program, (2) a program to meet community needs, and (3) a program to meet the needs of stu-dents as individuals. Let us examine briefly these three specific phases of an acceptable program.

A minimum foundation program. What does this mean? Every teen-ager needs help in acquiring the more important aspects of our culture. Even a super-genius, reared in an isolated area, is not likely to discover unaided the basic tools and values of modern living. Without effective education, could the average teen-ager grow up in your community and attain citizenship all by himself? On the contrary, lacking good schools, he probably will be dwarfed or distorted in personality by being cut off from an understanding of science, American government, art, music, literature, and moral values. Our records of juvenile delinquency give abundant proof that it can and does happen in America.

But how is this related to high school education? It simply means that there are educational experiences which all teen-agers must have because they are human beings who live in America. A minimum foundation program is justified on the grounds that all of us must adequately adjust to our culture. This need will become more intense as we continue to increase in population—through mounting birth rates and extended life span. There can be no turning back to the primitive days when a limited education met the need of the moment for a few of the more fortunate. Neither the Federal Government nor the states should permit any local community to ignore a minimum foundation program of education. What type of subject matter should be included in this minimum foundation program? It would surely include the most important areas of our cul-tural heritage.

What are the more important areas of our cultural heritage? We suggest that you stop here. What do you think are the most important areas? Formulate a short list of them; then compare your list with the one which follows. Your listing may be better than that given here, for we have no monopoly on the interpretation of the American heritage. What would you add to this list?

1. Every teen-ager should understand the meaning of the democratic way of life, as it has become a part of the process of government.

2. Every teen-ager should understand the structure and the operation of our economic system and be aware of how it affects his well-being as producer, consumer, and citizen.

3. Every teen-ager should understand the scientific method and the influence of science on human life and thought and should make those facts his own that are essential for an understanding of the world in which he lives.

4. Every teen-ager should grow constantly in his capacity to enjoy beauty and to understand and appreciate the best in literature and art.[9]

Such terms as *general education, common learnings,* and *core curriculum* have been employed in this textbook as synonyms: all have similar meanings. How have you applied them in your listings?

A program to meet local community needs. Every community must have some way of earning a living, such as agriculture, commerce, manufacturing, mining, food processing, and fishing; even in resort areas, where people live out their years on earned income and savings, these livelihoods are reflected. The high school can guide students in an honest orientation to a community vocation and in the acquisition of specific vocational skills. Students, thus prepared, may benefit considerably and win rapid advancement due to their preliminary preparation. For many parents, students, and employers, vocational education is the real reason for the high school. There are specific requests for courses or programs; these come from parents and the community, as well as from students. Such courses often depart from vocational training and may include the teaching of a language, driver education, family life education, consumer education, and similar areas. Since the community pays the bill, it has full right to request such additions to the basic foundation program.

An elective program to meet the needs of individual students. Although students have many needs in common, as individuals they differ widely in specific needs. Hence, many elective courses must be made available if the school is to serve youth and the community. Teen-agers have personal and social problems, as well as vocational problems. Many individual needs have been met through student activities and guidance programs. Through interviews and questionnaires, some principals identify the specific courses desired by individual students. For the most part, however, these individual needs are met by making every course offered in the high school a possible elective for individual students. This is recognition of the fact that every youth has a wide range of interests and must explore to establish those interests which are most closely in accord with his true potentialities, whether latent or developed.

[9] Educational Policies Commission, *Education for All American Youth—A Further Look,* rev. ed. (Washington, D. C., National Education Association, 1952), pp. 215-221.

When these three essentials are provided, a community can be justifiably proud of its superior high school system. But these superior schools are found much more frequently in those states where the wealth of the state is used as a tax base for the support of a minimum foundation program. This permits the local district to use the property tax for supporting those courses especially desired by the local community. Schools cost money; but in terms of the human wreckage which results when industrialization does not serve youth, schools in the long run save money.[10]

The Fundamental Problem. Can we honestly say that our teen-agers are being cheated? Are we cheating ourselves? What are the facts? One-fifth of our teen-agers attend inferior rural high schools. A higher mill levy on farmland produces less than one-fourth as much income per student as does a lower mill levy on industrial areas. The real wealth of many individual states and of the entire United States is not being tapped for the support of rural high schools. Here are the facts:

1. There are more children per family in rural areas than in urban and village areas.

2. For each one dollar available to be invested in a rural high school student, there are four and one-half dollars available for investment in the urban high school student.

3. Northeastern states receive 42 per cent of the national income for 27 per cent of the children; southeastern states receive 2 per cent of the national income for 13 per cent of the children.

4. Seventy-five per cent of America's 7 million children attend high schools with enrollments of less than 300 students. Nearly all of the small high schools are located in farm or rural areas.

5. The salary schedules for urban high schools exceed those for rural high schools by 50 to 200 per cent. The city schools, thus, take the better teachers away from rural areas.

6. In a period of teacher shortage, good teachers are attracted to urban high schools by higher pay and more favorable conditions for effective teaching; rural high school replacements are recruited from those who were not considered earlier. At least one-third of the rural teachers have emergency teaching certificates.

7. Many of the rural high schools lack instructional supplies that are now considered essential for learning; in some schools, science, for example, is presented without any laboratory equipment whatsoever.

8. It should not be assumed, however, that all rural high school teachers are necessarily incompetent; a few are superior teachers who, through makeshift measures and innovations, are able to maintain a superior pro-

[10] It is currently estimated that each inmate of a penitentiary, a reform school, or any institution designed to restrain human behavior, costs society more than $4,000 per annum: this is about ten times the per-pupil investment made by Delaware, Oregon, New York, Washington, and similar states where school costs seem to be highest.

gram. There are outstanding exceptions in America's rural areas, where high schools are located in attractive surroundings and the teachers are highly qualified and alert. Students in and from these schools are active, intelligent, confident, and poised; they are completely at home in our modern, complex world. Unfortunately, this cannot be said of all rural teachers, schools, and teen-agers.

All our youth are citizens of the state, as well as of the community. The education of its youth is a state responsibility. About one-half of the states of the American commonwealth already have accepted this responsibility by tapping the total wealth of the state, wherever it exists, to provide for an equal quality of education by a more equitable distribution of the income from taxes to all high schools within the state. It is a logical step.

The very process of industrialization has brought about a need for change in the high school program. Industry, more and more, is dependent upon the high school for the vocational orientation of many of its employees, who will be drawn not only from the community where the industry is located but also from many other communities. This has required an expansion of the high school program to include practical courses, in addition to the older academic courses. Since industry is asking the high school to produce technicians, who in time become a part of industry, industry should carry its share of the educational expense or investment. In its new program of automation, industry will depend even more upon the high school to train its employees. To do this, certain new subject-matter content will require an expansion of the high school program. Whether we like it or not, the contemporary high school is wedded to our new technology.

Federal aid is, actually, only a small part of the major problem today. The basic cause for an inadequate program in a large number of our high schools is the district's inability to support an adequate program. This does not mean that the state is without sufficient industrial resources. Short-sighted forces within such states have continued to lay down what Fine[11] termed a "smoke screen" that appeals strongly to legislators, who are not always objective in their decisions. In other states, however, there is too little industry to provide any degree of aid for schools that are inadequate; the only alternative is for such states to seek Federal aid. Again, this is a logical step. Teen-agers of such states are also citizens of the United States. They enter military service, they vote, and they ultimately contribute their share to the Federal Treasury. At least 10 per cent of these teen-agers will spend their adult lives in states that are more highly industrialized than were their own; they will be in some form of competition with other citizens who have had the advantage of a better high school background.

[11] Fine, *op. cit.*, p. 210.

Yet, the issue is controversial, and many honest Americans are not in favor of Federal aid under any circumstances; and some do not even favor state aid under any circumstances.

Trends Toward Equalization. Have there been any trends in the United States toward equalization of educational opportunity? What is the status of Federal aid? The financial support of the public high school has been, since early times, derived chiefly from a local property tax. It remains so today even when such new taxes as income, sales, motor fuel, ton mile, customs, poll, excise, inheritance, gift, and many others are reserved for the states and the Federal Government. Some states, in recent years, have made substantial grants to local high schools. Previous to 1920, these revenues were allocated to all of the high schools within the state and were flat grants made without regard to the needs of individual schools. While such apportionments helped every school, they tended to accentuate rather than to reduce differences in the quality of programs

Table 18. Proportion of Revenue for Public Education, Elementary and Secondary, Derived from Federal, State, and Local Sources over Two-Year Period

SCHOOL YEAR	PER CENT FROM FEDERAL SOURCES	PER CENT FROM STATE SOURCES	PER CENT FROM LOCAL SOURCES	PER CENT TOTAL
1935-36	.50	29.34	70.16	100
1939-40	1.76	30.27	67.97	100
1945-46	1.35	34.71	63.94	100
1949-50	2.87	39.83	57.30	100
1953-54	2.55	41.44	56.01	100

between schools. However, the flat grant has been largely replaced by an equalizing grant under which aid is given to the schools that need it; thus, the program of the inadequate school is improved to a point where it becomes adequate. Financially embarrassed high school districts which are helped this way soon find it possible to establish a minimum foundation program.

A publication from the United States Office of Education[12] reveals certain trends in Federal and state aid during the last twenty years. Table 18, in a much abbreviated form, shows these trends. Federal aid, it may be noted, has increased twentyfold since 1935-36. The two important items, here, are vocational aid from Federal appropriations and Federal aid to local districts which were burdened by Federal activities. The latter resulted in greatly increased enrollments in local schools and the withdrawal of large amounts of wealth from local tax lists through Federal purchases. Table 18 shows that state support for local school districts, during the two decades, increased from 29 to 41 per cent. This means that 41 per cent of all revenue for the support of local schools came from state

[12] U. S. Department of Health, Education, and Welfare, *Public School Finance Programs* (Washington, D. C., Government Printing Office, 1955), p. 7.

governments. Here is proof that, gradually, ways are being found in our America to reduce the inequalities of educational opportunity brought about by industrialization within and among the states. But there is a long road ahead before the equality of the pre-industrialization period can again be established. This might be an excellent place for you to determine, from the latest statistical report available, the exact status of your community in terms of state support.

A Summarization. What is at the heart of the issue? Let us here summarize so that all the facts will become apparent.

1. If every community is to maintain a minimum foundation program, the total wealth of the state must be tapped to support the educational program in the poorer communities.

2. The Federal government has aided the public school in land and money grants since 1800 without at any time taking control of the schools.

3. In general, the public is entirely satisfied with local control of education by its locally elected board of education.

4. As yet, no supplementary aid method by either state or Federal government has been completely satisfactory.

5. State aid, and wherever necessary Federal aid, is believed to be the best method yet devised for supplementing the local high school program so that a minimum foundation program may be established and maintained.

6. There is widespread dissatisfaction with present methods of determining the value of property for assessment purposes. No common standard for assessing has as yet been devised.

7. On a statewide basis, it is recommended that 50 per cent of the revenue for public education come from the state and 50 per cent from the local community. The revenue from the state should be derived from other sources than the property tax, such as income, sales, and motor fuel, while those from the local community may be based upon a mill levy in terms of property evaluation.

8. Due to the neglect of school construction in the past and the heavy birth rate of recent years, local districts are now unable to provide the school plant expansion needed. Several states are including aid for school plant construction as an emergency item in their legislative appropriation bills. The Congress has considered, but has not approved any proposals for aid to school plant construction.

9. The Congressional division, over the Kelley Bill of 1956, brought to light a few factors about Federal aid. Two indirect factors that were very influential in the defeat of the bill were integration and religious education. Two direct factors were the powerful opposition groups that represented industry—the United States Chamber of Commerce and the National Association of Manufacturers. Two rival education groups united in favor of the bill—the National Education Association and the American

Federation of Teachers. Also favoring the bill was the newly merged AFL-CIO.

10. Federal aid to education is a highly controversial issue and will probably remain so. There are many honest people on both the pro and con sides of the problem. Definite progress has been made toward equalization during the last two decades; this has been especially true for state aid.

The real heart of this issue is, "What is better for youth?"—complete local support or local support plus equalizing aid from either state or Federal government, or both? No professional teacher can long avoid facing this issue. What do you think? Now is a proper time to make a decision on this issue. As a class, list the arguments pro and con. Try, especially, to relate this issue to some of the problems that have been thus far introduced.

A SUPERIOR HIGH SCHOOL FOR ALL YOUTH

How can all high schools be superior? Can there be effective high schools without competent teachers, adequate school buildings, a co-ordinated educational program, or suitable instructional facilities? Can teachers be found who are willing to work without reasonable compensation for their services?

The Heart of the Issue. Some citizens feel that anyone can teach. This was an old and stongly held idea which, in recent years, has begun to fade away. For the most part, an inevitable truth has now been accepted, "High aptitude for teaching is relatively rare." Only a limited proportion of our people have a potential for becoming competent teachers. Also, the men and women who are highly effective in the classroom possess many skills and aptitudes that qualify them for other vocational pursuits as well as teaching. And teachers, like other human beings, are attracted to those occupations through which prestige and recognition are accorded. In our way of life, certain material possessions are essential for prestige— a reasonably new car, a respectable home, and acceptable clothing. They want an opportunity to save toward giving their own children a college education. Teachers want insurance programs and other benefits which are provided without cost by most industries. School districts, with limited financial resources, are unable to compete with industry or to attract and hold the more desirable teachers. In such districts, the compensation is below average, the school building is poorly adapted to its purpose, and instructional aids are limited or nonexistent. Under these conditions, the program of the school is of an inferior grade. Occasionally, because of personal circumstances, a superior teacher will continue to serve on such a school staff; but, on the whole, the teachers to be found in such schools are mediocre and inflict untold damage on those teen-agers who remain a part of their daily "captive audience."

What is needed? If more money can be made available, the high schools can be improved. From what sources can this money be obtained? Under our system of financing public education, there are just two sources aside from local support—the state and the Federal Government. And both sources are obligated to help, if the local community is unable to provide a good school. Consider, however, the general agreement among business men and organized labor that proper schools are essential, and the general disagreement on how this might be achieved, Chart 29.

Two Illustrations. How can equalization of educational opportunity, which existed prior to the coming of industrialization, be restored? An illustration of how this has been done in two industrialized states, Delaware and California, will be cited. In some highly industrialized states, the

Chart 29. Comparison of the Stands of Business and Labor on Public Education

U. S. Chamber of Commerce*	AFL-CIO**
"A considerable amount of space has been dedicated to telling the story of increased enrollments and the need for additional teachers and classrooms. State and local communities are doing something about these shortages. As was pointed out in recent Office of Education and Bureau of the Census releases, there was a 3.8 increase in enrollments last year in elementary and secondary schools and a 12 per cent increase in school funds.	"In 1938, labor approved Federal grants-in-aid for vocational education . . . endorsed the recommendations of the President's Advisory Committee on Education, favoring general Federal grants, assistance for facilities to improve teacher training, and aid to construct school buildings. In following years . . . gave consistent, active, and concrete support for Federal aid legislation, emphasizing money for better teacher's salaries as of prime importance.
"This money is being spent for building new schools, for other capital outlays and to raise teachers' salaries. The National Chamber has never doubted that, given the facts about school needs, the American taxpayer would take necessary action. The action now being taken is far preferable to anything the advocates of Federal intervention have yet dreamed up."	"Organized labor has continued its policy of urging needed Federal aid for education coupled with local control of the school system.
	"Today's rapidly increasing school population is faced by a selfish minority who would 'save' on taxes by denying our children the means for a good education. These forces, with great political power, would deny society the money needed to pay fair salaries to obtain qualified teachers. They would continue to permit thousands of our children to attend 'school' in dirty and dilapidated fire-traps."

* "News and Cues," Education Department, Chamber of Commerce of the United States, September, 1956, Vol. II, No. 2, p. 1.

** "Crusade for Public Schools," John D. Connors, Director of Education, American Federation of Labor and Congress of Industrial Organizations, February, 1956, pp. 7-9.

revenue for the support of schools is derived largely from legislative appropriations.

Delaware. The state with the highest per capita income serves as an example. In 1953-54, 87 per cent of all revenue to the public schools in Delaware was derived from appropriations by the state legislature. Through budgets prepared by local districts and approved by local and state boards of education, the monies alloted to each of 60 districts were made available to each without any additional supervision on the part of the state. The revenues provided by the state were sufficient to support a minimum foundation program for every high school within the state. If any local community desires a superior program, it may levy upon local property as extensively as a referendum vote will permit. Beyond a minimum foundation program, the local community is given complete freedom in determining the educational program. In 1953-54, 13 per cent of the total revenue for education in Delaware was derived from levies by the local districts.

Delaware provides an illustration of one way to restore equality of opportunity to teen-aged Americans. All of the state's wealth is taxed to support all of the high schools of the state; the whole state comprises a single taxing unit. Industry in Delaware carries its fair share of the tax load for the education of youth. With the exception of local taxes on property for the support of superior schools, all school revenues come from sources other than the property tax.

But in other areas of the United States, there are states where as much as 96 per cent of all revenue for the support of the high school comes from a levy on the property of the district in which the school is located. In general, where the development of industry has lagged and the per capita income is low, the *in*equality of educational opportunity is greatest. Studies of per capita income indicate that Mississippi has the lowest per capita income of any state. Hobbled by a sharecropper system of agriculture and the support of two separate school systems, Mississippi finds it difficult, and perhaps burdensome, to support its high schools adequately or to maintain equality of educational opportunity. Likewise, other Southern states are similarly handicapped. To some students of the problem of equalizing educational opportunity *for all youth,* aid of some type is essential at once, and Federal aid seems to be the only immediate solution. Industry is developing in the South, and some years hence the margin of wealth, as between the South and the North, will be decidedly narrowed. But what of the young Americans who look to their Southern states for a functional education at this moment?

California. The equalization program of California has been repeatedly praised by students of educational finance. Its essential plan is as follows:

1. In 1953-54, the total educational budget of the State of California was $780,000,000.

2. Of this budget, $15,000,000 came from the Federal Government, $415,000,000 came from the state government, $7,000,000 came from the county government, and $350,000,000 came from the local districts.

3. All revenues, aside from incidental fees and fines, are derived from income, sales, or motor fuel. All revenues for the county and local districts are from the property tax.

4. State aid is provided through (1) general-purpose flat grants, (2) general-purpose equalization grants, (3) special-purpose flat grants, and (4) special-purpose equalization grants.

5. Equalizing funds are employed to balance educational opportunity throughout the state; the size of the grant is varied in accordance with the financial aid a high school must have to provide a minimum foundation program.

The plan of state aid for high schools in California is as follows:

1. There is a flat grant of $120 per student. This is to assist all high schools in establishing a minimum program.

2. If a high school is unable to establish and maintain a minimum foundation program on the flat grant, the state guarantees an addition of $350 per student provided the district will levy 7.5 mills on the assessed evaluation of the district; or $280 if the levy is only 4.5 mills. This is the widely acclaimed equalization grant of California. Note that the state requires the district to put forth some effort before the equalization grant is made available. However, the state does not prescribe what is to be taught; the community is free to determine the curriculum of the school. Minimum requirements are those that the most mediocre teacher in the poorest school would automatically follow anyway. Rather than restrict, the state department of education carries on experimentation and research for the possible benefit of all school communities.

3. In addition, the high school district is expected to raise supplemental revenue by a mill levy on local property to provide for the specific needs of the local community, as well as the specific needs of individual students.

Thus, in California a minimum foundation program is the heart of the high school curriculum. Without this, the high school lacks vitality, meaning, and breadth.

CHARACTERISTICS OF A SUPERIOR HIGH SCHOOL

What makes a high school superior? We speak often of superior, good, and inferior high schools. In what ways do they differ? In the final analysis, the quality of service provided will determine the difference. No community deliberately seeks a poor quality of service; all communities desire superior teachers, since they provide a fine quality of service. Invariably, when one studies the superior schools, they are found in wealthy communities with a high investment per pupil; however, an expensive investment does not automatically assure that there will be a superior school.

Some of the most important characteristics of a superior high school are:

1. A principal who qualifies as having those qualities required for leadership. Such men understand how to work effectively with professional people; they do not insist that teachers work for them. They are skilled in developing fine human relations among students, teachers, and supervisors; they are able to create a permissive atmosphere in which teachers can achieve their best. They see clearly how to guide the learning of teen-agers, and they have an aptitude for doing it. However, to attract them, the high school must pay salaries equivalent to those paid by industry for men of equal abilities. These principals are accepted by the status leaders of the community as their equals; they may even be accepted as counselors by men of business, industry, and labor.

2. Superior teachers are attracted to the high school by salaries above those paid by other high schools and equal to those paid by industry for equivalent abilities. Working conditions are just as attractive; the number of classes per day is held to four or five, instead of six, seven, or eight as is common in inferior schools. Class sizes are set at 20-25; excellent conditions exist for effective work. There is an abundance of instructional materials; and a permissive atmosphere gives opportunity for experimentation and planning.

3. The curriculum of the high school meets (1) the common needs of all students through the common learnings or the general education program, (2) the specific needs of the community, and (3) the specific needs of individual students. It is a planned curriculum, tailored to the community which it was designed to serve. It is a flexible curriculum so that there will be little cultural lag between needs of modern living and the service provided by the school.

4. The program of the high school recognizes and makes specific provisions for the slow and rapid learners and similar individual differences among students. This is a characteristic that stands out among superior schools. Those who teach the slow and rapid learners must have the qualities of the superior teacher plus a specific aptitude for special instruction. Because there are few persons so qualified, these teachers command high salaries.

5. A superior high school will have a superior counseling and guidance service. The change from the agrarian to the industrial economy has greatly multiplied the types of jobs available and has handicapped parents in guiding their teen-age children toward the selection of a vocation. The rapidly changing customs, as between the younger and older generations, has led to considerable conflict between parents and teen-agers. The superior school has an effective service to guide teen-agers in their personal

and social problems, as well as in vocational and academic orientation. But this is a costly service. It requires highly capable people with specific aptitudes and special training.

6. The superior school has established a functional public relations program. Through it, all members of the community know that all, or nearly all, of our teen-agers are being urged to stay in school until graduation. A positive public relations program acts as liaison between school and community so that both may function and prosper with a minimum of ill will. It answers for the community those questions which parents and citizens always ask about the school.

7. The superior high school reports student progress to parents so that they have a clear understanding of what has been attempted, of why it has been attempted, and of the progress made. Since the person-to-person report is highly desirable, the superior school will provide for this with a marked degree of frequency.

8. The superior high school assists the student to make a realistic self-evaluation.

9. The superior high school through the extension of its counseling service assists employers in making a realistic evaluation of graduates. Accurate reports of student achievement are provided by the high school.

In its relationships with the community, the superior high school will recognize all factors that must be faced by the graduate of the modern high school—political problems, the question of unionization, community, county, state, national, and international policies will be discussed freely, with marked attention to the facts. Through this, the student will be better equipped to determine his own worth and place in our society.

These characteristics of the superior high school emphasize the important part that finance plays. The quality service of the superior high school costs more, which is true of any superior service. This type of service is the responsibility of the state, where state resources permit, or of the United States if state resources are inadequate.

DISCUSSION PROBLEMS

1. Why have public schools in many communities turned to the Federal Government for financial support?
2. Ideally, from what sources should school support come? List the real dangers that arise in (*a*) obtaining improved support within a community, (*b*) obtaining improved support within a state, and (*c*) obtaining improved support from the Federal Government.
3. Senators and members of the House of Representatives are paid $22,500 yearly, plus allowances for expenses. Are these sums provided from local budgets or from the Federal Treasury? Why is this process acceptable? Relate it to school finances.

   Discuss how the following factors have made it imperative that all American youth be given equal educational opportunity: (*a*) military service, (*b*) increased communication, (*c*) spread of industrialism throughout the world, and (*d*) discovery of atomic energy.

5. Under what circumstances should a metropolitan high school offer courses in agriculture? Similarly, when should a rural high school offer courses in retail sales and general office practice?

6. Much emphasis is placed upon athletic competition in all states. Upon what basis are the various divisions established? Why do the winning teams of each division seldom meet in statewide competition that would find a "Class A" school playing a "Class D" school? Do such differences extend to academic achievement?

7. By research determine the salaries paid the best high school teachers and also the salaries paid the best salesmen employed by industry. Which receives the greatest financial reward for the service rendered?

8. For the local high school what portion of the monies for the support of the high school are derived from (1) the local community, (2) the state, (3) the Federal Government?

RELATED REFERENCES

Association for Supervision and Curriculum Development, *Forces Affecting American Education,* 1953 Yearbook (Washington, D.C., National Education Association, 1953).

————, *What Shall the High Schools Teach?* 1956 Yearbook (Washington, D.C., National Education Association, 1956).

Burke, Arvid, *Financing the Public School* (New York, Harper & Brothers, 1951).

Crusade for Public Schools, John D. Connors, Director of Education, American Federation of Labor and Congress of Industrial Organizations (Washington, D.C., February, 1956).

Cyr, Frank W., Burke, Arvid J., and Mort, Paul M., *Paying for Our Schools* (Scranton, Pa., International Textbook Co., 1938).

Educational Policies Commission, *Public Education and the Future of America* (Washington, D.C., National Education Association, 1955).

————, *Education for All American Youth—A Further Look,* revised, (Washington, D.C., National Education Association, 1952).

Edwards, Newton B., *Equal Educational Opportunity for Youth* (Washington, D.C., National Education Association and the American Council on Education, 1939).

Ehlers, Henry, ed. *Critical Issues in Education* (New York, Henry Holt & Co., Inc., 1955).

Fine, Benjamin, *Our Children Are Cheated* (New York, Henry Holt and Co., Inc., 1947).

Hales, Dawson W., *Federal Control of Education* (New York, Bureau of Publications, Teachers College, Columbia University, 1954).

Holmes, Henry W., *The Last Best Hope* (Cambridge, Mass., Harvard University Press, 1955).

Johns, R. L., *The Property Tax and Public School Financing* (Washington, D.C., National Education Association Research Division, National Education Association, 1958).

Mort, Paul E., and Reusser, Walter C., *Public School Finance* (New York, McGraw-Hill Book Co., 1951).

National Association of Secondary-School Principals, *Planning for American Youth* (Washington, D.C., National Education Association, 1951).

National Education Association, Committee on Tax Education and School Finance, *Guides to the Development of State School Finance Programs* (Washington, D.C., National Education Association, 1949).

United States Department of Health, Education and Welfare, *Public School Finance Programs* (Washington, D.C., Government Printing Office, 1955).

Chapter 21

WHAT IS BETTER FOR YOUTH?

And glady wolde he lerne, and gladly teche.—Chaucer

The years 12 to 18 for youth vibrate with life, teem with ideas, and produce ideals and purposes. If the environment is a stimulating one, character, interests, habits, and insights begin to be established.

When we ask the question, "What is better for youth?" we desire to find guideposts by which to construct the best possible program for youth in the midst of a welter of contemporary conflicts. Whose among the protesting voices of our day represent false prophets and whose voices represent real prophets? Who protests to protect self-interest, to reduce taxes, or to provide more students for a particular subject? Who speaks for the type of program best suited to development of youth? Is the critic ignorant of how our youth develop, or has he a broad understanding of the adolescent years? Many who shout the loudest are the least informed; however, we may be assured that whatever is the best for youth is also the best for America.

Four institutions are of supreme importance in these years from 12 to 18. They are the home, the school, the church, and the community. If a consensus can be reached or a partnership formed among these four institutions as to "what is best for youth," teen-agers are likely to make much wiser choices and, in adult years, to be better citizens and better men. These choices which youth are helped to make should be guided by men of wisdom rather than by men of folly. Men who advise must speak from a fullness of understanding rather than from bias or ignorance. He who advises in ignorance is indeed guilty of offending youth.

ASSUMPTIONS AS TO WHAT IS BETTER FOR YOUTH

Adults, steeped in earlier traditions, may be moved to favorable action by the mention of an earlier custom which has been repeated many times in their presence. For example, in campaigns for public office, both public speakers and the newspapers believe that they influence voters favorably by reference to the lowly birth and difficult early life of the candidates for office.

Perhaps the "log cabin" myth will partly account for the hesitance of great segments of America to bring school plants and school offerings up to date. Those who prepare biographies of presidential candidates make the most of this traditional sentiment; indeed, a lowly origin is considered to be an excellent asset for anyone who seeks public office. James D. Hart[1] has written:

A lowly birthplace is a boon to both the presidential candidate and his campaign biographer, second only to such sure-fire vote-getters as a widowed mother and rural upbringing.

With curious reasoning, many Americans do feel that, because Lincoln was born in a log cabin, all leadership should start in humble surroundings. We are inclined to overlook the more obvious explanation of the emphasis upon Lincoln's limited environment—that he succeeded in spite of such a heritage. But the myth goes on, and schools do not always receive support that is proportionate to the contemporary living standards in the various school districts.

Some Assumptions Relative to American High Schools. School leadership, striving to interpret the will of the supporting public and to blend it with factual evidence of what is best for youth, must of necessity seek to establish certain assumptions.[2] The statements which follow comprise a list of some of the basic assumptions of American secondary education. How valid are these assumptions? What proof is there that they are or are not valid? A high school faculty must hold certain beliefs in common, if the institution they serve is to remain stable and function efficiently.

Yet, in the evaluation of an assumption one fixed standard must be observed—it must be realistic. Each assumption must represent, as accurately as possible, the current community, state, national, and world[3] outlook. American secondary education must meet these essential standards. It must teach students to co-operate with others and to acquire the common attitudes and ideals by which our nation becomes unified and to establish common loyalties to the community, the state, and the nation. To meet these obligations, the high school has developed a curriculum in general education (the core or common-learnings curriculum). It must provide an adequate elective program for those who wish to utilize their acquired skills immediately upon graduation. To develop the required competency, such students elect from both academic and vocational

---

[1] James D. Hart, "They All Were Born in Log Cabins," *American Heritage* 7:32-33 (August, 1956).

[2] *Assumption* defined: the supposition that an apparent fact or principle is true in light of available evidence.

[3] *World outlook* is a new approach for American high schools. Yet, a *world power* must accept and maintain a *world outlook.*

courses (the special curriculum). It must provide a satisfactory program for those students whose vocations will require subsequent education in college or university (the special curriculum). Any adequate educational program will include both socialization (general education, core curriculum, or common learnings) and specialization (special education) for all students.

Some basic assumptions of American secondary education.[4]

TEACHER SPECIALIZATION IS BEST. Secondary school teachers function best as specialists in one or two fields of knowledge in contrast to the wide range of elementary teachers. However, the core or common-learnings teachers are exceptions. They function in several fields.

SEVERAL SUBJECTS SHOULD BE TAKEN TOGETHER. A number of quite different subjects should be taken at the same time, and these should be scheduled over several semesters.

CLASS SIZE SHOULD BE SMALL. Without regard for the subject being studied, the size of a class should not be larger than from 25 to 30 for academic subjects and from 15 to 17 for vocational subjects where machinery is in operation.

ATTENDANCE SHOULD BE CONTINUOUS TO GRADUATION. Continuous, full attendance until graduation is the proper course for all students.

SOCIAL PROMOTION IS BEST. High standards of expectation and critical appraisal of student performance may create personal and social problems; social promotion has more positive results.

SCHOOL IS CONDUCTED AS A COMMUNITY. The school should be thought of and conducted as a community, even though the areas of activity are limited in scope and the basic source of authority and sanction are not in the hands of the students.

TEACHERS ARE MEMBERS OF A PROFESSION. There should be no symbolic recognition of differences between teachers by such devices as titles; it is further assumed that all teachers of the same section and the same level will generally teach in the same manner.

SCHOOL IS JUDGED BY INDIVIDUALS. The schools are made up of individuals each of whom accepts or rejects the values of the school as an individual.

PEER VALUES DOMINATE. Peer groups are assumed to dominate the life of the adolescent with parental values being of secondary importance.

TEACHER JUDGMENT IS SUPERIOR. The judgments which adolescents make of each other and which parents make of their children with reference to academic competence are of secondary importance in comparison with the judgments of teachers.

ALL STUDENTS ARE OF EQUAL IMPORTANCE. All students should associate freely with all other students, differences between students should be minimized, and egalitarian relations should prevail.

---

[4] Association for Supervision and Curriculum Development, *What Shall the High Schools Teach?* 1956 Yearbook (Washington, D. C., National Education Association, 1956), pp. 59-61.

THE SAME DIPLOMA SHOULD BE GIVEN ALL STUDENTS. A most common symbolic representation of the completion of the secondary school program—a high school diploma—must be given, even if the range of courses taken has been very great and of quite different kinds, and in spite of any major differences in the level of attainment in these subjects.

THE DIPLOMA IS PROTECTED. In order to protect the diploma, originally set up to mark the completion of the college preparatory program, the work must be done in the school and under the supervision of teachers, all of whom have been duly certified by the state.

These assumptions are largely a product of the twentieth century; they have evolved very slowly and in some instances through conflict and compromise. They are not all well established. In the matter of social promotion, for example, a clear recognition of the differences between general education (education for citizenship) and special education (education for acquiring specific skills) is not always made. In general education, all students pass a course who co-operate and put forth effort. In special education, however, only those students pass who acquire the skills and understandings being taught above a set minimum standard. Social promotion is simply an adjustment that must be made in a unique institution—the American comprehensive high school. Even though this sharp differentiation between promotion in general, as distinct from special education, has been fully explained many times, most citizens and some educators are not aware of it.

Similarly, efforts are being made to establish a variety of diplomas that would indicate the type of education or the degree of proficiency attained. The single diploma for all students is a product of our democratic traditions. This issue of a variety of diplomas versus a single diploma for all has been debated many times by the National Association of Secondary-School Principals at its annual meetings. A majority of the high school principals have always favored the single diploma. However, the movement to have each diploma show the type of education or the degree of proficiency attained seems to be gaining support. In the following discussion, the authors constantly have kept in mind the central theme of this chapter—"What Is Better for Youth?" High school teachers also are divided on the issue of the single diploma versus a variety of diplomas. Both sides of the issue are represented by teachers with very positive opinions. However, no studies of this issue revealing the relative strength of teachers' opinions on this issue have been found by the authors.

Teacher specialization. The assumption that high school teachers should be subject-matter specialists is now being violated about as frequently as it is being observed. During the present emergency of greatly increased enrollments in the high school, which now promises to continue for a decade or more, the pre-service teacher must anticipate being called upon to do substitute work for a single period or to actually teach for a full year in areas that are new and strange. This is a normal result of (1) increasing student populations, and (2) decreasing availability of special teachers in some areas. A single illustration given wide circulation by the National Chamber of Commerce shows how emergencies are bound to arise in the selection of a teacher of mathematics:

Mathematic Instruction in U.S. Found Inadequate—A year-long survey finds teachers deficient in mathematics. The Carnegie Corporation gave $21,000 to the Educational Testing Service of Princeton to find out how our students are being taught mathematics.

The survey found that many mathematics teachers were unable to teach this subject effectively. In many cases they were barely able to keep ahead of the students. Sixty teachers were tested in this survey; only ten were found competent—fifty were "confused." Many students were indifferent to mathematics; some were hostile to it.

The survey found that half of 370 candidates for elementary school positions failed to solve a simple problem in fractions.

The survey continues—Future teachers pass through the elementary school learning to detest math. They drop it in high school as early as possible. They avoid it in Teachers' Colleges because it is not required. They return to the elementary school to teach a new generation to detest it.[5]

In earlier studies, the Education Committee of the United States Chamber of Commerce revealed that schools frequently had only two choices in the matter of science: (1) to continue the subject under leadership of teachers who were not trained in science, or (2) to discontinue the subject altogether. This situation also exists in regard to the core curriculum. The teacher of core must be highly trained to succeed. Because of a shortage of core teachers, the core-curriculum movement (common learnings) has been greatly retarded. This deficiency probably has resulted from a failure of colleges of teacher education to develop an adequate curriculum in this specialty.

While it is quite possible for a certified teacher to take over a class in any subject for just a few days during an emergency brought about by the illness or absence of the regular teacher, there is every reason to suspect that no one person can be a specialist in every subject-matter area. The quality of such instruction, certainly in college preparatory and vocational subjects, will not be of equal quality throughout an entire year. There have been rare occasions when unprepared teachers schooled themselves in new areas and became superior teachers in these new fields. Inferences from the surveys by the Carnegie Corporation indicate that the average teacher does far better as a specialist in the one or two fields of knowledge in which he has majored in college.

Arguments against the employment of the specialist on the high school level are the same as those that are commonly discussed on the college

[5] *News and Cues*, U. S. Chamber of Commerce Bulletin (Washington, D. C., June, 1956).

campus. Will the instructor be so engrossed in his subject that he will be unable to explain it adequately to beginners who know very little about it? A clear answer for this, especially for the high school teacher, is that such a person is not regarded as a teacher at all, but rather as a research specialist.

There has been a continuing debate in the newspapers and magazines over the controversy of "knowing *what* you teach versus knowing how to teach." High school principals resolve such a controversy by stating that one cannot teach what one does not know and that one must know how to teach even that subject matter that he knows well. They believe that a high school teacher should be a specialist in educational leadership as well as in subject matter. Actually, this is the heart of the controversy between the liberal arts colleges and the colleges of education. As revealed in Chart 30, it is fairly common in certain states to permit pre-teachers to qualify in three distinct teaching fields. And, sometimes, especially in the small secondary school, teachers are actually assigned a teaching schedule that includes courses in three separate subject-matter fields. This practice violates the basic assumption that high school teachers are specialists wherever such teaching assignments are made.

Chart 30. Sample Teaching Assignments in 18 States, Alaska,* the District of Columbia, and Hawaii*

MAJOR	SECOND SUBJECT	THIRD SUBJECT
Agriculture	General Science	Chemistry
Commerce	Social Studies	Mathematics
English	Social Studies	Foreign Language
Industrial Arts	Physical Education	Mathematics
Mathematics	General Science	Social Studies
Physical Education	Social Studies	General Science
Social Studies	English	Physical Education

Adapted from a study by Ray C. Maul, *Teacher Supply and Demand in the United States,* National Commission on Teacher Education and Professional Standards, (Washington, D. C., National Education Association, 1950), p. 15.
* Prior to statehood.

Separate subjects. All high schools offer what is believed to be better for youth, tempered by the nature of the community and its degree of support. This is clearly reflected by a comparison of the course offerings in the metropolitan high school and in the rural or consolidated high school.

Separate subjects, or the academic disciplines, which originated with the puberty rites, were given order and meaning by the Greeks, and have become a part of our American heritage via Rome, the Middle Ages, the Renaissance, and recent Western culture. The basic assumption that separate subjects should comprise the total program of the high school is quite firmly established in our American heritage. It is yet for many honest and sincere people the only way to transmit our heritage.

As the program operates, students register for four or five courses. Usually, each course is one-half year's work in a separate subject-matter field. Upon the satisfactory completion of 32 semester courses or 16 units, the student meets the requirements for graduation. Upon graduation a diploma is awarded, which officially certifies to the completion of the high school program.

In recent years, many new subjects have been added to the original eight, such as homemaking, industrial arts, personal living, agriculture, aerodynamics, conservation, and general business. Cultural and technological changes have required new subjects and modification in the subject-matter content of the old disciplines. Progress and research are causing these older disciplines to undergo a face-lifting; even the long-honored discipline of mathematics is in for an overhauling.

But on the other hand, the number of separate and distinct subjects has been greatly reduced by fusion. For example, such separate subjects in the early high school as grammar, rhetoric, spelling, reading, writing, composition, and literature have been fused into a single subject, English. While English has been cited as an example, fusion has been common to all of the older disciplines—even the well-established title of arithmetic is being supplanted by the title, "mathematics," in both junior and senior high schools.

The number and kind of separate subjects offered by a high school depends upon where the school is located, the size of the school, the vision of the community, the principal and staff, and many other factors. Local and personal biases cause some high schools to put emphasis upon the academic disciplines. Others put emphasis upon meeting community needs, such as agriculture and homemaking in rural communities. Still other communities put emphasis upon meeting the needs of individual students. Of course, most high schools attempt to maintain a balance between all three of these pressures. By and large, the assumption that many different subjects should be taken at the same time is accepted by American high schools as sane and valid.

Until recently, it has been taken for granted that several subjects will be taken at the same time, but some high school teachers and principals have challenged this assumption. Experimentation is going on with a program in which the student may take only one subject at a time, concentrate upon it, and complete it within a six-weeks' period. It is believed that such an arrangement will provide a better program for youth. Incidentally, for some subjects such as social studies and science, this plan[6] does seem to have advantages. It permits field trips, extensive labor-

---

[6] This plan is called the block system. There are many variations of the block system in practice.

atory work, intensive library research, and decided emphasis upon problem-solving and the development of study habits and skills without
interrupting other classes. However, for such subjects as physical education, music, and vocational training, the intensified longer period may
serve youth less well.

By and large, the assumption that a number of different subjects taken
at the same time and scheduled over several semesters is best for youth
remains dominant in the American high school, although it is being challenged. Experimentation with the core program and the block system may,
in time, supplant the present subject system in part.

It has been said that a workable change in educational processes often
comes about only after twenty years of study. For at least that long, the
core curriculum has been discussed and has been subjected to experimentation. It consists primarily of the so-called common learnings, and it
is centered about two or more subjects that are closely related. In junior
high school, the core is receiving much attention, and combinations of
English with social studies and mathematics with science are no longer
innovations. There is difficulty, however, in finding teachers who are
trained adequately for this curriculum; school boards, also, seem reluctant
to provide the changes in classrooms and workshop areas that are necessary for a successful core program. In those regions of our country where
unusual growth is being met through marked expansion in the building
program, provisions are ordinarily made for core development.

Class size. Will the size of a class affect the quality of instruction? When
does a class get too large for youth to profit most from classroom instruction? There are many factors involved in an answer to these two questions.
But both the National Education Association and the American Federation
of Teachers have held that a maximum number of 25 students in a class
provides the best opportunity for youth, as well as for the teacher. The
several associations of vocational teachers recommend strongly that in
shop areas, especially where machinery is involved, classes should not
be larger than 17.

Trends shown by a National Education Association study[7] place the
teacher load, student-teacher ratio, at 37 in 1900, nearly 32 in 1920, nearly
28 in 1940, and nearly 27 in 1950. However, the practice by high school
principals of counting all members of the high school staff—the principal,
the assistant principal, the counselor, the deans, the school nurse, the
registrar, the treasurer, the attendance officer, and the medical staff—as
teachers makes the teaching load meaningless for reporting the actual
average teaching load of classroom teachers for a school. As announced
by the principal, it may be 25 when the actual average teaching load of a
classroom teacher is 35.

[7] See: U. S. Office of Education, Biennial Survey of Education, 1948-1950, Ch. 1;
"Teachers for Tomorrow," Fund for Advancement of Education, Bulletin No. 2, p. 70.

In average-sized classes, the drop-out rate is usually much lower because the teacher has time to know his students as individuals. Also, the teacher has time for more careful planning and for recreation which makes him a more competent teacher. But the predicted expansion of high school enrollments and the continuing shortage of teachers means that the teacher must anticipate larger classes and must develop new techniques to meet the crisis as successfully as possible. A class larger than 25 for most subjects is not desirable for youth.

Continuous attendance to graduation. Practically every study of school attendance indicates that the teen-ager who completes four years of high school wiil be more successful in life because of improved income. Russell B. Dickerson,[8] Pennsylvania State College, has written the following for the farm boy of America:

You'll get paid $40 a day for every day you go to high school.

Boys who graduate from high school can expect to earn $33,000 more during their lifetime than grammar school grads. And college graduates can expect to earn $72,000 more than high school grads.

The farm boy who invests $4,000 in a college education may reasonably expect a cash return of 18 times his investment.

Completion of the four-year high school by the teen-ager is best for him. Is it best for the nation? Dr. Lawrence R. Hafstad, an executive officer of General Motors, has suggested:

Americans must learn mathematics and science—OR Russian. Here are some unpalatable facts: In Russia, all elementary students take mathematics and basic science. Those with special aptitudes are given every encouragement to proceed to advanced study. In our country, all too often basic science and mathematics are merely elective courses—and unpopular ones at that.[9]

Although custom and law support the assumption of continuous attendance to graduation for all high school students, there has been some challenge as to the validity of the assumption for all students. Such questions as these are being raised by true friends of a high school for all youth. Are all students actually profiting by attending high school? Why not encourage those who are not profiting to drop out and work for a time and then to return to school again? Could not high school attendance and work be interspersed so that an individual will spend part-time in school and part-time at work?

One can infer from these questions the underlying assumption that some students might profit more by a flexible plan combining work and high school attendance. For these students, continuous attendance to gradu-

[8] Russel B. Dickerson, "Should a Farm Boy Go to College?" quoted in *Ford Almanac*, 1955, p. 166.

[9] On the occasion of the dedication of the General Motors Technical Center. Quoted in the national press.

ation may be less profitable in acquiring understandings, skills, habits, and interests than interspersing attendance at school with work. However, it will take longer for such students to complete a high school program. The movement just described may be classified as a strong protest movement. However, it must be emphasized that, in the long run, graduation from high school is best both for our youth and for America.

Social promotion. By custom in all and by law in many states, teenagers are compelled to attend high school until their eighteenth birthday. This is one proof of the American belief in universal education and of our rejection of a school system for the elite only. We are committed to the over-all principle of equal educational opportunity for all. Yet, America has provided for flexibility, through a pattern of local control, in what might otherwise have been a very rigid system.

Since all must attend high school and all must register for core-curriculum courses—although there is a wide range in student ability to achieve in these "must take" courses—the high school has for these "must take" courses *only* a flexible system of promotion sometimes called social promotion. These "must take" courses are planned to develop good citizenship, better family relations, ethical character, and the common learnings desired by society for all youth. Any student who shows an interest in the work, participates in class discussion, and hands in all assigned work receives a passing grade for the course. The final and quarterly examinations are employed, in part, to provide evidence for essential variations in semester marks. The basic assumption is that a student who registers for "must take" courses and works up to his ability should receive credit for courses completed. But, when a student registers for an elective course, (more than half of the program is elective) all academic standards must be met to earn a credit.

At the present time, a conflicting assumption is being promoted which will make mathematics and science "must take" subjects. In addition, the promoters of this assumption demand that the rigid academic standards for credit, which have been applied previously to the elite, now be applied to *all* students. There is little justification for this proposal.

As yet, the assumption that all youth can be held to the same academic standards in science and mathematics, as were the elite at an earlier period, is unrealistic. To compel all to attend and all to meet the academic standards of a select group makes the assumption too rigid for application to the modern high school, which offers general education for all youth. Some degree of flexibility must be introduced before this assumption is practical.

The high school is a community. The high school is recognized as a youth community. When it is functioning at its best, classes, laboratories, student activities, and especially the student council permit youth to function in groups and as groups. The adults of the high school deliberately seek to aid youth in the establishment of loyalties, and they encourage participation in the classroom, the laboratory, and student activities. It is assumed that such devices as the assembly, the school newspaper, a winning football or basketball team strengthen school and community loyalties; hence, it tends to establish a school-community *esprit de corps*. Of course, the students retain a loyalty to their families and to their common community—the city, town, or district. While they attend the high school, it is the youth community where they feel wanted and accepted.

Both teachers and parents recognize this relationship as a highly desirable one. The community atmosphere in which students live has a strong appeal to the gregarious activity of normal youth. However, gregariousness is not innate or inherited, but rather, a learned response to a conditioning environment. When a favorable community spirit fails to arouse a teen-ager, some understanding of the psychological basis for this may provide an explanation. Dashiel[10] has suggested the following:

An annoying brother or sister or tyrannizing parent will come to arouse negative reactions. Both Allport and Cason have shown gregariousness to be only a common social habit, learned as all habits are learned.

High schools that are themselves the result of a high-spirited adult community usually receive the utmost in support and understanding. When high schools are apart from a specific community, usually because of their largeness or smallness, they tend to be accepted as nothing more than institutions. The coldness and objectivity of institutional habitation can do little to attract teen-agers or adults. In such schools, the need to foster school-community relationships is paramount.

Teachers are realists. It is usually assumed that the public in general and the press in particular consider teachers to be conformists. Traditionally, the teacher has been an employee of the community and subject to public criticism for behaviors that displease parents. Hence, teachers conform to public demands in dress, behavior, and subject matter to be taught. Also, since they are professional people, they will all teach the same subject in a similar manner. And, in addition, the subject matter in the same subject will be nearly identical because all teachers will use like courses of study. In the more conservative schools, and especially in the small communities, parents may be critical and the community may object vigorously when the teacher departs even in minor details from the material found in the textbook.

High school graduates, when queried, usually cite two or three teachers as outstanding among the 10 to 15 with whom they come in contact during their high school experience. There seems to be no single factor to explain such differences in competency, for age, sex, education, experience,

[10] John F. Dashiel, *Fundamentals of Objective Psychology* (Boston, Houghton Mifflin Co., 1928), p. 225.

motherhood, character traits, appearance, mannerisms, and other factors have been fully explored with no one factor proving to be constant with well-rated teachers. An American Council on Education study identified three major areas of competence: "(1) the teacher behavior that suggests warmth, friendliness, and responsiveness in associations with pupils; (2) the teacher behavior that appears to indicate stability and awareness of responsibility; and (3) the teacher behavior that seems to challenge and stimulate pupils to do their best."[11]

The following condensed summary of teacher competency may contain some hint as to what may constitute a desirable teacher.

1. The competent teacher provides for the learning of students.
   Uses psychological principles of learning
   Uses principles of child growth and development
   Maintains a conducive atmosphere in the classroom
   Plans effectively
   Uses varied teaching procedures
   Uses diagnostic and remedial procedures effectively
   Adequately evaluates the achievement of students
   Manages the class effectively
2. The competent teacher counsels and guides students wisely.
   Uses psychological principles concerning growth and development
   Maintains effective relationships with parents
   Collects and uses significant counseling data
   Uses suitable counseling procedures
   Maintains appropriate relationships with guidance specialists
3. The competent teacher aids students to understand and appreciate our cultural heritage.
   Organizes the classroom for effective democratic living
   Makes significant applications of classroom learning
   Elicits the cultural growth of individuals and groups
   Helps students to apply democratic principles
4. The competent teacher participates effectively in the activities of the school.
   Plans the means of achieving educational objectives
   Assumes his share of responsibilities
   Maintains harmonious personal relations with his colleagues
5. The competent teacher assists in maintaining good relations between school and community.
   Uses community resources in classroom activity
   Obtains co-operation of parents in classroom activities
   Aids in defining and solving community problems
   Takes part in community affairs and projects
   Observes professional ethics in discussing school problems.[12]

[11] Alfred C. Jensen, "Definition of Teacher Behavior Encompasses Many Traits," *Educational Horizons* (Winter, 1953), p. 128.

[12] Condensed from *The Evaluation of Student Teaching*, Twenty-eighth Annual Yearbook, The Association for Student Teaching (Lock Haven, Pa., State Teachers College, 1949), pp. 7-11.

To be respected, a teacher must be more than a conformist who has insight into the purposes of the high school and a broad grasp of the subject he teaches. What you are will always speak more loudly than what you say. The teen-ager is more discerning than the adult; the high school is no place for the teacher who is "a stuffed shirt," "a fake," "a prude," or "a tattler."

Students are likely to make some effort to reduce the beginning teacher to their level or below. The wise teacher will conduct "private" interviews only during school hours and with the door to the office or classroom wide open. In no instance will he be alone in an automobile or school bus with any student. In rooms darkened for the presentation of films or slides, he will sit or stand apart from the students. Thus, anticipation may remove any source of gossip that might have devastating consequences.

From the discussion of seven of the thirteen assumptions, it is evident that an assumption can not be accepted literally, but should be studied carefully before it is accepted as an established truth. Also, the location of a high school and the mores of the community where it is located may indirectly affect an assumption that has been found practical in another community. Service to youth will always remain an ideal; at all times, the real test of what is better for youth is to observe with care whether the desired behavior changes actually occur. When we do this, we are indeed being guided in our instructional activity as teachers by the assumption that certain behavior changes will happen. And we test the assumption by determining whether the predicted changes have taken place.

YOUTH AND OUR TECHNOLOGICAL REVOLUTION

Throughout this textbook, the problem of the adjustment of our educational program to the rapid changes in technology has been stressed. During and since World War II, the pressure to discover new concepts in science and mathematics has been continuous and unavoidable if America is to maintain and continue to build its prestige. The application of these new science concepts to war and industry has required many more physicists and mathematicians than were being provided by our American school system. Since scientists and mathematicians were in short supply, the available men went where the rewards in income were greatest. The military and industry could easily outbid the colleges and high schools for highly qualified and available scientists and mathematicians. Hence, there is and has been a shortage of qualified science and mathematics teachers for both high school and college. And incidentally, in the elementary school also, where children first obtain a favorable impression of science and mathematics, there has been a dearth of elementary teachers who could teach science and mathematics with insight and vision.

Social and Educational Changes. In November, 1957, the Russian government launched the first of the satellites that challenged American progress in science and mathematics. It is most interesting to refer to a sociological pattern supplied by Burton and Brueckner[13] which shows how this event was bound to bring about social change and, in turn, marked change in our educational endeavors. Factors affecting change are given in Chart 31. Emphasis is added in the two lists which follow.

Chart 31. Factors Affecting Change

FACTORS RESISTING CHANGE	FACTORS FACILITATING CHANGE
Geographical isolation	Diffusion of culture traits
Severe or extreme climate	Temperate climate
Coercive universal language	Permissive vernacular
Conservative education	Creative education
Authoritarian leadership	Democratic leadership
Fundamentalist religion	Social religion
Dogma and scholasticism	*Science: Invention and discovery*
Homogeneous cultural grouping	Heterogeneous cultural grouping
Familial and racial ties	Cosmopolitan and universal experience
Rural social forces	Urban social forces
Centripetal forces (dominance by older persons, vested interests, rules of order, and succession of officers)	Centrifugal forces (war, literature, radio, movies, travel)
Private property (when conceived as private advantage, special privilege, and exploitation)	Private property (when conceived as a public trust or regulated in the public interest; when accompanied by social responsibility)
Monopoly	Division of labor
Epicurean mode of life	Saving and planning mode of life

Educational changes cited by Burton and Brueckner include the following:

1. Changes in philosophy of education
2. *Changes in social temper toward education*
3. Changes in knowledge of the nature of the learner, and of the teacher
4. Changes in knowledge of the nature of learning
5. Changes in goals and accompanying changes in evaluative measures
6. Changes in curriculum and methods of instruction.

Some psychologists might readily add *fear,* as the great motivating force in the change resulting from the Russian challenge. This force has been quite apparent in the press and radio-TV. If the American people have not actually been afraid, they have at least been troubled. Whether through pride or hysteria, the public has loudly called for a change. *Social temper toward education* is not the same as it was prior to November, 1957.

There is little need to review here the tremendous pressures that have been exerted to bring about change quickly. Some analysis of the true

[13] William H. Burton, and Leo J. Brueckner, *Supervision: A Social Process,* 3rd ed. (New York, Appleton-Century-Crofts, Inc., 1955), p. 36.

steps and the false starts may be helpful in understanding the very large number of changes under way and under discussion. One factor stands out clearly:

Through sheer ignorance and neglect, educational leadership had failed to establish in the public mind that schools were offering general rather than special education; that more youth were getting more schooling than ever before; and that the identification and training of those qualified for higher academic work was a costly process—more costly than any school budget could permit.

In the emergency, it seemed that everyone had a solution, and the following measures were proposed:

1. Solve the teacher shortage by eliminating all requirements for certification.

2. Put retired military personnel in charge of classes.

3. Hold more "teacher recognition" days.

4. Eliminate all frill subjects.

5. Establish a twelve-month school year.

6. Let teachers return, without pay, for extra classes on Saturday mornings.

7. Have industry provide more scholarships.

8. Teach algebra in the sixth grade.

9. Adopt the Russian system of education.

10. Throw out those students who were unable to do academic work.

11. Get the Federal Government to launch a vast school construction program.

From these suggestions, a few were selected and tried. Industry did provide additional scholarships—primarily in science and mathematics—only to learn that qualified candidates were in short supply. This brought about a logical return to the source of such students, the high school itself. When it became clear that identification of capable students is expensive, Federal funds were provided. By 1959, guidance and counseling services were getting as much attention as science and mathematics teaching. The road ahead seems clear, and the public appears to be gaining the understanding that from the general education courses will come the talented leadership so greatly needed.

The true steps that must be taken appear to be as follows, and in the sequence given:

1. Establish salary schedules and status privileges for teachers at least comparable to those granted by business and industry so as to attract promising recruits to the teaching profession.[14]

2. Replace the 75,200 obsolete or otherwise unsatisfactory school buildings[15] and provide modern facilities.

[14] *Teachers for Tomorrow*, Bulletin No. 2, Fund for the Advancement of Education, 655 Madison Ave., New York 21, pp. 68-69.

[15] *AFL-CIO Education News and Views*, AFL-CIO, 815 Sixteenth St., N.W., Washington 6, D.C. (May, 1959), p. 3.

3. Continue a program of general education in which all youth are encouraged to remain in school until the age of graduation.

4. Continue special grants to outstanding teachers of mathematics, science, and foreign languages, for summer study.

5. Enlarge the guidance and testing services so that qualified youth may be identified, as early as possible, and given adequate academic preparation.

6. Expand the scholarship offerings so that every capable student in need of such assistance may have the opportunity to develop fully those unique abilities so vital in today's world.

Other true steps are indicated and include modernization of all curriculum offerings, expansion of the social sciences and language arts curricula, continued experimentation with the testing programs in use to select candidates for scholarships, and inquiry into the teaching qualifications of specialists on college faculties. These adjustments are now under way in response to a change in social temper toward education which has been brought about by the invention and development of the satellite.

Turmoil Within the Educational Profession. In the process of change, citizens usually divide into two groups—the conservatives and the progressives—according to how they are affected personally; the conservatives oppose change and the progressives favor change. Frequently, though not always, the conservatives oppose change because of a limited insight, and the progressives favor change because they profit by it or believe that it is best for all. Conservatives claim that they keep society stable and on an even keel, while liberals and progressives assert that they are the prime movers of progress to get society going somewhere. Educators are not exempt from this division of group attitude.

Educators differ. There are many differences of opinion among educators as to what is best for youth. The over-all consensus is apparent in the current policies expressed by the National Education Association and the American Federation of Teachers as described earlier in this text. Despite the group opinion, there are many individual teachers and several small associations of teachers who hold contrary views. And in the local community, where the majority opinion is reflected in the actions taken by the board of education, there is always a minority group of citizens who hold contrary views as to what is better for youth. If the minority group of citizens has prestige and wealth, which it normally does, marked influence may be exerted upon the nature of the educational program—particularly when this is linked with the minority group of educators. A few typical issues over which such battles are being fought are indicated in Chart 32.

Old ways versus new ways. While a close analysis of the six statements above might seem to indicate that high school education is experiencing an active effort to revive conservatism, data presented in parts 1 and 2 of the text indicate that secondary education is on the move toward the

Chart 32. Typical Educational Issues Within the Profession

CONSERVATIVE POSITION	LIBERAL POSITION
1. Only pre-service teachers who are approved and recommended by the college of arts and sciences should be granted a license to teach.	1. Only pre-service teachers who are approved by the teachers college should be granted a license to teach.
2. High school education is for the children of the well-to-do and the intellectually competent.	2. High school education is for *all* youth.
3. The high school offers only one academic program.	3. The high school should offer academic, vocational, and general education programs.
4. The high school should be a private school.	4. The high school should be a public school.
5. A teacher is qualified to teach who knows his subject.	5. A teacher is qualified to teach who knows and can teach his subject-matter field.
6. Authoritarian control is best even in a democratic state.	6. In a democratic state democratic control is best.

maintenance of the status quo and its improvement so as to develop a more vital and a more essential program. Industrial, political, and educational leadership in America have become aware of the fact that the high school must advance to qualify our youth for participation in the new technology and in the changed world which that technology will create. Carefully re-read the six issues listed in Chart 32. What specific changes are proposed by the conservatives? (The conservative position has always been presented first.) How would the proposed changes affect our educational system? Chart 33 answers these questions very briefly. However, it is significant that the conservatives never mention the selection of teachers on the basis of personality factors or the necessity of financial reward for attracting competent teachers to the profession.

In Chart 34, some effort has been made to show the effect of liberal proposals. Neither chart is intended to be exhaustive, though both do indicate the differences among educators. The American check-and-balance system is functioning here; as a result, no radical or extreme theory dominates the problem of what is better for youth.

The technological revolution is probably with us to stay; hence, mathematics and science will retain and extend their importance in the vocational education of a goodly number of teen-age youth. Owing to the fact that mathematics and science have become so essential in the everyday life of all of us, these subjects will be included to a much greater extent in the common learnings or general education. In a way, the emphasis being put upon science and mathematics by the conservatives

Chart 33. Conservative Proposals and Their Probable Effect on the Program of the Contemporary High School

PROPOSED CHANGES[*]	EFFECT OF CHANGE
Right to approve applicants for teacher license resides in the college of arts and sciences.	Would put the approval of teacher qualifications in the hands of an authority who accepts the academic program as the only essential of a good high school program.
Restrict high school education to the children of the well-to-do and the intellectually competent.	Would reduce high school enrollments to one-fourth the present number. By inference, this is a major purpose of certain conservatives.
The high school has one purpose only—the intellectual development of students.	Would eliminate vocational and general education.
With extreme conservatives, only the private and parochial high school should be retained.	The cost of high school education would be transferred from the public to the individual parent.
Eliminate colleges of education.	Would tend to eliminate education as a profession: reduce the status of the teacher.
Emphasize the authoritarian type of discipline in the high school.	Would de-emphasize democracy as the American way of life.

[*] These changes would probably result if the conservatives were to become entirely dominant. As of now, the authors predict that liberals will retain all present achievements and make additional gains in the decade ahead.

may in the long run strengthen rather than weaken the present tripartite curriculum of academic, vocational, and common learnings. It is entirely in accord with the present practice for the public to insist that subject matter considered essential for all should be incorporated in either the vocational or the general education program.

It is entirely probable that the public will discuss and weigh the propaganda of the conservatives and separate chaff from wheat. For there are essential truths embodied in our old customs and ways which must be retained and kept inviolate as the core of our way of life; the academic program must be strengthened by adding to and eliminating from so as to adapt it to the technological revolution. Qualified teachers will be made available, and a more equitable income for teachers will attract better talent, so that the increase in teacher prestige will reach a point where the comic-strip symbols for teachers will be favorable rather than derogatory.

The sustained debate about the purposes and outcomes of high school education would not have persisted from 1945 to 1960, had there not been

Chart 34. Liberal Proposals and Their Probable Effect on the Program of the
Contemporary High School

PROPOSED CHANGES*	EFFECT OF CHANGE
Right to approve applicants for teacher certification should be within the college of education.	Puts the approval of teacher qualifications in the hands of an authority who understands the nature of general education with provisions for academic specialties.
Co-operation should be encouraged between college of education and major teaching fields in which college of arts and sciences specializes.**	Represents a logical compromise step away from an original premise that any certified teacher could teach any subject.
The high school has many purposes—and should accept responsibilities declined by home and society.	Curriculum is broadened and rate of retention is improved.
School plants and services should be expanded, teacher salaries should be doubled, and community colleges should be supported.	The quality of education is improved, but taxation processes would have to be drastically changed.
Colleges of education should become traditional as a source of good teachers, properly screened and trained. Furthermore, college teachers themselves should receive certification.	Education would then be recognized as a full-fledged profession. Many promising students would not leave college because of inept teaching by subject-matter specialists.
Should emphasize the democratic type of leadership in the high school.	Establishes by example the truth that the American way of life is functional and worthwhile.
Through experimentation and testing, should grant high school credits without regard for semester hours. Restrictive requirements removed.	Educational opportunity would then become alive and real; more youth could explore additional courses. Total learnings would increase.

* If liberals had been permitted to establish these aims at the outset, the degree of the present emergency might have been less critical. But, to illustrate, would citizens have taxed themselves so heavily at the local level as they are now being taxed at the national level?

** It seems likely that this change will establish the desirability of five years of pre-service preparation for secondary school teachers.

some weak spots in the program of the high school. The conservatives have served education and youth competently by keeping the debate alive; they have emphasized some weak spots in the educational program of the high school, which can now be eliminated.

As of now, the conflicts between the liberals and the conservatives appear to be in deadlock. However, some of our most astute educators, who have predicted educational trends accurately, state that secondary education is in the grip of profound changes. These educators predict that the same forces that brought reform to the elementary school in the first quarter of the twentieth century are now about to cause the same reform in the secondary schools and the colleges. To these educators the conservatives have already lost the battle. The sound and valid changes professed by the liberals will become accepted features of both the secondary school and the college in the next two decades.

PARENTS, TOO, WRESTLE WITH THE PROBLEM

Most parents, too, are much concerned with what is better for youth—their own teen-agers and those other teen-agers who influence their own sons and daughters. They grapple with a problem which is being made very difficult because of the technological revolution. Preparation must be made now, as far as possible. We know that our ways of earning a living and our very attitude toward life have changed markedly between 1950 and 1960. Can marked changes in our ways of earning a living, also, be as great or greater during the next decade? What subject matter pursued through high school will be the most valuable to youth? What type of high school will serve teen-agers best? In America these decisions must be made by the parents of teen-agers who are now in high school.

The Private and the Parochial High School. A century ago, parents faced the problem, not of what is better for youth, but of what can we afford. To most parents then, the private school, for some the parochial, was by tradition and custom accepted as better for youth. It took time for the public school to be accepted as a worthy competitor of the private and/or the parochial high school. In New England, along the Eastern Seaboard, and in many sections of the Old South, the tradition of the private high school being a superior school for youth is still strong. In the great Central Plains and to some extent throughout the United States, parents, especially parents of certain religious groups, struggle with the problem of whether the public or the parochial school will serve youth best.

In the United States approximately 10 per cent of the high school population attend either a private or a parochial secondary school. In many communities, there is a constant transfer of students from private and parochial secondary schools to the public high school and vice versa. Hence, teachers in all three types of schools need to have an understanding of and an appreciation for all three types of schools. In general, the private and parochial secondary schools seem to place greater emphasis upon the academic subjects and to stress authoritarian procedures more than do most public high schools.

Usually, the private secondary school is not co-educational, that is, each school is planned for girls only or boys only. A number of these private secondary schools are old—Phillips Academy was founded prior to the American Revolution. These private secondary schools vary widely in type; some are military, while others are civilian. Some are day schools, while others are boarding schools, and some are endowed, while others are not. They also vary widely in the quality of their educational program from superior to average or below.

Do private secondary schools provide a superior type of educational program? The assumption that they do has been kept alive during the years in which the public secondary school developed. Only three studies were found which employed a research method in investigating the relative superiority of the private and the public high school graduate. There follows a brief excerpt from each of the three studies. Two of these studies were done at Harvard and the other one at Princeton. The first excerpt below is from the investigation made at Princeton.

It was found that on the average the public school graduate made a higher academic average for the freshman year, in relation to ability as measured by the Scholastic Aptitude Test—Verbal Section, than did the private school graduates. The same was true for the sophomore year.[16]

A similar study for the freshman year record of Harvard College classes in 1943 and 1944 developed results similar to those at Princeton.[17]

President Conant of Harvard states as a matter of statistics the high school graduate does better than the private school boy in Harvard.[18]

The three statements above indicate that the private high school is not necessarily always superior to the public high school as a college preparatory institution. However, this evidence is sufficient to raise a doubt as to the superiority of all private high schools. Perhaps, a valid inference might be that among both private and public high schools there are some in both groups that are superior, average, and poor. The quality of leadership in the co-ordination of a superior program and in the selection of an excellent staff remains always an important factor.

Can the private secondary school be justified? Our private free-enterprise system permits any legitimate type of business activity to operate. The very fact that the private high schools have survived in competition with the public high school is one sound justification for them. Up to now, the public high school has attempted to provide a good education for a wide range of student abilities. Under the crowded classroom conditions and with the limited staff found in the public high school, it seems reasonable to assume that a school organized to serve the superior student only might provide a superior program. But is it always true that only superior students attend the private schools? The private high school is less subject to certain local and political pressures than are the public high schools. The private high school can and usually does provide acceptable substitutes for an unsavory home environment for some students and a good

---

[16] Junius A. Davis, and Norman J. Frederiksen, "Public and Private School Graduates in College," *The Journal of Teacher Education* 6:18-22 (March, 1955).

[17] William M. French, *American Secondary Education* (New York, Odyssey Press, 1957), p. 268.

[18] James B. Conant, *Education and Liberty* (Cambridge, Mass., Harvard University Press, 1953), p. 131.

substitute environment for the children of parents living in foreign countries. Also, it can teach religion in a forthright manner impracticable in public schools.

The parochial high school is a school maintained and operated by a religious body. Although almost all religious groups have operated parochial schools in the past, with some exceptions, only the Roman Catholics, Lutherans, and the Seventh-Day Adventists still do. The parochial schools for these groups are growing, though the ratio of increase in enrollments for the parochial schools is less than for the public schools.

Those who believe in parochial schools take the position that education without religion is incomplete or that it is the duty of the home and the church to see to it that each child from a Christian home receives a sound education in Christianity. Usually, there is an implication, not often stated, that without indoctrination in the creed of their particular church many of the young people will fall away from the church.

Since certain religious groups are strongly committed to the policy of parochial education, it seems probable that parochial schools will remain a permanent part of our educational system. Although many denominations have discontinued their parochial schools, it is unlikely that the Catholics, Lutherans, or Seventh-Day Adventists will do so. In fact, the Roman Catholic Church seems committed to a complete program of education from the kindergarten through higher education.

The Attainment of the Good Life. It is apparent that all members of a society, under any form of government, will not be scholars—nor will all subject themselves to scholarly discipline. In fact, the scholar is currently held in such low esteem among us that many parents are unaware that the good life may be attained in that way. But parents do wrestle with this problem and do seek to use the high school as an instrument to help their teen-age sons and daughters move toward the attainment of the good life. Because of this, the program of the high school is under continuous evaluation by parents; they ultimately define the program of the high school in accordance with the attainment of the type of good life they seek for their children.

In an attempt to meet the demands of the parents, the program of the high school now has a tripartite program of (1) helping students acquire the understandings, attitudes, and skills to make each an acceptable member of society, (2) helping students acquire the vocational education requisite for the selection of and the orientation to a vocation, and (3) helping students achieve the mastery of the academic subject-matter content needed by each teen-ager to achieve his life goals.

An enemy nation has arisen that is giving a decided emphasis to science and mathematics—two disciplines that are vital to modern industry and modern warfare. Parents are now struggling with the problem of greater emphasis upon science and mathematics. They are asking themselves and others this question, "Is this an essential to the attainment of the good life?" They know that industrial superiority has been the key to our greatness as a people and that industrialization has been one of the keys to the good life as it is lived among us. However, are science, mathematics, and industry the only means for the attainment of the good life?

Parental consensus, as to what constitutes a high school program best suited to develop abilities essential to the attainment of the good life for their sons and daughters, has been explained many times. In essence, these are the basic elements: soundness in mind and body; ability to discriminate between the shoddy and the superior in goods and services; necessary qualifications to enter and succeed in a vocation or a profession; stable and upright behavior. Parents are confused by much of the current criticism of the public school. They know, as you and I do, that much of this criticism is a "smoke screen" to cover up real purposes. Yet, they also sense that there are some elements of real truth in the propaganda. Parents are striving to find the answer to one ever-present question, "What is better for youth?" This is a much-discussed question in any group of parents. It was through this constant discussion and sharing of opinions that the present stable program of the high school has been secured.

Please observe that the present tripartite division of the high school program is quite similar to the demands of parents as outlined above. In teacher language (not parent language), this is what parents seem to believe is better for youth:

1. The common learnings are designed to develop mental and physical health, stable and upright behavior, and the ability to discriminate between shoddy and superior goods and services. Incidentally, one who learns how to co-operate and share in ideas and activities becomes stable himself and helps to maintain a stable community and school.

2. The academic subjects are designed to develop the understandings, the interests, and the skills that are vital to vocational or professional success. Intellectual development may result through a vigorous pursuit of the academic subject areas. New basic concepts may be established that provide a key to unlock one's physical, linguistic, economic, and political world. Because of these experiences, one feels at home in the total universe.

3. Vocational education is designed to develop essential basic skills, habits, and understandings that will orient the student to a vocation. The selection of the vocational family for which one has an aptitude is becoming much more complicated with each passing decade.

Although parents accept these divisions as being valid, yet they see (very indistinctly, to be sure) that a synthesis among the three divisions has not yet been attained. High schools are like weather vanes, they vary in the emphasis placed upon common learnings, vocational education, and academic subjects according to the pressures from the climate of opinion in the supporting community. We know that a high school program that has stability, flexibility, and balance will be better for youth. The achievement of such a true synthesis to best serve youth and the nation is a professional obligation. While parents are qualified to judge when this synthesis has been achieved, they are not technically able to do what must be done to achieve it. That is the teacher's task.

DISCUSSION PROBLEMS

1. The public demands that public schools must provide the best that is educationally known. Is this a cultural demand or is it the result of fear?
2. Might it be possible to judge the intangible quality of a public education? On what basis would you build such an evaluation?
3. Assuming that universal education may one day become a reality, and by "universal" we mean more than "national," should we be concerned by Napoleon's words: "Let China sleep. When she awakens, the world will be sorry"?
4. Parochial schools often manage to achieve victory in contests with public schools. Explain fully.
5. It has been said that democracy tends to defeat itself. What must leaders in public education do to prevent this happening?
6. What arguments might you present for a return to the "good old days" during which only the classical subjects constituted the school program? Justify or condemn the public demand for a broadened curriculum—has it helped or harmed youth?
7. Review the thirteen basic assumptions of American secondary education presented in this chapter. Are there any of them which you would reject? Why?
8. How do you feel about teaching out of your major field? Is it more important to know your subject field or how to teach?
9. Have you noticed any important changes in the American secondary school since you were a high school student? What are they?

RELATED REFERENCES

American Council on Education, *Teachers for Our Time*, Commission on Teacher Education (Washington, D.C., National Education Association, 1944).

Association for Student Teaching, *Evaluation of Student Teaching*, Twenty-Eighth Annual Yearbook, The Association for Student Teaching (Lock Haven, Pa., State Teachers College, 1949).

Association for Supervision and Curriculum Development, *What Shall the High Schools Teach?* 1956 Yearbook (Washington, D.C., National Education Association, 1956).

———, *Forces Affecting American Education*, 1953 Yearbook (Washington, D.C., National Education Association, 1953).

BAKKE, E. Wight, *Labor Mobility and Economic Opportunity* (New York, John Wiley & Sons, Inc., 1954).

———, *Adaptive Human Behavior* (New Haven, Conn., Yale University Press, 1950).

BRIGGS, Thomas H., "The Secondary-School Curricula—Yesterday, Today, and Tomorrow," *Teachers College Record* 52:399-448 (April, 1951).

BURTON, William H., and BRUECKNER, Leo J., *Supervision: A Social Process* 3rd ed. (New York, Appleton-Century-Crofts, Inc., 1955).

CASWELL, H. L., "Unfinished Business in Curriculum Development," *Teachers College Record* 50:360-69 (February, 1949).

CONANT, James B., *Education and Liberty* (Cambridge, Mass., Harvard University Press, 1953).

COREY, Fay L., *Values of Future Teachers* (New York, Bureau of Publications, Teachers College, Columbia University, 1955).

COUNTS, George S., *Education and American Civilization* (New York, Bureau of Publications, Teachers College, Columbia University, 1952).

CREMIN, Lawrence A., and BARROWAN, Merle L., *Public Schools in Our Democracy* (New York, The Macmillan Co., 1956).

CUMMINGS, Howard H., and others, *Factors Affecting the Improvement of Secondary Education,* Office of Education Circular No. 404 (Washington, D.C., United States Department of Health, Education, and Welfare, 1954).

DASHIELL, John F., *Fundamentals of Objective Psychology* (Boston, Houghton Mifflin Co., 1928).

DAVIS, Junius A., and FREDERIKSEN, Norman J., "Public and Private School Graduates in College," *The Journal of Teacher Education* 6:18-22 (March, 1955).

DRUCKER, Peter, "America's Next Twenty Years," *Harper's Magazine* 210:27-32, March; 41-47, April; 39-42, May; 52-59, June, 1955.

Educational Policies Commission, *Education and the Future of America* (Washington, D.C., National Education Association, 1955).

————, *Education and Manpower* (Washington, D.C., The National Education Association, 1956).

FAUNCE, Roland C., and BOSSING, Nelson L., *Developing the Core Curriculum,* 2nd ed. (Englewood Cliffs, N.J., Prentice-Hall, Inc., 1958).

FRENCH, William M., *American Secondary Education* (New York, Odyssey Press, 1957).

GAVIAN, Ruth A., GRAY, A. A., and GROVES, Ernest R., *Our Changing Social Order* (Boston, D. C. Heath & Company, 1953).

HART, James D., "They All Were Born in Log Cabins," *American Heritage* 7:32-33 (August, 1956).

HAVIGHURST, Robert J., *Human Development and Education* (New York, Longmans, Green & Co., Inc., 1953).

HEELY, Allen V., "The Case of Private Schools," *School Executive* 75:19-21 (October, 1955).

HUGGETT, A.J., and STINNETT, F. M., *Professional Problems of Teachers* (New York, The Macmillan Co., 1956).

JENSEN, Alfred C., "Definition of Teacher Behavior Encompasses Many Traits," *Educational Horizons* (Winter, 1953).

MAUL, Ray C., *Teacher Supply and Demand in the United States* (Washington, D.C., National Commission on Teacher Education and Professional Standards and the National Education Association, 1950).

The National Society for the Study of Education, *Adapting the Secondary-*

School Program to the Needs of Youth, Part I, (Chicago, The University of Chicago Press, 1953).

QUILLEN, I. James, and HANNA, Lavonne A., *Education for Social Competence* (Chicago, Scott, Foresman & Company, 1948).

RICE, Theodore D., "What Are the Issues in Secondary Education," *Educational Leadership* 10:473-477 (May, 1953).

ROSENBERGER, Homer T., *What Should We Expect of Education?* reprint, National Association of Secondary-School Principals, No. 217, Washington, D.C. (February, 1956).

RUGG, Harold, *Foundations of American Education* (Yonkers, N.Y., World Book Co., 1947).

Teachers for Tomorrow, Bulletin No. 2, Fund for the Advancement of Education, 655 Madison Ave., New York 21, N.Y., 1955.

ULICH, Robert, *History of Educational Thought* (New York, American Book Company, 1945).

WHITNEY, Frank C., *The Changing High School: Studies in Secondary Education* (New York, The Exposition Press, 1955).

ZERAN, Franklin R., ed. *The High School Teacher and His Job* (New York, Chartwell House, Inc., 1953).

Index

Abrams, Irving, 34, 45
Academic program: as basic education, 182-183; becoming more functional, 137; in a period of transition, 178-179; understanding principles and laws, 172
Academic and vocational education, 178
Academic subjects prepare for college, 183; vocation, common learnings, 183; status of, 183
Academic vs. functional subject matter, 42, 144
Academy, 9
Achievement of goals, 427-430
Activities: advantages to students, 238-239; advantages to teachers, 239-240; calendar, 391; endless list, 237; have purposes, 228; in the home room, 341; integral part of the instructional program, 238-240; many varieties needed, 230
Activity (an) is born, 231
Activity movement, 222-229
Adams, James T., 27, 32, 45
Adams, John, 331, 332
Adaptation of instruction to individual differences, 174; the class, 211-212; the organization of the school, 87-88; youth, 87-89
Adjustment to school life, 353
Adler, Alfred, 230
Adolescent psychology, 82
Adult recognition and respect, 360
Advertising: commercial printing, 382; face-to-face relations, 384; home visitation, 384; media for schools, 380-385; necessary for schools, 379; news notes for good cheer, 381; newsletters, 381; Parent-Teacher Association, 384; personal notes, 382; professional limitations, 380; start-to-school booklets, 382; sympathy notes, 380; teacher membership in local organizations, 384; other printed media, 383
AFL-CIO Education News and Views, 470

Agrarian (an) society becomes an industrial society, 26
Agricultural college, 28
Agriculture (vocational) in high school, 28-29
Aids and resources: building readiness for children, 256-257; conservatives object, 253-259; growth experiences, 254-255; increased intellectual and moral growth, 253
Allen, Charles M., 72
Allen, Frederick Lewis, 6, 24
American customs: fundamentals are changing, 232; in a period of flux, 222-223
American Federation of Teachers, AFL-CIO, 106-109
American society transformed: education for workers, 179; interdependent economic structure, 180; mechanization, 178
American Youth Commission, 20, 79
Ames, Louise B., 237
Andrews, Dean C., 288, 342
Anecdotal records, 271
Apprenticeship system, trade and industrial education, 122
Articulation: attacks on, 77-78; meaning of, 1, 97-98; teacher's role in achieving, 98
Association for Supervision and Curriculum Development, 4, 14, 182, 458
Association for Student Teaching, 467
Attitudes: development, 387; formation, 389
Autocratic leadership; dominant in high school, 419; produces hostility and apathy, 417
Automation, changes produced by, 28
Average and slow learners less adapted to academic subjects, 184-185
Ayers, Eugene, 303

Baker, Harry, J., 78, 294

Barnard, Henry, 135
Basic Education, 183
Batchelder, Howard T., 364
Beard, Charles, 24
Behavior: and curriculum, 140; code of, 356; disruptive, methods for checking, 367; reveals needs, 225; undesirable for a teacher, 110
Bell, Howard M., 72, 90, 410
Bellack, Arno A., 142
Benjamin, Harold, 14
Bennett, George L., 268
Bestor, Arthur E., 59, 72
Better schools, 111
Big Business and big unions, 56
Birth rates, 71
Blair, Glenn M., 319
Bloch, Herbert A., 288
Block system, 462
Boarding school, 9
Boaz, Franz, 39
Boaz, G., 72
Bossing, N. L., 159, 345
Bratton, Patrick J. 417
Breckman, B., 72
Briggs, Thomas H., 91, 173
Broad fields curriculum, 146
Brown Francis J., 27, 45
Brown vs. Board of Education, 51
Brubacher, John S., 133
Brueckner, Leo J., 8, 24, 47, 426, 469
Building and site as instructional tools, 407
Burke, Arvid J., 438
Burks, Arthur J., 296, 297, 302, 303
Buros, O. K., 317
Burton, William H., 8, 24, 47, 73, 80, 110, 217, 247, 272, 426, 469
Burton check list of teacher personality, 109-110
Bush, N. S., 366
Business courses, 316
Business-Industry-Education Days, 31
Buswell, Guy T., 62
Butts, R. Freeman, 48, 52, 73

Caldwell, Otis W., 63, 73
Calisher, Hortense, 6
Campbelle, Clyde M., 425
Carter, Alexander, 386
Carter, James G., 135
Castillo, Bernal Diaz del, 416
Caswell, H. L., 24, 45
Cattell, James McKeen, 62
Caudill, William W., 397
Census, 388

Chamber of Commerce, 29, 30, 45
Chamberlin, Dean C., 64, 73
Chapman, A. Hunter, 400
Chase, Stewart, 73
Chaucer, 456
Chesterton, G. K., 155
Childs, H. L., 73
Chisholm, Leslie L., 76
Churchill, Winston, 32, 46
Citizenship development through the high school, 4
Citizenship Education Study (Detroit), 73
Civic competence, 16
Civic duties, (tribal life), 130
Class size, 463
Classical curriculum, American version, 172
Classroom personality, 116
Classroom teacher and guidance, 332
Classrooms: appropriate work in, 363-367; become laboratories, 399; building morale, 363; new features in, 400; techniques for improving teacher-student relationships, 364-365
Clinton, DeWitt, 135
Commercial printing, 382
Commission on the Reorganization of the High School, 20
Commission on the Reorganization of Secondary Education, 79, 138, 167
Commission on Teacher Education, 271
Committee on the Orientation of Secondary Education, 20
Committee of Ten, 20, 79, 80, 138
Committee of Ten Report, 78, 80
Common learnings program: what is taught, 158, 478-479; essential attributes and characteristics, 160; in modern curriculum, 165-166; new to the high school, 156; and general education, 157-158; purposes, 155-157; advantages of, 158-159; guidance in, 345-346
Common learnings unit: building and evaluating, 162-164; course of study for, 166-167; introduced to a class, 165
Communication channels, 392
Community, 367-368; as laboratory, 408; improvement of, 29; surveys, 408; wants, 117
Comprehensive high school, 139-140
Compton, Arthur, 266
Compulsory attendance, 97
Conant, James B., 45, 59, 73, 79, 87, 172, 476
Conant Report, 21

Conformity, enforced, 352-355
Confucius, 407
Continuing crosscurrents in American education since 1600, 47-48
Continuous attendance to graduation, 464
Contractual obligations, 115
Co-ordinators (qualified) and work experience, 346
Correlation of the curriculum, 147
Cost of attending high school, 411
Counseling: defined, 331; way of keeping the curriculum functional, 172-173
Counselors: in guidance, 331; work illustrated, 332
Counts, George S., 26, 31, 35, 45, 79, 90, 185
Course of study, 214-215
Course of study for the common learnings, 166-167
Creative teaching, 197-198
Criticism counteracted by formulating an educational platform, 67; (specific), how to meet them, 68-69
Critics and operation stork, 70-71
Critics, crisis, and criticism, 51
Cronbach, Lee J., 83, 218
Crosby, Otis A., 73
Cubberly, Ellwood P., 136-137
Culture-molding process, 27
Culture patterns, predictions about, 181
Curriculum: and change, 120; as college preparation, 137; defined, 212; development, 133; induces changes in behavior, 141; in early cultures, 129-133; limited by the purposes of the high school, 144; meaning in, 145; modern, 54, 148; more practical, 136; new subjects, 181-182; provides rich experiences, 141-142
Curriculum patterns: broad fields, 146; common learnings, 147; correlation, 147; fusion, 146; separate subjects, 146
Cyr, Frank W., 438

Daily recitation method, 213
Dale, Edgar, 244
Dance band or orchestra as a new activity, 231-232
Danger card, 381
Dashiel, John F., 466
Davis, Allison, 73, 93, 94, 430
Davis, Junius A., 476
Debate club, 237
Decentralized education for early teenagers, 399

Defects of the district system, 437-438
Defense against criticisms, 67-69
DeHaan, R. F., 296, 300
Delinquency and individual differences, 292
Democracy, extended to minority groups, 39-40; through extension of suffrage, 41-42
Democracy in the high school, some guideposts, 3-5
Democratic administration, steps for attaining, 423-424
Democratic: discipline, 421; leader, 421; leadership, 417; society and the high school, 36
Demonstration (the), 245, 384
Design the school plant to serve youth, 398
Deutsch, Albert, 229
Development of reading ability, 313
Development of a unit in science, 204-205
Developmental tasks, 353
Developmental tasks and youth, 12-14
Dewey, John, 3, 79, 81, 84, 142, 174, 229, 334
Dezouche, Dorothy, 272
Diagnostic and remedial procedures, 317-318; diagnosis of reading ability, 317-318
Dickerson, Russell B., 414
Dickson, W. J., 418
Dictionary of Occupations, 186
Differentiated assignment for a heterogeneous class, 294-295
Dillon, Harold J., 409
Dining service, decentralization of, 399
Diploma mills, 118
Director of reading, 321
Discipline: and limits, 361; and the group, 370; can be taught, 354; causes of, 354-360; defined, 352-353; essential to society, 354; problems, 355-359
Discussion as a guidance technique, 336
Disruptive acts; contrived accidents, 357; curbs to check, 367
District system: and industrialization, 438-440; defects of, 437; strengths of, 437
Doob, Leonard W., 389
Dorsey, Mattie F., 120, 370, 418
Douglass, Harl R., 24, 38, 45, 189
Drake, William E., 24
Dramatic participation, 245
Dramatics, 236
Drop out rate: and class size, 464; for students of low ability, 94; largely from underprivileged homes, 92

Drop-outs, woefully unprepared, 90-91
Drucker, Peter F., 73, 202, 222
Duel, Leo, 45
Dugan, Lucille, 25
Dulles, Foster Rhea, 233
Dunn, Joan, 6, 25

Eckert, R. E., 90, 409
Economic independence, 16
Edgerton, A. H., 191
Education and business, 29, 30; conflict over, 1869-1918, 49, 50; for all American youth, 22, 25, 155, 156; in 1845 and 1919, 63; value of, 29, 30, 105-106; vocational, see vocational education
Educational inequality: caused by industry, 438-440; intrastate as well as interstate, 439-440
Educational opportunities: procedures to equalize, 435-443
Educational platform, a defense against criticisms, 67-68
Educational Policies Commission, 16, 18, 19, 22, 25, 33, 37, 45, 79, 165, 267, 443
Educational program (an), controversies over, 52; to fit the new culture, 181
Edwards, Newton, 420
Egypt (ancient) schools for leaders, 131
Elementary education influences the high school, 81; reduced to six years, 81
Eliot, Chas. W., 79, 81, 138, 139
Elsbree, Willard, 419
English, course of study in, 213; reading problems, 315
Empathic communication, 368
English, general classes, 322
Enrollments in high school, 11
Equal educational opportunity: minimum foundation program, 442-444
Ethical concepts, 106; a code of ethics for education, 106
Evaluation of student teaching, 467
Eves, Howard, 132
Evraiff, William, 90
Exhibits, 246
Experience: contrived, 245; defined, 141; through doing, 244; through observation, 245-246; through word symbols, 247-248
Experiencing vs. learning subject matter, an illustration, 150
Experimental High Schools, 64-65
Experimentation, 63

Faculty talent, 385
Failure and retardation, 96

Faunce, Ronald C. 159, 345, 428
Featherstone, W. B. 294
Federal aid to education, 440-441
Federal support of education, 446
Field trips, 245, 409
Films: *Broader Concepts of Method,* 409; *Freedom to Learn,* 390; *Learning to Understand Children,* 361
Finck, Edgar M., 336
Fine, Benjamin, 440, 441, 445
Flynn, Frank T., 288
Formal discipline, 82
Forms of organization, 86
Foster, Emery N., 73
Frazer, James G., 130, 155
Freeman, Frank, 62, 83
French, William, 476
Freud, Sigmund, 230
Fuller, Harry J., 59, 73
Fusion pattern, the curriculum, 146

Gallup, George, 387
Garfield, James A., 395
General Education: essential characteristics and attributes, 160; new to high school, 156; required of all students, 172
Gesell, Arnold, 62, 84, 237
Gifted learner: must be challenged, 304; identified, 304-305
Gifted and rapid readers, 318
Gittler, J. B., 45
Glueck, Eleanor T., 229
Glueck, Sheldon, 229
Good, Carter V., 50, 73
Grambs, Jean D., 276, 320
Gray, Thomas, 298
Gray, William S., 65, 73, 323
Greece (ancient), schools for leaders, 132
Greene, Harry A., 317
Griffiths, Daniel E., 426
Group dynamics: and leadership, 426-427; in the home room, 342-343
Group process and discipline, 370
Growth experiences (kinds of), 254-255
Guidance: and the common learnings, 345-346; counselors, 331-332; defined, 330; essential to good teaching, 336; function of teacher, 329-332; orientation in, 339; plan of organization, 331-332; program in operation, 346-348; services, 330-334; specialists, 331; techniques, 336-349

Hafstad, Lawrence R., 464
Hales, Dawson W., 439

Hall, G. Stanley, 62, 83
Hamilton, Allen T., 268
Hand, Harold C., 13, 15, 54, 73, 97, 410, 411, 412
Hanna, Paul R., 73
Harper, William R., 81
Harris, W. T., 79, 81
Hart, James D., 457
Hartford, Ellis F., 17, 25
Harvard and Chicago universities press for reorganization, 81
Harvard Committee Report, 21
Havighurst, Robert J., 13, 17, 25, 93, 430
Hawthorne Plant, Western Electric experiment, 418
Health factors affecting attendance, 100
Heidbredder, Edna, 267
Henderson, Kenneth B., 73
Hendry, Charles E., 338
Hennings, Thomas C., 73
Henry, George W., 145
Henry, Patrick, 222
Heterogeneous grouping defined, 294; vs. homogeneous grouping, 293-295
Hicks, John D., 41, 45
High school: a common school, 95-96; and the nation, 31-33; discrimination in, 410-412; history of, 10-11, 82; modern, 55, 267-270; population of, 71; preparation for college, 137; promotes the common welfare, 37; superior, 448-449, 451-453, 475-477
High school (junior) a transition school, 98
Hildreth, Gertrude H., 294, 299
Hill, Sam R., 166
Hippocrates, 105
Holbrook, Stewart H., 49, 73
Hollingshead, A. B., 17, 90, 92, 275
Homemaking, 192
Homeroom activities: a variety of approaches to, 343-344; guidance, 340; guideposts, 341; visitation, 384
Homogeneous grouping: defined, 175, 284; inadequate as a grouping technique, 176
Hopkins, Mark, 395
Horn, Gunnar, 25
Horsman, Gwen, 323
Hovet, Kenneth, 182
Hu, Shih, 407
Hymes, James L., Jr., 8, 25, 353, 354, 381

Ilg, Frances L., 237
Illustrations: building readiness for resource material, 256-257; of unit introductions, 199-200, 256

Immigrants: a select group, 35; possessed many deep loyalties, 35
Imperative needs of youth, 22
Individual differences, 82, 173, 267-269
Individual differences and instruction, 174-175
Indoctrination, 3-4
Inductive procedure, 63
Industrial arts: interprets the machine age, 191; offered in all grades, 191; reading problem in, 316
Industrial society, 26
Industrialization and the district system, 437; a probable cause of the upward extension of general education, 438
Industry has brought about educational inequality, 437-440
Inglis, Alexander, 36, 44, 279
In-Service education helps solve teacher problems, 166; workshops are procedures employed in common learnings, 168
Instruction: 1845 and 1919 compared, 63; guideposts to, 149
Instructional material: analyze need for, 249; selection of, 248-252; study cumulative records, 249; study all test data, 249
Instructional tools: for the classroom, 407; better selection for better teaching, 407-409
Instructional staff develops the common learnings course of study, 166
Integration, a stage in getting meaning from what is taught, 151
Intelligence, 90, 94
Interviews, 271
I. Q.: inadequate as a grouping device, 175; specific aptitude vs. I.Q., 174
Iverson, William, 276, 320

Jacobson, Paul B., 34, 46
James, William, 62, 82, 84
Jefferson, Thomas, 135
Jefferson's bill to establish a public school system, 48
Jenkins, Gladys G., 5, 25, 421
Jensen, Alfred C., 467
John Dewey Society, 21
Johnson, George, 275
Johnston, Edgar G., 428
Jorgensen, A. N., 317
Judd, Charles, H. 62, 84, 266
Junior high school as a transition school, 98
Justman, Joseph, 91, 173

Kalamazoo case, 75, 136
Keller, Franklin J., 140, 155
Keller, Helen, 166
Kelley, Bill of, 317
Kentucky Experiment in developing moral values, 17
Keppel, Francis, 25
Knight, Edgar W., 76, 133
Koopman, Robert G., 426
Koskey, Thomas A., 407
Kough, Jack, 296, 300
Krutch, Joseph, 254
Kurt, Lewin, 62

Laboratories in the outdoors, 400
Landis, Paul H., 17, 25
Laotzu (Laotse or Laotsze), 416
Latin Grammar school, 9
Laws of learning, 223
Lawshe, C. H. Jr., 135
Leadership: analysis, 427; and basic goals, 427-430; and group dynamics, 426-427; autocratic and democratic, 427; competing concepts, 416-417; control patterns, 418; for learning, 416, 430-432; guidance, 421-423; laissez-faire, 417; qualifications, 425
Leader-teacher: influences fellow teachers, 431; understands human nature, 431
Learner, rapid, identified, 299; slow, identified, 295-296
Learners, rapid and gifted possess vast potentialities, 298; the bright need to be challenged, 288; average, 185; slow, 185; percentage of slow, average, and rapid, 290
Learning: by units versus teaching by units, 211; is informal, not formal, 229-232
Lee, Edwin, 191
Leonard, J. Paul, 63, 73, 90, 173
Letter marking system, 273
Lewin, Kurt, 417
Librarian: services rendered, 402; skills possessed, 402
Library, high school, 401-402
Lieberman, Myron C., 58, 108
Lilienthal, David, 46, 74
Lincoln, Abraham, 135
Lippitt, Ronald, 338
Lippmann, Walter, 389
Literature and religion (tribal life), 130
Living standards improved by school attendance, 29

MacConnell, C. M., 46
McMahill, Don R., 121
McMahill, Don R., Jr., 404
Maladjusted student, 360
Mann, Horace, 61, 135
Mark, symbol, indicates differences in performance, 272
Marks: and marking, 270-273; exclude non essential factors in determination of, 275; define symbols concisely, 275; establish validity of tests, 276; reveal understanding achieved, 276; based on standing in class vs. individual growth, 265; purposes of, 272
Marriage, as a cause for leaving school, 99
Marshall, T. O., 409
Maskelyne, 267
Mass education motive, 139
Materials, availability of, 252
Mathematics: and science become popular, 472; reading problem in, 315; in tribal life, 130
Maturity, attainment of, 360-363
Maul, Ray C., 461
Mead, Margaret, 74
Melby, Ernest O., 60, 74
Mental discipline, challenged, 223
Mentally retarded: can learn and earn a living, 302-303; comprise from 1 to 3 per cent of the population, 302; learner, 302-303; special room for, 303
Merging marking systems, 275
Merit pay plans, 113; opposed by NEA and AFT, 111-211
Merrill's Marauders, 12
Meyer vs. Nebraska, 51
Miel, Alice, 426
Miller, Franklin A., 234
Military service, preparing for, 404-406
Mills, Caleb, 135
Minority groups: intellectual equals and productive, 39-40
Misner, Paul J., 426
Monitorial schools, 135
Monroe, Marion, 323
Moore, Hollis, 397
Moore, Raymond, 423
Moral values (Kentucky experiment), 17
Morale: School, 368; how to build, 363
Morgan, Owen W., 74, 90, 91
Morrill and Smith-Hughes Acts, 28-29
Mort, Paul M., 438
Motion pictures, 246
Moyer, James H., 234
Muir, Sarah T., 106
Myers, Robert M., 417
Myth, Lincoln, 457

National Association of Secondary School Principals, 94; Bulletin of, 22

National Education Association, 11, 390; addresses and proceedings of, in 1887, 78; in 1892, 18; in 1899, 78, 82

National Society for the Study of Education, 84

NEA and AFT oppose merit rating plan, 111

NEA offers important services, 108-109

Nebraska Department of Public Instruction, 214

Needs of youth: behavior indicates, 225-226; determine the nature of the program, 396-400; wants, lacks, deficiencies, 225

Newkirk, Louis, 191

Newsletters, 381

News and Cues, 449-460

News notes of good cheer, 381

New York Regents Inquiry, 20

Non-readers, definition of, 324

North-Central Association of Colleges and Secondary Schools, 20

Oberteuffer, Delbert, 233

Objectives of the high school: determined by public demand, 18; formulated by national commissions and the local community, 19-21

Observations, 271

Ogburn, Charleton, Jr., 12, 25

Oliva, Peter F., 74

Ortega, y Gasset, 53, 74

Orwell, George, 74

Overstreet, H. A., 13, 25

Oxtoby, O., 71, 74

Parent-Teacher Association, 384

Parent-teacher co-operation vs. divided responsibility, 61

Parker, Col. Francis W., 79

Parker and Harris propose ideas, 81

Parochial high school, 475-477

Part-time attendance and part-time work plan, 464

Pasadena Plan of Organization, 86

Patrick, Robert, 224

Pederson, Kenneth, 420

Percentage marking system, 274

Percentile rank system of marking, 274

Personal needs of students revealed in class, 162

Personal notes, 382

Personality, evaluation, 271

Physical education, 232-233

Physical fitness, 403-405

Physical fitness program, 403-406

Planning and developing a subject, 212-216

Planning student-teacher participation, 216

Policies and programs, 221-222

Political: concepts and forces created the public school system, 135; conflicts of today are inherited from our past, 35; motive for curriculum development, 134-135; special insterests prevent free inquiry, 56

Population, high school, will double between 1954 and 1966, 70

Population maps, 387

Practical (the) vs. the theoretical, 58

Practice (Cronbach), 219

Practices: common marking, 273-274

Preparation for college, 59

Pressey, S. L., 82

Principal, the, 420

Printed word, 80

Private high school, 475-477

Proceedings of the National Education Association, 78

Process unit, 213; vs. subject matter unit, 203

Productive study, 219

Professional education: a high calling, 105-106; professional standards, 117; professional teacher, 109

Program, 383-389, 391-392, 396-400, 475, 478-479

Progressive Education Association, 79

Prosser, Charles A., 189

Prosser resolution, 79

Puberty rites in tribal life, 129-130

Public affairs committee, 383

Public demand: determines subjects offered, 5-6; indicated by surveys, 387

Public high school education, 49

Public relations: a business principle, 377; good for the school, 377; meaning of, 389; neglected by the school, 377-378; program for, 391-392; the problem, 389-391

Public school: achieves the American dream, 27; creates a culture-molding process, 27; produces change, 27

Public school system established, 1830-1850, 48-49

Publicity, welfare of children central theme in, 386

Quality of education revealed by holding power, 88
Questionnaire to parents, 21
Questionnaires, 388
Quiggley, Thomas A., 189

Radio and TV, 385
Radio recordings, 247
Rank order system of marking, 274
Rapid learner 290; and the teacher, 300; identification of, 299-300; potential for contribution to society, 299; teaching problems with, 301-302
Rating scale, 271
Reader: gifted and rapid, 318; identification of the retarded, 318; retarded, 319; teaching the retarded, 318-319
Reading: for non-readers, 324; improvement of, 315; in the regular classroom, 324; remedial and the regular classroom teacher, 319; retardation in, 317; textbook use, 325; vocabulary of separate subjects, 325
Reading, nature of the problem, 313-314
Reading, skills and abilities, 314
Reading ability: diagnosis by teacher test, 317; general classes in, 322; in core classes, 323; laboratory, 321; of students, 313-314
Reading achievement, 1952, superior to that of earlier decades, 65
Reading improvement: nature of the problem, 313-314; new movement, 310; proposals for, 313; teachers for, 320-321
Reading problems, in business courses, 316; in separate subjects, 325
Reading Program: laboratory, 321; outline of, 320-324
Rebels, 353
Recognition: and adjustment to individual differences, 266-270 and respect by adults, 360-362; versus tolerance, 227
Regional accrediting associations, 117
Reid, John, 398
Reisner, Edward H., 41, 42, 46
Religion: for curriculum development, 133; prevents free inquiry into moral and spiritual issues, 56
Remedial classes for retarded readers, 319
Reorganization: agitation for, 77-79; alternative forms of, 87; and the secondary school, 77; indicated by psychological principles, 82-84; meaning of, 76; present status, 87; slow evolution of the high school, 1821 to 1880, 75-76

Report cards as advertising, 380; the least helpful method, 282
Reports to parents: 277-278, 280-284; by letter, 283; by report card, 282; by teacher-parent conference, 283; adequate, 280-281; improvement of, 277-280; standards for, 280-282
Research, defined and described, 62, 63
Resource material, sources of, 257-259
Retardation and failure, 96
Retardation, gifted, and talented learners, 302-306
Retarded reader: help for, 318; identification of, 318; role of the regular teacher, 319
Retention, 75
Rickover, H. G., 74
Roethlisberger, F. J., 418
Romine, Stephen A., 159
Roper, Elmo, 387
Rosenberger, Homer T., 310
Ross, C. C., 265
Routine: and classroom work, 365; role of, 364
Rugg, Earl U., 27, 46
Rugg, Harold, 27, 63, 74
Rules and regulations of the School District of Omaha, 119

Sayen, C. N., 107
Science in tribal life, 130; problems in reading, 315
Scientific method, 62
School life, 11; factors affecting adjustment to, 367-368
School morale, 368
School (the) movement of 1830-1850, causes of, 437
School newspaper, 234, 383
School nurse, 403
School plant, designed to serve youth, 396-400
School program, 385
School provides an activity for every need, 226
School publicity, 385-388; constant and regular, 389
Schools: European, brought to America, 435; for leaders in ancient and modern times, 131; increase living standards, 29-30; supply services parents unable to provide, 157; transmit the American Way, 438
School-society relationships, 36-38
Schools, survive through public support, 386
Schorling, Raleigh, 364

Scott, C. Winfield, 53, 74

Schram, William, 323

Script for a guidance program, 346-347

Seashore, Harold G., 268

Secondary Education, cardinal principles of, 19

Secondary School, role of, 5, 8

Segel, David, 268

Self-discipline and self-control, development of, 362

Self-evaluation in role playing, 342-343

Separate subjects, 461-463; in the curriculum, 146

Services provided by the library, 401

Sex, changes in status, 99

Shores, J. Harlan, 180, 203, 213

Slide film, 246

Slides, 246

Slow learner, 290; and rapid learners, 290-291; finds the conventional curriculum too abstract, 184, 297-298; identification of, 295-296; teaching the, 296-297

Smith, B. Othaniel, 180, 203, 213

Smith, David E., 132

Smith, Marion, 296, 297, 302, 303

Smith, Mortimer, 59, 74

Social: activities in a typical high school, 227; and educational changes, 468-471; one important cause of drop-outs, 92-94; promotion, 465

Social science, reading problems in, 315-316

Society: and the high school, 36; and the individual, 37; in the maintenance of democratic schools, 37-38; what it asks of its teachers, 38, 39, 116

Sociodrama as a guidance technique, 337

Socio-economic background determines attitudes of people, 386-387

Sociogram, the, 271

Socrates, 123

Solicitation, in teacher guidance an essential, 226

Solomon, Frederick, 438

Space, humanization of, 399

Spears, Harold, 25, 74, 125, 129, 203, 235

Special: interest groups vs. free inquiry, 55; learning, 171-172; reports, 381; learnings elective, 174

Specialist in guidance, 331

Spitznas, James E., 155, 188

Standard scores system, 274

Stanley, William O., 180, 203, 213

Start-to-school booklets, 382

Statistical Abstract of the United States, 11

Statistics, high school population projected to 1966, 70, 71

Stiles, Lindley J., 120, 370, 418

Stout, Lydia, 74

Strang, Ruth, 281

Strecker, E. A., 74

Strecker, Edward P., 15, 25

Student: identification of his class role, 343; participation in planning, 216; talent, 385; unique individual, 270

Student activities: characteristics of, 228-230; development of, 226; in accord with modern viewpoint, 223; movement (curriculum outside regular curriculum), 223-224; replace extrcurriculor activities, 224

Student council, 235

Students: and discipline, 359; in modern high school are superior to those from conventional school, 63-65; many have personality problems, 357-358; many read with comprehension of grade 4 level, 311; one-third unable to read standard high school text, 310; rate themselves, 282; vary greatly in social maturity, 230; with low ability and status discriminated against, 410-413

Student-teacher relationship, techniques for improving, 364-365

Study habits and skills, 218, 291-319

Subject matter: alien, 355; of central importance to the student, 129; planning and developing, 212-216; selection of, 148; unit, 213; unit versus process unit, 203-204

Subjects of study: more practical introduced since 1890, 136-137; suggested by the colleges in 1890, 137

Sullivan, Anne, 162

Superintendent's Bulletin, Omaha, Nebr., 112

Superior high school, characteristics of, 451-453

Survey abstract of local criticisms, 66

Survival rate for U. S. high schools, 92

Swanson, Chester, 377

Taba, Hilda, 17

Talented learners: defined, 305; list, 306; may be latent, 305

Taylor, Bob L., 246

Teacher: adjustment to community, 113-114; a key to the creation of the common high school, 98; assumed superiority of the academic, 185; competencies, 467-468; conservative vs.

liberal, 472-473; function in guidance, 329; must know his students, 123; personal standards of, 118; study people, 430

Teacher education: method differentiated from technique, 58; steadily improving, 57; teaching as a profession, 58; theoretical vs. practical, 58-59

Teacher-leader: influences fellow teachers, 431; understands human nature, 431

Teacher personality, 369

Teacher specialization, 459-461

Teachers: and trade unions, 106-107; cause friction, 116; for tomorrow, 470; traits, compilation of, 111

Teachers are realists, 466

Teacher's guide, 213-214

Teaching: methods with rapid learners, 301; modern methods, 55; problems with rapid learners, 300; the rapid learner, 300; the slow learner, 296

Teaching as a guidance technique: discipline, 354; study habits and skills, 218

Teaching as a profession: defined, 58; is a high calling, 105-106

Teaching assignments in several states, 461

Teaching by units vs. learning by units, 211-212

Techniques: differentiated from method, 58; for guidance in the regular classroom, 336-346; for superior classroom work, 364; for surveys, 387-388

Technological (our) revolution, 468-471

Teen age: characteristics of, 12-14; developmental tasks of, 12-14; guideposts to understanding of, 14-18; junior high school youth, 396-397; senior high and junior college youth, 396-398

Teen-agers: 27, 310, 354

Terman, Lewis M., 62

Textbook: a controversial issue, 247; in the modern high school, 215, 401; teacher's manual, 216

Textbook (one) or a single assignment, undesirable, 248; unsuited to slow, average, and rapid learners, 289

Thayer, V. T., 74

Theisen, W. W., 386

Theoretical (the) vs. the practical, 58

Thompson, Warren S., 11, 25

Thorndike, Edward L., 29, 46, 62, 82, 84

Threats to democracy, 43

Thurstone, L. L., 268

Thurstone, Thelma G., 268

Trade and industrial education, 192-193

Trade unions and teaching, 106-107

Tyler, Ralph W., 46

Uhl, Willis L., 130

Ulich, Robert, 171

Umstattd, J. G., 110, 120, 125, 205

UNESCO Committee on Race, 39, 46

Unified high school, 82

Unit: evaluated, 164; illustration of how developed, 162-163; inadequate introduction of, 200-202; or laboratory method, 202-203; pre-planning before presentation, 204-205; steps in development of, 163-164

Urban employment and adjustment, 114

U. S. Dept. of Health, Education and Welfare, 446

U. S. Office of Education, 21, 88, 92, 96, 463

Van Loon, Hendrick W., 131

Vocal and instrumental music, 236

Vocation program: the role of vocational education, 187; vocational education a necessity, 185-186

Vocational Education: equal in status to academic education, 190; purpose, fit the boy for a job, 189

Vocational subjects: laboratory or shop method employed, 192; major subjects, industrial arts, homemaking, agriculture, business, 190

Washburne, Carlton, A., 408

Washington, George, 135

Wellman, Frank E., 268

Wesmann, Alexander, 268

White House Conference on Education, 386

Wickman, E., 292

Wilds, Elmer H., 133

Wiley, Calvin H., 135

Willey, Roy Deverl, 289, 342

Wilson, Sloan, 54, 74

Worcester, D. A., 304

Wrightstone, J. Wayne, 64, 74

Wrinkle, William L., 277, 278

Young, Kimball, 122, 125

Zander, Alvin, 338